AF819959

All in One®

Recommended by Teachers Trusted by Toppers

POLITICAL SCIENCE

Class 11

EVERYTHING YOU NEED TO SCORE

- Simplified NCERT Theory
- NCERT & Other Important Questions
- CBQs; MCQs, A-R, Case Based
- Sample Question Papers

CBSE Exams 2026

Author

Aditi Verma,
Deepanshu Pandey

arihant
SUCCESS AND NOTHING LESS

ARIHANT PRAKASHAN
(School Division Series)

卐 *ADMINISTRATIVE & PRODUCTION OFFICES*

Regd. Office

'Ramchhaya' 4577/15, Agarwal Road, Darya Ganj, New Delhi -110002
Tele: 011- 47630600, 43518550; Fax: 011- 23280316

卐 *Head Office*

Kalindi, TP Nagar, Meerut (UP) - 250002, Tel: 0121-7156203, 7156204

卐 *SALES & SUPPORT OFFICES*

Agra, Ahmedabad, Bengaluru, Bareilly, Chennai, Delhi, Guwahati, Hyderabad, Jaipur, Jhansi, Kolkata, Lucknow, Nagpur & Pune.

PO No : TXT-XX-XXXXXXX-X-XX

Published By Arihant Publications (India) Ltd.

For further information about the books published by Arihant, log on to www.arihantbooks.com or e-mail at info@arihantbooks.com

Follow us on

卐 *PRICE* ₹400.00

PRODUCTION TEAM

Publishing Managers	Cover Designer	Inner Designer
Mahendra Singh Rawat & Keshav Mohan	Salman Shaikh	Ankit Tyagi
Project Head	*Page Layouting*	*Proof Reader*
Monika Bhasin	Chintoo Kumar	Pravesh Bhagrwal

Index *cum* Study Planner

Part A : Indian Constitution at Work

Latest Course *Structure*

Part A : Indian Constitution at Work

No.	Chapter Name	No. of Periods	Marks Alloted
1	Constitution: Why and How?	12	8
2	Rights in the Indian Constitution	8	
3	Election and Representation	14	6
4	Executive	14	12
5	Legislature	14	
6	Judiciary	14	
7	Federalism	14	6
8	Local Governments	10	4
9	Constitution as a Living Document	6	4
10	The Philosophy of the Constitution	6	
	No. of periods & marks allotted to Indian Constitution at Work	**112**	**40**

Part B : Political Theory

No.	Chapter Name	No. of Periods	Marks Alloted
1	Political Theory: An Introduction	8	4
2	Freedom	10	12
3	Equality	12	
4	Social Justice	12	6
5	Rights	14	4
6	Citizenship	12	8
7	Nationalism	15	
8	Secularism	16	6
	No. of periods & marks allotted for Political Theory	**99**	**40**
	Total	**211**	**80**

PART A : Contemporary World Politics

1. Constitution: Why and How?

a) Why do we need a Constitution?
- Constitution allows coordination and assurance
- Specification of decision-making powers
- Limitations on the powers of government
- Aspirations and goals of a society
- Fundamental identity of a people

b) The authority of a Constitution
- Mode of promulgation
- The substantive provisions of a Constitution
- Balanced institutional design

c) How was the Indian Constitution made?
- Composition of the Constituent Assembly
- Procedures
- Inheritance of the nationalist movement
- Institutional arrangements

d) Provisions adapted from Constitutions of different countries

2. Rights in the Indian Constitution

a) The importance of rights
- Bill of Rights

b) Fundamental Rights in the Indian Constitution
- Right to Equality
- Right to Freedom
- Right against Exploitation
- Right to Freedom of Religion
- Cultural and Educational Rights
- Right to Constitutional Remedies

c) Directive Principles of State Policy
- What do the directive principles contain?

d) Relationship between fundamental rights and directive principles

3. Election and Representation

a) Elections and democracy

b) Election system in India
- First Past the Post System
- Proportional Representation

c) Why did India adopt the FPTP system?

d) Reservation of constituencies

e) Free and fair elections
- Universal franchise and right to contest
- Independent Election Commission

f) Electoral Reforms

4. Executive

a) What is an executive?

b) What are the different types of executives?

c) Parliamentary executive in India
- Power and position of President
- Discretionary Powers of the President

d) Prime Minister and Council of Ministers

e) Permanent Executive: Bureaucracy

5. Legislature

a) Why do we need a parliament?

b) Why do we need two houses of parliament?
- Rajya Sabha
- Lok Sabha

c) What does the parliament do?
- Powers of Rajya Sabha
- Special Powers of Rajya Sabha

d) How does the parliament make laws?

e) How does the parliament control the executive?

f) What do the committees of parliament do?

g) How does the parliament regulate itself?

6. Judiciary

a) Why do we need an independent judiciary?
  - Independence of Judiciary
  - Appointment of Judges
  - Removal of Judges

b) Structure of the Judiciary

c) Jurisdiction of Supreme Court
  - Original Jurisdiction
  - Writ Jurisdiction
  - Appellate Jurisdiction
  - Advisory Jurisdiction

d) Judicial Activism

e) Judiciary and Rights

f) Judiciary and Parliament

7. Federalism

a) What is Federalism?

b) Federalism in the Indian Constitution
  - Division of Powers

c) Federalism with a strong central government

d) Conflicts in India's federal system
  - Centre-State Relations
  - Demands for Autonomy
  - Role of Governors and President's Rule
  - Demands for New States
  - Interstate Conflicts

e) Special provisions
  - Jammu and Kashmir

8. Local Governments

a) Why local governments?

b) Growth of Local Government in India
  - Local Governments in Independent India

c) 73rd and 74th amendments

d) 73rd Amendment
  - Three Tier Structure
  - Elections
  - Reservations
  - Transfer of Subjects
  - State Election Commissioners
  - State Finance Commission

e) 74th Amendment

f) Implementation of 73rd and 74th Amendments

9. Constitution as a Living Document

a) Are constitutions static?

b) How to amend the Constitution?

c) Why have there been so many amendments?

d) Contents of amendments made so far
  - Differing Interpretations
  - Amendments through Political Consensus
  - Controversial Amendments

e) Basic structure and evolution of the Constitution

f) Constitution as a Living Document
  - Contribution of the Judiciary
  - Maturity of the Political Leadership

10. The Philosophy of the Constitution

a) What is meant by philosophy of the Constitution?
  - Constitution as Means of Democratic Transformation

b) Why do we need to go back to the Constituent Assembly?

c) What is the political philosophy of our Constitution?
  - Individual freedom
  - Social justice
  - Respect for diversity and minority rights
  - Secularism
  - Universal franchise
  - Federalism
  - National identity

d) Procedural Achievements

e) Criticisms

f) Limitations

PART B : Political Theory

1. Political Theory: An Introduction

a) What is politics?

b) What do we study in political theory?

c) Putting Political theory into practice

d) Why should we study political theory?

2. Freedom

a) The Ideal of freedom

b) The Sources of Constraints-Why do we need constraints?

c) The Harm Principle

d) Negative and Positive Liberty

3. Equality

a) Why does equality matter?

- Equality of opportunities
- Natural and Social Inequalities

b) Three dimensions of equality

c) Feminism, Socialism

d) How can we promote equality?

4. Social Justice

a) What is Justice?

- Equal Treatment for Equals
- Proportionate Justice
- Recognition of Special Needs

b) Just distribution

c) John Rawls Theory of Justice

d) Pursuing Social Justice

e) Free Markets versus State Intervention

5. Rights

a) What are Rights?

b) Where do rights come from?

c) Legal rights and the state

d) Kinds of rights

e) Rights and responsibilities

6. Citizenship

a) Introduction

b) Full and equal membership

c) Equal Rights

d) Citizen and Nation

e) Universal Citizenship

f) Global Citizenship

7. Nationalism

a) Introducing Nationalism

b) Nations and Nationalism

- Shared Beliefs
- History
- Shared National Identity

c) National self-determination

d) Nationalism and Pluralism

8. Secularism

a) What is Secularism?

- Inter-religious Domination
- Intra-religious Domination

b) Secular State

c) The western model of secularism

d) The Indian model of secularism

e) Criticisms of Indian secularism

- Western Import
- Minoritism
- Interventionist
- Vote Bank Politics

Prescribed Textbooks

1. Indian Constitution at Work, Class XI, Published by NCERT
2. Political Theory, Class XI, Published by NCERT
3. Added Reference Material available with the document in the Annexure

Note: The above textbooks are also available in Hindi and Urdu versions.

01 CHAPTER

The Constitution is the highest legal document of a country. It lays down the basic structure of the political system under which its people are to be governed.

Constitution: Why and How?

▼ YOUR STUDY GOALS

1.1 Constitution
1.2 The Authority of a Constitution
1.3 Making of the Indian Constitution

▼ YOUR PRACTICE GOAL

- Objective Type Questions (30 Qs ; MCQs, A-R, Statements, Matching, Passage Based)
- Subjective Questions (11 VSAs, 11 SAs, 6 LAs, 4 Picture Based)

1.1 Constitution

- Constitution consists of several articles. These articles specify how the state will be formed and what rules it should follow. It also decides how people should interact with their governments.
- It establishes certain values and guidelines in society. These guidelines help the citizens of various ethnic and religious groups to live in peace.
- The Constitution establishes the three main organs of the state i.e. the **Legislature,** the **Executive** and the **Judiciary** and defines their powers.
- To understand the need of a Constitution, it is important to study its different functions. These are given below

Constitution Allows Co-ordination and Assurance

- The **first function** of a Constitution is to provide a set of basic rules for the minimal co-ordination amongst members of the society.
- Every person needs some basic rules that are publicly promulgated (circulate) to achieve minimum co-ordination. These rules must also be enforceable. By making these rules legally enforceable[1], a guarantee to everybody is attained. It is ensured that others will also follow these rules and if they do not follow, they will be punished by the law.

1 Enforceable It means to put or keep in force or to enforce a rule.

Specification of Decision-Making Powers

- **The second function** of the Constitution is that, it is a set of fundamental principles according to which a state is formed and governed. The Constitution specifies who will have the decision-making powers in the country.
- For example, in a Monarchical Constitution, a monarch take the decisions. While as in some Constitutions like the old Soviet Union, one single party decides. However, in a democratic Constitution, the people get to decide.
- The Indian Constitution specifies that the Parliment has the power to decide laws and policies in most cases. If Parliment can make laws, there must be a law that gives it this power. This is the role of the Constitution, which establishes the authority to create the government.

Limitations on the Power of Government

- **The third function** of the Constitution is to set some limits on what a government can impose on its citizens. These limits are fundamental in the sense that the government may never cross them.
- The Constitution limits the power of the government in many ways. The most common way is to specify certain **Fundamental Rights**[2] that all the citizens will possess.
- Citizens generally have the right to certain liberties such as, freedom of speech, freedom of religion, freedom of conscience, freedom of association, etc., which are fundamental in nature.

Aspirations and Goals of a Society

- **The fourth function** of the Constitution is to enable the government to fulfill the aspirations of a society and create conditions for a just society.
- India aspires to be a society that is free from caste discrimination and to achieve this, the government will have to be enabled to take all the necessary steps. The framers of the Indian Constitution thought that every individual in the society should have all the things that are necessary for them to lead a life of dignity and social self-respect, minimum material well-being, education, etc.
- The Indian Constitution enables the government to take positive welfare measures, some of which are **legally enforceable**. Some such provisions have the support of the **Preamble** and some are found in the section on **Fundamental Rights**. The **Directive Principles of the State Policy** (DPSP) were also included to fulfill certain aspirations of the people.

Enabling Provisions of the Constitution

Constitution are not only rules and regulations controlling the powers of the government. They also give powers to the government for achieving collective good of the society.

- **Constitution of South Africa** assigns many responsibilities to the government. It wants the government to take measures to promote conservation of nature, make efforts to protect persons or groups subjected to unfair discrimination and provides that the government must progressively ensure adequate housing to all, health care, etc.
- In the case of Indonesia also, the government is empowered to establish and conduct national education system.
- The **Indonesian Constitution** ensures that the poor and destitute children will be looked after by the government.

Fundamental Identity of People

A Constitution expresses the fundamental identity of the people. It means that people as a collective entity come into being only through the basic Constitution. It is by agreeing to a set of basic rules about how one should be governed, and who should be governed that one forms a collective identity.

2 **Fundamental Rights** These are the basic human rights that are considered essential for human dignity and freedom.

The different types of identities provided by the Constitution to its citizens are

- By agreeing to certain basic norms and principles one constitutes one's basic **political identity**.
- Constitutional norms provide a framework within which one pursues individual aspirations, goals and freedoms. It also sets authoritative constraints that citizens must not **trespass**[3]. Hence, the Constitution also gives one a **moral identity**.
- The Constitution of every country is different from each other. Constitutions are also different in the ways they present the concept of **national identity**.
- Most of the nations are a mixture of a complex set of historical traditions. For instance, German identity was constituted by being ethnically German. So its Constitution gives expression to this identity. The Indian Constitution, on the other hand, does not make ethnic identity, a criterion for citizenship. Different nations have different concepts of what the relationship between different regions of a nation and the Central Government should be. This relationship constitutes the national identity of a country.

1.2 The Authority of a Constitution

- In most countries, the term **'Constitution'** refers to a compact document that includes a number of articles. These articles describe how the state should be constituted and what rules it should follow. However, certain countries, such as the United Kingdom, do not have a single document that can be referred to as the Constitution. Instead, they have a series of documents and the decisions that are taken together are known as the Constitution.
- Many Constitutions around the world exist only on paper, they are just words written on a document. But the real question is how effective they are. The effectiveness of a Constitution depends on several factors as disussed below

Mode of Promulgation

- Mode of **promulgation**[4] refers to how a Constitution comes into existence. It also refers to who crafted the Constitution and how much authority they have in the Constitution making process.
- In many countries, the Constitution was drafted by unpopular military leaders and thus remains defunct or unused. The most successful Constitutions in the world, like that of India, South Africa and the United States were drafted in the aftermath of popular national movements.
- The Indian Constitution was formally created by a **Constituent Assembly** between **December 1946 and November 1949**. Most of the members of India's Constituent Assembly were also leaders of the National Freedom Movement. Hence, the Constitution makers had the support and trust of the public.
- The Constitution makers did their best to accomodate the needs and interests of different sections of the society. They also convinced the people that the Constitution was not an instrument for personal gains or power consolidation. Instead, it was drafted in a way that focused on the public good. Hence, the Constitution reflected the broad national **consensus**[5] of that time.
- Some countries have subjected their Constitution to a full-fledged **referendum**[6]. The Indian Constitution was never subject to such a referendum. Instead, it was drafted by people who enjoyed immense public credibility. Therefore, the authority of the Constitution makers helps in determining the success of the Constitution.

---

3 **Trespass** It is an unlawful act committed on the person, property or rights of another.

4 **Promulgation** It means to announce publicly especially a new law.

5 **Consensus** It means a generally accepted opinion or decision among a group of people.

6 **Referendum** It means an occasion, when all people of a country can vote on a particular potitical question.

Substantive Provisions of a Constitution

- The hallmark of a successful Constitution is that it gives everyone in a society some reason to go along with its provisions. For example, if a Constitution allows majorities to oppress **minority**[7] groups or gives certain privileges to only some members and not to others, then, in such cases, the oppressed groups will have no reason to follow the provisions of the Constitution.
- So, it is the duty of a Constitution that it provides freedom and equality to all its members. It should provide the basic rules and regulations for pursuing basic justice in order to become a just and successful Constitution.

Debate over Constitution making in Nepal

- Making a Constitution is not an easy work. **Nepal** is an example of the complicated nature of Constitution making.
- Since 1948, Nepal has had five Constitutions(1948, 1951, 1959, 1962 and 1990).
- The 1990 Constitution introduced a multi party competition, but the king continued to hold final power.
- Some groups in Nepal wanted to abolish the institution of monarchy and establish republican form of government.
- The **Communist Party of Nepal (Maoist)** demanded elected Constituent Assembly.
- Under pressure of popular agitation, the king had to established a government and in 2008, Nepal emerged as a democratic republic after abolishing the monarchy.
- In 2015, Nepal adopted a new Constitution.

Balanced Institutional Design

A well crafted Constitution distributes the power in a society in such a way so that no single group can subvert (corrupt) the Constitution. There are two ways of such intelligent designing

- **Firstly**, it is often done by fragmenting power across different institutions to ensure that no single institution acquires total control of power.

  For example, the Indian Constitution has horizontally distributed its power across the Legislature, Executive, Judiciary and even independent bodies like the Election Commission. This has been done to ensure that if one institution tries to subvert the Constitution, it can be checked by other institutions. It is also called the system of **'checks and balances'** which makes the Indian Constitution a successful one.
- **Secondly,** the Constitution must be both **rigid** as well as **flexible**. It must strike the right balance between certain values, norms and procedures as authoritative. A Constitution must allow enough flexibility to adapt according to the changing needs and circumstances. While a rigid Constitution is likely to break under the weight of change. At the same time, being too flexible will give no security, predictability or identity to the people. Hence, successful Constitutions should maintain the right balance between preserving core values and adapting to new situations.
- The Indian Constitution has been referred to as **'a living document'**. A successful Constitution is one that strikes a fine balance between rigidity and flexibility on changing its provisions. It also guarantees that no section or party will defy the Constitution on its own.

Quick Test 1

1. Name the organs of the state established by the Constitution.
2. Who has the ultimate power in a democratic Constitution?
3. Does the Indian Constitution make ethnic identity a criterion for citizenship?
4. What is the hallmark of a successful Constitution?
5. The Constitution of which country is referred to as a 'living document'?

7 **Minority** It is a small group of people, who are of a different race or religion to most of the people in the community or country, where they live.

1.3 Making of the Indian Constitution

The Constitution of India was formally made by the **Constituent Assembly**. It held its first sitting on **9th December, 1946** and reassembled as Constituent Assembly for divided India on 14th August, 1947. Its members were chosen by **indirect elections** by the members, of the Provincial Legislative Assemblies that had been established under the Government of India Act, 1935.

The composition of the Constituent Assembly was proposed by the British cabinet, know as the **Cabinet Mission**. According to this plan

- Seats were allotted to the provinces and Princely States. Distribution of seats in each province was among the three main communities, Muslims, Sikhs and general, in proportion to their respective populations.
- Each Province and each Princely State or group of states were allotted seats proportional to their respective population roughly in the ratio of 1:10,00,000.
- Provinces were to elect 292 members. These Provinces were under the direct rule of the British. While the Princely States were allotted a minimum number of 93 seats.
- In the Provinces or the Provincial Legislative Assembly, members of each community elected their own representatives. They were elected by the **method of proportional representation** system with a single transferable vote.
- In the case of representatives of Princely States, the method of selection was to be decided by consultation.

Composition of the Constituent Assembly

- After the partition, under the plan of **3rd June, 1947,** the members elected from the territories of Pakistan ceased to be the members of the Constituent Assembly. Due to this reason, the number of members in the assembly were reduced to 299.
- The Constitution was adopted on **26th November, 1949**. However, out of the 299 members, 284 were actually present on 24th January, 1950 and appended (attached) their signature to the Constitution as finally passed. The Constitution came into force on **26th January, 1950**. It was written against the backdrop of the partition and the horrific violence caused by it.
- The Indian Constitution envisioned a new kind of citizenship under which minorities could be safe and religious identity could have no effect on citizenship rights.
- The members of the Constituent Assembly were not elected by universal suffrage. However, there was a serious attempt to make the assembly a representative body.
- Under the above-mentioned plan, members of all religions were represented and the assembly also included twenty-eight members from the Scheduled Castes. In terms of political parties, the Congress dominated the assembly occupying as many as 82 per cent of the seats in the assembly after the partition.

Principles of Deliberation Followed by Constituent Assembly

- The authority of the Constituent Assembly comes from the procedures in which they adopted to frame the Constitution and the values, which was brought by its members to their deliberation (observation).
- The Constituent Assembly represented the participation of all sections of the society.
- It is desirable that diverse sections of society claim to be representative in the assembly. Each member should consider the interest not only of his/her own identity, but also consider the interest of the whole nation.
- There were genuine differences about the opinions regarding the form of government, the division of powers and the Fundamental Rights of the people. But all these matters were discussed with great sophistication in shaping the foundation of the largest democracy of the world.

- However, the assembly members felt no need at all to discuss or debate the provision on 'Universal Suffrage'. **Universal Suffrage** means that all citizens of a certain age will be given the right to vote irrespective of their gender, religion, caste, income etc.
- Hence, the debates and discussions are a testament of the democratic nature of the Constituent Assembly.
- The Constitution drew its authority from the fact that members of the Constituent Assembly engaged in public reason. They placed a great emphasis on discussions and reasoned arguments. The members also valued and respected the opinion of each other.

Procedures

- The Constituent Assembly had **eight major committees** on different subjects. Usually, Jawaharlal Nehru, Rajendra Prasad, Sardar Patel and Dr. B. R. Ambedkar chaired these committees.
- Each committee usually drafted particular provisions of the Constitution which were then subjected to debate by the entire assembly. Some provisions were subject to the vote.
- The assembly met for 166 days spread over 2 years and 11 months. It had 11 sessions in total and those were open to press and public alike.

Inheritance of the Nationalist Movement

- The principles of the Constitution were developed during the long struggle for freedom and inherited by the assembly in shaping the Constitution.
- The best summary of the principles that the nationalist movement brought to the Constituent Assembly is the Objective Resolution. **The resolution was moved by Nehru in 1946.**
- This resolution summarised the aspirations and values behind the Constitution. Based on this resolution, our Constitution gave institutional expression to the fundamental commitments i.e. equality, liberty, democracy, sovereignty and a cosmopolitan identity.
- As a result, our Constitution is more than a set of laws and processes. It is a moral commitment to form a government that will fulfill the promises held before the people during the nationalist movement.

Main Points of the Objective Resolution

India is an independent, sovereign, republic.

- India shall be a union of erstwhile British Indian territories, Indian States and other parts outside British India and Indian states as are willing to be a part of the union.
- Territories forming the union shall be autonomous units and exercise all powers and functions of the government and administration, except those assigned to or vested in the union.
- All powers and authority of sovereign and an independent India and its Constitution shall flow from the people.
- All people of India shall be guaranteed and secured social, economic and political justice; equality of status and opportunities and equality before law and fundamental freedoms - of speech, expression, belief, faith, worship, vocation, association and action-subject to law and public morality.
- The minorities, backward and tribal areas, depressed and other backward classes shall be provided adequate safeguards.
- The territorial integrity of the republic and its sovereign rights on land, sea and air shall be maintained according to justice and law of civilised nations.
- The land would make full and willing contribution to the promotion of world peace and welfare of mankind.

Institutional Arrangements

- Another important factor that ensures the effectiveness of a Constitution is a **balanced arrangement** of the institutions of the government. The basic principle is that the government must be democratic and committed towards the welfare of the people.
- The Constituent Assembly spent lots of time in evolving a clear balance between the various institutions like the Legislature, Executive and the Judiciary. This led to the adoption of the **Parliamentary form** of government and the **federal structure**[8]. It would describe complete separation of powers between legislature and executive and between states and the Central Government.
- For a balanced governmental arrangement, the makers of our Constitution borrowed many provisions from different countries. They borrowed the best features available everywhere in the world and adopted it to suit the Indian conditions.
- It is important to note that borrowing ideas was not the same as copying. Each provision of the Constitution had to be defended on the basis of its applicability to Indian problems and aspirations.

Provisions Adapted from Constitutions of Different Countries

Country	Provisions Adopted
British Constitution	▪ First past the post system ▪ Parliamentary form of government ▪ The idea of rule of law ▪ Institution of the speaker and his/her role ▪ Law making procedure
Irish Constitution	▪ Directive Principles of State Policy
United States Constitution	▪ Charter of Fundamental Rights ▪ Power of judicial review and independence of judiciary
French Constitution	▪ Principles of liberty, equality and faternity
Canadian Constitution	▪ A quasi-federal system with a strong Central Government ▪ An idea of residual powers.

Quick Test 2

1. When was the first meeting of the Constituent Assembly held?
2. What was the number of members in the Constituent Assembly after the plan of 3rd June, 1947?
3. Name the members who chaired the committees of the Constituent Assembly.
4. The institution of speaker is adopted from which Constitution?

8 **Federal Structure** It is a system of government in which power is divided between Central Government and State Government.

Mind Map

Constitution Why and How?

1 Constitution

It is the highest legal document defining governance and laws in a nation.

- It establishes certain values and guidelines in society.
- The three main organs of state are the Legislative, the Executive and the Judiciary.

2 Functions of a Constitution

Co-ordination and Assurance
- Provides basic rules for societal co-ordination.

Decision-making Powers
- It specifies who will have the power to make decisions.

Limitation of Government Powers
- It encourages Fundamental Rights to protect liberties. (e.g. speech, religion, etc.)

Aspiration and Goals of a Society
- It ensure that the government fulfill the aspirations of a society.

Fundamental Identity of People
- It empowers government for collective good. (e.g. education, health care etc.)

3 Authority of a Constitution

Mode of Population Promulgation
- It reflects legitimacy based on how it was created. (e.g. India via Constituent Assembly)

Substantial Provisions
- It gives everyone in a society some reason to go along with in provision.
- It provides freedom and equality to all its members.

Balanced Institutional Design
- Power fragmented among institutions for checks and balances.
- A Constitution must be rigid and flexible for adaptability.

4 Making of the Indian Constitution

Key Events
- On 9th Dec 1946, first Constituent Assembly meeting was held.
- The Constitution was adopted on 26th Nov 1949, and come into force on 26th January 1950.

Guiding Principles
- The principles that the nationalist movement brought to Constituent Assembly was objective resolution.

Composition of the Constituent Assembly
- Assembly comprises 299 members, which includes diverse community.

Procedures
- The Constituent Assembly had eight major committees on different subjects.
- The assembly met for 160 days spread over 2 years and 11 months.

5 Principles of Deliberation

- The procedures it adopted to frame the Constitution and the values its members brought to their deliberation.
- The assembly members felt no need at all to discuss or debate the provision on 'Universal Suffrage'.
- The debates and discussions are a testament of the democratic nature of the Constituent Assembly.

6 Institutional Arrangements

- The Constituent Assembly spent lots of time in evolving a clear balance between the various institutions like the Legislature, Executive and the Judiciary.
- Parliamentary form of government with federal structure was adopted by the assembly.
- It is important to note that borrowing ideas was not the same as copying.
- Its applicability to Indian problems and aspirations.

7 Provisions Adapted from Constitution of Different Countries

- **British Constitution** Parliamentary system, rule of law.
- **U.S.A Constitution** Fundamental Rights, Judicial Review.
- **Ireland Constitution** Directive Principle of policy.
- **France Constitution** Principle of liberty, equality and fraternity.
- **Canada Constitution** Federal structure with strong centre.

NCERT Folder

Intext Question

1. Here are some provisions of the Indian and other Constitutions. For each of these write the function that this provision performs. (pg 10)

The government cannot order any citizen to follow or not to follow any religion	**Limitations on the power of the government**
The government must try to reduce inequalities in income and wealth	
The President has the power to appoint the Prime Minister	
The Constitution is the supreme law that everyone has to obey	
Indian citizenship is not limited to people of any race, caste or religion	

Ans.

The government cannot order any citizen to follow or not to follow any religion	**Limitations on the power of the government**
The government must try to reduce inequalities in income and wealth	Imposing taxes on the rich and giving subsidies to the poor to reduce inequality in income.
The President has the power to appoint the Prime Minister	The President appoints a Prime Minister who is the leader of the majority party.
The Constitution is the supreme law that everyone has to obey	It contains fundamental rules that include the entity's powers and limits.
Indian citizenship is not limited to people of any race, caste or religion	The Constitution gave power to the Parliament of India to govern the right of citizenship by law.

Exercise

1. Which of these is not a function of the Constitution?

(i) It gives a guarantee of the rights of the citizen.

(ii) It marks out different spheres of power for different branches of government.

(iii) It ensures that good people come to power.

(iv) It gives expression to some shared values.

Ans. (iii) It ensures that good people come to power.

2. Which of the following is a good reason to conclude that the authority of the Constitution is higher than that of Parliament?

(i) The Constitution was framed before the Parliament came into being.

(ii) The Constitution makers were more eminent leaders than the members of Parliament.

(iii) The Constitution specifies how Parliament is to be formed and what are its powers.

(iv) The Constitution cannot be amended by the Parliament.

Ans. (iii) The Constitution specifies how Parliament is to be formed and what are its powers.

3. State whether the following statements about a Constitution are True or False.

(i) Constitution are written documents about formation and powers of government.

(ii) Constitution exist and are required only in democratic countries.

(iii) Constitution is a legal document that does not deal with ideas and values.

(iv) A Constitution gives its citizens a new identity.

Ans. (i) True (ii) False (iii) False (iv) True

4. State whether the following inferences about the making of the Indian Constitution are Correct or Incorrect. Give reasons to support your answer.

(i) The Constituent Assembly did not represent the Indian people since it was not elected by all citizens.

(ii) Constitution making did not involve any major decision since there was a general consensus among the leaders at that time about its basic framework.

(iii) There was little originality in the Constitution, for much it was borrowed from other countries.

Ans. (i) The inference about the making of the Indian Constitution is incorrect.

Though, the members of the Constituent Assembly were not elected on the basis of universal adult suffrage, they were chosen indirectly by the members of the Provincial Legislative Assemblies that had been established under the Government of India Act 1935.

Further, the Constituent Assembly represented members from every province, religious groups, community and even women from every community. In addition, the assembly had 28 members from Scheduled Castes.

(ii) The statement about the procedures in making of the Constitution is incorrect.

The statement is incorrect because there were arguments and queries on most of the provisions of the Constitution. Each clause of the Constitution was subjected to scrutiny and debate in the entire assembly. The members did not agree with each other on many matters and some provisions were also subject to vote in the assembly.

(iii) The statement is incorrect.

It will be wrong to state that there was little originality in the Indian Constitution and that it was mostly borrowed from other countries. Only the best features from the Constitutions of different countries have been borrowed in a way that best fits the Indian situation.

The Indian Constitution is a combination of French, British, Irish, Canadian, the US and other Constitutions in a way that meets Indian needs and demands.

For instance, Parliamentary form of government has been borrowed from the British Constitution, Fundamental Rights from the United States Constitution, DPSP from the Irish Constitution, etc.

5. Give two examples each to support the following conclusions about the Constitution.

(i) The Constitution was made by credible leaders who commanded people's respect.

(ii) The Constitution has distributed its power in such a way as to make it difficult to subvert it.

(iii) The Constitution is focus of people's hopes and aspirations.

Ans. (i) The two examples in support of the statement are

(a) The members of the Constituent Assembly represented all religions as well as all sections of the society. There were 28 members from the Scheduled Castes as well as members from Hindu, Sikh and Muslim communities from different provinces and Princely States.

Further, the members of the assembly were indirectly elected by the members of the Provincial Legislative Assemblies established under the Government of India Act, 1935.

(b) The Constituent Assembly also had members who have been a part of long struggle for freedom and gathered immense respect and credit among the masses, such as Pt. Nehru, Sardar Patel, Rajendra Prasad, Dr. Ambedkar, who were part of the National Movement and also headed the major committee's in framing the Constitution.

(ii) The following are two examples in support of the statement

(a) The Constitution of India has horizontally distributed its power among different institutions of Judiciary, Legislature and Executive. By doing so, no single institution can acquire control of power and the theory of checks and balances is uplifted. If one institution tries to exploit it, other institution can keep a check.

(b) The Constitution strikes a balance between the possibility of change and the limits placed upon the nature of changes that can be made. Thus, it is neither too rigid nor too flexible and survives as a living document that has the respect of the people.

(iii) The following reasons in support of the statement are

(a) The Constitution of India is formed on the basis of common goals and aspirations of the Indian people that were expressed during the nationalist movement. It is reflected in the objective resolution moved by Nehru, that defined the aims of the constituent assembly.

(b) The Constitution provides institutional expression to the ideas of equality, liberty, sovereignty, democracy and cosmopolitan identity. It has also incorporated some 'Directive Principles of State Policy' which are not justiciable but a moral duty of the government.

6. Why is it necessary for a country to have a clear demarcation of powers and responsibilities in the Constitution? What would happen in the absence of such a demarcation?

Ans. It is necessary for a country to have a clear demarcation of powers and responsibilities in the Constitution because

- Demarcation allows the institutions to work efficiently without any interference or overlapping of powers and responsibilities.
- The intelligent designing of the Constitution is to ensure that no single institution acquires monopoly of power which is achieved by fragmenting power across different institutions (Executive, Legislature and Judiciary).
- The Indian Constitution horizontally fragments power across different institution including independent bodies like Election Commission to ensure that even if one institution wants to subvert, others can check it and the theory of checks and balances is upheld.

- To specify, who plays important role in decision making power in the society.
- It shows how the government would be constituted.
- It stipulates certain limitations on both the government and the citizens which are fundamental in nature and should not be trespassed.

In the absence of such demarcation

- It would lead to a clash between the various institutions that derive their power from the Constitution and ultimately subvert it.
- There would be a problem to the citizens and laws will be proved to be unjust and unfair.

7. Why is it necessary for a Constitution to place limitation on the rulers? Can there be a Constitution that gives no power at all to the citizens?

Ans. It is necessary for a Constitution to place limitations on the rulers because

- Ruler would lead to authoritarian or dictatorship form of government that threatens human rights.
- The government can pass any law which will infringe or violate the basic Fundamental Rights guaranteed by the Constitution that all of us possess as citizens.
- Limitations are fundamental in the sense that the rulers may not trespass them except during national emergency or in the national interest.
- Citizens have also been granted some basic rights or liberties like, Right to Freedom of Speech and Expression, Freedom to form Trade Union and Associations, etc. which cannot be checked by the government except during emergency situations.

No, there cannot be any Constitution that gives no power at all to the citizens because

- The citizens make up the fabric of the state.
- Any authority cannot exist without the citizens. The citizens are the foundation of the Constitution and by virtue of the citizens plight the Indian Constitution is framed.
- The institutions of the state that are meant to serve the citizens would end up denying them their rights in such a scenario.
- In a democratic Constitution like India, the people are the real source of power where public mandate is required to enact the policies by the government.

8. The Japanese Constitution was made when the US occupation army was still in control of Japan after its defeat in the Second World War. The Japanese Constitution could not have any provision that the US Government did not like. Do you see any problem in this way of making the Constitution? In which way was the Indian experience different from this?

Ans. Indian experience was different from the experience of Japan in the following manner

- The problem with making this kind of a Constitution is that it is influenced by external factors or occupations.
- It does not represent the will, goals and aspirations of the citizen of the country. Citizens have little participation in this type of government and institutions that are imposed upon them.
- It also compromises with the sovereignty of the country. Thus, in many ways, it is an enforced Constitution.
- The Indian experience of Constitution making was different as it was based upon ideologies that were influenced by nationalist movements.
- Sovereignty and freedom were the main goals of the Indian nationalist movement that gave way to ideals of equality, fraternity and secularism.
- The framers of the Indian Constitution worked for leading a life of social dignity and respect for all the citizens.
- The Constituent Assembly framed Constitution after a long debates and discussions to provided political, social and legal equalities to the people.
- This is the reason behind the democratic, secular and sovereign character of the Indian Constitution.

9. Rajat asked his teacher this question: " The Constitution is a fifty year old and therefore outdated book. No one took my consent for implementing it. It is written in such tough language that I cannot understand it. Tell me why should I obey this document"? If you were the teacher, how would you answer Rajat? **Competency Based Que**

Ans. If I were the teacher, I would answer Rajat in the following ways

- The Constitution is not an outdated book as it represents universal values, ideals and rights that are relevant to the society in every age.
- The ideals of secularism, equality and fraternity are necessary for the creation of a just society. The democratic form of government provides representation to the collective will of the society.
- The Constitution is also the source of the rights and privileges that are enjoyed by all citizens of the state. It provides immunity against the arbitrary action by the state and makes it accountable for its decisions.
- It provides a stage to the citizens ensuring their participation in election, governance and national development.

- The Constitution has the provisions of amendments to ensure that it keeps up with requirements of the changing times, without compromising on its basic structure.

Thus, the Constitution is a necessary requirement for the smooth and orderly working of institution and maintenance of stability and continuity alongwith changes in the society. It creates conditions in which the ordinary citizens can live their life according to their individual choice. It upholds the Rule of Law, places limits on power and prevent the situation of anarchy.

10. In a discussion on the experience of the working of our Constitution, three speakers took three different positions.

(i) Harbans: The Indian Constitution has succeeded in giving us a framework of democratic government.

(ii) Neha: The Constitution made solemn promises of ensuring liberty, equality and fraternity. Since this has not happened, the Constitution has failed.

(iii) Nazima: The Constitution has not failed us. We have failed the Constitution. Do you agree with any of these positions? If yes, why? If not, what is your own position?

Ans. (i) The position of Harbans is correct. The Constitution has succeeded in creating a framework of democratic government within which people exercise their choice while electing the government. Elections are conducted at all levels of government and institutional arrangements have been largely successful in preventing the subversion of Constitution.

(ii) The position of Neha is not correct. While it is true that the country is yet to entirely achieve the stated goals of liberty, equality and fraternity, it must be also remembered that these goals are not a static but dynamic process since society is always evolving.

The inability to achieve these goals cannot be attributed to the Constitution but rather to the individual shortcomings and weakness of the people who are in position of power and the nature of politics in recent years.

(iii) The position of Nazima is correct. The Constitution has adequate principles for proper governance of the country. The people who are responsible for executing and implementing the principles of the Constitution have failed to do so because of their self-interest and dishonesty.

The tendency to subvert democratic processes for power has led to the state of affairs where elections are rigged, money and muscle power becomes important and political parties are run as family institutions without inner-party democracy.

All this is responsible for the rise in corruption as people who gain positions of power through money want to recover their expenditure.

Exam Pattern Questions

Objective Type Questions

Multiple Choice Questions (MCQs)

1. Which of the following is NOT a function of the Constitution? CBSE Diksha App

(a) It protects our natural rights.
(b) It sets out the rules under which the government is to operate.
(c) It makes laws and implements them.
(d) It constitutes the government.

2. Choose an enabling provision of the Indian Constitution out of the following options. Diksha App

(a) Parliamentary Democracy
(b) Residuary Powers
(c) Written Constitution
(d) Fundamental Rights

3. What specific responsibility does the Indonesian Constitution place on the government?

(a) To increase military spending
(b) To establish and run a national education system
(c) To control natural resources
(d) To enforce strict immigration policies

4. **A successful Constitution was created after a popular national movement in which of the following countries?**
(a) United Kingdom (b) South Africa
(c) China (d) Japan

5. **Given below are two statements:**

Statement I A Constitution expresses the fundamental identity of a people. **Competency Based Que**

Statement II The people as a collective entity come into being only through the basic Constitution.

In the light of above statements, choose the correct answer from the options given below
(a) Both Statement I and Statement II are true.
(b) Both Statement I and Statement II are false.
(c) Statement I is true, but Statement II is false.
(d) Statement I is false, but Statement II is true.

6. **Given below are two statements** **Competency Based Que**

Statement I Constitution of South Africa assigns many responsibilities to the government.

Statement II The government in Indonesia has the power to regulate the judicial system.

In the light of above statements, choose the correct answer from the options given below
(a) Both Statement I and Statement II are true.
(b) Both Statement I and Statement II are false.
(c) Statement I is true, but Statement II is false.
(d) Statement I is false, but Statement II is true.

7. **Which of the following countries does not have a Constitution as a single document?**
(a) United States (b) United Kingdom
(c) India (d) France

8. **How many Constitutions has Nepal had since 1948?**
(a) Three (b) Four (c) Five (d) Six

9. **Which of the following groups in Nepal wanted to abolish the monarchy?**
(a) Those who supported the king
(b) Republican groups
(c) Military leaders (d) Political elites

10. **How many seats were allotted to the provinces under direct British rule?**
(a) 93 seats (b) 292 seats
(c) 500 seats (d) 640 seats

11. **Consider the following statements about the Constituent Assembly.**
I. **The first meeting was held on 9th December, 1946.**
II. **Its composition was based on the Cabinet Mission Plan.**
III. **Its members were directly elected by the people of India.** **Competency Based Que**

Which of the statement(s) is/are correct?
(a) Only I (b) Only II (c) I and II (d) I, II and III

12. **The composition of the Constituent Assembly was based on the proposals of which of the following?**
(a) Wavell Plan (b) Cabinet Mission Plan
(c) Cripps Mission (d) August Offer

13. **The Constitution of India was adopted on ...., and it came into force on ....**
(a) 26th November, 1949, 26th January, 1950
(b) 26th January, 1949, 26th January, 1950
(c) 26th January, 1950, 26th January, 1949
(d) 27th November, 1949, 28th January, 1950

14. **Which group had twenty-eight members in the Constituent Assembly?**
(a) Muslims (b) Scheduled Castes
(c) Sikhs (d) Princely States

15. **The Constitution of India is based on the principles enshrined in the ...., which was moved by Nehru in 1946.**
(a) Cabinet Mission Plan (b) Wavell Plan
(c) August Offer (d) Objective Resolution

16. **The provisions of Directive Principles of State Policy were adopted from which Constitution?**
(a) Irish Constitution (b) French Constitution
(c) United States Constitution (d) British Constitution

17. **Which of the following Constitutional provision of Indian Constitution is borrowed from the British Constitution?**
(a) Judicial Review
(b) Directive Principles of State Policy
(c) Parliamentary form of Government
(d) Charter of Fundamental Rights

18. **Identify the provision of the Indian Constitution which is adapted from the Constitution of Canada.**
Competency Based Que; Diksha App
(a) Rule of Law (b) First Past the Post
(c) Judicial Review (d) Quasi-federal

19. **Which of the following statements is correct about the Constitution?** **Competency Based Que**
(a) The Constitution is a written document about the formation of government and its powers.
(b) Constitution is required only in democratic countries.
(c) The Constitution cannot be amended by the Parliament.
(d) All of the above

20. **Consider the following statements regarding need of a Constitution in a democracy.** **Competency Based Que**
I. **It allows co-ordination between various organs of the government.**
II. **It puts limitations on the powers of government.**

III. It ignores aspirations and goals of a society.
IV. It specifies allocation of powers in a society.
Which of the following statement(s) is/are correct?
(a) Only I (b) I and II (c) I, II and III (d) I, II and IV

21. Arrange the following in chronological order **Competency Based Que**
I. Adoption of Constitution
II. Signatures by members on the Constitution
III. Constitution came into force
IV. Introduction of Objectives Resolution
Choose the correct option
(a) I, IV, III, II (b) IV, I, II, III
(c) IV, I, III, II (d) I, IV, III, II

22. Match the Constitutions in List I correctly with their provisions given in column List II and choose the appropriate code as the correct answer **Competency Based Que**

List I	List II
A. British Constitution	1. The idea of residual power
B. United States Constitution	2. Power of judicial review
C. Canadian Constitution	3. The idea of the rule of law
D. French Constitution	4. Principles of liberty

Codes

	A	B	C	D		A	B	C	D
(a)	2	4	3	1	(b)	3	2	1	4
(c)	2	1	3	4	(d)	4	2	3	1

Assertion-Reason Questions

Direction (Q. Nos. 23-26) In the questions given below, there are two statements marked as Assertion (A) and Reason (R). Read the statements and choose the correct option.

Codes
(a) Both A and R are true and R is the correct explanation of A.
(b) Both A and R are true, but R is not the correct explanation of A.
(c) A is true, but R is false.
(d) A is false, but R is true.

23. **Assertion (A)** Constitution provides the basic rules to prevent the states from having absolute power.
Reason (R) Constitution can give vulnerable people the power to achieve collective good.

24. **Assertion (A)** The Indian Constitution is described as 'a living' document.
Reason (R) It strikes a balance between the possibility to change the provisions and the limits on such changes.

25. **Assertion (A)** A successful Constitution is one that provides everyone in society with a reason to support its rules.
Reason (R) A Constitution that systematically privileged some members at the expense of others would command allegiance.

26. **Assertion (A)** The Constitution designers included a number of particular provisions to protect the interests of Scheduled Castes and Scheduled Tribes, such as legislative seat reservations.
Reason (R) The Constitution makers believed that simply granting the rights to equality would not be enough to overcome the age old injustices suffered by these groups.

Passage Based Questions

27. Read the given passage and answer the following questions.

Constitutions limit the power of government in many ways. The most common way of limiting the power of government is to specify certain Fundamental Rights that all of us possess as citizens and which no government can ever be allowed to violate. The exact content and interpretation of these rights varies from Constitution to Constitution. But most Constitutions will protect a basic cluster of rights. Citizens will be protected from being arrested arbitrarily and for no reason. This is one basic limitation upon the power of government.

(i) Which of the following reflects the role of Constitutions in a democratic society?
(a) Constitutions give governments unlimited power.
(b) Constitutions ensure that citizens have no rights that the government must respect.
(c) Constitutions set limits on government power by protecting Fundamental Rights.
(d) Constitutions allow governments to violate the rights of citizens.

(ii) Why are Constitutions necessary in limiting government power?
(a) Constitutions give governments the ability to ignore citizens' rights.
(b) Constitutions ensure that governments can arrest anyone they choose.
(c) Constitutions protect individuals by outlining rights that the government cannot violate.
(d) Constitutions allow governments to act without legal restrictions.

(iii) Why are Fundamental Rights mentioned in a Constitution important?
(a) They allow the government to become powerful
(b) They ensure citizens obey the government
(c) They protect citizens from government abuse of power
(d) They give the police full control

(iv) What can vary from constitution to Constitution?

(a) The exact content and interpretation of rights
(b) The number of laws made each year
(c) The power of the police
(d) The voting system

28. Read the given passage and answer the following questions.

Most of the older Constitutions limited themselves largely to allocating decision-making power and setting some limits to government power. But many 20th century Constitutions, of which the Indian Constitution is the finest example, also provide an enabling framework for the government to do certain positive things, to express the aspirations and goals of society. The Indian Constitution was particularly innovative in this respect. Societies with deep entrenched inequalities of various kinds, will not only have to set limits on the power of government, they will also have to enable and empower the government to take positive measures to overcome forms of inequality or deprivation.

(i) How did the Indian Constitution innovate compared to older Constitutions?

(a) It only focused on limiting government power.
(b) It provided a framework for the government to express societal aspirations and goals.
(c) It removed the concept of rights from its framework.
(d) It allocated all decision-making power to the government without limitations.

(ii) What role do modern Constitutions play in societies with entrenched inequalities?

(a) They simply set limits on government power without addressing social inequalities.
(b) They enable the government to take actions to overcome inequalities.
(c) They only focus on economic growth, without considering social justice.
(d) They provide no specific framework for government action.

(iii) What did older Constitutions mainly focus on?

(a) Providing an enabling framework for the government
(b) Limiting government power and allocating decision-making power
(c) Creating new laws for society
(d) Removing inequalities in society

(iv) Which constitution is described as the finest example of 20th century Constitution?

(a) The American Constitution (b) The British Constitution
(c) The Indian Constitution (d) The French Constitution

29. Read the given passage and answer the following questions.

The members of the assembly placed a great emphasis on discussion and reasoned argument. They did not simply advance their own interests, but gave principled reasons to other members for their positions. The very act of giving reasons to others makes you move away from simply a narrow consideration of your own interest because you have to give reasons to others to make them go along with your view point. The voluminous debates in the Constituent Assembly, where each clause of the Constitution was subjected to scrutiny and debate, is a tribute to public reason at its best. These debates deserved to be memorialised as one of the most significant chapters in the history of Constitution making.

(i) Why did members of the Constituent Assembly give principled reasons for their positions?

(a) To impose their own views on others
(b) To advance narrow personal interests
(c) To persuade others and build consensus
(d) To avoid conflict and opposition

(ii) Why does the passage describe the debates in the Constituent Assembly as "a tribute to public reason"?

(a) Because they focused on the interests of the elite
(b) Because they involved careful, principled discussions that benefited the public goal
(c) Because they were brief and to the point
(d) Because they only focused on the protection of individual rights

(iii) Discuss why the debates in the Constituent Assembly are considered one of the most significant chapters in the history of Constitution-making.

30. Read the given passage and answer the following questions.

An Assembly as diverse as the Constituent Assembly of India could not have functioned if there was no background consensus on the main principles the Constitution should enshrine. These principles were forged during the long struggle for freedom.

In a way, the Constituent Assembly was giving concrete shape and form to the principles it had inherited from the nationalist movement.

(i) What allowed the diverse members of the Constituent Assembly to function effectively?

(a) Strong political party alignment
(b) Background consensus on key Constitutional principles
(c) The absence of ideological differences
(d) A unified leadership without opposition

(ii) How did the nationalist movement influence the Constituent Assembly's work?

(a) By restricting the assembly's powers
(b) By providing concrete guidelines for decision-making
(c) By creating conflicts among members
(d) By making the assembly ignore the needs of the people

(iii) How did the principles from the nationalist movement influence the Constituent Assembly?

Answers

1. (c) It makes laws and implements them.
2. (d) Fundamental Rights
3. (b) To establish and run a national education system
4. (b) South Africa
5. (a) Both Statement I and Statement II are true.
6. (c) Statement I is true, but Statement II is false.
7. (b) United Kingdom
8. (d) Six
9. (b) Republican groups
10. (b) 292 seats
11. (c) I and II
12. (b) Cabinet Mission Plan
13. (a) 26th November, 1949, 26th January, 1950
14. (b) Scheduled Castes
15. (d) Objective Resolution
16. (a) Irish Constitution
17. (c) Parliamentary form of Government
18. (d) Quasi-federal
19. (a) The Constitution is a written document about the formation of government and its powers.
20. (d) I, II and IV
21. (b) IV, I, II, III
22. (b) 3 2 1 4
23. (b) Both A and R are true, but and R is not the correct explanation of A.
24. (a) Both A and R are true and R is the correct explanation of A.
25. (a) Both A and R are true and R is the correct explanation of A.
26. (a) Both A and R are true and R is the correct explanation of A.
27. (i) (c) Constitutions set limits on government power by protecting Fundamental Rights.
    (ii) (c) Constitutions protect individuals by outlining rights that the government cannot violate.
    (iii) (c) They protect citizens from government abuse of power.
    (iv) (a) The exact content and interpretation of rights
28. (i) (b) It provided a framework for the government to express societal aspirations and goals.
    (ii) (b) They enable the government to take actions to overcome inequalities.
    (iii) (b) Limiting government power and allocating decision-making power
    (iv) (c) The Indian Constitution
29. (i) (c) To persuade others and build consensus
    (ii) (b) Because they involved careful, principled discussions that benefited the public goal
    (iii) The debates in the Constituent Assembly are considered significant because they involved thorough scrutiny of every clause, with each decision being carefully debated and reasoned. This thoughtful and democratic process played a crucial role in shaping the Indian Constitution, reflecting the aspirations of the people and addressing the country's diverse needs.
30. (i) (b) Background consensus on key Constitutional principles
    (ii) (b) By providing concrete guidelines for decision-making
    (iii) The principles from the nationalist movement provided a foundation for the Constituent Assembly's work. These principles, developed through the struggle for freedom, guided the members in creating a Constitution that reflected the values of justice, equality and democracy, ensuring the transition from colonial rule to a sovereign nation.

Subjective Questions

Very Short Answer Type Questions

1. Why do we need a Constitution?

Ans. We need a Constitution because

- Constitution is a set of legal documents according to which a nation is governed.
- Constitution guarantees Fundamental Rights to citizens against any subvertion of power.

2. Constitution of India is based on a vision. Comment. **Competency Based Que**

Ans. When the Constitution was made, the leaders and the people of our country shared a common vision of India. The vision was dignity and freedom of the individuals, social and economic equality, well-being of the people and unity based on national integrity.

Therefore, the Constitution based on this vision has remained an object of respect and authority even after, more than half-a century.

3. 'India is a democratic state'. Explain. **Competency Based Que**

Ans. India is a democratic state means Indian Polity is governed by democratic principles such as

- The people in a democracy like India elect their representatives to form a government and work on behalf of the people periodically.
- That is to say, that, the government is of the people, for the people and by the people.

4. What do you understand by the term Constitution?

Ans. The Constitution of a country is a compact document consisting of the supreme laws of that country which decide the composition, powers and functions of the government as well as the rights and duties of the citizens.

5. How were the members of the Constituent Assembly elected?

Ans. The members of the Constituent Assembly were chosen by indirect election by the members of the Provincial Legislative Assemblies that had been established under the Government of India Act, 1935.

6. The framers of the Indian Constitution wanted it to be 'flexible' as well as 'rigid'. Explain. **Competency Based Que**

Ans. The framers of our Constitution wanted the Constitution to be 'flexible' as well as 'rigid'. Flexible means open to changes and rigid means resistant to changes.

The framers were aware that there may be some faults or mistakes in the Constitution and it could not be totally free of errors.

7. When was the Constituent Assembly established and why?

Ans. The Constituent Assembly was established on 9th December, 1946 along the lines suggested by the Cabinet Mission. The Constituent Assembly was formed for framing the Constitution of Independent India in the aftermath of a long freedom struggle.

8. Mention any two factors ensuring effectiveness of a Constitution.

Ans. The factors ensuring effectiveness of a Constitution are

- Balanced arrangement between the various the institution of government, like the executive, the legislature and the judiciary.
- Government must be democratic and committed to the welfare of the people.

9. How many major committees were formed and who headed the committees?

Ans. There were eight major committees formed for the purpose of framing the Constitution of India. Pandit Nehru, Dr. Ambedkar, Sardar Patel and Dr. Rajendra Prasad were the Chairman of the major committees.

10. Who headed the drafting committee to frame the Constitution of India?

Ans. A Constituent Assembly framed the Constitution of our country. The assembly constituted a drafting committee which consists of seven members and it was headed by Dr. B.R. Ambedkar.

11. What are the main organs or institutions of the Government of India?

Ans. The three main organs or institutions of the Government of India are

- Legislature
- Executive
- Judiciary

Short Answer Type Questions

1. Critically examine the features of the Indian Constitution.

Ans. The features of the Indian Constitution are as follows

- The Constitution is the supreme law of the land according to which the nation is governed.
- It has provisions of Fundamental Rights and Duties for the citizens of India.
- It establishes a Parliamentary form of Government in India.
- There is a clear demarcation of powers between the various institutions of the government (Legislature, Executive and Judiciary) for its smooth functioning.

2. What are some common ways that Constitutions limit the power of government?

Ans. Constitutions limit government power by specifying Fundamental Rights that all citizens possess, such as the right to freedom of speech, conscience and protection from arbitrary arrest.

These rights create a framework for what the government can and cannot do, ensuring that citizens are protected from abuses of power.

3. What kind of society does India aspires to be? What role does the government needs to play?

Ans. India aspires to be a society that is free of caste discrimination, economic inequality and social injustice etc.

This is the aspiration of India, and the government will have to be enabled or empowered to take all the necessary steps to achieve this goal such as

- To ensure that every individual in the society should have all that is necessary for them to lead a life of minimal dignity and self-respect.
- Upholding the essence of the Directive Principles of State Policy to fulfill the aspirations of a society and create conditions for a just society.
- Minimise the inequalities prevailing in the society and at the same time uphold the rule of law.

4. How does the Constitution expresses the fundamental identity of a people.

Ans.
- A Constitution expresses the fundamental identity of people, which means the people as a collective entity come into being only through the basic Constitution.
- By agreeing to certain basic norms and principles, one constitutes one's **political identity**.
- Constitutional norms are the enveloping framework within which one pursues individual aspirations, goals, freedoms and simultaneously sets authoritative constraints that we may not tresspass. So, the Constitution also gives one a **moral identity**.
- Different nations embody different conceptions of the relationship between different regions of a nation and the central government, this relationship constitutes the **national identity** of a country.

5. Write a note on Constituent Assembly.

Ans. The Constituent Assembly was composed along the lines suggested by the committee of British Cabinet known as the Cabinet Mission Plan for framing the Constitution of Independent India in 1946.

The members of the Constituent Assembly represented all religions as well as sections of the society. There were members from Hindu, Muslim and Sikh communities and 28 members from Scheduled Castes including all provinces and Princely States. Even women from all the sections were included.

The members of the assembly were indirectly elected by the members of the Provincial Legislative Assemblies established under the Government of India Act, 1935.

6. The Constitution of India encourages equal respect between communities. Discuss. **Competency Based Que**

Ans. India is the largest liberal democratic country of the world. Since the day it started working, the Indian Constitution has been ecouraging equal regard among all the communities of the country.

This was a very big challenge for the framers of the Indian Constitution to make communities liberal in their approach and foster a sense of equal respect among them under existing social conditions of hierarchy of intense rivalry.

India is a land of multiple cultural communities, it was important to ensure that no one community systematically dominates others.

This made it mandatory for our Constitution to recognise community based rights. One such Fundamental Right is the Right of Religious Communities to establish their own educational institutions to preserve and carry forward their own culture and traditions.

In this way, the Constitution of India encourages equal respect between communities.

7. Why did the Constitution of India came into force on 26th January 1950?

Ans. The Constitution of India came into force on 26th January 1950, because of the fact that 26th January had a great significance in India's struggle for freedom.

At its Lahore Session on December 1929, the Congress had passed a resolution declaring 'Purna Swaraj' as India's goal. It was also decided in the session that 26th January shall be observed all over India as complete Independence day.

In order to keep the memory of the day alive, it was decided to enforce the Constitution on this day. Now this day is celebrated as 'Republic Day' every year.

8. What is public reason in context of the Constitution?

Ans. Public reason refers to a common mode of deliberation that individuals may use for issues of public concern. It involves justifying a particular position by way or reasons that people of different moral or political backgrounds could accept.

In context of the Constitution

- Public reason is a distinctive political idea which mainly involves the laws and other political institutions of our society.

- It is the outcome of the miseries and sufferings of the people faced during the long struggle for freedom.
- Public reason was the common and the vocal platform for debate in framing the provisions of the Constitution in the Constituent Assembly.
- Public reason involves the Fundamental Rights, equality of opportunity, protection of minorities against the majority, socio-economic development of the cross-sections of the society, etc.

9. Explain the significance of the Objectives Resolution. Diksha App

Ans. The Objectives Resolution is significant because it incorporated principles of the nationalist movement to the Constituent Assembly. This resolution encapsulated the aspirations and values behind the Constitution.

On the basis of Objectives Resolution, our Constitution gave institutional expression to fundamental commitments such as equality, liberty, democracy, sovereignty and a cosmopolitan identity.

10. The Constitution of India is 'People's own Constitution'. Discuss. Competency Based Que

Ans. The Constitution of India is people's own Constitution as it has been framed by the Constituent Assembly of India. The Constitution has not been imposed on us, it originates from the people of India and is promulgated in the name of the people.

The Preamble emphasises the ultimate sovereignty of the people. The people are thus, the source of all authority and all power lies with them.

Since, the Constitution is founded on the authority of the people, no state or group of states can destroy it.

11. Why is Indian Constitution bulky? Give reasons.

Ans. The India Constitution is one of the lengthiest Constitution in the world, consisting of 446 articles and 13 schedules and many amendments.

- **Borrowing from various Constitutions** The Indian Constitution was adopted from various Constitutions of different countries because the framers of the Constitution wanted to insure that Indian Constitution should have the best features of each of the Constitution.
- **Diverse population and complex social issues** India is a diverse country with a complex social structure, and our Indian Constitution had addressed all these issues.
- **Federal structure** The distribution of powers between Central and State Government is discussed in detail in the Constitution.
- **Amendments** Our Constitution has been amended many times, according to the needs of the country, which has further added to the length of the Constitution.

Long Answer Type Questions

1. Summarise four functions of the Constitution. Diksha App

Ans. The functions of the Constitution are as follows

(i) To provide a set of basic rules that allow for minimal co-ordination amongst members of a society.

(ii) To specify who has the power to make decisions in a society. It decides how the government will be constituted.

(iii) To set some limits on what a government can impose on its citizens. These limits are fundamental as government may never trespass them.

(iv) To enable the government to fulfill the aspirations of a society and create conditions for a just society.

2. Balanced institutional design of the Indian Constitution makes it an effective Constitution. Validate the statement with the help of appropriate examples. Competency Based Que; Diksha App

Ans. Balanced institutional design of the Indian Constitution makes it an effective Constitution in many ways.

The Indian Constitution horizontally fragments power among different institutions like the Legislature, Executive and the Judiciary and even independent statutory bodies like the Election Commission. This ensures that even if one institution wants to subvert the Constitution, others can check its transgression.

An intelligent system of checks and balance has facilitated the success of the Indian Constitution. A balanced institutional design is also ensured as the Indian Constitution strikes the right balance between certain values, norms and procedures as authoritative and at the same time allows enough flexibility in its operations to adapt to changing needs and circumstances.

Too rigid Constitution is likely to break under the weight of change. A Constitution that is, on the other hand, too flexible, will give no security, predictability or identity to people.

Indian Constitution strikes right balance between preserving core values and adapting them to new circumstances.

Thus, Indian Constitution is described as a living document.

3. **What were the main provisions of the Cabinet Mission Plan?**

Ans. The Constituent Assembly was roughly composed along the lines suggested by the plan proposed by the committee of the British Cabinet, known as the Cabinet Mission Plan.

According to this plan

- Each province and Princely State or group of states were allotted seats proportional to their respective population (i.e. 1 : 1000000).
- As a result, the province were to elect 292 members while the Princely States were allotted 93 seats.
- The seats in each province were distributed among three main communities i.e. Muslims, Sikhs and general in proportion to their respective populations.
- Members of each community in the Provincial Legislative Assembly elected their own representatives by the method of proportional representation with single transferable vote.
- The method of selection in the case of representative of Princely States was to be determined by consultation.

4. **Critically examine the objectives resolution and the provisions of the Constituent Assembly.**

Ans. The Objectives Resolution was introduced by Jawaharlal Nehru in 1946 that laid the foundation for India's Constitution by emphasising sovereignty, justice, equality and liberty. It aimed to establish a republic ensuring Fundamental Rights, a federal structure and international peace. However, it was criticised for being idealistic and lacking specifics on implementation.

The Constituent Assembly was formed to draft the Constitution and comprised of elected representatives from provincial assemblies. Despite challenges like partition and refugee crises, it worked democratically through debates and committees. Leaders, like Dr. B.R. Ambedkar and Nehru played key roles in shaping a secular, inclusive and democratic Constitution.

Critics argue the assembly was not directly elected, dominated by elites and limited representation of marginalised groups. Moreover, concerns also arose over the Central Government's dominance.

Nevertheless, the assembly successfully delivered a progressive Constitution that upheld India's unity, democracy, and diversity, laying the foundation for a modern nation.

5. **The Constitution of India is 'a bag of borrowing'. Discuss.** Competency Based Que

Ans. The Indian Constitution is generally described as 'Borrowed Constitution', because it is drawn extensively from the major Constitution of the world.

The framers of the Constitution were interested in making a fine and workable Constitution which should work efficiently and prove to be a living document. The framers included best features from the various Constitutions to address the issues and needs of the people of the country. The Constitution of India is borrowed from the following

Sources	Provisions Adopted
British Constitution	▪ Parliamentary form of government. ▪ Rule of Law. ▪ Institution of Speaker and his/her role. ▪ First Past the Post.
United States Constitution	▪ Fundamental Rights. ▪ Powers of judicial review and independence of the judiciary.
French Constitution	Principle of liberty, equality and fraternity.
Canadian Constitution	A quasi-federal form of government (a federal system with a strong Central Government). The idea of residual powers.
Irish	Directive Principles of State Policy.

Thus, we can say it is 'a Bag of Borrowing'.

6. **Discuss the special features of the Indian Constitution considered as an important achievements.**

Ans. The special features considered as an achievement of the Indian Constitution are as follows

- Our Constitution emphasises on liberal individualism and is an important achievement because this is done in the backdrop of a society which have different community values or hostile to individual autonomy.
- Our Constitution upholds the principle of social justice without compromising on individual liberties.
- Constitution upholds its commitment to group rights against the background of internal communal disputes.
- Secularism, according to our Constitution means freedom of religion to both individuals and communities and the state has the power to intervene in religiously sanctioned customs which deprive individuals of basic dignity and self respect.

Picture Based Questions

1. Observe the cartoon given below and answer the questions that follow.

(i) What has been depicted in the above cartoon?

(a) Failure of European Constitution
(b) Framing of European Constitution
(c) Election Committee of European Constitution
(d) None of the above

Ans. (a) Failure of European Constitution

(ii) In the above cartoon, who has been refer to a 'feuding father'?

(a) Political leaders of world
(b) Political leaders of Soviet Union
(c) Political leader of European Nations
(d) None of the above

Ans. (c) Political leader of European Nations

(iii) A body of fundamental principles, according to which a state is constituted is known as ....

(a) Convention (b) Constitution
(c) Law (d) Tradition

Ans. (b) Constitution

(iv) Which of these is not a function of the Constitution?

(a) It gives a guarantee of the rights of the citizen.
(b) It marks out different spheres of power for different branches of government.
(c) It ensures that good people come to power.
(d) It gives expression to some shared values.

Ans. (c) It ensures that good people come to power.

2. Observe the cartoon given below and answer the questions that follow.

(i) Can you identify what these different groups stand for?

(ii) Who was conciliating the above situation?

(iii) Who do you think prevailed in this balancing act?

Ans. (i) The cartoon refers to the different religions, cultures, caste and regions having different preferences of two different groups.

(ii) Pandit Jawaharlal Nehru was conciliating the above situation.

(iii) By accepting the demands of both the nationalist group, Nehru balanced the diversity of India as both the songs 'Jana Gana Man' and 'Vande Mataram' were accepted as National Anthem and National Song respectively.

3. Observe the cartoon given below and answer the questions that follow.

(i) Which event is being depicted in the above cartoon?

(a) Writing of the new Iraqi Constitution
(b) Protest against US invasion of Iraq
(c) Beginning of the operation Iraqi freedom
(d) The establishment of a unified Iraqi Government

Ans. (a) Writing of the new Iraqi Constitution

(ii) What do the different ethnic groups in Iraq represent according to the cartoon?

(a) Different political parties
(b) Different religions and beliefs
(c) Their own philosophies, ideologies and interests
(d) Different regional interests only

Ans. (c) Their own philosophies, ideologies and interests

(iii) The primary theme of the cartoon could be ....

(a) the conflict between different ethnic groups.
(b) the co-operation between Iraq's ethnic groups.
(c) the unification of Iraq under a single ideology.
(d) the peaceful coexistence of different religions in Iraq.

Ans. (a) the conflict between different ethnic groups.

(iv) The new Constitution in Iraq was written in the backdrop of ....

(a) the peaceful unification of Iraq
(b) the collapse of Saddam Hussein's regime
(c) the rise of a democratic government in Iraq
(d) the invasion of Kuwait by Iraq

Ans. (b) the collapse of Saddam Hussein's regime

4. Observe the cartoon given below and answer the questions that follow.

(i) What do the cards in the cartoon symbolise?

(a) Weak foundation of the new Iraqi Constitution
(b) The diversity of ethnic groups in Iraq
(c) The negotiation between Iraq's political factions
(d) The role of individual leaders in the Constitution-making process

Ans. (a) Weak foundation of the new Iraqi Constitution

(ii) What is implied about the representation of ethnic groups in the Iraqi Constitution in the cartoon?

(a) The Constitution fully represents all ethnic groups in Iraq.
(b) The Constitution was imposed without representing all the ethnic groups.
(c) Only one ethnic group had the power to write the Constitution.
(d) The ethnic groups worked together to create a unified Constitution.

Ans. (b) The Constitution was imposed without representing all the ethnic groups.

(iii) In the above cartoon, what does the weak foundation of a Constitution imply?

(a) It is built on clear and universally accepted principles.
(b) It is vulnerable to being undone or easily changed.
(c) It has widespread support from all sections of society.
(d) It has a strong legal framework.

Ans. (b) It is vulnerable to being undone or easily changed.

(iv) How does the Indian Constitution differ from the Iraqi Constitution, based on the cartoon?

(a) The Indian Constitution represents only one ethnic group.
(b) The Indian Constitution was written under foreign influence.
(c) The Indian Constitution is representative and has the support of its citizens.
(d) The Indian Constitution was drafted more hastily than the Iraqi Constitution.

Ans. (c) The Indian Constitution is representative and has the support of its citizens.

SELF ASSESSMENT TEST

Objective Type Questions

1. "Principles of Liberty, Equality and Fraternity" is borrowed from which Constitution?
   (a) French Constitution (b) Irish Constitution (c) British Constitution (d) United States Constitution
2. Who were the members of Constituent Assembly?
   (a) Jawaharlal Nehru (b) Sardar Patel (c) Rajendra Prasad (d) All of these
3. Select the incorrect statement.
   (a) The basic structure has been defined in the Constitution.
   (b) As of 2020, the Constitution has been amended 104 times.
   (c) The Constitution of India came into force on 26th January, 1950.
   (d) Constitution of India is a framework for the democratic governance of the society.

Very Short Answer Type Questions

4. How did older Constitutions typically approach the allocation of power?
5. Why is the Indian Constitution considered innovative compared to earliers Constitutions?
6. Give any two reasons for the bulkiness of the Indian Constitution.
7. Is the Constitution of India flexible or rigid? Give reason.
8. When was the Constituent Assembly of India formed and how much time did it take to draft the Constitution?

Short Answer Type Questions

9. The most successful Constitutions were created in the aftermath of the freedom struggle. Explain with examples.
10. India has adopted Parliamentary form of government. Explain.
11. How is the Constitution a living document?
12. Why can some Constitutions be ineffective despite being written down?
13. Describe the influence of various other Constitution in the formation of Indian Constitution.

Long Answer Type Questions

14. Critically examine the objectives of the Indian Constitution.
15. 'The Indian Constitution provides on enabling framework for the government to be certain positive things'. Justify the statement.

02

CHAPTER

Rights in the Indian Constitution

Rights are the conditions of social life without which no human being can develop itself.

▼ **YOUR STUDY GOALS**

2.1 Importance of Fundamental Rights
2.2 Fundamental Rights in the Indian Constitution
2.3 Directive Principles of State Policy (DPSP)
2.4 Fundamental Duties

▼ **YOUR PRACTICE GOAL**

- Objective Type Questions (27 Qs ; MCQs, A-R, Statements, Matching, Passage Based)
- Subjective Questions (13 VSAs, 8 SAs, 5 LAs) 3 Picture Based

2.1 Importance of Fundamental Rights

- A Constitution sets limits on the powers of the government. It ensures a democratic system in which all the citizens enjoy certain **Rights.**
- These rights are guaranteed and protected by the Constitution to all its citizens without any discrimination of caste, creed, colour, sex etc.
- **Part three of the Indian Constitution** lists the **Fundamental Rights** (Article 12-35).
- Fundamental Rights are a set of basic human rights that are guaranteed to the citizens by the Constitution. These rights uphold the equality of all the citizens, the dignity of the individual, the larger public interest and the unity of the nation.
- The Constitution also mentions certain limits on these rights.
- The Fundamental Rights are meant for promoting the ideas of political democracy.
- They prevent the establishment of an **authoritarian**[1] rule in the country.

---

1 **Authoritarian Rule** A political system where power is concentrated in single leader or a small group only.

- They also protect the liberties and freedom of the people in achieving the goals and aspirations of the society against the violation of their rights by the organs of the government.

Bill of Rights

- A democracy must ensure that individuals have certain rights and that the government will always recognise these rights.
- Such a list of rights mentioned and protected by the Constitution itself is called the **'bill of rights'**.
- The bill of rights prohibits the government from acting against the rights of the individuals.
- Its purpose is to protect the citizens' rights against invasion from other individuals as well as public officials. It also ensures a remedy in case there is a violation of these rights.

Bill of Rights in the South African Constitution

- The South African Constitution was inaugurated in December 1996. Its creation and promulgation took place at a time when South Africa faced the threat of a civil war after the dissolution of the apartheid government.
- The South African Constitution says that its "Bill of Rights is a cornerstone of democracy in South Africa".
- It forbids discrimination on the grounds of "race, gender, pregnancy, marital status, ethnic or social origin, colour, age, disability, religion, conscience, belief, culture, language and birth". It grants perhaps the most extensive range of rights to its citizens.
- A special Constitutional Court enforces the rights enshrined in the Constitution.

Some of the Rights included in the Constitution of South Africa

- Right to Dignity
- Right to fair labour practices
- Right to adequate housing
- Children's rights
- Right to Information
- Right of cultural, religious and linguistic communities
- Right to Privacy
- Right to healthy environment and right to protection of environment
- Right to health care, food, water and social security
- Right to basic and higher education

2.2 Fundamental Rights in the Indian Constitution

- The Fundamental Rights in the Indian Constitution is the result of our long struggle for freedom. The leaders of the freedom movement had realised the importance of certain basic rights in the lives of the people. They demanded that the British rulers should respect the rights of the people.
- For instance, the demand for a **Bill of Rights** was presented by the **Motilal Nehru Committee** in 1928.
- Hence, there were no two opinions on the inclusion and protection of rights in the Indian Constitution after India became independent.
- The Constitution listed the rights that would be specially protected and called them 'Fundamental Rights'. These rights are so important that the Constitution has separately listed them and made special provisions for their protection. The Constitution itself ensures that they are not violated by the government.
- Fundamental Rights are different from the ordinary legal rights available to the citizens.
- The judiciary has the powers and responsibility to protect the Fundamental Rights of the citizens from violations by actions of the government. It can declare the executive and legislative actions as illegal if they violate or unreasonably restrict the Fundamental Rights of the people.
- However, Fundamental Rights are not absolute or unlimited rights. The government can put reasonable restrictions on the exercise of these rights.

Difference between Fundamental Rights and Ordinary Rights

Fundamental Rights	Ordinary Rights
Protected and guaranteed by the Constitution of the country.	Protected and enforced by ordinary law.
Can only be changed by amending the Constitution.	Can be changed by the legislature by ordinary process of law making.

The various Fundamental Rights in the Indian Constitution are as follows

Right to Equality

- The Right to Equality **prohibits discrimination** on the grounds of religion, caste, race, sex and place of birth. It provides its citizens with equal access to public places like shops, hotels, places of entertainment, wells, bathing ghats and places of worship. It also prohibits any discrimination in public employment on any of the above mentioned basis.
- The right to equality is very important because our society did not practise equal access to all in the past.
- Untouchability is one of the most harsh forms of inequality that has existed in Indian society. It has now been abolished under the right to equality.
- This right also provides that the state shall not confer any title on a person except those who excel in the military or academic fields.
- Thus, Right to Equality strives to make India a true democracy by ensuring a sense of equality of dignity and status among all its citizens.

Equality in Preamble

- The Preamble of the Indian Constitution mentions two things about equality i.e. **equality of status** and **equality of opportunity**.
- Equality of opportunity means that all sections of the society enjoy equal opportunities. To achieve this right, the Constitution clarifies that the government can implement special schemes and measures for improving the conditions of certain sections of the society such as children, women, socially and educationally backward classes.
- Therefore, **Article 16(4)** of the Constitution clarifies that a policy like reservation is not be seen as a violation of Right to Equality.

- **Article 16(4) Nothing in this article shall prevent the state from making any provision for the reservation of appointments or posts in favour of any backward class of citizens which, in the opinion of the state, is not adequately represented in the services under the state.**

Right to Freedom

Equality and freedom are the two rights that are most essential to a democracy to uphold the aspirations and goals of the society. Both the rights are interlinked. Liberty means freedom of thought, expression and action. However, freedom must be practised in a manner that does not threaten the freedom of others and should not endanger the law and order situation.

Right to Life and Personal Liberty

- Right to life and personal liberty is the essence of the foundation of all the other rights because there is no right without life and that is why it is the foremost right among the rights to freedom.
- For instance, under this right no citizen can be arrested without being told the reason. If a person is arrested, then he/she has the right to defend himself by a lawyer of his choice.

- It is also necessary that the police will take the person to the nearest Magistrate within 24 hours. The Magistrate who is not a part of the police will decide whether the arrest is justified or not.
- Various judgement of the Supreme Court have expanded the scope to this right. They have included the **right to live with human dignity** and to be free from exploitation. The Supreme Court has also included the **right to shelter and livelihood** because no person can live without the means of livelihood.

- **Article 21** Protection of life and personal liberty. No person shall be deprived of his life or personal liberty except according to procedure established by law.

Preventive Detention

- Normally, an individual is arrested after he/she has reportedly committed some crime. However, there are, exceptions to this rule. Sometimes, an individual can be arrested simply because he/she is suspected of engaging in an illegal activity and detained for a period of time without following normal procedure. This is known as **Preventive Detention**. It means that if the government feels that a person can be a threat to the law and order or to the peace and security of the nation, it can detain or arrest that person.
- Preventive detention can only be extended for three months, after which the case is reviewed by an advisory board. While it seems like a useful tool for the government against anti-social individuals but it has often been misused by the government.

Other Freedoms

- Under the Right to Freedom, there are some other rights as well, however, these rights are not absolute. Restrictions can be imposed by the government to these rights.
- For instance, the **freedom of speech and expression** and **freedom to assemble in public** are subject to restrictions imposed by the government. However, such powers can be misused easily by the administration.
- For example, a genuine protest by the people against an act or policy of the government may be denied permission. Some of the members of the Constituent Assembly too had expressed their dissatisfaction about such restrictions on rights of the people.

Rights of Accused

The Constitution of India has also ensured that a person who is accused of various offences also get sufficient protection. No person is guilty unless the court has found that person guilty of an offence. It is therefore necessary that the accused person should get adequate opportunity to defend himself/herself.

To ensure a **fair trial** in the court, the Constitution provides the following three rights

(i) No person would be punished for the same offence more than once.
(ii) No law shall declare any action as illegal from a backdate.
(iii) No person shall be asked to give evidence against himself/herself.

Quick Test 1

1. Define Fundamental Rights.
2. When was the South African Constitution inaugurated?
3. What are the two things that the Preamble mentions about equality?
4. Which Article of the Constitution allows the government to make reservations for the backward classes?

Right Against Exploitation

- In our country, there are a number of people who are under-privileged and deprived.
- They are often subjected to **exploitation**[2] by their fellow human beings. These are some form of exploitation such as **begar**[3] human trafficking, child labour and bonded labour.
- These are all various forms of exploitation that are strictly prohibited under the Constitution. These acts have been declared as a crime and are punishable by law.
- The Constitution also forbids (prohibits) employment of children below 14 years of age in dangerous jobs like factories and mines. The **Right against Exploitation** has become more meaningful after the Constitution has declared child labour as illegal and made the **Right to Education** as a Fundamental Rights for children.

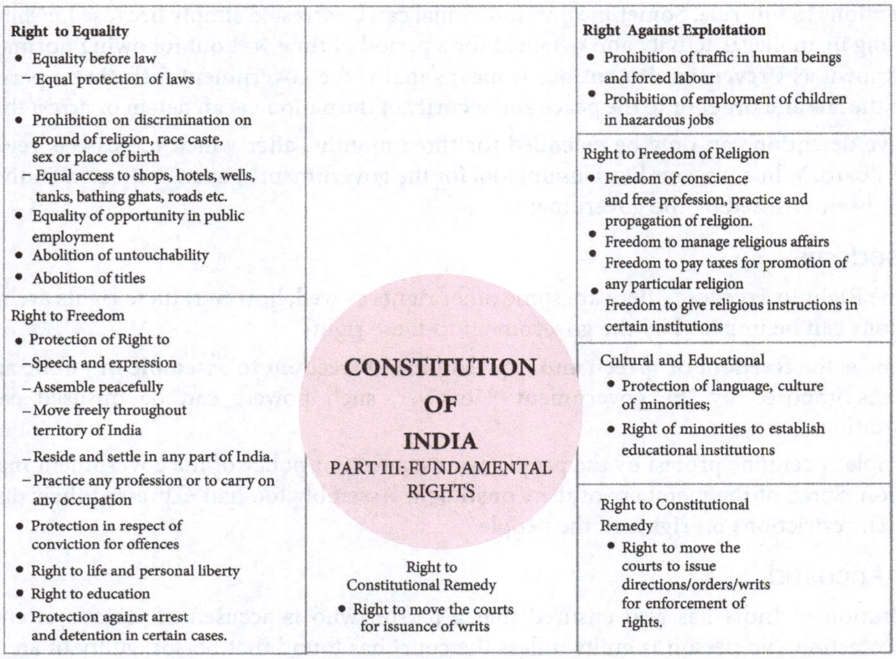

▲ *Constitution of India*

Right to Freedom of Religion

According to our Constitution everyone has the right to practice the religion of their choice. This liberty is regarded as a defining feature of democracy. A core principle of democracy is to allow its citizens to practice the religion of one's choice.

Freedom of Faith and Worship

- The Constitution of India has provided every individual in the country the right to practice, **profess**[4], follow and propagate freely any religion.
- Freedom of religion also includes **freedom of conscience**. This means that a person may or may not choose to follow any religion. However, freedom of religion is subject to certain limitations.
- The government can impose restrictions on the practice of freedom of religion in order to protect public order, morality and health. Therefore, the freedom of religion is not an unlimited right. The government can interfere in religious matters to remove social evils.

2 **Exploitation** It is the act of doing injustice to others in any form.
3 **Begar** It is a type of forced labour done without any payment for the work done.
4 **Profess** It means to make an open declaration.

- Such restrictions cannot be opposed in the name of interference in the Right to Freedom of Religion. For instance, the government has in the past taken measures to ban practices like sati, bigamy or human sacrifice.
- The Constitution has also guaranteed the right to propagate one's religion. This includes persuading people to convert from one religion to another. However, the Constitution does not allow forcible conversions.
- It only gives people the right to spread information about a particular religion.

Equality of All Religions

- As India is a country where diverse religions and culture accommodate together, it is necessary for the government to extend equal treatment to all religions.
- The government will not favour any particular religion as **India does not have any official religion.**
- The Right to Equality also guarantees non-discrimination on grounds of religion by the government in giving employment.
- The institution run by the state will not preach any religion or give religious education nor will they favour persons of any religion.
- Therefore, the objective of these provisions is to sustain and nurture the **principles of secularism.**

Cultural and Educational Rights

- Indian society is diverse, with many different groups, some of which are smaller in number.
- Our Constitution values diversity and protects the right of minorities to maintain their culture, language and traditions. Minorities, whether based on religion, language or culture, have the right to preserve and promote their identity.
- Minorities can also establish their own schools and the government cannot discriminate against them when providing financial support.

Right to Constitutional Remedies

- The Constitution of India contains a list of Fundamental Rights. It is not merely a written list of Foundamental Rights but it also provides a way in which these rights could be realised in practice. It defends against any attack on these rights through the **Right to Constitutional Remedies.**
- According to Dr. B. R. Ambedkar, the Right to Constitutional Remedies[5] is the **'Heart and soul'** of the Constitution.
- It gives every individual the right to approach to the High Court or the Supreme Court in case there is a violation of their Fundamental Rights. The Supreme Court and High Courts issue orders and give directives to the government for the enforcement of rights through special order known as **writs.**

The various writs provided by the Indian Constitution are as follows

- **Habeas Corpus** A writ of habeas corpus means that the court orders that the arrested person should be presented before it. It can also order to set free an arrested person if the manner or grounds of arrest are not lawful or satisfactory.
- **Mandamus** This writ is issued by the court when it finds that a public official is unable or failed to perform his official duties, thereby violating the right of an individual.
- **Prohibition** This writ is issued by a higher court (Supreme Court and High Court) to a lower court in order to prevent the case going beyond its jurisdiction.
- **Quo-Warranto** If the court finds that a person is holding office but is not entitled to hold that office, the court issues the writ of Quo-Warranto to restrict the person from acting as an office holder.

5 **Constitutional Remedies** It refers to the legal mechanisms provided by the Constitution of a country to safeguard and enforce the Fundamental Rights of individuals.

- **Certiorari** It is issued by higher court to lower court or authority to transfer a pending case to the higher authority or court.
  - Many other mechanisms have been created for the protection of rights apart from judiciary like, National Commission for Minorities, National Commission for Women, National Commission for Scheduled Castes and Scheduled Tribes and National Human Rights Commission.
  - These institutions protect the Rights of Minorities, Women, Scheduled Castes and Scheduled Tribes and other kinds of human rights. The **National Human Rights Commission** (NHRC) has been established by law to protect fundamental and other kinds of rights.

National Human Rights Commission (NHRC)

The real test of the rights given by any Constitution is in their actual implementation. The poor, illiterate and the deprived sections of the society must be able to exercise their rights. In this background, the government has established an institution, the National Human Rights Commission, in 1993.

- The National Human Rights Commission (NHRC) is composed of a former Chief Justice of the Supreme Court of India, a former judge of the Supreme Court, a former Chief Justice of a High Court and two other members who have knowledge and practical experience in matters relating to human rights.
- The commission's duties **include investigating human rights violations,** visiting jails to assess conditions, and promoting research on human rights.
- It receives thousands of complaints each year, covering issues like custodial deaths, police abuse, disappearances and violence against women.
- Notably, the commission has intervened in cases like the disappearances in Punjab and the Gujarat riots.
- However, the commission does not have the power to prosecute. It can only make recommendations to the government or suggest court to take actions based on its investigations.

2.3 Directive Principles of State Policy (DPSP)

- The Directive Principles of State Policy (DPSP) is one of the novel features of the Indian Constitution. The DPSP denotes the ideals such as **'equality'** and **'well being'** of all citizens. The state should keep in mind these ideals while formulating policies and enacting laws.
- The Fundamental Rights along with Directive Principles of State Policy constitute the **soul of the Constitution**. These are incorporated to achieve the aspirations and goals of the society for the all round development of the nation and the individuals. The Directive Principles of State Policy are non-justiciable or not-enforceable by court in case of their violation.

  The Directive Principles of State Policy lists mainly three goals/objectives, which are
  - The goals and objectives that a society should adopt.
  - Certain rights that individuals should enjoy apart from Fundamental Rights.
  - Policies that the government should adopt to fulfill their duties.
- According to the vision of the Constitution makers, the government from time to time has tried to give effect to some Directive Principles of State Policy by passing certain bills and making laws like, zamindari abolition bills, nationalised banks, enacted factory laws, fixed minimum wages, promotion of small and cottage industries and provisions for reservation for the upliftment of Scheduled Castes and Scheduled Tribes.
- Beside the above policies, certain Directive Principles, like Right to Education, formation of Panchayati Raj Institutions all over the country and mid-day meal scheme, etc, were also given effect.

  The goals, policies and non-justiciable rights of Directive Principles are mentioned below in the table

Directive Principles of State Policy

Goals	Policies	Non-justiciable Rights
Welfare of the people; social, economic and political justice.	Uniform Civil Code	Adequate livelihood.
Raising the standard of living; equitable distribution of resources.	Prohibition of consumption of alcoholic liquor.	Equal pay for equal work for men and women.
Promotion of international peace.	Promotion of cottage industries.	Right against economic exploitation.
	Prevention of slaughter of useful cattle.	Right to work.
	Promotion of village panchayat.	Early childhood care and education to children below the age of six years.

Relationship between Fundamental Rights and Directive Principles

- The Fundamental Rights and Directive Principles of State Policy share a complementary relationship with each other.
- The Fundamental Rights restrains (control) the government from doing certain things. While the Directive Principle of State Policy urges the government to do certain things.
- Fundamental Rights mainly protect the rights of individuals, while Directive Principles ensure the well-being of the society as a whole.
- However, when the government intends to implement Directive Principles of State Policy, it can come in conflict with the Fundamental Rights of the citizen.
    - For instance, when the government wanted to pass laws to abolish the zamindari system, it was opposed on the ground that they violated the right to property.
- However, the government amended the Constitution to prioritise societal needs over individual interests by implementing the Directive Principles of State Policy.

Brief Background : Change in the Status of Right of Property

- The relationship between the Fundamental Rights and DPSP resulted in a long legal battle and a feud between the executive and judiciary. The government claimed that rights can be abridged for giving effect to the Directive Principles. While as, the court was of the opinion that Fundamental Rights are so important and sacred that they cannot be limited, not even for implementing the DPSP.
- Consequently, in 1978, the 44th amendment to the Constitution **removed the right to property** from the list of Fundamental Rights. It was converted into a simple legal right under **Article 300 A.** This resulted in another complicated debate related to the amendment of the Constitution. The government was of the opinion that Parliament can amend any part of the Constitution. However, the court said that the Parliament cannot make an amendment that violated the Fundamental Rights.
- This controversy was settled by an important decision of the Supreme Court in the famous **Kesavananda Bharati case, in 1973.** In this case, the court said that there are certain basic features of the Constitution which cannot be changed by the Parliament.

2.4 Fundamental Duties

- The 42nd **Constitutional Amendment** passed in 1976 inserted a list of **ten Fundamental Duties** of citizens.
- However, Fundamental Duties[6] are not enforceable. As citizens, we must abide by the Constitution, to defend our country, promote harmony among all citizens and protect our environment. The Indian Constitution does not make the enjoyment of rights dependent or conditional upon fulfilment of duties. By the insertion of Fundamental Duties the status of Fundamental Rights has not changed.
- The 11th **Fundamental Duty** was added by the 86th **Amendment in 2002**, which stated to provide opportunities for education to children between 6-14 years of age and duty as parents to ensure that such opportunities are being awarded to their child.

  The ten fundamental duties are as follows
  - To oblige with the Indian Constitution and respect the National Anthem and Flag.
  - To cherish and follow the nobel ideas that inspired the national struggle for freedom.
  - To protect the integrity, sovereignty and unity of India.
  - To defend the country and perform national services if and when the country requires.
  - To promote the spirit of harmony and brotherhood amongst all the people of India and renounce any practices that are derogatory to women.
  - To cherish and preserve the rich national heritage of our composite culture.
  - To protect and improve the natural environment including lakes, wildlife, rivers, etc.
  - To develop scientific temper, humanism and spirit of inquiry.
  - To safeguard all public property.
  - To strive towards excellence in all genres of individual and collective activities.

Quick Test 2

1. What is the age for employment of children according to the Constitution?
2. What do you mean by Habeas Corpus?
3. Who can issue writs for the enforcement of Fundamental Rights?
4. Name any two institutions created for the protection of rights.
5. Right to property comes under which article?

6 Duties It is a set of obligations towards society or nation that complements rights.

Mind Map

RIGHTS IN THE INDIAN CONSTITUTION

1 Importance of Fundamental Rights

- Limits government power to ensure democracy.
- Protects all citizens from discrimination.
- Fundamental Rights are meant for promoting the ideas of political democracy.
- Prevents authoritarian rule in the country.

2 Bill of Rights

- It ensures government respects individual rights.
- It protects citizens from abuse by others or officials.
- For example, South Africa Bill of Rights.

3 Bill of Rights in the South African Constitution

Some of the Rights included in the Constitution of South Africa

- Right to Dignity
- Right to Privacy
- Right to fair labour practices
- Right to healthy environment and right to protection of environment
- Right to adequate housing
- Right to health care, food, water, social security and children's rights
- Right to basic and higher education
- Right of cultural, religious and linguistic communities
- Right to Information

4 Fundamental Rights in the Indian Constitution

Rights to Equality

- Equality before law and equal protection of laws
- Prohibition on discrimination on certain grounds
- Equal access to public place
- Equality of opportunity in employment
- Abolition of untouchability
- Abolition of titles

Rights to Freedom

- Right to speech and expression
- Assemble peacefully
- Move freely throughout the territory of India
- Reside and settle in any part of India
- Right to life and liberty
- Right to education
- Protection against arrest and detention in certain cases

Right Against Exploitation

- Prohibition of forced labour.
- Prohibition of employment of children in hazardous jobs.

Right to Freedom of Religion

- Freedom to pay taxes for promotion of any particular religion.
- Freedom to manage religion affairs.

Cultural and Educational Rights

- Protection of language, culture of minorities.
- Right of minorities to establish educational institutions.

Right to Constitutional Remedy

- Right to move the courts for issuance of writs.

5 Directive Principles of State Policy

Aims

- Welfare and justice for all.
- Equal pay, education and prevention of exploitation.
- Balances societal welfare and individual rights.

6 Fundamental Duties

- Introduced by the 42nd Amendment (1976).

Duties includes

- Protecting environment and culture.
- Promoting harmony and unity.
- Ensuring education for children.
- To safeguard all public property.
- Develop scientific temper humanism and spirit of inquiry.

7 National Human Rights Commission

- The government has established in 1993 an institution, the National Human Rights Commission.
- Independent organisations have been working as watchdogs against the violations of rights.
- It is composed of a former Chief Justice of the Supreme Court of India, a former judge of the Supreme Court, a former Chief Justice of a High Court and two other members.

NCERT Folder

Intext Questions

1. Compare the Fundamental Rights in the Indian Constitution with the Bill of Rights in the South African Constitution. Make a list of rights that are

(i) Common to both the Constitutions

(ii) Available in South Africa but not in India

(iii) Clearly granted in South Africa but implicit in the Indian Constitution. (Pg 30)

Ans. (i) **Common Rights** Rights such as dignity, equality, non-discrimination, privacy, education and children's rights are recognised in both Constitutions.

(ii) **Unique to South Africa** Rights such as fair labor practices, the right to a healthy environment, the right to adequate housing and the right to information are more explicitly stated in South Africa's Bill of Rights.

(iii) **Implicit in India, clearly granted in South Africa** Rights related to dignity, labor practices, environmental protection, and privacy are implicit in the Indian Constitution, while they are more directly stated in the South African Constitution.

2. Do you think that the following situations demand restrictions on the right to freedom? Give reasons to support your answer. (Pg 37)

(i) People have assembled for a peace march after communal riots in the city.

(ii) Dalits are denied entry in a temple. A march is being organised to forcibly enter the temple.

(iii) Hundreds of Adivasis blocked the road demanding that the land taken away from them for an industry be returned.

(iv) A caste panchayat is meeting to decide the punishment to a young couple for marrying outside their caste.

Ans. (i) No, this situation does not necessarily demand restrictions on the right to freedom of assembly, as long as the march is peaceful and does not disturb public order. The right to peaceful assembly is guaranteed under Article 19(1)(b) of the Indian Constitution. However, if the assembly turns violent or poses a threat to public safety, the government may impose restrictions.

(ii) Yes, this situation could demand restrictions on the Right to Freedom of movement and assembly. While the demand for social justice and the removal of caste-based discrimination is legitimate and forcibly entering a temple (or any private or religious space) could lead to violence, unrest and law and order problems.

The right to freedom of movement and assembly is subject to reasonable restrictions under Article 19(2), particularly if the assembly could incite violence or disturb public peace.

(iii) This situation demands careful consideration. While the Adivasis have the right to protest , blocking roads and causing disruption to traffic or essential services could violate the public interest and disrupt the functioning of society. In such a case, the government might impose restrictions on the protest if it threatens public order, safety or disrupts essential services.

(iv) Yes, this situation demands restrictions on the right to assembly. The actions of a caste panchayat, if they involve threats of violence or coercion, or if they promote caste-based discrimination, violate Fundamental Rights, particularly the right to equality (Article 14) and the right to live with dignity (Article 21).

Exercise

1. Write true or false against each of these statements.

(i) A Bill of Rights lays down the rights enjoyed by the people of a country.

(ii) A Bill of Rights protects the liberties of an individual.

(iii) Every country of the world has a Bill of Rights.

(iv) The Constitution guarantees remedy against violation of rights.

Ans. (i) True (ii) True (iii) False (iv) True

2. Which of the following is the best description of Fundamental Rights?

(i) All the rights an individual should have.

(ii) All the rights given to citizens by law.

(iii) The rights given and protected by the Constitution.

(iv) The rights given by the Constitution that cannot ever be restricted.

Ans. (iii) The rights given and protected by the Constitution.

3. Read the following situations. Which Fundamental Right is being used or violated in each case and how?

(i) Overweight male cabin crew are allowed to get promotion in the national airlines but their women colleagues who gain weight are penalised.

(ii) **A director makes a documentary film that criticises the policies of the government.**

(iii) **People displaced by a big dam take out a rally demanding rehabilitation.**

(iv) **Andhra society runs Telugu medium schools outside Andhra Pradesh.**

Ans. (i) The right being violated is the Right to Equality of opportunity in employment.

(ii) The right being used is the Right to Freedom of speech and expression.

(iii) The right being used is the freedom of expression and freedom to assemble peacefully.

(iv) The right being used is the cultural right to represent and protect one's own language and culture.

4. Which of the following is the correct interpretation of the Cultural and Educational Rights?

(i) **Only children belonging to the minority group that has opened educational institution can study there.**

(ii) **Government schools must ensure that children of minority group will be introduced to their belief and culture.**

(iii) **Linguistic and religious minorities can open schools for their children and keep it reserved for them.**

(iv) **Linguistic and religious minorities can demand that their children must not study in any educational institution except those managed by their own community.**

Ans. (iii) Linguistic and religious minorities can open schools for their children and keep it reserved for them. This statement is correct for the interpretation of the Cultural and Educational Rights.

5. Which of the following is a violation of Fundamental Rights and why?

(i) **Not paying minimum wages.**

(ii) **Banning of book.**

(iii) **Banning of loudspeakers after 9 pm.**

(iv) **Making a speech.**

Ans. (i) Not paying minimum wages is a violation of a Fundamental Rights of an individual because this violation is included in the Right against Exploitation followed by the other violations like beggar or forced labour, not paying minimum wages, bonded labour child labour, etc. This kind of violation is a crime and punishable by law.

6. An activist working among the poor says that the poor don't need Fundamental Rights what they need are Directive Principles to be made legally binding. Do you agree with this? Give your reasons.

Ans. Every individual in the world needs both their Fundamental Rights as well as the Directive Principles to support their rights. However, from the view of the activist, **I do not agree** with this statement because

- Fundamental Rights are the basis of the Constitution and hence cannot be denied to any section of the society, whether the rich or the poor.
- While implementation of Directive Principles is required for improving the condition of the poor, Fundamental Rights are universal as they ensure dignity to every citizen and form the basis for equality among people.
- Only by ensuring the basic Fundamental Rights such as food, shelter, clothing under Right to Life and Personal Liberty can the larger Directive Principles be given effect.
- Certain rights such as the Right to Constitutional Remedies are important for the protection of the poor and weak sections of the society from the arbitrary action of the state.

7. Several reports show that caste groups previously associated with scavenging are forced to continue in this job. Those in positions of authority refuse to give them any other job. Their children are discouraged from pursuing education. Which of their Fundamental Rights are being violated in this instance?

Ans. In this instance, the following rights are violated

- Right against Exploitation is being violated as forced labour is one of the prohibitions in this article.
- Right to Education is being violated by discouraging the children from pursuing education.
- Right to practise any profession is violated, as they are refused to do any other job by the authorities.
- Right to Equality is also being violated as it prohibits discrimination on grounds of caste and provides for equality of opportunity in public employment.

8. A petition by a human rights group drew attention of the court to the condition of starvation and hunger in the country. Over five crore tonnes of food grains was stored in the godowns of the Food Corporation of India. Research shows that a large number of ration cardholders do not know about the quantity of food grains they can purchase from fair price shops. It requested the court to order the government to improve its public distribution system.

(i) **Which different rights does this case involve? How are these rights interlinked?**

(ii) **Should these right form part of the right to life?**

Ans. (i) The case involves different rights as follows

(a) Right to Speech and Expression and the Right to Constitutional Remedy are used by the human rights group to inform the court about the prevailing condition of the hunger and starvation.

Thus, requesting the court to order the government to improve the public distribution system.

(b) The Right to Life of people is also involved as right to life includes everything necessary to support life i.e., food, water, shelter, etc. These rights are interlinked as freedom of speech provides the basis for the Right to Constitutional Remedies.

(ii) Yes, these rights should form part of the right to life, as they are necessary for the sustenance of life and people.

9. I feel that many of these Fundamental Rights have been framed from the point of view of a police constable… you will find that very minimum rights have been conceded and are almost invariably followed by a proviso. Almost every article is followed by a proviso which takes away the right almost completely,. ... What should be our conception of Fundamental Rights? ..... We want to incorporate every one of those rights which our people want to get.

Read the statement by Somnath Lahiri in the Constituent Assembly quoted above.

Do you agree with him? If yes, give instances to prove it. If not, give arguments against his position.

Ans. Yes, I agree with Somnath Lahiri's statement that minimum rights have conceded are almost invariably followed by a provision and have been framed from a police constable point of view. This is visible in certain provisions that are invoked to place restrictions on judgments right seen as

- The provision of preventive detention contradicts the Right to Life and Personal Liberty and has often been misused by the government.
- There are several other rights that are restricted by the government. For example, the provision of restriction over assembly of five or more people in certain areas can be misused by the administration.

10. Which of the Fundamental Rights is in your opinion the most important right? Summarise its provision and give arguments to show why it is most important.

Ans. The Right to Constitutional Remedies is the most important right guaranteed by the Constitution, as the provisions of this right includes the right to move to courts for issuance of writs in violation of any of the Fundamental Rights.

- The Right to Constitutional Remedies provides a legal solution within the framework of the Constitution, to the violation of Fundamental Rights and it also checks the state power.
- It also safeguards the other Fundamental Rights, ensures realisation of other rights as well as provide a defence for them.
- According to Dr. Ambedkar, this right is the 'Heart and Soul' of the Constitution'.

Exam Pattern Questions

Objective Type Questions

Multiple Choice Questions (MCQs)

1. Which committee demanded a Bill of Rights in 1928?
(a) The Simon Commission
(b) The Motilal Nehru Committee
(c) The Salt March Committee
(d) The Khilafat Committee

2. Which part of the South African Constitution is described as the "cornerstone of democracy"?
(a) The Preamble
(b) The Bill of Rights
(c) The Fundamental Duties
(d) The Judicial Review

3. The Fundamental Rights are meant for promoting the ideas of which of the following?
(a) Monarchy
(b) Political democracy
(c) Anarchy
(d) Military dictatorship

4. How long can a person be detained under preventive detention without a trial?
(a) One month (b) Three months
(c) Six months (d) One year

5. According to our Constitution, everyone enjoys the right to follow the religion of his or her choice. This freedom is considered as a hallmark of democracy. Democracy has always incorporated the freedom to follow the religion of one's choice as one of its basic principles. Competency Based Que

Name the Fundamental Rights mentioned above.
(a) Cultural and Educational Rights
(b) Right to Freedom of Religion
(c) Right to Equality
(d) Right to Constitutional Remedies

6. "It means that the court orders that the arrested person should be presented before it. It can also order to set free an arrested person if the manner or grounds of arrest are not lawful or satisfactory".
Name the writ mentioned above. Competency Based Que
(a) Mandamus (b) Prohibition
(c) Habeas Corpus (d) Quo-Warranto

7. Some guidelines were incorporated in the Constitution but they were not made legally enforceable: this means that if a government did not implement a particular guideline, we cannot go to the court asking the court to instruct the government to implement that policy. Thus, these guidelines are 'non-justiciable'.
The Rights mentioned above are known as ....
Competency Based Que
(a) Fundamental Rights
(b) Fundamental Duties
(c) Directive Principles of State Policy
(d) None of the above

8. How many Fundamental Duties of citizens were listed in the 42nd amendment?
(a) 5 (b) 10
(c) 15 (d) 20

9. Figure out the incorrect statement.
Competency Based Que; Diksha App
(a) Fundamental Rights are non- justiciable whereas Directive Principles are justiciable.
(b) Fundamental Rights ensure political equality whereas Directive Principles ensure social and economic equality.
(c) Fundamental Rights are in Chapter III whereas Directive Principles are in Chapter IV of the Constitution.
(d) Fundamental Rights restrain the government from doing certain things whereas Directive Principles exhort the government to do certain things.

10. .... mainly protect the rights of individuals while Directive Principles ensure the well-being of the entire society.
(a) Fundamental Rights (b) Fundamental Duties
(c) Preamble (d) None of these

11. Which of the statement is correct?
(a) Fundamental Duties are justiciable in nature.
(b) Directive Principles of State Policy are justiciable in nature.
(c) Fundamental Rights are justiciable in nature.
(d) All of the above

12. The Right to property is a ....
(a) Economic Right (b) Fundamental Right
(c) Moral Right (d) Legal Right

13. In which of the following cases, the court said that basic features of the Constitution cannot be altered by Parliament. **Diksha App**
(a) Shah Bano case (b) Kesavananda Bharati case
(c) Minerva Mills case (d) Vishakha guidelines

14. .... enforce limitations on the functioning of the government and ensure democratic governance of the country.
(a) Freedom (b) Duties (c) Rights (d) Liberty

15. Given below are two statements

Statement I The Jawaharlal Nehru committee had demanded a bill of rights as far back as in 1929.

Statement II Fundamental Rights are protected and guaranteed by the Constitution of the country.

In the light of above statements, choose the correct answer from the options given below
(a) Both Statement I and Statement II are true.
(b) Both Statement I and Statement II are false.
(c) Statement I is true, but Statement II is false.
(d) Statement I is false, but Statement II is true.

16. Given below are two statements

Statement I The practice of untouchability has been abolished under the Right to Equality.

Statement II Article 20 of the Constitution explicitly clarifies that a policy like reservation will not be seen as a violation of the Right to Equality.

In the light of above statements, choose the correct answer from the options given below
(a) Both Statement I and Statement II are true.
(b) Both Statement I and Statement II are false.
(c) Statement I is true, but Statement II is false.
(d) Statement I is false, but Statement II is true.

17. Identify and write the incorrect pair
(a) Article 17- Personal life and liberty
(b) Article 16- Equality of opportunity
(c) Article 25- Freedom of conscience
(d) Article 32- Right to Constitutional Remedies

18. Consider the following statements.
I. Fundamental Rights are granted and protected by the Constitution.
II. Only Supreme Court has the power to use writs for the enforcement of Fundamental Rights.
III. Right to property has been removed from the list of Fundamental Rights.

Which of the following statement(s) is/are correct?
(a) Only I (b) Only II (c) I and III (d) II and III

19. Arrange the following in chronological order
I. Insertion of Fundamental Duties
II. 44th amendment act
III. Inauguration of South African Constitution
IV. Establishment of NHRC

Choose the correct option
(a) I, II, IV, III (b) IV, I, II, III
(c) IV, I, III, II (d) I, IV, III, II

20. Match the writs in List I correctly with their correct description given in List II and choose the appropriate code as the correct answer

List I		List II	
A.	Certiorari	1.	A writ issued to transfer the pending case.
B.	Mandamus	2.	A writ issued to prevent a lower court from hearing a case beyond its jurisdiction.
C.	Prohibition	3.	A writ issued when a person is holding an office without being legally entitled to it.
D.	Quo Warranto	4.	A writ issued to compel a public official to perform their legal duties.

Codes

	A	B	C	D		A	B	C	D
(a)	1	4	2	3	(b)	3	2	1	4
(c)	2	1	4	3	(d)	4	2	3	1

Assertion-Reason Questions

Direction (Q. Nos.21-25) In the questions given below, there are two statements marked as Assertion (A) and Reason (R). Read the statements and choose the correct option.

Codes
(a) Both A and R are true and R is the correct explanation of A.
(b) Both A and R are true, but R is not the correct explanation of A.
(c) A is true, but R is false.
(d) A is false, but R is true.

21. Assertion (A) A democracy must ensure that individuals have certain rights and that the government will always recognise these rights.

Reason (R) The government can violate the rights of individuals unless there is a system in place to protect them.

22. Assertion (A) Article 25 stipulates that all persons have the right to follow any religious belief and to propagate it.

Reason (R) The state cannot regulate or restrict the economic, financial, political or other secular activities associated with religious practices.

23. Assertion (A) Dr. B.R. Ambedkar called the Right to Constitutional Remedies right as the "Heart and Soul of the Constitution".

Reason (R) This right empowers citizens to approach the Supreme Court or High Courts to restore any of their Fundamental Rights in case of violation.

24. Assertion (A) The Indian Constitution clearly states the Fundamental Duties of citizens.

Reason (R) The Fundamental Rights are also granted by the Indian Constitution to the citizens of India.

25. Assertion (A) The Right to Property was removed from the list of Fundamental Rights.

Reason (R) The Right to Property stood in the way of land reform scheme.

Passage Based Questions

26. Read the given passage and the following questions.

Independent organisations like the People's Union for Civil Liberties (PUCL) or People's Union for Democratic Rights (PUDR) have been working as watchdogs against the violations of rights. In this background, the government has established in 1993 an institution, the National Human Rights Commission. The National Human Rights Commission (NHRC) is composed of a former chief justice of the Supreme Court of India, a former judge of the Supreme Court, a former chief justice of a High Court and two other members who have knowledge and practical experience in matters relating to human rights. The Commission's functions include inquiry at its own initiative or on a petition presented to it by a victim into complaint of violation of human rights; visit to jails to study the condition of the inmates; undertaking and promoting research in the field of human rights, etc.

(i) What is the role of organisations like the People's Union for Civil Liberties (PUCL) and People's Union for Democratic Rights (PUDR)?

(a) To draft new laws for human rights protection.
(b) To act as intermediaries between the government and citizens.
(c) To monitor and act as watchdogs against violations of human rights.
(d) To provide financial support to the government.

(ii) Which of the following functions is most likely to be carried out by the National Human Rights Commission (NHRC)?

(a) Organising political rallies.
(b) Conducting investigations into human rights violations based on complaints.
(c) Providing financial support to businesses.
(d) Formulating laws related to human rights.

(iii) Who among the following can be the Chairperson of the National Human Rights Commission (NHRC)?

(a) A sitting judge of the Supreme Court
(b) A former Chief Justice of the Supreme Court
(c) A Member of Parliament
(d) A Chief Minister of any state

(iv) How many members, apart from the Chairperson, are there in the NHRC?

(a) Two (b) Three
(c) Four (d) Five

27. Read the given passage and the following questions.

The South African Constitution was inaugurated in December 1996. Its creation and promulgation took place at a time when South Africa still faced the threat of a civil war after the dis-solution of the Apartheid government. The South African Constitution says that its "Bill of Rights is a cornerstone of democracy in South Africa". It forbids discrimination on the grounds of "race, gender, pregnancy, marital status, ethnic or social origin, colour, age, disability, religion, conscience, belief, culture, language and birth". It grants perhaps the most extensive range of rights to the citizens. A special Constitutional Court enforces the rights enshrined in the Constitution.

(i) Why was the South African Constitution inaugurated in December 1996?

(a) It was established to protect the political rights of citizens in South Africa.
(b) It was created to address the threat of civil war.
(c) It aimed to provide a legal framework for a new political party.
(d) It was created to increase economic development in South Africa.

(ii) What can be inferred about the stance of the South African Constitution on equality?

(a) The Constitution promotes inequality in the treatment of citizens based on their background.
(b) The Constitution aims to ensure equality and prevent discrimination on several grounds, such as race, gender, and age.
(c) The Constitution focuses solely on economic equality.
(d) The Constitution allows for limited discrimination in cases of national security.

(iii) What is the significance of the "Bill of Rights" in the South African Constitution?

Answers

1. (b) The Motilal Nehru Committee
2. (b) The Bill of Rights
3. (b) Political Democracy.
4. (b) Three months
5. (b) Right to Freedom of Religion
6. (c) Habeas Corpus
7. (c) Directive Principles of State Policy
8. (b) 10
9. (a) Fundamental Rights are non- justiciable whereas Directive Principles are justiciable.
10. (a) Fundamental Rights
11. (c) Fundamental Rights are justiciable in nature.
12. (d) Legal right
13. (b) Kesavananda Bharti case
14. (c) Rights
15. (d) Statement I is false, but Statement II is true.
16. (c) Statement I is true, but Statement II is false.
17. (a) Article 17- Personal life and liberty
18. (c) I and III
19. (a) I, II, IV, III
20. (a) 1 4 2 3
21. (a) Both A and R are true and R is the correct explanation of A.
22. (c) A is true, but R is false.
23. (a) Both A and R are true and R is the correct explanation of A.
24. (b) Both A and R are true, but R is not the correct explanation of A.
25. (a) Both A and R are true and R is the correct explanation of A.
26. (i) (c) To monitor and act as watchdogs against violations of human rights.
    (ii) (b) Conducting investigations into human rights violations based on complaints.
    (iii) (b) A former Chief Justice of the Supreme Court
    (iv) (b) Three
27. (i) (b) It was created to address the threat of civil war.
    (ii) (b) The Constitution aims to ensure equality and prevent discrimination on several grounds, such as race, gender and age.
    (iii) The "Bill of Rights" in the South African Constitution is a cornerstone of the country's democracy, serving as a guarantee for the protection of a broad range of Fundamental Rights for all citizens. It ensures that every person, regardless of race, gender, or other characteristics, is entitled to equal rights and freedoms. The Bill of Rights plays a crucial role in the transformation of South Africa post-apartheid, laying the foundation for a just and inclusive society.

Subjective Questions

Very Short Answer Type Questions

1. Mention two discriminations present in the society?

Ans. The two discriminations present in the society are

(i) Inequality of opportunity among various sections of the society.

(ii) Inequality towards women in the pay scale.

2. State the difference between Fundamental Rights and Ordinary Rights.

Ans. Fundamental Rights are different from Ordinary Rights in many ways such as

- Fundamental Rights are guaranteed and enforced by the Constitution, but Ordinary Rights are provided and protected by Ordinary Laws.
- Ordinary Rights can be changed by the legislature without amending the Constitution, while the Fundamental Rights can only be changed by amending the Constitution.

3. Which country's Constitution has given the most extensive rights in the world?

Ans. Constitution of South Africa has given the most extensive rights in the world.

4. What is Preventive Detention?

Ans. Preventive detention is the practice of detaining someone before a trial or conviction to prevent them from committing crimes. It's a Constitutional approach that's intended to keep the community safe by preventing individuals from committing crimes.

Preventive detention can also involve detaining a convicted criminal who has served their sentence but is considered too dangerous to release.

5. Why the Right to Freedom of Religion is an important right?

Ans. The Right to Freedom of Religion is an important right because

- It is the basic principle of the Constitution provided according to the diverse nature of our country.
- It gives the citizens the right to manage their own religion affairs.

6. Mention the Fundamental Rights which makes India a secular state.

Ans. **Right to Equality (Article 14-18)** Prohibits discrimination based on religion, race, caste, sex, or place of birth and abolishes untouchability and any discrimination on religious grounds.

Right to Freedom of Religion (Article 25-28) Guarantees freedom of conscience and free practice of religion.

Cultural and Educational Rights (Article 29-30) Protects the rights of minorities to conserve their language, script and culture. It allows minority religious communities to establish and administer educational institutions and prevents discrimination in state-funded educational institutions based on religious background.

7. How does Right to Constitutional Remedies work?

Ans. Constitutional remedy allows citizens to directly approach the Supreme Court or High Court if their Fundamental Rights are violated, seeking legal protection and justice through writs like habeas corpus, mandamus or prohibition.

8. 'The courts can issue writs'. Define.

Ans. The Supreme Court and High Court issue orders and give directives to the government and other public officials for the enforcement of rights through special order known as writ.

9. Name the writs issued against the lower courts.

Ans. The writs issued against the lower courts are

- **Prohibition** This writ is issued by the High Court or by the Supreme Court to the lower court in order to prevent the case going beyond its jurisdiction.
- **Certiorari** Issued by High Court to lower court to transfer a pending case.

10. Mention the various writs of the Supreme Court.

Ans. The various writs of the Supreme Court are

- Habeas corpus
- Mandamus
- Prohibition
- Certiorari
- Quo-warranto

11. What do you understand by the term 'non- justiciable'?

Ans. The term 'non-justiciable' means that a person cannot approach the court for implementation of the directives of the Constitution.

12. What is the aim of Directive Principles of State Policy?

Ans. The main aim of Directive Principles of State Policy is to create social and economic conditions for the citizens to achieve their aspirations and goals and lead a good life.

13. What do the Directive Principles of State Policy contain?

Ans. The Directive Principles of State Policy contains the following

- The goals and objectives, the society should adopt.
- Certain rights that individuals should enjoy apart from Fundamental Rights.
- Policies that the government should adopt in discharge of their duties.

Short Answer Type Questions

1. Indian democracy faces the challenge of harmonising two essentially contradictory political concepts such as equality before law and social justice. Assess the effectiveness of the Right to Equality in the light of the above statement. **Diksha App**

Ans. Equality before Law and Equality of Opportunity are two important components of Right to Equality and also mentioned in the preamble.

- In the Indian Constitution the Right to Equality provides for equal access to public places and places of worship. There can not be any discrimination in this access on the grounds of religion, race, cast, sex or place or birth.
- This also prohibits any discrimination in public employment on the above mentioned basis. Right to Equality is important as our society did not practice equal access to all in the past.
- The practice of untouchability has been abolished under the Right to Equality. This right also provides that the state shall confer no titles on a person except for military or academic achievement.
- Thus Right to Equality strives to make India a true democracy by ensuring equality of dignity and status among all its citizens.
- Equality of opportunity means that all sections of the society enjoy equal opportunities. Therefore the Constitution clarifies that the government can implement special schemes and measures such as reservation in jobs and in admissions to improve the conditions of certain sections of society: children, women and socially and educationally backward classes.
- Article 16(4) of the Constitution clearly states that a policy like reservation will not be seen as a violation of Right to Equality.

- This is protective discrimination and affirmative action to ensure justice, equality of all citizens before Law and Equality of Opportunity.

2. Discuss how does the Constitution of India ensures that persons accused of various offences get sufficient protection?

Ans. The Indian Constitution ensures that persons accused of various offences would also get sufficient protection. It is important that a person accused of any crime should get adequate opportunity to defend himself/herself. To ensure a fair trial in courts, the Indian Constitution has provided three rights

- No person would be punished for the same offence more than once,
- No law shall declare any action as illegal from a backdate, and
- No person shall be asked to give evidence against himself or herself.

3. What are the Constitutional Provisions given to safeguard the cultural rights of the society?

Ans. India is country where people of different or diverse religions and culture resides and accommodate. Our Constitution believes in the strength of the diversity and manifested various Constitutional provisions to safeguard the cultural rights of the society, which are as follows

- It has made the right to maintain the culture of the minorities fundamental and also justiciable.
- The minority status not only includes religion but also linguistic and cultural minorities in the provisions.
- It has provided the communities with the right to conserve and develop their own languages, script and culture.
- All minorities, religious or linguistic can set up their own educational institutions to preserve and develop their culture.
- The government cannot discriminate in granting aid to these educational institutions on any basis.
- These are provisions which served as the cornerstone in upholding the principles of democracy in the Constitution of India.

4. "Supreme Court is the protector of Fundamental Rights". Support the statement with any three arguments. **Competency Based Que**

Ans. The Constitution has given the title of a protector to the Supreme Court and made the institution a watchdog of the Fundamental Rights. It is said so because of the following reasons

- Supreme Court of India is the most powerful court all over the country guaranteed by the Constitution.
- In case of violation of any of the Fundamental Right, the aggrieved person can approach the Supreme Court in first instance.
- The Constitution has given the power of judicial review to the Supreme Court to check the legality of the amendment made to the Fundamental Rights.

5. Infer the significance of the theory of basic structure of the Constitution in evolution of the Indian Constitution with reference to conflict between implementation of Directive Principles and Fundamental Rights. **Diksha App**

Ans. At times when the government intends to implement Directive Principles, it can come in conflict with the Fundamental Rights. For example, when the government sought to pass laws to abolish the zamindari system , these measures were opposed on the ground that they violated the Right to Property.

The government amended the Constitution to give effect to the Directive Principles of State Policy as societal needs are greater than individual interests. This led to conflict between the executive and judiciary. The government claimed that rights can be abridged for giving effect to Directive Principles. On the other hand the court held the view that Fundamental Rights are so important that they cannot be limited even for the purpose of implementing Directive Principles.

The government said that parliament can amend any part of the Constitution. The court said that parliament cannot make an amendment that violated Fundamental Rights.

In Kesavananda Bharati case the court said that there are certain basic features of the Constitution which cannot be amended by Parliament. The theory of basic structure is itself an example of a living and evolving Constitution as there is no mention of this theory in the Constitution. It has emerged from judicial interpretation.

Thus, the judiciary and its interpretation have practically amended the Constitution without a formal amendment.

6. What is the relation between Fundamental Rights and Directive Principles of State Policy?

Ans. The Fundamental Rights and Directive Principles shares a complementary relationship with each other, as the Fundamental Rights restrain the government from doing certain thing, while the Directive Principles of State Policy urge the government to do certain things.

Secondly, Fundamental Rights mainly protect the rights of individuals in the society, while Directive Principles ensures the well-being of the society as a whole. However, the government can come into conflict with the judiciary for the Fundamental Rights violation, when the government intends to implement the Directive Principles.

7. Examine some efforts made by the government to give effect to the Directive Principles.

Ans. The government from time to time has tried to give effect to the Directive Principles of State Policy in following ways

- It passed several zamindari abolition bills, nationalised banks, enacted numerous laws like factory laws etc.
- It formulated policy of fixed minimum wages, promoted cottage and small scale industry and provision for reservation for the Scheduled Caste and Scheduled Tribes were made.
- It enacted rights like Right to Education, formation of Panchayati Raj Institutions all over the country and the mid-day meal scheme, etc.

8. State the difference between 'Justiciable' and 'Non-Justiciable' in context of the Constitution.

Ans. The difference between justiciable and non-justiciable rights are

- Fundamental Rights are justiciable, while Directive Principles of States Policy are non-justiciable.
- Fundamental Rights are justiciable, so it is legally enforceable by the court, while the Directive Principles are non-justiciable in nature, so they are not legally enforceable by the court for their violation.
- Fundamental Rights are justiciable and incorporated in part-III of the Constitution, while the fundamental duties are non-justiciable and incorporated in part-IV(A) of the Constitution.
- In case of violation of the Fundamental Rights, the court can compel the government to implement justiciable part but the court cannot compel the government to implement the non-justiciable part that is the Directive Principles of State Policy.

Long Answer Type Questions

1. Highlight the salient features of the Fundamental Rights?

Ans. The salient features of the Fundamental Rights are

- The Fundamental Rights are very detailed and comprehensive. Fundamental Rights forms part-III of the Constitution of India.
- Fundamental Rights are justiciable in nature. It meany if these rights are violated, the citizens can approach the court for their enforcement.
- Fundamental Rights have been given to every citizen of India irrespective of caste, creed, religion, sex or place of birth.
- They are limited and restrictions can be imposed on their enjoyment by the Constitution and can be suspended during emergency.
- Fundamental Rights can only be changed by amending the Constitution.
- Fundamental Rights set limits on the power of the government and upholds the principles of democracy.

2. Right to Freedom is a cluster of several rights. Explain.

Competency Based Que

Ans. Right to Freedom is one of the most focal Fundamental Rights which has upheld the principles of democracy in India by giving explicit meaning to the aspirations and goals of the society for a welfare state and at the same time ensuring secularism in India.

The Right to Freedom guarantees various freedoms or rights to the citizens of India which are as follows

- **Freedom of Speech and Expression** Every citizen of India enjoys the Right to Freedom of speech and expressions of his/her ideas and views freely either orally or in written form.
- **Freedom to Assemble Peacefully** The citizens have the right to assemble to express their ideas and to understand others views but only peacefully and without arms.
- **Freedom to Form Associations** The citizens have the right to form unions and associations to safeguard their rights and interest. Such a right is very essential for the sake of securing justice and equal opportunities.
- **Freedom to Practice any Profession or Occupations** Every citizen of the country has right to choose one's professions as per his/her choice. Further, he/she also his/her the right to change his/her profession according to will and circumstances.
- **Freedom to Move Freely within the Territory of India** Citizens of the country have the right to move freely within the territory of India with subject to certain reasonable restrictions in the interest of public order and for safeguarding the interest of any scheduled tribe.
- **Freedom to reside and settle in Any Part of India** Citizens of the country have the right to reside in any part of the country with subject to certain restrictions of public order and for protecting the Rights of Scheduled Tribes.

3. The Supreme Court and the High Court can issue orders and give directions to the government for the enforcement of Fundamental Rights. Support the statement.

Competency Based Que

Ans. The Supreme Court and the High Courts can issue orders and give directives to the government for the enforcement of Fundamental Rights. They can issue various spicial orders known as writs.

- **Habeas Corpus** It is an order of the court to present the arrested or detained person before the court to examine the cause and legality of arrest. The court would free the arrested person, if the arrest is found illegal.

- **Mandamus** This writ is issued by the court when it finds that a public official is unable or failed to perform his official duties, thereby violating the right of an individual.
- **Prohibition** This right is issued by higher court (Supreme Court and High Court) to lower court to prevent the latter from exceeding its jurisdiction or capacity which it does not possess.
- **Quo-Warranto** If the court finds that a person is holding office but is not entitled to hold that office, the court issues the writ of Quo-Warranto to restrict the person from acting as an office holder.
- **Certiorari** It is issued by higher court to lower court to transfer the pending case to the higher authority or court.

4. 'Right to Constitutional Remedies is the hallmark of democracy'. Justify the statement. **Competency Based Que**

Ans. Ariticle 32 of the Indian Constitution provides for Constitutional Remedies against the violation of Fundamental Rights. As we know that the Fundamental Rights are the of highest importance to the individuals, as they are the basic conditions for the fullest development of one's personality.

That is why Dr. B.R. Ambedkar stated that the Right to Constitutional Remedies is the 'Heart and Soul' of the India Constitution.

This right is the bullwork of the Fundamental Rights, guaranteed by the Constitution because as per the provisions of this article, the citizens have the rights to move directly to the Supreme Court in violation of any of the Fundamental Rights. The Supreme Court in case of violation or transgression of Fundamental Rights issue directives to the government for the implementation or the rights.

Hence, Supreme Court act as the 'Protector and Guarantor' of the Fundamental Rights.

Right to Constitutional Remedies is itself a Fundamental Right. It provides a legal solution within the framework of the Constitution and a check on state power. It also safeguards the other Fundamental Rights and ensures the realisation of other rights as well as provides a defence.

Hence, Right to Constitutional Remedies is the hallmark of democracy.

5. State the difference between the Fundamental Rights and Directive Principles.

Ans. The Fundamental Rights and Directive Principles are distinct entities in an integrated system which focus on the liberly of individuals in a welfare state.

The difference between them are

- The Fundamental Rights are concerned directly to each and every individual, whereas the Directive Principles are directly concerned to the state in formulating policies and enacting laws to achieve the goal of a welfare state.
- Fundamental Rights constitutes limitations on the power of government, while the Directive Principles are the instrument of instruction to the government.
- Fundamental Rights are justiciable, means it can be enforced by the court in case of their violation, whereas the Directive Principles are non-justiciable and cannot be enforced by the court.
- Fundamental Rights are suspended during emergency, whereas the Directive Principles are not suspended during emergency.
- Fundamental Rights are concerned with the overall development of an individual, whereas the Directive Principles are concerned with the overall development of the society, to create a society by the state where everyone enjoys social and economic justice.
- The Directive Principles are required to be implemented by the legislation, while the Fundamental Rights are already enshrined in the Constitution.

Picture Based Questions

1. Observe the picture given below and answer the questions that follow.

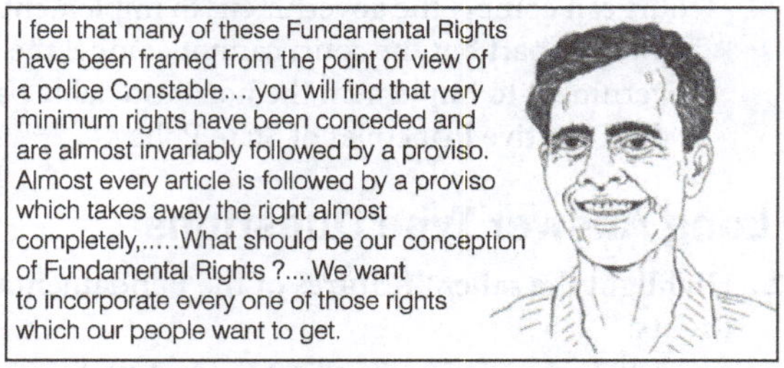

(i) Whose words is being referred to here?
(ii) What should be our conception of Fundamental Rights? When does the Fundamental Rights get suspended?
(iii) Do you agree with the statement? Give reason to support your answer.

Ans. (i) The words of Somnath Lahiri is being referred here.

(ii) The conception of Fundamental Rights should be the words mentioned in the preamble of our Constitution which is the essense and bedrock of the Constitution. The Fundamental Rights should give each and evey right which the citizens want for fulfillment of their aspirations and goals.

The Fundamental Rights are suspended during National emergency.

(iii) Yes, I agree with the statement because this is visible in certain provisions that are invoked to place restrictions on Fundamental Rights such as.

- The provision of preventive detention contradicts the Right to Life and Personal Liberty and has often been misused by the government.
- The provision of restriction over assembly of five or more people in certain areas can be misused by the government.

2. Study the cartoon given below and answer the question that follow.

(i) Which Fundamental right has been violated in above picture?

(a) Right to Equality
(b) Right against Exploitation
(c) Right to Constitutional Remedy
(d) Right to Freedom

Ans. (b) Right against Exploitation

(ii) What are the various forms of exploitation in our country?

(a) Forced labour (b) Human slavery
(c) Buying and selling human beings
(d) All of the above

Ans. (d) All of the above

(iii) The Constitution forbids employment of children below age of .... in dangerous jobs like factories and mines.

(a) 14 years (b) 18 years
(c) 15 years (d) Below 10 years

Ans. (a) 14 years

(iv) Which of the following right/rights does Child Labour violate?

I. Right to Constitutional Remedies
II. Right to Education
III. Cultural and Educational Right
IV. Right against Exploitation

Options

(a) I only (b) II and III (c) II and IV (d) IV only

Ans. (c) II and IV

3. Study the picture given below and answer the questions that follow

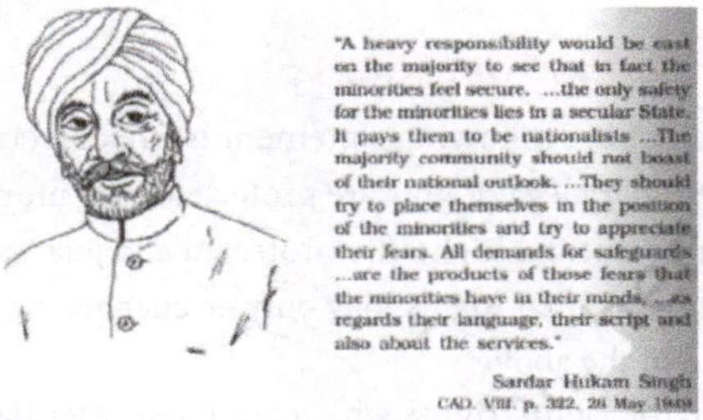

(i) What is the significance of a secular state for minorities, as suggested in the image?

(a) It makes it easier for the majority to dominate.
(b) It ensures that minorities have a safe and equal place in society.
(c) It limits the rights of minorities.
(d) It eliminates all fears regarding religion or culture for minorities.

Ans. (b) It ensures that minorities have a safe and equal place in society.

(ii) How should the majority community approach the demands of the minorities, according to the image?

(a) By disregarding their concerns as unfounded.
(b) By asserting their cultural superiority.
(c) By limiting the rights of minorities to avoid conflict
(d) By acknowledging and appreciating the fears of the minorities regarding language, script and services.

Ans. (d) By acknowledging and appreciating the fears of the minorities regarding language, script and services.

(iii) What should the majority community avoid in terms of their national outlook?

(a) They should avoid any discussion on cultural differences.
(b) They should not boast of their national outlook, as it may alienate minorities.
(c) They should focus only on their own national identity.
(d) They should assert their dominant position in the state.

Ans. (b) They should not boast of their national outlook, as it may alienate minorities.

(iv) What underlying fear do minorities have?

(a) Fear of economic inequality.
(b) Fear of political dominance.
(c) Fear of losing their cultural identity, including language, script and access to public services.
(d) Fear of losing their rights as citizens.

Ans. (c) Fear of losing their cultural identity, including language, script and access to public services.

SELF ASSESSMENT TEST

Objective Type Questions

1. Which of the following statement is/are correct?
   (a) Ordinary legal Rights are protected and enforced by ordinary law.
   (b) Fundamental Rights are protected and guaranteed by the Constitution of the country.
   (c) Fundamental Rights may only be changed by amending the Constitution itself.
   (d) All of the above
2. Name the rights/rights which are most essential to a democracy to uphold the aspirations and goals of the society.
   (a) Right to Equality (b) Right to Freedom (c) Both (a) and (b) (d) Neither (a) nor (b)

Very Short Answer Type Questions

3. What do you understand by "Bill of Rights"?
4. Give any two characteristics of Fundamental Rights given in the Indian Constitution.
5. Discuss how are Fundamental Rights different from other rights.
6. When was the South African Constitution inaugurated?
7. Which Fundamental Right states that reservation will not be seen as a violation of Right to Equality?
8. What is the 'writ of Habeas Corpus'?

Short Answer Type Questions

9. Why is Right to Freedom of Religion is considered as a hallmark of democracy? Give reasons.
10. Various judgements of Supreme Court have expanded the scope of Right to Life and Personal Liberty. Justify the statement.
11. List three rights provided by the Constitution to ensure a fair trial in courts.
12. Write a note on National Human Rights Commission.
13. Elucidate Right to Property in context of conflict between Fundamental Rights and Directive Principles of state policy.

Long Answer Type Questions

14. Freedom of Religion is not an unlimited right. Express your opinion.
15. Explain the provision of 'preventive detention' under Right to freedom. What are some of the rights of an accused given by the Indian Constitution?
16. Describe the various writs which can be issued to guarantee the rights to the people.

Competency Based Que

03
CHAPTER

An election is a formal decision-making process through which the citizens of a country chooses an individual to hold public office.

Election and Representation

▼ **YOUR STUDY GOALS**

3.1 Elections and Democracy
3.2 Election System in India
3.3 Free and Fair Elections
3.4 Electoral Reforms

▼ **YOUR PRACTICE GOAL**

- Objective Type Questions (39 Qs ; MCQs, A-R, Statements, Matching, Passage Based)
- Subjective Questions (12 VSAs, 9 SAs, 5 LAs, 3 Picture Based)

There are different rules and systems for conducting elections. The outcome of the elections depend upon the rules we have adopted. Further, we also need some machinery to conduct the election in an impartial manner. Therefore the elections uphold the principles of democracy in a state and are the most visible symbol of a democratic process.

3.1 Elections and Democracy

In a country with a vast population like India, it is not possible for all its citizens to take direct part in making every decision. Therefore, **representatives** are elected by the people.

Direct Democracy

- A **direct** democracy[1] is one where the citizens directly participate in the day to day decision-making process and in the running of the government.

  For example: Ancient city-states in Greece were an example of direct democracy.
- However, the direct democracy system cannot be practised when a decision has to be taken by lakhs and crores of people.

1 Democracy It is a system of government where the people hold the power to make decisions and choose their leader through elections.

Indirect Democracy

- In an indirect democracy, people do not take part in the decisions of the government directly. Rather, they participate indirectly through their elected representatives.
- The method followed to choose these representatives is referred to as an **election**. The representatives then make the key decisions that govern the country.
- Therefore, **'rule by the people'** in a democracy usually means, **'rule by people's representatives'**.
- In an indirect democracy, citizens have a limited role in the decision-making and running the administration. They are not actively involved in the policy-making process.
- The mechanism by which people elect their representatives becomes extremely essential as all the critical decisions are made by the elected representatives.
- Not all elections are democratic. Many countries that are not democratic also hold elections. In fact, non-democratic rulers often want to appear democratic for which they organise elections in a way that does not challenge their power.

3.2 Election System in India

- The Constitution of India lays down the system of conducting elections, authorities and rules about do's and don'ts in the election process and various other guidelines.
- In a democratic election, people vote and their preference decides the result of the contest. However, there can be different ways in which people make their choice and their preferences can be counted.

Following are the different systems of elections

First Past the Post System (FPTP)

- In the FPTP system, whoever secures the highest number of votes than all other candidates in that constituency[2] is declared **elected.**
- The winning candidate need not secure a majority of the votes.
- The candidate who is ahead of the others and crosses the winning post first, wins the election. The method of FPTP is also called the **Plurality System.**
- India is divided into a total of 543 constituencies in Lak Sabha elections and each constituency elects one representative.

Proportional Representation (PR) System

- The PR system is the second type of election system. When the votes are counted, each party is allotted the share of seats in the Parliament in proportion to its share of votes.
- Each party fills its quota of seats with its nominees from a preference list declared before elections. This is called the **Proportional Representation System.**

  In the Proportional Representation system, there could be two variations. These are

  - In some countries, the entire country is treated as **one constituency** and seats are allotted to each party according to its share of votes in the national election. For example, Israel and Netherlands.
  - The other method is when the country is divided into **several multi-member constituencies** and each party prepares a list of candidates for each constituency. For example, Argentina and Portugal.
- Depending on how many people must be elected from each constituency, every party produces a list of candidates.
- In both of these cases, voters express their choice for a **political party** rather than a specific candidate.
- The seats in a constituency are distributed on the basis of votes polled by a party.

2 **Constituency** It is an area or seat fixed for a particular election (like Lok Sabha and Vidhan Sabha).

- As a result, representatives of a constituency belong to multiple political parties.

Proportional Representation In Israel

- Elections in Israel to the legislature (knesset) take place in every four years.
- Israel follows the proportional representation system, which allows smaller parties with very small support base to get representation in the legislature.

Comparison of FPTP and PR System of Election

FPTP System	PR System
The country is divided into small geographical units called constituencies or districts.	Large geographical areas are demarcated as constituencies. The entire country may be a single constituency.
Every constituency elects one representative.	More than one representative may be elected from one constituency.
Voter votes for a candidate.	Voter votes for the party.
A party may get more seats than votes in the legislature.	Every party gets seats in the legislature in proportion to the percentage of votes that it gets.
Candidate who wins the election may not get majority (50%+1) votes.	Candidate who wins the elections gets majority of votes.
Examples are UK and India	Examples are Israel and Netherland.

Proportional Representation System in India

- India has adopted the PR system on a limited scale for **indirect elections.**
- The Constitution prescribes a complex variation of the PR system for the election of the President, Vice-President and election to the Rajya Sabha and Vidhan Parishads. It is called **Single Transferable Vote System** (STV).
- In this system, to declare a winner, a candidate must secure a minimum quota of votes, which is determined by a formula given below

$$\left[\left(\frac{\text{Total votes polled}}{\text{Total number of candidates to be elected } +1}\right)+1\right]$$

- For example, if 4 Rajya Sabha members have to be elected by the 200 MLAs in Rajasthan, the winner would require (200/4 + 1 = 40 + 1) i.e., 41 votes.
- The votes are counted on the basis of first preference votes secured by each candidate, of which the candidate has secured the first preference votes.
- If the required number of candidates fail to fulfill the quota, the candidate who secured the lowest votes of first preference is eliminated. Then his/her votes are transferred to those who are mentioned as second preference on the ballot papers.
- This process continues till the required number of candidates are declared elected.
- However, the PR system is a little complicated and may work well in a small country and might be difficult to work in a sub-continental country, like India.

Reasons for Adoption of FPTP System in India

The reasons for the popularity and success of the FPTP system in India is its simplicity. Some other reasons for India to adopt FPTP system are as follows

- The FPTP system offers voters a **clear choice between parties and specific candidates** in giving importance. However, in the other electoral systems such as the PR system, voters are asked to choose a party only. As a result, there is no one representative, who represents and is responsible for one locality. But in FPTP, the voters know their representatives and can hold them accountable.
- The FPTP system may **produce a majority** in the legislature. While as the PR system may not produce a clear majority in the legislature because seats in the legislature would be divided on the basis of shares of votes. FPTP makes it possible for the Parliamentary Government to function smoothly and effectively by facilitating the formation of a stable government.
- The FPTP system encourages voters from different social groups to come together to win an election in a locality. Whereas the PR system would encourage each community to form its own nation-wide party, in a diverse country, like India.
- The FPTP has helped larger parties to win clear majorities at the centre and state level. But it discouraged political parties that get all their votes only from one community.
- Normally, the working of the FPTP system results in a **two-party system**. It is difficult for new parties or a third party to enter the competition. In this respect, the experience of FPTP in India is slightly different.
- India has been experiencing the function of a multiparty coalition since 1989. Simultaneously, two party system is also increasingly developing in several states.
- However, despite the FPTP structure, India's party system is unique in that the **proliferation of coalition** has made it possible for new and similar parties to enter in the electoral competition.
- The makers of our Constitution also felt that the PR system may not be suitable for giving a stable government in a parliamentary system.

Reservation of Constituencies

- In the FPTP system, the candidate who secures the highest votes is declared elected. So, it may be possible that only dominant social groups and castes can win everywhere and the weak and oppressed social groups will remain un-represented.
- To overcome this problem, our Constitution has introduced the system of reservation.
- In this system, all voters in a constituency are eligible to vote but the candidate must belong to only a particular community or social section for which the seat is reserved. This system is necessary to ensure their proper representation in the Parliament and state legislature.
- The Constitution provides reservation of seats for the Scheduled Castes and Scheduled Tribes in the Lok Sabha and State Legislative Assemblies in proportion to their share in the population of India.
- Out of 543 elected seats in Lok Sabha, 84 seats are reserved for Scheduled Castes and 47 seats are reserved for Scheduled Tribes. The provision of reservation was initially made for a period of 10 years. Now it has been extended till 2030.

Quick Test 1

1. Give one example of a direct democracy.
2. Under the FPTP system, India is divided into how many constituencies?
3. Which election system does Israel follow?
4. What is the Single Transferable Vote System used for?
5. How many seats are reserved for Schedules Tribes?

3.3 Free and Fair Elections

- In order to achieve democracy in its true sense, it is important that the election system is **impartial** and **transparent**. The true test of any election system is its ability to ensure a free and fair electoral process. Only a fair conduct of elections allows the aspirations of the voter to find a legitimate expression through the electoral results.

Universal Adult Franchise

- Universal Adult Franchise means that all adults, that is, those who are above the age of **18 years** are eligible to vote in the elections irrespective of caste, creed, colour or sex.
- In many countries, citizens had to fight long battles with their rulers to get this right.
- One of the important decisions of the framers of the Indian Constitution was to guarantee every adult citizen in India, **the right to vote**.
- Until 1989, eligibility to vote was 21 years of age. However, the amendment to the Constitution in **1989**, reduced the eligibility age to vote to **18 years**.
- The idea behind the universal adult franchise is to ensure that all the citizens are able to participate in the process of selecting their representatives. It upholds the principle of equality and non-discrimination as mentioned in the Fundamental Rights.

Right to Contest

Similarly, all the citizens in the country have the right to contest elections and become a representative of the people. However this is subject to a certain eligibility criteria. These are as follows

- In order to stand for a Lok Sabha or assembly election, the minimum age is 25 years.
- A person who has undergone imprisonment for two or more years is not eligible for contesting elections.
- There is no restriction on income, education, class or gender to contest elections. This indicates that the election system is open to all its citizens.

Independent Election Commission

- The Election Commission (EC) of India is an **independent body** under **Article 324** of the Indian Constitution. It has been created to supervise and conduct elections to ensure a free and fair election system.
- The Election Commission plays the key role in **superintendence, direction** and **control** of the electoral roll and the conduct of elections in India.
- Hence, the Constitution has given important powers to the Election Commission.
- It plays a decisive role in the entire election process. The Supreme Court has also agreed with this interpretation of the Constitution.

Article 324 (1) The superintendence, direction and control of the preparation of electoral rolls for and conduct of, all elections to Parliament and to the legislature of every state and of elections to the offices of President and Vice-President held under this Constitution shall be vested in a commission (referred as the Election Commission).

Features of Election Commission of India

Features of Election Commission of India are as follows

- The Election Commission of India is assisted by a **Chief Electoral Officer** in every state.
- The Election Commission is not responsible for the conduct of local body elections.
- The State Election Commissioners work independently and have their own sphere of operation.

- The Election Commission of India can either be a multi-member or a single member body. This has been a subject to some changes before. However, it has remained a **multi-member body** since 1993.
- The Chief Election Commissioner (CEC) presides over the Election Commission. However, it does not have more powers than the other Election Commissioners. The CEC and the two Election Commissioners have **equal powers** to take all decisions related to elections as a collective body.
- The CEC and the other Election Commissioners are appointed by the **President of India** on the advice of the Council of Ministers.
- The Constitution ensures the security of tenure to the Chief Election Commissioner and the Election Commissioners. They are appointed for a term of **six years or till the age of 65 years**, whichever is earlier.
- The CEC can be removed from office before the expiry of the term, by the President. This process of impeachment of the CEC takes place when both the houses of Parliament make such a recommendation with a **special majority**. This is done to ensure that a ruling party cannot remove a CEC who refuses to favour it in elections.

Special Majority
- Two-third majority of the members present, and voting, and
- A simple majority of the total membership of the house.

Functions of Election Commission of India

The functions of Election Commission are as follows

- The Election Commission supervises the preparation of the **updated voters' list**. It ensures that the voters' list is free of errors.
- It determines the timing of elections and **prepares the election schedule**. This schedule includes the notification of elections, date from which nominations can be filed, last date for filing elections, last date of scrutiny, last date of withdrawal of nomination, date of polling and counting and declaration of results.
- The Election Commission has to take decisions to ensure **free and fair part**. It has also **the power to postpone or cancel the elections** in the entire country or in a state of a constituency on grounds of a vitiated (corrupted) atmosphere, where free and fair elections are impossible.
- The commission implements **the model code of conduct** for parties and candidates. It can order a re-poll in a specific constituency and it can also order for a recount of votes when it feels the counting process is unfair and unjust.
- The Election Commission confirms **recognition to political parties** and **allots symbols** to each of them.
- The administrative officers of the State and Central Governments are assigned election duty and the EC has full control over them during the process of elections. The Election Commission can transfer the officers or stop their transfer or take action against them for misconduct.
- Thus, it is correct to state that over the years the Election Commission of India has emerged as an independent authority. It has ensured fairness in the election process by acting in an impartial and unbiased manner.

Problems Faced by Election Commission

- Since 1951-52, eighteen Lok Sabha elections have been held in India, The Election commission of India has performed its duties effectively but it also faced many difficult situations to conduct the elections. Such as
  - The Election commission has difficult situations to conduct elections in militancy affected areas like Assam, Punjab and Jammu and Kashmir.

- The Election Commission also faced a difficult situation in 1991, when the ex-Prime Minister Rajiv Gandhi was assassinated during campaigning. The Commission had to postpone the election process mid-way.
- In 2002, the Election Commission faced another critical situation when the Gujarat Assembly was dissolved and elections had to be conducted. The EC realised that un-precedented violence in the state had made it impossible to hold free and fair elections immediately. It thus, decided to postpone elections to the State Assembly by a few months. The Supreme Court upheld this decision of the Election Commission.

3.4 Electoral Reforms

India has always tried various mechanisms to make the election process free and fair. However, the experience from the past has given rise to many suggestions and proposals for reforming the electoral system of the country. Some of the suggestions for reforms are as follows

- The system of elections should be changed from the First Past the Post System (FPTP) to some form of the Proportional Representation (PR) system. This will ensure that parties get seats in proportion to the votes secured.
- One-third seats should be **reserved for women** in Parliament and the State Assemblies.
- There should be strict provisions to **control the role of money** in electoral politics. The election expenses should be paid by the government out of a special fund.
- Candidates with any criminal background should be barred from contesting elections, even if their appeal is pending before a court.
- There should be a complete **ban on the use of caste and religious appeals** in the campaign.
- A law should be enacted to oversee the functioning of political parties and to ensure that they are accountable and democratic.

One Nation One Election

One nation one election means holding elections to the house of the people, and the state legislative assemblies together.

- **Need for One Nation One Election**
  - Reduce the massive expenditure incurred for conduct of separate elections every year.
  - Reduce identity politics like caste and religion based identity.
  - Reduce the diversion of human resources like security forces, electoral officers (such as teachers) from their primary duties.
- Thus, 'One Nation, One Election' aims to bring efficiency and reduce cost.

Quick Test 2

1. What is the minimum voting age in India?
2. What is the minimum age for contesting Assembly Elections?
3. The election commission was creacted under which article of the Indian Constitution?
4. Who appoints the Chief Election Commissioner?
5. Why election commission supervises the voters list?

Mind Map

ELECTIONS AND REPRESENTATION

1 Democracy

Direct Democracy
- In this citizens participate directly (e.g. Gram Sabha, Ancient Greece).
- Citizens participates in day to day decision making and in the running of the Government.

Indirect Democracy
- In this citizens elect representatives to make decisions. (e.g. Most modern democracies).
- Citizens have a limited role in the decision-making and running administration.

2 Election Systems in India

First Past the Post System (FPTP)
- This is Constituency based.
- Candidates with the most votes wins.
- Voter votes for a candidates.
- Simplicity and clarity.
- India is divided into a total of 543 constituencies
- For example, U.K., India.

Proportional Representation (PR)
- Each party is allotted the share of seats in the Parliament in proportion to its share of votes.
- Variants of (PR) - National or Multi-member.
- Voter votes for the party.
- For example, Israel and Netherlands.

Reservation of Constituencies in India
- Our Constitution has introduced the system of reservation.
- The candidate who secures the highest votes is declared elected.
- All voters in a constituency are eligible to vote but the candidate must belong to only a particular community.
- Out of 543 elected seats in Lok Sabha, 84 are reserved for Scheduled Castes and 47 are reserved for Scheduled Tribes.
- Provision of reservation was made for a period of 10 years.

3 Free and Fair Elections

Universal Adult Franchise
- Adults above 18 years are eligible to vote.
- Citizens had to fight long battles with their rulers to get this right in many countries.
- Important decision of the Indian Constitution assembly was to guarantee every adult citizen in India, 'the right to vote'.

Right to Contest
- All citizens have the right to contest elections and become representative.
- All citizens can stand for a Lok Sabha or assembly election and the minimum age requirement is of 25 years.

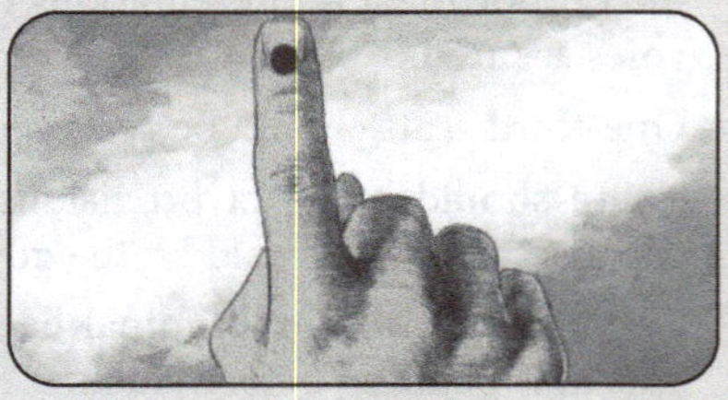

Election

4 Election Commission of India (ECI)

Roles
- Supervises elections and ensures impartiality.
- Manages voters lists and election schedule.
- Implements the model code of conduct.

Problems faced by EC
- Conducting Elections in conflict zones.
- Handing major incidents (e.g. 1991 elections after Ex-Prime Minister Rajiv gandhi's was assassination during compaigning.

Features of ECI
- It is a independent body under Article 324.
- Assisted by Chief Election Commissioner .
- Election Commissioner is not responsible for the conduct of local body election .

5 Electoral Reforms

- Transition from FPTP to proportional representation.
- Reservation of seats for women.
- Restrictions on money and criminal influences.
- Ban on caste-religious appeals in campaigns.

NCERT Folder

Intext Question

1. Here are the results of the Tamil Nadu Assembly Election held in 2016.

(i) What would be the composition of the assembly if it was a PR system like, in Israel? Which party would have a majority?

(ii) Who would form the government?

(iii) What would be the effect of this system on the relationship of political parties? (Pg. 62)

Total Seats 234 (Election held in 232)			
Party	**% of total votes**	**Number of seats**	**Seats in PR**
AIADMK	40.77	135	
DMK	31.64	88	
INC	6.42	8	
PMK	5.32	0	
BJP	2.84	0	
DMDK	2.39	0	
CPI	0.79	0	
IUML	0.73	1	
Other Parties	6.37	0	
Independents	1.43	0	
NOTA	1.30	-	

Ans. (i) The composition of the assembly if it was a PR system like in Israel would be more proportional to the votes each party receives. AIADMK would likely still be the largest party, but smaller parties would have more seats. The majority would depend on the coalitions formed. AIADMK or DMK-led alliances would likely form the government depending on vote shares.

(ii) Government would be formed by coalition talks and smaller parties would play a significant role in the process.

(iii) This system would lead to more co-operation between parties but could also result in more fragmentation and complex coalition dynamics.

2. The proportion of Muslims in the population of India is about 14.2 per cent. But the number of Muslim MPs in the Lok Sabha has usually been less than 6 per cent, less than half of their share in population. A similar situation prevails in most State Assemblies. Three students drew different conclusions from this fact. Write down whether and why you agree or disagree with each of them. (Pg. 66)

(i) Hilal: This demonstrates the unfairness of the FPTP system. We should have opted for PR system.

(ii) Arif: This shows the wisdom of granting reservations to SC and ST. What is needed is a reservation of seats for Muslims on the same lines as for SC and ST.

(iii) Saba: There is no point in talking about Muslims as a whole. Muslim women are not going to get any share in any of these systems. We need a separate quota for Muslim women. (Pg. 66)

Ans. (i) I agree with Hilal as he makes a valid point regarding the dis-proportionality of the FPTP system and the benefits of the PR system for fair representation.

(ii) I do not agree with Arif's suggestion of reservations based on religion as it may not be the best approach and it could lead to religious division.

(iii) I agree with Saba as she rightly identifies the unique challenges faced by Muslim women, but I don't think that creating a separate quota for them would be the most appropriate approach. A more inclusive strategy addressing both gender and socio-economic disparities could be more effective.

3. Why do you think does the Election Commission have the following powers and privileges? What could have happened if these did not exist?

(i) The Commission can issue orders to government employees engaged in any election related duty.

(ii) The government cannot remove the Chief Election Commissioner.

(iii) The Commission can cancel an election if it thinks that it was not fair. (Pg. 72)

Ans. (i) The Election Commission must ensure fair and impartial elections. To achieve this, it needs the authority to direct government employees who are involved in election-related tasks, such as polling officers, election officials and law enforcement. This helps maintain the integrity and smooth operation of the election process.

Without this power, there would be no way to ensure that government employees involved in elections remain neutral or follow election guidelines.

(ii) The independence of the Election Commission is essential to ensure that elections are free from political influence or manipulation. If the Chief Election Commissioner could be easily removed by the government, it could lead to the appointment of someone who might favor the government in power, which would compromise the fairness of the elections.

(iii) The Election Commission must safeguard the fairness of the election process. If an election is conducted in an unfair or biased manner, such as through rigging, violence or other forms of malpractice, the Commission needs the authority to cancel the election to protect the legitimacy of the democratic process.

If the Election Commission did not have the power to cancel a flawed election, there could be situations where unfair elections are allowed to stand, resulting in the election of illegitimate representatives.

Exercise

1. Which of the following resembles most a direct democracy?

(i) Discussions in family meeting
(ii) Election of the class monitor
(iii) Choice of a candidate by a political party
(iv) Decisions taken by Gram Sabha
(v) Opinion polls conducted by the media

Ans. (iv) Decisions taken by Gram Sabha

2. Which of the following tasks are not performed by the Election Commission?

(i) Preparing the electoral rolls
(ii) Nominating the candidates
(iii) Setting up polling booths
(iv) Implementing the model code of conduct
(v) Supervising the Panchayat elections

Ans. (v) Supervising the Panchayat elections

3. Which of the following is common to the method of election of the members of Rajya Sabha and Lok Sabha?

(i) Every citizen above the age of 18 is eligible voter.
(ii) Voter can give preference order for different candidates.
(iii) Every vote has equal value.
(iv) The winner must get more than half the votes.

Ans. (iii) Every vote has equal value.

4. In the First Past the Post System, that candidate is declared winner who

(i) secures the largest number of postal ballots.
(ii) belongs to the party who has highest number of votes in the country.
(iii) has more votes than any other candidate in the constituency.
(iv) attains just position by securing more than 50% votes.

Ans. (iii) has more votes than any other candidate in the constituency.

5. What is the difference between the system of reservation of constituencies and the system of separate electorate? Why did the Constitution-makers reject the latter?

Ans. In the system of reservation of constituencies, all the voters in a constituency are eligible to vote but the candidate must belong to only a particular community or social section for which the seat is reserved.

Whereas in the system of separate electorates, the candidate of a particular community can only be elected by the voters of his/her community.

The Constitution makers rejected the separate electorate system because it went against the principles of democracy and it is against the purpose of unity, equality, secularism and state which is free from discrimination.

6. Which of the following statements are incorrect? Identify and correct them by substituting, adding or re-arranging only one word of phrase.

(i) FPTP system is followed for all the elections in India.
(ii) Election Commission does not supervise Panchayat and Municipal elections.
(iii) President of India cannot remove an Election Commissioner.
(iv) Appointment of more than one Election Commissioner in the Election Commission is mandatory.

Ans. (i) Incorrect → FPTP system is only followed for elections to Lok Sabha, Legislative Assemblies and the Panchayats.

(ii) Correct → This statement is correct.

(iii) Incorrect → President of India can remove an Election Commissioner on the recommendation of both the house of Parliament with special majority.

(iv) Incorrect → Appointment of more than one Election Commissioner in the Election Commission is not mandatory, but it is an established practice through consensus to ensure accountability.

7. Indian electoral system aims of ensuring representation of socially disadvantaged sections. However we have only 12 per cent women members in our legislatures.

What measures would you suggest to improve the situation?

Ans. The measures to improve the situation are

- Proportional Representation system of election would be better, as this ensures proper representation of women according to their percentage of population in India.
- Reservation of seats for women candidates in the electoral constituencies.
- The system of reservation should be rotated among all constituencies to ensure proper representation of women from all parts of the country.

8. Here are some wishes expressed in a conference to discuss a Constitution for a new country. Write against each of these whether FPTP or Proportional Representation system is more suited to meet each of these wishes.

(i) **People should clearly know who is their representative, so that they can hold him or her personally accountable.**

(ii) **We have small linguistic minorities who are spread all over the country; we should ensure fair representation to them.**

(iii) **There should be no discrepancy between votes and seats for different parties.**

(iv) **People should be able to elect a good candidate even if they do not like his/her political party.**

Ans. (i) FPTP system

(ii) Proportional Representation system

(iii) Proportional Representation system

(iv) FPTP system

9. A former Chief Election Commissioner joined a political party and contested elections. There are various views on the issue. One view is that a former Election Commissioner is an independent citizen and has a right to join any political party and to contest election. According to the other view, leaving this possibility open can affect the impartiality of the Election Commission. So, former Election Commissioners must not be allowed to contest any elections.

Which position do you agree with and why?

Ans. The Election Commission should not contest election after they leave office because the Election Commission is a constitutional body that requires the highest standards of integrity to ensure impartiality in its conduct.

The task of Election Commissioner is to impartially supervise and safeguards the conduct of elections and not become a part of electoral process. Any future prospect of this kind would seriously compromise the integrity and impartiality of the institution that is cornerstone of a democracy.

10. 'Indian democracy is now ready to shift from a crude First Past the Post System (FPTP) to a system of Proportional Representation (PR)'. Do you agree with this statement? Give your reasons for or against this statement.

Ans. Indian democracy is not yet ready to replace the FPTP system with PR system because

- FPTP is more suitable for political parties rather than Indian society because it has a large number of social groups.
- The system of PR system is very complex and difficult for an ordinary person to understand easily.
- It would lead to conflict of demand between the social groups and the dominant social group would continue to exercise power and create a new social alliance to maintain it.
- It would endanger the social fabric of a country which according to the Constitution is the strength of the country.
- Proportional Representation can be adopted in due course of time with the maturing of Indian democracy.

Exam Pattern Questions

Objective Type Questions

Multiple Choice Questions (MCQs)

1. .... is a formal decision-making process by which population chooses an individual to hold public office?

(a) Election (b) Democracy
(c) Adult Franchise (d) Communism

2. What is the universal tool for selecting people's representative in modern representatives' democracies?

(a) Referendum (b) General Election
(c) Autocracy (d) None of these

3. .... is the type of government for the people, of the people and by the people?

(a) Bureaucracy (b) Autocracy
(c) Democracy (d) Military

4. Who among the following is not involved in policy making process in representative democracy.

(a) Executive (b) Bureaucracy
(c) Citizens (d) None of these

5. A .... is one where the citizens directly participate in the day-to-day decision-making and in the running of the government.

(a) Direct democracy (b) Indirect democracy
(c) Elected democracy (d) None of these

6. In India who gets elected through an indirect election system?

(a) President (b) Lok Sabha member
(c) Legislative Assembly (d) None of these

7. Who among the following is elected directly by the election system in India?

(a) President (b) Vice-President
(c) Lok Sabha members (d) None of these

8. In the 1984 elections to Lok Sabha , the Congress Party got 48% of the votes. This means that only 48% of those who voted, voted in favour of the candidates put up by the Congress Party, but the party still managed to win more than 80% of the seats in the Lok Sabha. The BJP got 7.4 % votes but less than one per cent seats. Identify the above election system. Competency Based Que

(a) Single Transferable Vote System
(b) Proportional Representation System
(c) Special Majority System
(d) First Past The Post System

9. Consider the following statements regarding election of Lok Sabha in India. Competency Based Que

I. There are a total of 543 Constituencies.
II. Each constituencies elects one representative.
III. The candidate who scores the highest number of votes is declared elected.

Which of the following statement(s) is/are correct?

(a) Only I (b) Only II
(c) I and II (d) I, II and III

10. Consider the following statements regarding the merits of FPTP system Competency Based Que

I. It secures the rights of minorities.
II. It ensures that votes are not wasted.
III. It is easy to operate.

Select the correct statement using the codes given below.

(a) Only I (b) Only III
(c) I and II (d) I, II and III

11. In how many constituencies the entire country is divided?

(a) 545 (b) 543
(c) 540 (d) 535

12. In which of the following systems is the candidate ahead of others in election who crosses the winning post first of all?

(a) Federal system (b) Plurality system
(c) Parliamentary system (d) None of these

13. Which among the following system of election is known as Plurality system?

(a) FPTP system (b) PR system
(c) Single Transferable Vote (d) None of these

14. What are the systems of elections in India?

(a) First Past the Post System
(b) Proportional Representation System
(c) Both (a) and (b)
(d) Neither (a) nor (b)

15. The system of election practiced in Argentina and Portugal is known as

(a) Preferential Representation
(b) First Past the Post System
(c) Proportional Representation
(d) None of the above

16. **In which of the following countries are divided into several multi-member constitutiencies?**

(a) Argentina (b) Portugal
(c) Both (a) and (b) (d) Netherland

17. **In India, the PR system is followed for the election of President and ....**

(a) Vidhan Sabha (b) Vidhan Parishad
(c) Panchayat (d) Lok Sabha

18. **Which system is followed for the elections of Rajya Sabha to the offices of President and Vice-President?**

(a) First Past The Post System
(b) Proportional Representation
(c) Preferential Representation
(d) None of the above

19. **Select the criteria for a reserved constituencies.** **Competency Based Que; Diksha App**

(a) For electing a representative from a particular community, only those voters would be eligible who belongs to that community.
(b) A reserved constituency should be a single member constituency.
(c) A reserved constituency has the majority of population belonging to reserved category.
(d) All voters in a constituency are eligible to vote but the candidates must belong to a particular community or social section for which the seat is reserved.

20. **The provision for the reservation of ST and SC in Lok Sabha has been extended till ....**

(a) 2020 (b) 2025
(c) 2030 (d) 2040

21. **Who decides which constituency is to be reserved? Choose the correct option from the following** **Diksha App**

(a) Election Commission
(b) State Election Commission
(c) Delimitation Commission
(d) Chief Election Commissioner

22. **Universal Franchise is which type of right?**

(a) Constitutional Right (b) Legal Right
(c) Fundamental Right (d) Natural Right

23. **What is the minimum age for contesting elections in the Lok Sabha?**

(a) 25 years (b) 30 years
(c) 35 years (d) 20 years

24. **Select the article of the Indian Constitution which provides for an independent Election Commission for the superintendence, direction and control of the electoral roll and the conduct of elections in India.** **Diksha App**

(a) Article 324 (b) Article 321
(c) Article 323 (d) Article 325

25. **Who appoints the Chief Election Commissioner in India?**

(a) Chief Justice of India (b) President of India
(c) Lok Sabha Speaker (d) Prime Minister of India

26. **There should be a special provision to ensure that at least .... women are elected to the Parliament and Assemblies.**

(a) two-fourth (b) two-third
(c) one-fourth (d) one-third

27. **Consider the following statements related to the Electoral Reforms.** **Competency Based Que**

I. **Our system of elections should be changed from FPTP to some form of the PR system to ensure that parties get seats in proportion to the votes secured.**
II. **Ceiling on election expenditure ₹20-28 lakhs for the Lok Sabha election.**

Select the correct answer using the codes given below.

(a) Only I (b) Only II
(c) Both I and II (d) None of these

28. **Given below are two statements**

Statement I Elections have today become the most visible symbol of the democratic process.

Statement II The ancient city-states in Greece were considered examples of indirect democracy.

In the light of above statements, choose the correct answer from the options given below **Competency Based Que**

(a) Both Statement I and Statement II are true.
(b) Both Statement I and Statement II are false.
(c) Statement I is true, but Statement II is false.
(d) Statement I is false, but Statement II is true.

29. **Given below are two statements**

Statement I Israel follows proportional representation system of election

Statement II The legislature of Israel is known as Knesset. **Competency Based Que**

In the light of above statements, choose the correct answer from the options given below

(a) Both Statement I and Statement II are true.
(b) Both Statement I and Statement II are false.
(c) Statement I is true, but Statement II is false.
(d) Statement I is false, but Statement II is true.

30. **Consider the following statement?**

I. **The Chief Election Commissioner can be removed from his office is the same manner as a judge of the Supreme Court.**
II. **Election Commission advices the President on matters related to the disqualification of the member of Parliament.** **Competency Based Que**

Which among the following statement(s) above is/are correct?

(a) Only I (b) Both I and II
(c) Only II (d) None of these

31. Arrange the following in chronological order

I. Election Commission once again became multimember body.
II. Separate electorates introduced in British India.
III. India creates an independent Election Commission.
IV. The minimum age for voting is reduced to 18 years.

Choose the correct option. **Competency Based Que**

(a) I, IV, III, II (b) IV, I, II, III
(c) IV, I, III, II (d) II, III, IV, I

32. Match the Constitutions in List I correctly with their descriptions given in List II and choose the appropriate code as the correct answer **Competency Based Que**

List I		List II	
A.	FPTP System	1.	Clear accountability to a representative for each locality.
B.	Proportional Representation (PR)	2.	Ensures that all citizens, irrespective of class or caste, can vote.
C.	Reserved Constituencies	3.	Voters select political parties, not candidates, with multiple representatives per constituency.
D.	Universal Adult Franchise	4.	Aimed at improving representation for marginalised social groups in legislative bodies.

Codes

	A	B	C	D		A	B	C	D
(a)	1	3	4	2	(b)	3	2	1	4
(c)	2	1	4	3	(d)	4	2	3	1

Assertion-Reason Questions

Direction (Q. Nos. 33-37) In the questions given below, there are two statements marked as Assertion (A) and Reason (R). Read the statements and choose the correct option.

Codes

(a) Both A and R are true and R is the correct explanation of A.
(b) Both A and R are true, but R is not the correct explanation of A.
(c) A is true, but R is false.
(d) A is false, but R is true.

33. **Assertion (A)** In India, people elect their own representatives to govern the nation.

Reason (R) India is a democratic country.

34. **Assertion (A)** In India political parties which formed the government represent the majority of seats secured in the elections to the house of the People at the Centre and the Legislative Assemblies in the States but not the majority of votes.

Reason (R) The elections based on the majority vote system decide the result on the basis of relative majority of votes secured.

35. **Assertion (A)** India adopted Proportional Representation system for the election of Lok Sabha and State Legislative Assembly as it is easier for the public and people have experienced it during the freedom struggle.

Reason (R) In Proportional Representation system voter votes for the party.

36. **Assertion (A)** The FPTP system offer voters a choice between parties and specific candidates in giving importance.

Reason (R) In PR system voters are asked to choose a party only.

37. **Assertion (A)** An open electoral competition might be unfair to weaker sections.

Reason (R) The weaker sections of the society lack what their influential counterparts have in terms of resources, education and political connections.

Passage Based Questions

38. Read the given passage and answer the following questions.

When the votes are counted, each party is allotted the share of seats in the Parliament in proportion to its share of votes. Each party fills its quota of seats by its nominees from a preference list declared before elections. The seats in a constituency are distributed according to a party's vote totals. As a result, members of a constituency would and do belong to multiple political parties. In both these forms, the voters exercise their preference for the party and not for a candidate.

(i) Which election system is being referred in the above passage?

(a) FPTP system (b) PR system
(c) Plurality system (d) Both (b) and (c)

(ii) Which of the following country has adopted PR system in their election?

(a) USA (b) UK
(c) Poland (d) Israel

(iii) In India which of the following election takes place through the PR system.
(a) Election of the Vice-President
(b) Rajya Sabha
(c) Both (a) and (b)
(d) Election of the Governor of the State

(iv) In .... voters exercise their preference for the party and not for a candidate.
(a) PR system (b) Parliamentary system
(c) Presidential system (d) Plurality system

39. Read the given passage and answer the following questions.

No system of election can ever be perfect. And in actual election process, there are bound to be many flaws and limitations. Any democratic society has to keep searching for mechanisms to make elections free and fair to the maximum. With the acceptance of adult suffrage, freedom to contest elections, and the establishment of an independent Election Commission, India has tried to make its election process free and fair. However, the experience of the last fifty five years has given rise to many suggestions for reforming our election system. The Election Commission, political parties, various independent groups, and many scholars have come up with proposals for electoral reform. Some of these suggestions are about changing the Constitutional Provisions.

(i) What is being referred in this passage?
(a) Democracy (b) Electoral Reforms
(c) Legislature (d) Executive

(ii) What mechanism(s) has/have been adopted by India to make free and fair elections?
(a) Acceptance of adult suffrage
(b) Freedom of contest elections
(c) Establishment of an independent Election Commission.
(d) All of the above

(iii) Explain the role played by the Election Commission in ensuring the fairness of elections in India.

Answers

1. (a) Election
2. (b) General Election
3. (c) Democracy
4. (c) Citizens
5. (a) Direct Democracy
6. (a) President
7. (c) Lok Sabha members
8. (d) First Past The Post System
9. (d) I, II and III
10. (b) Only III
11. (b) 543
12. (b) Plurality system
13. (a) FPTP system
14. (c) Both (a) and (b)
15. (c) Proportional Representation
16. (c) Both (a) and (b)
17. (b) Vidhan Parishad
18. (b) Proportional Representation
19. (d) All voters in a constituency are eligible to vote but the candidates must belong to a particular community or social section for which the seat is reserved.
20. (c) 2030
21. (c) Delimitation Commission
22. (a) Constitutional Right
23. (a) 25 years
24. (a) Article 324
25. (b) President of India
26. (d) one-third
27. (a) Only I
28. (c) Statement I is true, but Statement II is false.
29. (a) Both Statement I and Statement II are true.
30. (b) Both I and II
31. (d) II, III , IV, I
32. (a) 1 3 4 2
33. (a) Both A and R are true and R is the correct explanation of A.
34. (a) Both A and R are true and R is the correct explanation of A.
35. (d) A is false, but R is true.
36. (b) Both A and R are true, but R is not the correct explanation of A.
37. (a) Both A and R are true and R is the correct explanation of A.
38. (i) (b) PR system (ii) (d) Israel
(iii) (c) Both (a) and (b) (iv) (a) PR System
39. (i) (b) Electoral Reforms
(ii) (d) All of the above
(iii) The Election Commission plays a key role in overseeing and managing the election process to ensure it is free, fair and impartial.
    - It supervises the preparation of the updated voters list.
    - It prepares the election schedule.
    - It implements the model code of conduct.
    - It confirms the recognition of political parties and allots symbols.
    - It has power to postpone the election or cancel the election.

Subjective Questions

Very Short Answer Type Questions

1. What do you understand by election system?

Ans. An election system is a medium to elect the representatives especially in an indirect democracy to form the government. The representatives are elected by the people to act in accordance with the wishes of the people.

2. Explain the type of elections prevailing in India.

Ans. There are following two types of election practised in India

Direct Election People of the country vote by a secret ballot to elect their representatives to Lok Sabha, State Assembly and local bodies.

Indirect Election In this, the elected representative of the people vote to elect a person for the position of President, Vice-President and members of Rajya Sabha and Vidhan Parishad.

3. Discuss the advantages of FPTP System?

Ans. The advantages of the FPTP system are as following

- It is easy to operate.
- It establishes a clear link between representatives and constituencies.
- It allows governments that are formed to have a clear mandate.

4. How has the experience of FPTP in India been different?

Ans. After independence, India saw one-party dominance along with many smaller parties. After 1989, multiparty coalitions started functioning and in many states, a two-party competition started.

5. What do you mean by constituency?

Ans. The division of the the country or a state into a number of representative area is called Constituencies. So, a constituency is a fixed area with a body of voters or residents with voting rights.

6. What is Proportional Representation?

Ans. It is an electoral system where the political parties get representation (number of seats) in the legislature in proportion to the share of votes they get in the elections. It fairly represents political parties based on their share of the vote.

7. Name the institutions in India elected by proportional system of election.

Ans. The institutions or organs elected by the PR system are the President, Vice-President, members of Rajya Sabha and Vidhan Parishad.

8. Define Separate Electorate.

Ans. The system in which the candidate of a particular community can only be elected by the voters of his/her community is called Separate Electorate.

9. Why is the system of reserved constituency necessary in India?

Ans. The makers of the Constitution found necessary to reserve the constituency to ensure the proper representation of seats of a particular community or social group to the Parliament and State Legislature.

Thus, the Constitution provides for reservatio of seats in Lok Sabha and state legislative assemblies for the scheduled castes and scheduled tribes.

10. Is there any provision of reserving seats for women? How it would be done?

Ans. Yes, there is a provision for reserving seats for women. The 73rd and 74th Amendments mandate 33% reservation in local bodies. The Women's Reservation Act (2023) reserves 33% of seats in the Lok Sabha and State Assemblies which will be effective after the next delimitation process.

11. What do you understand about the Delimitation Commission?

Ans. The Delimitation Commission is constituted by the President. It works in collaboration with the Election Commission of India. The Commission is appointed for the purpose of drawing up the boundaries of constituencies all over the country.

12. Mention any two drawbacks in Indian electoral system.

Ans. The two drawbacks in Indian electoral system are

(i) The absence of representation for women in the legislature.

(ii) Mis-representation of seat-vote ratio in the legislatures.

Short Answer Type Questions

1. What is the importance of elections?

Ans. An election is a formal decision making process by which a population chooses an individual to hold public office. Elections are the most important process conducted in any democracy as

- Elections provide opportunities to the people to participate actively in the functioning of the democratic government.
- Elections is the tool to widen the scope of political awakening among the masses and educate them by acquainting with the issue of public concern.

- It enables peaceful transfer of power from one political party to another and legitimise the working by justifying the authority of representative to lead people.
- Elections provide the citizens opportunity to react against the unjust policies and implementation of the government.

2. Analyse reasons for adopting the FPTP system in India. Diksha App

Ans. The reasons for adopting the FPTP system in India are

- The entire election system is extremely simple to understand even for common voters who may have no specialised knowledge about politics and elections.
- There is also a clear choice presented to the voters at the time of elections. Voters have to simply endorse a candidate or a party while voting. The FPTP system offers voters a choice not simply between parties but specific candidates.
- In constituency based systems like the FPTP, the voters know who their own representative is and can hold him or her accountable.
- The FPTP system has helped larger parties to win clear majorities at the centre and the state level and facilitates the formation of stable governments.

3. Compare and contrast FPTP and PR system of elections. Diksha App

Ans. For answer refer to under the text Comarison of FPTP and PR System of Election on page no. 49.

4. In the PR system there could be two variations. Support the statement with examples.

Ans. In the PR system there could be two variations as discussed below

- In some countries, like Israel or Netherlands, the entire country is treated as one constituency and seats are allocated to each party according to its share of votes in the national election.
- The other method is when the country is divided into several multi-member constituencies as in Argentina and Portugal. Each party prepares a list of candidates for each constituency, depending on how many have to be elected from that constituency.
- In both these variations, voters exercise their preference for a party and not a candidate. The seats in a constituency are distributed on the basis of votes polled by a party. Thus, representatives from a constituency, would and do belong to different parties.

5. What is the procedure of reserving seats for SCs and STs in India?

Ans. The Delimitation Commission is an independent body appointed by the President of India. It is vested with the authority of reserving seats for SCs and STs in the country.

The procedure followed for reserving seats for SCs and STs is

- A quota of constituencies to be reserved in each state is fixed on the proportion of SCs and STs in the state.
- Those constituency that have the highest proportion of Scheduled Tribes population are reserved for STs.
- In case of Scheduled Caste two things are figured out (i) It picks the constituency that have the highest population of SCs. (ii) It spreads these constituencies in different regions of the state because the SCs population is evenly distributed throughout the country.

These reserved constituencies can be rotated each time when delimitation is exercised.

6. 'The true test of any election system is its ability to ensure a free and fair electoral process'. Justify the statement by giving the importance for free and fair elections. Competency Based Que

Ans. In order to achieve democracy in a true sense, it is crucial that the election system is impartial and transparent. The true test of any election system is its ability to ensure free and fair electoral process. Free and fair elections are important because

(i) It allows the aspirations of the voters to find a legitimate expression through the electoral results.
(ii) Elections serves as a tool for the citizens to hold the government accountable.
(iii) It is a process through which a stable government is formed at the centre, state and local level.
(iv) Election provides the right to caste vote and the right to contest elections to all the citizens of the country.
(v) Elections serves as the tool for the democratic setup of a country.

7. Suggest two electoral reforms to control the use of money and muscle power in elections. Diksha App

Ans. Two electoral reforms to control the use of money and muscle power in elections are as follows

(i) The elections expenses should be paid by the government out of a special fund (State funding of elections)
(ii) Candidates with any criminal case should be barred from contesting elections, even if their appeal is pending before a court.

8. Mention the electoral reforms suggested by the various groups and organs of India.

Ans. The Election Commission, various independent groups, scholars and political parties have come up and suggested about changing the Constitutional Provisions such as

- Our system of election should be changed from FPTP to some form of the PR system to ensure that parties get seats in proportion to the votes secured.
- One-third seats are to be reserved for women in Parliament and State Assemblies.
- Provisions to control the role of money in electoral politics and election expenses should be paid by the government out of special funds.
- Complete ban on the use of caste and religious appeals in the campaign.
- Candidates with any criminal background should be barred from contesting elections, even if the appeal is pending in court.

9. Analyse any four drawbacks of Indian electoral system?

Ans. The drawbacks of Indian electoral system are

- **Distortion of Seat-Vote Ratio** The foremost defect of the present electoral system is that there is no relationship between the votes secured by a party and its strength in the assembly or in the Parliament.
- **Expensive Elections** The growing influence of money power has led to the downfall of the electoral system in India. In India, elections are very expensive and a common man of integrity cannot fight elections. As a result, only rich people can fight elections and first serve their own interest.
- **Use of Caste and Religion in Election** In India, a large number of votes are cast on the basis of caste and religion, as a result people get divided on this basis which is very detrimental to the social fabric of the nation.
- **Independent Candidates** Independent candidates are also proving to be a distraction in the electoral system and wastes a large number of votes.

Long Answer Type Questions

1. How does the First-Past-The-Post (FPTP) system disadvantage smaller social groups, and why is this significant in the Indian context? How did the Indian Constitution makers ensure fair representation for oppressed social groups?

Ans. In the FPTP system, the candidate with the highest number of votes in a constituency is declared the winner. This often works to the disadvantage of smaller social groups because it can result in a situation where the dominant social or caste groups win in most constituencies.

The system favors the larger, more influential groups, which can ignore or marginalise the smaller and oppressed social groups. In the Indian social context, where caste-based discrimination has been historically prevalent, this is particularly significant.

The dominant castes can continue to control political power, leaving the marginalised or oppressed castes under-represented.

This issue became an important concern for India's Constitution makers, who sought to ensure that such groups received fair and just political representation.

To ensure fair representation for oppressed social groups, the Constitution makers decided not to continue with the British system of separate electorates. Instead, they opted for a system of reserved constituencies.

2. There has been a strong demand seeking reservation of seats in the Lok Sabha and State Assemblies for women. Justify the statement with relevant arguments.

Competency Based Que

Ans. In recent years, there has been a strong demand for the reservation of seats for women in the Lok Sabha (Lower House of Parliament) and State Legislative Assemblies. This is because women remain significantly under-represented in India's representative bodies. Despite the large number of women voters and the progress made in other areas of gender equality, very few women are elected to positions of political power. This disparity has led to growing calls for reserving a one-third quota of seats in both the Lok Sabha and State Assemblies for women, ensuring their fair participation in the political process.

While the reservation of seats for women has been successfully implemented in rural and urban local bodies (such as Panchayats and Municipalities), the reservation for the higher legislative bodies, like the Lok Sabha and State Assemblies, has not yet been realised.

The Constitution of India would need to be amended to implement such a reservation system at the national and state levels.

3. Elucidate in brief the functions of Election Commission.

Diksha App

Ans. The functions of Election Commission are as follows

- It supervises the preparation of up to date voters list.
- It determines the time of elections and prepares the election schedule such as notification of elections, date of nomination, last date of scrutiny and withdrawal of nomination, date of polling, counting and declaration of results.
- It has the power to postpone or cancel the elections in the entire country of a particular state of constituency on the grounds of vitiated (corrupted) atmosphere.
- The commission implements the model code of conduct for the party's candidates.

- It can order a re-poll in a specific constituency and can order a recount of votes when it feels the counting process is unfair and unjust.
- The commission accords recognition to political parties and allots symbols to each of them.
- The administrative officers of centre and state are assigned election duty and the commission have full control over them.

4. Describe the challenges the Election Commission of India has faced while conducting elections in difficult situations. **Competency Based Que**

Ans. The Election Commission of India (EC) has faced several challenging situations while conducting elections in different regions

- One of the most difficult situations occurred in the militancy-affected areas of India, such as Assam, Punjab, and Jammu and Kashmir, where the EC had to conduct elections in regions facing violence and instability.
- In such areas, ensuring the safety and security of voters and election officials was a major challenge.
- Another critical challenge occurred during the 1991 Lok Sabha elections, when Rajiv Gandhi, the former Prime Minister, was assassinated during the election campaign. The assassination led to a temporary halt in the election process as the country faced significant political and social turmoil.
- The Election Commission had to manage the situation and ensure that the elections could continue with proper security measures in place.
- In 2002, the Election Commission faced another difficult decision when it had to conduct elections in Gujarat after the state assembly was dissolved. However, unprecedented violence in the state made it impossible to hold free and fair elections at that time. In this case, the EC took the significant step of postponing the elections by a few months, ensuring that they would be held only when the situation in the state had stabilised enough to allow for a peaceful and fair electoral process.
- This decision was challenged but was upheld by the Supreme Court, which supported the Election Commission's right to ensure fair elections in the state.

5. "Government has taken many steps in the Electoral System but still there are some lacunae in the electoral system". Suggest some suggestion to make election more effective. **Competency Based Que**

Ans. Government has taken many steps to make election more transparent and effective such as use of Electronic Voting Machine, Voter Verifiable Paper, Audit Trail and NOTA. Restriction on exit polls, ceiling on election expenditure (₹ 50-70 lakhs for the Lok Sabha election and ₹ 20-28 lakhs for the assembly election) and the use electoral bonds in election funding are some of the major reforms initiated by the Election Commission of India that have sought to bring about revolutionary changes in the electoral process and the voter behavior in contemporary India.

However, there are some problems in the election system which need to be solved. The various committees have worked on electoral reforms, i.e., The Goswami Committee and Tarkunde Committee, but these have not brought substantial changes in electoral system and law. It seems that political parties are indifferent to electoral reforms because in some cases, political parties have neutralised the steps taken by the Election Commission to bring in some desired changes.

It is now widely recognised to preserve and strengthen the democratic setup. A comprehensive agenda of reforms is necessary in system, structure and processes. Some of the measures that can be adopted are as follows

- Criminalisation should be checked in politics.
- Political parties functions should be regulated.
- Voters participation and awareness should be ensured.
- Make the election machinery effective and credible.
- The use of money and muscle power should be stopped.
- A proportionate share to every class, section and society should also be provided in the parliament.

Picture Based Questions

1. Observe the cartoon given below and answer the questions that follow.

(i) What does the cartoon about elections depict?

(a) Peace and unity (b) Chaos and disorder

(c) Celebrations and joy (d) Silence and calm

Ans. (b) Chaos and disorder

(ii) What does the phrase 'carnival of democracy' mean?

(a) Elections are chaotic

(b) Elections are celebrations of democracy

(c) Elections are always peaceful

(d) Elections are boring

Ans. (b) Elections are celebrations of democracy

(iii) Can chaos during elections be good for democracy?

(a) Yes, it always helps democracy

(b) No, it is always harmful to democracy

(c) It depends on whether chaos allows people to express their opinions freely

(d) Chaos has nothing to do with democracy

Ans. (c) It depends on whether chaos allows people to express their opinions freely

(iv) Why are elections important in a democracy?

(a) They allow leaders to choose the people

(b) They allow people to choose their leaders

(c) They create disorder in society

(d) They help end democracy

Ans. (b) They allow people to choose their leaders

2. Observe the cartoon given below and answer the questions that follow.

(i) What does the cartoon represent?

(ii) These members of the ruling party are trying to listen to the 'tiny' opposition. Was this the effect of our electoral system?

(iii) Is the participation of the opposition necessary and why?

Ans. (i) The cartoon represents the unheard voice of the small opposition party and the ruling party is making efforts to hear its voice.

(ii) Yes, it is the effect of our electoral system, as there was only one political party that dominated in the Lok Sabha or Rajya Sabha. The opposition was not so big to play any role. This might be due to adoption of First Past the Post System of elections where all communities do not get proper representation.

(iii) In a democratic set-up like India, the leader of opposition is like second Prime Minister of the country. Without an opposition in the legislature, it would make the political system un-responsive.

The participation of the opposition is the focal point in formulating the policies of the government and an enactments of an acts.

3. Study the cartoon given below and answer the question that follow.

(i) What does the cartoon represents?

(a) Criminal taken to court in public

(b) Criminal turned politician facing public

(c) Politician turned criminal facing public

(d) None of the above

Ans. (b) Criminal turned politician facing public

(ii) Why should a person accused of a serious crime be barred from contesting an election?

(a) He/She can do illegal practices

(b) He/She can harm the voters and candidates contesting election

(c) He/She can use money muscle power to win the election

(d) All of the above

Ans. (d) All of the above

(iii) State the provision of electoral reform regarding above cartoon.

(a) Any candidate with any criminal background should be barred from contesting election.

(b) Freedom to contest elections

(c) Complete ban on the use of caste and religion

(d) All of the above

Ans. (a) Any candidate with any criminal background should be barred from contesting election.

(iv) The minimum age of voting was 21 years till

(a) 1984 (b) 1987 (c) 1989 (d) 1990

Ans. (c) 1989

SELF ASSESSMENT TEST

Objective Type Questions

1. What is the general outcome of the FPTP system in terms of party competition?
   (a) It leads to a multi-party system.
   (b) It results in a two-party system.
   (c) It ensures that no party dominates.
   (d) It makes it difficult for any party to win.
2. Arrange the following in chronological order
   I. Amendment reducing the voting age to 18 years
   II. Creation of a multi-member Election Commission
   III. Reservation of seats for SC/ST extended up to 2030
   IV. Lok Sabha elections of 1984

   Choose the correct option
   (a) I, IV, III, II (b) IV, I, II, III (c) IV, I, III, II (d) II, III, I, IV
3. **Assertion (A)** The Election Commission of India has conducted numerous elections since 1951, including 18th Lok Sabha elections and many state assembly elections.

   Reason (R) The Election Commission is responsible for ensuring the conduct of free and fair elections across India.

   Codes
   (a) Both A and R are true, and the R is the correct explanation of the A.
   (b) Both A and R are true, but the R is not the correct explanation of A.
   (c) A is true, but R is false.
   (d) A is false, but R is true.

Very Short Answer Type Questions

4. Why is direct democracy not feasible for large populations?
5. What distinguishes a democratic election from a non-democratic election?
6. Examine the key feature of the First Past The Post (FPTP) system regarding the winner?

Short Answer Type Questions

7. What makes the FPTP system easier to understand compared to other electoral systems like Proportional Representation (PR)?
8. The FPTP system encourages voters from different social groups to come together to win an election in a locality. Justify the statement. **Competency Based Que**
9. Explain how voters participate in the Proportional Representation system.
10. Evaluate the general eligibility criteria for a citizen to contest in elections in India. **Competency Based Que**

Long Answer Type Questions

11. What is FPTP system and why was this system adopted in india?
12. Describe the changes in the structure of the Election Commission of India over time. **Competency Based Que**
13. Enumerate the procedure followed for conduct of elections in India. **Competency Based Que**
14. How does the Indian electoral system ensure equal opportunities for all citizens to stand for election, regardless of their social or economic background?

04

CHAPTER

Legislature, Executive and Judiciary are the three main organs of the government which together perform the functions of the government, maintain law and order and work for the welfare of the people.

▼ YOUR STUDY GOALS

▼ YOUR PRACTICE GOAL

- Objective Type Questions (35 Qs ; MCQs, A-R, Statements, Matching, Passage Based)
- Subjective Questions (12 VSAs, 14 SAs, 4 LAs, 3 Picture Based Questions)

Executive

In a Parliamentary form of government, the executive and the legislature are interdependent where the legislature controls the executive and vice-versa. The Constitution mandates that they collaborate and maintain a sense of balance among themselves.

4.1 Meaning of Executive

The organ of the government that primarily looks after implementation of policies and administration is called the executive. The executive takes important policy decisions, supervises and co-ordinates with the routine administrative functioning. In a government, one institution takes important policy decisions and decides about the rules and regulations. While, the other is in charge of implementing those rules.

Functions of the Executive

- Executive is the institution of the government which holds the responsibility of **implementation of laws and policies** adopted by the legislature.
- It is involved in the framing of policies of the government.
- The official designation of executive varies from country to country, according to the form of government, which has adopted by the country.

- The executive branch includes the President, Prime Minister and ministers and also includes the administrative machinery such as the civil servants.
- The head of the government and their ministers charged with the overall responsibility of the government policy and together they known as **Political Executive.** The body responsible for the day to day administration is called the **Permanent Executive.**

Types of Executives

The types of executives in Parliamentary system, Presidential system and Semi-Presidential system are discussed below

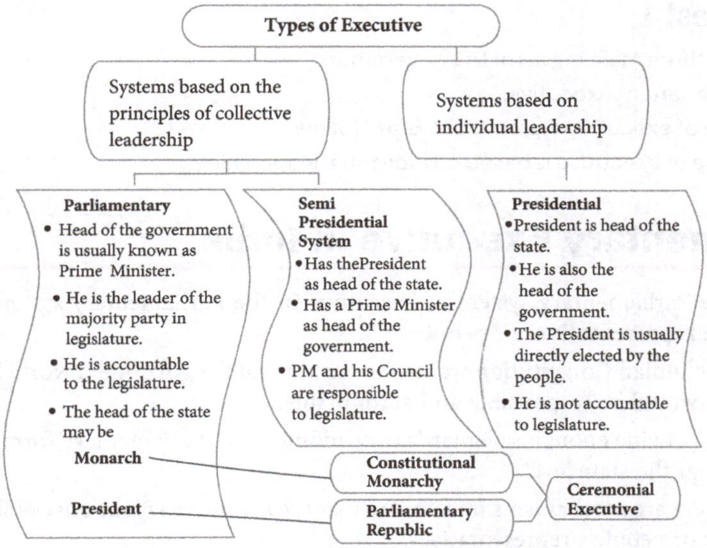

▲ *Types of Executive*

Parliamentary System

- The Parliamentary system is one where the formulation of policies and enactment of the laws of a country are done by the Parliament. In this system, the **Prime Minister is the head** of the government while the President or monarch is the nominal head of the state.
- The role of President or monarch is primarily ceremonial and the Prime Minister with the cabinet exercises effective power. For example, Germany, Italy, Japan, UK, Portugal, India are some of the countries which follow the Parliamentary system.

Presidential System

- In this system, the **President is the head** of the state as well as the head of the government. For example, the USA, Brazil and most nations of Latin America have adopted the Presidential system.
- In this system, the President is directly elected by the people and he is not responsible to the legislature.

Semi-Presidential System

- A Semi-Presidential system is the form of government which has both the President and Prime Minister. In this system, the **President is the head of the state** and the **Prime Minister is the head of the government.**
- Prime Minister and the Council of Ministers are responsible to the legislature. But, unlike the Parliamentary system, the President may possess significant day to day powers.

- In this system, it is possible that the President and Prime Minister, sometimes may belong to the same party and at times belong to two different parties and thus, would confront each other. For example, France, Russia, Sri Lanka, etc., are the countries which follow the Semi-Presidential System.

Semi-Presidential Executive in Sri Lanka

- In 1978 the Constitution of Sri Lanka was amended and the system of Executive Presidency was introduced. Under the system of Executive Presidency, people directly elect the President. It may happen that both the President and the Prime Minister belong to the same political party or to different political parties.

Quick Test 1

1. Name the three main organs of the government.
2. Define Permanent executive.
3. What type of executive system does Brazil follow?
4. Which type of executive is based on individual leadership?

4.2 Parliamentary Executive in India

- India follows the Parliamentary system of executive. In the Parliamentary system, the executives are controlled by the **representatives of people**.
- The makers of the Indian Constitution wanted to ensure that the goverment world be sensitive to public expectations and would be responsible and accountable.
- Thus, in order to provide enough safeguards they adopted the Parliamentary form of government both at the centre and at the state level.
- In this system, there are mechanisms that ensure that the executive will be answerable to and controlled by the legislature or people's representatives.
- According to the Parliamentary form of government, executive at the national level comprises of the President (a formal Head of the State) and the Prime Minister with his Council of Ministers. At the state level, the Governor and the Chief Minister with his Council of Ministers run the government.

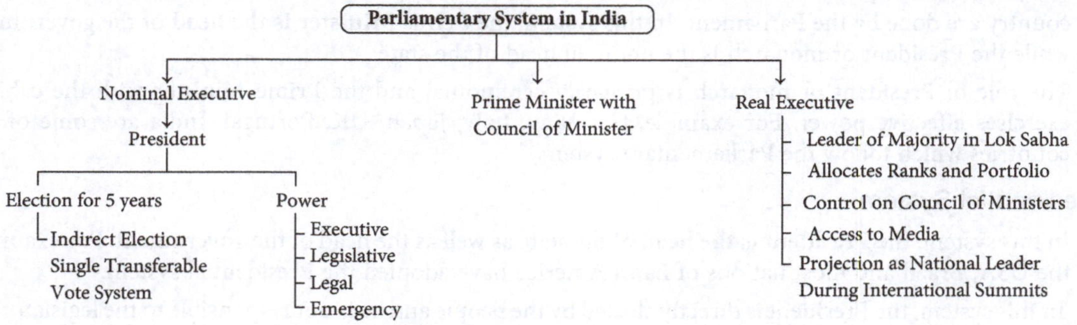

President

- The President is the **nominal head** of the state. The Constitution of India vests the executive powers of the union formally in the President. The President exercises these powers through the Council of Ministers headed by the Prime Minister. The President is **elected indirectly** for a period of **five years**.
- The President is elected by the elected MLAs and MPs, according to the principle of **proportional representation** with single transferable vote.

- The President can be removed from office only by the Parliament by following the **impeachment**[1] procedure. This requires the special majority of both the houses of Parliament and the only ground for impeachment is the violation of the Constitution.

Power and Position of President

- In the Parliamentary system, the President has a wide range of executive, legislative, judicial and emergency powers which can be exercised only on the advice of the Council of Ministers headed by the Prime Minister.
- The Prime Minister and the Council of Ministers have support of the majority in the Lok Sabha and they constitute the true executive. In most cases, the President has to follow the advice of the Council of Ministers'.

- **Article 74 (1)** of the Indian Constitution states that there shall be a Council of Ministers headed by the Prime Minister to aid and advise the President who shall exercise his functions in accordance with such advice.

Discretionary Powers of President

Constitutionally, the President has the right to be informed of all matters and deliberations (discussions) of the Council of Ministers. The Prime Minister is obliged to furnish all the information that the President may call for.

Besides this, there are three situations where President exercises his **discretionary**[2] powers

(i) When the President thinks that the advice rendered to him has certain flaws or legal breakdown or it is not in the best interest of the country, the President can ask the Council of Ministers to reconsider the decision. However, if the Council of Ministers send back the same advice, then the President would be bound to consider that advice or decision.

(ii) The President also has a **veto power** by which he can withhold or refuse to give consent to bills passed by the Parliament other than **money bill**. Every bill passed by the Parliament goes to the President for his approval to become law. The President can send the bill back to the Parliament for re-consideration. However, if the Parliament passes the same bill again and sends it back to the President, then the president is bound to give consent to the bill, as the veto power is limited.
The President can just keep the bill pending with him without any time limit and enjoys informal power to use this veto in an effective manner which is referred to as **pocket veto**.

(iii) In a situation after an election where no leader has acquired majority in the Lok Sabha to form government, then the President exercises his discretion in judging who may have the support of the majority or who can actually form and run the government.

However, this discretion comes out of political circumstances. In ordinary circumstances, if the Council of Ministers are removed as they depend on the support of the majority in legislature, then the President has the power to make a choice in appointing the Prime Minister to run the government of the country.

Vice-President

- The Vice-President is elected for a term of **five-years**. The only difference between his election and that of the President is that representatives of state legislatures are not included. The Vice-President may be removed from his office by a resolution of the Rajya Sabha passed by a majority and agreed to it by the Lok Sabha.

1 **Impeachment** It is a legal process that involves a legislative body which formally charging a public official with misconduct.
2 **Discretionary** It means the right to decide something based on one's own judgement.

- When the President's office becomes vacant due to death, resignation, expulsion by impeachment, or by other reasons, the Vice-President acts as the President only until a new President is elected. **B.D. Jatti** acted as President on the death of Fakhruddin Ali Ahmed until a new President was elected. Vice-President serves as the **Ex-officio Chairman of the Rajya Sabha.**

4.3 Prime Minister and Council of Ministers

- As the head of the Council of Ministers, the Prime Minister is the most important functionary of the government in our country. In a Parliamentary system, it is essential for the Prime Minister to enjoy the support of the majority in the Lok Sabha.
- A leader who has the **support of the majority** is appointed by the President as Prime Minister and then the Prime Minister decides the Council of Ministers. However, the Prime Minister loses his office if the majority is lost.
- It is required for the Prime Minister and all the Ministers to be members of the Parliament. In case someone becomes the Prime Minister or minister without being an MP, such person needs to get elected to the Parliament within a period of **six months.**

President's Role in Choosing the Prime Minister

After 1977, India's party politics grew more competitive and there have been numerous instances in which no single political party has held a clear majority in the Lok Sabha. In such circumstances, what does the President do?

In the March 1998 elections, no political party or coalition received a majority. The BJP and its partners won 251 seats, falling short of a majority by 21 votes. President K.R. Narayanan followed the procedure.

He asked the leader of the alliance, to furnish the document in support of his claim to form the goverment and also advised to secure a vote of confidence within 10 days of being sworn in.

Powers and Functions of Prime Minister

In India, the Prime Minister enjoys a pre-eminent place in the government by following ways

- The allocation of **ranks and portfolios to the ministers** is done by the Prime Minister depending upon the seniority and political importance.
- The ranks of Cabinet Minister or Minister of state or Deputy Minister are assigned by the Prime Minister. The same role is performed by the Chief Minister in the state level government.
- The Council of Ministers comes into existence only after the Prime Minister has taken oath of office. Hence, the **Council of Ministers cannot exist without the Prime Minister.**
- The death or resignation of the Prime Minister automatically dissolves the Council of Ministers but the death, dismissal, resignation of minister only creates a ministerial vacancy.
- The Prime Minister acts as a link between the Council of Ministers on one hand and the President and Parliament together on the other hand.
- It is Constitutionally mandatory for the Prime Minister to communicate to the President about all decisions of the Council of Ministers relating to the administrative affairs of the union and proposals of legislation. The Prime Minister is involved in all crucial decisions of the government and decides on the policies of the government.
- Thus, the power exercised by the Prime Minister flows from various sources, such as, control over the Council of Ministers, leadership of Lok Sabha, command over bureaucratic machinery, etc. Pt. Nehru described the Prime Minister as the **'Linchpin of Government'**[3].

3 **Linchpin of Government** It refers to the Prime minister, who is considered the essential element in the government structure.

Quick Test 2

1 Define the process through which the President is removed from office?
2 What is pocket veto?
3 How long does the Vice-President hold their position?
4 Which authority allocates ranks and portfolios to the ministers?
5 Who described the Prime Minister as the 'Linchpin of Government'?

Council of Ministers

- The Council of Ministers is also appointed by the President on the advice of the Prime Minister and is **collectively responsible** to the Lok Sabha, which means that a minister who loses confidence of the Lok Sabha is obliged to resign.
- Collective responsibility implies that a vote of no confidence even against a single minister, leads to the resignation of the entire Council of Ministers and further, it also indicates that if a minister does not agree with a policy or decision, the minister either accept the decision or resign.

Size of Council of Ministers

91st Amendment Act, 2003 stated that the size of the Council of Ministers shall not exceed 15 per cent of total number of members of the Lok Sabha or the State Legislative Assembly.

Coalition Government

If none of the parties wins an absolute majority in the general election, the government is formed by a coalition[4] of more than one party.

Since 1989, the system of Coalition Government was introduced in India and many of such governments could not remain in power for the full term of Lok Sabha. These developments have affected the working of the Parliamentary executive in the following ways

- It resulted in the growing discretionary role of the President in selection of the Prime Minister.
- The coalition nature of Indian politics requires much more consultation between political partners. This leads to erosion of Prime Ministerial authority.
- It has also brought restrictions on the privileges of the Prime Minister, like choosing the ministers and deciding their ranks and portfolios.
- The policies and programmes of the government cannot be decided by the Prime Minister alone, as the political parties of different ideologies come together to form government.
- It has led to a lot of negotiations and compromises in policy formulation.
- At the state level, there is a similar parliamentary system, but with some differences.

4.4 Permanent Executive: Bureaucracy

- Bureaucracy or administrative machinery is one of the executive organs of the government who works as a permanent employee. They are assigned the task of **assisting the ministries** in formulating policies and implementing these policies.
- The bureaucracy is politically neutral which means that the bureaucracy will not take any political position on policy matters.
- In a democracy, the elected representatives and the ministers are incharge of the government and the administration is under their control and supervision.

4 **Coalition** It is an alliance between two or more political parties to form a government.

- In the Parliamentary system, the legislature also exercises control over the administration.
- The administrative officers cannot violate the policies adopted by the legislature and the machinery.

Indian Bureaucracy

- The Indian bureaucracy is an enormously complex system consisting of the All India Services, State Services, employees of the local governments technical and managerial staff.
- It is the duty of the bureaucracy to faithfully and efficiently participate in drafting policy and its implementation. In order to make the bureaucracy more representative, the Constitution also ensures that all the sections of the society including the weaker sections have the opportunity to be a part of the bureaucracy.
- For this purpose, the Constitution has provided **reservation in jobs** for Dalits, Adivasis, women and backward classes.This ensures that social inequalities will not come in the way of recruitment to the civil service.
- The Union Public Service Commission (UPSC) selects people for the Indian Administrative Service and the Indian Police Service, which forms the **backbone of the country**. The Collector of a district is the most powerful government official in the district. An IAS or IPS official is allocated to a specific state and works under the direction of the State Government.
- The IAS or IPS officers, on the other hand, are appointed by the Central Government, can return to the service of the Central Government. Most importantly, only the Central Government can take action against them.

Classification of Civil Services

All India Services
- Indian Administrative Services
- Indian Police Service

Central Services
- Indian Foreign Services
- Indian Custom Service

State Services
- Provincial Civil Services

- This means that the Central Government supervises and controls the main administrative officers of the states. Apart from the IAS and IPS officers recruited by the UPSC, officers appointed by the State Public Service Commissions are in charge of the State's Government.
- The members of civil services of the bureaucracy are impartially selected on the basis of merit by the Union Public Service Commission (UPSC) at the centre. A similar kind of Public Service Commission (PSC) is provided for the states also. For recruitment into services of state, the members of the commission are appointed for a fixed term and their removal or suspension is subject to a thorough enquiry made by a judge of the Supreme Court.
- Therefore, bureaucracy is an important instrument through which welfare policies of the government reach to the people.

Quick Test 3

1. Who appoints the Council of Ministers?
2. Which amendment stated that the size of the Council of Ministers shall not exceed 15 per cent of total members of the Lok Sabha?
3. When did the system of Coalition Government started in India?
4. Who is responsible for the recruitment of All India Service Officers?

Mind Map

EXECUTIVES

1 Definition

- The organ of the government that primarily looks after implementation of policies and administration.
- Mandates that they collaborate and maintain a sense of balance among themselves.

2 Functions of Executives

- It is Involved in framing of policies of the government.
- They enforces the law.
- Executive branch includes the President, Prime Minister and ministers.
- Overall responsibilities of the government policy are given to political executive while day to day administration is given to permanent executive.

3 Types of Executive

Presidential System
- President holds the executive power for both state and government (e.g. USA, Brazil).

Parliamentary System
- President is the head of state and Prime Minister is the head of government (e.g. India, UK, Germany).

Semi-Presidential System
- President is the head of state.
- Prime Minister is the head of government (e.g. France, Russia).

4 Parliamentary Executive in India

President
- Executives are controlled by the representative of people.
- Nominal head of the state.
- Executes powers on advice of Council of Ministers.
- He is elected indirectly for a period of five years.

Vice-President
- Plays important role in the event of vacancy of President's office.
- He is elected for five years.

Prime Minister
- Leader of Council of Minister.
- Decides portfolio and policy direction.
- The most important functionary of the government in our country.

Council of Ministers
- Appointed by President on advice of the Prime Minister.
- Collective responsibility implies that a vote of no confidence even against a single minister leads to the resignation of the entire Council of Ministers.

5 Coalition Government

- These developments have affected the working of the Parliamentary executive are growing discretionary role of the President in selection of the Prime Minister.
- Restrictions on the privileges of the Prime Minister.
- Negotiations and compromises in policy formulation.
- At the state level, there is a similar Parliamentary system, but with some differences.

6 Permanent Executive: Bureaucracy

- The executive organs of the government who works as a permanent employee.
- It is politically neutral.
- The legislature also exercises control over the administration.
- The policies adopted by the legislature are implemented by the administrative machinery which also made them politically accountable.

Indian Bureaucracy
- An enormously complex system consisting of the All India Services.
- India has developed a professional administrative infrastructure.
- Efficiently participates in the policy making and its implementation.
- The Constitution has provided reservation in jobs for Dalits, Adivasis, women and backward classes.

NCERT Folder

Intext Questions

1. Procure a photograph of the SAARC summit meeting or the meeting of G-7 countries and list those who attended the meeting. Can you imagine why these people and not some others are attending the meeting? (Pg 80)

Meeting of G-7 Countries

Ans. These leaders and not others are attending the meeting because of the following reasons

- **Economic Power and Influence** The heads of the most economically powerful nations or regional organisations are the ones attending because they have the capacity to shape global or regional policies. Their decisions affect international trade, security and development.
- **Decision-Making Authority** Only the highest-ranking leaders, like Presidents and Prime Ministers, are given the authority to make significant decisions that affect their countries' foreign policies and international co-operation.
- **Regional or Global Significance** The attendees of such summits are leaders whose countries play crucial roles in regional or global stability.

The people attending summits like SAARC or G-7 are those who hold the highest positions of authority in their countries, representing their nations in important discussions about regional or global co-operation. These leaders have the decision-making power and influence necessarily to shape policies and agreements, which is why they are chosen to attend.

2. Neha: It is really very simple. A country having a President has a Presidential executive and one with a Prime Minister has a Parliamentary executive.

How would you explain to Neha that this is not always the case? (Pg 83)

Ans. According to Neha, a country having a President has a Presidential executive and one with a Prime Minister has a Parliamentary executive. But this is not always the case

- In some countries, the executive is a mix of both Presidential and Parliamentary systems. This is called a Semi-Presidential system. In such systems, a country may have both a President and a Prime Minister, where the President is the head of state, and the Prime Minister is the head of government. Example-France.
- Some countries have a President but they still follow a Parliamentary system. In these countries, the President may hold a largely ceremonial role, while the Prime Minister and the Parliament hold the real executive power. Example- Germany and India
- There are some countries where the President holds significant power as the head of state and government, but there is still a Prime Minister. The Prime Minister may have a more limited or symbolic role. Example-Russia

3. Imagine that the Prime Minister wants to impose 'President's rule' in ones state because the State Government has failed to effectively curb atrocities against the Dalits in that state. The President has a different position. He is saying that the provision regarding the President's rule should be used only sparingly. (Pg 89)

In this situation which of the following courses are open to the President?

(i) Tell the Prime Minister that he will not sign on the order promulgating President's rule.
(ii) Dismiss the Prime Minister.
(iii) Ask the Prime Minister to send CRPF to that state.
(iv) Make a press statement about how the Prime Minister is wrong.
(v) Discuss the matter with the Prime Minister and try to dissuade him from taking this action, but if he insists, agreeing to sign the said order.

Ans. (i) While the President has the Constitutional power to promulgate President's rule (under Article 356), this action is done on the advice of the Prime Minister and the Council of Ministers (Article 74). The President cannot act on his own against the advice of the Prime Minister and the Council of Ministers.

The President is expected to respect the advice given by the Prime Minister in this matter, even if they may have reservations.

(ii) The President does not have the authority to dismiss the Prime Minister uni-laterally unless the Prime Minister has lost the confidence of the Lok Sabha.

So, in this case, the President cannot dismiss the Prime Minister just because of a difference in opinion about invoking President's Rule.

(iii) The President has the power to recommend measures for addressing issues like law and order, but this specific action of sending the CRPF is typically within the jurisdiction of the Prime Minister and the Union Government.

The President can suggest or recommend action, but cannot order the Prime Minister to take this specific step unless the situation is dire and requires a central response.

(iv) The President is expected to maintain a position of neutrality and Constitutional propriety. Publicly criticising the Prime Minister or making political statements about the Prime Minister's actions would undermine the office of the President and the Constitutional framework. Such actions would not align with the President's role as a neutral Constitutional head.

(v) The President should discuss the matter with the Prime Minister and express concerns if they believe the President's Rule is being invoked prematurely or unnecessarily.

The President has the discretion to advise and discuss with the Prime Minister, but ultimately, the Prime Minister has the final say on the advice to be given to the President. If the Prime Minister insists on taking the action of imposing President's rule, the President must respect the advice of the Council of Ministers and proceed with signing the order.

4. Suppose the Prime Minister is to select the Council of Ministers. What will he/she do? (Pg 94)

(i) Select those who are experts in the various subjects.

(ii) Select only those who are from his/her party.

(iii) Select those who are personally loyal and dependable.

(iv) Select those who are supporters of the government.

(v) Take into account the political weight of the various aspirants and choose from among them

Ans. (i) While expertise in various subjects (such as finance, foreign affairs, defense, etc.) is certainly important for ministers, the Prime Minister does not always select ministers based purely on expertise.

Expertise is often balanced with other factors, such as political considerations, the need to represent different states or regions, etc.

(ii) The Prime Minister typically selects members from their own political party to form the Council of Ministers. This ensures party unity and the support of the majority in the Lok Sabha.

However, sometimes members from coalition partners can also be included if the government is a Coalition Government.

(iii) Personal loyalty is an important factor in ministerial selection. A Prime Minister may choose individuals who are loyal to them and can be trusted to support their leadership in the cabinet. However, this is not the only criterion.

(iv) Support for the government's policies is important, but it's a broader concept than just selecting people who support the Prime Minister personally.

The Prime Minister will choose those who are aligned with the government's ideology, agenda and the party's manifesto, but they will also need to consider coalition partners, balance within the party and regional representation.

(v) When selecting the Council of Ministers, the Prime Minister typically takes into account the political weight of various aspirants, such as their influence within the party, loyalty, the regions or communities they represent and their ability to maintain the government's majority in Parliament.

The Prime Minister will choose individuals who can help maintain political stability, represent important constituencies and strengthen the government's position.

Exercise

1. A Parliamentary executive means

(i) Executive where there is a Parliament.

(ii) Executive elected by the Parliament.

(iii) Where the Parliament functions as the executive.

(iv) Executive that is dependent on support of the majority in the Parliament.

Ans. (iv) Executive that is dependent on support of the majority in the Parliament.

2. Read this dialogue. Which argument do you agree with? Why?

(i) Amit : Looking at the Constitutional provisions, it seems that the President is only a rubber stamp.

(ii) Shama : The President appoints the Prime Minister, so he must have the powers to remove the Prime Minister as well.

(iii) Rajesh : We don't need a President. After the election, the Parliament can meet and elect a leader to be the Prime Minister.

Ans. (i) The argument raised by Amit is correct because despite having certain discretionary powers, the President is bound to the advice given by the Council of Ministers. Even the veto power of the President is limited. The President is bound to give his assent to the bill which is sent for re-consideration to the Parliament.

3. Match the following.

A. Works within the particular state in which recruited.	1. Indian Foreign Services
B. Works in any Central Government office located either at the national capital or elsewhere in the country.	2. State Civil Services
C. Works in a particular state to which allotted; can also be sent on deputation to the centre.	3. All India Services
D. Works in Indian missions abroad.	4. Central Services

Ans. A-2 B-4 C-3 D-1

4. Identify the ministry which may have released the following news items. Would this be a ministry of the Central Government or the State Government? Why?

(i) An official release said that in 2004-05, the Tamil Nadu Textbooks Corporation would release new versions for standards VII, X and XI.

(ii) A new railway loop line bypassing the crowded Tiruvallur-Chennai section to help iron-ore exporters. The new line, likely to be about 80 km long, will branch of at Puttur and then reach Athipattu near the port.

(iii) The three member sub-divisional committee formed to verify suicide by farmers in Ramyampet mandal has found that the two farmers who committed suicide this month have had economic problems due to failure of crops.

Ans. (i) It is the Ministry of education under the State Government. This is because the textbooks related to education in a particular state are published by the Government of the State.

(ii) It is the Ministry of Railways under the Central Government. This is because the Indian Railways Sector is an All-India Organisation that is managed by the Central Government.

(iii) It is the Ministry of Agriculture under the State Government. This is because agriculture at the sub-divisional level is supervised by the Agricultural Department of the State Government.

5. While appointing the Prime Minister, the President selects

(i) Leader of the largest party in the Lok Sabha.

(ii) Leader of the largest party in alliance which secures a majority in the Lok Sabha.

(iii) The leader of the largest party in the Rajya Sabha.

(iv) Leader of the alliance or party that has support of the majority in Lok Sabha.

Ans. (iv) Leader of the alliance or party that has support of the majority in Lok Sabha.

6. Read the discussion and say which of these statements applies most to India.

(i) Alok : Prime Minister is like a king, he decides everything in our country.

(ii) Shekhar : Prime Minister is only the 'first among equals', he does not have any special powers. All ministers and the Prime Minister have similar jobs.

(iii) Bobby : Prime Minister has to consider the expectations of the party members and other supporters of the government. But after all, the Prime Minister has a greater say in policy making and in choosing the ministers.

Ans. (iii) The statement made by Bobby applies to India as the Prime Minister of India is real executive and also heads the executive and is accountable to the legislature at the same time.

7. Why do you think is the advice of the Council of Ministers binding on the President? Give your answer in not more than 100 words.

Ans. The advice of the Council of Ministers is binding on the President in a Parliamentary executive because

- The Council of Ministers is an elected executive that has the support of the majority in the legislature.
- It also emphasises the supreme authority of elected representatives in a republic.
- This arrangement distinctively projects the President as a ceremonial head and limits the powers vested in him/her to avoid conflict within the executive.

Thus, the executive, legislative, judicial and emergency powers of the President are exercised only on the advice of the Council of Ministers.

8. The Parliamentary system of executive vests many powers in the legislature for controlling the executive. Why do you think is it necessary to control the executive?

Ans. It is necessary for the legislature to control the executive for the following reasons

- To ensure its accountability to the legislature.

- The various mechanisms ensures that the executive is answerable and controlled by the people's representatives so that there is transparency and accountability.
- The control on the executive is must so that it works according to the laws and checks deviation of any kind.
- It also prevents the domination of personality cult and provides a check on arbitrary functioning and concentration of power into a single source.

9. It is said that there is too much of interference in the working of the administrative machinery. It is suggested that there should be more and more autonomous agencies which do not have to answer to the ministers.

(i) Do you think this will make administration more people friendly?

(ii) Do you think this will make administration more efficient?

(iii) Does democracy mean full control of elected representatives over the administration?

Ans. (i) This will not make administration more people friendly as it would function arbitrarily and thus, lose accountability without checks and balances.

(ii) This will not make administration more efficient as it would lead to non-compliance by bureaucratic executives with government policies. Thus, it would lead to contradiction of the bureaucracy with the objectives of the government. Efficiency in this situation is not valid as social welfare would be compromised.

(iii) Democracy does not mean full control of elected representatives over the administration. The task of elected representatives is to make laws and keep the administration accountable. Administration is a specialised task that is best handled by the administrative machinery.

Therefore, it requires a certain degree of autonomy to carry out its task.

10. Write an essay of two hundred words on the proposal to have an elected administration instead of an appointed administration.

Ans.
- If the administration is elected instead of appointed, it can give rise to chaos. To handle administrative task, the executives should have deep knowledge of the nation, its problems, its future prospects and the various perspective to approach them should be clear.
- Only a person with deep knowledge of the facts and analytical skills can make out the possible consequences of any provision, policies and programmes of the government.
- Thus, skilled candidates need to be selected to ensure smooth working of the administrative machinery at ground level. This can be done through various written exams that test a broad range of skills as it is not otherwise possible to judge the knowledge and eligibility of a candidate only through elections.
- More money and time would be required in election of the executive and the selection criteria to judge the candidates would become very difficult.
- Electoral process is more suited for legislatures, as they give representation to people in law making. The domain of execution needs expertise even though it can be monitored by elected representatives.
- Elected representative may succeed in administration at smaller levels but large scale administration at the national level required an appointed administration.

Exam Pattern Questions

Objective Type Questions

Multiple Choice Questions (MCQs)

1. Which of the following is/are part of Executive? Competency Based Que

I. President
II. Prime Minister
III. Civil Servants
IV. Council of Ministers

Codes

(a) I and II (b) II and III
(c) I, II and IV (d) All of these

2. Identify the country having a Semi-Presidential system. Diksha App

(a) France (b) Canada
(c) Japan (d) India

3. The Presidential executive puts much emphasis on the President as the .... and as source of all executive power.

(a) Chief Executive (b) Political leader
(c) President (d) None of these

4. Which of the following statements about the President of India is incorrect? Competency Based Que

(a) He/she is the head of the state.
(b) He/she is accountable to the legislature.
(c) He/she is the Commander in chief of the Indian Armed Forces.
(d) He/she does not appoint the Chief Minister of the states.

5. Select the correct statement regarding the Parliamentary system. Competency Based Que Diksha App

(a) The President is the head of the government and the Prime Minister is the head of the state.
(b) The Prime Minister is the head of the government and the President is the head of the state.
(c) There is no distinction between the head of the state and the head of the government.
(d) Head of the state is always elected.

6. The Constitution of India vests the executive power of the Union formally in the ....

(a) Prime Minister (b) Chief Minister
(c) President (d) Vice-President

7. The President of India can be removed by .... Diksha App

(a) Parliament (b) Prime Minister
(c) Judiciary (d) Council of Ministers

8. Which type of veto power used by the President in this statement? Competency Based Que

The President can just keep the bill pending with him without any time limit

(a) Qualified Veto (b) Suspensive Veto
(c) Pocket Veto (d) Absolute Veto

9. If no political party or coalition received a majority in the general election then how does the President appoint the Prime Minister?

(a) By consultation with his secretary
(b) By consultation with the last ruling party
(c) By his own discretion
(d) None of the above

10. The tenure of the cabinet is .... but it can be removed earlier by the President.

(a) 10 years (b) 7 years (c) 5 years (d) 6 years

11. Who is the Ex-officio Chairman of the Rajya Sabha?

(a) Speaker of the House of People
(b) Person appointed by the member of Rajya Sabha.
(c) Person nominated by the President
(d) Vice-President

12. It shall be the duty of .... to aid and advise the President who shall exercise his functions in accordance with such advice.

(a) Cabinet Minister
(b) Council of Minister headed by the Prime Minister
(c) Speaker of the House of People
(d) Vice-President

13. According to 91st Amendment Act 2003, it was decided that the size of the Council of Ministers shall not exceed Diksha App

(a) 15 per cent of the total number of members of the House of the People.
(b) one-third of the total number of members of the House of the People.
(c) one-fourth of the total number of members of the House of the People.
(d) 20 per cent of total number of members of the House of the People.

14. What is the total strength of the Council of Minister?

(a) 10 per cent (b) 20 per cent
(c) 15 per cent (d) There is no limit

15. Who is collectively responsible to the Lok Sabha?
(a) President (b) Member of Parliament
(c) Council of Ministers (d) Speaker of the House

16. Which of the following is/are the characteristic(s) of the Cabinet System?
(a) Collective liability (b) Political Uniformity
(c) Responsibility of Lok Sabha on Council of Ministers
(d) All of the above

17. Who enjoys a pre-eminent place in the government?
(a) The Prime Minister (b) The President
(c) The Governor
(d) The Chief Minister of the state

18. Who allocates ranks and portfolios to the ministers?
(a) Prime Minister (b) President
(c) Vice-President (d) None of these

19. The policies and programmes of the government cannot be decided by the .... alone.
(a) Judges of Supreme Court (b) Prime Minister
(c) Speaker of Lok Sabha (d) Vice President

20. Which of the following government organs is responsible for the implementation of rules and regulation? Competency Based Que

I. Legislature **II. Judiciary**
III. Executive **IV. Parliament**

Codes
(a) Only I (b) III and II
(c) III and IV (d) Only III

21. Which organisation is responsible for conducting the process of recruitment of the Civil Servants for the Government of India? Diksha App
(a) Indian Administrative Service
(b) Union Public Service Commission
(c) Competition Commission of India
(d) Indian Commission

22. Which of the following categories of the Civil Service is under the Central Service?
(a) Indian Police Service (b) Indian Administrative Service
(c) Indian Forest Service (d) India Foreign Service

23. Choose the wrong statement. Competency Based Que
(a) The Prime Minister allocates ranks and portfolios to the ministers.
(b) The Council of Ministers is collectively responsible to the Lok Sabha.
(c) Collective responsibility is based on the principle of the solidarity of the cabinet.
(d) Chief Minister, unlike the Prime Minister is the leader of the majority party in the assembly.

24. Who is the part of electoral college to election of the President Competency Based Que
I. Elected member of the both the House of Parliament
II. Nominated member of the both the House of Parliament
III. Elected member of the State Legislative Assembly
IV. Elected member of Legislative Council.

Codes
(a) I and II (b) I, II and III
(c) I and III (d) All of these

25. Consider the following statements related to Indian bureaucracy
I. The Indian bureaucracy consisting of the All-India Services, state services, employees of the local governments technical and managerial staff.
II. There is no provision in the Constitution which ensures that all the sections of the society including the weaker sections have the opportunity to be a part of the bureaucracy.

Select the incorrect statements?
(a) Only I (b) Only II
(c) Both I and II (d) None of these

26. Given below are two statements Competency Based Que
Statement I The official designations of the executive vary from country to country.
Statement II The executive is not involved in framing policies.
In the light of above statements, choose the correct answer from the options given below
(a) Both Statement I and Statement II are true.
(b) Both Statement I and Statement II are false.
(c) Statement I is true, but Statement II is false.
(d) Statement I is false, but Statement II is true.

27. Match the Constitutions in List I correctly with their descriptions given in List II and choose the appropriate code as the correct answer

List I	List II
A. Political Executive	1. The primary responsibility of this group is to draft and implement policies decided by elected representatives.
B. Permanent Executive	2. The Prime Minister, along with the Council of Ministers, is responsible for the day to day administration and governance.
C. Presidential System	3. The President serves as both the head of state and the head of government, holding significant power.
D. Parliamentary System	4. A Prime Minister is the head of government and the President or Monarch is usually the ceremonial head of state.

Codes

	A	B	C	D		A	B	C	D
(a)	1	3	4	2	(b)	3	2	1	4
(c)	2	1	3	4	(d)	4	2	3	1

Assertion-Reason Questions

Direction (Q. Nos. 28-32) In the questions given below, there are two statements marked as Assertion (A) and Reason (R). Read the statements and choose the correct option. **Competency Based Que**

Codes

(a) Both A and R are true and R is correct explanation of A.
(b) Both A and R are true, but R is not the correct explanation of A.
(c) A is true, but R is false.
(d) A is false, but R is true.

28. Assertion (A) India follows the Parliamentary system of executive.

Reason (R) India already had some experience of running the Parliamentary system under the Government of India Acts of 1919 and 1935.

29. Assertion (A) The President also has a veto power by which he can withhold or refuse to give assent to bills passed by the Parliament.

Reason (R) If the Parliament passes the same bill again after re-consideration and sends it back to the President, then the President is not bound to give assent to the bill.

30. Assertion (A) The Constitution vests the executive powers of the union in the Prime Minister.

Reason (R) The Prime Minister of India is the head of the government.

31. Assertion (A) Council of Minister is collectively responsible to the Lok Sabha.

Reason (R) Collective responsibility implies that a vote of no confidence even against a single minister leads to the resignation of the entire Council of Ministers.

32. Assertion (A) A body of persons that looks after the implementation of rules and regulations of an organisation is known as the executive.

Reason (R) The executive branch includes the President, Prime Minister and ministers and also extends to the administrative machinery, like the Civil Servants.

Passage Based Questions

33. Read the given passage and answer the following questions.

President is the formal head of the government. In this formal sense, the President has wide ranging executive, legislative, judicial and emergency powers. In a Parliamentary System, these powers are in reality used by the President only on the advice of the Council of Ministers. The Prime Minister and the Council of Ministers have support of the majority in the Lok Sabha and they are the real executive. In most of the cases, the President has to follow the advice of the Council of Ministers. "We did not give him any real power but we have made his position one of authority and dignity. The Constitution wants to create neither a real executive nor a mere figurehead, but a head that neither reigns nor governs it wants to create a great figurehead...".

(i) Which organ of the executive is mentioned in the passage?
(a) Authority of the President
(b) Legitimacy of Prime Minister
(c) Both (a) and (b)
(d) None of the above

(ii) .... is the formal head of the government.
(a) Vice-President
(b) President
(c) Chief Minister
(d) Council of Minister

(iii) President follows the advice of ....
(a) Council of Ministers
(b) Parliamentary Secretaries
(c) Chief Minister
(d) Prime Minister

(iv) Consider the following statement. **Competency Based Que**

I. Constitution makers did not give any real power to the Prime Minister but they have made his position one of authority and dignity.

II. The real executive is Council of Minister headed by the Prime Minister.

Which of the statements given above is/are correct
(a) Only I (b) Only II
(c) Both I and II (d) None of these

34. Read the given passage and answer the following questions.

There were some members in the Constituent Assembly who felt that ministers should be elected by the legislature and not selected by the Prime Minister or Chief Minister: "Swiss system under which the legislature elects the executive for a certain period ...is to my mind the best form of government for the provinces... The system of the single transferable vote is ...the best system that can be adopted for the appointment of the executive because in that all interests will be represented and no party in the legislature will have any occasion to feel that it is not represented"

(i) **What form of government is practiced in Switzerland?**
(a) Democratic Federal Republic
(b) Monarchical Government
(c) Parliamentary Government
(d) None of the above

(ii) **The Executive organ of the government which includes the Prime Minister, the ministers and a large organisation is called the ....**
(a) Bureaucracy (b) Administrative machinery
(c) Both (a) and (b) (d) Neither (a) nor (b)

(iii) **Who proposed that ministers should be elected by the legislature and not selected by the Prime Minister or Chief Minister?**

35. Read the given passage and answer the following questions.

While efficiency and merit are the norms for recruitment, the Constitution also ensures that all sections of the society including the weaker sections have an opportunity to be part of the public bureaucracy. For this purpose, the Constitution has provided reservation in jobs for Scheduled Castes and Scheduled Tribes. Subsequently, reservations have also been provided for women, Other Backward Classes (OBC) and Economically Weaker Sections (EWS).

(i) **Which of the following is a key feature of the recruitment process for Civil Servants in India?**
(a) The recruitment process is based on the seniority system.
(b) Civil Servants are recruited without considering merit.
(c) The UPSC conducts the recruitment based on merit.
(d) Political affiliations are considered in the recruitment process.

(ii) **Which process ensures the impartiality of the members of the Public Service Commissions in India?**
(a) A judicial enquiry by a Supreme Court judge for their removal or suspension.
(b) The Prime Minister personally reviews their work.
(c) The Parliament evaluates their performance.
(d) Both A and C.

(iii) **Discuss the significance of a merit-based recruitment system for the Indian bureaucracy.**

Answers

1. (d) All of these
2. (a) France
3. (a) Chief Executive
4. (b) He/she is accountable to the legislature.
5. (b) The prime Minister is the head of the government and the President is the head of the state.
6. (c) President.
7. (a) Parliament
8. (c) Pocket Veto.
9. (c) By his own discretion
10. (c) 5 Years
11. (d) Vice-President
12. (b) Council of Minister headed by the Prime Minister
13. (a) 15 per cent of the total number of members of the House of the People.
14. (c) 15 per cent
15. (c) Council of Ministers
16. (d) All of the above
17. (a) The Prime Minister
18. (a) Prime Minister
19. (b) Prime Minister
20. (d) Only III
21. (b) Union Public Service Commission
22. (d) Indian Foreign Service
23. (d) Chief Minister, unlike the Prime Minister is the leader of the majority party in the assembly.
24. (c) I and III
25. (b) Only II
26. (c) Statement I is true, but statement II is false.
27. (c) 2 1 3 4
28. (a) Both A and R are true and R is the correct explanation of A.
29. (c) A is true, but R is false.
30. (d) A is false, but R is true.
31. (a) Both A and R are correct and R is the correct explanation of A.
32. (a) Both A and R are true and R is the correct explanation of A.
33. (i) (c) Both (a) and (c) (ii) (b) President
(iii) (a) Council of Ministers (iv) (b) only II
34. (i) (a) Democratic Federal Republic
(ii) (c) Both (a) and (b)
(iii) Some members of the Constituent Assembly proposed that ministers should be elected by the legislature, similar to the Swiss system, where the legislature elects the executive for a certain period. They also suggested using the system of the single transferable vote to ensure all interests are represented.
35. (i) (c) The UPSC conducts the recruitment based on merit
(ii) (d) Both (a) and (c)
(iii) A merit-based recruitment system is essential for maintaining the professionalism and effectiveness of the Indian bureaucracy. By selecting candidates based on their qualifications, knowledge, skills and aptitude, the system ensures that only the most capable individuals are inducted into public service.

Subjective Questions

Very Short Answer Type Questions

1. Why did India opted for Parliamentary system?

Ans. India adopted for the Parliamentary form of government because

- India had the experience of Parliamentary system during pre-independence era.
- The makers of the Constitution wanted a strong executive branch and at the same time provide enough safeguards to check against the personality cult and work for the welfare of people.

2. Mention the forms of government in a democracy with examples.

Ans. The various forms of government in a democracy are

- Presidential system of government in USA and Brazil.
- Parliamentary form of government prevalent in UK and India.
- Semi-Presidential form of government practiced in Russia and France.

3. How is President elected in India? How is President elected in India.

Ans. The President of India is indirectly elected by the representatives of people such as MPs and MLAs of the country by the method of proportional representation with a single transferable vote.

4. How can a president be removed from office?

Ans. The President can be removed from the office only by the impeachment procedure of the Parliament with special majority of both the Houses of Parliament and the only ground for impeachment is the violation of the Constitution.

5. How is pocket veto availed by the President?

Ans. The veto in which the President can keep the bill pending with him without any time limit and enjoys informal power to use this veto in effective manner is referred to as pocket veto.

6. Council of Ministers 'floats and sinks' together. Explain.

Competency Based Que

Ans. The council of ministers is collectively responsible to Lok Sabha, collective responsibility of the Council of Ministers implies that

- A vote of no-confidence even against a single ministry leads to the resignation of the entire Council of Ministers.
- If a minister does not agree with a policy or decision of the council, the minister either accepts the decision or resigns.

Thus, we can say that Council of Ministers 'floats and sinks' together.

7. How is the Governor of a state appointed?

Ans. The Governor of a state shall be appointed by the President by warrant under his hand and seal. Generally, President of India on the advice of the Council of Ministers headed by the Prime Minister of India appoint a Governor of a state for a period of 5 years.

8. How are ranks and portfolios allocated to the ministers?

Ans. The allocation of rank and portfolios are done by the Prime Minister depending upon the seniority and political importance.

9. Define Bureaucracy.

Ans. Bureaucracy is one of the executives of the government who works as a permanent employee of the government and are assigned the task of assisting the ministers in formulating policies and implementing these policies.

10. What does the Constitution provide for the re-presentation of all sections of the society into the civil services?

Ans. For the re-presentation of all sections of the society into the civil services, the Constitution provided the reservation of jobs for Dalits and Adivasis and reservation for women and backward classes into the bureaucracy.

11. State the classification of the civil services in India.

Ans. The classification of civil services in India are

All India Services It includes the Indian Administrative Services and Indian Police Services.

Central Services It includes Indian Foreign Services and Indian Revenue Services.

State Services It includes Sales Tax Officers among others.

12. Name the body who is assigned the task of recruiting civil servants.

Ans. The bodies that are assigned the task of recruiting civil servants are

- Union Public Service Commission at the centre.
- State Public Service Commission for the respective states.

Short Answer Type Questions

1. Write down the merits of a good executive.

Ans. The organ of the government that primarily looks after the functions of implementation and administration is called the executive.

The merits of a good executive are

- It looks after the administration of law and order in the country, so that the law breakers do not find an opportunity to carry out their evil intentions.
- It should avoid financial fluctuations in the country to maintain stability in economy.
- A good executive sees that the national boundaries are preserved and there is no danger from external aggression.
- It should have the capacity to accommodate all the sections of the society in policy and law.

2. Explain the functions of the executive.

Ans. The functions of the executive are

- It is involved in framing the policies of the government.
- The executive branch includes the President, Prime Minister and ministers and which also extends to the administrative machinery, like the civil servants.
- These are two division of executive, one is the political executive charged with the overall responsibility of the government policy and the other is the permanent executive that looks after the day to day administration.

3. Distinguish between Parliamentary and Presidential executive citing appropriate examples. Diksha App

Ans. The difference between Political executive and Permanent executive are as follows

Parliamentary Executive	Presidential Executive
System based on the principles of collective leadership	System based on individual leadership
Head of Government is usually known as Prime Minister	President is head of the state as well as Head of the government
Prime Minister is the leader of the majority party in Legislature	The President is usually directly elected by the people
Prime Minister is accountable to the legislature	President is not accountable to the legislature
Examples: India, Canada, Japan, Italy , Germany, UK, Portugal	For example, United States, Brazil and most nations in Latin America, Belarus, Cyprus, Argentina

4. Discuss the Presidential system of government.

Ans. Presidential system is the form of government where the President is the head of the state as well as the head of the government and the office of the President is very powerful in theory and practice is known as Presidential system of government.

In this system, the President is directly elected by the people and he is not accountable to the legislature.

For example, USA, Brazil and most nations of Latin America opted the Presidential system of government.

5. 'The President is an essential part of Parliament in India'. Do you agree with this statement? Competency Based Que

Ans. Yes, the President is an essential part of the Parliament. The Parliament consist of President, Lok Sabha and Rajya Sabha. Similar to the British emperor, the President is an integral part of the Parliament.

The President can call both the houses for session. He can dissolve the Lok Sabha.

Any bill passed by the Parliament cannot become an act unless it is signed by the President. He has the authority to address both the houses jointly or separately. He can issue ordinance if both the houses are not in session and the circumstances are compelling for the law.

6. Examine whether the President can become a dictator during emergency?

Ans. The President cannot become a dictator during emergency due to the following reasons

- He can declare emergency only when the Council of Ministers sends such a recommendation to him in writing.
- The proclamation of emergency made by the President must be approved by the Parliament within one month. If the Parliament does not give its approval, it will cease to operate at the expiry of one month from the date of its declaration.
- If the President tries to become dictator, he can be removed by the Parliament by the method of impeachment.

7. Discuss the importance of the position of President in a Parliamentary system, even though the President is mainly a ceremonial figure. Competency Based Que

Ans. In a Parliamentary system, the position of President is important to fulfill specific Constitutional and ceremonial roles. Although the President is largely a formal power holder and serves as a ceremonial head of state, their position becomes crucial for maintaining the stability and continuity of government.

In a Parliamentary system, the Council of Ministers, headed by the Prime Minister, is dependent on the support of the majority in the legislature. This means that the government can be removed at any time if it loses the confidence of the legislature, requiring the formation of a new government. To manage such situations effectively, a President with a fixed term is needed to ensure a consistent, neutral head of state.

8. What do you understand by the dominance of executive leadership?

Ans. The dominance of executive can be understood by following ways

- In the Parliamentary system, the legislature is formed mainly by the elected representatives because the leader of political party who gets the majority is called upon by the President to form the government.
- The Prime Minister forms the Council of Ministers. In the ministry mostly the members of his own party are taken.
- The Prime Minister leads the Parliament. Whenever, he wants he can dissolve the Lok Sabha. Hence, it is considered as dominance of executive leadership.

9. Discuss the relationship between the President and the Prime Minister.

Ans. The relationship between the President and the Prime Minister is as follows

- According to the Constitution, the President calls upon the leader of the majority party to form government and appoints the Prime Minister.
- President is the nominal head of state while the Prime Minister is the real head of the state.
- The Prime Minister serves as a link between the President and the Council of Ministers.
- The President is indirectly elected, while the Prime Minister is directly elected and leads the nation.

10. Write a short note on individual responsibility of ministers.

Ans. Along with collective responsibility, a minister is individually responsible for handling the charge of his department efficiently and in accordance with the accepted policies. He is responsible for the cases in the department incurred due to mishandling and due to mis-management. The minister is morally bound for it.

A railway accident prompted late Lalbahadur Shastri, then the Railway Minister to resign on moral ground following the dictate of his conscience.

Similarly, if a minister is involved in corrupt practices or misuse of public money or some criminal case or murder, etc. he is individually responsible for it.

11. Write a short note on Vice-President?

Ans. The Vice-President is elected for a five-year term. The only difference between his election and that of the President is that representatives of State Legislatures are not included in the electoral college.

- The Vice-President may be removed from his office by a resolution of the Rajya Sabha passed by a majority and agreed to it by the Lok Sabha.
- When the President's office becomes vacant due to death, resignation, expulsion by impeachment, or other factors, the (removal).
- The Vice-President acts as the President only until a new President is elected.

12. Discuss the powers and functions of the Prime Minister.

Ans. As the head of the Council of Ministers, the Prime Minister becomes the most important functionary of the government in our country. It is essential for the Prime Minister to enjoy the support of the majority in the Lok Sabha.

The powers and functions of the Prime Minister are

- The council comes into existence only after the Prime Minister has taken oath of office, hence the Council of Ministers cannot exist without the Prime Minister.
- The death, resignation of the Prime Minister automatically dissolves the Council of Ministers.
- The Prime Minister acts as a link between the Council of Ministers on one hand and the President and the Parliament on the other hand.
- It is mandatory, constitutionally for the Prime Minister to communicate to the President all decisions regarding the administrative affairs of the union and purpose of legislation.

13. What do you mean by Coalition Government?

Ans. A Coalition Government is a form of a Parliamentary government in which multiple political parties co-operate, together.

The usual reason given for this arrangement is that no party on its own achieves a majority in the Parliament.

The system of Coalition Government in India is prevalent since 1989 but many such governments could not remain in power for the full term of Lok Sabha.

14. What are the outcomes of Coalition Government? Briefly Explain.

Ans. The outcomes of Coalition Government are as follows

- It resulted in the growing discretionary role of the President in selection of the Prime Minister.
- In the Indian politics, it has necessitated much more consultation between political partners, leading to erosion of Prime Ministerial authority.
- It has also brought restrictions on the privileges of the Prime Minister like, choosing the ministers and deciding their ranks and portfolios.
- The policies and programmes of the government cannot be decided by the Prime Minister alone, as the political parties of different ideologies come together to form government.
- It has led to a lot of negotiation and compromise in policy formulation.

Long Answer Type Questions

1. Describe the various forms of government systems in details.

Ans. The various forms of government are

Presidential System In the Presidential system, the office of the President is very powerful in theory and practice as the President is the head of the state as well as the head of the government.

In this system, the President is directly elected by the people and he is not answerable to the legislature. For example, USA, Brazil, etc.

Parliamentary System The system in which the formulation of policies and enactment of the laws are done by the Parliament is called Parliamentary system.

In this system, the Prime Minister is the real head of the government, while the President or Monarch is the nominal head of the state. For example, UK, Portugal, etc.

Semi-Presidential System This is the form of government which has both the President and Prime-Minister, where the President is the head of the state and Prime Minister is head of the government, with his council responsible to the legislature.

But, unlike the Parliamentary system, the President may possess significant day to day powers. It is possible that the President and Prime Minister belong to the same party and at times belong to different parties. For example, Russia, Sri Lanka, etc.

2. How does the Parliamentary system of government in India ensure accountability and prevent the concentration of power in the hands of one individual?

Ans. The Parliamentary system of government in India ensures accountability and prevents the concentration of power in the hands of a single individual through

(i) **Collective Responsibility** In the Parliamentary system, the entire Council of Ministers, headed by the Prime Minister, is collectively responsible to the Lok Sabha (the lower house of Parliament).

If the government loses the confidence of the majority in the Lok Sabha, the entire cabinet, including the Prime Minister, must resign. This collective responsibility ensures that the executive branch remains answerable to the legislature and to the people.

(ii) **Leadership by the Prime Minister** The Prime Minister, although the head of government, does not hold absolute power. His position depends on the continued support of the majority in the Lok Sabha.

This ensures that decisions are made collectively and that the Prime Minister is not able to make decisions on his own.

(iii) **Role of the Opposition** The presence of a vibrant opposition in the Parliamentary system also ensures that the government remains accountable. The opposition has the right to question the government's actions, propose alternative policies and hold the government to account through various Parliamentary procedures such as debates, question hours and votes of no confidence.

This acts as a check on the power of the ruling party and its leaders.

(iv) **Regular Elections** The system ensures that the government is directly answerable to the people through regular elections.

At both the national and state levels, the electorate has the power to choose its representatives. If the people are dis-satisfied with the government's performance, they can vote in new representatives during elections, ensuring that the government remains responsive to the public.

3. State the discretionary powers of the President.

Ans. There are three situations where the President exercises his discretionary powers

(i) Firstly, when the President thinks that the advice rendered to him has certain flaws or legal breakdown, or it is not in the best interest of the country, then the President can ask the Council of Ministers to reconsider the decision.

However, if the Council of Ministers send back the same advice, then the President would be bound to consider that advice or decision.

(ii) Secondly, every bill passed by the Parliament goes to the President for his assent to become law. The President can sent the bill back for re-consideration, and if the bill is send back to the President for the second time, then the President is bound to give assent to the bill as his veto power is limited.

The President can just keep the bill pending with him without any time limit and enjoys informal power to use this veto in effective manner which is referred to as 'pocket veto'.

(iii) Thirdly, in a situation after election when no leader has acquired majority in the Lok Sabha to form government, then the President exercises his discretion in judging who really may have the support of the majority or who can actually form and run the government.

However, this discretion comes out of political circumstances.

4. In India, the Prime Minister enjoys a pre-eminent place in the government and is called the Linchpin of Government. Validate the statement.

Competency Based Que; Diksha App

Ans. In India, the Prime Minister enjoys a pre-eminent place in the government and is called as the linchpin of Government due to the following reasons

- In India, the Prime Minister enjoys a pre-eminent place in the government. The Council of Ministers cannot exist without the Prime Minister.
- The council comes into existence only after the Prime Minister has taken the oath of office.
- The death or resignation of the Prime Minister automatically brings about the dissolution of the Council of Ministers but the demise, dismissal or resignation of a minister only creates a ministerial vacancy.
- The Prime Minister acts as a link between the Council of Ministers on the one hand and the President as well as the Parliament on the other.
- It is also the Constitutional obligation of the Prime Minister to communicate to the President all decisions of the Council of Ministers relating to the administration of the affairs of the union and proposals for legislation.
- The Prime Minister is involved in all crucial decisions of the government and decides on the policies of the government.
- Thus, the power wielded by the Prime Minister flows from various sources, control over the Council of Ministers, leadership of the Lok Sabha, command over the bureaucratic machine, access to media, projection of personalities during elections, projection as national leader during international summitry as well as foreign visits.

Picture Based Questions

1. Observe the cartoon given below and answer the questions that follow.

(i) What does the above cartoon represent?

(a) Walk out in Parliament House
(b) Council of Minister headed by Prime Minister
(c) Protest against leading government
(d) None of the above

Ans. (b) Council of Minister headed by Prime Minister

(ii) What is the implication of the statement 'There is no Council of Ministers without the Prime Minister'?

(a) The Prime Minister is merely a ceremonial figure.
(b) The Prime Minister is essential to the functioning of the Council of Ministers.
(c) The Prime Minister has no real power in the Council.
(d) The Prime Minister can operate without the Council of Ministers.

Ans. (b) The Prime Minister is essential to the functioning of the Council of Ministers.

(iii) Who is collectively responsible to the Lok Sabha?

(a) President (b) Member of Parliament
(c) Council of Minister (d) Speaker of the House

Ans. (c) Council of Minister

(iv) Which of the following is not the power function of Prime Minister?

(a) Allocation of ranks and portfolios to ministers.
(b) PM acts as a link between the Council Minister and President.
(c) PM can keep bill pending with him without any time limit.
(d) None of the above.

Ans. (c) PM can keep bill pending with him without any time limit.

2. Observe the cartoon given below and answer the questions that follow.

(i) Why do people generally want to become ministers?

(a) For financial rewards only

(b) For the power and influence associated with the position

(c) To have more responsibilities

(d) To travel abroad

Ans. (b) For the power and influence associated with the position

(ii) There is competition for certain portfolios within a government because

(a) They provide greater status, influence and control over resources

(b) They are considered prestigious and offer strategic decision-making power

(c) They come with higher financial rewards and benefits

(d) They involve critical responsibilities that shape national policies

Ans. (a) They provide greater status, influence and control over resources

(iii) What is a key factor that determines the power of the Prime Minister in India?

(a) The Prime Minister's ability to influence the media

(b) The Prime Minister's personal popularity with the public

(c) The support of the majority in the Lok Sabha

(d) The Prime Minister's control over the military

Ans. (c) The support of the majority in the Lok Sabha

(iv) What role does the Prime Minister play in the functioning of the government?

(a) The Prime Minister only serves a ceremonial role with limited powers

(b) The Prime Minister is the central figure in government, leading the Council of Ministers

(c) The Prime Minister oversees foreign affairs exclusively

(d) The Prime Minister's role is limited to controlling the media

Ans. (b) The Prime Minister is the central figure in government, leading the Council of Ministers

3. Observe the cartoon given below and answer the questions that follow.

(i) What does the cartoon represents?

(ii) The Chief Minister is not happy after winning the confidence motion. Can you imagine, why this is so?

(iii) How is the Chief Minister appointed when there is no single majority?

Ans. (i) The cartoon represents the challenge that come along with the responsibility of Chief Ministerial position. The real challenge of running the government (especially coalition government) begins after winning the trust vote.

(ii) The Chief Minister is not happy because after the Chief Minister gets the confidence vote of MLAs, he is bound by the limitation set by members in place of independent decision taken by himself or has to make some compromises also to compensate the confidence vote of members. This is particularly true for Coalition Government.

(iii) When there is no single majority party or absolute majority in the assembly, the Governor uses his discretion and appoints the Chief Minister and directs the Chief Minister to prove his majority in the assembly.

SELF ASSESSMENT TEST

Objective Type Questions

1. In which among the following countries is the Parliamentary system followed?
   (a) Italy (b) Sri Lanka
   (c) Brazil (d) Russia
2. The body responsible for the day to day administration is called .... Executive.
   (a) Permanent (b) Political
   (c) Social (d) None of these
3. Select the correct statement. **Competency Based Que; Diksha App**
   (a) The President has veto power regarding both ordinary bill and money bill.
   (B) The President has veto power regarding the amendment bill.
   (c) The President has veto power regarding the Finance bill.
   (d) The President has veto power regarding bills other than money bill.
4. Point out the term not associated with bureaucracy. **Diksha App**
   (a) Hierarchy (b) Permanent nature
   (c) Politically biased (d) Specialisation

Very Short Answer Type Questions

5. Define the three organs of the government.
6. Who elects the President of India?
7. What is the position of Prime Minister in the Council of Ministers?
8. Mention any two powers of Vice-President.
9. Briefly explain the collective responsibility of ministers?
10. Name the All India Services.

Short Answer Type Questions

11. Why was Parliamentary system adopted in India?
12. Mention the discretionary powers of the President.
13. Discuss the relationship between Governor and the State Council of Ministers.
14. 'Bureaucracy a little more responsible and accountable'. Justify. **Competency Based Que**

Long Answer Type Questions

15. Critically examine the emergency powers of the President.
16. Prime Minister is the head of the government'. Analyse this statement and also explain the functions of the Prime minister. **Competency Based Que**
17. 'The Indian bureaucracy today is an enormously complex system'. Examine this statement. **Competency Based Que**

05

CHAPTER

Legislature is the law making organ of the government. The legislature of the Indian union is known as the Parliament, while the legislatures of the states are known as State Legislative Assemblies. The Parliament in India consists of the President and two houses called as the Rajya Sabha and the Lok Sabha.

YOUR STUDY GOALS

5.1 Introduction
5.2 Need for Two Houses of Parliament
5.3 Functions of the Parliament
5.4 Making of Laws by the Parliament
5.5 Parliament's Control Over Executive
5.6 Committees of the Parliament

YOUR PRACTICE GOAL

- Objective Type Questions (39 Qs ; MCQs, A-R, Statements, Matching, Passage Based)
- Subjective Questions (13 VSAs, 8 SAs, 5 LAs 3 Picture Based) 1 Map Based

Legislature

5.1 Introduction

- Parliament is important for carrying out democratic political processes and holding the representatives accountable. This function is the basis of a **representative democracy**[1].
- A true democracy could function only when there is a representative with efficient and effective legislature.

Democratic Capacity of the Parliament

- Legislatures in most democracies are losing their position over the **executive**[2] branch. For example, In India, cabinet makes policies, sets the governance agenda and implements them.
- However, the Parliament exercises control over the cabinet by making them answerable to the Parliament and mandating them to maintain a majority in the legislature.

House of the Parliament

- Legislature exists at both, the **national level** (The Parliament or National legislature) and **state level** (the State legislature).
- The Parliament of India is a **bicameral**[3] legislature as there are two houses.

1 Representative democracy It is a political system where citizens elect representatives to make decisions on their behalf.
2 Executive It is a powerful branch of the government, who is responsible for implementing of laws and policies.
3 Bicameral It is a legislature having two houses.

- The two houses of the Indian Parliament are the **Council of States (Rajya Sabha)** and the **House of the People (Lok Sabha)**.
- The Constitution has given the states the option of establishing either a unicameral or a bicameral legislature. Only six states in India have a bicameral legislature at present.
- The six states in India which have a bicameral legislature are **Andhra Pradesh, Bihar, Karnataka, Maharashtra, Telangana and Uttar Pradesh**.

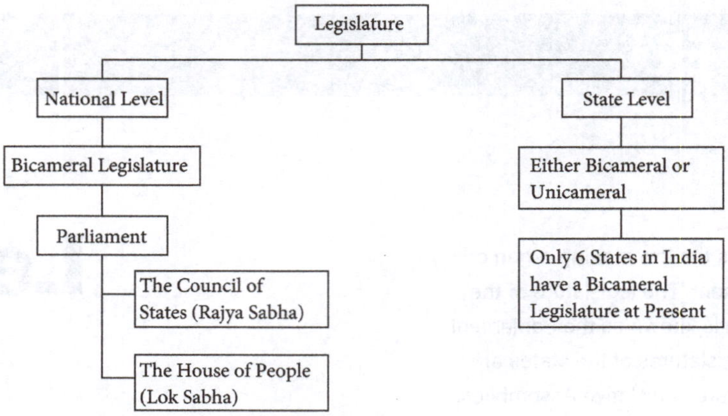

▲ *Houses of The Parliament*

Benefits of a Bicameral Legislature

A bicameral legislature has the following benefits

- It gives representation to all the sections of the society and geographical regions of the country.
- It gives scope for re-considering every decision.
- It ensures double check on every matter, means every bill and policy discussed twice.

Bicameralism in Germany

Bundestag (Federal Assembly)	**Bundesrat** (Federal Council)
▪ This is elected by direct and proportional representation for 4 years period.	▪ It represent the 16 federal states of the country.
	▪ There are 69 seats, which are divided among states on the basis of population.
	▪ The members are ministers in the state level government.
	▪ The members are appointed by the government of the federal states.

Working of the Bundesrat

- All members from one state have to vote together as a bloc on the basis of the instructions given by their State Government.
- If a state has Coalition Government and can't agree on a vote, then they might have to abstain (discard) from voting.
- The bundesrat doesn't vote on every law, but all the policy areas on which the federal states have concurrent powers and are responsible for federal regulations must be passed by it. It also has the power to veto laws in these areas.

5.2 Need for Two Houses of Parliament

We need two houses of Parliament to ensure balanced representation of all the citizens of the society. The Lok Sabha represents the people, while the Rajya Sabha protects state's interests.

Rajya Sabha

Rajya Sabha represents the states of India in the Parliament. It is an **indirectly elected** body where its members are elected by the members of the State Legislative Assembly.

- There are commonly two principles of representation in the second house of the legislature
  - The first principle of representation is **symmetrical representation,** which means giving equal representation to all the parts of the country irrespective of their size or population. For example, in the USA, every state has equal representation in the Senate.
  - The second principle of representation has been adopted where states with larger population get more representatives than states with smaller populations.
- The number of members to be elected from each state has been fixed by the **fourth schedule** of the Constitution.
- Apart from elected members, the Rajya Sabha also has **12 nominated members** from the fields of literature, science, art and social service nominated by the President.

Term of the Rajya Sabha

- The members are elected for a term of six years.
- One-third of the members retire in every two years.
- Thus, the Rajya Sabha is also known as the **permanent house** of the parliament. It never fully dis-solves and elections are held in every two years to fill the vacant one-third seats.
- This arrangement allows the Rajya Sabha to carry out urgent work of the Parliament in cases when the Lok Sabha has been dis-solved and elections have not yet been held.

Powers of the Rajya Sabha

- Considers and approves non-money bills.
- Suggests amendments to money bills but cannot initiate, reject or amend such bills.
- Approves Constitutional Amendments.
- Exercises control over executive by asking questions, introducing motions and resolutions.
- Participates in the election and removal of the President, Vice-President, Judges of the Supreme Court and High Court.
- **Only Rajya Sabha can initiate the procedure for removal of Vice-President.**
- It empowers the Union Government to make laws on matters included in the state list.

Special Power of the Rajya Sabha

The approval of Rajya Sabha is necessary before removing or transferring a matter from state list to either the union or concurrent list.

Lok Sabha

- The Lok sabha and the State Legislative Assemblies are **directly elected** by the people through the **universal adult suffrage**[4].
- The entire country is divided into territorial constituencies, having almost equal population and the value of vote of each individual is the same. One representative is elected from each constituency[5]. There are 543 constituencies in the country since 1971.

Term of the Lok Sabha

- The maximum term of the Lok Sabha is **five years.**
- However, it can be dissolved before the expiry of this term if
  - No party or coalition can form the government.
  - The Prime Minister advises the President to dissolve the Lok Sabha and hold fresh elections.

Powers of the Lok Sabha

- Makes laws on matters included in union list and concurrent list.
- Introduce and enact both the money and non-money bills.
- Approves bills on taxation, budget and annual financial statements.
- Controls the executive by asking questions and moving motions.
- Amends the Constitution.
- Approves the proclamation (declaration) of emergency.
- Can remove the government as the Council of Ministers is responsible only to the Lok Sabha.
- Elects the President and Vice-President.
- Removes the judges of the Supreme Court and High Court.
- Establishes committees and commissions.

Difference in the Powers of the Rajya Sabha and the Lok Sabha

There are some differences in powers of the two houses of the Parliament.

- **Money bills** can only be introduced in the Lok Sabha, while the Rajya Sabha cannot initiate, reject or amend the money bills. If the Rajya Sabha takes no action on a money bill within 14 days then the bill is deemed to have been passed.
- The Rajya Sabha cannot remove the government as the **Council of Ministers is responsible only to the Lok Sabha.**

Quick Test 1

1. How many houses are there in the Parliament of India? Name them.
2. Name any two states which have a bicameral legislature.
3. What is the total strength of Lok Sabha?
4. Name any two powers of Lok Sabha.
5. Which house approves the declaration of emergency?

4 Universal adult suffrage It means every adult citizen has the right to vote regardless of their social status, education, gender etc.
5 Constituency It is a geographical area, which is represented by a member of the state assembly or the Parliament.

5.3 Functions of the Parliament

The Parliament is the **chief law-making body** of India, but apart from this, it also have other functions such as

- **Legislative Function** The Parliament makes laws for the country but no major bill can be introduced in the parliament without the approval of the cabinet.
- **Control of Executive and ensuring its Accountability** The Parliament controls the executive and prevent it from overstepping its authority and remains responsible to the people who have elected them.
- **Financial Function** The Parliament controls taxation and usage of money by the government. It prevents the misuse of money by keeping a check through the budget and annual financial statements.
- **Representation** Parliament represents the divergent views and opinions of members from different parts of the country.
- **Debating Function** The Parliament is the **highest forum of debate** in the country and the members are free to speak on any matter without fear.
- **Constituent Function** The Parliament has the power to enact changes to the Constitution and such changes has to be approved by special majority of both the houses.
- **Electoral Functions** It elects the President and Vice-President of India.
- **Judicial Functions** The Parliament can remove the President, Vice-President and the judges of High Courts and Supreme Court.

5.4 Making of Laws by the Parliament

The basic function of any legislature is to make laws for its people. A specific procedure is followed in the process of making law. Some of the procedures of law-making are given in the Constitution, while some have evolved over a period of time.

Process of Making Laws in The Parliament

- The process of making laws involves several steps. A bill passes through three stages in each house of the Parliament. In case of a deadlock, a **joint session** is called upon to resolve it. Finally, the bill is sent for the approval of the President.

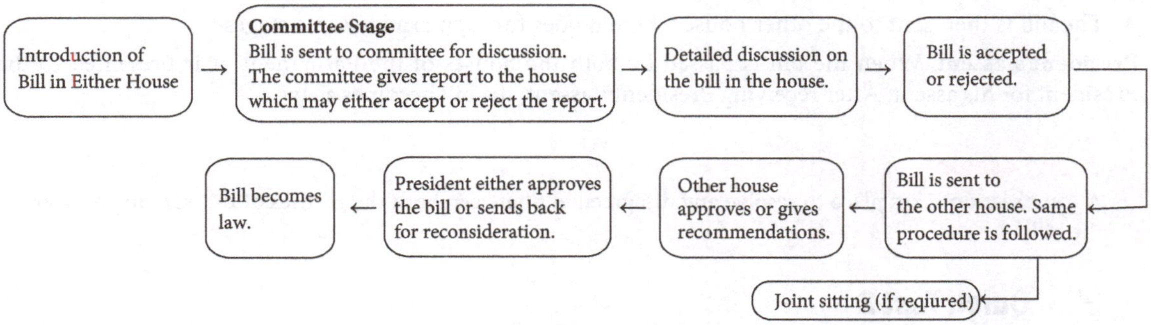

▲ *Law-Making Process*

Various stages in the passage of the bill in the Parliament are summarised as follows

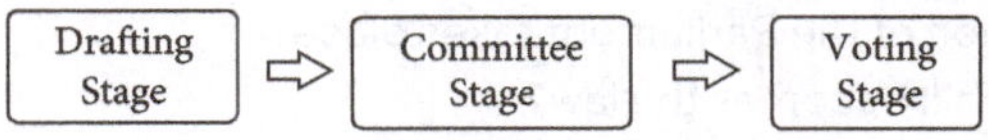

▲ *Stages of bill in The House*

First Stage (Drafting Stage)

- A draft of the proposed legislation is called as a **bill**.
- Sometimes a lot of debate is held before the introduction of a bill and also the government is pressurised by political parties or other groups to initiate a bill.
- The aspects such as the resources required to implement the law, the amount of support and its impact etc. are studied before introducing the bill.

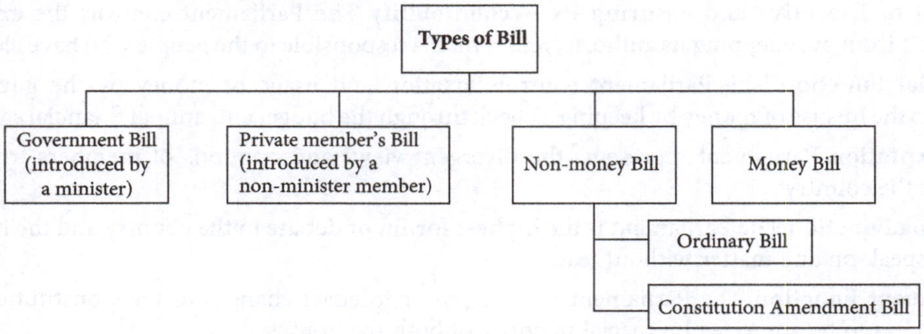

▲ *Types of Bill*

- Drafting of the bill starts after it gets approval from the cabinet.
- The draft of any bill is prepared by the concerned ministry.
- The bill is then introduced either in the Lok Sabha or in the Rajya Sabha by a member (usually a minister). In case of money bills , it is introduced only in the Lok Sabha.

- According to Article 109 of the Constitution 'Lok Sabha' has special procedure in respect of money bills.

Second Stage (Committee Stage)

- Committees are called as **mini legislatures** as here, a large part of discussions on the bill takes place.
- The Committees prepare a report on the bill and make several recommendations.
- The bill is then transmitted to the house.

Third Stage (Voting Stage)

- This is the final stage in the house in which the voting on bill takes place.
- The bill is then sent to the other house where it goes through exactly same stages.

President's assent When the bill is passed by both the houses of the Parliament, it is presented to the President for his assent. After receiving President's assent, the bill becomes a law.

Joint Session

A Joint session takes place to resolve any disagreement between both the Houses of the Parliament over the bill.

Quick Test 2

1. Which is the chief law making body of India?
2. How many stages does a bill goes through in a house ?
3. A bill introduced by a minister is called.
4. When the joint session of the Parliament takes place?
5. After whose assent, bill becomes the law?

5.5 Parliament's Control Over Executive

- In a Parliamentary democracy, the Parliament plays a crucial role in controlling the executive and preventing it from abusing its powers. At the same time legislators are provided with certain privileges that allow them to do their work as people representatives effectively without any fear.

Parliamentary Privileges

- These is a set of rules for the members, that prevents actions against a member of the Parliament for whatever the member may have said in the legislature.
- The presiding officer of the legislature is the deciding authority in case of breach of privilege.

The legislature in Parliamentary system ensures executive accountability at various stages through the use of a variety of devices,which are as follows

Deliberation and Discussion

- The legislature can exercise its control over the executive during the law-making process by scrutinising the policy direction and its implementation by the executive.
- Various instruments such as the **question hour** (where ministers have to respond to the question raised by the member), **zero hour** (where members are free to raise any matter that they think is important), **half an hour discussion** (this discussion is on the matters of public importance), **adjournment motion** (suspension of proceeding), helps in maintaining control of the legislature over the executive during general discussions in the house.
- Most of the questions aim at gaining information form the government on issues of public interest such as price rise, availability of food grain, black-marketing etc.

Approval or Refusal of Laws

- A bill can become an act only after receiving approval from both the houses of the Parliament, thus, Parliamentary control is also exercised through the power of ratification.
- Although, a government having majority in the legislature faces no difficulty in receiving such approvals however, then also the bill undergoes lots of discussions and negotiations.
- Sometimes, government has to make concessions when it has majority in Lok Sabha but not in the Rajya Sabha. For example during Janta Party rule in 1977 and NDA rule in 2000.

Financial Control

- A government has to prepare and present the budget in the Parliament to get it approved. In this way, the Parliament exercises control over the finances of the government.
- Parliament studies the report of the **comptroller and auditor general of India and Public accounts committee** to check misuse of funds by the government.

No Confidence Motion

- It is the most powerful weapon in the hands of the Parliament to control the executive. It helps to maintain the **executive accountability** as the government can be dismissed if they lost the confidence of the Lok Sabha.
- After 1989, several governments have been forced to resign due to lack of confidence in the Lok Sabha.

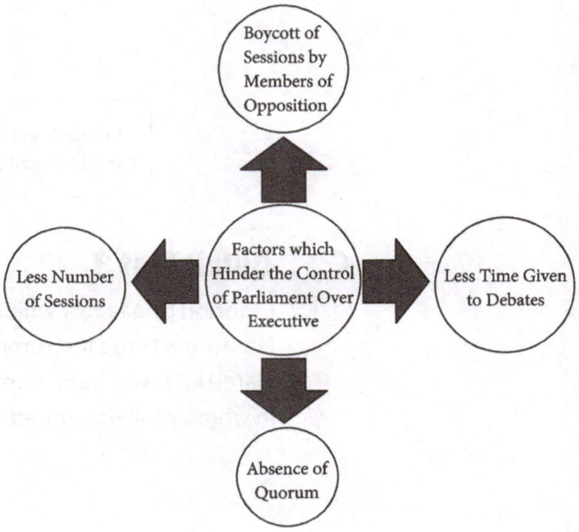

5.6 Committees of the Parliament

- The Parliament has numerous work at its disposal which makes it difficult to handle all of them on its own, thus various Parliamentary Committees are appointed to help in day to day business of the house. The two major type of such Parliamentary Committees are the **Parliamentary Standing Committees** and **Joint Parliamentary Committees.**
  - (i) **Parliamentary Standing Committees (PSC)** The system of Parliamentary Standing Committees started in India since 1983. These are over twenty in number. The important functions performed by these committees are
    - Supervision of work of various departments.
    - Supervise the budget and expenditure of various departments.
    - Supervise the bills initiated in the house relating to department.
  - (ii) **Joint Parliamentary Committees (JPC)** They are set up for various purposes like discussing a particular bill, investigating financial irregularities etc. Its members are selected from both the houses.

Regulation of the Parliament

- The Parliament needs to function smoothly in ordered way so that it become an effective platform for discussion and debates.
- The Constitution contains certain provisions that help attain this objective. The presiding officer has the final say in regulating the legislative proceedings to ensure orderly conduct and maintaining Parliamentary decorum.

Anti-Defection Law

- The Anti-defection law was enacted in 1985 to **prevent elected members from switching parties,** which was a major issue in India after independence.
- This law (also known as the **52nd Amendment Act**) restricts legislators from defecting to another party after being elected on the ticket of a specific party.
- It has also been subsequently modified by the **91st Amendment.** The presiding officer of the house is the authority to take final decisions in all such cases.
- If a member is found guilty of defection, they lose their membership in the house and are dis-qualified from holding any political office.

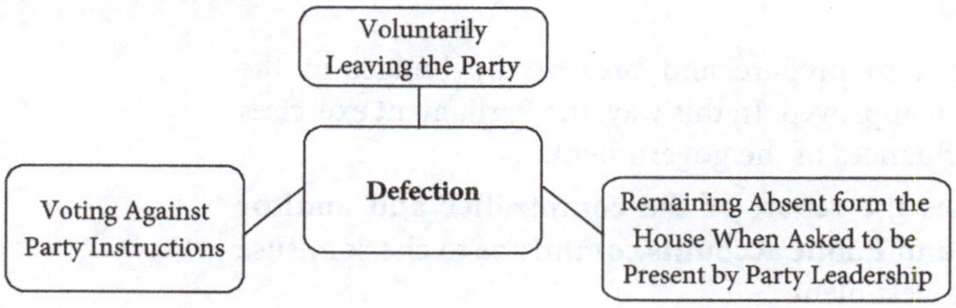

Quick Test 3

1. Mention one factor which hinder the control of Parliament over executive.
2. Name any three instruments which parliament uses to control the executive.
3. Name any two major committees of the Parliament.
4. In which year was anti-defection law passed?

Mind Map

LEGISLATURE

1 Need of the Parliament

Democratic Capacity of the Parliament
- Losing their position over the executive branch.
- Maintain a majority in the legislature.
- Ensures democracy and accountability.
- Represents people's will and balances power with the executives.

House of the Parliament
- Legislature exists at both the national level and the state level .
- Two houses of the Indian Parliament Rajya Sabha and Lok Sabha.

2 Structure of the Parliament

Unicameral Legislature

Bicameral Legislature

Lok Sabha (House of the people)
- It is directly elected by the people.
- It is elected for a period of five years.
- It can be dissolved if no party or coalition form the government.

Rajya Sabha (Council of State)
- It represent the State of India.
- It is an indirectly elected body.
- Rajya Sabha is never fully dissolved.
- Rajya Sabha has 12 nominated members.

3 Functions of the Parliament

- **Legislative Function** The Parliament enacts legislation like the money bill, finance bill etc.
- **Financial Function** The Parliament control taxation and usage of money by the government.
- **Representation** Represents the divergent views and opinions of members from different parts of the country.
- **Debating Function** The highest forum of debate in the country.
- **Constituent Function** Parliament has the power to enact changes of the Constitution.
- **Electrical Function** It elects the president and Vice-President of India.
- **Judicial Function** It look into all judicial functions of the Parliament.

4 Low-making Process

- **Drafting** 'Bill' is prepared by the ministry.
- **Committee Review** Detailed examination by Parliamentary.
- **Voting** Debated and passed in both houses.
- **Presidents Assent** Becomes law after approval.

5 Parliamentary Control over Executive

- **Tools** Question hour., zero hour.
- **Challenges** Lack of time for debates, low attendance in session.

6 Committees of Parliament

- **Standing Committee** Supervises the budget and expenditure of various departments.
- **Joint Parliamentary Committee** Discussing a particular bills, investigates financial irregularities.

Regulation of the Parliament
- An effective platform for discussion and debates.
- It contains certain provision that help to align this objective.

Anti-Defection Law
- **Objectives** Prevents members from switching political parties.
- **Consequences** Defectors lose membership.

Parliament of India

NCERT Folder

Intext Questions

1. Do you think that composition of Rajya Sabha has protected the position of states of India? (Pg 107)

Ans. Yes, the composition of the Rajya Sabha has helped to protect the position of states in India. By allocating seats based on the population of states and ensuring representation for smaller states through a minimum seat allocation, the Rajya Sabha balances the interests of larger and smaller states. Additionally, it allows states to voice their concerns on national policies and laws, thereby maintaining the federal structure of governance in India.

2. Should indirect election of Rajya Sabha be replaced by direct elections? What would be its advantages and dis-advantages? (Pg 107)

Ans. Replacing the indirect election of the Rajya Sabha with direct elections would fundamentally alter its role and influence. Some of the advantages and dis-advantages of this are

Advantages of Direct Elections

- Increases accountability and democratic legitimacy.
- Encourages greater public participation in governance.
- Reduces political manipulation in indirect elections.

Dis-advantages of Direct Elections

- Undermines the Rajya Sabha's role in representing states' interests.
- Risks overlapping with the Lok Sabha's functions.
- Marginalises smaller states and promotes majoritarianism.
- Adds to the electoral and administrative burden.

3. Since 1971 census the number of seats in the Lok Sabha has not increased. Do you think that it should be increased? What should be the basis for this? (Pg 107)

Ans. Yes, the number of Lok Sabha seats should be increased to ensure better representation as India's population has grown significantly since the 1971 census. The basis for this should be

- **Population Proportionality** Seats should reflect current population figures to ensure fair representation for all regions.
- **Balanced Federalism** Maintain adequate representation for smaller states to prevent dominance by larger states.
- **Improved Governance** More representatives can address diverse local issues effectively and reduce the burden on existing MPs.

4. From the discussion of the law-making process, do you think that Parliament can devote enough time for thorough discussion of the bills? If not, then what remedies would you suggest to overcome this difficulty? (Pg 114)

Ans. Parliament often struggles to devote enough time for thorough discussion of bills due to a packed legislative agenda, disruptions and limited sessions.

Remedies

- **Increase Parliamentary Sessions** Extend the duration and frequency of sessions to allow more time for debate.
- **Strengthen Committee System** Refer bills to standing or select committees for detailed examination and expert consultation.
- **Limit Disruptions** Enforce strict rules to minimise disruptions and ensure productive use of time.
- **Digitise Bill Review** Use digital platforms for MPs to study and share feedback on bills before formal discussions.
- **Allocate Specific Time** Reserve time slots exclusively for discussing important legislation.

Exercise

1. Alok thinks that a country needs an efficient government that looks after the welfare of the people. So, if we simply elected our Prime Minister and ministers and left to them the task of government, we will not need a legislature. Do you agree? Give reason for your answer.

Ans. I do not agree with Alok because

- Leaving the whole task of government with Prime Minister and ministers would hamper the essence of democracy. Such a set up would reduce the representation of people in the govenment.
- The members of the legistature who do not represent the majority would not have the opportunity to present their point of view.
- The decisions made by the cabinet would not be accountable, as the minister will not be answerable to the legislature, thus the executive would become more powerful. The task of legislature also includes law-making.
- It is a complex process that requires the opinion of all sections of the society. So legislature is required for this purpose.

2. **A class was debating the merits of a bicameral system. The following points were made during the discussion. Read the arguments and say if you agree or disagree with each of them, give reasons.**
   (i) **Neha said that bicameral legislature does not serve any purpose.**
   (ii) **Shama argued that experts should be nominated in the second chamber.**
   (iii) **Tridib said that if a country is not a federation, then there is no need to have a second chamber.**

Ans. (i) I do not agree with Neha as bicameral legislature is necessary for a democratic country with large population for the re-consideration of every decision along with a thorough debate.
(ii) I do agree with Shama that experts should be nominated into the second chamber, as they can provide inputs on subjects that require technical knowledge and give rational suggestions for policy-making.
(iii) I do not agree with Tridib, as federalism is not a pre-condition for having bicameral legislature. Therefore, the statement that a country without federalism need not have second chamber is incorrect.

3. **Why can the Lok Sabha control the executive more effectively than the Rajya Sabha?**

Ans. Lok Sabha exercises control over the executive more effectively than Rajya Sabha because
- It is a directly elected body.
- The Council of Ministers is responsible to Lok Sabha and not the Rajya Sabha.
- The Lok Sabha has the power to make laws, ask question and amend the constitution.
- The Lok Sabha can remove the government by expressing no-confidence motion but Rajya Sabha cannot remove any government.
- The Lok Sabha has crucial power in controlling the finances, as it can reject money bill but Rajya Sabha cannot.

4. **Rather than effective control of the executive, the Lok Sabha is a platform for the expression of popular sentiments and people's expectations. Do you agree?**

Ans. I do not agree with the statement that the Lok Sabha is only a platform for the expression of popular sentiments and people's expectations because
- The members of the legislature are free to express their views and no action can be taken against any member for anything said inside the house. The main purpose of the Parliamentary privilege is to enable the members to control the executive and to work for people effectively.
- The Lok Sabha holds the Union Cabinet accountable for its decisions, it has the power to make laws, control finances and amend the Constitution. The Council of Ministers continues in office only as long as it enjoys the confidence of the Lok Sabha. Therefore, Lok Sabha functions as an effective control of the executive.

5. **The following are some proposals for making the Parliament more effective. State if you agree or disagree with each of them and give your reasons. Explain what would be the effect if these suggestions were accepted.**
   (i) **Parliament should work for longer period.**
   (ii) **Attendance should be made compulsory for members of Parliament.**
   (iii) **Speakers should be empowered to penalise members for interrupting the proceedings of the house.**

Ans. (i) I agree with the proposal that Parliament should work for longer period, as there are large number of issues that require debate and legislation. These are delayed sometimes because of the other Parliamentary proceedings. To overcome this, the Parliament needs to work for a longer time.
(ii) I agree with the proposal, as compulsory attendance would lead to presence of members for crucial decisions that require the support of majority. It would also encourage presentation of views across the political spectrum.
(iii) I agree with the proposal for penalising members for interrupting the proceedings of house, as it would lead to less wastage of time and maintain the dignity of the Parliament.

6. **Arif wanted to know that if ministers propose most of the important bills and if the majority party often gets the governmental bills passed, what is the role of the Parliament in the law-making process? What answer would you give him?**

Ans. Parliament is an important component of the law-making process even though most of the important bills are proposed by minister. This is because
- The provisions of the proposed law are required to be debated and these debates can only be conducted in Parliament. Various committees comprising of members of Parliament study these bills and present their recommendations.
- The opposition also participates in the framing of laws by suggesting changes and thus, it is necessary for legislative procedure to take place in Parliament. Differences between Rajya Sabha and Lok Sabha over proposed bills are only resolved through Joint sitting of both the houses of Parliament.

7. Which of the following statements you agree with the most? Give your reasons.

(i) Legislators must be free to join any party they want.

(ii) Anti-defection law has contributed to the domination of the party leaders over the legislators.

(iii) Defection is always for selfish purposes and therefore, a legislator who want to join another party must be dis-qualified from being a minister for the next two years.

Ans. (i) Legislators should not be free to join any party they want, as this would encourage corrupt practice particularly at the time of confidence motions. There should be certain restrictions outlining the conditions under which they are allowed to join another party.

(ii) It is incorrect that anti-defection law has led to domination of party leaders over legislators. The legislators are allowed to defect as long as they have the support of a minimum number of members from their own party.

(iii) In all the three statement, I agree most with the third statement. Most of the time, defection may be for selfish purposes. However, a legislator who wishes to join another party must seek re-election plan from his/her constituency before being eligible for ministerial post. A period of two years of dis-qualification is appropriate in this situation.

8. Dolly and Sudha are debating about the efficiency and effectiveness of the Parliament in recent times. Dolly believed that the decline of Indian Parliament is evident in the less time spent on debate and discussion and increase in the disturbances of the functioning of the house and walkouts, etc. Sudha contends that the fall of different governments on the floor of Lok Sabha is a proof of its vibrancy.

What other arguments can you provide to support or oppose the positions of Dolly and Sudha?

Ans. Dolly's position about the decline of Parliament is correct upto some extent. The time spent on debates has decreased and infact on many occasions, entire session of Parliament have passed without discussions due to disruption by one party or the other. This has somewhat hindered the law-making process, as many progressive legislations have been pending for a long period of time.

However, the effectiveness of Parliament as an institution is un-diminished, as it remains the supreme law-making body in the country. Crucial policy decisions like of nuclear agreement with the United States that was debated in the Parliament is proof of the relevance of the body. Thus, major decisions related to national interest still required the approval of the Parliament.

Sudha's position that the fall of different government on the floor of Lok Sabha is a proof of its vibrancy, is also partially correct.

The fall of different governments on the floor of Lok Sabha is a reminder that no government can afford to take its existence for granted. It has to be accountable for its actions. The Lok Sabha is the body that controls the finances of the government and scrutinies its every action.

A government cannot survive by acting against the wishes of the majority of elected representatives. This has checked the excess concentration of power in the Council of Ministers. However, instability must not be mistaken with vibrancy. In the age of coalition governments at the centre, stability is important for achieving the goal of development.

9. Arrange the different stages of passing of a bill into a law in their correct sequence.

(i) A resolution is passed to admit the bill for discussion.

(ii) The bill is referred to the President of India- write what happens if she/he does not sign it.

(iii) The bill is referred to other house and is passed.

(iv) The bill is passed in the house in which it was proposed.

(v) The bill is referred to the sub-committee, the committee makes some changes and sends it back to the house for discussion.

(vi) The concerned ministry proposes the need for a bill.

(vii) Legislative departments in ministry of law, drafts a bill.

Ans. The stages of passing a bill into a law are

(i) The concerned ministry proposes the need for a bill.

(ii) Legislative departments in ministry of law, drafts a bill.

(iii) A resolution is passed to admit the bill for discussion.

(iv) The bill is referred to the sub-committee, the committee makes some changes and sends it back to the house for discussion.

(v) The bill is passed in the house in which it was proposed.

(vi) The bill is referred to other house and is passed.

(vii) The bill is referred to the President of India- if she/he does not sign it then the bill does not become a law.

10. How has the system of Parliamentary Committe affected the overseeing and appraisal of legislation by the Parliament?

Ans. The system of Parliamentary Committee has influenced the overseeing and appraisal of legislation by the Parliament, as most of decisions regarding the technical points of legislation are referred to these committees.

- The Parliament rarely rejects any of the suggestions made by the committee.
- There are over twenty standing committees related to various departments that works on the issue of budget and its expenditure related to their respective departments.
- These committees also supervise the bills related to their department that comes in the house.
- The joint Parliamentary Committees investigate financial irregularities.
- Thus, Parliamentary Committees have reduced the burden on the legislature and saved time, as the Parliament meets only for a limited time during its sessions.
- However, on most occasions, the Parliament makes only minor alterations to the draft of the bills, while approving them. This has diluted the Parliament's appraisal of legislation to a large extent.

Exam Pattern Questions

Objective Type Questions

Multiple Choice Questions (MCQs)

1. What is legislature? Diksha App

(a) Law-making body (b) Law implementing body
(c) Law enforcing body (d) Law interpreting body

2. Why are legislatures losing central place to the executive in democracies like India? Diksha App

(a) Cabinet initiate the policies
(b) Cabinet sets the agenda for governance
(c) Both (a) and (b)
(d) None of the above

3. Which among the following is the highest deliberative body in a democracy?

(a) Cabinet (b) Parliament
(c) Supreme Court (d) High Court

4. The term 'Parliament' refers to the .... legislature.

(a) state (b) international
(c) national (d) None of these

5. Parliament consist of two houses in India. What is the term which is used to describe such legislature?

(a) Uni-cameral (b) Bicameral
(c) National (d) Dual

6. The Council of States is called ...., and the House of People is called ....

(a) Lok Sabha, Rajya Sabha
(b) Rajya Sabha, Lok Sabha
(c) Vidhan Sabha, Vidhan Parishad
(d) Vidhan Parishad, Vidhan Sabha

7. 'Indian states have both bicameral and unicameral legislature'. Mention the number of state having bicameral legislature in India. Competency Based Que

(a) 6 (b) 8 (c) 9 (d) 10

8. Which of the following state does not have Bicameral legislature?

(a) Uttar Pradesh (b) West Bengal
(c) Karnataka (d) Telangana

9. Which among the following Indian states doesn't have a bicameral legislature? Diksha App

(a) Telangana (b) Andhra Pradesh
(c) Punjab (d) Karnataka

10. Which house of the Indian Parliament is indirectly elected ? Diksha App

(a) Lok Sabha (b) Rajya Sabha
(c) Both (a) and (b) (d) None of these

11. Rajya Sabha members are ....

(a) nominated by the member of Lok Sabha.
(b) directly elected by the member of Lok Sabha.
(c) indirectly elected by the elected members of the State Legislative Assembly.
(d) indirectly elected by the elected members of the State Legislative Council.

12. Name two houses of German legislature. Diksha App

(a) Lower house–Lok Sabha and upper house Rajya Sabha.
(b) House of commons and house of lords.
(c) House of representatives and debates.
(d) Federal assembly (Bundestag) and federal council (Bundesrat).

13. The system of representation adopted for the Rajya Sabha is different from that in ....

(a) the USA (b) the UK
(c) Germany (d) Australia

14. The number of members to be elected from each state has been fixed by the ...... schedule of the Constitution.

(a) second (b) ninth (c) fifth (d) fourth

15. What is the tenure of the member of the Rajya Sabha?

(a) Five (b) Four
(c) Six (d) No fixed term

16. Consider the following statements. Competency Based Que

I. Every two years, one-fourth members of the Rajya Sabha complete their term and elections are held for one-fourth seats only.

II. The Rajya Sabha is never dissolved and is called the Permanent House of the Parliament.

Which of the statements given above is/are correct?

(a) Only I (b) Only II
(c) Both I and II (d) None of these

17. How many nominated members are there in Rajya Sabha?

(a) Eleven (b) Fifteen (c) Twelve (d) Ten

18. Nominated members of Rajya Sabha are appointed by

(a) Chairman of the Rajya Sabha
(b) The President
(c) Speaker of the Rajya Sabha
(d) Chief Justice of India

19. The .... and .... are directly elected by the people on the basis of Universal Adult Suffrage.

(a) Lok Sabha, Rajya Sabha
(b) Legislative Council, Rajya Sabha
(c) Rajya Sabha, State Legislative Assemblies
(d) Lok Sabha, State Legislative Assemblies

20. What is the total strength of the House of People?

(a) 543 (b) 554 (c) 535 (d) 550

21. The house can be dissolved by the President on which of the following advice?

(a) Leader of the Opposition
(b) Speaker of the House of the People
(c) Chairman of the Rajya Sabha
(d) Council of Minister-PM

22. What do you understand by the constituent function of the Parliament? Diksha App

(a) It is the power of the Parliament to perform electoral functions.
(b) It is the power of the Parliament to discuss and enact changes to the Constitution.
(c) Both (a) and (b)
(d) None of the above

23. Which of the following persons can be removed by the Parliament? Diksha App

(a) President of India
(b) Vice-President of India
(c) Judges of the High Court and Supreme Court
(d) All the above

24. Consider the following statements related to the power of Rajya Sabha? Competency Based Que

I. Exercise control over executive by asking questions, introducing motions and resolutions.

II. It participates in the elections and removal of the President, Vice-President, Judges of Supreme Court and High Court.

III. It cannot alone initiate the procedure for removal of Vice-President.

Which of the statements given above is/are correct?

(a) I and II
(b) II and III
(c) I and III
(d) All of the above

25. In which hour Parliamentarians are free to raise any matter that they think is important though the ministers are not bound to reply? Diksha App

(a) Question hour (b) Zero Hour
(c) Last hour (d) First hour

26. When did India develop a system of organising parliamentary standing committees? Diksha App

(a) 1983 (b) 1984
(c) 1988 (d) 1980

27. 'Anti-Defection law in India prohibits the elected representatives from switching parties'. Which of the following is incorrect regarding the Anti-Defection law? Competency Based Que

(a) A member of Parliament automatically loses the membership of the house when he votes against the instruction of his party.
(b) A member disqualified under the Anti-Defection law can hold any other political office.
(c) Anti-Defection law was enacted in the year 1985.
(d) Anti-Defection law is also known as the 52nd Constitutional Amendment Act.

28. Choose the incorrect answer. Competency Based Que

(a) The legislature of the states is described as state legislature.
(b) The Rajya Sabha represents the state of India.
(c) The Lok Sabha is called as the lower house of the Parliament.
(d) The Parliament can remove the Prime Minister from office through impeachment.

29. Given below are two statements. **Competency Based Que**

Statement I Legislature is the most representative of all organs of the government on the basis of its composition.

Statement II The Parliament can effectively control the executive and ensure a more responsive government.

In the light of the above statements, choose the correct answer from the options given below.

(a) Both Statement I and Statement II are true.
(b) Both Statement I and Statement II are false.
(c) Statement I is true, but Statement II is false.
(d) Statement I is false, but Statement II is true.

30. **Study the picture given below and answer the question that follows.**

What does this picture refer to? **Competency Based Que**

(a) Discussion among the members on bill
(b) Individual discussion of ministers
(c) Both (a) and (b)
(d) None of the above

31. **Match the following** **Competency Based Que**

List I (Term)	List II (Explanation)
A. Bicameral Legislature	1. Ensures double-checking of decisions and debates.
B. Rajya Sabha	2. Represents the states in the Parliament.
C. Lok Sabha	3. Directly elected body.
D. Committees of Parliament	4. Miniature legislatures for detailed examination.
E. Anti-Defecti-on Law	5. Prevents legislators from switching parties unfairly.

Codes

	A	B	C	D	E		A	B	C	D	E
(a)	1	2	5	4	3	(b)	4	2	1	3	5
(c)	2	5	1	4	3	(d)	1	2	3	4	5

Assertion-Reason Questions

Direction (Q. Nos. 32-36) In the questions given below, there are two statements marked as Assertion (A) and Reason (R). Read the statements and choose the correct option.

Codes

(a) Both A and R are true and R is the correct explanation of A.
(b) Both A and R are true, but R is not the correct explanation of A.
(c) A is true, but R is false.
(d) A is false, but R is true.

32. **Assertion (A)** Legislature is the highest deliberative organ in a democracy.

Reason (R) Legislatures are elected by the people and work on behalf of the people.

33. **Assertion (A)** The Rajya Sabha is elected by MLAs rather than the general public. As a result, the Rajya Sabha was not given certain powers under the Constitution.

Reason (R) The Rajya Sabha can criticise the government, but not overthrow it.

34. **Assertion (A)** Members of the Rajya Sabha are elected by the elected member of the State Legislative Assembly.

Reason (R) There is a provision for a nominated member of the Rajya Sabha so in that case President appoint 2 members from Anglo-Indian Community if it is not well represented in the Rajya Sabha.

35. **Assertion (A)** The Rajya Sabha is referred to as the Permanent House of Parliament.

Reason (R) One-third of Rajya Sabha members retire every two years, ensuring that the house is never fully dissolved.

36. **Assertion (A)** Anti-Defection law, means that a legislator who is elected on one party's ticket is restricted from defecting to another party.

Reason (R) Anti-Defection law is mention in the ninth schedule of the Constitution.

Passage Based Questions

37. Read the given passage and answer the following questions.

Countries with large size and much diversity usually prefer to have two houses of the national legislature to give representation to all sections in the society and to give representation to all geographical regions or parts of the country. A bicameral legislature has one more advantage. A bicameral legislature makes it possible to have every decision re-considered. Every decision taken by one house goes to the other house for its decision. This means that every bill and policy would be discussed twice. This ensures a double check on every matter. Even if one house takes a decision in haste, that decision will come for discussion in the other house and re-consideration will be possible.

(i) Countries with a large population and a diverse population typically tend to have two houses of the .... legislature to ensure that all parts of society are represented.

(a) national
(b) state
(c) dual
(d) bicameral

(ii) The advice of upper house is not binding on the lower house in relation to the ....

(a) money bill
(b) ordinary bill
(c) constituent amendment bill
(d) private members' bill

(iii) Which kind of legislature makes it possible to have every decision re-considered?

38. Read the given passage and answer the following questions.

What is defection? If a member remains absent in the House when asked by the party leadership to remain present or votes against the instructions of the party or voluntarily leaves the membership of the party, it is deemed as defection. Experience of the past twenty years shows that the Anti-Defection Amendment has not been able to curb defections, but it has given additional powers to the party leadership and the presiding officers of the legislatures over the members.

(i) What does defection mean?

(a) Moving of a person from the ruling party to opposition party.
(b) Moving of a person from the party to another party by which he got elected.
(c) Moving of a person from opposition party to ruling party.
(d) Leaving all the parties.

(ii) Which of the following Acts is known as Anti-Defection Amendment?

(a) 56th Amendment Act (b) 51st Amendment Act
(c) 52nd Amendment Act (d) 54th Amendment Act

(iii) What has been the impact of the Anti-Defection law in India since it was enacted?

39. Read the following passage carefully and answer the questions that follow.

The 16 federal states of Germany are represented in the Federal Council. The 69 seats of the Bundesrat are divided among states on the basis of a range of populations. These members are generally the ministers in the governments at the state level and are appointed, not elected, by the governments of the federal states. According to the German law, all the members from one state have to vote as a bloc as per the instructions of the state governments. Sometimes due to coalition government at the state level, they fail to reach an agreement and may have to abstain.

The Bundesrat does not vote on all legislative initiatives but all the policy areas on which the federal states have concurrent powers and are responsible for federal regulations must be passed by it. It can also veto such legislation.

(i) How are the 69 seats of the Bundesrat divided among the states of Germany?

(a) Based on the economic strength of each state.
(b) Based on the geographical area of each state.
(c) Based on the population range of each state.
(d) Based on the number of ministers in each state government.

(ii) Who appoints the members of the Bundesrat?

(a) The President of Germany
(b) The Chancellor of Germany
(c) The governments of the federal states
(d) The German Parliament

(iii) How do members from the same state vote in the Bundesrat?

(a) Independently, based on their personal opinions.
(b) As a bloc, based on the instructions of the state governments.
(c) Based on the decision of the federal government.
(d) Based on the decision of the opposition parties.

(iv) What is the Bundesrat's role in legislation?

(a) It votes on all legislative initiatives.
(b) It only votes on policy areas where the federal states have concurrent powers.
(c) It has no role in legislation.
(d) It only votes legislation proposed by the opposition parties.

Answers

1. (a) Law-making body
2. (c) Both (a) and (b)
3. (b) Parliament
4. (c) national
5. (b) Bicameral
6. (b) Rajya Sabha, Lok Sabha.
7. (a) 6
8. (b) West Bengal
9. (c) Punjab
10. (b) Rajya Sabha
11. (c) indirectly elected by the elected members of the State Legislative Assembly.
12. (d) Federal assembly (Bundestag) and federal council (Bundesrat).
13. (a) the USA
14. (d) fourth
15. (c) Six
16. (b) Only II
17. (c) Twelve
18. (b) The President
19. (d) Lok Sabha, State Legislative Assemblies
20. (a) 543
21. (d) Council of Minister-PM
22. (b) It is the power of the Parliament to discuss and enact changes to the Constitution.
23. (d) All the above
24. (a) I and II
25. (b) Zero Hour
26. (a) 1983
27. (b) A member disqualified under the Anti-Defection law can hold any other political office.
28. (d) The Parliament can remove the Prime Minister from office through impeachment
29. (a) Both Statement I and Statement II are true.
30. (a) Discussion among the members on bill
31. (d) 1 2 3 4 5
32. (b) Both A and R are true, but R is not the correct. explanation of A.
33. (a) Both A and R are true and R is the correct explanation of A.
34. (c) A is true, but R is false.
35. (a) Both A and R are true and R is the correct explanation of A.
36. (c) A is true, but R is false.
37. (i) (a) national (ii) (a) money bill

    (iii) A bicameral legislature makes it possible to have every decision re-considered. This type of legislative system consists of two houses, typically an upper and lower house, which provide checks and balances on each other.

    The bicameral structure allows for revisions and reviews of proposed laws, enabling more thorough deliberation and ensuring that hasty decisions are avoided.
38. (i) (b) Moving of a person from the party to another party by which he got elected.

    (ii) (c) 52nd Amendment Act

    (iii) Experience shows that the Anti-Defection law, enacted in 1985 has not been able to completely stop defections but it has given more powers to party leadership and the presiding officers which has reduced defections to certain extent and increased the control over the members.

    By disqualifying MPs/MLAs who switch parties, the law has checked the trend of legislators changing parties for personal gain.
39. (i) (c) Based on the population range of each state.

    (ii) (c) The governments of the federal states

    (iii) (b) As a bloc, based on the instructions of the state governments.

    (iv) (b) It only votes on policy areas where the federal states have concurrent powers.

Subjective Questions

Very Short Answer Type Questions

1. Analyse the declining importance of Parliament in Current time. Competency Based Que

Ans. Parliament is losing its importance because
- There has been frequent walkouts, dharna, protests and no Parliamentary work is done on time.
- In India, cabinet initiates policies, sets the agenda for governance and carries them through.
- A lot of time is wasted with no real work being done.

2. What is a bicameral legislature? Explain.

Ans. A bicameral legislature is a system with two separate chambers or houses, typically an upper and a lower house. In India, the lower house (Lok Sabha) represents the people, while the upper house (Rajya Sabha) represents states and regions.

3. Name the states having bicameral legislature.

Ans. The states having bicameral legislature are Uttar Pradesh, Bihar, Maharashtra, Karnataka, Andhra Pradesh and Telangana.

4. 'Rajya Sabha is called as the permanent house of Parliament'? Explain why Rajya Sabha is called as permanent house of Parliament as it do not dissolves. Competency Based Que

Ans. All members of Rajya Sabha do not retire at the same time. After every two years, one-third of the members retire and elections are held for that one-third. Therefore, Rajya Sabha is never fully dis-solved. That is why, it is called as the permanent house of Parliament.

5. How is Lok Sabha formed?

Ans. The Lok Sabha is the lower house of the Parliament having 543 members. Its members are elected by the people who have the right to vote. To conduct its elections, the country is divided into constituencies and members are elected from these constituencies.

6. Mention some important functions of the legislature.

Ans. The important functions of the legislature are
- To enact laws.
- To control the finance of the country.
- To amend the Constitution.

7. What are the judicial functions of Parliament?

Ans. The judicial functions of the Parliament include considering the proposals for removal of President, Vice-President and judges of High Courts and Supreme Court. It performs quasi-judicial or semi-judicial functions.

8. Analyse the statement that the Lok Sabha is more powerful than Rajya Sabha. Competency Based Que

Ans. Lok Sabha is more powerful than Rajya Sabha because
- The members of Lok Sabha are directly elected, while the members of Rajya Sabha are indirectly elected.
- Money bill can only be introduced in Lok Sabha. It is sent to Rajya Sabha just for recommendation and the recommendation is not binding.
- Council of Ministers is responsible to the Lok Sabha and not to the Rajya Sabha.

9. Explain the Lok Sabha control the executive more effectively than Rajya Sabha. Competency Based Que

Ans. The Lok Sabha control the executive more effectively than Rajya Sabha because
- The government is formed by the party who gets majority in the Lok Sabha.
- The Lok Sabha enjoys the power to remove any executive from the office, while the Rajya Sabha cannot remove any executive from the office.

10. What is a bill ? How can we broadly categorise the types of the bill? Diksha App

Ans. A bill is the draft of the proposed law. There can be different types of bill.
- When a parliamentarian other than the ministers of the ruling party proposes a bill it is called private member bill.
- A bill proposed by the minister is described as a government bill.
- Other categories of bills are non money bill and money bill.
- The bills can also be categorised into ordinary bills and Constitution Amendment Bill.

11. Enumerate the devices with which the Parliament control the executive. Diksha App; Competency Based Que

Ans. The devices with which the Parliament control the executive are as under

(a) Deliberation and discussion

(b) Approval or refusal of laws

(c) Financial control

(d) No confidence motion

(e) Asking questions to the concerned ministers

12. 'Parliament exercises control over the purse strings of executive'? Comment. Competency Based Que

Ans. A budget is an estimation of revenue and expenses over a specified future period of time. Budget cannot be passed unless it is approved by majority in Parliament. This Constitutional obligation allows the legislature to exercise control over purse strings of government.

13. What is defection?

Ans. If a member remains absent in the house when asked by the party leadership to remain present or votes against the instructions of the party or voluntarily leaves the membership of the party, it is known as defection.

Short Answer Type Questions

1. Parliament is the supreme law-making body of the government. Explain its need? Competency Based Que

Ans. For the following reasons, we require a Parliament

- The Parliament enables citizens of India to participate in decision-making and control the government.
- It contributes to the legislative process and, from time to time introduces new legislation.
- It maintains financial control over the government's revenue, i.e., the government cannot spend public funds without Parliament's permission.
- It is incharge of the government's executive branch. This means that in order for the organ to function, it must have a mandate from Parliament.

2. Discuss the main features of the Indian Parliament.

Ans. Following are the main features of India Parliament

- The Parliament of India is a bicameral legislature.
- The Parliament consists of President, Lok Sabha and Rajya Sabha.
- The upper house of the Parliament is the permanent chamber i.e. it does not dissolve.
- Lower house of the Parliament can be dissolved before expiry of its term.
- The membership of both the houses is not equal.
- A person cannot have the membership of both the houses.
- Parliament is the supreme law-making body in India.
- Powers of both the houses are not equal.
- Lok Sabha is more powerful than Rajya Sabha but, in few matters Rajya Sabha has special powers.

3. State your arguments in favour of uni-cameral legislature. Competency Based Que

Ans. Arguments in favour of uni-cameral legislature are as follows

- **Uniformity in Legislature** It is believed by the pro-unicameral supporters that this system helps to maintain uniformity and unity in the legislature.
  Laws express the opinion of the people and the people cannot have two opinions on the same subject. Thus, there should be only one chamber to represent the public opinion properly.
- **Saving of Time and Money** Uni-cameral System leads to saving of time and money. The expenditure to be incurred on the payment of salary and allowances of the members of the other house can be utilised for other useful purposes.
  When a bill has to be passed only in one house, it saves time.

4. "Rajya Sabha has some special powers that is not there with the Lok Sabha". Explain. Competency Based Que

Ans. The special powers of the Rajya Sabha are as follows;

(i) **Permanent House** The Rajya Sabha can never be dissolved. In Every two years, one-third of its members retire so it always continues to function, even if the Lok Sabha is dissolved.

(ii) **Making Laws on State list Subjects** If the Rajya Sabha agrees with a two-thirds majority only then Parliament can make laws on subjects that usually belong to the states list.

(iii) **Removal of the Vice President** The Rajya Sabha has the power to initiate the removal of the Vice President.

5. Elucidate the powers of Lok Sabha.

Ans. The powers of Lok Sabha are as follows

- Makes laws on matters including in the union list and concurrent list.
- It can introduce and enact money bill and ordinary bills.
- Approves proposal for taxation, budget and annual financial statement.
- Controls the executive by asking questions, supplementary questions, resolutions, motions and through no-confidence motion.
- Amends the Constitution.
- Approves the proclamation of emergency.
- Elects and removes the President, Vice-President and the judges of Supreme Court and High Court.
- Establishes committees and commissions and consider their reports.

6. What are the different types of committees. Describe the role of committees.

Ans. There are two types of committees

- **Standing committees** who supervise the work of various departments, their budget, their expenditure and bills that come up in the house. They are permanent in nature.
- **Joint committees** They are appointed for a specific purpose of discussing a particular bill or for investigating financial irregularites. They are temporary in nature. They are appointed for specific purpose only.

The committees play a vital role in providing in depth information about the provisions of a bill. It requires expertise and great research to draft the provisions of a bill.

Since, the houses do not have much time to deliberate on every provision of a bill, committees discuss a bill in great length. Also, it reduces the burden of Parliament. It helps in the day to day business of the house.

7. How does the Parliament regulate itself?

Ans. The Parliament regulates itself through the amendments which are made from time to time.

For example, 52nd Amendment: this is anti-defection amendment. With the help of this amendment the members are restricted from defecting.

It means that if a member remains absent in the house when asked by the party leadership, or votes against the instructions of the party or voluntarily leaves the membership of party, he is said to have been defected. If it is proved that the member has defected then he loses membership of the house and is dis-qualified from holding any political office.

8. What is Anti-Defection law?

Ans. Members of Parliament and state legislatures could be dis-qualified for switching political parties under the 52nd Amendment Act of 1985 as a result anti-defection legislation was enacted.

The presiding officer of the House is the authority who takes final decisions on all such cases. If it is proved that a member has 'defected', then such member loses the membership of the house.

Defection occurs when a member fails to appear in the House when asked by the party leadership to do so, votes against the party's instructions or willingly departs the party's membership.

Long Answer Type Questions

1. Many states in India are in favour of establishing a bicameral legislature. Why do we need a bicameral legislature? **Competency Based Que**

Ans. A bicameral legislature means having two houses in the legislative system, which plays a key role in ensuring a fair and balanced law-making process. In India, the Parliament consists of two houses: the Lok Sabha (House of the People) and the Rajya Sabha (Council of States). Similarly, many states in India are considering a bicameral legislature for their own assemblies for several important reasons.

Having two houses allows for better representation of different groups. The lower house (like the Lok Sabha) represents the people directly, based on population. This ensures that the majority's views are heard. The upper house (like the Rajya Sabha) represents regions, smaller communities or states. This helps in protection of the interests of states or groups that might otherwise be overlooked in a population-based system.

A bicameral system encourages more careful law-making. Bills have to pass through both houses, which mean they are scrutinised more thoroughly. This reduces the chance of hasty or poorly thought-out laws being passed.

A bicameral legislature allows for the balancing of power between different regions and interest groups, promoting fairness and stability. It also ensures that states with diverse needs and concerns have a platform to voice their opinions, which is essential in a large, diverse country like India.

2. Describe in detail about the upper house or Rajya Sabha. Also discuss about its powers.

Ans. Rajya Sabha is the representation of states of India to the Parliament. Its members are indirectly elected by the elected members of the State Legislative Assembly. Representation of seats to the second chamber is done according to the size of the population of the states, that means states with large population will have more seats than the states with less population. Members of the Rajya Sabha are elected for a term of six years and can be re-elected.

All members of the Rajya Sabha do not complete their term at the same time. Every two years, one-third members of the Rajya Sabha complete their term and elections are held for one-third seats only.

Thus, the Rajya Sabha is never dissolved and is called the Permanent House of the Parliament.

Power of Rajya Sabha

- It considers and approves non-money bill and suggests amendments to money bills.
- It approves Constitutional Amendments.
- Exercise control over executive by asking questions, introducing motions and resolutions.
- It participates in the elections and removal of the President, Vice-President, Judges of Supreme Court and High Court.
- It can alone initiate the procedure for removal of Vice-President.
- It can give Union Parliament powers to make laws on matters included in the state list.
- The Rajya Sabha is the re-presentation of states and its purpose is to protect the powers of states, thus, the Union Parliament needs the approval of the Rajya Sabha to alter the matter prescribed in the state list. This provision adds to the strength of the Rajya Sabha.

3. Elucidate the functions of the Parliament.

Competency Based Que

Ans. The powers and functions of the Parliament are as follows

Legislative Function The Parliament is the chief law making body in the country and often merely approves legislations. The task of drafting the bill is done by the bureaucracy under the supervision of the minister concerned. The substance and timing of the bill are decided by the cabinet and no major bill is introduced in the Parliament without the approval of the cabinet.

Control of Executive and Ensuring its Accountability The most vital function of the Parliament is to ensure that the executive does not overstep its authority and remains responsible to the people who have elected them.

Financial Function In a democracy, legislature controls the taxation and its use by the government. No new tax can be introduced without the approval of Lok Sabha. The financial powers of the Parliament involves the grant of resources to the government to implement its programmes. The government has to give an account to the legislature about the expenditure and resources. In order to ensure that the government does not overspend, the budget and annual financial statements are prepared.

Re-presentation Parliament represent the divergent views of members from different regional, social, economic and religious groups of different parts of the country.

Debating Function The Parliament is the highest forum of debate in the country without any limitation on its power of discussion and the members are free to speak on any matter without fear. These discussions constitute the heart of democratic decision-making.

Constituent Function The Parliament has the power to enact changes to the Constitution and both the houses are similar in constituent powers. All the amendments have to be approved by a special majority of both the houses of Parliament.

Electoral Functions The Parliament also performs some electoral functions, as it elects the President and Vice-President of India.

Judicial Functions The judicial function of the Parliament includes considering the proposals for removal of President, Vice-President and judges of High Courts and Supreme Court. It performs quasi-judicial or semi-judicial functions.

4. Describe the law-making procedure in the Parliament of India.

Ans. The detailed procedure followed by Parliament is given below

First Stage Introduction of a bill in the Parliament constitute the first stage. A bill can either be introduced in the Lok Sabha or Rajya Sabha, except the money bill which can only be introduced in Lok Sabha. A bill introduced or proposed by a minister is called a government bill, whereas a bill proposed by a non-minister is called a private member's bill.

Second Stage The bill is sent to committee for recommendation and then sent back to the house.

Third Stage The bill is voted upon and if a non-money bill is passed by one house, it is sent to the other house where it goes through the same procedure.

Final Stage A bill has to be passed by both the houses for enactment and if there is disagreement between the house on the proposed bill, then a Joint session of the Parliament is held to resolve the deadlock.

If it is money bill, the Rajya Sabha has to give its suggestion or it could delay the passage by 14 days and after that it is deemed to have been passed.

Any amendments suggested by Rajya Sabha may or may not be accepted by the Lok Sabha. When the bill is passed by both the houses, it is sent to the President for his assent.

Finally, the assent of the President results in the enactment of bill into a law.

5. Lok sabha is a very powerful house. What are the different powers of Lok Sabha and how its are power different from Rajya Sabha?

Competency Based Que; Diksha App

Ans. The different between the power of Lok Sabha and Rajya Sabha are as follows

Aspect	Powers of Lok Sabha	Powers of Rajya Sabha
Money Bills	Money Bills can only be introduced in Lok Sabha.	Rajya sabha can only discuss and suggest amendments in money bill but cannot reject it.
Control Over Government	The government stays in power only if it has the support of Lok Sabha. It can remove the government by passing a No-Confidence Motion.	Rajya sabha is less powerful than loksabha, as it Cannot pass a No-Confidence Motion or remove the government.
Dissolution	Lok Sabha can be dissolved anytime before five years by passing no confidence motion in loksabha.	Rajya sabha is the permanent house where one-third of its members retire in every two years.
Removal of Vice President	Lok sabha can not initiate the impeachment motion against the vice president.	Rajya sabha an initiate the impeachment motion against the Vice President.

Picture Based Questions

1. Observe the cartoon given below and answer the questions that follow.

(i) What is the main theme of the cartoon?

(a) Ministers have full control over financial decisions.
(b) Parliament has the power to approve funds for ministries.
(c) Ministers can directly access funds without approval.
(d) Parliament has no financial authority.

Ans. (b) Parliament has the power to approve funds for ministries.

(ii) What does the ministers' humble attitude in the cartoon represent?

(a) Their fear of elections.
(b) Their dependence on Parliament for financial grants.
(c) Their willingness to donate money to Parliament.
(d) Their dissatisfaction with the Parliament's control.

Ans. (b) Their dependence on Parliament for financial grants.

(iii) What document is the Parliament official holding in the cartoon?

(a) A bill of expenses.
(b) A budget allocation report.
(c) A 'Demand for Grants' document.
(d) A resignation letter from ministers.

Ans. (c) A "Demand for Grants" document.

(iv) Which part of the Parliamentary process is depicted in this cartoon?

(a) Passing of a constitutional amendment.
(b) Approval of the annual budget.
(c) The election of the Prime Minister.
(d) Conducting Parliamentary debates.

Ans. (b) Approval of the annual budget.

2. Study the cartoon given below and answer the question that follow.

(i) What does the above cartoon depicts?

(a) Walkout by opposition party
(b) No confidence motion
(c) Refusal of laws
(d) All of the above

Ans. (a) Walkout by opposition party

(ii) Why does such conditions occur?

(a) If opposition party wants to protest
(b) On grounds of defection
(c) Misbehaving
(d) All of the above

Ans. (a) If opposition party wants to protest

(iii) **The .... of the legislature is the final authority in matters of regulating the business of the legislature**

(a) Prime Minister
(b) Presiding Officer
(c) President
(d) Council of Minister

Ans. (b) Presiding Officer

(iv) **Which of the following is the power of Lok Sabha?**

(a) Controlling executive by asking questions
(b) Amend Constitution
(c) Approves the procalamation of Emergency
(d) All of the above

Ans. (d) All of the above

3. **Observe the cartoon given below and answer the questions that follow.**

(i) **Why do member of Parliament sometimes get ordered out of the Parliament?**

Ans. Member of Parliament may be ordered out if they break rules, disrupt the proceedings or engage in inappropriate behaviour.

(ii) **How does the Speaker of the House handle disruptions during Parliament sessions?**

Ans. The Speaker can ask MPs to leave if they are causing disruptions or not following the rules of the house.

(iii) **What can MPs do if they disagree with the way a session is being conducted?**

Ans. MPs can protest, walk out, or raise their concerns through official channels, but they must do so within the rules.

Map Based Question

1. **On an outline map of India mark the five states having a bicameral legislature.**

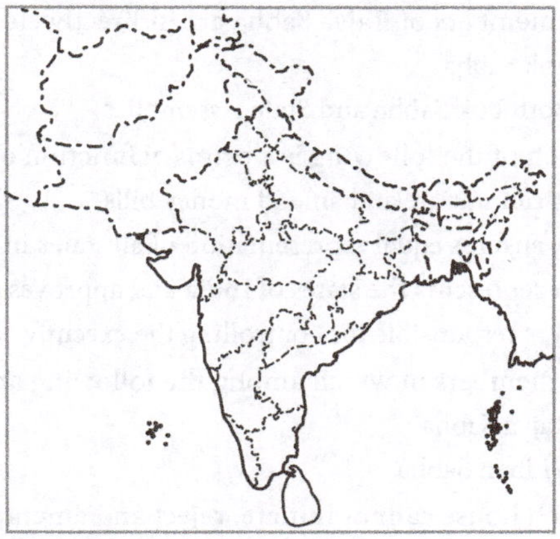

Ans.

SELF ASSESSMENT TEST

Objective Type Questions

1. The members of Rajya Sabha are indirectly elected by the elected members of ....
   (a) Lok Sabha
   (b) State Lagislative Assemblies
   (c) Both Lok Sabha and State Assemblies
   (d) They are elected directly by the people
2. Which of the following is a primary function of the Rajya Sabha in the Indian Parliament?
   (a) It can initiate and amend money bills.
   (b) It ensures equal representation of all states in the country.
   (c) It represents the states of India and approves constitutional amendments.
   (d) It is responsible for controlling the executive through no-confidence motions.
3. The members of which among the following are elected on the basis of Universal Adult Suffrage?
   (a) Rajya Sabha
   (b) Lok Sabha
   (c) Vidhan Sabha
   (d) President
4. Which house cannot initiate, reject and amend the money bills? **Diksha App**
   (a) Lok Sabha
   (b) Rajya Sabha
   (c) Both (a) and (b)
   (d) None of these

Very Short Answer Type Questions

5. Who is the presiding officer of the lower house and how he/she is elected?
6. What can be the maximum strength of the House of People?
7. Explain the process of election of members of Lok Sabha. **Competency Based Que**

Short Answer Type Questions

8. Explain the need and importance of Parliament in a democracy?
9. Analyse the composition of the Parliament. **Competency Based Que**
10. 'The Rajya Sabha is elected by the MLAs and not directly by the people'? Explain. **Competency Based Que**
11. Describe the committee system in Indian Parliament.

Long Answer Type Questions

12. Describe the limitations on the powers of the Parliament.
13. Analyse the mutual relations between the two houses of Parliament. **Competency Based Que**
14. Describe the powers and functions of the Indian Parliament.
15. 'The legislature in Parliamentary system ensures executive accountability at various stages through variety of devices'. Justify the statement. **Competency Based Que**

06

CHAPTER

In this chapter, you will learn about the role and importance of the judiciary, which plays a key role in protecting our rights.

Judiciary

▼ **YOUR STUDY GOALS**

6.1 Need of an Independent Judiciary
6.2 Structure of the Judiciary
6.3 Judicial Activism
6.4 Judiciary and Rights
6.5 Judiciary and Parliament

▼ **YOUR PRACTICE GOAL**

- Objective Type Questions (34 Qs ; MCQs, A-R, Statements, Matching, Passage Based)
- Subjective Questions (9 VSAs, 11 SAs, 4 LAs, 3 Picture Based)

Judiciary is an important organ of the government. Apart from acting as an arbitrator in disputes between individuals and private parties, it also performs judicial functions. It plays an important role in interpreting and protecting the Constitution and the rights of the individuals. The Supreme Court of India is one of the powerful courts in the world, which safeguards the rights of the individual.

6.1 Need of an Independent Judiciary

- Disputes are bound to happen in every society. Such disputes need to be settled by an independent body according to the **rule of law**[1]. This function is performed by an independent judiciary.
- Apart from protecting the rule of law and ensuring supremacy of law, the judiciary plays other important roles such as
  - Safeguarding the rights of individuals
  - Settling disputes in accordance with law
  - Prevent individual or group dictatorship
  - Securing democratic values
- In order to performs all these functions, the judiciary needs to be an independent body. It is also necessary that the judiciary remains independent of any political pressures.

1 **Rule of law** It means everyone including government officials and citizens, is subject to the law and no one is above the law.

Independence of Judiciary

- Judiciary is a part of the democratic political structure of the country, which makes it accountable to the Constitution and the people of the country. However, it is independent at the same time.

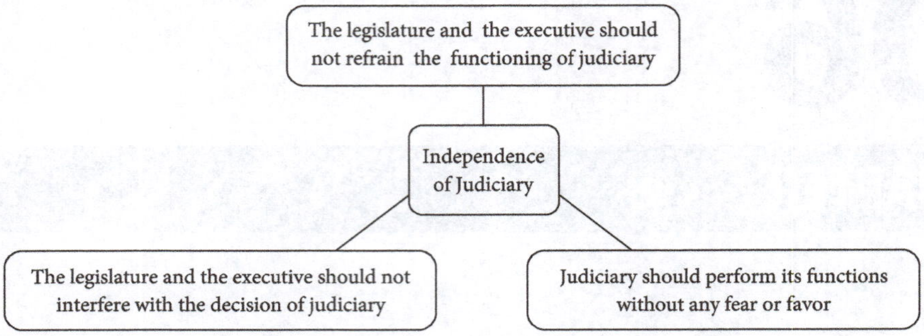

Protection of the Independence of the Judiciary

The Constitution of India contains several provisions that ensures the independence of judiciary. These are as follows

- **No involvement of legislature in the appointment of judges.**
- A person to be appointed as a judge must have an experience as a lawyer or must be well versed in law.
- The judges have the **fixed tenure**. They hold office until they retire.
- They have security of tenure[2] which ensures that judges could function without fear.
- They are **financially independent** from legislature and executive. The salaries and allowances of the judges are not subjected to the approval of the legislature.
- There judgements are **secure** from personal criticism. Judiciary has the power to penalise for the contempt of court[3].
- The **conduct of judges cannot be discussed in the Parliament**. The only exception to this is when the removal proceeding of a judge is being carried out.

Appointment of Judges

The process of judicial appointment is influenced by the Council of Ministers, Governors, Chief Ministers and the Chief Justice of India.

- **Appointment of Chief Justice of India (CJI)** It is a convention that the **senior-most judge** of the Supreme Court will be elected as the Chief Justice of India. However, this convention was broken twice
  - In 1973, when **A.N. Ray** was appointed by superseding three senior judges.
  - In 1975 when **M.H. Beg** was appointed by superseding Justice **H.R. Khanna.**
- **Appointment of Other Judges** The other judges of the Supreme Court and the High Court are appointed by the President in consultation with the CJI. In practice, this means that the final decision on appointments was made by the Council of Ministers.

Principle of Collegiality

- The Chief Justice of India gives recommendation of the names of persons to be appointed as the judges of the Supreme Court and the High Court in consultation with four senior-most judges in case of the Supreme Court and with 2 senior most judges in case of High Court judge. This is known as the principle of collegiality, developed by the Supreme Court of India.

---

2 Security of tenure It is a guarantee that a public official, such as judge, cannot be removed from office arbitrarily, ensuring independence and impartiality.

3 Contempt of court It is an actions or words that disrespect or disobey court orders, undermining the authority and dignity of the judiciary.

Removal of Judges

- The process of removal of judges is extremely difficult and unless there is a common consensus among the members of the Parliament, a judge cannot be removed.
- A judge of the Supreme Court or High Court can be removed only on the round of proven misbehavior.
- A **special majority**[4] of both the Houses of Parliament is required to pass the motion containing charges against the judge.
- Till date, only one case of removing a Supreme Court judge has been brought before the Parliament. Although the motion gained a two-third majority, but it lacked the support of the majority of the total strength of the house and hence, the judge retained.

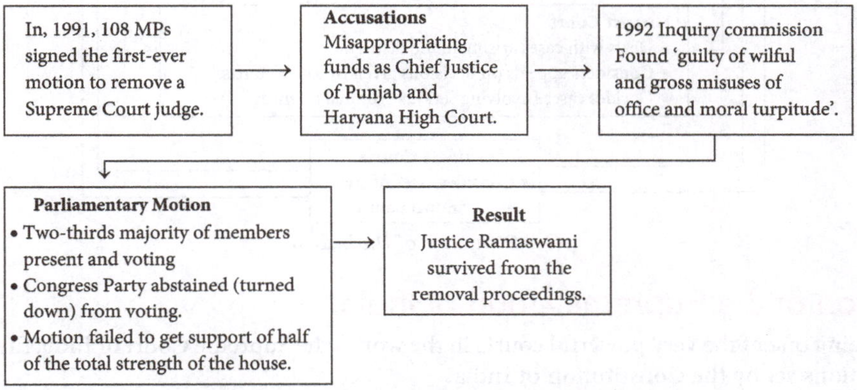

▲ *Justice V. Ramaswami's Removal Proceedings*

Quick Test 1

1. Define the system of courts that interprets the laws and Constitutional Provisions.
2. Who appoints the judges of the Supreme Court?
3. Which kind of majority is required for the removal of judges?
4. Name the judge, whose removal was brought before the Parliament?

6.2 Structure of the Judiciary

- The Constitution provides for a **Single-Integrated Judicial System** in India. This means that unlike some other federal countries of the world, India does not have separate state courts.
- The structure of judiciary is **pyramidal** with the Supreme Court at the top, High Courts below them and district and subordinate courts at the lowest level.
- The lower courts function under the guidance and superintendence of the higher courts.

---

4 **Special majority** It refers to a majority of 2/3rd members present and voting supported by over 50 per cent of the total strength of the house.

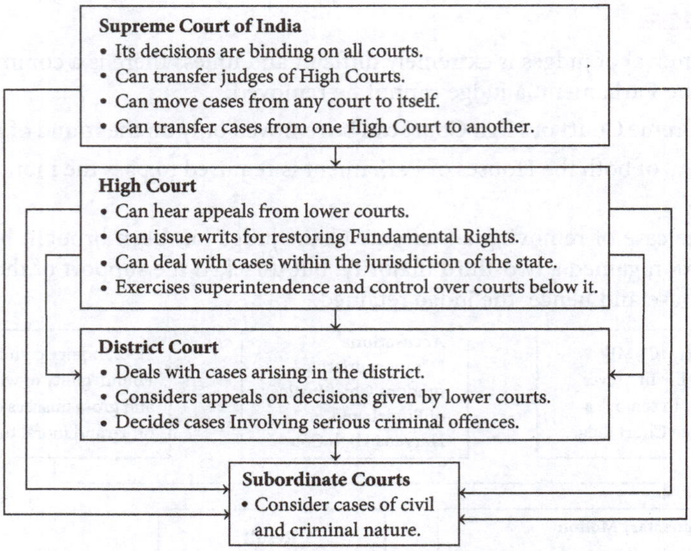

▲ *Structure of Judiciary*

Jurisdiction of the Supreme Court of India

- Despite being one of the very powerful courts in the world, the Supreme Court of India functions within the limitations set by the Constitution of India.
- The Constitution defines the functions, responsibilities, scope of powers and jurisdiction of the Supreme Court.

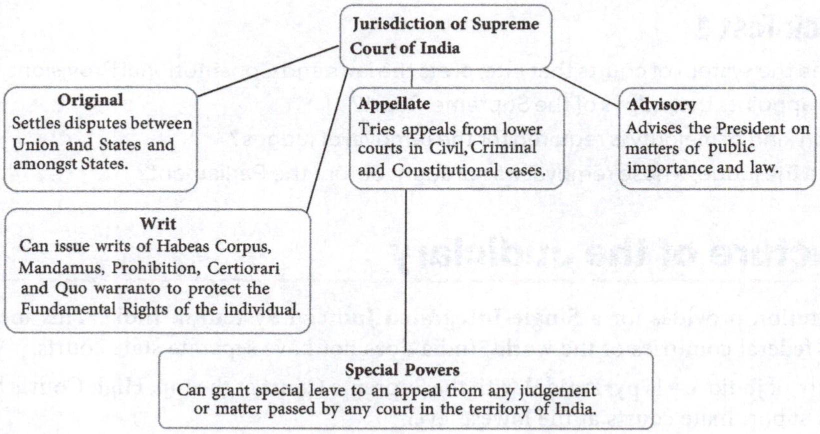

▲ *Jurisdiction of Supreme Court*

Original Jurisdiction

- It contains cases directly considered by the Supreme Court without going to lower courts. This **jurisdiction**[5] establishes Supreme Court as an umpire in **federal disputes**[6].
- Original jurisdiction means that Supreme Court has exclusive power to resolve such cases. No lower courts or High Courts can deal with these cases.

5 **Jurisdiction** It is the official power of the courts to make legal decisions and judgements.
6 **Federal disputes** It means legal conflicts between the Central Government and States, or between states.

Writ Jurisdiction

- In case of violation of Fundamental Rights, individuals can either directly approach to the Supreme Court or the High Court.
- Supreme Court and High Court can **issue writs to enforce Fundamental Rights**. The courts can give orders to executive to act or not act in a particular way.

Appellate Jurisdiction

- The Supreme Court is the India's **highest court of appeal**. It hears appeals against the decision of the High Court.
- An appeal can be made to both the High Court and the Supreme Court if the lower court has given death sentence to a person. The Supreme Court can admit appeals even if High Court does not give certification.
- The appellate jurisdiction allows the Supreme Court to reconsider the case and legal issues involved. It can change the rulings and give new interpretations of the Constitution.
- High court also have appellate jurisdiction over lower court decisions.

Advisory Jurisdiction

- The Supreme Court possess advisory jurisdiction which means the President of India can refer any matter of public importance or matter which involves interpretation of Constitution to Supreme Court for advice.
- However, neither Supreme Court is bound to give advice, nor the President is bound to accept such advice. But, this jurisdiction serves the following utility
  - The government has the option to seek legal opinion on a matter of importance before taking action on it to prevent unnecessary **litigations**[7].
  - The government can make suitable changes in its actions or legislation.

Article-137

The Supreme Court shall have the power to review any judgement pronounced or order made by it.

Article-144

All authorities, civil and judicial, in territory of India shall act in aid of Supreme Court.

6.3 Judicial Activism

- Judicial activism or **Public Interest litigation (PIL) or Social Action Litigation** (SAL) have revolutionised the functioning of judiciary and made it more people-friendly.
- PIL and SAL are the legal instruments that allows individuals or organisations to file cases on behalf of others, promoting public interest, protecting rights and secure social-economic justice.
- This concept emerged in 1979, when the Supreme Court heard a case filed by others on behalf of aggrieved persons (means unhappy and angry because of unfair treatment), marking a shift from traditional litigation.

The key features of PIL are as follows

- It allows public spirited citizens and organisations to seek judicial intervention.
- Allow judiciary to consider cases based on newspaper reports and postal complaints.
- It focusses on **issues of public importance,** such as the protection of rights, environmental protections and betterment of life conditions for the poor.

7 **Litigation** It is the process of taking legal actions.

Impact of Judicial Activism

Judicial activism in India has transformed the concept of rights as now the citizens can seek justice for issues like clean air, unpolluted water and decent living conditions, which are considered rights for the entire society. Judicial activism has a major role in protecting rights, especially for those who cannot easily access the courts.

Positive Impact	Negative Impact/Challenges
▪ Democratisation of the judicial system : Both the individuals and groups can access courts.	▪ Overburdened courts : Excessive PILs have overburdened the judiciary.
▪ Executive accountablity : Judiciary holds the executive branch accountable.	▪ Blurred lines of distinction: Judiciary has encroached on executive and legislative domains by resolving issues that belong to them.
▪ Free and fair elections : Courts asked the candidates to disclose assets, income and educational qualifications.	▪ Threat to democratic balance : Some argue that judicial activism disrupts the balance among the branches of government.

Quick Test 2

1. Which is the highest court of appeal?
2. Which court adjudicate a dispute between the Union and the state?
3. Name any two writs which can be issued by the Supreme Court of India.
4. Which article of the Indian Constitution says that the Supreme Court can review its own judgement?

6.4 Judiciary and Rights

- The judiciary has been entrusted with the task of protecting rights of individuals. The Supreme Court is the **protector of Fundamental Rights** of the citizen as well as the **interpreter of the Constitution.** The Constitution empowers the Supreme Court to
  - Issue writs to restore Fundamental Rights. The Supreme Court issue writs under **Article 32** and the High Courts issue writs under **Article 226.**
  - Declare laws unconstitutional through judicial review **(Article 13).**
- The writ power and the review power of the court together make judiciary very powerful.

Judicial Review

- It means that the Supreme Court or High Courts have the power to examines laws for Constitutionality and strike down those that are inconsistent with the provisions of the Constitution.
- The judicial review power of the Supreme Court extends to legislations that violate both
  - The Fundamental Rights and
  - The federal distribution of powers.
  - Thus, by this Supreme Court can declare them unconstitutional.
- The judicial review power also extends to the laws passed by the state legislatures.

The term 'Judicial review' is nowhere mentioned in the Constitution. The fact that India has a **written Constitution** and power given to the Supreme Court to strike down a law inconsistent with the Fundamental Rights indirectly provides the power of judicial review to the Supreme Court.

6.5 Judiciary and Parliament

The Indian Constitution has clearly demarcated the functioning of every part of the government. Despite this, conflicts arise between the Parliament and judiciary as well as between the executive and judiciary.

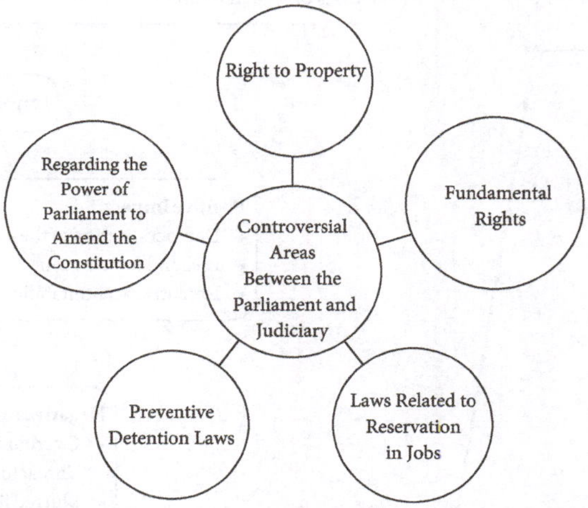

Decision of Supreme Court in 1973

- Judgement given by the Supreme Court in the **Kesavananda Bharati case (1973)** changed the nature of conflicts between the legislature and the judiciary. The court ruled that
  - The Constitution has a **'basic structure'** that cannot be altered.
  - **Right to property** is not a part of this basic structure and it can be suitably abridged.
  - Judiciary has the right to decide what constitutes the basic structure.
- In 1979, the Right to Property was removed from the list of Fundamental Rights which also helped in changing the legislature–judiciary relationship.

Unresolved Issues Between Judiciary and Legislature

- There are some issues that still remain unresolved like
  - The legislature has the power to punish a person who is held guilty for breach of Parliamentary privilege. But it is still unclear whether the judiciary can intervene in such case and whether the aggrieved person can seek protection of courts.
  - The Constitution does not allow the discussion on the conduct of the judges in the Parliament but there are several instances where such discussions have taken place.
  - Judiciary in some instances has remarked on the functioning of the legislature and criticised it. This was seen as the violation of **Parliamentary sovereignty**[8].

These instances reflect how important it is in a democracy for each organ of the government to respect the authority of other organs.

Quick Test 3

1 Under which article the Supreme Court can issue writ?
2 Define Judicial review.
3 Which judgement of the Supreme Court provided the basic structure of the Constitution of India?

8 **Parliamentary sovereignty** It is the doctrine that Parliament has absolute authority to make laws and its decisions cannot be challenged in court.

Mind Map

JUDICIARY

1 Concept

- Judiciary is an important organ of the government.
- Judiciary play an important role in interpreting, protecting the Constitution and the rights of the individuals.

Role of Judiciary

- Safeguarding the rights of individual.
- Securing democratic value.
- Prevent from individual and group dictatorship.
- Setting disputes in accordance with law.

Independence of Judiciary

- The legislature and the executive should not refrain the functioning of judiciary.
- The legislature and the executive should not interfere with the decision of judiciary.
- Judiciary should perform its functions without any fear or favour.

Appointment of Judges

- Appointment of Chief Justice of India (CJI) conterversy
  – A.N. Ray in 1973
  – M.H. Beg in 1975
- Appointed by the President in consultation with the CJI

Removal of Judges

- A judge of the Supreme Court or High Court can be removed.
- A special majority of 2/3rd majority of members present and voting of both the Houses of Parliament is required to pass the motion containing charges against the judge.

2 Structure of the Judiciary

Supreme Court

- It is the highest court of appeal.
- Its decisions are binding on all courts.
- Can transfer judges of High Court.
- It can move case from any court to itself.

High Court

- Can hear appeal from lower court.
- Can issues writs for enforcing Fundamental Rights.

District Court

- Deals with cases of district level.
- Deals case involving serious criminal offences.

Subordinate court

- Consider cases of civil and criminal nature.

3 Judicial Activism

PIL and SAL are the legal instruments that allows individual and organisation to file cases on behalf of others.

Impact of Judicial Activism

Positive Impact

- Democratisation of the judicial system.
- Free and fair election.
- Executive accountability.

Negative Impact

- Overburdened courts.
- Threat to democratic balance.
- Blurred lines of distinction.

4 Judiciary and Rights

- The Supreme Court issues writs to restore Fundamental Rights (Article 32). The High Court can also issue writs under (Article 226).

5 Judiciary and Parliament

Controversial Areas between Parliament and Judiciary

- Regarding the power of Parliament to amend the Constitution.
- Right to property.
- Fundamental Rights.
- Preventive detention laws.
- Laws related to reservation in jobs.

Supreme Court Decision (1973)

- Basic structure of Constitution can not be changed.
- Right to property is not a part of Fundamental Rights.

Jurisdiction of Supreme Court of India.

Original

- Settles disputes between union and states and amongst state.

Writ

- Supreme Court and High Court can issue writs to enforce Fundamental Rights.

Appellate

- Tries appeals from lower courts in civil, criminal and Constitutional cases.

Advisory

- Advises the President on matters of public importance and law.

NCERT Folder

Intext Questions

1. Why is independence of the judiciary important? (Pg 129)

Ans. The independence of the judiciary is important because it ensures that disputes, whether between individuals, groups, or between individuals/groups and the government, are settled fairly and impartially.

An independent judiciary operates without political interference, allowing it to uphold the rule of law. This means that all individuals, regardless of their social or economic status, are subject to the same laws, ensuring equality and justice.

2. Do you think that executive should have the power to appoint judges? (Pg 129)

Ans. The involvement of the executive in judicial appointments raises concerns about potential political influence over the judiciary, which is meant to be an independent body. It is important that this role is limited to a formal, procedural capacity, with the final decision-making power resting with the judiciary itself.

The involvement of the Chief Justice and senior judges in recommending candidates should ensure that political interference is minimised.

The judiciary must remain as independent as possible to protect its role as an interpreter of the Constitution and the law.

3. If you were asked to make suggestions for changing the procedure of appointing judges, what changes would you suggest? (Pg 129)

Ans. Suggestions for changing the procedure of appointing judges are as follows

- The process of appointing judges should be more transparent. Transparency would help build public trust in the fairness and impartiality of the appointments.
- The establishment of an independent, non-political judicial appointments commission could be considered. This would reduce political influence in the appointment process.
- The executive should still play a role, but it should be limited to formal approval rather than decision-making.
- The final selection should be primarily based on judicial recommendations, ensuring the independence of the judiciary while keeping the executive's role ceremonial and procedural.

4. Match the following

A.	Dispute between state of Bihar and union of India will be heard by	1.	High Court
B.	Appeal from District Court of Haryana will go to	2.	Judicial review
C.	Single Integrated Judiciary	3.	Supreme Court
D.	Declaring a law unconstitutional	4.	Single Constitution

Ans. A-3, B-1, C-4, D-2

5. Find out the details about at least one case involving a PIL and study the way in which that case helped in serving public interest. (Pg 137)

Ans. One of the landmark PIL cases in India is the 'M.C. Mehta Vs. Union of India' case.

In 1986, environmentalist M.C. Mehta filed a PIL before the Supreme Court regarding the pollution caused by tanneries in the city of Kanpur, particularly around the Ganga river. He sought the enforcement of environmental laws to control pollution and protect public health. The PIL highlighted the illegal discharge of untreated toxic waste into the river.

The Supreme Court issued several orders to the government and local authorities, compelling them to shut down polluting tanneries, enforce stricter environmental regulations and implement waste treatment processes.

The case helped in serving public interest as

- It played a crucial role in raising awareness about environmental issues and pollution in India.
- It led to stricter enforcement of environmental laws, particularly in industrial zones, benefiting public health and the environment.
- It also set a precedent for PILs being used to address public health and environmental concerns, showing the power of judicial intervention for the public good.

6. When does the court use the review powers? (Pg 140)

Ans. The court uses its review powers in the following situations

- To examine the Constitutionality of laws passed by the legislature. If a law contradicts or violates the Constitution, the court can declare it unconstitutional and strike it down.
- To determine if any law or action violates the Fundamental Rights guaranteed by the Constitution.

If a law infringes upon these rights, the court can declare the law invalid and protect the rights of individuals.

- The court can also use its review powers to check whether a law encroaches on the powers allocated to the states or the Central Government under the Constitution.

7. What is the difference between judicial review and writ? (Pg 140)

Ans.

Judicial Review	Writ
It is the power of courts to examine the Constitutionality of laws, actions and policies.	It is a formal order issued by a court to protect Fundamental Rights.
It aims to ensure that laws and actions comply with the Constitution.	It aims to provide specific relief in cases of Fundamental Rights violations.
It applies to laws, executive actions and judicial decisions.	It is specific to individual cases where rights are violated.

Exercise

1. What are the different ways in which the independence of the judiciary is ensured? Choose the odd ones out.

(i) Chief Justice of Supreme Court is consulted in the appointment of other judges of Supreme Court.

(ii) Judges are not generally removed before the age of retirement.

(iii) Judges of High Court cannot be transferred to another High Court.

(iv) Parliament has no say in the appointment of judges.

Ans. The independence of judiciary is ensured in following ways

- Chief Justice of Supreme Court is consulted in the appointment of other judges of Supreme Court.
- Judges are generally not removed before the age of retirement. They are removed in exceptional cases.
- Parliament has no say in the appointment of judges.

Therefore odd ones are

- Judges of High Court cannot be transferred to another High Court.

2. Does independence of judiciary mean that the judiciary is not accountable to any one? Write your answer in not more than 100 words.

Ans. The independence of judiciary does not mean that the judiciary is not accountable to anyone as the judiciary has to work according to the law written in the Constitution. Any kind of misbehaviour and incapacity of the judges can lead to their removal from the office.

The judges have to write and explain the grounds of their decision made in the court. They cannot rule one way today and the opposite tomorrow in the same case. The judiciary cannot interfere in the sphere of legislature and executive.

Thus, the judicial system has to function independently, while having accountability to the Constitution.

3. What are the different provisions in the Constitution in order to maintain the independence of judiciary?

Ans. The different provisions in the Constitution in order to maintain the independence of judiciary are

- The conduct of judges cannot be discussed in the Parliament.
- The legislature is not involved in the process of appointment of judges.
- The judges have fixed tenure that ensures that they can work without fear and favour. They can be removed only in exceptional cases. The procedure for the removal of judges of Supreme Court and High Court is extremely difficult.
- The approval of the legislature is not required for salaries and allowances of the judges.
- The instructions of the judiciary has to be followed by the legislature and executive of the country.

4. Read the news report below and identify, the following aspects

(i) What is the case about?

(ii) Who has been the beneficiary in the case?

(iii) Who is the petitioner in the case?

(iv) Visualise what would have been the different arguments put forward by the company?

(v) What arguments would the farmers have put forward?

Supreme Court orders REL to pay ₹ 300 crore to Dahanu farmers.

Our Corporate Bureau 24th March, 2005 Mumbai.

The Supreme Court has ordered Reliance Energy Limited to pay ₹ 300 crore to farmers who grow the chikoo fruit in the Dahanu area outside Mumbai. The order comes after the chikoo growers petitioned the court against the pollution caused by Reliance's thermal power plant. Dahanu, which is 150 km from Mumbai, was a self-sustaining agricultural and horticultural economy known for its fisheries and forests just over a decade ago, but was devastated in 1989 when a thermal power plant came into operation in the region. The next year, this fertile belt saw its first crop failure. Now, 70 per cent of the crop of what was once the fruit bowl of Maharashtra is gone. The fisheries have shut and the forest cover has thinned. Farmers and environment alists say that fly ash from the power plant entered ground water and polluted the entire eco-system.

The Dahanu Taluka Environment Protection Authority ordered the thermal station to set up a pollution control unit to reduce sulphur emissions and inspite of a Supreme Court order backing the order, the pollution control plant was not set up even by 2002. In 2003, Reliance acquired the thermal station and re-submitted a schedule for installation process in 2004. As the pollution control plant is still not set up, the Dahanu Taluka Environmental Protection Authority asked Reliance for a bank guarantee of ₹ 300 crores.

Ans. (i) The case is about the loss borne by the farmers in the production of chikoo because of the pollution generated by the thermal power plant of Reliance Energy Limited.

(ii) The farmers have been the beneficiary in the case.

(iii) The chikoo growing farmers of Dahanu are the petitioner in the case.

(iv) The different arguments that would have put forward by the company are as follows

- Thermal power plant is needed to produce electricity to meet growing energy needs.
- The thermal power plant is set up outside the main city, so least pollution affects large area and population.
- The thermal power plant has generated employment in the region.
- Therefore, it has helped in solving the problem of employment upto some extent and also has contributed in the economy.

(v) The arguments that the farmers would have put forward are as follows

- The loss in the production of chikoo has adversely affected the agriculture and economy of the region.
- The shutting down of fishing has created un-employment in the region.
- The increased pollution has affected the agricultural and fishing industries as well as healthy people and animals of the region.
- The forests have been destroyed as a result of pollution.

5. Read the following news report and

(i) Identify the governments at different levels.

(ii) Identify the role of Supreme Court.

(iii) What elements of the working of judiciary and executive can you identify in it?

(iv) Identify the policy issues, matters related to legislation, implementation and interpretation of the law involved in this case.

Centre, Delhi join hands on CNG issue.

By Our Staff Reporter, The Hindu 23rd September, 2001.

NEW DELHI, 22nd September. The Centre and the Delhi government today agreed to jointly approach the Supreme Court this coming week... for phasing out of all non-CNG commercial vehicles in the capital. They also decided to seek a dual fuel policy for the city instead of putting the entire transportation system on the single-fuel mode 'which was full of dangers and would result in disaster'.

It was also decided to discourage the use of CNG by private vehicle owners in the capital. Both governments would press for allowing the use of 0.05 per cent low sulphur diesel for running of buses in the capital. In addition, it would be pleaded before the court that all commercial vehicles, which fulfil the Euro-II standards, should be allowed to play in the city. Though both the centre and the state would file separate affidavits, these would contain common points. The centre would also go out and support the Delhi government's stand on the issues concerning CNG.

These decisions were taken at a meeting between the Delhi Chief Minister, Mrs. Sheela Dikshit, and the Union Petroleum and Natural Gas Minister, Mr. Ram Naik.

Mrs. Dikshit said the Central Government would request the court that in view of the high powered committee appointed under Dr. R.A. Mashelkar, to suggest an 'Auto Fuel Policy' for the entire country, it would be appropriate to extend the deadline, as it was not possible to convert the entire 10,000-odd bus fleet into CNG during the prescribed time frame. The Mashelkar Committee is expected to submit its report within a period of six months.

The Chief Minister said time was required to implement the court directives. Referring to the co-ordinated approach on the issue, Mrs. Dikshit said this would take into account the details about the number of vehicles to be run on CNG, eliminating long queues outside CNG filling stations, the CNG fuel requirements of Delhi and the ways and means to implement the directive of the court.

The Supreme Court had refused to relax the only CNG norm for the city's buses but said it had never insisted on CNG for taxis and auto-rickshaws. Mr. Naik said the centre would insist on allowing use of low sulphur diesel for buses in Delhi as putting the entire transportation system dependent on CNG could prove to be disastrous. The capital relied on pipeline supply for CNG and any disruption would throw the public transport system out of gear.

Ans. (i) The government at different levels are the Central and the State Government, represented by the Union Petroleum Ministry and Chief Minister, respectively.

(ii) The Supreme Court has played an active role in upholding public interest by instructing authorities to take steps to curb pollution.

(iii) The action of the judiciary is an example of judicial activism and writ jurisdiction. The executive is concerned with the implementation of the directives of the judiciary.

(iv) The main policy issue in this case was the transition of public and commercial transport vehicle to a cleaner fuel of CNG. The government also sought to implement a dual policy instead of a single fuel for the entire transportation system.

The legislature aspect was mandating the switching of all commercial vehicles to CNG and setting standards for the same.

The debatable part was the interference of judiciary directing this action. The Supreme Court interpreted the law to provide for a clean environment to the citizens of Delhi. Judicial activism pressurised the executive to implement them at the earliest. The issues related to implementation were norms for pollutants and the time frame for converting the transport to CNG that was the domain of the executive.

6. The following is a statement about Ecuador. What similarities or differences do you find between this example and the judicial system in India?

"It would be helpful if a body of common law or judicial precedent, existed that could clarify a journalist's rights. Unfortunately, Ecuador's courts don't work that way. Judges are not forced to respect the rulings of higher courts in previous cases. Unlike the US, an appellate judge in Ecuador (or elsewhere in South America, for that matter) need not provide a written decision explaining the legal basis of a ruling. A judge may rule one way today and the opposite way, in a similar case, tomorrow, without explaining why?"

Ans. There are differences between the judicial review system of India and Ecuador, which are as follow

- Unlike the judges in Ecuador's Court, Indian judges have to follow the instructions and rulings of higher courts in previous cases. Indian judges have to provide written decision that explains the legal basis of a ruling.
- An Indian judge may not rule one way today and in the other way tomorrow in the same case and he has to give explanation of the decision of every ruling in written form as compared to judges in Ecuador.

7. Read the following statements: Match them with the different jurisdictions the Supreme Court can exercise - Original, Appellate and Advisory.

(i) The government wanted to know if it can pass a law about the citizenship status of residents of Pakistan-occupied areas of Jammu and Kashmir.

(ii) In order to resolve the dispute about river Cauvery, the government of Tamil Nadu wants to approach the court.

(iii) Court rejected the appeal by people against the eviction from the dam site.

Ans. (i) Advisory jurisdiction

(ii) Original jurisdiction

(iii) Appellate jurisdiction

8. In what way can Public Interest Litigation help the poor?

Ans. Public Interest Litigation can help the poor in following ways

- It can seek to protect the Fundamental Rights and the living conditions of the poor.
- It can allow public spirited citizens, social organisations and lawyers to file cases on behalf of those who cannot approach the courts.
- The judiciary can also consider the cases on the basis of newspaper reports and postal complaints received by the courts.
- The courts can direct the executive to comply with its orders and provide remedial action to the aggrieved person whose rights have been violated.
- PILs have also expanded the idea of rights and thus, have led to formation of new norms for public good like, clean air and water that have benefitted the entire society.

9. Do you think that judicial activism can lead to a conflict between the judiciary and executive.

Ans. Yes, judicial activism can lead to conflict between the judiciary and the executive because of the interference of the judiciary in the domain of the executive. Issues related to pollution, investigation of cases against corruption and electoral reforms that are ordinarily handled by the executive under the control of the legislature are being resolved by the judiciary.

Judicial activism also violates the democratic principle of respecting the powers, and jurisdiction of each organ of the government, as it confers extraordinary powers on the judiciary.

Thus, the balance between the three organs of the government has become very delicate.

10. How is judicial activism related to the protection of Fundamental Rights? Has it helped in expanding the scope of Fundamental Rights?

Ans. Judicial activism is related to the protection of the Fundamental Rights as

- It has made the judiciary more approachable by the common people seeking justice.
- The Supreme Court has the power to remedy the violation of Fundamental Rights by issuing writs or by reviewing and declaring certain laws as unconstitutional.
- The PIL helps the poor to fight against discrimination.
- Inhumane working conditions, sexual exploitation of the children, blinding of jail inmates by the police are some of the cases that have been considered by the courts, which have made rights meaningful and useful for the poor and dis-advantaged people.
- Issues related to better living conditions, like clean air and water and pollution free environment, have also helped in the expansion of the scope of Fundamental Rights.

Thus, by these ways, judicial activism has it helped in expanding the scope of Fundamental Rights.

Exam Pattern Questions

Objective Type Questions

Multiple Choice Questions (MCQs)

1. Which of the following government organs provides a mechanism for the resolution of disputes between individuals or private parties?

(a) Legislature (b) Judiciary
(c) Executive (d) Bureaucracy

2. Who among the following is not a principle function of judiciary?

(a) Ensure supremacy of law
(b) Protect Fundamental Right of individual
(c) Settle disputes
(d) Promote personality cult

3. What does independence of judiciary mean?

(a) It is not under the control of the legislature or the executive.
(b) The judges do not act on the direction of the government.
(c) The judges do not act according to the wishes of the party in power.
(d) All of the above

4. Which of the following organ of the government is not involved in the process of appointment of judges?

(a) Executive (b) Legislature
(c) Judiciary (d) None of these

5. Who among the following does not influence the process of judicial appointment?

(a) Chief Justice of India (b) Council of Ministers
(c) President (d) Bar Council of India

6. Who appoints the judges of the Supreme Court and the High Courts?

(a) The President
(b) The Prime Minister
(c) The Chief Justice of the Supreme Court
(d) The President on the advice of the Prime Minister and in consultation with the Chief Justice of the Supreme Court.

7. Under collegium system of judicial appointment in Supreme Court how many seniors-most judges are consulted apart from Chief Justice?

(a) Four (b) Five
(c) Six (d) Two

8. The .... plays a crucial role in appointment process, while the .... has the powers of removal?

(a) President, executive (b) executive, legislature
(c) legislature, executive (d) Speaker, Vice-chairman

9. Structure of the Judiciary in India is ....

(a) pyramidal (b) square
(c) circle (d) rectangle

10. .... majority is required in procedure of removal of Judges.

(a) Simple (b) Special
(c) Effective (d) Absolute

11. The Constitution of India provides for a .... integrated judicial system.

(a) quasi (b) single
(c) multi (d) None of these

12. **Who has the power to deal cases that are arising between union and the states and among the states themselves?**
(a) Civil Court (b) District Court
(c) Supreme Court (d) High Court

13. **Who has the power to issue writs for enforcement of Fundamental Rights?**
(a) Supreme court (b) High Courts
(c) President (d) Both (a) and (b)

14. **Which Article of Indian Constitution stipulates the Supreme Court shall have power to review any judgement pronounced by it?**
(a) Article 144 (b) Article 142
(c) Article 137 (d) Article 135

15. **Public Interest Litigations has become the most important vehicle of ....**
(a) judicial review (b) judicial activism
(c) judicial overreach (d) None of these

16. **In which year did the Supreme Court gave judgement in Keshvananda Bharti case?**
(a) 1971 (b) 1973 (c) 1975 (d) 1977

17. **Who has defined the basic structure of the Constitution?**
(a) Executive (b) Legislature
(c) Supreme Court (d) High Court

18. **The Constitution of India has provided for a single integrated judiciary. Which of the following is incorrect related to the structure and integration of judiciary?** Competency Based Que
(a) Sub-ordinate Courts can consider cases of civil and criminal nature.
(b) High Courts can issue writs for restoring Fundamental Rights.
(c) District Courts cannot decide cases involving serious criminal offences.
(d) Supreme Court can transfer cases from one High Court to another.

19. **Which of the following statement about the Supreme Court is incorrect?** Competency Based Que
(a) Supreme Court can move cases from any court to itself.
(b) It can transfer judges of High Court.
(c) It can deal cases within the jurisdiction of the foreign state.
(d) It can transfer cases from one High Court to another.

20. **Consider the following statements related to the High Courts.** Competency Based Que
I. It can hear appeal from lower courts.
II. It cannot issue writs for enforcing Fundamental Rights.
Select the correct statements?
(a) Only I (b) Only II
(c) Both I and II (d) None of these

21. **Consider the following statements related to advisory jurisdiction of the Supreme Court?** Competency Based Que
I. The Supreme Court is obligated to provide advice on such matter as referred by the President.
II. President is obligated to take such advice.
Select the correct statements?
(a) Only I (b) Only II
(c) Both I and II (d) None of these

22. **Consider the following statements related to judges.** Competency Based Que
I. The judges have a fixed tenure of office till reaching the age of retirement.
II. The salaries and allowances of the judges are subjected to the approval of the legislature.
Select the correct codes.
(a) Only I (b) Only II
(c) Both I and II (d) None of these

23. **Given below are two statements** Competency Based Que
Statement I All the judges in India have been given security of tenure.
Statement II There is no ground mentioned in the Constitution of India for the removal of the judges.
In the light of above statements, choose the correct answer from the options given below
(a) Both Statement I and Statement II are true.
(b) Both Statement I and Statement II are false.
(c) Statement I is true, but Statement II is false.
(d) Statement I is false, but Statement II is true.

24. **Given below are two statements.** Competency Based Que
Statement I PIL is the chief instrument through which judicial review has flourished in India.
Statement II Social Action Litigation (SAL) have revolutionised the functioning of judiciary and made it more people friendly.
In the light of above statements, choose the correct answer from the options given below
(a) Both Statement I and Statement II are true.
(b) Both Statement I and Statement II are false.
(c) Statement I is true, but Statement II is false.
(d) Statement I is false, but Statement II is true.

25. **Match the List I with List II.** Competency Based Que

List I		List I	
A.	Supreme Court	1.	It issue writs under Article 226
B.	High court	2.	It's decisions are binding on all courts.
C.	District Court	3.	It operates under the supervision of High Courts.
D.	Subordinate Court	4.	It deals with the cases arising in the districts.

Codes

	A	B	C	D		A	B	C	D
(a)	2	1	4	3	(b)	1	2	3	4
(c)	2	1	3	4	(d)	2	3	4	1

Assertion-Reason Questions

Directions (Q. Nos. 26-31) In the questions given below, there are two statements marked as Assertion (A) and Reason (R). Read the statements and choose the correct option.

Codes

(a) Both A and R are true and R is the correct explanation of A.
(b) Both A and R are true, but R is not the correct explanation of A.
(c) A is true, but R is false.
(d) A is false, but R is true.

26. **Assertion (A)** The actions and decisions of judges are immune from personal criticisms.

Reason (R) Parliament is allowed to discuss the conduct of judges at any time to ensure accountability.

27. **Assertion (A)** In the only case of a Supreme Court judge's removal, the motion received a two-third majority in Parliament but the judge was not removed.

Reason (R) The motion did not have the support of the majority of the total strength of the house, which is required for the removal of a judge.

28. **Assertion (A)** The Constitution of India provides for a single integrated judicial system.

Reason (R) Supreme Court decisions are binding for lower Subordinate Courts and it can ask to transfer any cases to any other High Court or can call cases to itself.

29. **Assertion (A)** The role of judiciary became more popular by judicial activism.

Reason (R) Judiciary can consider cases on the basis of newspaper reports and postal complaints received by the court.

30. **Assertion (A)** Constitution of India prescribe separation of power between three organs of the government.

Reason (R) Judiciary favours the government and helps in the implementation of its plans.

31. **Assertion (A)** The Parliament cannot amend the basic structure of the Constitution.

Reason (R) Supreme Court in the Kesavananda Bharati Case ruled there are some basic structures of the Constitution such as secularism, rule of law etc.

Passage Based Questions

32. **Read the given passage and answer the following questions.**

The judges have a fixed tenure. They hold office till reaching the age of retirement. Only in exceptional cases, judges may be removed. But otherwise, they have security of tenure. Security of tenure ensures that judges could function without fear or favour. The Constitution prescribes a very difficult procedure for removal of judges. The Constitution makers believed that a difficult procedure of removal would provide security of office to the members of judiciary.

(i) The judiciary is not financially dependent on ....

(a) executive (b) legislature
(c) Both (a) and (b) (d) Neither (a) nor (b)

(ii) The other judges of the Supreme Court and the High Court are appointed by the .... after 'consulting' the CJI.

(a) Chief Minister (b) President
(c) Governor (d) Prime Minister

(iii) What is the role of legislature in the process of appointment of judges?

33. **Read the given passage and answer the following questions.**

It must be remembered that the problems of the poor …are qualitatively different from those which have hitherto occupied the attention of the court and they need ….a different kind of judicial approach. If we blindly follow the adversarial procedure in their case, they would never be able to enforce their Fundamental Rights.

Judicial activism has had manifold impact on the political system. It has democratised the judicial system by giving not just to individuals but also groups access to the courts. It has forced executive accountability. It has also made an attempt to make the electoral system much free and fair. The court asked candidates contesting elections to file affidavits indicating their assets and income along with educational qualifications so that the people could elect their representatives based on accurate knowledge.

(i) In first three lines of the passage whose words are being referred?

(a) Justice Bhagwati (b) Alladi Krishnaswami Ayyar
(c) Mahatma Gandhi (d) Jawaharlal Nehru

(ii) Judicial activism has had a lot of implications for the ....

(a) social system (b) economic system
(c) political system (d) industrial system

(iii) .... has been forced as a result of judicial activism.
(a) Executive accountability
(b) Legislation
(c) Judiciary
(d) None of the above

(iv) .... has overburdened the courts.
(a) Judicial activism (b) Judicial overview
(c) Judicial review (d) All of these

34. **Read the given passage and answer the following questions.**

Perhaps the most important power of the Supreme Court is the power of judicial review. Judicial review means the power of the Supreme Court (or High Courts) to examine the Constitutionality of any law if the court arrives at the conclusion that the law is inconsistent with the provisions of the Constitution, such a law is declared as un-constitutional and inapplicable. The term judicial review is now here mentioned in the Constitution.

(i) What allows the Supreme Court to exercise the power of judicial review?
(a) The Parliament's authority to pass any law.
(b) The written nature of India's Constitution and the ability to strike down laws against Fundamental Rights.
(c) The executive's permission to review laws.
(d) The Constitution explicitly grants judicial review to the Supreme Court.

(ii) What role does judicial review play in protecting Fundamental Rights?
(a) It allows the Parliament to change Fundamental Rights.
(b) It prevents the Constitution from being amended.
(c) It grants the executive the power to restrict Fundamental Rights.
(d) It allows the judiciary to ensure laws do not violate Fundamental Rights.

(iii) Explain how judicial review applies to federal relations and the distribution of powers between the central government and states.

Answers

1. (b) Judiciary
2. (d) Promote personality cult
3. (d) All of the above
4. (b) Legislature
5. (d) Bar Council of India
6. (d) The President on the advice of the Prime Minister and in consultation with the Chief Justice of the Supreme Court.
7. (a) Four
8. (b) executive, legislature
9. (a) pyramidal
10. (b) Special
11. (b) Single
12. (c) Supreme Court
13. (d) Both (a) and (b)
14. (c) Article 137
15. (b) judicial activism
16. (b) 1973
17. (c) Supreme Court
18. (c) District Courts cannot decide cases involving serious criminal offences.
19. (c) It can deal cases within the jurisdiction of the foreign state.
20. (a) Only I
21. (d) None of these
22. (a) Only I
23. (c) Statement I is true, but Statement II is false.
24. (a) Both Statement I and Statement II are true.
25. (a) 2 1 4 3
26. (c) A is true, but R is false.
27. (a) Both A and R are true and R is the correct explanation of A.
28. (a) Both A and R are true and R is the correct explanation of A.
29. (a) Both A and B are true and R is the correct explanation of A.
30. (c) A is true, but R is false.
31. (a) Both A and R are true and R is the correct explanation of A.
32. (i) (c) Both (a) and (b) (ii) (b) President
(iii) There is no involvement or role of legislature in the appointment of judges. A person to be appointed as a judge must have an experience as a lawyer or must be well versed in law. The process of judicial appointment is influenced by the Council of Ministers, Governors, Chief Ministers and the Chief Justice of India.
33. (i) (a) Justice Bhagwati (ii) (c) political system
(iii) (a) executive accountability (iv) (a) Judicial activism
34. (i) (b) The written nature of India's Constitution and the ability to strike down laws against Fundamental Rights.
(ii) (d) It allows the judiciary to ensure laws do not violate Fundamental Rights.
(iii) Judicial review plays a critical role in maintaining the balance of power between the Central Government and the States.
According to the Constitution, certain subjects are exclusively under state jurisdiction, while others are within the jurisdiction of the Central Government. If the Central Government passes a law on a state subject, states can challenge this law in the Supreme Court. If the court agrees that the law infringes on the state's powers, it can declare the law unconstitutional.

Subjective Questions

Very Short Answer Type Questions

1. Mention any two factors responsible for independence of judiciary.

Ans. The factors responsible for independence of judiciary are

- Appointment of judges on the basis of merit.
- The judiciary should be kept free from the influence of the executive.

2. Define the collegium system.

Ans. The system where the group of senior-most judges are consulted for the appointment of judges is known as collegium system.

3. Mention the jurisdictions of the Supreme Court.

Ans. The jurisdictions of Supreme Court are

- Original jurisdiction
- Writ jurisdiction
- Appellate jurisdiction
- Advisory jurisdiction

4. Briefly explain the utility of advisory powers of Supreme Court.

Ans. The utility of the advisory powers of the Supreme Court is two fold

(i) It allows the government to seek legal opinion on a matter of importance before taking action on it.

(ii) The government can make suitable changes in its action or legislations in the light of the advice of Supreme Court.

5. Mention the various writs of the Supreme Court.

Ans. The various writs of Supreme Court for the implementation of Fundamental Rights are as follows

- Habeas Corpus
- Mandamus
- Prohibition
- Certiorari
- Quo-Warranto

6. Describe the appellate jurisdiction of Supreme Court.

Ans. The Supreme Court is the highest court of appeal. Appellate jurisdiction means that the Supreme Court will reconsider the decisions made by the High Court in the Constitutional matters and decisions made by the lower court involving death sentence or criminal matters, etc.

7. Describe the PIL system.

Ans. PIL stands for Public Interest Litigation. A person can file a case in court on behalf of the aggrieved person of society on the matters of public interest and not for personal benefit. Such a case is known as Public Interest Litigation.

8. 'Judicial review is the power of courts'. Explain briefly. **Competency Based Que**

Ans. Judicial review is the power of the Supreme Court (or High Courts) to examine the Constitutionality of any law. If the court arrives at the conclusion that the law is inconsistent with the provisions of the Constitution, such law is declared unconstitutional and inapplicable.

9. Write a short note on High Courts power of Judicial Review.

Ans. Like the Supreme Court of India, the High Courts have also been vested with the power of judicial review. High Courts can strike down any law of the state or any order of the executive if it violates any provision of the Constitution or takes away any of the Fundamental Rights of the people.

Short Answer Type Questions

1. Explain in brief the meaning of independence of judiciary.

Ans. Independence of judiciary means that

- The executive and legislature must not restrict the functioning of judiciary.
- The other organs of the government should not interfere with the decisions of the judiciary.
- Judges must be able to function without any fear or favour.

Independence of judiciary does not imply anti-democratic or absence of accountability. Judiciary is also the part of democratic political structure of the country and therefore, accountable to the Constitution and people of the country.

2. Analyse Constitutional provisions through which independence of judiciary is protected. **Competency Based Que; Diksha App**

Ans. The Constitutional provisions through which independence of judiciary is protected are as follows

- The legislature is not involved in the process of appointment of judges so that party politics does not play a role in the process of appointments.
- The judges have a fixed tenure. They holds office till reaching the age of retirement.
- Security of tenure ensures that judges could function without fear or favour.
- The salaries and allowances of the judges are not subjected to the approval of the legislature.
- The actions and decisions of the judges are immune from personal criticisms.

- Parliament cannot discuss the conduct of the judges except when the proceeding to remove a judge is being carried out.

3. Examine how the Supreme Court's interpretation of the consultation process evolved between 1982 and 1998. **Competency Based Que**

Ans. Between 1982 and 1998, the Supreme Court addressed the issue of judicial appointments repeatedly.

- Initially, the court viewed the role of the Chief Justice of India in the appointment process as purely consultative, meaning the Chief Justice's opinion was considered but not binding. However later, the court modified its stance, asserting that the opinion of the Chief Justice must be followed by the President.
- The court's final stance introduced a significant change: it suggested that the Chief Justice should recommend the names of judges to be appointed, but this recommendation should be made in consultation with the four senior-most judges of the Supreme Court.
- This process emphasised the importance of collective decision-making among the senior-most judges.

4. What is the procedure for the removal of the judges?

Or **Explain the procedure for removal of a judge of the Supreme Court.** **Diksha App**

Ans. The removal of judges of the Supreme Court and the High Courts is also extremely difficult. A judge of the Supreme Court or High Court can be removed only on the ground of proven misbehaviour or incapacity.

A motion containing the charges against the judge must be approved by special majority in both Houses of the Parliament. It should also be noted that while in making appointments, the executive plays a crucial role; the legislature has the powers of removal.

5. When does the Supreme Court of India advises the President? Is that advise binding on him?

Ans. Under Article 143 of the Constitution, the Supreme Court exercises advisory or consultative functions also. Article 143 provides that if any time it appears to the President that a question of law has arisen or is likely to arise which is of public importance, he may refer the matter to the Supreme Court for consideration and opinion.

Such a question is heard by a bench consisting of atleast five judges and the court follows the procedure of an ordinary trial. The majority opinion is sent to the President. The judges can hold dissenting opinion as well.

The opinion of the Supreme Court is not binding on the President as it is not of the nature of a judicial pronouncement. Nor is it obligatory for the Supreme Court to give its opinion.

6. 'PIL is an important tool of Judicial Activism'. Support the statement with any three arguments. **Competency Based Que**

Ans. Judicial activism or Public Interest Litigation have revolutionised the functioning of judiciary and made it more people friendly. The chief instrument through which judicial activism has flourished in India is PIL.

Importance of PIL are as follows

- A person or a group can file a litigation in court on behalf of an individual of society in matters of public interest and not for personal cause.
- This has opened the gates for large number of cases where public spirited citizens and voluntary organisations sought judicial intervention for protection of existing rights, betterment of life conditions of poor, protection of the environment and many other issues in the interest of public.
- Judiciary began considering cases merely on the basis of newspaper reports and postal complaints received by the court and the role of judiciary became more popular by judicial activism.

7. Discuss the role of judiciary in context of the rights.

Ans. Judiciary is entrusted with the task of protecting the rights of individuals and the Supreme Court or High Court can provide remedy against the violation of rights in two ways as

(i) Firstly, it can restore Fundamental Rights by issuing various writs.

(ii) Secondary, the Supreme Court can declare the concerned law un-Constitutional and therefore, non-operational.

The second of the two ways involves judicial review, which means the power of the Supreme Court to examine the Constitutionality of any law, if the court arrives at the conclusion that the law is inconsistent with the provision of the Constitution.

8. Does the Supreme Court's power of judicial review apply only to laws that violate Fundamental Rights, or does it extend to other matters as well?

Ans. The Supreme Court's power of judicial review is not limited to laws that violate Fundamental Rights. While the court certainly has the authority to strike down laws that infringe on Fundamental Rights, its power extends beyond that also.

The Supreme Court has the authority to review laws to ensure that they do not violate the federal distribution of powers as defined by the Constitution. This means that the court can review both central and state laws to check if they respect the division of legislative powers between the central and state governments.

Thus, the court's power of judicial review covers both the protection of Fundamental Rights and the safeguarding of the federal structure of the Constitution.

9. Examine the ruling of the famous Keshavananda Bharti case?

Ans. The famous case of Keshavananda Bharti (1973) was very controversial and dealt with issue that was bone of contention between the judiciary and legislature.

The Supreme Court ruled out following in this case

- The basic structure of the Constitution cannot be violated even by the Parliament.
- It declared that right to property is not part of the basic structure.
- The court reserved to itself the right to decide whether any matter is a part of the basic structure or not.

10. 'Judiciary plays an important role in importing justice, Examine. Competency Based Que

Ans. Judiciary plays an important role in imparting justice to people. It also performs the following functions

- The judiciary act as the guardian of the Constitution by interpreting it in a proper manner as it can declare any law passed by legislature unconstitutional, if it is inconsistent with the Constitution.
- The judiciary performs administrative functions by keeping check on the functioning of each courts.
- The judiciary act as the protector of Fundamental Rights in case of its violation and issue orders for its implementation.
- The judiciary performs legislative functions by giving judgements and making laws to fill up the gap between the legislature and society.

11. Give some suggestions to ensure fast and inexpensive justice in India. Competency Based Que

Ans. Some suggestions to ensure fast and inexpensive justice in India are as follows

- India has a high case backlog and the current judge-to-population ratio is insufficient. Increasing the number of judges, especially at the lower courts, would help in reducing delays.
- Encouraging the use of Alternative Dispute Resolution (ADR), with trained mediators and arbitrators, can help in quick resolutions, particularly for civil cases.
- Simplifying legal procedures, especially in civil and family matters, would make the justice system more accessible and affordable.
- Establishing fast-track courts for specific categories of cases would ensure quicker trials and reduce delays in critical matters.
- Expanding legal aid services and conducting awareness campaigns can make justice more accessible, especially for the underprivileged sections of society.

Long Answer Type Questions

1. 'The Constitution of India has ensured the independence of judiciary'. Discuss the means to provide and protect the independence of judiciary. Competency Based Que

Ans. The Constitution of India has ensured the independence of judiciary through various measures

- The legislature is not involved in the process of appointment of judges. Thus, party politics are not involved in the process of appointment.
- A person must have experience as a lawyer and/or must be versed, in law, to be appointed as judge. His/Her political opinions or political loyalty should not be the criteria for appointment to 'judiciary'.
- The judges have a fixed tenure of office till the age of retirement in order to function without fear. The Constitution prescribes very difficult procedure for the removal of judges to provide security of office to the members of judiciary.
- The judiciary is not financially dependent on either the executive or legislature. The salaries and allowances of the judges are not subjected to the approval of the Parliament as prescribed by the Constitution.
- The actions and decisions of the judges are immune from personal criticism and the judiciary has the power to penalise those guilty of contempt of court.
- Parliament cannot discuss the conduct of judges except when the proceedings for removal is carried out.

2. Describe the various jurisdictions of Supreme Court.

Or **Describe the power and jurisdistion of the Supreme Court of India.** Diksha App

Ans. The jurisdictions of Supreme Court are as follows

Original Jurisdiction It means when the cases are directly considered by the Supreme Court and it alone has the power to deal with such cases. Neither the High Court nor the Lower Courts has the power to deal with such cases. For instance, disputes between union and states and amongst the states.

Writ Jurisdiction When the Fundamental Rights of an individual is violated and the aggrieved person approach the Supreme Court directly, the Supreme Court issues a special order to be followed in the form of writs. This jurisdiction is known as writ jurisdiction.

Appellate Jurisdiction The Supreme Court is the highest court of appeal. Appellate jurisdiction means that Supreme Court will reconsider the decisions made by the High Court in various matters and the Lower Courts involving death sentence or criminal matters. However, the High Court must certify the fitness of appeal and the Supreme Court holds the power to decide whether to admit appeal even when the appeal is not allowed by the High Court.

Advisory Jurisdiction The Supreme Court of India possesses advisory jurisdiction which means that President of India can refer any matter of public importance or Constitutional interpretation to Supreme Court for advice. However, the Supreme Court is not bound to give advice and the President is not bound to accept such advice.

3. Evaluate the reasons for the growth of judicial activism in India. **Competency Based Que; Diksha App**

Ans. The chief instrument through which judicial activism has flourished in India is Public Interest Litigation (PIL) or Social Action Litigation (SAL). In normal course of law, an individual can approach the courts only if he/she has been personally aggrieved.

- This concept underwent a change around 1979. In 1979, the court set the trend when it decided to hear a case where the case was filed not by the aggrieved persons but by others on their behalf. As this case involved a consideration of an issue of public interest, it and such other cases came to be known as Public Interest Litigations. Around the same time, the Supreme Court also took up the case about rights of prisoners.
- This opened the gates for large number of cases where public spirited citizens and voluntary organisations sought judicial intervention for protection of existing rights, betterment of life conditions of the poor, protection of the environment, and many other issues in the interest of the public. PIL has become the most important vehicle of judicial activism.
- Judiciary, which is an institution that traditionally confined to responding to cases brought before it, began considering many cases merely on the basis of newspaper reports and postal complaints received by the court. Therefore, the term judicial activism became the more popular description of the role of the judiciary.
- Through the PIL, the court has expanded the idea of rights. Clean air, unpolluted water, decent living, etc., are rights for the entire society.
- Therefore, (i) It was felt by the courts that individuals as parts of the society must have the right to seek justice wherever such rights were violated.
  (ii) Secondly, through PIL and judicial activism of the post-1980 period, the judiciary has also shown readiness to take into consideration rights of those sections who cannot easily approach the courts.
- For this purpose, the judiciary allowed public spirited citizens, social organisations and lawyers to file petitions on behalf of the needy and the deprived.

4. Judicial activism has had manifold impact on the political system. Comment. **Competency Based Que**

Ans. For answer refer to text under the heading Impact of Judicial Activism on page no. 120.

Picture Based Questions

1. Observe the cartoon given below and answer the questions that follow.

(i) What does the above cartoon signify?

(a) A judgement in a criminal case.
(b) Judgement by court during emergency period.
(c) Judicial activism by the court.
(d) Court helping the dacoits.

Ans. (c) Judicial activism by the court.

(ii) What message is being conveyed through the cartoon?

(a) Bandh and hartal make functioning of judiciary efficient.
(b) Bandh and hartal are illegal.
(c) Bandh and hartal make judiciary more people friendly.
(d) Only bandh and hartal could provide speedy justice.

Ans. (b) Bandh and hartal are illegal.

(iii) Which of the following are the instruments of judicial activism?

(a) Public Interest Litigation (b) Social Interest Application
(c) Social Action Litigation (d) Both (a) and (c)

Ans. (d) Both (a) and (c)

(iv) Which of the following is not a negative impact of judicial activism?

(a) Overburdened judiciary
(b) Financial dependence of judiciary on legislature
(c) Judicial overreach in the executive sphere
(d) Executive accountability

Ans. (d) Executive accountability

2. Study the picture given below and answer the questions that follow

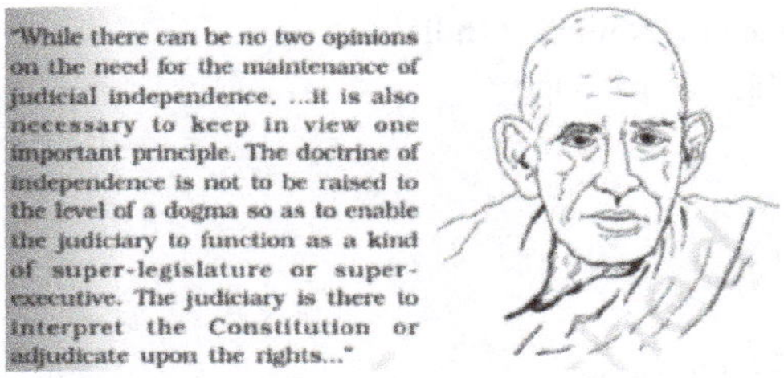

(i) Identify the speaker of the above lines.

(a) Alladi Krishnaswami Ayyar
(b) B. R. Ambedkar
(c) Jyotirao Phule
(d) Jawaharlal Nehru

Ans. (a) Alladi Krishnaswami Ayyar

(ii) What would happen if judicial independence is treated as a dogma?

(a) The judiciary would only interpret the Constitution.
(b) The judiciary could act as a super-legislature or super-executive.
(c) The judiciary would have no power to adjudicate on rights.
(d) The judiciary would remain independent without any restrictions.

Ans. (b) The judiciary could act as a super-legislature or super-executive.

(iii) Despite the clear division of powers, which issue has remained in Indian politics?

(a) Conflict between the executive and Parliament.
(b) Conflict between the judiciary and the executive.
(c) Conflict between the judiciary and Prime minister.
(d) Conflict between the judiciary and the President.

Ans. (b) Conflict between the judiciary and the executive.

(iv) Based on the picture, which of the following best describes the role of the judiciary?

(a) The judiciary should make laws and enforce them.
(b) The judiciary should only interpret laws without any limitations.
(c) The judiciary's role is limited to interpreting the Constitution and adjudicating rights.
(d) The judiciary should control the actions of the executive branch.

Ans. (c) The judiciary's role is limited to interpreting the Constitution and adjudicating rights.

3. Observe the cartoon given below and answer the questions that follow.

(i) Identify the values shown in the above picture.
(ii) Discuss the weakness of Indian judicial system.
(iii) How active is the judiciary in combating corruption in the public sector?

Ans. (i) The values shown in the above picture are independent judiciary, integration and protection of citizens.

(ii) The weaknesses of Indian judicial system are as follows

- Justice is very costly in India. It is difficult for a poor man to get justice from the court. Very high fee is demanded by the lawyers and there are various other expenses which a poor man cannot afford.
- The judicial system of India is very time consuming, where cases are running from 10 years, 15 years, etc.
- There are lack of judges in courts, seats are running vacant and files of cases are getting piled-up day by day.

(iii) The judiciary is a powerful institution that prides itself on its independence. Many people's rights have been preserved by diverse interpretations of the Constitution. The Supreme Court frequently participates in the administration of justice by issuing directives to governmental authorities.

SELF ASSESSMENT TEST

Objective Type Questions

1. Who among the following is appointed by the President as the Chief Justice of India?
   (a) Senior-most judge of Supreme Court
   (b) As recommended by Council of India
   (c) President of Bar Council of India
   (d) Senior-most High Court judge
2. The judges of the High Court are appointed by the ....
   (a) Governor
   (b) President
   (c) Prime Minister
   (d) Chief Minister
3. What is PIL?
   (a) Public Information Letter
   (b) People's Interest Litigation
   (c) Public Interest Litigation
   (d) People's Information Law

Very Short Answer Type Questions

4. 'The Constitution formulated to preserve the independence of the judiciary'. Explain **Competency Based Que**
5. How long do judges hold office in India?
6. Discuss briefly the procedure to remove the judge of Supreme Court or High Court.
7. Which two judges were superseeded in the appointments of Chief Justice of India in 1973 and 1975?
8. When can Parliament discuss the conduct of judges?

Short Answer Type Questions

9. 'The Court use the review power'. Examine. **Competency Based Que**
10. Discuss why it is important for each organ of the government to respect the authority of others in a democracy?
11. 'Judicial activism can lead to conflict between the executive and the judiciary'. Justify. **Competency Based Que**
12. Comment on the relationship between the judiciary and Parliament.

Long Answer Type Questions

13. 'The appointment of judges has never been free from political controversy'. Discuss. **Competency Based Que**
14. 'Supreme Court is the guarantor of Fundamental Rights'. Explain. **Competency Based Que**
15. 'Judicial intervention in legislative principles relate to the principle of Parliamentary sovereignty'. Explain. **Competency Based Que**

07

CHAPTER

Federalism

This chapter explains the concept of federalism in India. Federalism refers to division of power between the Central and State Government by the Constitution.

▼ YOUR STUDY GOALS

▼ YOUR PRACTICE GOAL

- Objective Type Questions (32 Qs ; MCQs, A-R, Statements, Matching, Passage Based)
- Subjective Questions (12 VSAs, 10 SAs, 3 LAs, 2 Picture Based, 2 Map Based)

India has adopted a federal structure of governance in its Constitution. Despite having enormous diversity, our country has managed to stay united. This is in contrast with other countries like **USSR, Czechoslovakia, Yugoslavia, Pakistan** which had to face division despite being a federation.

India is a land of continental proportions and immense diversities. There are more than 20 major languages and several hundred minor ones. It is the home of many major religions. There are several million indigenous people's living in different part of the country.

7.1 Meaning of Federalism

- Federalism is the idea of staying organised. It does not consist of a set of fixed principles which can be applied as it is. Rather, it has evolved uniquely in different countries and historical contexts.
- For example, the federalism in America is different from the one in Germany or India. The actual working of a federation depends upon the politics, culture, ideology and the history of the country. **The concept of federalism first started with America.**

Federalism in West Indies

The West Indies federation was formed in 1958 by uniting the Caribbean islands colonised by the British. However, its weak Central Government and independent economies led to its dis-solution in 1962. Later, the independent islands created the **Caribbean community** through **the Treaty of Chiguaramas in 1973**. This community has the following features

- **Common Institutions** A shared legislature, Supreme Court and executive.
- **Economic Integration** A common currency and a shared market
- **Co-operative Governance** Heads of government from member countries participate in the executive.

Features of Federalism

The following key features of federalism are

- **Two Sets of Polities** Federalism is an institution, which accommodates two set of politics-one at the regional level and the other at the national level. Each government is autonomous. In some federal countries, there is **single citizenship**.

  For example, India, while some federal countries have dual citizenship e.g, USA.
- **Two Sets of Identities** People have both regional and national identities and loyalties. Each level has different powers and responsibilities and also separate system of government.

  For example, we are Delhites or Jharkand as well as Indians.
- **Written Constitution** The Constitution is considered supreme source of power to both the governments. It detailed about certain subjects related to national matters and state matters.

  For example, defence matters or currency matters, are the responsibility of the Central Government and land revenue is the responsibility of the State Government.
- **Independent Judiciary** Judiciary settles disputes between the centre and states.

Failure of Federalism in Nigeria

- Nigeria's experience with federalism is a prime example of how lack of trust among regions and communities can hinder unity.
- Federal Constitution of Nigeria was formed by following the **Ibadan Constitutional Conference in 1950.**
- The federal arrangement failed due to mistrust among ethnic groups[1] – **Yoruba, Ibo and Hausa-Fulani.**
- In the military-supervised Constitution of 1979, no state was allowed to have any civil police.
- The federal Constitution could not overcome conflicts fueled by ethnic, religious and economic differences.
- The country even went into military regime. Democracy was restored in 1999 but, Nigeria still struggles with unity.

7.2 Federalism in the Indian Constitution

- The word 'Federation' is nowhere mentioned in the Constitution. **Article-1** in the Constitution says that **India that is Bharat, shall be a union of states.** It also says about the states and union territories specified in the first schedule.
- India's founding leaders during the course of national movement recognised the need for power division between the provinces and the Central Government due to vast size and diverse society of the country. Their key considerations were
  - Regional diversity
  - Linguistic diversity
  - Power sharing between central and regional authorities
  - Ensuring a representative government through democratic governance.

1 **Ethnic group** It is a social category of people who share common cultural, linguistic, national or regional characteristics.

- After the partition of the country, the Constituent Assembly decided to form the Indian federal system based on co-operation between the union and the states. This system emphasises on unity while acknowledging diversity.

Indian federalism has following characteristics which are as follows

- Division of Power
- Written Constitution
- Supremacy of the Constitution
- Independent judiciary

Division of Power

- Indian Constitution provides for the two sets of government – **The Union Government (Central Government) and State Government.** Both the government have Constitutional status and defined areas of activity. If there is dispute related to power division then it is resolved by the judiciary based on Constitutional provisions.
- The Constitution divides the powers between the union and State Government by demarcates subjects into **three lists.**
- Union Government has exclusive authority over the **union list** while the states have exclusive authority over the **state list**. Also both the governments share authority over the subjects mentioned in the **concurrent list**.
- The economic and financial powers are concentrated in the hands of Central Government while despite having immense responsibilities, states have limited revenue resources.

Constitution of India

Union List
Includes subjects like,
- Defence
- Atomic Energy
- Foreign Affairs
- War and Peace
- Banking
- Railways
- Post and Telegraph
- Airways and Ports
- Foreign Trade
- Currency and Coinage

Union Legislature alone can make laws on these matters.

State List
Includes subjects like,
- Agriculture
- Police
- Prison
- Local Government
- Public Heath
- Land
- Liquor
- Trade and Commerce
- Livestock and Animal
- Husbandry
- State Public Services

Normally only the State Legislature can make laws on these matters.

Concurrent List
Includes subjects like,
- Education
- Transfer of Property other than Agricultural land
- Forests
- Trade Unions
- Adulteration
- Adoption and Succession

Both Union and State Legislature alone can make laws on these matters.

Residuary Powers
Include all other matters not mentioned in any of the lists.
Cyber Laws
Union Legislature alone has the power to legislate on such matters.

7.3 Federalism with a Strong Central Government

- The vast size, diversity and social problems in India necessitated a strong Central Government to maintain unity and facilitate social and political change.
- During the time of independence there were over 500 Princely States that needed to be integrated into existing or new states. This task could only be performed by a strong Central Government.
- The socio-economic challenges like poverty, illiteracy and wealth inequalities demanded the co-ordinated planning and action from the Central Government.

  Provisions that create a strong Central Government are
  - Parliament has the power to alter the boundaries of any state, change its name and form a new state.
  - Emergency[2] provisions turn the federal polity into a unitary one.
  - Parliament gets the power to make laws within the jurisdiction of the states. The financial powers and responsibilities are under the control of the Central Government. States are dependent on grants and financial assistance from the centre.
  - Governor has the power to recommend dis-solution of the State Government and assembly.

2 Emergency It refers to a situation when the administration of the country is under the rule of the President on account of threat to nation from internal and external sources or from critical financial situation.

- The Governor has the power to reserve a bill passed by the state legislature for the assent of the President. This gives the Central Government an opportunity to delay the state legislation and can also veto them.
- Central Government can legislate on matter in the state list if Rajya Sabha ratifies (approves) the move.
- **Article 257 (1)** says that executive powers of the centre are superior to the executive powers of the state. Central Government may give instructions to the State Government.
- There is an **Integrated Administrative System** in India. Officers of All India Services are under the control of the Central Government. States have no power regarding their removal or taking disciplinary action.
- **Article 33 and 34** of the Constitution empower the Parliament to safeguard individuals to serve the union or state during martial law[3].

Quick Test 1

1. Define federal government.
2. Education as a subject comes under which list?
3. Name the matters which are not included in any of the list.
4. Give names of any two provisions that create a strong Central Government.

7.4 Conflicts in India's Federal System

- The Constitution of India grants strong powers to the Central Government while recognising the unique identities of the states. This has led to an imbalance, where states feel they deserve more autonomy and a greater role in governing themselves and the country.
- As a result, states have been demanding more powers and autonomy, causing tension and conflict between the Central Government and States.
- Legal disputes between the centre and the states can be settled by the judiciary, but **demands for autonomy are political issues** that should be resolved through discussions and negotiations.

Some areas of conflict between Central and State Government are as follows

Centre-State Relations

- Federalism in India, to a large extent has been influenced by the changing nature of the political process. In the 1950s and early 1960s the foundation of our federalism was laid under Jawaharlal Nehru.
- The Constitution of India, being federal in structure, divides the legislative, executive and financial powers between the centre and the states. However, there is no division of judicial power, as the Constitution has established an **integrated judicial system** to enforce both central and state laws.
- Though the centre and the states have powers in their respective fields, but maximum harmony and co-ordination between them is essential for the effective operation of the federal system. Hence, the Constitution contains elaborated provisions to regulate the various dimensions of the relations between the centre and the states.

Demand for Autonomy

States and even political parties keep demanding more autonomy from time to time. The term 'autonomy' has various dimensions

- **Demand for Division of Power in Favour of States** States demands that, more power and important subjects should be assigned to them. Many states and parties have made demand of autonomy from time to time.

3 Martial law It is a temporary and extreme measure where military authorities take control of a government or area.

- **Demand for Financial Autonomy** State Governments have been demanding independent sources of revenue and greater control over resources.
- **Demand for Administrative Autonomy** States oppose greater control of centre over the administrative machinery and demand more autonomy in matters of daily administration.
- **Demand for Cultural and Linguistic Issues** Many states oppose the domination and encouragement of Hindi over other regional languages.

Role of Governor and President's Rule

- The Governor is **not elected but appointed** by the Central Government and his actions are often seen as interference by the Central Government in the functioning of the State Government.
- The most Controversial article of our Constitution is **Article 356**. According to this article President's rule is imposed in the state. During the President's rule Union Government takes over the State Government, Governor can even recommend the dismissal of the State Government and suspension or dissolution of the State Assembly. This often creates tensions when this provision is used unfairly.

The **Sarkaria Commission** (appointed in 1983) recommended in his report (1988), which was based on centre-state relations that the appointment of the Governors should be **strictly** **non-partisan**[4].

Demand for New States

- New states were created after independence on the basis of linguistic and cultural diversity of the country emphasised during the national movement.
- The **States Re-organisation Commission** established in 1953 recommended to form the states based on linguistic identity. This was followed by several re-organisations and creation of new states. For example, formation of Telangana from Andhra Pradesh in 2014.
- Despite these changes, some regions like **Vidarbha in Maharashtra** continue to demand separate statehood.

Inter-state Disputes

Apart from the centre-state disputes, there are inter-state disputes too in a federal system. Broadly two kinds of inter-state dispute are very common, which are as follows

- **Border disputes** It is not easy to divide the states strictly on the basis of language because in border areas there have people who speaks more than one language. Hence, tensions arise between states over these regions. For example, Dispute between Maharashtra and Karnataka over Belgaum.
- **River water sharing dispute** Disputes over sharing of river water is more serious as water is used for drinking purpose, agriculture and other vital purposes. For example, Cauvery water dispute between Tamil Nadu and Karnataka.

7.5 Special Provisions for Some States

- The federal system of India has a unique feature, where states receive different treatment due to their varying sizes, populations and historical circumstances.
- This is reflected in the **Rajya Sabha**, where smaller states have minimum representation, while larger states have more representation.

4 **Non-partisan** It refers to an individual, organisation or activity that remains neutral and impartial without allegiance or bias towards any political party, ideology or interest group.

Special Provisions for North-Eastern States

- The Constitution provides special provisions to the North-Eastern states, such as Assam, Nagaland, Arunachal Pradesh, Mizoram and Meghalaya.
- These states have significant indigenous tribal populations with distinct history and cultures. However, these provisions have not fully addressed the regional alinenation and insurgency[5].

Special Provisions for Some Other States

- Some hilly states and other regions also have special provisions, including such as, Himachal Pradesh, Andhra Pradesh, Goa, Gujarat, Maharashtra, Sikkim and Telangana.
- These special provisions aim to address the unique social, economic and cultural needs of each state, **promoting unity and diversity** within the federal system of India.

Special Provisions for Jammu and Kashmir

- Jammu and Kashmir had a special status under **Article 370** of the Indian Constitution due to its unique history. After India gained independence in 1947, Pakistan sent tribal infiltrators to capture Kashmir, forcing **Maharaja Hari Singh** to seek Indian help and join the Indian Union.
- According to Article 370, the concurrence of the state was required for making any laws in matters mentioned in the union and concurrent list.

Special Autonomy Provisions

- Jammu and Kashmir had greater autonomy due to its special status. Some key provisions included
  - The state's consent was necessary for making laws in matters listed in the union and concurrent lists.
  - The Central Government had limited powers, which could only be exercised with the State Government's consent.
  - Jammu and Kashmir had its **own Constitution and flag.**
  - No emergency due to internal disturbances could be declared without the state's concurrence.
  - Union government couldn't impose a financial emergency in the state.
  - The Directive Principles of the Indian Constitution didn't apply in Jammu and Kashmir.
  - Amendment to the Indian Constitution under **Article-368** could be applied to Jammu and Kashmir only with the concurrence of State Government.

Repeal of Special Status

The Jammu and Kashmir Re-organisation Act, 2019, repealed the special status, which was given under the Article 370, and bifurcated the state into two Union Territories i.e. Jammu and Kashmir and Ladakh, effective from **October 31, 2019.**

Quick Test 2

1. Which commission recommended that Governor should be non-partisan?
2. State Re-organisation Commission recommended to form the states based on which factor?
3. Name any four states that enjoy special provisions.
4. Article 370 is related to which state?

5 **Insurgency** It refers to an organised, violent and sustained rebellion against an established government or authority.

Mind Map

FEDERALISM

1 Meaning
- Division of powers between Central and State Government.
- The USA is one of the earliest founding country of federalism.
- It evolved differently based on different political, cultural and historical context.

2 Key Features of Federalism
- Two sets of polities.
- Written Constitution.
- Two sets of Identities.
- Independent judiciary

3 Federalism in Indian Constitution
- Mentioned in Article-I that India shall be a Union of States.

Characteristics of Indian Federalism
- Division of Power
- Written Constitution
- Supremacy of the Constitution
- Independent Judiciary

4 Division of Power
Union Government
- It can make laws relating to the subjects like defence foreign affairs etc.

State Government
- Looks into subject of state and local importance, which includes police, trade etc.

5 Constitution of India
Union List Includes
- Defence
- Railways
- Foreign affairs
- Atomic energy
- Banking
- War and peace

State List Includes
- Police
- Land
- Liquor
- Agriculture
- Public health
- Prison

Concurrent List Includes
- Education
- Adulteration
- Transfer of property.
- Trade unions
- Adoption and succession
- Forests

Residuary Powers
Cyber laws
- Maintained by Union Legislature.

6 Challenges in India's Federal System
Division of power
- Financial and administrative powers are more centralised.
- Emergency powers allow Parliament to legislate on state matters.

Centre-state Conflicts
- Demands for more state autonomy. (e.g. financial, cultural).
- Disputes over administrative control and resources.

Inter-state Conflict
- **Border Disputes** Divide the states strictly on the basis of language as border areas.(e.g. dispute between Maharashtra and Karnataka over Belgaum).
- **Water-sharing Disputes** Sharing of river water is more serious as water is used for drinking purpose and other vital purpose (e.g. Cauvery water disputes between Tamil Nadu and Karnataka).

7 Special Provisions
Provisions for North-Eastern States
- Addresses indigenous tribal population.
- Constitution provides special treatment to some states like, Assam, Nagaland, Arunachal Pradesh, Mizoram, Meghalaya.

Provision for Jammu and Kashmir
- At present special status given to Jammu and Kashmir under Article 370 does not exist.

Provision for Some-other States
- Addresses the unique social, economic and cultural needs of each states, and also promote unity and diversity within the federal system
- Some other special provision states include, Himachal Pradesh, Andra Pradesh ,Goa, Gujarat, Maharashtra, Sikkim, Telangana.

NCERT Folder

Intext Questions

1. Who decides the powers of the Central Government in a federation? (Pg 156)

Ans. In a federation, the powers of the Central Government are decided by the country's Constitution. The Constitution outlines the division of powers between the Central and State Governments, ensuring a balance.

Any changes usually require a Constitutional Amendment, which often involves approval from Legislature.

2. How are conflicts between the Central Government and the States resolved in a federation? (Pg 156)

Ans. Conflicts between the Central Government and States in a federation are resolved through Constitutional provisions, judicial intervention by courts or through negotiation by ensuring supremacy to the Constitution.

3. Do you think that there is a need for mentioning residuary powers separately? Why? (Pg 158)

Ans. Yes, mentioning residuary powers separately is essential in India to clarify that matters not included in the union, State or concurrent lists fall under the Union Government's authority (Article 248). This ensures efficient governance and avoids conflicts in legislative powers.

4. Why do the States feel dissatisfied about the division of powers? (Pg 158)

Ans. States feel dissatisfied with the division of powers due to the dominance of the Central Government in financial and legislative matters, the allocation of residuary powers to the union and interference in state subjects through laws or policies.

5. Give two reasons for the claim that our Constitution has a unitary bias. (Pg 163)

Ans. Indian Constitution has unitary bias due to following claims

- **Residuary Powers** The Constitution grants residuary powers to the Union Government, favoring central authority.
- **Emergency Provisions** During emergencies, the Central Government can assume greater control over State government functions.

6. Do you think that (Pg 163)

(i) a strong centre makes the states weak?

(ii) strong states will weaken the centre?

Ans. (i) No, a strong center does not necessarily make states weak, nor do strong states weaken the center.

(ii) A balanced federal system ensures both strong center and empowered states, ensuring co-operation and mutual support. Over centralisation or excessive state autonomy, however, can disrupt this balance.

7. Collect information about at least one dispute about river waters involving two or more states. (Pg 169)

Ans. Kaveri River Water Dispute

- **States Involved** Tamil Nadu, Karnataka, Kerala and Puducherry.
- **Issue** Dispute over sharing Kaveri river water for agriculture and urban needs.
- **Historical Agreements** 1892 and 1924 favored Tamil Nadu, causing Karnataka's dissatisfaction.

Key Resolutions

- **1990** Cauvery Water Disputes Tribunal formed. Final award in 2007.
- **2018** Supreme Court allocated more water to Karnataka and also ensures Tamil Nadu's share.
- **Kaveri Management Authority (KMA)** Established for water release monitoring.
- **Current Status** Tensions persist during droughts, requiring interventions.

8. Why do states want more autonomy? (Pg 170)

Ans. States seek more autonomy to address their specific needs effectively, to manage their resources independently, and to reduce dependence on the Central Government for funds and decision-making.

Greater autonomy allows them to implement policies suited to their socio-economic and cultural contexts, ensuring better governance and development.

9. What is the difference between autonomy and secession? (Pg 170)

Ans. Autonomy refers to a state's right to self-govern within the Constitutional framework, allowing it to make decisions on specific matters without central interference.

Secession, on the other hand, is the act of a region or state breaking away from a country to form an independent nation, challenging the country's sovereignty.

Exercise

1. From the list of following events which one would you identify with the functioning of federalism? Why?

(i) The centre on Tuesday announced sixth schedule status to GNLF-led Darjeeling Gorkha Hill Council, which would ensure greater autonomy to the governing body in the hill district of West Bengal. A tripartite memorandum of settlement was signed in New Delhi between the centre, West Bengal government and the Subhas Ghising-led Gorkha National Liberation Front (GNLF) after two days of hectic deliberations.

(ii) **Government for Action Plan for Rain-hit States** Centre has asked the rain-ravaged states to submit detailed plans for reconstruction to enable it to respond to their demands for extra relief expeditiously.

(iii) **New Commissioner for Delhi** The capital is getting a new municipal commissioner. Confirming this, present MCD commissioner Rakesh Mehta said he has received his transfer order and that he is likely to be replaced by IAS officer Ashok Kumar, who is serving as the Chief Secretary in Arunachal Pradesh. Mehta, a 1975 batch IAS officer, has been heading the MCD for about three and a half years.

(iv) **CU Status for Manipur University** Rajya Sabha on Wednesday passed a bill to convert the Manipur University into a Central University with the Human Resource Development Minister promising such institutions in the North-Eastern states of Arunachal Pradesh, Tripura and Sikkim as well.

(v) **Funds Released** The centre has released ₹ 5.53 lakh to Arunachal Pradesh under its rural water supply scheme. The first instalment was of ₹ 466.81 lakh.

(vi) **Well Teach the Biharis How to Live in Mumbai** Around 100 Shiv Sainiks stormed JJ Hospital, disrupted daily operations, raised slogans and threatened to take matters into their own hands if no action was taken against non-Maharashtrian students.

(vii) **Demand for Dismissal of Government** The Congress Legislature Party (CLP) in a representation submitted to State Governor recently, has demanded dismissal of the ruling Democratic Alliance of Nagaland (DAN) government for its alleged financial mismanagement and embesslement of public money.

(viii) **NDA Government asks Naxalites to Surrender Arms** Amid a walkout by opposition RJD and its allies Congress and CPI (M), the Bihar government today appealed to the naxalites to shun the path of violence and reaffirmed its pledge to root out unemployment to usher in a new era of development in Bihar.

Ans. (i) Yes, the agreement between the Centre and State Government and GNLF involves the functioning of federal structure, as it allows autonomy in governance at the state and provincial level.

(ii) Yes, it involves the functioning of federalism because flood relief is undertaken by the states which is funded by the centre.

(iii) No, it does not involve functioning of federalism because this appointment reflects a centralised authority.

(iv) No, it does not reflect a federal structure as a central university comes under the control of the Central Government.

(v) Yes, it involves the functioning of federalism as the centre is providing funds to the state of Arunachal Pradesh under its Rural Water Supply Scheme. The state can then make use of the funds for its own development.

(vi) No, it does not involves the functioning of federalism because it is hampering the essence of federalism. The states have autonomy but they are tied in the bond financed by the central power. They are bound to work according to the instructions of the Central Government as it is superior to the state. This act of Shiv Sena is the violation of citizen's rights as well as spirit of federalism.

(vii) No, it does not involves the functioning of federalism, as demand for the dismissal of a duly elected State Government is an attack on the federal structure.

(viii) Yes, it involves the functioning of federalism as the problem of naxtionalism is being tackled by the government at state level and national level.

2. Think which of the following statements would be correct? State why?

(i) Federalism enhances the possibility of people from different regions to interact without the fear of one's culture being imposed upon them by others.

(ii) Federal system will hinder easier economic transactions between two different regions that have distinct types of resources.

(iii) A federal system will ensure that the powers of those at the centre will remain limited.

Ans. (i) The statement is correct because federalism provides unity while respecting the differences.

(ii) The statement is incorrect because federal system is not a hindrance to trade and commerce.

(iii) The statement is incorrect because, while a federal system ensures that the powers of those at the centre are limited, it has also provided for a strong Central Government.

3. Based on the first few articles of Belgium Constitution given below - explain how federalism is visualised in the country. Try and write a similar Article for the Constitution of India.

Title I On Federal Belgium, its components and its territory.

Article 1 Belgium is a Federal State made up of Communities and Regions.

Article 2 Belgium is made up of three communities. The French Community, The Flemish Community and The German Community.

Article 3 Belgium is made up of three regions. The Walloon Region, The Flemish Region and The Brussels Region.

Article 4 Belgium has four linguistic regions The French– speaking Region, The Dutch speaking Region, The Bilingual Region of Brussels capital and the German speaking Region. Each commune (country borough) of the Kingdom is part of one of these linguistic regions. ....

Article 5 The Walloon Region is made up of the following provinces: The Walloon Brabant, Hainault, Liege, Luxemburg and Namur. The Flemish Region is made up of the following provinces: Antwerp, The Flemish Brabant, West Flanders, East Flanders and Limburg. ....

Ans. The federal structure of Belgium is based upon communities, regions and languages. There are three communities and regions and four linguistic regions in the country

Title I On federal India, its components and its territory.

Article 1 India is federal state means it is a union of states.

Article 343 India has more than 20 major languages and several hundred minor languages.

Article 25 India has many religions and all the people have freedom to practice their religion.

Article 1 India is divided into 28 States and 8 Union Territories.

Article 246 It defines the distribution of legislative powers between the Central and State Governments.

4. Imagine that you were to rewrite the provisions regarding federalism. Write an essay of not more than 300 words making your suggestions about

(i) Division of powers among the Centre and the States,

(ii) Distribution of Financial Resources,

(iii) Methods of resolving Inter-State Disputes and

(iv) Appointment of Governors.

Ans. (i) **Division of Powers** The powers of the Central Government and State Government should be separated, where the states enjoy their autonomy and the Central Government has the advantage of having more power than that of State Government. Agriculture, employment, infrastructure and public health should come into concurrent list. Water distribution should come into union list.

Residuary power of the union legislature should be expanded and made flexible according to the need. The union legislature has to legally explain the decision and steps on exercising such power so that discrimination between states cannot take place. The states should be formed on the basis of administrative convenience and geographical continuity.

(ii) **Distribution of Financial Resources** The sources of revenue collection and the control of the resources should be in the hands of the Central Government. However, the states should be free to set up enterprises that attract investment locally.

(iii) **Methods of Resolving Inter-State Disputes** The Central Government has to take initiative to resolve inter-state disputes in a time bound frame or the order of the Supreme Court would be final in this regard. Encouragement of regional bias during inter-state disputes should be made a cognisable offence.

(iv) **The Appointment of Governors** The Governor should be appointed by the Central Government in consultation with the State Government. This would prevent the misuse of the office of the Governor.

The candidate for the post of Governor should not be from political background. The conditions for the imposition of President's rule should be made very strict to prevent the abuse of this provision. State Government should have the right to challenge their dismissal in Supreme Court.

5. Which of the following should be the basis for formation of a state? Why?

(i) Common language.

(ii) Common economic interest.

(iii) Common religion.

(iv) Administrative convenience.

Ans. (iv) The administrative convenience should be the basis of formation of states, as it helps in the better administration and welfare of the citizens or people of that area. This would automatically lead to development of a common economy and culture.

6. Majority of people from the states of North India—Rajasthan, Madhya Pradesh, Bihar— speak Hindi. If all these states are combined to form one state, would it be in tune with the idea of federalism? Give arguments.

Ans. No, the unification of four large states with sizeable population would not be in true with the idea of federalism because there are many regional variations in the local issues that affect people in these states. Addressing these issues require separate political and administrative set-up for each of them.

From administrative point of view, the creation of one very large state with a huge population would lead to imbalance in distribution of resources across the Territory. This would lead to unequal development and conflicts between various regions with the failure to fulfill the aspirations of all people.

7. List four features of the Indian Constitution that gives greater power to the Central Government than the State Government.

Ans. Four features of the Indian Constitution that gives greater power to the Central Government than the State Government are

(i) The union list has more important subjects than that in the state list. Also centre has overriding powers over subjects in the concurrent list.

(ii) During national emergencies, the Central Government can take control of the State Government legislative and executive powers.

(iii) States rely on the centre for loans and grants in aid.

(iv) Governors are appointed by the President and they are representative of the Central Government.

8. Why are many states unhappy about the role of the Governor?

Ans. Many states are unhappy about the role of the Governor because the Governor is not elected but appointed by the Central Government and work as an agent of the Central Government. Therefore, there is possibility of the Governor's office being used to control and remove the State Government.

9. President's rule can be imposed in a state if the government is not being run according to the provisions of the Constitution. State whether any of the following conditions are a fit case for imposition of President's rule in the state. Give reasons.

(i) Two members of the State Legislative Assembly belonging to the main opposition party have been killed by criminals and the opposition is demanding dismissal of the State Government.

(ii) Kidnapping of young children for random is on rise. The number of crimes against women are increasing.

(iii) No political party has secured majority in the recent elections of the State Legislative Assembly. It is feared that some MLAs from the other parties may be lured to support a political party in return for money.

(iv) Different political parties are ruling in the state and at the centre and they are bitter opponents of each other.

(v) More than 2000 people have been killed in the communal riots.

(vi) In the water dispute between the two states, one State Government refused to follow the decision of the Supreme Court.

Ans. (i) No, killing of two members of the State Legislative Assembly belonging to the main opposition party by the criminals is not the basis for removal of the State Government, as it is a law and order problem.

(ii) No, rise in kidnapping of young children for random and the number of crimes against women is a law and order problem but does not represent a breakdown of the Constitution.

(iii) No, President's rule cannot be imposed in a state without giving the largest political party or alliance a chance to prove their majority on the floor of legislative assembly.

(iv) No, ruling of two opponent and different political parties in the state and at the centre is not a criterion for implementing President's rule.

(v) Yes, if the state is unable to control the riots, then President's rule needed to be implemented, as it represents a complete failure of the administration.

(vi) Yes, if one state has refused to follow the decision of Supreme Court, then it is a case of Constitutional breakdown and fit for imposition of President's rule.

10. What are the demands raised by states in their quest for greater autonomy?

Ans. There are four demands raised by states in their quest for greater autonomy

(i) Demands for separation of state and central power.

(ii) Some states have demanded for independent revenue sources and greater control over resources, known as financial autonomy.

(iii) States have demanded that the centre should not have control over the administrative machinery of the state.

(iv) Some states have demanded for autonomy on the basis of language and culture.

11. Should some states be governed by special provisions? Does this create resentment among other states? Does this help in forging greater unity among the regions of the country?

Ans. It is essential that some states should be governed by the special provisions on the basis of history, cultural and social circumstances and administrative requirements. The special provisions are made according to the special requirements.

For example, the North-Eastern states of India have a unique history and tribal culture that needs to be protected. This has created resentment among other states, as there is a fear that these provisions would lead to separation in those areas.

Many people oppose these provisions because they believe that there should be equal division of powers in federal states. No, this does not forge unity among the regions of the country, as it leads to a feeling of biasedness.

Exam Pattern Questions

Objective Type Questions

Multiple Choice Questions (MCQs)

1. What was the major reason for the breakup of the USSR?
(a) Excessive centralisation and concentration of powers.
(b) Dominance of Russia over other regions.
(c) Independent language and culture of federation units.
(d) Separation of powers between legislature, executive and judiciary.

2. The governments are classified into unitary and federal on the basis of nature of relations between......... .
(a) Legislature and Executive
(b) Judiciary and Executive
(c) National Governments and Regional Governments
(d) Regional Governments and People

3. Which among the following country offer dual citizenship?
(a) India (b) Sri Lanka
(c) USA (d) Both (a) and (c)

4. Which among the following is not an essential feature of federalism?
(a) Written Constitution (b) Independent Judiciary
(c) Dual citizenship (d) Division of power

5. Which of the following statements is not true with respect to the idea and concept of federalism? Diksha App
(a) Federalism accommodates two sets of Polities one at the regional level and the other at the national level.
(b) People have two sets of identities and localities.
(c) Division of powers by the written Constitution.
(d) States are more powerful than the centre in all federal systems.

6. Who is responsible to settle or to prevent the disputes between centre and state, on legal matters about the division of power?
(a) Judiciary (b) Parliament
(c) President (d) Governor

7. Nigeria became a federation in the year ....
(a) 1950 (b) 1999
(c) 1958 (d) 1962

8. Which of the following factors was not responsible for the adoption of the Federal System in India? Diksha App
(a) Vast Geographical area (b) Regional diversity
(c) Linguistic diversity (d) Parliamentary democracy

9. Article 1 of the Indian Constitution declares India. Diksha App
(a) Federation (b) Union of States
(c) Co-federation (d) Common Wealth of Nations

10. The names of the states and union territorial and their territories extent are specified in ..... schedule.
(a) fourth (b) third
(c) second (d) first

11. Who can make laws on Concurrent List?
(a) Parliament (b) State Legislature
(c) Both (a) and (b) (d) President

12. Which of the following subject is in the State List?
(a) Defense (b) Atomic Energy
(c) Foreign Affairs (d) Police

13. Residuary powers are vested with............ .
(a) Executive (b) Parliament
(c) Judiciary (d) Local Government

14. **Why did Indian Constitution-makers create a strong Central Government?** **Diksha App**

(a) To stem disintegration and bring about social and political change.
(b) To make India a culturally homogenous society.
(c) To make India a unitary system.
(d) To ensure the success of Parliamentary democracy.

15. **The .... is empowered to "'Form a new state by separation of territory from any state or by uniting two of more states".** **Competency Based Que**

(a) State Legislature (b) Parliament
(c) Governor (d) President

16. **Parliament is not empowered by the Constitution to......... .** **Diksha App**

(a) from a new state.
(b) alter boundaries of the existing states or even their names.
(c) uniting two or more states.
(d) to settle all federal disputes.

17. **States have been demanding more powers and autonomy, causing tension and conflict between the Central Government and States. Which of the following is NOT correct regarding centre-state conflict?** **Competency Based Que**

(a) States demand for independent sources of revenue for them.
(b) Governor is not elected but appointed by the President.
(c) Language has never been an area of centre-state conflict.
(d) Inter-state dispute arises between states over border villages.

18. **Which of the following Articles of the Constitution proved the most controversial vis-Ã -vis center-state relations.** **Diksha App**

(a) Article 257 (b) Article 370
(c) Article 356 (d) Article 352

19. **Identify the incorrect statement.**

(a) President's rule in the state is imposed on the recommendations of the Governor.
(b) President's proclamation has to be ratified by the Parliament.
(c) President's rule can be extended up to three years.
(d) State Governments were dismissed only when they lost a majority in the legislature.

20. **What is not the reason behind providing special status to many North Eastern States?** **Diksha App**

(a) Sizeable indigenous tribal population.
(b) Distinct history.
(c) Distinct culture.
(d) To pacify separatist elements.

21. Consider the following statements

I. In a federation, the powers of the Union and State Governments are clearly demarcated.
II. In India, Union and State Governments have exclusive jurisdiction on their respective subjects under all circumstances. **Competency Based Que**

Which of the statement given above is/are correct?

(a) Only I (b) Only II
(c) Both I and II (d) Neither I nor II

22. Consider the following statements **Competency Based Que**

I. The Parliament has exclusive power to make laws with respect to any of the matters enumerated in the union list.
II. Both the Parliament and State Legislature can make laws with respect to any of the matters enumerated in the state list.

Which of the statement given above is / are correct?

(a) Only I (b) Only II
(c) Both I and II (d) Neither I nor II

23. **Given below are two statements** **Competency Based Que**

Statement 1 The Constitution of India provides special provisions for only the North-Eastern states.

Statement 2 Differential treatment between states is reflected in the Rajya Sabha.

In the light of the above statements, choose the correct answer from the options given below

(a) Both Statement I and Statement II are true.
(b) Both Statement I and Statement II are false.
(c) Statement I is true, but Statement II is false.
(d) Statement I is false, but Statement II is true.

24. **Match the List I with the List II.**

List I	List II
A. Banking	1. State list
B. Education	2. Union list
C. Land	3. Concurrent list

Codes

	A	B	C		A	B	C
(a)	2	1	3	(b)	3	2	1
(c)	2	3	1	(d)	1	2	3

Assertion-Reason Questions

Directions (Q.Nos. 25-29) In the questions given below, there are two statements marked as Assertion (A) and Reason (R). Read the statements and choose the correct option.

Codes

(a) Both A and R are true and R is the correct explanation of A.
(b) Both A and R are true, but R is not the correct explanation of A.
(c) A is true, but R is false.
(d) A is false, but R is true.

25. Assertion (A) India has a federal system.

Reason (R) Under a unitary system, either there is only one level of government or the sub-units are sub-ordinate to Central Government.

26. Assertion (A) Federalism is a system of government in which the power is divided between a central authority and various constituent units of the country.

Reason (R) In federalism all tier of governments enjoys their power independent of the other.

27. Assertion (A) In federalism, sources of revenue for each level of government are clearly specified to ensures its financial autonomy.

Reason (R) In India Central Government is more powerful than State Government in case of financial matter.

28. Assertion (A) States have the exclusive authority to make laws on the subjects enumerated in the state list.

Reason (R) Central Government can legislate on matter in the state list if Rajya Sabha ratifies the move.

29. Assertion (A) Federalism in India often faces challenges due to disputes between states over issues like borders and river water sharing.

Reason (R) Disputes over resources like river waters and border territories arise because they impact the livelihoods, sentiments and governance of the states involved.

Passage Type Questions

30. Read the given passage and answer the following questions.

"Let me tell my honourable friends in the house that the drift… in all Constitutions has been towards the centre... because of circumstances that have now come into being that the states have become, ...federal or unitary, welfare states from being polities states and the ultimate responsibility as for the economic well-being of the country has become the paramount responsibility of the centre. Besides the concern for unity, the makers of the Constitution also believed that the socio-economic problems of the country needed to be handled by a strong Central Government in co-operation with the states. Poverty, illiteracy and inequalities of wealth were some of the problems that required planning and co-ordination. Thus, the concerns for unity and development prompted the makers of the Constitution to create a strong Central Government".

(i) In first 3 lines of the passage whose words are referred?
(a) T.T. Krishnamachari (b) Mahatma Gandhi
(c) B.R. Ambedkar (d) Jawaharlal Nehru

(ii) Which of the following comes under the state list?
(a) Prison (b) Police
(c) Liquor (d) All of these

(iii) Why has the Constitution given more powers to the centre?

31. Read the given passage and answer the following questions.

You may have heard about the cricket team of West Indies. But is there a country called West Indies? Like India, West Indies was also colonised by the British. In 1958, the federation of West Indies came into being. It had a weak Central Government and the economy of each unit was independent.

These features and political competition among the units led to the formal dis-solution of the federation in 1962. Later, in 1973 by Treaty of Chiguaramas The Independent Islands established joint authorities in the form of a common legislature, Supreme Court, a common currency, and to a degree, a common market known as the Caribbean Community.

(i) When did the federation of West Indies came into being?
(a) 1958 (b) 1959 (c) 1960 (d) 1961

(ii) Who are the members of Caribbean Community?
(a) Common Executive (b) Chief Manager
(c) Executive Officer (d) None of these

(iii) Features of federation of West Indies includes …… .
(a) weak Central Government (b) independent economy
(c) Both (a) and (b) (d) Neither (a) nor (b)

(iv) Which of the following treaty established joint legislature?
(a) Treaty of Paris (b) Treaty of Salabai
(c) Treaty of Chiguaramas (d) Treaty of Mysore

32. Read the given passage and answer the following questions.

Federalism in Nigeria If the regions and various communities do not trust each other, even a federal arrangement can fail to produce unity. The example of Nigeria is instructive: Till 1914, Northern and Southern Nigeria were two separate British colonies. At the Ibadan Constitutional Conference of 1950 Nigerian leaders decided to form a federal Constitution. The three major ethnic groups of Nigeria—Yoruba, Ibo and Hausa Fulani—controlled the regions of the West, the East and the North respectively. Their attempt to spread their influence to other regions led to fears and conflicts, this led to a military regime. In the 1960 Constitution, both federal and regional governments jointly controlled the Nigerian police. In the military supervised Constitution of 1979, no state was allowed to have any civil police. Though democracy was restored in Nigeria in 1999, religious differences along with conflicts over who will control revenues from the oil resources continue to present problems before the Nigerian federation. Local ethnic communities resist centralised control of the oil resources. Thus, Nigeria is an example of overlap of religious, ethnic and economic differences among the units.

(i) In Nigeria's federal structure, what was a significant change introduced by the military supervised Constitution of 1979?

(a) Only federal and regional governments could control the police.
(b) States were allowed to maintain their own civil police forces.
(c) No state was allowed to have a civil police force.
(d) The federal government took complete control of oil revenues.

(ii) Which of the following is a key issue causing conflicts in Nigeria's federal system?

(a) Linguistic differences among regions.
(b) Religious differences and disputes over oil revenues.
(c) A lack of military presence in regions.
(d) Absence of democracy since 1999.

(iii) Discuss the challenges faced by Nigeria's federalism, focusing on the interplay of ethnic, religious and economic factors. How have these challenges affected the unity of the country?

Answers

1. (a) Excessive centralisation and concentration of powers.
2. (c) National Government and Regional Governments
3. (c) USA
4. (c) Dual citizenship
5. (d) States are more powerful than the centre in all federal systems.
6. (a) Judiciary
7. (a) 1950
8. (d) Parliamentary democracy
9. (b) Union of States
10. (d) first
11. (c) Both (a) and (b)
12. (d) Police
13. (b) Parliament
14. (a) to stem disintegration and bring about social and political change.
15. (b) Parliament
16. (d) To settle all federal disputes.
17. (c) Language has never been an area of centre-state conflict.
18. (c) Article 356
19. (d) State Governments were dismissed only when they lost a majority in the legislature.
20. (d) To pacify separatist elements
21. (a) Only I
22. (a) Only I
23. (d) Statement I is false, but Statement II is true.
24. (c) 2 3 1
25. (b) Both A and R are true, but R is not the correct explanation of A.
26. (a) Both A and R are true and R is the correct explanation of A.
27. (b) Both A and R are true , but R is not the correct explanation of A.
28. (b) Both A and R are true, but R is not the correct explanation of A.
29. (a) Both A and R are true and R is the correct explanation of A.
30. (i) (a) T.T. Krishnamachari (ii) (d) All of these
    (iii) The Constitution has given more powers in the hands of the centre due to the extent of diversity and varied form of socio-economic problems in our country. The Constitution intended to create a welfare state and for this the socio-economic problems need to be handled by the strong centre in co-operation with state.
31. (i) (a) 1958 (ii) (a) Common Executive
    (iii) (c) Both (a) and (b) (iv) (c) Treaty of Chiguramas
32. (i) (c) No state was allowed to have a civil police force.
    (ii) (b) Religious differences and disputes over oil revenues.
    (iii) Nigeria's federalism faces challenges from ethnic, religious, and economic divisions. Ethnic groups like Yoruba, Ibo and Hausa Fulani compete for influence, creating distrust. Religious tensions between the Muslim majority North and Christian majority South created conflicts. Control over oil revenues led to economic disparities, with local communities resisting centralised authority. Military regimes and centralised governance have reduced regional autonomy, further challenging unity.

Subjective Questions

Very Short Answer Type Questions

1. Why is federal system of government necessary for India?

Ans. India is a big country and there are people of several castes, religion, regions, language, dialects and geography and for the development of all the people , federal system is necessary which will generate unity in diversity.

2. Mention the factors which makes federalism successful.

Ans. The factors which makes federalism successful are

- A written Constitution.
- Co-operation and mutual trust.
- Independent judiciary.
- A clear distribution of powers in various lists.

3. Analyse the role of federalism in maintaining unity in a diverse country like India. Competency Based Que

Ans. India's federalism accommodates regional diversity by granting autonomy to states while maintaining a strong central authority. The history, cultural unity and Constitutional provisions like linguistic re-organisation and financial division ensure balance.

Unlike rigid models, India's flexible federalism adapts to changing needs, encouraging unity despite immense linguistic, religious and cultural diversity.

4. Comment on how India's federal structure helps to manage its diversity.

Ans. India's federal structure divides powers between the Central and State Governments, allowing each region to manage its own needs while working together as one country. This system respects the country's diversity of languages and cultures, ensuring local governance and unity at the same time, which helps in maintaining harmony and democracy.

5. Analyse why the Indian Constitution provides for a strong Central Government despite being a federal system.

Ans. The Indian Constitution ensures a strong Central Government to maintain unity in a diverse nation and address socio-economic challenges like poverty and inequality.

Provisions such as emergency powers, financial centralisation and control over state boundaries enable the center to integrate regions, plan development and ensure stability, crucial for India's vast size and diversity.

6. Explain briefly the role played by judiciary in federalism of India.

Ans. The role played by judiciary in federalism of India are

- To prevent conflict between the centre and the states, there is an independent judiciary to settle disputes.
- The judiciary enjoys the power to resolve the disputes between Central and State Government on legal matters and division of powers.

7. What is meant by the concurrent list? Name any four subjects of the concurrent list. Diksha App

Ans. The concurrent list includes subjects on which both union and state legislature can make laws.

Four subjects of the concurrent list are

(i) Education (ii) Forests
(iii) Trade unions (iv) Adoption and succession

8. Mention the provision of All India Services in connection with the states.

Ans. The officers recruited from All India Services such as IAS and IPS are under the control of the Central Government and States can neither take disciplinary action nor they can remove officers from services.

9. State the reasons of conflict between the centre and the states. Diskha App

Ans. The reasons for conflict between the centre and the states are

- Unnecessary interference by Central Government in state matters.
- Demands for autonomy.
- Role of Governors and President's rule.
- Demand for new states.
- Inter-state conflicts.

10. Explain why demands for greater autonomy from States have increased over time in India.

Ans. The demand for greater autonomy from states in India has increased over time due to a number of reasons, including

- **Uneven development** States and sub-regions within a state have developed at different rates, which have led to a sense of discrimination by the center.
- **Control over resources** States want to gain control over the resources and development process.
- **Cultural and linguistic issues** Some states demand autonomy based on their language and culture.

- **Central control** States resent the center's control over the administrative machinery.
- **Independent revenue** Some states demand independent sources of revenue.

11. What is financial autonomy?

Ans. The demand by some states for independent sources of revenue and greater control over the resources of the states is known as financial autonomy.

12. Define the provision of Article 356.

Ans. Under Article 356 of the Indian Constitution, the Governor can recommend President's rule in the state, if there is breakdown of Constitutional machinery. This results in the takeover of the State Government by the Union Government.

Short Answer Type Questions

1. Enumerate the unitary features of the Indian Constitution.

Ans. The unitary features of the Indian Constitution are

- The division of power between the centre and the state goes in favour of the centre by the Constitution. The union list consist of 97 subjects, state list consist of 66 subjects and concurrent list has 47 subjects.
- The Governor of a state is appointed by the President on the advice of the Central Government and he/she remain in office till the pleasure of the President.
- Every individual living in India enjoys single citizenship i.e. India only.
- There is integrated judiciary system.

2. Supremacy of judiciary is essential in a Federal Government. Explain. What is the role of judiciary in federal system? **Competency Based Que**

Ans. Judiciary plays an important role in the federal set up. It is the guardian of the Constitution of the country. In India, the Supreme Court and the High Courts have the power to interpret the Constitution. If a law, passed by the Central Government, is against any provision of the Constitution, the law can be declared as null and void by the Constitution.

Secondly in a federal set up, if any conflict arises between the Central Government and the State Government or between any two State Governments, the power to decide conflict rests with the Supreme Court.

3. Describe the relation between the Union Government and states. Mention the lists in Constitution.

Ans. India has a federal form of Government. The main characteristics of this form of government is the division of powers between the Central Government and Government of the States. The Indian Constitution also provides for division of legislative, administrative and financial powers between the union and the states.

The Indian Government is vested with strong centre. There are three list in the Constitution i.e. union, state and concurrent.

4. Analyse why Indian federalism is known as Quasi federal. **Competency Based Que**

Ans. Indian federalism is considered as Quasi federal because

- Parliament has wide scope of legislation, it can legislate on subjects given under state list if the Rajya Sabha passes a resolution, or when a proclamation of emergency is in operation.
- Parliament also has the power to legislate on residuary subjects. On subjects given in the concurrent list, the Parliamentary law is upheld in case of conflict with state law.
- Parliament can alter the boundaries of the states.
- Greater financial powers are vested with the Central Government and the States are dependent upon central grant.
- During an emergency, the federal policy is changed into unitary one. *(Any Four)*

5. 'Indian Constitution has created a strong Central Government'. Examine. **Competency Based Que**

Ans. It was necessary to have a strong Central Government because

- The framers of the Constitution believed that their is strong requirement of a federal Constitution to accommodate the diversities.
- To stem disintegration and bring about social and political change.
- There was a need for the centre to have such powers because India at the time of independence was not only divided into provinces, but there were more than 500 Princely States which had to be integrated into the existing states or new states had to be created.
- The framers of the Constitution believed that the socio-economic problems of the country needed to be handled by a strong Central Government in co-operation with the states.

6. Can the Union Parliament frame laws on the subjects mentioned in the state list? Explain. **Competency Based Que**

Ans. Yes, Union Parliament or Central Government can frame laws on the subjects mentioned in the state list in following circumtances

- If any subject has been referred to the Central Government as the subject of national importance by the Rajya Sabha through a resolution passed by 2/3 majority of members present on voting.

- If two or more states desires to frame laws by the Central Government.
- If President's rule has been imposed in the states.
- In order to implement some international treaty or convention, etc.

7. Explain the nature of centre-state relationship. **Competency Based Que**

Ans. The Constitution of India being federal in structure divides the legislature, executive and financial powers between the centre and the states.

However, there is no division of judicial powers, as the Constitution has established an integrated judicial system to enforce both central and state laws.

Though, the centre and the states are supreme in their respective field, maximum harmony and co-ordination between them is essential for effective operation of the federal system.

Hence, the Constitution contains elaborate provisions to regulate the various dimensions of relations between centre and the states.

8. What are the main causes of interstate conflicts? Explain with examples. **Diksha App**

Ans. The main causes of interstate conflicts are – Border disputes and inter-state river water sharing disputes.

- **Border disputes** states have certain claims over territories belonging to neighboring states.
  For example, dispute between Maharashtra and Karnataka over the city of Belgaum.
- **River water disputes** States have dispute with neighbouring states over sharing of water from rivers which is used for various functions like drinking, agrricIture etc.
  For example, the dispute between Punjab and Haryana over Chandigarh disputes related to the sharing of river waters, the Cauvery water dispute between Tamilnadu and Karnataka.
  The dispute among Gujarat, Madhya Pradesh and Maharashtra over the sharing of water of the Narmada river.

9. 'Many states and even many political parties have, from time to time demanded, that states should have more autonomy'. Analyse the reason. **Competency Based Que**

Ans. Reasons behind the increasing demands for greater autonomy by states in India are as follows

- **Political Shift** The decline of Congress dominance in the 1960s and the rise of opposition parties in several states led to demands for more autonomy, as regional parties sought control over their governance without central interference.
- **Coalition Politics** Since the 1990s, coalition politics at the center has increased state influence, leading to a stronger voice for regional governments in the political process.
- **Discontent Over Centralisation** States, especially those governed by opposition parties, viewed Central Government interference as a barrier to their development and decision making.
- **Respect for Diversity** The growing recognition of India's linguistic, cultural and regional diversity made autonomy a vital issue for many states seeking to preserve their unique identities.

10. Analyse the role of Governor in the state? **Competency Based Que**

Ans. The role of Governor has always been a controversial issue between centre and the state, as the Governor is not an elected office holder, but is appointed by the Central Government. Therefore, actions of the Governor are often viewed as interference by the Central Government in the functioning of the State Government.

The Governor has the power to recommend the dismissal of the State Government and suspension or dis-solution of State Assembly.

Long Answer Type Questions

1. Elucidate the ideas and concepts associated with federalism. **Competency Based Que**

Or **What are the basic features of the federal system?** **Diksha**

Ans. Ideas and concepts associated with federalism are

- Federalism is an institutional mechanism to accommodate two sets of polities i.e. one at the regional level and other at the national level. Each government is autonomous in its own sphere.
- In some federal countries like USA, there is even a system of dual citizenship, while India has only a single citizenship.
- The people have two identities and loyalties, they belong to the region as well as the nation. For example, Gujarati or Biharis as well as Indians.
- Each level of polity has distinct powers and responsibilities and a separate system of government.
- The details of the dual system of government are enshrined in the Constitution, which is the supreme source of power for both sets of government.
- Certain subjects which concern the nation as a whole are the responsibility of Central Government.

- Regional or local matters are the responsibility of the regional or State Government.
- There is an independant judiciary to settle or to prevent the disputes between centre and state, on legal matters about the division of power.

2. Analyse the provisions of the Indian Constitution deeply which create a strong Central Government? **Diksha App**

Ans. The provisions of the Indian Constitution which create a strong Central Government are as follows

- Parliament is empowered to alter boundaries even the names of the states, from new states to unite two or more states.
- Emergency provisions can turn our federal polity into a highly centralised system. Parliament also assumes the power to make laws on subjects within the jurisdiction of the states.
- The financial power-centre has very vast financial powers. The Central Government has many revenue sources and states are mostly dependent on grants and financial assistance from the centre.
- Planned economic development adopted after independence led to the centralisation of economic decision-making.
- Governor who is appointed by the centre can recommend dismissal of the State Government and imposition of the President's rule.
- If verified by the Rajya Sabha, Central Government can legislate on matters from the state list.
- Executive powers of the centre are superior to the executive powers of the state.

3. Comment on the role of Governors and President's Rule in India's federal system. **Competency Based Que**

Ans. Governors and President's Rule in India's federal system are as follows

- **Governors' Role** Governors are appointed by the Central Government, often from non-local backgrounds, leading to perceptions of interference in state matters. When different parties govern at the centre and state, Governors' actions are seen as reflecting central control, causing tension between the two.
- **Controversial Use of Article 356** Article 356 allows the President to impose President's rule in states when the government is unable to function according to the Constitution. This has often been used to dismiss State Governments, even when they hold a majority, raising concerns about misuse for political gain.

There role comes under the jurisdiction and the Supreme Court has ruled that the judiciary can review the Constitutional validity of President's rule, adding a layer of scrutiny to prevent arbitrary use.

The ensure impartiality in the federal system there was a committee called Sarkaria Commission formed in 1980. It suggested nonpartisan appointments of Governors to ensure impartiality and reduce political conflicts.

Picture Based Questions

1. Study the cartoon given below and answer the question that follow.

(i) 'Identify' the leader who is making appeal in the cartoon?

(a) Sardar Vallabhbhai Patel
(b) Ram Manohar Lohia
(c) Pt. Jawaharlal Nehru
(d) None of the above

Ans. (c) Pt. Jawaharlal Nehru

(ii) What appeal he is making to others?

(a) Stop making protest
(b) Show tolerance towards other language
(c) Appeal to make peace
(d) All of the above

Ans. (b) Show tolerance towards other language

(iii) The State Reorganisation Commission recommended the creations of

(a) Regional states (b) Religious states
(c) Ethnic states (d) Linguistic states

Ans. (d) Linguistic states

(iv) What is the main objective of the federal system?

(a) Accomodate regional diversity
(b) Promote diversity
(c) Make centre more powerful
(d) Distribute finance to different organs

Ans. (a) Accomodate regional diversity

2. **Observe the cartoon given below and answer the questions that follow.**

(i) **Whose image is referred to in the picture?**

(ii) **Who appoints Governor and Council of Ministers in State?**

(iii) **What is the role of Governor in the state?**

Ans. (i) The image of Jawaharlal Nehru and few ministers are referred to in the picture.

(ii) The Governor is appointed by the President on the advice of the Central Government. The Council of Ministers in the states are appointed by the Governor on the advice of the Chief Minister.

(iii) Governor is a nominal executive head of the state. He forms an important part of the state executive, where he acts as the chief executive head. At the same time, he is the agent of the Centre as the Union Government nominates Governor in each state.

Map Based Questions

1. **In the given outline map of India, five states been marked as (A), (B), (C), (D) and (E). Identify these states on the basis of the information given below and write their correct names in your answer book along with their respective serial number of the information used and the concerned alphabets as per format that follows**

(i) **Name the Princely State which covers the present day area of Karnataka.**

(ii) **What are the Princely States of Rajputana area? Name one.**

(iii) **Identify the Princely State marked with 'A'.**

(iv) **The state with Bicameral legislature.**

(v) **Identify Princely State marked with 'B'.**

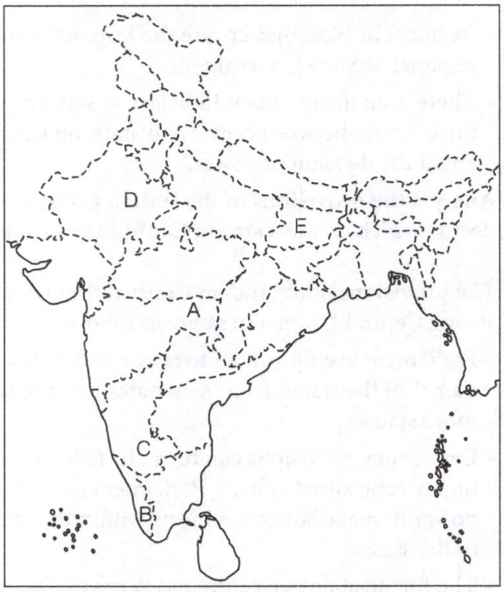

S.No.	Alphabet Concerned	Name of the State/City
(i)		
(ii)		
(iii)		
(iv)		
(v)		

Ans.

S.No.	Alphabet Concerned	Name of the State/city
(i)	(C)	Mysore
(ii)	(D)	Ajmer
(iii)	(A)	Nagpur
(iv)	(E)	Bihar
(v)	(B)	Travan Core

2. **In the given outline political map of India, four states have been marked as (A), (B), (C) and (D). Identify these states on the basis of the information given below and write their correct names in your answer book along with the respective serial numbers of the information used and the concerned alphabets as per the format that follows**

S.No.	Alphabet Concerned	Name of the State/City
(i)		
(ii)		
(iii)		
(iv)		
(v)		

(i) Identify state having dispute over the state of Belgaum.
(ii) Identify state carved out of state of Punjab.
(iii) Identify state having Kaveri water dispute.
(iv) Identify state involved in Narmada water dispute.

Ans.

S.No.	Alphabet Concerned	Name of the State/City
(i)	(C)	Maharashtra
(ii)	(D)	Haryana
(iii)	(B)	Tamil Nadu
(iv)	(A)	Madhya Pradesh

SELF ASSESSMENT TEST

Multiple Choice Questions

1. The United States of America has a system of .... citizenship.
   (a) single (b) dual
   (c) multiple (d) no
2. Whose ratification is must for Parliament to make laws on matters from state list?
   (a) President (b) Governor
   (c) Rajya Sabha (d) Lok Sabha
3. The Constitution has established on .... judiciary to enforce both central and state laws.
   (a) federal (b) fragmented
   (c) integrated (d) inclusive

Very Short Answer Type Questions

4. Define Federalism.
5. Why was federalism adopted in India?
7. Name any five subjects enumerated in the state list.
6. 'Indian federation called as Centralised Federation' Briefly Explain. **Competency Based Que**
8. What do you mean by the powers given in the concurrent list?

Short Answer Type Questions

9. Explain four features of Indian federal system.
10. 'The Union Parliament can make laws, on the subjects given in the state list'. Examine. **Competency Based Que**
11. Describe the administrative relations between the union and the states.

Long Answer Type Questions

12. Describe the development of federal system in India.
13. Discuss the reasons of conflict between the centre and the states.
14. 'The most extra-ordinary feature of the federal arrangement created in India, is that many states get a different treatment'. Justify with examples. **Competency Based Que**

08
CHAPTER

Democracy is based on the ideas of meaningful participation and accountability. Local governments make this possible by involving common citizens in making decisions that affects their lives.

Local Governments

YOUR STUDY GOALS

8.1 Local Government
8.2 Growth of Local Government in India
8.3 73rd and 74th Amendments
8.4 Implementation of 73rd and 74th Amendments

YOUR PRACTICE GOAL

- Objective Type Questions (40 Qs ; MCQs, A-R, Statements, Matching, 3 Passage Based)
- Subjective Questions (8 VSAs, 9 SAs, 4 LAs, 2 Picture Based)

Apart from the elected governments at the national and state level, a democracy requires an elected government at the local level too for dealing with local affairs.

Local government institution was given a Constitutional status in India in 1993. Since then, India is witnessing a larger transformation in the local governance.

8.1 Local Government

- Local government is the **lowest level of government** in a country and is responsible for the administration and governance of a specific area.
- Strong and vibrant local government ensure both active participation and purposeful accountability.
- In a democracy, local tasks should be handled by local people and their representatives, as they are most familiar with local needs and concerns. Local government is more familiar to people than State or National Government.

Characterstics of Local Government

- Local government refers to the administration and decision-making at the village and district levels. This form of government is **closest to the people** which addresses their immediate needs and concerns.
- It involves the day to day life and problems of ordinary citizens.

- It believes that local knowledge and local interest are important for democratic decision-making.
- It is essential for people-friendly administration.

Advantages of Local Government

There are various advantages of local government such as

- It is convenient for people to approach for problem solving.
- It provides quick and cost effective solutions.
- It protects local interests of the people.
- It fosters meaningful participation and accountability in democracy.

8.2 Growth of Local Government in India

The development of local government in India took the following course

- The history of local government in India dates back to ancient times when self-governing village communities, or **sabhas** existed. These village assemblies eventually evolved into panchayats, comprising of five persons who addressed local issues. Their role and functions changed at different points in time.
- After 1882, elected local bodies (called as **local boards**) were created by the initiative of **Lord Ripon,** the Viceroy of India at that time. However, the progress was slow in this area.
- The Government of India Act of 1919 and 1935 further established Village Panchayats across various provinces, laying the foundation for de-centralised power[1].
- During the course of national movement, the panchayats were seen as instruments of de-centralisation and participatory democracy.
- **Mahatma Gandhi** strongly advocated for de-centralising economic and political power and believed that powerful village panchayats were key for the effective de-centralisation. The leader equated independence with de-centralisation of decision-making, executive and administrative powers.
- The subject of local government was assigned to states in the Constitution. It was also made a part of the Directive Principles of State Policy (DPSP). This meant that being a part of DPSPs, the provision for local government was made non-justiciable and advisory.
- Local government in India did not get enough importance in the Constitution due to the following reasons
  - **Impact of Partition** The impact of partition led to a need of strong Central Government instead of localised power. Jawaharlal Nehru saw extreme localism as a threat to the unity of India.
  - **Concerns about Rural Dynamics** Dr. B.R. Ambedkar was worried that the factional and caste ridden nature of the rural society would undermine the effectiveness of the local government.

Local Government in Independent India

Local government in India gained significant momentum after the 73rd and 74th Constitution Amendment Acts. However, efforts to develop local government bodies began much earlier.

Early Initiatives

- The **Community Development Programme** was launched in 1952 to encourage people's participation in local development activities.
- This led to the recommendation of a three-tier Panchayat Raj system for rural areas. Some states like Gujarat and Maharashtra adopted elected local bodies around 1960.

1 De-centralised power It is the process of moving decision-making and authority from a Cental Government to the local institutions or lower levels of governments.

Challenges and Limitations

- Despite the efforts, local bodies faced significant challenges
  - Lack of sufficient powers and functions.
  - Heavy reliance on state and Central Governments for financial assistance.
  - Some states did not establish elected local bodies.
  - Some others dissolved the existing local bodies and handed over the control to government officers.
  - Indirect elections and frequent postponements of elections.

Reform Efforts

- A thorough review of Local Government Institutions began in 1987.
- The **P.K. Thungon Committee (1989)** recommended Constitutional recognition for local government bodies. The committee advocated for periodic elections and proper allocation of functions funds to the local government.
- These recommendations ultimately shaped the 73rd and 74th Constitution Amendment Acts.

Quick Test 1

1. When were village panchayats formed?
2. Name the Viceroy who initiated the local government in India.
3. Which programme was launched in 1952 to increase people participation in local developmental issues?
4. Mention the name of the committee who recommended Constitutional recognition for the local government bodies?

8.3 73rd and 74th Amendments

- Two Constitutional Amendments were introduced by the Central Government in 1989. These amendments were passed as the 73rd and 74th Constitutional Amendments in 1992.
- 73rd Amendment is related to the rural local government or **Panchayati Raj Institutions (PRIs)** and 74th amendment is related to urban local government or Nagarpalikas. Both these amendments came into force in 1993.
- After these amendments, states were required to bring their laws related to local bodies in conformity with the amended Constitution within one year.

Municipal Councils in Brazil

The Constitution of Brazil has created States, Federal Districts and Municipal Councils. Each of these is assigned independent powers and jurisdiction. Just as the Republic cannot interfere in the affairs of the States (except on grounds provided by the Constitution), states are prohibited from interfering in the affairs of the Municipal councils. This provision protects the powers of the local government.

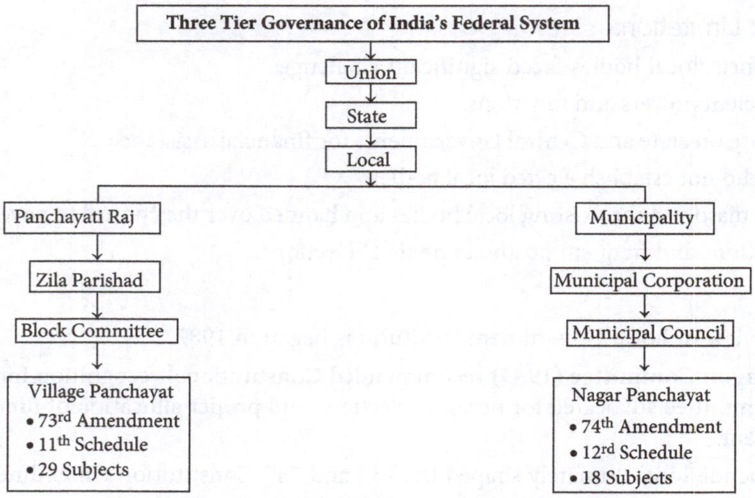

▲ *India's Federal System*

73rd Amendment

There were many changes brought about by the 73rd amendment in Panchayati Raj Institutions. Some of them are discussed below

Three Tier Structure

- 73rd Amendment in the Panchayati Raj Institutions brought a **three tier structure** comprised of Gram Panchayat, Mandal Panchayat and Zila Panchayat.
- The Amendment also created **Gram Sabha** which would comprise all the **adult members** registered as voters in the panchayat area. The role and function of Gram Sabha are decided by state legislation.

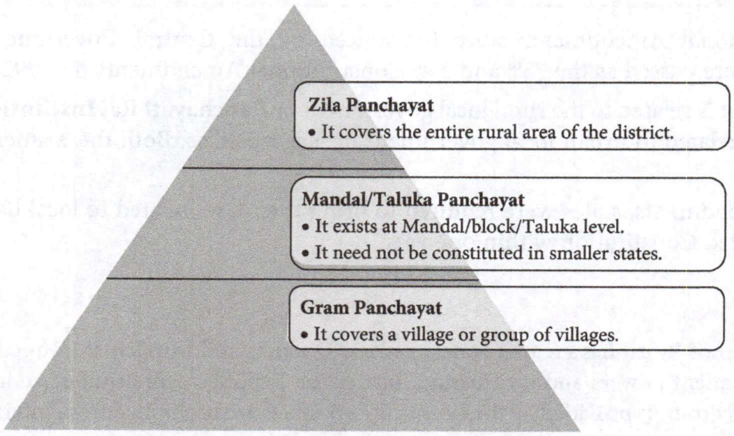

▲ *Three Tier Structure*

Elections

- All the three levels of Panchayati Raj Institutions are **elected directly** by the people.
- The term of each panchayat body is **five years** and if there is panchayat dis-solved before the expiry of five years term by the State Government, then fresh elections must be held within six months of such dis-solution. Before the 73rd Amendment, many states had indirect elections for district bodies and there was no provision for holding immediate elecions after their dis-solution.

Reservations

The provisions related to reservations in Panchayati Raj Institutions are as follows

- One third of the positions in all Panchayat institutions are reserved for **women**. This reservation is given not only in the general category but also within seats reserved for Scheduled Castes, Scheduled Tribes and Backward Castes.
- **Scheduled Caste** and **Scheduled Tribes** are given reservation at all three levels in proportion to their population.
- States can also provide reservation to **Other Backward Classes (OBCs)** if necessary.
- These reservations also apply to positions of chairpersons or 'Adhyakshas' at all three levels.

The 73rd amendment did not initially apply to areas inhabited by **Adivasi** populations. An Act in 1996 extended the panchayat provisions to these areas. This act protects **'Adivasi communities'** rights to manage resources like forests and water reservoirs according to their customs. It empowers Gram Sabhas, requiring elected panchayats to obtain consent from the Gram Sabha, preserving local self-governance traditions while introducing modern elected bodies.

Transfer of Subjects

- **Twenty-nine subjects** mostly related to local level development and welfare were identified and listed in the eleventh schedule of the Constitution.
- These subjects were earlier in the state list and are to be transferred to the Panchayati Raj Institutions. But the actual transfer depends on the state legislation as each state decide the number of subjects among the twenty nine subjects.
- Some of these subjects are
  - Agriculture
  - Small scale industries
  - Drinking water
  - Rural electrification
  - Education
  - Adult and non-formal education
  - Cultural activities
  - Health and sanitation
  - Women and child development
  - Welfare of weaker sections
  - Minor irrigation, water management and watershed development
  - Rural housing
  - Roads
  - Poverty alleviation programme
  - Technical training and vocational education
  - Libraries
  - Markets and fairs
  - Family welfare
  - Social welfare
  - Public distribution system

Aritcle 243G power, authority and responsibility of panchayats. .... the legislature of a state may, by law, endow the panchayats with such powers and authority .... with respect to .... the matters listed in the eleventh schedule.

State Election Commissioners

- State Election Commissioner appointed by the State Government conducts elections to the Panchayati Raj Institutions.
- It is an **autonomous office** and State Election Commissioner is an independent officer not under the control of Election Commission of India.
- Earlier, Panchayati Raj Elections were conducted by the state administration.

State Finance Commission

- State Finance Commission is appointed by the State Government **in every five years.** It is responsible for examining
  - Financial position of local government in the state.
  - Distribution of revenues between State and Local Government.
  - Distribution of revenues between Rural and Urban Local Government.

Quick Test 2

1. What is the base level of the Panchayati Raj System in India?
2. How many subjects are there in municipality?
3. Before the 73rd Amendment, how were district bodies in many states elected?
4. In which schedule Panchayati Raj is mentioned?

74th Amendment

- 74th Amendment deals with **the urban local bodies or Nagarpalikas.** An urban area can be big or small based on the population.
- Around 31 per cent of India's population lives in the urban areas as per the census 2011.
- The provisions relating to direct elections, reservations, transfer of subjects, State Election Commission and state Finance Commission in 74th Amendment is similar to 73rd Amendment.
- The list of functions transferred from the State Government to the urban local bodies are listed in twelfth schedule of the Constitution.

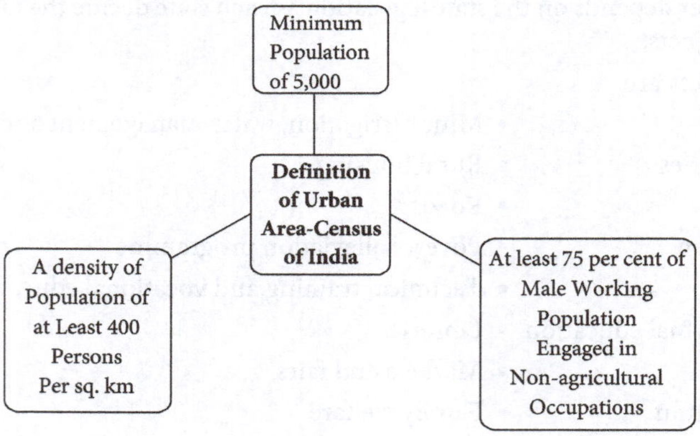

8.4 Implementation of 73rd and 74th Amendments

- All the states have passed a legislation to implement the provisions of these amendments and elections to local bodies have been held many times during this period.
- Today, the number of elected representatives at the local level is higher than the local representatives in the State Assemblies and Parliament.

Impact of 73rd and 74th Amendment

These amendments have created a uniformity in the structures of Panchayati Raj and Nagarpalika Institutions. These amendments have had the following impact

Impact on Women and Social Dynamics

Impact on Women	Impact on Social Dynamics
Reservation to women candidates has increased the number of elected women representatives.	These Constitutional Amendments mandates reservation of seats for Scheduled Castes and Tribes and many states also reserve seats for Backward Castes. This has made the local bodies more representative.
Women are gaining power and confidence by asserting their control over resources. They are gaining greater understanding of politics.	The dominant group sometimes resist this change because they do not want to give up their control leading to struggle for power.
Participation of women has brought a new perspective and sensitivity to discussions.	However, these tensions can be a positive sign of democracy becoming more inclusive.
There has been reduction in instances of women acting as proxies for male members of their families.	

Bolivia: A Shining Example of Democratic De-centralisation

Bolivia is a successful example of democratic de-centralisation in Latin America. It was brought about by its **1994 popular participation law**. This law divided the country into 314 municipalities, each with a popularly elected mayor and municipal council. Local elections take place nationwide in every five years.

Key features of Bolivia's de-centralisation

- Municipalities have control over building and maintaining local health and education facilities.
- 20 per cent of national tax collections are distributed among municipalities based on population size.
- Municipalities can levy taxes on motor vehicles, urban property and large agricultural properties, but most funding comes from fiscal transfers.

Problems of Local Governance

- They enjoy **limited autonomy** to perform functions assigned to them.
- Many states have not transferred most of the subjects to local bodies.
- Local bodies are not consulted in the decisions taken at central and state level.
- They do not enjoy much power of choosing welfare programmes or allocation of resources.
- They have very little funds of their own.
- Financial dependence on Central and State Government.
- Earn less than they spend.

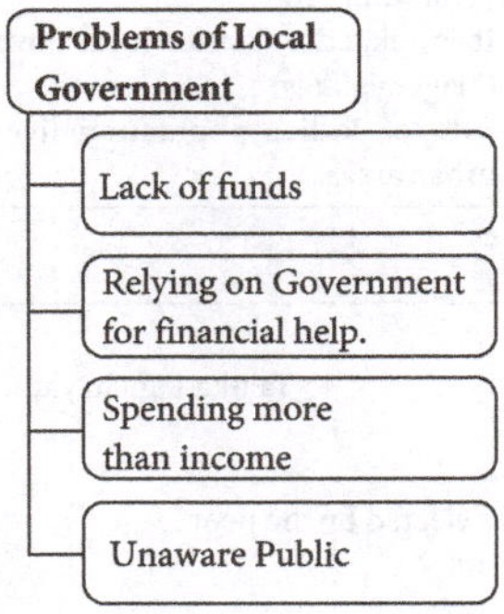

Quick Test 3

1 As per the 2011 Census, what percentage of India's population lives in urban areas?
2 What is the purpose of the reservation system for women in local bodies under the 73rd and 74th Amendments?
3 In which year did Bolivia implement the Popular Participation Law?
4 Mention any two problems faced by local governments.

Mind Map

LOCAL GOVERNMENTS

1 Meaning

- Local government refer to the governance at the village and district level.
- Closest to people addresses immediate and local concerns.
- Promotes meaningful participation and accountability.

2 Advantages of Local Government

- Provides quick and cost effective solutions.
- Protects local interests of people.
- Convenient for people to approach problem solving.
- Essential for people friendly administration.
- Involves the day to day life problems of ordinary citizens.

3 Evolution in India

Ancient Times
- Village assemblies called as 'Sabha' evolved into panchayats.

British Era
- Lord Rippon (1882) initiated elected local bodies.

Post-Independence
- **1952** Community development programme.
- Three tier Panchayati Raj system recommended

4 Constitutional Amendments

73rd Amendment
- It is related to rural local government. (Panchayati Raj Institution).

74th Amendment
- It is related to urban local government. (Nagar Palikas).
- 31% of India's population lives in the urban areas.

Key Features

Three Tier System
- Zila Panchayat
- Taluka Panchayat
- Gram Panchayat

Elections
- Gram Panchayat is elected by the people .
- Held every five years.

Reservations
- 33% seats for women
- Seats for SC/ST

State Finance Commission
- Financial position of local government in the state.
- Distribution of revenues between state and local government (rural and urban local government).

Transfer of Subject
- Twenty-nine subject mostly related to local level development are listed in the eleventh schedule of the Constitution.

5 Impact and Callenges

Impact
- Increased representation of women and marginalised groups.
- Strengthened democratic participation.
- Woman has brought a new perspective and understanding of the working of politics.

Challenges
- **Limited Autonomy** Lack of resources and folding.
- Dependence on State-Central Government for finances.
- Spending more than income.
- Transfer most of the subject to local bodies.

In the interests of democracy, the villages maybe trained in the art of self-government, even autonomy... We must be able to reform the villages and introduce democratic principles of government there..."

Ananthasayanam Ayyangar

Local Sarkar

NCERT Folder

Intext Questions

1. How does local government strengthen democracy? (Pg 179)

Ans. Local government strengthens democracy by fostering meaningful participation and ensuring accountability, both of which are foundational to a vibrant democratic system. As democracy is about empowering citizens to actively participate in decision-making, local governments provide the most direct platform for such involvement. People are more familiar with and impacted by the actions of their local governments, making it easier for them to engage and hold their representatives accountable.

2. Both Nehru and Dr. Ambedkar were not very enthusiastic about local government bodies. Did they have similar objections to local governments? (Pg 182)

Ans. Both Nehru and Dr. Ambedkar were not very enthusiastic about local government bodies. Both of their concerns were rooted in different aspects of governance and society.

Jawaharlal Nehru was wary of extreme localism, as he saw it as a potential threat to the unity and integration of the nation. He believed that local governments, particularly in a newly independent India, could become fragmented and lead to a lack of national cohesion. Nehru feared that emphasising local autonomy too much might weaken the Central Government and hinder the country's overall development.

Dr. Ambedkar was concerned about the social structure of rural India, which he believed was deeply influenced by caste divisions and factionalism. He feared that local government bodies, particularly in rural areas, would be dominated by caste-based politics and entrenched inequalities, which could undermine the democratic goals of local governance.

3. What was the Constitutional provision about local governments before 1992? (Pg 182)

Ans. Before 1992, there was limited Constitutional provision regarding local governments in India. The framework for local governance was not well defined and local governments did not have significant Constitutional recognition or authority.

- The Constitution of India initially did not provide specific provisions for the establishment of local governments. There were no clear Constitutional guarantees for the existence or functioning of local bodies.
- The Constitution had provisions in the Directive Principles of State Policy (Article 40), which encouraged the establishment of Panchayats at the village, intermediate and district levels. However, these were not mandatory.
- In 1952, the Community Development Programme was launched to encourage people's participation in local development. This was one of the early attempts to promote local governance, particularly in rural areas, but it lacked the Constitutional backing to make local bodies fully functional and empowered.

4. Which were the states that had established local government during the 1960s and 1970s? (Pg 182)

Ans. During the 1960s and 1970s, several states such as Gujarat, Maharashtra, Rajasthan and Andhra Pradesh took steps to establish local government bodies. These states adopted the Panchayati Raj system based on the recommendations of the Balwant Rai Mehta Committee (1957), which recommended a three-tier system to ensure local participation in governance.

5. Identify some of the powers that your State Government has delegated to panchayats. (Pg 187)

Ans. The State Government delegates several powers and responsibilities to panchayats to promote local governance and de-centralised decision-making. These powers vary from state to state in India which are as follows

- Panchayats are empowered to implement State and Central Government schemes aimed at rural development, poverty alleviation, health, sanitation and education. For example, schemes like the **Mahatma Gandhi National Rural Employment Guarantee Act** (MGNREGA).
- Panchayats oversee the construction and maintenance of rural infrastructure such as roads, schools, health centers and water supply systems.
- Panchayats are often given the responsibility to manage and conserve local water resources and oversee irrigation facilities for agricultural use.
- Panchayats are involved in the management and protection of local forests, ensuring that community resources are sustainably utilised.
- Panchayats regulate local markets, such as determining prices, ensuring the availability of essential goods and maintaining market infrastructure.

- Panchayats are authorised to collect taxes and fees on local services, such as property taxes and allocate funds for local development projects and social-welfare programmes.

Exercise

1. Constitution of India visualised Village Panchayats as units of self-government. Think over the situation described in the following statements and explain how do these situations strengthen or weaken the panchayats in becoming units of self-governments.

(i) Government of a state has allowed a big company to establish a huge steel plant. Many villages would be adversely affected by the steel plant. Gram Sabha of one of the affected villages passed a resolution that before establishing any big industries in the region, village people must be consulted and their grievances should be redressed.

(ii) The government has decided that 20 per cent of all its expenditure would be done through the panchayats.

(iii) A Village Panchayat kept on demanding funds for a building for village school, the government officials turned down their proposal saying that funds are allocated for certain other schemes and cannot be spent otherwise.

(iv) The government divided a village Dungarpur into two and made a part of village Jamuna and Sohana. Now village Dungarpur has ceased to exist in government's books.

(v) A village panchayat observed that water sources of their region are depleting fast. They decided to mobilise village youth to do some voluntary work and revive the old village ponds and wells.

Ans. (i) It strengthens the Village Panchayat, as the Gram Sabha can take decisions independently for the welfare of the village people.

(ii) It strengthens the Village Panchayat, as it makes more resources available at their disposal. It allows them to spend to their local needs.

(iii) It demoralises or weakens the Village Panchayats, as it does not have enough funds to maintain and carry out welfare projects in the village. It has to depend on the government official's for funds.

(iv) It strengthens the panchayat, as it creates new unit of self-government and allows more power in the hands of people.

(v) It strengthens the self-governance of the village, as it shows the ability of the Village Youth Panchayat to mobilise the village to utilise their own resources without any help from the State Government.

2. Suppose you are entrusted to evolve a local government plan of a state, what powers would you endow to the village panchayats to function as units of self-government? Mention any five powers and the justification in two lines for each of them for giving those powers.

Ans. The powers which should be endowed to the village panchayats to function as unit of self-governance are

(i) **Allowing panchayats to raise their own funds** This would reduce their dependency on the higher levels of government and make active, the development process.

(ii) **Starting village co-operatives at panchayat level** This would lead to the development of village economy and co-operation between various panchayats. It would also generate employment and allow panchayats to directly market village produce and get better prices for the same.

(iii) **Authority to create and maintain infrastructure in village** This would lead to less dependency on government officials for funds and consequently, lead to autonomy.

(iv) **Control of village panchayat over local resources** like water and pastureland enable their maintenance and prevent their degradation. This would engage the entire community in their conservation.

(v) **Direct engagement of village panchayats with State Government** in matters related to development projects, as this would allow them to get adequate compensation for development projects and acquisition and reduce the role of middle men.

3. What are the provisions for the reservations for the socially disadvantaged groups as per the 73rd Amendment? Explain how these provisions have changed the profile of the leadership at the village level.

Ans. In 1992, two Constitutional Amendment Acts, were passed to recognise local self-government at the grass-root level. 73rd amendment made the following provisions.

- The socially dis-advantaged groups like the women, SCs and STs have been given reservations for various posts in the local government of rural India according to the proportion of their population.
- One-third of all positions in panchayats are reserved for women, while SCs and STs have seats reserved as per the proportion to their population.
- States can also provide reservation to the other backward classes, if they think it is necessary.

This has changed the profile of the leadership at the village level by transferring the leadership from the earlier dominant social groups to groups that were previously unable to have a say in the decision-making process. There is now a greater representation of all social groups in the Panchayat Institutions.

Thus, more women and people belonging to SCs and STs are now able to play important role in making decisions that can bring benefits for their community.

4. What were the main difference between the local governments before 73rd amendment and after that amendment?

Ans. The main difference between local governments before 73rd amendments and after the amendment can be listed as

- After the implementation of 73rd amendment, the local government has been divided into a uniform Three-Tier Panchayati Raj structure.
- Earlier the state administration was responsible for conducting elections to the Panchayati Raj Institutions but now the State Government has to appoint a State Election Commissioner for this purpose.
- After the dis-solution of Panchayati Raj before its term of five years, a fresh election has to be conducted within six months. This was not the case before 73rd amendment was passed.
- Distribution of revenue between the State Government and local government and between rural and urban government is done by the State Finance Commission. This was not the case before the 73rd amendment was implemented.
- Reservation for women, SCs, STs and OBCs (if necessary) is implemented for various positions in local government according to the proportion of their population. This provision was not made before the 73rd amendment.
- Twenty nine subjects that were earlier in the state list has been transferred to the Panchayati Raj Institutions under the eleventh schedule of the Constitution before the 73rd, amendment such subjects were not defined.

5. Read the following conversation. Write in two hundred words your opinion about the issues raised in this conversation.

Alok : Our Constitution guarantees equality between men and women. Reservations in local bodies for women ensure their equal share in power.

Neha : But it is not enough that women should be in positions of power. It is necessary that the budget of local bodies should have separate provision for women.

Jayesh : I don't like this reservations business.
A local body must take care of all people in the village and that would automatically take care of women and their interests.

Ans. It is correct that the Constitution has guaranteed equality between men and women. Reservation has ensured the participation of women in decision-making process at the local level. Women have gained more power and confidence in the society by acquiring positions at various levels of Panchayati structures. They have developed better understanding of politics and have helped other women to know about their rights.

However, the social status of women can only be increased through their economic independence and funds are required for this purposes. Therefore, the budget of local bodies should have provisions for women, particularly for their health, education, livelihood, etc.

It is also correct to say in theory that reservation go against the nature of equality. However, there are certain issues that are best represented by the members of the particular groups which is affected by them.

Reservation also provides a chance to these groups to make their voice heard. Thus, reservation for women is required in the context of their socio-economic status.

6. Read the provisions of the 73rd amendment. Which of the following concern does this amendment address?

(i) Fear of replacement makes representatives accountable to the people.

(ii) The dominant castes and feudal landlords dominate the local bodies.

(iii) Rural illiteracy is very high. Illiterate people cannot take decisions about the development of the village.

(iv) To be effective the village panchayats needs resources and powers to make plans for the village development.

Ans. (iv) To be effective the village panchayats needs resources and powers to make plans for the village development.

7. The following are different justifications given in favour of local government. Give them ranking and explain why you attach greater significance to a particular rationale than the others. According to you, on which of these rationales the decision of the Gram Panchayat of Vengaivasal village was based? How?

(i) Government can complete the projects with lesser cost with the involvement of the local community.

(ii) The development plans made by the local people will have greater acceptability than those made by the government officers.

(iii) People know their area, needs, problems and priorities. By collective participation they should discuss and take decisions about their lives.

(iv) It is difficult for the common people to contact their representatives of the state or the national legislature.

Ans. These can be ranked as follows

1st Rank (iii) People know their area, needs, problems and priorities. By collective participation, they should discuss and take decisions about their lives. Local government by definition is meant of the local people of a particular area. It is based upon the assumption that the problems of an area are best understood and resolved by the local people. Thus, it is the most important aspect of local government.

2nd Rank (ii) The development plans made by the local people will have greater acceptability than those made by government officers. This is because the decisions of local people are based upon an accurate knowledge of local requirements. This makes it the most important aspect of local government.

3rd Rank (iv) It is difficult for the common people to contact their representatives of the state or the national legislature. This is because common people may not have the time or resources to approach authorities at state or even district level about issues that have been pending for a long time.

4th Rank (i) Government can complete the projects with lesser cost with involvement of the local community. Community involvement lessens the cost of projects. However, it is a less important aspect compared to the relevance of the development activities for local people.

The decision of the Gram Panchayat of Vengaivasal village was based upon the knowledge of people about their local area, needs, problems and priorities. Collective participation enabled the people to discuss and take decisions about issues that affected their lives. The decision of the government was taken without the consent of the panchayat. Thus, it was violation of the rights of the people to decide upon issues that affected them.

8. Which of the following according to you involve de-certralisation? Why are other options not sufficient for de-centralisation?

(i) To hold election of the Gram Panchayat.

(ii) Decision by the villagers themselves about what policies and programmes are useful for the village.

(iii) Power to call meeting of Gram Sabha.

(iv) A Gram Panchayat receiving the report from the Block Development Officer about the progress of a project started by the State Government.

Ans. (ii) Decision by the villagers themselves about what policies and programmes are useful for the village.

Rest of the three options do not involve de-centralisation because elections can be held, meeting can be called and projects can be monitored even in a certain form of government. These features are not related to the decision-making process, which is the most important aspect of de-centralisation.

9. A student of Delhi University, Raghavendra Parpanna, wanted to study the role of de-centralisation in decision -making about primary education. He asked some questions to the villagers. These questions are given below. If you were among those villagers, what answer would you give to each of these questions?

A meeting of the Gram Sabha is to be called to discuss what steps should be taken to ensure that every child of the village goes to the school.

(i) How would you decide the suitable day for the meeting? Think who would be able to attend/not attend the meeting because of your choice.

(a) A day specified by the BDO or the collector.
(b) Day of the village haat.
(c) Sunday
(d) Naag panchami/sankranti

(ii) What is a suitable venue for the meeting? Why?

(a) Venue suggested by the circular of the district collector.
(b) Religious place in the village.
(c) Dalit Mohalla
(d) Upper caste Tola
(e) Village school

(iii) In the Gram Sabha meeting, firstly a circular sent by the District Collector was read. It suggested what steps should be taken to organise an education rally and what should be its route. The meeting did not discuss about the children who never come to school or about girls' education or the condition of the school building and the timing of the school. No women teacher attended the meeting, as it was held on Sunday.

What do you think about these proceedings as an instance of people's participation?

(iv) Imagine your class as the Gram Sabha. Discuss the agenda of the meeting and suggest some steps to realise the goal.

Ans. (i) (c) Sunday, as it would allow the adults of the village to attend the meeting.

(ii) (e) Village school would be the suitable place for the meeting because the meeting is regarding education, irrespective of caste, gender and religion of the children.

(iii) It is not an instance of people's participation, as women teachers did not attend the meeting, girls' education was not discussed and children who has never been to school were not considered. The condition of the building and timing of the school were also ignored.

Thus, most issues that were vital to the participation of people were ignored, as issues related to all groups were not considered.

(iv) Agenda of Gram Sabha

Agenda of the Meeting	Steps to Achieve the Goal
Age of Enrolment	All children of the village from the age of 5 years should be enrolled in the school.
School Building	The school building should be renovated with proper seats and black boards in all classrooms.
Water and Sanitation Facility	The Gram Pradhan is held responsible for the water supply and better separate sanitation facility for boys and girls.
Syllabus	Sports and extra co-curricular activities will be included to lessen the pressure of the study and cultivate physical development.
Mid-Day Meal	School Principal will be responsible for the quality and quantity of the food provided to the students.
Free Education	Every child till 14 years of age is eligible for free education.
Appointment of Staff	Helping staff can be recruited from the village and secretary would be responsible for the appointment of teachers.
Compensation	Villagers whose land will be taken should be provided with appropriate compensation by the government.

Exam Pattern Questions

Objective Type Questions

Multiple Choice Questions (MCQs)

1. Where are local governments found? Diksha App

(a) Village level and district level
(b) State level
(c) Central level
(d) Regional level

2. Which of the following has been created to strengthen democracy at grass-root level in India? Diksha App

(a) Central Government
(b) State Governments
(c) Inter-State Government
(d) Local self-government

3. Self governing village communities existed in India from the earliest times in the form of ....

(a) Samiti
(b) Ur
(c) Sabhas
(d) Gramam

4. What was the position Lord Rippon held in India?

(a) Viceroy of India
(b) Commander in Chief
(c) Secretary of State
(d) National Security Advisor to the British Government in India

5. Village panchayats were formed in a number of provinces following the ....

(a) Government of India Act, 1919
(b) Government of India Act, 1909
(c) Government of India Act, 1942
(d) India Independence Act, 1947

6. Identify the leader who advocated for de-centralisation of economic and political control during India's independence struggle? Competency Based Que

(a) Jawaharlal Nehru (b) Subhash Chandra Bose
(c) Mahatma Gandhi (d) Sardar Patel

7. Who was assigned the subject of local self-government when the Constitution was prepared? Diksha App

(a) State Governments (b) Central Government
(c) District Governments (d) Presidency towns

8. A dominant voice in the Constituent Assembly, headed by ...., believed that the rural society's factionalism and casteism would undermine the noble intent of local government at the rural level. Competency Based Que

(a) Dr. B.R. Ambedkar
(b) Alladi Krishnaswami Ayyar
(c) C. Rajagopalachari
(d) M.N. Roy

9. Which of the following initiatives was taken by the Government of India for local self-government in 1952?
(a) Introduced amendment for the local bodies
(b) Community Development Programme
(c) Planning development
(d) None of the above

10. Mark the state who adopted the first Panchayati Raj System.
(a) Gujarat (b) Rajasthan
(c) Madhya Pradesh (d) Andhra Pradesh

11. Which among the following Committee recommended Constitutional recognition for the local government bodies?
(a) Kelkar Committee (b) Swaminathan Committee
(c) P.K. Sinha Committee (d) P.K. Thungon Committee

12. Which Amendment Acts gave Constitutional status to local bodies?
(a) 71st and 72nd Amendments
(b) 72nd and 73rd Amendments
(c) 73rd and 74th Amendments
(d) 74th and 75th Amendments

13. When was the 73rd and 74th Amendment Acts were passed by the Parliament for Panchayati Raj Institution and Urban Local Governments?
(a) 1992 (b) 1990 (c) 1987 (d) 1993

14. 73rd amendment to the Constitution of India provides for
(a) Two Tiers of Panchayati Raj Institutions at the village and district levels.
(b) Two Tiers of Panchayati Raj Institutions at the village and block levels.
(c) Two Tiers of Panchayati Raj Institutions at the block and district levels.
(d) Three Tiers of Panchayati Raj Institutions at the village, block and district levels.

15. What is the basic unit of local government at village level in the Panchayati Raj structure?
(a) Zila Panchayat (b) Village Panchayat
(c) Mandal Panchayat (d) Taluka Panchayat

16. Which of the following doesn't come under the Three Tier System of Panchayati Raj? **Diksha App**
(a) Gram Panchayat at village
(b) Block Samiti at block level
(c) Town Committee at town level
(d) Zilla Parishad at district level

17. The Gram Sabha is composed of .... and its creation is ....
(a) all registered voters in panchayat area, mandatory
(b) all residents of the village, voluntary
(c) all registered voters in panchayat area, voluntary
(d) all residents of the village, mandatory

18. What is the tenure of the elected member of the Local Government?
(a) Four years (b) Five years
(c) Six years (d) Two years

19. Women have been provided with one-third reservation in the local bodies. Which of the following is NOT TRUE regarding impact of women reservation in panchayats? **Competency Based Que; Diksha App**
(a) Women reservation has decreased the number of elected women representatives.
(b) Reservation has increased the Instances of women as proxies for male members.
(c) Reservation has helped women to assert more control over resources.
(d) Reservation has helped women in greater understanding of politics.

20. Which of the following is not included in the eleventh schedule to the Constitution? **CBSE Diksha**
(a) Rural housing (b) Rural electrification
(c) Public Distribution System (d) Village industrial

21. The provisions of 73rd amendment was extended to the scheduled (Adivasi) areas in ....
(a) 1993 (b) 1996 (c) 2000 (d) 2006

22. Who is responsible to conduct the election at the Local Government?
(a) Zila Panchayat
(b) State Election Commission
(c) Election Commission of India
(d) State Legislature

23. State Finance Commission is appointed by a State Government every five years to determine **Competency Based Que**
(a) Financial resources of the state for placing state's requirement before the Union Government.
(b) Development requirements of the state for formulating state Five Year Plan.
(c) Budgetary requirements of various departments of the State Government.
(d) Pattern of distribution of state's tax revenue between the State Government and local bodies (both rural and urban) and the pattern of grants in aid to local bodies.

24. What does the 74th amendment of Indian Constitution deal with? **CBSE Diksha**
(a) Panchayats (b) Parliament
(c) Legislative assemblies (d) Urban local bodies

25. Which of the following statements regarding the 74th Amendment to the Constitution of India is/are correct?
I. It provides for the insertion of a new schedule to the Constitution.
II. It restructures the working of the municipalities.

III. It provides for the reservation of seats for women and Scheduled Castes in the municipalities.

Select the correct answer using the codes given below. **Competency Based Que**

(a) I and II only (b) Only II
(c) I and III (d) All of these

26. Which of the following provisions of the 73rd amendment is not incorporated in the 74th amendment? **Diksha App**

(a) Direct elections (b) Reservation
(c) State election commission (d) Rural electrification

27. In which one of the following schedules of the Constitution of India, is urban Local self-government mentioned?

(a) Seventh Schedule (b) Eighth Schedule
(c) Eleventh Schedule (d) Twelfth Schedule

28. How many subjects are assigned to the Local Governments by Constitution Amendments? **CBSE Diksha**

(a) 29 subjects (b) 30 subjects
(c) 103 subjects (d) 6 subjects

29. Which of the following are the Grounds of criticism of the Local self-government?

(a) The states have not transferred most of the subjects to local bodies.
(b) Local self-government give more autonomy to villages.
(c) Local self-government have subjects of local importance.
(d) Local self-government give reservation to women.

30. Consider the following statements the 73rd Constitutional Amendment Act provided

I. For 27 per cent reservation of seats in the panchayats for the Other Backward Castes (OBCs).
II. That the chairpersons of the panchayats at intermediate or district level, shall be elected by and from amongst the elected members thereof.

Which of the statements given above is/are correct? **Competency Based Que**

(a) Only I (b) Only II
(c) Both I and II (d) None of these

31. Given below are two statements

Statement I The eleventh schedule was inserted in the Constitution of India by the Constitution (73rd amendment) Act, 1992.

Statement II The eleventh schedule of the Constitution of India contains 11 items. **Competency Based Que**

In the light of the above statements, choose the correct answer from the options given below

(a) Both Statement I and Statement II are true
(b) Both Statement I and Statement II are false.
(c) Statement I is true, but Statement II is false.
(d) Statement I is false, but Statement II is true.

32. Match the List I with List II.

List I		List II	
A.	Mahatama Gandhi	1.	Localism is a threat to unity and integration of the nation.
B.	J.L. Nehru	2.	Independence must began at the bottom.
C.	B.R. Ambedkar	3.	Villages trained in the art of self government.
D.	Anan then Sayanam Ayyangar	4.	Fraction in society would harm for the local government

Codes

	A	B	C	D		A	B	C	D
(a)	1	2	3	4	(b)	2	1	3	4
(c)	2	1	4	3	(d)	1	2	4	3

Assertion-Reason Questions

Directions (Q. Nos. 33-37) In the questions given below, there are two statements marked as Assertion (A) and Reason (R). Read the statements and choose the correct option. **Competency Based Que**

Codes

(a) Both A and R are true and R is the correct explanation of A.
(b) Both A and R are true, but R is not the correct explanation of A.
(c) A is true, but R is false.
(d) A is false, but R is true.

33. **Assertion (A)** Local governments are formed to solve local problems by the people themselves.

Reason (R) The local government reduces the burden of the Central and State Governments by de-centralising power.

34. **Assertion (A)** Local government did not have any power and the sources of their own.

Reason (R) The Constitution was amended in 1992 to make third tier of democracy more powerful.

35. **Assertion (A)** There is no provision of reservation of seats for women in Panchayati Raj bodies.

Reason (R) Empowerment of women is essential for the achievement of democracy and development.

36. **Assertion (A)** The 73rd Constitutional Amendment Act is the culmination of the process of democratic de-centralisation.

Reason (R) The state should take steps to organise Village Panchayats and endow them with such powers and authority as may be necessary to enable them to function as units of self-government.

37. Assertion (A) The Panchayati Raj Institutions have been greatly handicapped in the performance of their assigned duties because of the lack of funds.

Reason (R) The Constitution of India now provides a mechanism for regular flow of funds to Panchayati Raj Institutions.

Passage Based Questions

38. Read the given passage and answer the following questions.

In modern times, elected local government bodies were created after 1882. Lord Ripon, who was the Viceroy of India at that time, took the initiative in creating these bodies. They were called the local boards. However, due to slow progress in this regard, the Indian National Congress urged the government to take necessary steps to make all local bodies more effective. Following the Government of India Act 1919, village panchayats were established in a number of provinces. This trend continued after the Government of India Act of 1935. During India's freedom movement, Mahatma Gandhi had strongly pleaded for de-centralisation of economic and political power.

(i) Name the Viceroy of India who supported the formation of local bodies in India.

(a) Lord Mayo (b) Lord Chelmsford
(c) Lord Rippon (d) Lord Lytton

(ii) .... laid the framework for the establishment of Village Panchayats.

(a) Government of India Act, 1919
(b) Government of India Act, 1935
(c) Democratic De-centralisation Act, 1882
(d) Morley-Minto Act, 1909

(iii) What is the history of local self-government in India?

39. Read the given passage and answer the following questions.

In 1992, the 73rd and 74th Constitutional Amendments were passed by the Parliament. The 73rd Amendment is about rural local governments which are also known as Panchayati Raj Institutions or PRIs and the 74th Amendment made the provisions relating to urban local government (Nagarpalikas). The 73rd and 74th Amendments came into force in 1993. States are free to make their own laws on this subject. But once the Constitution was amended, the States had to change their laws about local bodies in order to bring these in conformity with the amended Constitution. They were given one year's time for making necessary changes in their respective state laws in the light of these amendments.

(i) The 73rd and 74th Constitutional Amendments Act dealt with......................

(a) Panchayats and Municipalities respectively.
(b) Municipalities and Panchayats respectively.
(c) Official language and Anti-defection.
(d) Panchayats and Co-operatives.

(ii) The Constitutional Amendment Act provided for establishment of .... structure in rural and urban local bodies.

(a) two-tier (b) three-tier
(c) four-tier (d) single-tier

(iii) What is the provision for Adivasis in the 73rd and 74th Constitutional Amendments?

40. Read the given passage and answer the following questions.

"Gandhiji believed that strengthening of Gram Panchayats is an effective means of decentralisation of power. Every initiative of development should involve the participation of local people so that it can succeed. The independence of India as a whole must begin from the very bottom, in this way every state will be a republic".

(i) What does decentralisation of power mean?

(a) Strengthening of Gram Panchayats
(b) Participation of local peoples in developmental works
(c) Reaching of Power up to the people
(d) All of the above

(ii) What does republic mean?

(a) Election of the head of the state by the People
(b) Hereditary selection of head of state
(c) Dictatorial head of the state
(d) King or queen being the head of the state.

(iii) How can Panchayats be strengthened?

a) They should not have a lack of money
b) Support of Centre & State must be given
c) People should be well aware
d) All of the above

(iv) Who gave this statement "Freedom should start from the bottom"

(a) Mahatma Gandhi
(b) Pandit Nehru
(c) Sardar Patel
(d) Netaji Subhash Chandra Bose

Answers

1. (a) Village level and district level
2. (d) Local self-governments
3. (c) Sabhas
4. (a) Viceroy of India
5. (a) Government of India Act, 1919
6. (c) Mahatma Gandhi
7. (a) State Governments
8. (a) Dr. B.R. Ambedkar
9. (b) Community Development Programme
10. (a) Gujarat
11. (d) P.K. Thungon Committee
12. (c) 73rd and 74th Amendments
13. (a) 1992
14. (d) Three Tiers of Panchayati Raj Institutions at the village, block and district levels.
15. (b) Village Panchayat
16. (c) Town Committee at town level
17. (a) all registered voters in panchayat area, mandatory
18. (b) Five years
19. (c) Reservation has helped women to assert more control over resources.
20. (d) Village industrial
21. (b) 1996
22. (b) State Election Commission
23. (d) Pattern of distribution of state's tax revenue between the State Government and local bodies (both rural and urban) and the pattern of grants in aid to local bodies
24. (d) Urban local bodies
25. (d) All of these
26. (d) Rural electrification
27. (d) Twelfth Schedule
28. (a) 29 subjects
29. (a) The states have not transferred most of the subjects to local bodies.
30. (b) Only II
31. (c) Statement I is true, but Statement II is false.
32. (c) 2 1 4 3
33. (a) Both A and R are true and R is the correct explanation of A.
34. (a) Both A and R are true and R is the correct explanation of A.
35. (d) A is false, but R is true.
36. (a) Both A and R are correct and R is the correct explanation of A.
37. (b) Both A and R are true, but R is not the correct explanation of A.
38. (i) (c) Lord Ripon
    (ii) (a) Government of India Act, 1919
    (iii) The history of Local government in India dates back to ancient times when self-governing village communities or 'sabhas' existed. These village assemblies eventually evolved into panchayats, comprising of five persons who addressed local issues. Their role and functions changed at different points in time.
39. (i) (a) Panchayats and Municipalities respectively.
    (ii) (b) three-tier
    (iii) The 73rd Amendment did not initially apply to areas inhabited by Adivasi populations. An act in 1996 extended the panchayat provisions to these areas. This act protects Adivasi communities' rights to manage resources like forests and water reservoirs according to their customs.
    It empowers Gram Sabhas, requiring elected panchayats to obtain consent from the Gram Sabha, preserving local self-governance traditions while introducing modern elected bodies.
40. (i) (d) All of the above
    (ii) (a) Election of the head of the state by the people.
    (iii) (d) All of the above
    (iv) (a) Mahatma Gandhi

Subjective Questions

Very Short Answer Type Questions

1. Why are local governments important for a democracy?

Ans. The local governments are important for a democracy because

- It is a government at the village and district level.
- It is government closest to the people and involves the day to day life and problems of an ordinary citizen.

2. 'Mahatma Gandhi pleaded regarding local governments'. Briefly discuss. **Competency Based Que**

Ans. During India's freedom movement, Mahatma Gandhi strongly pleaded for de-centralisation of economic and political power, as the panchayats are the instrument of de-centralisation and participatory democracy.

3. Discuss the effort made in developing local governments after independence?

Ans. The first effort in the direction of developing local governments bodies was the Community Development Programme in 1952, it sought to promote people's participation in local development in range of activities, for which three-tier Panchayati Raj system of local government was recommended.

4. Why was the reform in local body government was introduced in 1992?

Ans. The reform in local body government by the 73rd and 74th amendment was introduced to strengthen local government and ensure an element of uniformity in their structure and functioning across the country.

5. Briefly explain the composition of Gram Sabha.

Ans. The Gram Sabha consists of all the registered voters residing in the jurisdiction of a panchayat (either one or group of villages), who should meet twice in a year.

6. Why a separate act was passed for extending the provisions of panchayat system to Adivasi areas?

Ans. A separate act was passed for extending the provisions of panchayat system to Adivasi areas because many adivasi communities have their traditional customs of managing common resources.

Therefore, to safeguard the rights of these communities and to manage their resources in way acceptable to them, this act was passed.

7. Discuss the role of State Finance Commission?

Ans. The State Government is required to appoint a State Finance Commission once in five years to examine the financial position of local body of government and also to review the distribution of revenues between the state and local government and between rural and urban local government.

8. Define the urban area.

Ans. As per the census of India, an area having a minimum population of 5000, where atleast 75 per cent male working population engaged in non-agricultural occupations and the density of population is atleast 400 persons per sq km, is known as urban area.

Short Answer Type Questions

1. 'Local government strengthen the democracy'. Explain? **Competency Based Que**

Ans. Democracy is about a constructive participation and accountability.

- The local government is the government at village and district level and closest to the common people.
- A local government involves itself with day to day life and problems of ordinary citizen.
- Strong and vibrant local governments ensure both active participation and purposeful accountability.
- Local government strengthen democracy as they work at local level. So common people can be involved in decision-making concerning their lives, needs, priorities and development.
- It also educate the people in matters of importance and also form co-operatives.
- Thus, local governments strengthen democracy.

2. Discuss the recommendations made by P.K. Thungon Committee for local government.

Ans. The recommendations made by P.K. Thungon Committee for local government are

- It recommended for Constitutional status or recognition for local government bodies.
- A Constitutional Amendment to provide for periodic elections.
- Enlistment of appropriate functioning along with funds was recommended for local governments.
- Zila Parishad should be the only planning and development agency in district.

3. Enumerate the structure of Panchayati Raj system.

Ans. All the states now have a uniform Three-Tier Panchayati Raj structure, at the base is the Gram Panchayat which covers a village or groups of village. The intermediary level is the Mandal or Taluka Panchayat or Block and at the apex is the Zila Parishad or panchayat covering the entire rural area of the district.

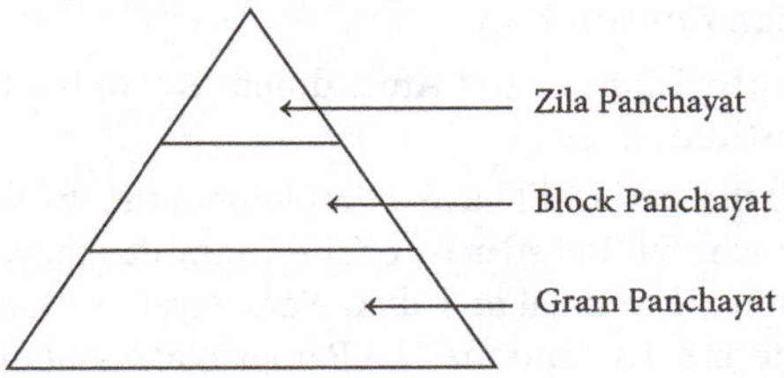

Further, the provision for creation of Gram Sabha is also mandatory and it would consists of all the adult voters registered in the panchayat area.

4. Write a note on the reservation in the Panchayati Raj Institution. CBSE Diksha

Ans. One third of the positions in all Panchayati Raj Institutions are reserved for women. Reservation for Scheduled Caste and Scheduled Tribes are also proof provided for at all the three levels in proportion to their population. If the states find it necessary they can also provide for reservation for the other backward classes.

It is important to note that these reservations apply not nearly to ordinary members in panchayat but also to positions of chair-persons at all three levels.

5. Write a short note on State Election Commissioners. Diksha App

Ans. The State Government is required to appoint a State Election Commissioner who would be responsible for conducting elections to the Panchayati Raj Institutions. Earlier this task was performed by the state administration which was under the control of the State Government.

Now the office of the State Election Commissioner is like the Election Commissioner of India.

However the State Election Commissioner is an independent officer and is not linked to nor is this officer under the control of the Election Commission of India.

6. Explain the main functions of panchayats?

Ans. The main functions of panchayats are as follows

- To call upon the meetings of Gram Sabha and to preside over them.
- To settle down disputes with the help of other members.
- To make plan for the welfare of the people.
- To obtain grants from the State Government for development projects of village.
- It is the mediator between the villages and the State Government.

7. 'The Panchayati Raj System improved the conditions of villages'. Discuss the achievements of Panchayati Raj Institutions. Competency Based Que

Ans. The achievements of Panchayati Raj Institutions are

- The system has succeeded in improving the conditions of villages by providing welfare schemes.
- The system has brought political awakening among the villagers as they elect their representatives and take part in decision-making.
- It has succeeded in drawing the attention of government officials to their problems.
- It has helped in community and people's participation in all round development of villages.
- It has helped the people in educating them about their rights and preserve their culture.
- It also ensures purposeful accountability and upheld the principles of democracy at the grass-root level.

8. 'Some people criticse the formation of local bodies'. Justify. Competency Based Que

Ans. Some people criticise the formation of local bodies due to following reasons

Ineffectiveness of Gram Sabha Gram Sabha which is the basic and most important unit of Panchayati Raj is the most ineffective but many people do not even know about it. Its meetings are never held regularly and very few people attend these meetings.

Lack of Financial Resources In comparison to the functions assigned to Panchayati Raj Institutions, its source of income are quite in-adequate. As a result, they fail to achieve their objectives.

Excessive Government Control There is excessive control of government over these institutions. As a result, they are not able to work properly. All the polices made by Panchayati Raj Institutions require the government's approval.

9. 'Village community prepare better citizens'? Explain. Competency Based Que

Ans. The village community prepares better citizens in the following manner

- The villagers help and co-operate one-another in the joys and sorrows of their village people.
- They are more tolerant and co-operative towards their neighbours.
- The villagers come to know about their rights and duties from the very beginning and they are very careful in performing their duties.
- They are more loyal towards the society and their country.

Long Answer Type Questions

1. What is the need and importance of local government in a democracy?

***Or* What is the importance of local government in a democracy.** Diksha App

Ans. The need and importance of local government in a democracy are as follows

- It is a government closest to the people and involves the day to day life and problems of ordinary citizen.
- It is necessary for efficient and people-friendly administration.
- It is convenient for the people in solving their problems at minimum cost.
- It gives meaning to democracy by participation and also ensures accountability.
- It is a legal platform where common citizen are involved in decision-making concerning their needs, lives and their development.
- The local bodies provides the right solution of the local problems due to participation of local people.
- Local bodies develop the qualities of citizens to awaken the political consequences and to experience the sense of liberty and equality which is essential for the success of democracy.

2. Elucidate the system of local governments in independent India.

Ans. In independent India, many steps were taken in the direction of development of local government bodies and the outcome was Community Development Programme in 1952.

This sought to promote people participation in local development in range of activities, for which a three-tier Panchayati Raj system of local government was recommended for rural areas. However, this system was not adopted by all the states and some did not had enough powers and functions to look after the local development.

They were even much dependent on the State and Central Government for financial assistance. Elections were also not held regularly and in some states the members of panchayat were even elected indirectly. In 1987, a thorough review of the functioning of Local Government Institutions was initiated. In 1989, the PK Thungon Committee recommended Constitutional recognition for the local government bodies.

A Constitutional Amendment to provide for periodic elections enlistment of appropriate functioning along with funds was recommended. In 1992, the 73rd and 74th Amendment Act was passed, which made local government mandatory for the states.

3. Discuss the provisions of 73rd Amendment Act of the Indian Constitution.

Ans. The provisions of 73rd Amendment Act of the Indian Constitution are

- All the states will have to implement the three-tier Panchayati Raj structure. The Gram Panchayat at the base, the Mandal or Taluka Panchayat or Block at the intermediary and the Zila Parishad at the apex level.
- It made the provision mandatory, for creation of Gram Sabha which comprises of all the adult voters in the panchayat area.
- The State Election Commission is to be appointed by the State Government as a autonomous body for conducting elections to rural and urban local bodies.
- Reservations of seats for SCs and STs in proportion to their population at all the three levels. One-third positions are reserved for women in all the Panchayat Institutions. Further, if necessary the states can provide reservation to OBCs also.
- All the three levels of Panchayati Raj Institution should be directly elected by the people for a term of five years. If the state legislature dissolves the panchayat before its term, fresh elections are to be conducted within six months of dis-solutions.
- The subjects which were earlier in the states list were transferred to the eleventh schedule of the Constitution for Panchayati Raj Institutions.
- The State Government is also require to appoint a State Finance Commission once in five years to review the distribution of revenues and examine the financial position of local governments.

4. Mentions some subjects included in the eleventh schedule.

***Or* Enumerate any ten subjects listed in the eleventh schedule of the Constitution.** Diksha App

Ans. Article 243G describes the power, authority and responsibilities of panchayat. The legislatures of the state may by law endow the panchayats with such powers and authority.

Some matters listed in the eleventh schedule are given below

(i) Agriculture and agricultural extension.
(ii) Minor irrigation, water management and watershed development
(iii) Rural housing
(iv) Drinking water
(v) Roads, culverts (water course)
(vi) Rural electrification
(vii) Poverty alleviation programmes

(viii) Primary and Secondary education
(ix) Technical training and vocational education
(x) Adult and non-formal education.
(xi) Libraries
(xii) Cultural activities
(xiii) Markets and fairs
(xiv) Health and sanitation
(xv) Family welfare
(xvi) Women and child development
(xvii) Social welfare
(xviii) Welfare of weaker sections especially SCs and STs
(xix) Public Distribution System
(xx) Fuel and Fodder
(xxi) Non-conventional energy resources
(xxii) Maintenance of community assets
(xxiii) Fisheries
(xxiv) Animal husbandry, dairy, poultry
(xxv) Soil forestry
(xxvi) Implementation of land reforms, soil conservation, etc
(xxvii) Khadi village and cottage industries
(xxviii) Minor forest produce
(xxix) Small scale industries including food processing

Picture Based Questions

1. Observe the picture below and answer the questions that follow.

(i) Explain 'We are the government here in the village'.
(ii) Why this statement is mentioned in the flag?
(iii) What was the first step towards local government after independence?

Ans. (i) It means the development of the village is under the control of the village panchayat who is the government in the village across the country. The presence of Panchayati Raj and Nagarpalika institutions would create atmosphere and platform for people's participation in government.

(ii) This statement is mentioned in the flag because it is the Constitutional right of the people or the village to govern themselves and this right has also been made fundamental by nature.

(iii) Community Development Programme of 1952, with a three-tier system was the first step towards local governments.

2. Study the cartoon given below and answer the question that follow.

(i) Is there any feature that strikes you in the picture given above?
(a) Presence of women in local institution
(b) Reservation of women in government jobs
(c) Women's participation in strikes
(d) All of the above

Ans. (a) Presence of women in local institution

(ii) The ......and .... Amendments have created uniformity in the structures of Panchayati Raj and Nagarpalika Institution in India.
(a) 61st and 63rd
(b) 73rd and 74th
(c) 84th and 90th
(d) None of the above

Ans. (b) 73rd and 74th

(iii) Which Constitutional Amendment provided reservation to women in panchayats?
(a) 72nd
(b) 73rd
(c) 74th
(d) 75th

Ans. (b) 73rd

(iv) What is the percentage of reservation assigned to women?
(a) 15 per cent
(b) 20 per cent
(c) 25 per cent
(d) 33 per cent

Ans. (d) 33 per cent

SELF ASSESSMENT TEST

Objective Type Questions

1. Which Article of the Constitution defines powers, authority and responsibilities of the Panchayats?
   (a) 243G (b) 243Z (c) 242G (d) 242Z
2. The district level Panchayati Raj Institution is called ....
   (a) Village Panchayat (b) Mandal Panchayat (c) Rajya Panchayat (d) Zila Panchayat
3. Who decided the roles and functions of the Gram Sabha.
   (a) Constitution itself (b) Parliament (c) State legislature (d) Governor of a state

Very Short Answer Type Questions

4. Name the states which have local governments during 1960s and 1970s.
5. What are the three organs of Gram Panchayat?
6. What is the role of State Election Commissioner in elections?
7. Mention the source of income of local bodies.
8. What is Nagar Panchayat?

Short Answer Type Questions

9. Mention the powers of village panchayat as a unit of local self-government.
10. Explain the importance of local bodies in modern times?
11. What are the main functions of Gram Sabha?
12. How does government exercise control over local bodies?
13. Why was local government not given adequate importance in the original Constitution?
14. 'In many ways, the 74th amendment is a repetition of the 73rd amendment'. Justify the statement.

Competency Based Que

Long Answer Type Questions

15. Where does the municipal corporation get its income from? Is this money sufficient to solve the problem of the citizens. Why?
16. Describe the composition and functions of Zila Parishad.
17. 'The limited autonomy of local governments affected the effectiveness of the democratic process at the grass-root level'. Justify.

Competency Based Que

09

CHAPTER

In this chapter, you will learn how the Constitution of India has worked over the past 75 years and how India has continued to be governed by the same Constitution throughout this time.

Constitution as a Living Document

▼ **YOUR STUDY GOALS**

9.1 Our Constitution

9.2 Constitutional Amendments in India so Far

9.3 Basic Structure and the Evolution of the Constitution

▼ **YOUR PRACTICE GOAL**

- Objective Type Questions (21 Qs ; MCQs, A-R, Statements, Matching, Passage Based)
- Subjective Questions (10 VSAs, 6 SAs, 4 LAs, 1 Picture Based)

- Many nations around the world have rewritten their Constitutions according to the changing situations. For example, **Soviet Union** had four Constitution in 74 years (1918, 1924, 1936 and 1977) and in 1993 Russian federation adopted new Constitution and **France** had five Constitutions (1793, 1848, 1875, 1946 and 1958).
- However, In India, the Constitution that was adopted on **26th November, 1949** and implemented on **26th January, 1950** continues to guide the functioning of the government till today.

9.1 Our Constitution

- Although our Constitution makers were very farsighted and framed a robust Constitution that provided many solutions for future situations, but no document can be such accurate that it needs no change. A Constitution must balance the contemporary needs with long term importance.
- Constitutions are **dynamic**[1], made by humans and may require revisions. They reflect dreams and aspirations of a society while serving as a framework for democratic governance.
- A Constitution faces dual challenge such as
  - Addressing current societal issues
  - Providing a framework for future governance

1 **Dynamic** It refers to some key concepts in systems that are characterised by constant change, progress or reform.

- The makers of the Indian Constitution struck a balance between the needs of the present generation and the future generation and made our **Constitution sacred and adaptable**.
- They recognised differences of opinion that may arise and the need for future modifications, ensuring the Constitution remains a living document.

Amendment of the Constitution

- The Indian Constitution is a blend of **flexibility** and **rigidity**. This feature allows it to adapt with the changing times while maintaining its core principles. It is open to changes when needed, yet protected from unnecessary or frequent modifications.
- **Flexibility of Constitution** It refers to how easily a Constitution can be changed or modified. The Constitution makers were aware that mistakes or faults might arise and they wanted to allow for easy amendments to correct these errors. Some provisions were temporary which needed to be altered later.
- **Rigidity of Constitution** It means a Constitution is harder to change, requiring special procedures. The Constitution makers had to ensure that the rights and powers of states could not be changed without their consent because Constitution was framing a federal polity. Some features formed the core principles of Constitution which needed protection from change.
- The balance between rigidity and flexibility has been maintained in the Indian Constitution through different ways of amendment.

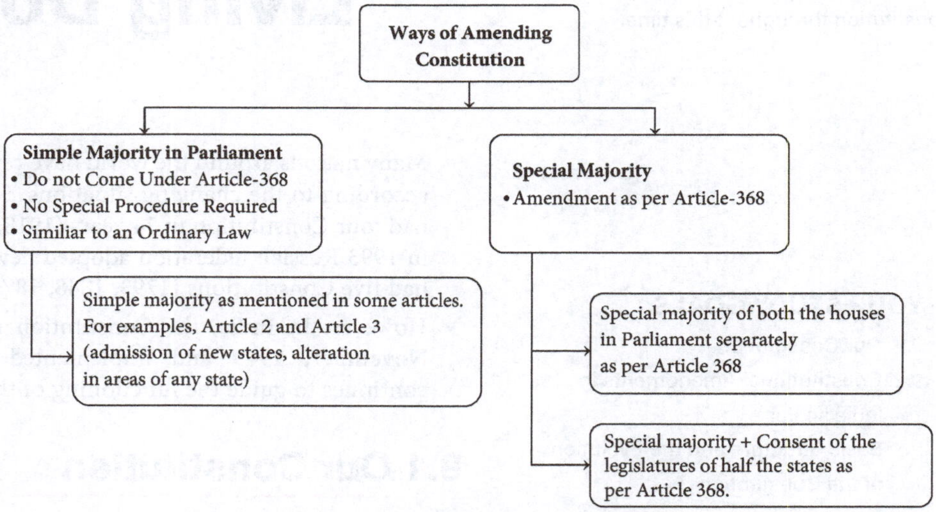

▲ *Ways of Amending Constitution*

Process of Amendments to the Constitution

There are three process of amendments to the Constitution

Simple Majority

- There are many articles in the Constitution which can be amended by simple law of the Parliament and with a simple majority.
- These parts of the Constitution are very flexible and can be amended by the Parliament without following the procedure laid down in Article 368.
- It requires a simple majority of members present and voting i.e. more than 50 per cent. For example, formation of new states, altering the areas of state, etc are matters that can be amended without Article 368.

Special Majority

- Amendment to the Constitution requires two different kinds of special majority
  - **Firstly** The bill must be supported by at least half of the total strength of the house.
  - **Secondly** The bill must also recieve 2/3rd of votes from members present and voting.
- For example, in Lok Sabha, there are 545 members. Any amendment requires support from at least 273 members and if 400 members are voting, then the bill need 2/3rd support i.e., 267 members.
- To amend the Constitution by special majority, the party in power needs support of other political parties and Parliamentarians.

Two principles dominate the procedure of amendment of the Constitution in a most modern countries.

(i) One is the principle of special majority: Some countries like USA, Russia, South Africa have employed this principle.

(ii) The other principle is the participation of people in the process of amending the Constitution. For example, Switzerland.

Ratification by States

- For certain amendments, a special majority is not enough, especially when an amendment is related to modification of an article related to distribution of powers between the States and the Central Government. In such cases, rectification and **consent of states** is required in the following manner
  - Half of the state legislatures must pass the amendment bill.
  - A simple majority in the state legislature is sufficient.
- The key points related to amendment procedure are as follows
  - The amendments **can only be initiated in Parliament.**
  - The amendments require the special majority of the Parliament without needing approval from outside agencies or commissions.
  - No ratification[2] is required for ratification of the amendment.
  - The President must give assent to the Constitutional Amendment bill and cannot send it back for re-consideration.
  - Only elected representatives can consider and take final decisions in matters related to amendment thus maintaining Parliamentary sovereignty.

Article 368

Article 368 (1) of the Constitution of India grants constituent power to make formal amendments. It empowers Parliament to amend the Constitution by way of addition, variation or repeal of any provision according to the procedure laid down therein, which is different from the procedure for ordinary legislation.

In this article, there are following two methods of amending the Constitution

- Amendment can be made by special majority of the two houses of the Parliament.
- It requires special majority of the Parliament and consent of half of the State legislatures.

Quick Test 1

1. When did Constitution of India come in force?
2. How many process of amendment to the Constitution are there?
3. Which article of Indian Constitution grants power to the Parliament to make amendments?
4. Define, what kind of majority is required to amend federal provisions?

2 **Ratification** It is the approval from the state required to validate government agreements.

9.2 Constitutional Amendments in India so Far

- The Indian Constitution has undergone **106 amendments** in its 75 years of existence. This number is high considering the tough amendment process.

History of Amendments

1970-1990 This period saw surge in amendments. Also there was dominance of congress in the Parliament.

1974-1976 Ten amendments occurred in just three years. It was a period of congress domination.

2001-2003 Again ten amendments in three years. It was a period of coalition politics and also different parties were in power in different states.

- The history of amendments tells the following facts
  - Amendments are not solely influenced by the dominance of the ruling party.
  - Every decade, except the first has seen a steady stream of amendments.
- This suggests that amendments are necessary regardless of politics or party in power.

Types of Amendments

The amendments made so far in our Constitution can be divided into the following groups

Administrative Amendments

- These require minor modifications, clarifications or explanations that don't significantly alter the original provisions.
- The following are the examples of this type of amendment
  - **15th amendment** increased the retirement age of High Court judges from 60 to 62 years.
  - **54th amendment** increased the salaries of the High Court and Supreme Court judges.
  - Extension of reserved seats for scheduled castes and tribes by ten years every decade.
  - Amendment to the **Article 74(1)** that clarified that the advice of the Council of Ministers will be binding on the President.

Amendments Relating to the Differing Interpretations of the Constitution

- The Indian Constitution has undergone amendments due to differing interpretations by the judiciary and government.
- When these interpretations clashed, the Parliament clarified the **authentic interpretation** through amendment.
- Between 1970 and 1975, Parliament frequently made amendments to address judicial interpretations.
- Key areas of disagreement in interpretations between the Parliament and judiciary are as follows
  - **Fundamental Rights Vs. Directive Principles** Balancing individual rights with state directives.
  - **Right to private property** Defining the scope of private property ownership.
  - **Parliament's power to amend** Determining the limits of Parliament's amendment authority.

Amendments Arising from Political Consensus

- The Constitution of India has undergone numerous amendments due to consensus among political parties, reflecting the evolving political philosophy and societal aspirations of our country.
- Notably, the post-1984 period saw significant amendments despite **Coalition governments**[3] because of growing consensus on key issues.

3 **Coalition government** It is a form of government in which political parties co-operates to from a government.

- Key amendments due to political consensus are as follows
  - **52nd amendment (1985) Anti-defection law,** which made it illegal to switch parties after election.
  - **61st amendment (1989)** Bringing down the minimum age for voting from 21 to 18 years.
  - **73rd and 74th amendments** Strengthened local self-governance through Panchayati Raj Institutions.
  - **77st, 81st and 82nd amendments** Expanded the scope of reservation in jobs and admissions.

Controversial Amendments

- The amendments in the Indian Constitution between 1970 to 1980 were highly contentious and sparked intense legal and political debate.
- The opposition parties saw these changes, particularly the **38th, 39th and 42nd amendments** as attempts by the ruling party to undermine the Constitution, because these three amendments were made in the background of internal emergency declared in June, 1975.

42nd Amendment Act, 1976

- Extended the term of the Lok Sabha from five to six years.
- Introduced fundamental duties.
- Restricted the judicial review powers.
- Over-rode the Supreme Court's ruling given in the Kesavananda case.
- These amendments were passed during internal emergency of 1975 and many opposition MPs were jailed at that time.
- However, the 1977 elections brought a new government which repealed most of these changes through the **43rd and 44th amendments.**

9.3 Basic Structure and the Evolution of the Constitution

- The theory of the basic structure of the Indian Constitution was established by the landmark case of **Kesavananda Bharati** (1973).
- The case has profoundly impacted the evolution of the Constitution in the following ways
  - This ruling set limits on the amendment power of the Parliament and states that no amendment can compromise the basic framework of the Constitution.
  - The judiciary has final say in determining if an amendment breaches the basic structure.
  - Parliament can amend any part of the Constitution, but not violate its basic structure.
  - The theory of basic structure is itself an example of **living Constitution**. This theory is not mentioned in the Constitution, rather it has evolved from judicial interpretations.

Thus, in this case judicial interpretation effectively amended the Constitution without a formal amendment.

Contribution of Judiciary in the Evolution of the Constitution

The Indian Constitution has evolved significantly since 1973 through debates, arguments and practical politics, and in this evolution process the Supreme Court played a crucial role in shaping its interpretations.

Key Contributions of Judicial Interpretations

- **Reservation Limits** The Supreme Court ruled that reservations in job and educational institution cannot exceed 50 per cent of total seats.
- **Creamy Layer Concept** Excludes creamy layer category from other backward classes from benefits under reservation.
- **Informal Amendments** Judicial interpretation has effectively amended the Constitution by clarifying provisions related to Right to Education, Right to Life and Liberty, Right to Establish and manage minority educational institutions.

Constitution as a Living Document

- The Constitution is a dynamic document and it has the ability to respond to changing situations.
- It is open to interpretations and allows for evolving and understanding.
- Our Constitution protects democracy and at the same time allows for evolution of new practices and ideas that keep evolving in a democracy.
- It maintains checks and balances among the organs of the government and uphold the **rule of law**.

Contribution of the Judiciary

- The success of the Indian Constitution lies in resolving tensions between the judiciary and Parliament, particularly regarding the power to make laws and amendments. The judiciary has emphasised that pro-people measures must adhere to Constitutional frameworks and legal procedures to prevent arbitrary power use.
- The basic struture theory introduced by the suprem court in the Kesavananda Bharati case puts emphasis on understanding the **spirit of the Constitution** rather than literal meaning of the text part.
- This approach has ensured that the Constitution remains a living document and responsive to the changing circumstances of the nation.

Maturity of Political Leadership

- The political parties, political leaders, the government and the Parliament accepted the idea of basic struture of the Constitution despite several controversy between 1967 and 1973.
- After the Kesavananda ruling, the parliament tried to reassert its supremacy through the 42nd Amendment Act but the court again reiterated its stand in the **Minerva Mills case** (1980). Thereafter, the Parliament and the execuitve realised that a balanced and long term view is necessary.

Quick Test 2

1. How many times the Indian Constitution has been amended in 75 years?
2. In which case was the theory of basic structure given?
3. Define, 52nd amendment of the Indian Constitution.
4. Which amendment extended the term of Lok Sabha from five to six years?

Mind Map

CONSTITUTION AS A LIVING DOCUMENT

1 Key Characteristics

Dynamic and Adaptable
- It can be modified as per the need.
- It offers flexibility.

2 Amendment of the Constitution

- It is open to changes when needed.
- Adapt to changing times while maintaining its core principles.
- **Flexibility of Constitution** Easily a Constitution can be changed or modified.
- **Rigidity of Constitution** A Constitution is harder to change, requiring special procedures.

3 Amendment Process

Simple Majority
- It requires a simple majority of members present and voting.

Special Majority
- Require
  - 50% of total house strength.
  - 2/3rd of members present and voting.

Ratification by States
- Requires consent from half the states legislatures.
- This type of bill can only be initiated in Parliament.

4 History

CI 1970-1990
- Dominated by Congress in the Parliament.

1974-1976
- Ten amendment occured in just three years.

2001 - 2003
- It was a period of coalition politics.

5 Types of Amendment

- **Administrative** These are minor changes (e.g. raising retirement age for judges)
- **Interpretation Conflict** It balances judiciary and government views (e.g. Fundamental Rights Vs. Directive Principles)
- **Political Consensus** Broad agreements due to political consensus (e.g. 73rd and 74th amendments)
- **Controversial Amendments** These amendments were made during the emergency period. (e.g. 42nd amendment- extended the team of Lok Sabha to 6 years.

6 Basic Structure of Doctrine

- Introduced in Kesavananda Bharati case (1973).
- Example of contribution
  - Reception limits
  - Creamy layer's concept
  - Right to education expanded

7 Role of Judiciary

- It is a dynamic document.
- Maintains checks and balances.
- Shapes the Constitution with judicial interpretation.
- Ensures pro-people measures align with Constitution.
- Evolution of new practices and idea that keep it evolving.

Contribution of the Judiciary
- Regarding the power to make laws and amendment.
- Ensure that the Constitution remains a living document and responsive to the changing circumstances.

Maturity of Political Leadership
- Accepted the idea of basic structure of the Constitution despite several controversy between 1967 and 1973.
- After the Kesavananda ruling, the Parliament tried to re-assert its supremacy through the 42nd Amendment Act.

TIMELINE FOR THE EVOLUTION OF THE BASIC STRUCTURE

- Constitution 1st Amendment
- Pre Golak Nath
- Golak Nath v. State of Punjab
- Constitution 24th Amendment
- Kesvananda Bharati v. State of Kerala

Doctrine of Basic Structure of Constitution

NCERT Folder

Intext Questions

1. After reading the section given in NCERT (from page no. 197 to 199). What would you say about the following? (Pg 199) (Modified)

(i) The Constitution is like any other law. It simply tells us what are the rules and regulations governing the government.

(ii) The Constitution is the expression of the will of the people, so there must be a provision to change the Constitution after every ten or fifteen years.

(iii) The Constitution is a statement of the philosophy of the country. It can never be changed.

(iv) The Constitution is a sacred document. Therefore any talk of changing it is against democracy.

Ans. (i) This statement is partially true but oversimplified. While the Constitution does lay down the rules and regulations for governance, it is much more than just a set of laws.

It is the foundational document that defines the structure, powers and responsibilities of the government and guaranteed rights to citizens.

It provides a framework for governance and democracy and its flexibility allows for changes over time to meet the evolving needs of society.

(ii) This statement is not entirely correct. While the Constitution is indeed an expression of the will of the people, it does not require amendments in every ten or fifteen years.

A good Constitution should be stable enough to provide continuity while also being adaptable to societal changes.

India's Constitution provides for amendments when necessary, but it is not designed to be frequently altered. Amendments should be made when required to address specific needs, not on a fixed schedule.

(iii) This statement is not accurate. While the Constitution does reflect the philosophy and ideals of the country, it is not a static document.

The Constitution was designed with flexibility in mind. The framers understood that societal needs change over time and they included provisions for amendments. It is not meant to remain unchanged forever; instead, it is a living document that can evolve to meet the demands of the future.

(iv) This statement is not correct. While the Constitution is certainly a sacred document in the sense that it embodies the foundational values of the country, it is not unalterable. Democracy is about responding to the needs and will of the people. The Constitution allows for amendments to reflect changes in society, ensuring that it remains relevant and effective.

Therefore, discussing or implementing changes to the Constitution, when necessary, is not against democracy but rather a part of its ongoing evolution.

2. For making the following amendments to the Constitution of India, what conditions need to be fulfilled? Place a tick mark in the chart wherever applicable. (Pg 204)

Subject of amendment	Special Ratification	Majority by States
Citizenship Clause		
Right to Freedom of Religion		
Changes in the Union List		
Changes in State Boundaries		
Provision regarding Election Commission		

Ans.

Subject of amendment	Special Ratification	Majority by States
Citizenship Clause	✗	✗
Right to Freedom of Religion	✓	✗
Changes in the Union List	✓	✗
Changes in State Boundaries	✗	✗
Provision regarding Election Commission	✓	✗

3. Find out the amendments about the Right to Education (RTE) and the Goods and Services Tax (GST). What do you think is the importance of these amendments? (Pg 210)

Ans. **The Right to Education Act** The Right to Education (RTE) Act was introduced in 2002 to ensure free and compulsory education for children between the ages of 6 and 14. The 86th Constitutional Amendment was a crucial step in enshrining the right to education in the Indian Constitution.

Importance of this amendment are as follows

- The inclusion of the Right to Education as a Fundamental Right guaranteed that every child, regardless of socio-economic background, would have access to education.
- It empowered the state and government to focus on expanding educational facilities and improving the quality of education.
- This amendment helped to address inequalities in access to education and aimed to eliminate barriers to education such as child labor, poverty and discrimination.

GST The 101st Constitutional Amendment laid the foundation for the implementation of the Goods and Services Tax (GST) in India in 2016. GST is a single indirect tax levied on the manufacture, sale and consumption of goods and services across the country. It aimed to streamline the tax system, eliminate the cascading effect of taxes and create a unified market in India.

Importance of this amendment are as follows

- It simplified the tax structure in India by replacing multiple indirect taxes like excise duty, VAT and service tax with a single unified tax.
- It made the tax system more transparent and efficient, reducing the complexity of tax administration.
- It facilitated the creation of a common national market, thereby improving interstate trade.
- It improved tax compliance and broadened the tax base, contributing to economic growth.

4. State whether the following statements are correct or not (Pg 213)

(i) After the basic structure ruling, Parliament does not have power to amend the Constitution.

(ii) The Supreme Court has given a clear list of the basic features of our Constitution, which cannot be amended.

(iii) Judiciary has the power to decide whether an amendment violates basic structure or not.

(iv) The Kesavananda Bharati ruling has set clear limits on Parliament's power to amend the Constitution.

Ans. (i) This statement is incorrect. The basic structure ruling in 1973 did not strip Parliament of its power to amend the Constitution entirely. Parliament still has the power to amend the Constitution, but this power got limited by the basic structure doctrine. This means that Parliament cannot amend the Constitution in a way that alters or destroys its fundamental features or basic structure.

(ii) This statement is incorrect. While the Kesavananda Bharati case established the basic structure of the Constitution, but the Supreme Court did not provide an exhaustive or fixed list of the basic structure of the Constitution. Instead, the court mentioned certain features like secularism, democracy, rule of law, judicial review, etc., but left it open-ended, implying that the basic structure can evolve over time based on judicial interpretation.

(iii) This statement is correct. Under the Kesavananda Bharati ruling, the judiciary, particularly the Supreme Court, has the power to review and decide if a Constitutional Amendment violates the basic structure of the Constitution. This judicial review power ensures that any amendment passed by Parliament is consistent with the basic principles of the Constitution.

(iv) This statement is correct. The Kesavananda Bharati case (1973) established that Parliament can amend the Constitution but cannot alter or destroy its basic structure. The ruling set a limit on the extent of amendments that Parliament can make, ensuring that certain fundamental aspects of the Constitution remain unchanged.

Exercise

1. Choose the correct statement from the following.

A Constitution needs to be amended from time to time because,

(i) Circumstances change and require suitable changes in the Constitution.

(ii) A document written at one point of time becomes outdated after sometime.

(iii) Every generation should have a Constitution of its own liking.

(iv) It must reflect the philosophy of the existing government.

Ans. (i) A Constitution needs to be amended from time to time because circumstances change and require suitable changes in the Constitution.

2. Write True/false against the following statements.

(i) The President cannot send back an amendment bill for re-consideration of the Parliament.

(ii) Elected representatives alone have the power to amend the Constitution.

(iii) The Judiciary cannot initiate the process of Constitutional Amendment but can effectively change the Constitution by interpreting it differently.

(iv) The Parliament can amend any section of the Constitution.

Ans. (i) True (ii) True
(iii) True (iv) True

3. Which of the following are involved in the amendment of the Indian Constitution? In what ways are they involved?

(i) Voters **(ii) President of India**
(iii) State Legislatures **(iv) Parliament**
(v) Governors **(vi) Judiciary**

Ans. (ii) **President of India** He/she has to give assent to the amendment bill to become an act.

(iii) **State Legislatures** Half of the state legislature has to vote in favour of the amendment bill along with a special majority in the Parliament.

(iv) **Parliament** It has to initiate an amendment bill. In both the houses of Parliament, the amendment bill will be passed only if half of the total strength of house voting in favour of the bill and the supporter of the bill must constitute two-third majority present and voting.

(vi) **Judiciary** It has interpreted various provisions that concern Right to Education, Right to Life, etc to an informal amendment. It helps in the matter by balancing the spirit and letter of the Constitutions.

4. You have read in this chapter that the 42nd amendment was one of the most controversial amendments so far. Which of the following were the reasons for this controversy?

(i) It was made during national emergency and the declaration of that emergency was itself controversial.
(ii) It was made without the support of special majority.
(iii) It was made without ratification by state legislatures.
(iv) It contained provisions, which were controversial.

Ans. (i) It was made during national emergency, and the declaration of that emergency was itself controversial.

(iv) It contained provisions which were controversial.

5. Which of the following is not a reasonable explanation of the conflict between the legislature and the judiciary over different amendments?

(i) Different interpretations of the Constitution are possible.
(ii) In a democracy, debates and differences are natural.
(iii) Constitution has given higher importance to certain rules and principles and also allowed for amendment by special majority.
(iv) Legislature cannot be entrusted to protect the rights of the citizens.
(v) Judiciary can only decide the Constitutionality of a particular law; cannot resolve political debates about its need.

Ans. (iv) Legislature cannot be entrusted to protect the rights of citizens.

6. Identify the correct statements about the theory of basic structure. Correct the incorrect statements.

(i) Constitution specifies the basic tenets.
(ii) Legislature can amend all parts of the Constitution except the basic structure.
(iii) Judiciary has defined which aspects of the Constitution can be termed as the basic structure and which cannot.
(iv) This theory found its first expression in the Keshavananda Bharati case and has been discussed in subsequent judgements.
(v) This theory has increased the powers of the judiciary and has come to be accepted by different political parties and the government.

Ans. (i) **Incorrect** The Constitution does not specify the basic tenets as it does not mention anywhere about the basic structure. This theory is given by the judiciary of India that looks into the spirit of the Constitution.

(ii) Correct

(iii) **Incorrect** The judiciary has not explicitly defined the basic structure of the Constitution. However, it has given various interpretations from time to time in its judgements.

(iv) Correct

(v) Correct

7. From the information that many amendments were made during 2000-2003, which of the following conclusions would you draw?

(i) Judiciary did not interfere in the amendments made during this period.
(ii) One political party had a strong majority during this period.
(iii) There was strong pressure from the public in favour of certain amendments.
(iv) There were no real differences among the parties during this time.
(v) The amendments were of a non-controversial nature and parties had an agreement on the subject of amendments.

Ans. (v) The amendments were of a non-controversial nature and parties had an agreement on the subject of amendments.

8. Explain the reasons for requiring special majority for amending the Constitution.

Ans. Special majority is required in the different manner.

(i) Half of the total strength of the house, who are in favor of the amendment bill.

(ii) Two-third of these supporters, who participate in voting.

(iii) Both the houses of the Parliament must pass the bill separately also.

The above mentioned majorities are required because

- To take some opposition parties into confidence due to majority.
- On the issues of distribution of powers, some articles are needed to be consulted with the states.
- Through wide consensus and limited participation of states, the Constitution can be amended.

To maintain partial flexibility and rigidity, consent of half of the states and simple majority of State Legislature is sufficient.

9. Many amendments to the Constitution of India have been made due to different interpretations upheld by the judiciary and Parliament. Explain with examples.

Ans. Certain amendments have been made as a result of the different interpretations upheld by the judiciary and the Parliament. For e.g.

(i) The most prominent among them was related to the basic structure of the Constitution. It led to 42nd amendment to the Constitution that took place during the period of emergency.

(ii) Prior to this, in its judgement in the Kesavanada Bharati case in 1973, the Supreme Court had upheld certain features of the Constitution to be fundamental in nature and making up the basic structure of the Constitution. It also placed the judiciary as the final authority in interpreting the Constitution and its basic structure has prohibited the legislature from passing any amendments that were contrary to this.

10. If amending power is with the elected representatives, judiciary should not have the power to decide the validity of amendments. Do you agree? Give reasons in 100 words.

Ans. I do not agree with the statement because the judiciary is authorised to interpret the Constitution. It is more acquainted with the fundamentals of the Constitution than any other body. This power of judiciary checks the inappropriate and arbitrary use of the amendments by any political party that is in power. It also defends the Fundamental Rights of the people.

Judiciary as an institution involved actively in interpreting the provisions of the Constitution while pronouncing its judgements. Further, the Supreme Court is the guardian of the Constitution and protector of the Fundamental Rights, as specified by the provisions of the Constitution.

Exam Pattern Questions

Objective Type Questions

Multiple Choice Questions (MCQs)

1. Why is the Indian Constitution a living document?

(a) It has existence today (b) It can be amended
(c) It is non changeable (d) All of these

2. Which of the following statements is not true?

Competency Based Que; Diksha App

(a) The Constitution provides the framework of the government.
(b) The Constitution is an unalterable document.
(c) The Constitution reflects the dreams and aspirations of the society.
(d) Indian Constitution is a mix of rigidity and flexibility.

3. Which article of the Indian Constitution lays down the procedure to amend the Constitution? **Diksha App**

(a) Article 370 (b) Article 352
(c) Article 368 (d) Article 1

4. Which of the following statements is not true with respect to the Indian Constitution?

Competency Based Que; Diksha App

(a) The Constitution accepts the necessity of modifications according to the changing needs of the society.
(b) Flexibility of interpretations.
(c) Constitution fulfills the aspirations of the people.
(d) Constitution is extremely rigid and static.

5. Which of the following statements is not true?

Competency Based Que

(a) State legislatures can initiate a Constitutional Amendment.
(b) Only Parliament can initiate Constitutional Amendments.
(c) Some provisions of the Constitution can be amended by a simple majority in the Parliament.
(d) There are provisions in the Constitution that can be amended by a special majority.

6. Some amendments come under Article-368 while other amendments are just like ordinary laws. Which of the following is NOT TRUE regarding amendment of the Constitution under Article -368?

(a) Requires special majority of both the houses of Parliament.
(b) Requires simple majority in half of state legislature if amendment is related to federal provisions.
(c) Requires simple majority in both the houses of Parliament.
(d) Some times require special majority in Parliament and consent of half of the state legislatures.

7. Given below are two statements

Statement 1 Amendments arising from political consensus are minor modifications, clarifications, or explanations that don't significantly alter the original provisions.

Statement 2 15th amendment that increased the retirement age of High Court judges from 60 to 62 years is a type of administrative amendment.

In the light of the above statements, choose the correct answer from the options given below

(a) Both Statement I and Statement II are true.
(b) Both Statement I and Statement II are false.
(c) Statement I is true, but Statement II is false.
(d) Statement I is false, but Statement II is true.

8. Which Constitutional Amendments brought down the minimum age for voting from 21 to 18 years?

(a) 73rd amendment
(b) 52nd amendment
(c) 61st amendment
(d) 74th amendment

9. Which of the following amendments has been the most controversial amendment so far? **Diksha App**

(a) 42nd amendment
(b) 44th amendment
(c) 73rd amendment
(d) 74th amendment

10. Which of the following statements is not true with respect to the basic structure theory of the Constitution? **Diksha App**

(a) It has set specific limits to parliament's power to amend the Constitution.
(b) It places the judiciary as the final authority in deciding Constitutionality of the amendment.
(c) Basic structure theory was pronounced in the Kesavanand Bharati case.
(d) Parliament is the final authority to decide the basic structure of the Constitution.

11. Which of the following statements is not correct with respect to the Supreme Court ruling in the Kesavananda Bharati case?

Competency Based Que; Diksha App

(a) Basic structure doctrine was pronounced.
(b) The Supreme Court ruled that certain parts of the Constitution cannot be amended.
(c) In the Minerva Mills case Supreme Court reaffirmed the Kesavananda Bharati ruling.
(d) By Kesavananda Bharati ruling Parliament got absolute power to amend any part of the Constitution.

12. Which of the following statements is not true?

Competency Based Qu; eDiksha App

(a) In the Minerva Mills case (1980) Supreme Court repeated the basic structure doctrine.
(b) Supreme Court ruling in the Minerva Mills case was contrary to Kesavananda Bharati's case judgment.
(c) There was consensus among political leaders, political parties and government regarding basic structure doctrine.
(d) Basic structure theory sets limits on Parliament's power to amend the Constitution.

13. Constitution as a living document does not imply that.........

Diksha App

(a) it keeps responding to the situations and circumstances.
(b) it responds to experiences.
(c) it's dynamic and open to interpretation.
(d) it's static.

14. Match the List I with List II

List I		List II	
A.	Article 2	1.	Parliament can make law to increase the area of any state.
B.	Article 3	2.	Parliament can admit new state into Union of India.
C.	Article 74	3.	Parliament amend the Constitution by special majority.
D.	Article 368	4.	Advice of Council of Minister will be binding on the President.

Codes

	A	B	C	D		A	B	C	D
(a)	1	2	3	4	(b)	2	3	4	1
(c)	2	1	4	3	(d)	2	3	1	4

Assertion-Reason Questions

Directions (Q.Nos. 15-19) In the questions given below, there are two statements marked as Assertion (A) and Reason (R). Read the statements and choose the correct option. **Competency Based Que**

Codes

(a) Both A and R are true and R is the correct explanation of A.
(b) Both A and R are true, but R is not the correct explanation of A.
(c) A is true, but R is false.
(d) A is false, but R is true.

15. Assertion (A) The Indian Constitution has undergone numerous amendments since its adoption in 1949.

Reason (R) The Constitution's dynamic nature allows it to respond to changing situations.

16. Assertion (A) The Indian Constitution is entirely rigid.

Reason (R) Article 368 allows Parliament to amend the Constitution.

17. Assertion (A) The Supreme Court plays a crucial role in shaping the Indian Constitution's interpretations.

Reason (R) Basic structure of the Constitution theory was inserted in the Constitution through an amendment.

18. Assertion (A) The theory of basic structure has impacted the Indian Constitution's evolution.

Reason (R) The Parliament can use its amending power in limits as mentioned under the basic structure theory.

19. Assertion (A) The Indian Constitution protects democracy by allowing for the evolution of new practices.

Reason (R) The Constitution prioritises individual rights over national interests.

Passage Based Questions

20. Read the given passage and answer the following questions.

"Those who are dissatisfied with the Constitution need only two-third majority. If they are not able to obtain even that their dissatisfaction with the Constitution cannot be deemed to be shared by the general public".

Dr. Ambedkar is talking here not only of Parliamentary majority. He refers to 'sharing (of the views) by the general public'. This indicates that behind the majority there is the principle of public opinion that governs decision-making.

(i) **According to Dr. Ambedkar what is required for dissatisfaction with the Constitution to be considered shared by the general public?**
(a) A simple majority in Parliament
(b) A two third majority in Parliament
(c) Endorsement from the Supreme Court
(d) Approval from the President

(ii) **According to Dr. Ambedkar , what principle governs decision-making behind the Parliamentary majority?**
(a) Principle of Judicial review
(b) Principle of Public opinion
(c) Principle of Parliamentary supremacy
(d) Principle of Federalism

(iii) **When is the special majority required?**

21. Read the given passage and answer the following questions.

Even within the Constituent Assembly, there were some members who felt that this constitution was not suited to the Indian situation: "The ideals on which this ..... Constitution is framed have no manifest relation to the spirit of India. .... this Constitution .... would not prove suitable and would break down soon after being brought into operation". Lakshminarayan Sahu.

(i) **Who expressed dissatisfaction with the Constitution in the Constituent Assembly?**
(a) Dr. B.R. Ambedkar (b) Jawaharlal Nehru
(c) Lakshminarayan Sahu (d) Mahatma Gandhi

(ii) **What was Lakshminarayan Sahu's concern about the Constitution?**
(a) It gave too much power to the states
(b) It did not adequately protect individual rights
(c) It was not suited to the Indian situation
(d) It was too long and complex

(iii) **What did Lakshminarayan Sahu predict would happen to the Constitution?**
(a) It would be amended frequently
(b) It would remain unchanged
(c) It would be replaced soon
(d) It would break down soon after being brought into operation

(iv) **What aspect of the Constitution did Lakshminarayan Sahu feel was lacking?**
(a) Western ideals
(b) Indian spirit
(c) Economic principles
(d) Social justice

Answers

1. (b) It can be amended
2. (b) The Constitution is an unalterable document.
3. (c) Article 368
4. (d) Constitution is extremely rigid and static.
5. (a) State legislatures can initiate a Constitutional Amendment.
6. (c) Requires simple majority in both the houses of Parliament.
7. (d) Statement I is false, but Statement II is true.
8. (c) 61st amendment 9. (a) 42nd amendment
10. (d) Parliament is the final authority to decide the basic structure of the Constitution.
11. (d) By Kesavananda Bharati ruling Parliament got absolute power to amend any part of the Constitution.
12. (b) Supreme Court ruling in the Minerva Mills case was contrary to Kesavananda Bharati's case judgment.
13. (d) it's static.
14. (c) 2 1 4 3
15. (a) Both A and R are true, and R is the correct explanation for A.
16. (d) A is false, but R is true.
17. (c) A is true, but R is false.
18. (a) Both A and R are true and R is the correct explanation for A.
19. (c) A is true, but R is false.
20. (i) (b) A two third majority in Parliament
(ii) (b) Principle of public opinion
(iii) Special majority is required to pass the Constitutional Amendments Bill and various other bills concerning division of powers between the centre and the states.
21. (i) (c) Lakshminarayan Sahu
(ii) (c) It was not suited to the Indian situation
(iii) (d) It would break down soon after being brought into operation
(iv) (b) Indian spirit

Subjective Questions

Very Short Answer Type Questions

1. How the framers wanted the Constitution to be amended?

Ans The framers of our Constitution wanted the Constitution to be 'flexible' as well as 'rigid'. Flexible means open to changes and rigid means resistant to changes. The framers were aware that there may be some faults or mistakes in the Constitution and it could not be totally free of errors.

2. Name the amendments which can be passed by simple majority.

Ans. The amendments which can be passed by simple majority are formation of new states, altering the boundary or area of a state, etc.

3. What is simple majority?

Ans. A bill passed by more than 50 per cent of the members present and voting in the house is called a simple majority.

4. Who enjoys the power to amend the Constitution and how?

Ans. The Parliament of India enjoys the power to amend the Constitution by the procedure laid down in Article 368 i.e:

- By simple majority in Parliament.
- By special majority in both the houses of Parliament.
- By special majority of half of the states.

5. When is the ratification of states is necessary for amendments?

Ans. When an amendment aims to modify an article related to distribution of powers between the States and the Central Government or articles related to representation, the consent of half of the states is necessary.

6. Why the reservations of SCs and STs in the legislature is always extended by amendments?

Ans. The reservation of SCs and STs in the legislature is always extended, in order to ensure fair representation of these castes in the legislature.

7. State any three contents of amendments so far.

Ans The contents of amendments are

- Differing interpretations.
- Amendments through political consensus.
- Controversial amendments.

8. Which is the most controversial amendment in the history of India and why?

Ans The 42nd Amendment Act, 1976 is the most controversial amendment of India because it was passed during emergency. This amendment sought to make basic changes in many crucial parts of the Constitution.

9. State the provision of 61st Amendment Act.

Ans. The 61st Amendment Act brought down the minimum age of voting from 21 to 18 years.

10. How does the Constitution continue to serve the country even after so many years?

Ans. The reason for the Constitution continuity to serve the country even after so many years is that our Constitution accepts the necessary modifications according to changing needs of the society and for the future generations.

Short Answer Type Questions

1. 'Constitution is not static, it is a living document'. justify the statement by giving these arguments.

Competency Based Que; Diksha App

Ans. Nations need to rewrite and amend the Constitution according to changed circumstances. Like a living being, the Constitution keeps representing the situation and circumstances arising from time to time. Even after so many changes in society, the Constitution continues to work effectively because of this ability to be dynamic, to be open.

In a democracy, practices and ideas keep evolving over time. A Constitution that protects democracy and yet allows for the evolution of new practices is more durable. Over hundreds of amendments in our Constitution prove its dynamism Constitution fulfills the changing aspirations of the people

2. What are the main characteristics of the method of amendment to the Constitution of India?

Ans. The main characteristics of the method of amendment to the Constitution of India are as follows

- Each and every part of the Constitution can be amended but the basic structure of the Constitution cannot be changed.
- Amendment bill can be introduced in either house of the Parliament.
- Article 368 of the Constitution which deals with procedure of amendment can be amended.
- The power of initiating the procedure lies with the Parliament and the states have not been given such powers.
- No time limit is fixed for ratification by states. There is no Constitutional limitations on their power of delay.

3. What special majorities are required to amend the Constitution? What is meant by ratification by states?

Ans Amendment to the Constitution requires two different kinds of special majorities

- Firstly, those voting in favour of the amendment bill should constitute atleast half of the total strength of that house.
- Secondly, the supporters of the amendment bill must also constitute two-third of members taking part in voting.
- When an amendment aims to modify an article related to distribution of powers between the States and the Central Government or articles related to representation, it is necessary to consult the states and they give their consent by passing bill through state legislature. This is known as ratification by states.

4. The ruling of Kesavananda Bharati case has contributed to the evolution of the Constitution Explain.
Competency Based Que; Diksha (Modified)

Ans. The ruling of Kesavananda Bharati case has contributed to the evolution of the Constitution by following ways

- It has set specific limits on the Parliament's power to amend the Constitution.
- It allows the Parliament to amend any and all parts of the Constitution, within the limits of basic structure of the Constitution.
- It places the judiciary as the final authority in deciding the violation of basic structure by amendments and what constitutes the basic structure.

5. Mention any two factors which make the Constitution of India a living document.

Ans. The factors which make the Constitution of India a living document are

- The required modification can be made as per the changing needs and aspirations of the society.
- There has been enough flexibility of interpretations. Both political parties and judicial rulings have shown majority and flexibility in implementing the Constitution.
- The Indian Constitution has been amended 106 times in the 75 years. The various amendments were made not only due to political considerations but it was also made due to the need of the situation and exigencies from time to time.

6. Constitution of India is based on a vision. Comment.

Ans. When the Constitution was made, the leaders and the people of our country shared a common vision of India. The vision was dignity and freedom of the individuals, social and economic equality, well-being of the people and unity based on national integrity.

Therefore, the Constitution based on this vision has remained an object of respect and authority even after, more than half-a century.

Long Answer Type Questions

1. Discuss the processes of amendments to the Constitution.

Or Explain three different procedures to amend the Constitution **Diksha App**

Ans. There are three processes of amendments to the Constitution

(i) **Simple Majority** There are many articles in the Constitution which can be amended by simple law of the Parliament and with a simple majority. These parts of the Constitution are very flexible and can be amended by the Parliament without following the procedure laid down in Article 368.

It requires a simple majority of members present and voting i.e. more than 50 per cent. For examples, formation of new states, altering the areas of state, etc are matters that can be amended without Article 368.

(ii) **Special Majority** Amendment to the Constitution requires two different kinds of special majorities. Firstly, those voting in favour of the amendment bill should constitute atleast half of the total strength of that house.

Secondly, the supporters of the amendment bill must also constitute two-third of members taking part in voting. Both houses of Parliament must pass the amendment bill separately in the same manner.

This means that unless there is sufficient consensus over the proposed amendment, it cannot be passed. So, the basic principle behind the amending procedure is to take the opposition into confidence.

(iii) **Ratification by States** When an amendment aims to modify an article related to distribution of powers between the states and the central government, or articles related to representation, it is necessary to consult the states and their consent.

In order to upheld the principle of federalism, the Constitution ensures that the legislatures of half of the states have to pass the amendment bill before it comes into effect.

In this way, Fundamental Rights are also protected. Further, the consent of only half the states is required and simple majority of the states legislature is sufficient.

2. Mention any three criticisms against the procedure of amendments in the Constitution.

Ans The methods of amendments are criticised on the following grounds

(i) The power of initiating an amendment lies only with the Parliament, the states have not been given any such power of initiating amendments. Besides, the approval of the states are not essential for all the amendments.

(ii) The procedure suffers from other defect such as no time limit is fixed in the Constitution for the approval of the states. They may take as much time as they like. There is no Constitutional limitation on their power to delay.

(iii) Nothing about the veto power of the President is given in the procedure of amendments. It is also not mentioned in the Constitution that an amendment which is approved by the states require the assent of the President or not.

(iv) The President cannot send the amendment bill for reconsideration to the Parliament, and has to give his assent.

3. What were the major areas of contention between Parliament and the judiciary? How were issues resolved?

Ans. The major areas of contention between Parliament and the judiciary are as follows

- Relationship between the Fundamental Rights and Directive Principles of State Policy.
- Social change demands the implementation of Directive Principles and it sometimes leads to putting restrictions on Fundamental Rights.
- Issues related to the right to property became a bone of contention.
- Scope of Parliament's power to amend the Constitution.

These issues were resolved by

- Basic structure doctrine was given by the Supreme Court after Kesavananda Bharati 1973 judgment and repeated in the Minerva Mills case 1980

4. Judiciary plays important role in the growth of the Indian Constitution. **Competency Based Que**

Ans. There has been controversies between the judiciary and the Parliament in making and amending the laws, but the judiciary has always guided the Parliament to function within the framework of the Constitution and not to bypass the laws.

The success or working of the Indian Constitution lies in resolving these tensions, which was visualised in the famous Keshavananda Bharati ruling and the invention of basic structure.

- The judiciary has been entitled to the responsibility of interpretating the Constitution and to uphold its supremacy and the power of the judiciary has checked the inappropriate and arbitrary use of amendments by any political party that is in power and the Fundamental Rights of the people.
- Judiciary as an institution involved actively in interpreting the provisions of the Constitution while pronouncing judgements.
- The Supreme Court as the guardian of the Constitution have safeguarded its violation and upheld its supremacy in various judgements like the Keshavanada Bharti case, Golaknath case, etc.

Picture Based Question

1. Study the picture given below and answer the questions that follow.

"If those who are dissatisfied with the Constitution have only to obtain a 2/3 majority and if they cannot obtain even (that)..., their dissatisfaction with the Constitution cannot be deemed to be shared by the general public."

(i) What happens if those dissatisfied with the Constitution cannot secure a 2/3 majority?

(a) Their dissatisfaction is considered justified
(b) Their dissatisfaction cannot be regarded as shared by the general public
(c) The Constitution must be amended
(d) The public will eventually agree with their dissatisfaction

Ans. (b) Their dissatisfaction cannot be regarded as shared by the general public

(ii) According to the image, what does the 2/3 majority signify?

(a) The need for an agreement among states
(b) The general will of the people
(c) A requirement for Constitutional Amendments or changes
(d) A decision by the judiciary

Ans. (c) A requirement for Constitutional Amendments or changes

(iii) What is the significance of "sharing by the general public" in the above image statement?

(a) It indicates that public opinion should influence decisions on Constitutional matters
(b) It shows that public opinion is irrelevant to Constitutional changes
(c) It suggests that public opinion must be enforced through law
(d) It means that only Parliament's majority counts, not public opinion

Ans. (a) It indicates that public opinion should influence decisions on Constitutional matters

(iv) Identify the speaker of the above lines.

(a) Jawaharlal Nehru (b) Mahatma Gandhi
(c) Dr. B.R. Ambedkar (d) Sardar Patel

Ans. (c) Dr. B.R. Ambedkar

SELF ASSESSMENT TEST

Objective Type Questions

1. Which amendment was specifically made to restore the Constitutional balance after the 42nd amendment?
   (a) 40th amendment (b) 43rd amendment
   (c) 44th amendment (d) 45th amendment
2. Which amendments were related to the anti-defection law?
   (a) 52nd and 91st amendments (b) 61st and 77th amendments
   (c) 73rd and 74th amendments (d) 81st and 82nd amendments
3. Who developed the 'basic Structure' of the Constitution?
   (a) Executive (b) Legislature
   (c) Judiciary (d) Municipality

Very Short Answer Type Questions

4. What do you understand by technical amendments?
5. The amendments made after, 1984 passed without much differently Explain. **Competency Based Que**
6. Which amendment increased the salaries of judges of High Court and Supreme Court?
7. What was a common feature of the amendments made by Parliment in the 1970s?
8. Define basic structure of the Constitution?

Short Answer Type Questions

9. How has the Supreme Court influenced the right of minority educational institutions?
10. Write a short note on 42nd amendment to the Constitution.
11. 'The judiciary determines whether an amendment violates the basic structure of the Constitution'? Justify. **Competency Based Que**
12. On what grounds the procedure of amendments in the Indian Constitution has been criticised?

Long Answer Type Questions

13. Describe some of amendments in Indian Constitution through political consensus.
14. Analyse the difference between simple majority and special majority. **Competency Based Que**

10
CHAPTER

A Constitution consists of not only laws but also moral values. For example, an anti-discrimination law embodies the principle of equality. This concept is known as the political philosophy of the Constitution.

▼ **YOUR STUDY GOALS**

▼ **YOUR PRACTICE GOAL**

- Objective Type Questions (20 Qs ; MCQs, A-R, Statements, Matching, Passage Based)
- Subjective Questions (12 VSAs, 7 SAs, 4 LAs, 1 Picture Based)

The Philosophy of the Constitution

10.1 Political Philosophy Approach to the Constitution

A political **philosophy**[1] approach to the Constitution refers to examining the fundamental moral principles, values and ideals that shape the various provisions and overall character of the Constitution. This approach has three key aspects

- **Justification of Values** Reading the Constitution alongside Constituent Assembly debates to provide detailed justifications for its values and principles acknowledging the reasoning and intentions of the framers.
- **Understanding Conceptual Structure** Analysing the meaning of the terms used in the Constitution, e.g,-rights, democracy etc.
- **Understanding of Constitutional ideals** Having a clear understanding of society and politics based on the key concepts of the Constitution. It is important to have a deeper understanding of the ideals that the Constitution promotes.
- Thus, a political philosophy approach to the Constitution helps in
    - Understanding its moral content.
    - Deviding what is right and wrong.
    - Resolve conflicting interpretations of core values.

1 **Philosophy** A theory of attitude that acts as a guiding principle for behaviour.

- Conflicting interpretations arise because
  - The core values of the Constitution are debated in various arenas like legislatures, press, schools etc. It leads to differing interpretations and manipulations.
  - Sometimes, the same ideal is interpreted differently by different institutions.
- The philosophical authority of the Constitution helps to clarify these differing interpretations and align them with Constitutional values.

The Japanese Constitution of 1947 is also known as the **Peace Constitution** as it embodies a philosophy of peace, reflected in its Preamble and Article-9.

Key aspects

- **Preamble**[2] Expresses desire for eternal peace, emphasising human relationship ideals.
- **Article-9**
  - Renounces war as a national right and threat/use of force in international disputes.
  - Prohibits maintaining land, sea, air forces and war potential.

Constitution as a Means of Democratic Transformation

A Constitution is necessary because it helps to safeguard democracy, empowers marginalised groups and promote collective well being. It establishes rules for guiding the conduct of the state.

Social Transformation Potential of the Constitution

- Restrict state power to prevent abuse
- Provide democratic means for social transformation
- Protect individual and group interest
- Prevent states from turning tyrannical

Nehru envisioned the Constituent Assembly as

- A symbol of India's self-determination
- A force for achieving freedom, equality and justice
- A catalyst for breaking traditional social hierarchies

Importance of Revisiting History of Our Constitution

Studying the history of our Constitution is important because its values and ideas are still relevant today.

- Unlike America, where the Constitution is based on 18th century values, India's Constitution reflects values that remain relevant even today.
- Our beliefs have not changed much since the time of the Constituent Assembly.
- Over time, we may have forgotten the original purpose behind the creation of many of our laws and political practices. Although the original ideas of the Constituent Assembly is relevant even today in shaping our system.
- Ignoring the underlying principles can be harmful when these practices are questioned.
- To understand our current Constitutional practices, we may need to revisit the Constituent Assembly debates and even the colonial era.

2 **Preamble** It is an introduction that explains the objectives, guiding principles and main ideas of a document, such as a Constitution.

Quick Test 1

1 Give an example of a law that reflects deeply held values.
2 Which value is directly connected to the law prohibiting discrimination on grounds of religion or language?
3 According to the preamble of the Japanese Constitution, what do the Japanese people desire?
4 How did Nehru describe the Constituent Assembly?

10.2 Political Philosophy of Our Constitution

- The Constitutional philosophy of India is multifaceted embracing **liberalism, democracy, egalitarianism[3], secularism[4]** and **federalism[5]**. The key aspects of India's Constitutional philosophy include
  - Protecting minority rights (religious, linguistic)
  - Empowering disadvantaged groups
  - Fostering national unity
  - Upholding freedom, equality and **social justice[6]**

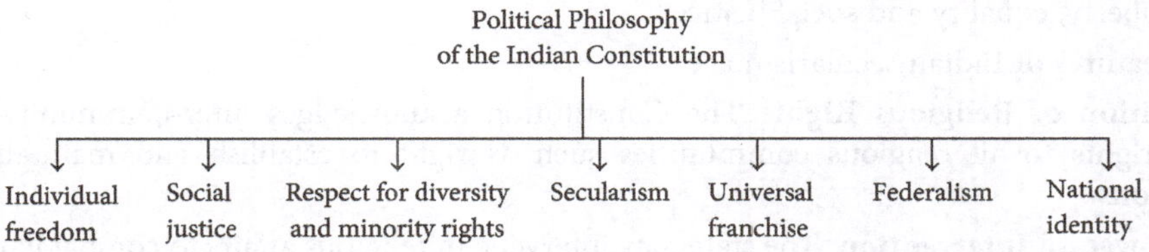

▲ *Fundamental Concepts of the Political Philosophy of the Indian Constitution*

Individual Freedom

- The Constitution's commitment to individual freedom has its roots in centuries of intellectual and political activism.
- Visionaries like **Rammohan Roy** fought against British colonial restrictions by advocating for liberty of publication and freedom of expression.
- This liberal ideology has shaped the Constitution by ensuring us freedoms like
  - Freedom of expression
  - Freedom from arbitrary arrest
  - Freedom of conscience
- The **Indian National Congress** consistently gave priority to individual rights for over 40 years before the adoption of the Constitution.
- The Preamble of the Constitution embodies these values by aiming to secure justice, liberty, equality and fraternity for all Indians.

Social Justice

- Liberalism in the Indian Constitution gives priority to both social justice and community values along with individual rights. Whereas the classical Western liberalism gives priority to individual rights.
- This is evident in provisions for **Scheduled Castes and Scheduled Tribes** such as reservation in legislature and government jobs.
- The Constitution makers recognised the historical injustice and sought to empower marginalised groups through special measures thus ensuring meaningful equality and voting rights.

---

3 **Egalitarianism** Philosophical and political ideology that advocates for equality among all individuals.
4 **Secularism** It is a principle that ensures the separation of state and religion where the state does not officially favour any particular religion.
5 **Federalism** It is a system of government where power is divided between a Central Government (or union) and smaller regional governments (states).
6 **Social Justice** It is a justice in terms of wealth, opportunity and privileges within a society.

Respect for Diversity and Minority Rights

- The Indian Constitution aims to promote equal respect among diverse communities which is a challenging task due to historical hierarchies and rivalries.
- India is a land of multiple cultural communities and each community has its own unique values, traditions and languages.
- The Constitution of India recognised this by acknowledging community based rights such as religious communities establishing and running educational institutions with the help of funding from the government.
- This approach differs from Western liberal Constitutions which often overlook community identities.

Secularism

- The Indian Constitution's approach to secularism differs from the western model. While Western concept of secularism emphasises **mutual exclusion**[7] between the state and religion, India's Constitution adopts a 'principled distance' approach.
- This means the state maintains a balance between intervening or abstaining from interference to promote liberty, equality and social justice.
- The key features of Indian secularism are
  - **Recognition of Religious Rights** The Constitution acknowledges inter-community equality and grants rights to all religious communities such as right to establish and maintain educational institutions.
  - **State Power of Intervention** The state may intervene in religious affairs to combat harmful customs like untouchability or it may provide aid to community-run institutions.
  - **Principled Distance** The state maintains a balance by neither helping nor hindering religions to promote individual freedom and social justice.
- The key Constitutional achievements of our Constitution are
  - **Liberal Individualism** Reinforces individual autonomy in a society where community values often ignore individual freedom.
  - **Social Justice** Upholds **social justice**[8] without compromising individual liberties which is evident in caste-based actions.
  - **Group Rights** Protects cultural identity, addressing inter-communal strife and promoting multiculturalism.

Universal Franchise

- The commitment of the Indian Constitution to universal franchise is a significant achievement. This is despite the fact that traditional hierarchies were deeply prevalent in India whereas voting rights to women and working class were only extended recently in Western democracies.
- This commitment has its roots in the idea of democratic self-government which emerged alongside Indian nationalism.
- This concept was further solidified through the **Constitution of India bill (1895)** and the **Motilal Nehru Report (1928)**. These documents emphasised the right of every citizen to vote and participate in the affairs of the country regardless of sex or social status.

---

7 **Mutual exclusion** It means that religion and state must be strictly separated. The state does not interfere with religious matters, nor does religion interferes with state affairs.

8 **Social justice** It refers to the fair and equitable distribution of resources, opportunities and privileges within a society regardless of race, gender, class or other social characteristics.

Federalism

- The Constitution of India provides for asymmetric federalism[9] **(Article-371)** unlike Constitutional symmetry of American federalism.
- This means it provides special status for certain states like **Nagaland (under Article 371A)**, to address unique regional needs.
- This approach balances unity with diversity and recognises regional identities.
- India's democratic federalism combines unity with cultural recognition, allowing multiple identities to coexist and complement each other.

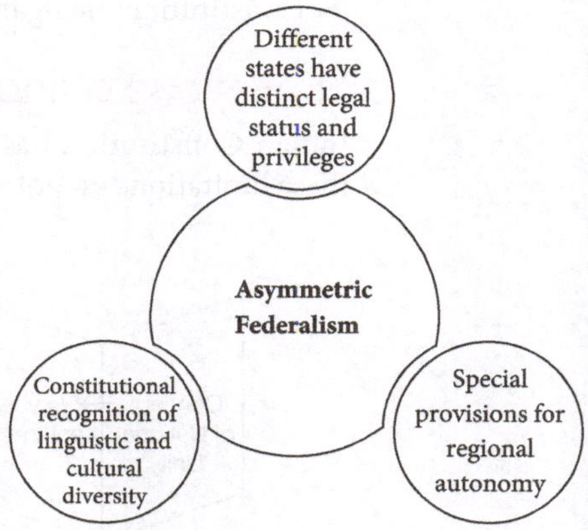

National Identity

- The Indian Constitution promotes a common national identity while respecting regional, religious and linguistic diversity. It strikes a balance between individual freedoms, social justice and community rights.
- The Constitution rejects separate electorates[10] based on religious identity, not to suppress differences but to ensure a healthy national life and foster fraternity.

10.3 Procedural Achievements of Indian Constitution

The procedural achievements of the Constitution are

- **Commitment to Political Deliberation** Including diverse groups despite some not being fully represented in the Constituent Assembly. It encourages people to change their opinions based on reasons instead of self interest and disagreements.
- **Reflection of a Spirit of Compromise and Accommodation** Not all compromises are bad; when values are balanced through open, equal discussions, they are morally acceptable. It emphasises consensus over majority decisions on important issues.

10.4 Criticisms of the Indian Constitution

The Indian Constitution majorly faces three criticism

- **It is unwieldy** The size of the Indian Constitution is very large due to its comprehensive nature incorporating various documents and practices. It is not a compact document like the one in US.
- **It is unrepresentative** Constituent Assembly members were chosen by restricted franchise and not by universal adult franchise. However, despite this the Constituent Assembly of India represented diversity of opinions.
- **It is alien** The Constitution of India is accused of being entirely inspired by West and is disconnected from Indian cultural ethos.

Various arguments were put forward to counter these criticisms

- The complexity of the Constitution reflects the diverse needs of India.
- Constituent Assembly debates showcased diversity of opinions and social concerns.
- Indian Constitution reflects **innovative borrowing,** adaptation and hybridisation of Western and Indian values.

9 Asymmetric federalism A federal system where power and autonomy are distributed unevenly among constituent units.
10 Separate electorate It refers to an electoral system where different social groups have separate voting constituencies or representation.

- Modernity was embraced by Indians, especially Dalits as a tool for dignity and justice.
- Constitution amalgamates Western and traditional Indian values through selective adaptation.

Limitations of Indian Constitution

Indian Constitution has several limitations due to its historical context and social conditions. However, these limitations do not undermine the philosophy of the Constitution.

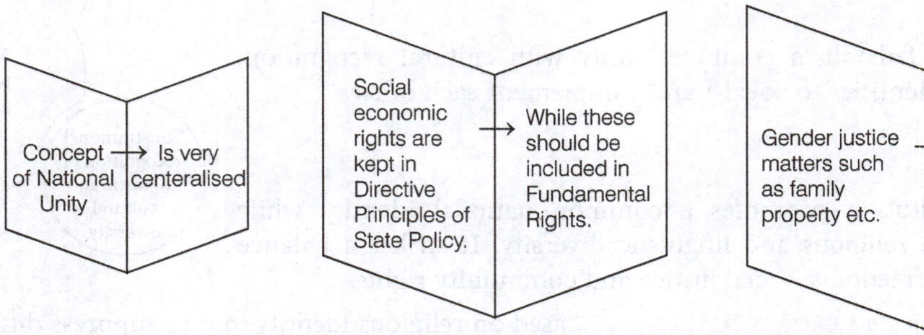

▲ *Major Limitation Seen in Indian Constitution*

Quick Test 2

1. What is secularism?
2. Define mutual exclusion.
3. What is the significance of the Nehru report of 1928?
4. Give any one of the special achievement of our Constitution.

Mind Map

THE PHILOSOPHY OF THE CONSTITUTION

1 Political Philosophy Approach to the Constitution

- **Justification of Values** Provide detailed justification for its values and principles.
- **Understanding Conceptual Structure** Analysing the meaning of terms used in Constitutions. (e.g. democracy, rights).
- **Understanding of Constitutional Ideals** Based clear understanding of society and politics.

2 Constitution as a Means of Democratic Transformation

Social Transformation Potential of the Constitution

- Restrict state power to prevent abuse.
- Protect individual and group interest.
- Provide democratic means for social transformation.
- Prevent states from turning tyrannical.

3 Importance of Revisiting History of Our Constitution

- Our beliefs have not changed much since the time of the Constituent Assembly.
- The original purpose behind many of our laws and political practices.
- Ignoring the underlying principles can be harmful when these practices are questioned.
- To understand our current Constitutional practices.

4 Political Philosophy of Our Constitution

Key aspects of India's constitutional Philosophy.

Procedural Achievements of Indian Constitution

- Commitment to political deliberation.
- Reflection of a spirit of compromise and accommodation.

Individual Freedom

- Freedom of expression.
- Freedom from arbitrary arrest.
- Freedom of conscience.

Social Justice

- Gives priority to both social justice and community value.
- Constitution makers recognised the historical injustice.

Respect for Diversity and Minority Rights

- Indian Constitution aims to promote equal respects.
- India is a land of multiple cultural communities and communities has its own unique values.

Secularism

- Secularism emphasises mutual exclusion between the state and religion.
- State maintains a balance between intervening or abstaining.

Universal Franchise

- It is a significant achievement.
- This commitment has its roots in the idea of democratic self-government.

Federalism

- It provides for asymmetric federalism.
- It provides special status for certain states like Nagaland.

National Identity

- It promotes a common national identity.
- It rejects separate electorates based on religious identity.

5 Criticism of Indian Constitution

- Very long and detailed.
- Representative of all the groups were not present in the framing of Constitution.
- It is disconnected from Indian cultural ethos.

6 Limitations of Indian Constitution

- **Concept of National Unity** It is very centeralised.
- **Social Economic Rights are kept in Directive Principles of State Policy** While these should be included in Fundamental Rights.
- **Gender Justice Matters such as Family Property** etc Such matters were not included in Fundamental Rights.

NCERT Folder

Intext Questions

1. **State which of the following rights are part of individual freedom (Pg. 227)**
   (i) **Freedom of expression**
   (ii) **Freedom of religion**
   (iii) **Cultural and educational rights of minorities**
   (iv) **Equal access to public places**

Ans. The following rights are part of individual freedom
   (i) **Freedom of expression** This is a fundamental right, that allows individuals to express their opinions, ideas and beliefs freely.
   (ii) **Freedom of religion** This is also a key individual freedom, granting people the right to practice, propagate or change their religion without interference.

Exercise

1. The following are certain laws. Are they connected with any value? If yes, then what is the underlying value? Give reasons.
   (i) **Both daughters and sons will have share in the family property.**
   (ii) **There will be different slabs of sales tax on different consumer items.**
   (iii) **Religious instructions will not be given in any government school.**
   (iv) **There shall be no begar or forced labour.**

Ans. (i) **Idea of equality and social justice,** as it treats both children equally by giving inheritance to them irrespective of their gender.
   (ii) **Economic justice,** as it reflects the importance of certain consumer items for people and seeks to discourage the consumption of other items deemed as non-essential.
   (iii) **Secularism,** as it shows that government does not give importance to any religion in particular.
   (iv) **Idea of social justice,** as it strives to end forced labour and protect workers from exploitation.

2. Which of the options given below cannot be used to complete the following statement?

Democratic countries need a Constitution to
   (i) **Check the power of the government.**
   (ii) **Protect minorities from majority.**
   (iii) **Bring independence from colonial rule.**
   (iv) **Ensure that a long-term vision is not lost by momentary passions.**
   (v) **Bring social change in peaceful manner.**

Ans. (iii) Bring independence from colonial rule.

3. The following are different positions about reading and understanding Constituent Assembly debates.
   (i) **Which of these statements argues that Constituent Assembly debates are relevant even today? Which statement says that they are not relevant?**
   (ii) **With which of these positions do you agree and why?**
      (a) **Common people are too busy in earning livelihood and meeting different pressures of life. They can't understand the legal language of these debates.**
      (b) **The conditions and challenges of today are different from the time when the Constitution was made. To read the ideas of Constitution makers and use them for our new times is trying to bring past in the present.**
      (c) **Our ways of understanding the world and the present challenges have not changed totally. Constituent Assembly debates can provide us reasons why certain practises are important. In a period when Constitutional practises are being challenged, not knowing the reasons can destroy them.**

Ans. (i) The statement that argues that Constituent Assembly debates are relevant even today is
      (c) Our ways of understanding the world and the present challenges have not changed totally. Constituent Assembly debates can provide the reasons why certain practices are being challenged, not knowing the reason can destroy them.

      The statement that argues that constituent debates are not relevant today is
      (b) The conditions and challenges of today are different from the time when the Constitution was made. To read the ideas of Constitution makers and use them for our new times is trying to bring the past in present.

   (ii) (c) I agree with statement (c). The statement is correct because the values that are enshrined in the Constitution are universal in nature and constitute a safeguard for the rights of the citizen. It is necessary to uphold these values, as they are relevant to society in all ages. The break down of Constitutional values would lead to chaos and endanger the rights of the citizens as well as the integrity of the country.

4. Explain the difference between the Indian Constitution and Western ideas in the light of
(i) Understanding of secularism
(ii) Articles 370 and 371
(iii) Affirmative action
(iv) Universal Adult Franchise

Ans. (i) Indian secularism is based on principled distance, whereas Western secularism is based on mutual exclusion. In India, the states can intervene in religious matters so that the citizens are treated equally and can enjoy a life of dignity. While in the Western countries, religion cannot interfere in matters of the state and state cannot interfere in the matters of religion.

(ii) The Articles 370 and 371 give special rights to the state of Jammu and Kashmir and North-Eastern states respectively according to their peculiar social and historical back ground. This type of provision of accommodation is not found in Western countries.

(iii) Affirmative action in India is based on the principle of social justice without compromising on individual liberties. Affirmative action in India was introduced two decades before as it was introduced in US.

(iv) Every Indian citizen whose age is 18 years or above, is eligible to vote, whereas in established democratic countries, right to vote was not enjoyed by every eligible voters. This right was extended to women and working class in some democratic nations around 20th century after a long struggle.

5. Which of the following principles of secularism are adopted in the Constitution of India?
(i) That state will have nothing to do with religion.
(ii) That state will have close relation with religion.
(iii) That state can discriminate among religions.
(iv) That state will recognise rights of religious groups.
(v) That state will have limited powers to intervene in affairs of religions.

Ans. (iv) That state will recognise rights of religious groups.
(v) That state will have limited powers to intervene in affairs of religions.

6. Match the following

A.	Freedom to criticise treatment of widows.	1.	Substantive achievement.
B.	Taking decisions in the Constituent Assembly on the basis of reason, not self interest.	2.	Procedural achievement.
C.	Accepting importance of community in an individual's life	3.	Neglect of gender justice.
D.	Article 370 and 371.	4.	Liberal individualism.
E.	Unequal rights to women regarding family property and children.	5.	Attention to requirements of a particular region.

Ans. A-4 B-2 C-1 D-5 E-3

7. This discussion was taking place in a class. Read the various arguments and state which of these do you agree with and why?

Jayesh: I still think that our Constitution is only a borrowed document.

Saba: Do you mean to say there is nothing Indian in it? But is there such thing as Indian and Western in the case of values and ideas? Take equality between men and women. What is Western about it? And even if it is, should we reject it only because it is Western?

Jayesh: What I mean is that after fighting for independence from the British, did we not adopt their system of Parliamentary Government?

Neha: You forget that when we fought the British, we were not against the British as such, we were against the principle of colonialism. That has nothing to do with adopting a system of government that we wanted, wherever it came from.

Ans. The arguments of Saba and Neha are correct that an idea of equality cannot be rejected merely because it is of Western origin. The values that are part of Constitution are universal and thus cannot be discriminated as Indian or Western.

It is also correct that while the British were unjust in their policy of colonialism, there were certain principles of governance that were modern and suitable, as they allowed people to choose their own representatives. Thus, the positive values of British system should not be ignored on the basis of negative impact of British colonialism.

8. Why is it said that the making of the Indian Constitution was unrepresentative? Does that make the Constitution unrepresentative? Given reasons for your answer.

Ans. It is said that making of the Constituent Assembly was unrepresentative because the members of the Constituent Assembly were chosen by a restricted franchise and not by universal suffrage. It does not make the Constitution unrepresentative because it constrains the aspirations and voice of every section of the nation. The Constitution has also provided for a democratic system of government with a head of the republic.

9. **One of the limitations of the Constitution of India is that it does not adequately attend to gender justice. What evidence can you give to substantiate this change? If you were writing the Constitution today, what provisions would you recommend for remedying this limitation?**

Ans. It is true that there are inadequate provisions for gender justice in the Constitution. Though, it is a Fundamental Right of every citizen to be treated equally but their is no specification on the basis of gender but specification is made on religion, caste and class.

Citizens cannot be discriminated on the basis of their caste, class, religion and language but there is no mention of gender. Respect for women has been confirmed to the Directive Principles and women's rights are not specified, so that they can be interpreted and defended by the judiciary.

The status of women with family has also been ignored in the Constitution. Thus, it makes no special privileges for almost half of the population, while there are provisions for affirmative action for other socially backward groups and minorities.

10. **Do you agree with the statement that "It is not clear why in a poor developing country, certain basic socio-economic rights were relegated to the section on Directive Principles rather than made an integral feature of our Fundamental Rights"? Give reasons for your answer. What do you think are the possible reasons for putting socio-economic rights in the section of Directive Principles?**

Ans. It is correct that the socio-economic rights were relegated to Directive Principles. These rights should have been incorporated particularly for backward classes in the same manner as the cultural rights of minorities. A developing country like India requires the fulfillment of the potential of human resources. For this reason, it is essential that the socio-economic requirements of all sections of society are met and all groups have equal opportunities.

The possible reason was the lack of adequate resources in a newly independent nation. Making socio-economic rights a Fundamental Right would have placed a burden on the state. Besides, the economic development path of newly independent country was already concerned with planned development whose benefits were to be made available to all sections of the society.

Exam Pattern Questions

Objective Type Questions

Multiple Choice Questions (MCQs)

1. **Philosophy of Constitution doesn't refer to............** Diksha App

(a) values and ideals enshrined in the Constitution.
(b) vision of the Constitution makers .
(c) conceptual structure of the Constitution.
(d) structure of political parties.

2. **Who termed Constitution Assembly as "Nation on Move"?** Diksha App

(a) J.L. Nehru (b) Dr. B.R. Ambedkar
(c) Dr. Rajendra Prasad (d) M.K. Gandhi

3. **Individual freedom doesn't refer to......... .** Diksha App

(a) free press
(b) freedom of expression
(c) freedom from arbitrary arrest
(d) freedom to do anything

4. **Which of the following best explains the Western conception of secularism?** Diksha App

(a) Treats religion as a private matter.
(b) Religion is not given public or official recognition.
(c) Mutual exclusion, means both religion and state must stay away from the internal affairs of one another.
(d) Prohibition of religion.

5. **Which of the following statements is NOT TRUE?** Diksha App

(a) Indian Constitution reflects faith in political deliberations.
(b) All groups and interests were adequately represented in the Constituent Assembly.
(c) Approach of Constitution makers was inclusive.
(d) Constituent Assembly recognised the creative value in difference and disagreement.

6. Which of the following statements is NOT correct?

(a) Constituent Assembly worked with the spirit of compromise and accommodation.

(b) Compromises are bad and unacceptable in all circumstances.

(c) In the open process of free deliberation one value can be traded off for another.

(d) Compromise and accommodation should always be in the common interest.

7. Which among the following is NOT a ground, the Indian Constitution is criticised for? Diksha App

(a) It is unwieldy.

(b) It is unrepresentative.

(c) It is alien to our conditions.

(d) It is non-democratic.

8. Which of the following statements doesn't reflect the limitations of the Indian Constitution? Diksha App

(a) It has a centralised idea of national unity.

(b) It didn't accept socio-economic rights as Fundamental Rights.

(c) It glossed over some important issues of gender justice.

(d) It provided universal adult franchise.

9. Given below are two statements

Statement I Liberal individualism is one of the key Constitutional achievements.

Statement II Liberal individualism reinforces individual autonomy in a society where community values often prevail.

In the light of the above statements, choose the correct answer from the options given below

(a) Both Statement I and Statement II are true.

(b) Both Statement I and Statement II are false.

(c) Statement I is true, but Statement II is false.

(d) Statement I is false, but Statement II is true.

10. Indian Constitution provides for asymmetric federalism unlike the Constitutional symmetry in America. Which of the following is NOT TRUE regarding asymmetric federalism in India?

(a) Different states have distinct legal status and privilege.

(b) There are special provisions for regional autonomy.

(c) Any state can become an autonomous state according to its will.

(d) Constitution gives recognition to linguistic and cultural diversity.

11. Arrange the following in chronological order

I. Constitution of India Bill

II. Japan Constitution

III. Civil Rights Act in US

IV. Motilal Nehru Report

Choose the correct option

(a) I, IV, II, III (b) IV, I, II, III

(c) IV, I, III, II (d) I, IV, III, II

Assertion-Reason Questions

Directions (Q.Nos. 12-16) In the questions given below, there are two statements marked as Assertion (A) and Reason (R). Read the statements and choose the correct option.

Codes

(a) Both A and R are true and R is the correct explanation of A.

(b) Both A and R are true, but R is not the correct explanation of A.

(c) A is true, but R is false.

(d) A is false, but R is true.

12. Assertion (A) A political philosophy approach to the Constitution involves working out a coherent vision of society and polity.

Reason (R) The Constitution's ideals should be interpreted as a coherent set of concepts that guide society and politics.

13. Assertion (A) The ideals in the Constitution are rarely discussed or contested in political arenas.

Reason (R) Political arenas such as legislatures, party forums, the press and universities are the primary spaces where Constitutional ideals are debated and contested.

14. Assertion (A) The Indian Constitution's provision for reservations for Scheduled Castes and Scheduled Tribes was designed to make sure that they have real equality, especially in political and economic spheres.

Reason (R) The Constitution makers believed that merely providing the right to equality was inadequate to achieve real equality for historically oppressed groups.

15. Assertion (A) The Indian Constitution does not recognise communities and treats all individuals equally, like most Western liberal Constitutions.

Reason (R) The Indian Constitution recognises the value of communities and acknowledges the importance of community-based rights due to India's diverse cultural landscape.

16. Assertion (A) The Indian Constitution ensures that the state does not intervene in religious matters and that religious organisations do not dictate state policies.

Reason (R) Secularism in India means the separation of state and religion, ensuring that the state does not assist religious organisations, nor does it interfere with their internal affairs.

Passage Based Questions

17. Read the given passage and answer the following questions.

Indian liberalism has two streams. The first stream began with Rammohan Roy. He emphasised individual rights, particularly the rights of women. The second stream included thinkers like K.C. Sen, Justice Ranade and Swami Vivekananda. They introduced the spirit of social justice within orthodox Hinduism. For Vivekananda, such a reordering of Hindu society could not have been possible without liberal principles.

K.M. Panikkar, In Defence of Liberalism, Bombay, Asia Publishing House, 1962.

(i) Who is considered the pioneer of the first stream of Indian liberalism, emphasising individual rights, particularly women's rights?

(a) K.C. Sen (b) Justice Ranade
(c) Swami Vivekananda (d) Rammohan Roy

(ii) According to Swami Vivekananda, what was essential for reordering Hindu society?

(a) Conservative traditionalism
(b) Liberal principles
(c) Social conservatism
(d) Religious fundamentalism

(iii) Define liberalism in Indian context.

18. Read the given passage and answer the following questions.

"The assembly has adopted the principle of adult franchise with an abundant faith in the common man and the ultimate success of democratic rule, and in the full belief that the introduction of democratic government on the basis of adult suffrage will ... promote well-being ..."

(i) What principle did the assembly adopt with faith in the common man and democratic rule?

(a) Universal Adult Franchise
(b) Limited Suffrage
(c) Monarchy
(d) Oligarchy

(ii) What is expected to be promoted by the introduction of democratic government based on adult suffrage?

(a) Social unrest (b) Economic instability
(c) Well-being (d) Authoritarianism

(iii) Why Adult Franchise is needed in a democracy?

19. Read the given passage and answer the following questions.

"But in the long run, it would be in the interest of all to forget that there is anything like majority or minority in this country and that in India there is only one community..."

(i) What is the desired outcome for India, according to the passage?

(a) Emphasis on majority-minority divisions
(b) Recognition of multiple communities
(c) Unity as one community
(d) Segregation of social groups

(ii) Whose words are referred to in the passage promoting unity and inclusivity?

(a) Jawaharlal Nehru (b) Mahatma Gandhi
(c) B.R. Ambedkar (d) Sardar Patel

(iii) What is to be forgotten, according to the passage, for India's benefit?

(a) Religious differences
(b) Caste distinctions
(c) Majority-minority divisions
(d) Economic disparities

(iv) What is the underlying theme of this passage?

(a) Social exclusion (b) Political fragmentation
(c) National unity (d) Sectarianism

20. Read the given passage and answer the following questions.

".... we wanted the music of Veena or Sitar, but here we have the music of an English band. That was because our Constitution makers were educated that way. .... That is exactly the kind of Constitution Mahatma Gandhi did not want and did not envisage".

(i) What is the speaker expressing dissatisfaction with?

(a) India's cultural heritage
(b) The Constitutional framework
(c) Educational system
(d) Economic policies

(ii) Why did India adopt Western-inspired governance, according to the speaker?

(a) Influence of British colonialism
(b) Education of Constitution makers
(c) Economic necessity
(d) Social revolution

(iii) Who did not envision the adopted Constitution, according to the speaker?

(a) Jawaharlal Nehru (b) B.R. Ambedkar
(c) Mahatma Gandhi (d) Sardar Patel

(iv) What does the "Music of an English band" symbolise in the context?

(a) India's cultural heritage
(b) Western influence on governance
(c) National unity
(d) Social reform

Answers

1. (d) Structure of political parties.
2. (a) J.L. Nehru
3. (d) Freedom to do anything
4. (c) Mutual exclusion, means both religion and state must stay away from the internal affairs of one another.
5. (b) All groups and interests were adequately represented in the Constituent Assembly.
6. (b) Compromises are bad and unacceptable in all circumstances.
7. (d) It is non-democratic.
8. (d) It provided universal adult franchise.
9. (a) Both Statement I and Statement II are true.
10. (c) Any state can become an autonomous state according to its will.
11. (a) I, IV, II, III
12. (a) Both A and R are true and R is the correct explanation of A.
13. (d) A is false, but R is true.
14. (a) Both A and R are true and R is the correct explanation of A.
15. (d) A is false, but R is true.
16. (a) Both A and R are true and R is the correct explanation of A.
17. (i) (d) Rammohan Roy
    (ii) (b) Liberal principles
    (iii) Liberalism in Indian context means, to grant individual rights by linking the demand of social justice and community values and not only by privileging individual rights.
18. (i) (a) Universal Adult Franchise
    (ii) (c) Well-being
    (iii) Adult Franchise is needed in a democracy for the following reasons
    - To promote the well-being of the society and the nation.
    - To provide the ultimate power into the hands of the people as democratic rule is of the people, for the people and by the people.
19. (i) (c) Unity as one community
    (ii) (d) Sardar Patel
    (iii) (c) Majority-minority divisions
    (iv) (c) National unity
20. (i) (b) The Constitutional framework
    (ii) (b) Education of Constitution makers
    (iii) (c) Mahatma Gandhi
    (iv) (b) Western influence on governance

Subjective Questions

Very Short Answer Type Questions

1. Constitution of which country is known as 'Peace Constitution?

Ans. Japanese Constitution is known as 'Peace Constitution'.

2. Why do we need a Constitution?

Ans. We need a Constitution because
- It provides the basic rules to prevent the states from turning tyrannical or despotic.
- It provides peaceful democratic means to bring about social transformation.

3. Why do we need to think back about the Constituent Assembly debates?

Ans. We need to think back about the Constituent Assembly debates in order to get a handle on the current Constitutional practices and to understand the values and meaning of philosophy underlying our Constitution.

4. Which rights are considered as part of individual freedom?

Ans. The rights considered as part of individual freedom are
- Right to life and personal liberty
- Equal access to public places
- Freedom of speech and expressions
- Freedom of religion and faith

5. What is Classical liberalism?

Ans. The liberalism which privileges rights of the individuals over demands of social justices and community values are called as Classical liberalism.

6. Mention the difference between Classical liberalism and Indian liberalism.

Ans. Classical liberalism always privileges individual rights over social justice and community values whereas the Indian liberalism is always linked to social justices and community values.

7. What is secularism?

Ans. Secularism means that the state will treat religion as only a private matter and refuse to give religion a public or official recognition in order to protect values.

8. What do you understand by 'Mutual Exclusion'?

Ans. The concept of mutual exclusion is followed in terms of secularism, which means religion and state must be separate from the internal affairs of one another, in order to safeguard the freedom of individuals.

9. When was the demand of universal suffrage was demanded for the first time?

Ans. The demand for universal suffrage was demanded for the first time in the Nehru report of 1928.

10. What is the significance of Article 371?

Ans. The Constitution of India provides for asymmetric federalism under Article 371. Under this it provides special status for certain states like Nagaland, Maharashtra, Manipur etc.

11. Why was the concept of separate electorate rejected by the framers of the Constitution?

Ans. The concept of separate electorate was rejected by the framers of the Constitution because it endangers a healthy national life.

12. Why is the Constitution of India is criticised as an alien document?

Ans. The Constitution of India is criticised as an alien document because most of the provisions are borrowed from Western Constitutions and it is not in parity with the Indian people.

Short Answer Type Questions

1. What is meant by the political philosophy approach to the Constitution? Diksha App

Ans. (i) By political philosophy approach we try to understand the conceptual structure of the Constitution and to get the possible meaning of terms like, rights, citizenship, minority, democracy etc.

(ii) It gives a better understanding of ideals embedded in the Constitution.

(iii) It enables us to understand the provisions of the Constitution in the context of Constituent Assembly debates. It helpes in finding moral content expressed in the Constitution.

2. What things come in mind to adopt the political philosophy approach to the Constitution?

Ans. Three things should come in mind to adopt the political philosophy approach to the Constitution which are

(i) First, we need to understand the conceptual structure of the Constitution and understand the words mentioned in the Constitution such as rights, citizenship, minority or democracy.

(ii) Second, we must attempt to work out a logical and reasonable vision of society and polity with interpretation of the key concepts of the Constitution.

(iii) Third, the Indian Constitution must be read in conjunction with the Constituent Assembly debates, in order to refine and raise to a higher theoretical plane i.e. the justification of values embedded in the Constitution.

3. What is the significance of going back to Constituent Assembly debates? Diksha App

Ans. (i) Constituent Assembly debates help us to understand legal and political ideas from which various provisions of the Constitution emerged.

(ii) We come to know about the intentions and concerns of the Constitution makers.

(iii) To understand the vision, ideals and basic principles behind our Constitution.

4. The Constitution of India pays equal respect to different communities. How?

Ans. Every community wants to dominate the other community, if they are not given the equal treatment by the states. It was a great challenge before the Constitution makers to foster a sense of equal respect in the conditions of hierarchy of interest rivalry.

India is a land of multiple cultural communities which ensure community based right to be mandatory.

Hence, there are Fundamental Rights of religious communities to establish and run their own educational institutions as well to receive money from the government for the same. In this way, the Constitution of India pays equal respect to different communities.

5. India is a secular state. Explain.

Ans. The Preamble of the Indian Constitution declares India to be a secular state. A secular state is a state which is not based on any religion. There is no state religion and every citizen is free to practise and propagate the religion of his/her choice.

There can be no discrimination among citizens on the basis of religion. No one can be refused admission in any educational institution maintained wholly or partly by state funds on the basis of religion.

6. Give two contrasting features regarding secularism in India and in the West.

Ans. The secularism in India is different from those of the Western conception in two ways

(i) Firstly, the framers of the Constitution recognised that inter-community equality was as necessary as equality between individuals because a person's freedom and sense of respect was directly dependent upon the status of his/her community. So, freedom of religion in India means the freedom of religion of both individuals and communities, but in the Western conception, it is only the freedom of individuals.

(ii) Secondly, separation in India could not mean 'mutual exclusion' because some religiously sanctioned customs deprived individuals of the most basic dignity and self-respect, such as untouchability and states intervention is necessary for its dissolution. The states interferes for positive aspects but the Western states does not interfere in religious matters.

7. State the limitations to the Constitution of India.

Ans. The limitations to the Constitution of India are

- The Indian Constitution has a centralised idea of national unity.
- It appears to have concealed over some important issues of gender justice, particularly within the family.
- It is not clear why certain basic socio-economic rights were downgraded to Directive Principles rather than making it our Fundamental Rights.

Long Answer Type Questions

1. Examine the Constitution as a means of democratic transformation. Diksha App

Ans. The Constitution is a means of democratic transformation due to following reasons

(i) Reason for having Constitution is the need to restrict the exercise of the power.

(ii) Modern states are excessively powerful, various institutions are created for our safety but without a Constitution, there is no guarantee that these same institutions are not used against us.

(iii) The Indian Constitution was designed to break the shackles of traditional social hierarchies and to usher in a new era of freedom, equality and justice.

(iv) Individual freedom democracy, universal adult franchise etc. are the basic principles that bring about democratic transformation.

2. What is meant by the secular state? How Indian concept of secularism different from that of the West? Diksha App

Ans. States which treat religion as private matters and refuse to give religion public or official recognition, in other words, there is no state religion, such a state is called a secular state.

Indian concept of secularism is different from Western concept in the following ways

(i) In the Western concept of secularism, there is mutual exclusion, meaning both state and religion must stay away from the internal affairs of one another.

(ii) Indian Constitution on the other hand adopted alternative conception of secularism, In the Indian Constitution ensures freedom of religion to both individuals and communities.

(iii) In India, the state can intervene in religious matters, can sanction social customs which are against the interests of any section of the society and gender.

(iv) State also gives aid to religious communities to run educational institutions.

(v) Indian state ensures equal respect to all religions.

3. Discuss the special features of the Indian Constitution considered as an important achievements.

Ans. The special features considered as an achievement of the Indian Constitution are

- Our Constitution emphasises on liberal individualism and is an important achievement because this is done in the backdrop of a society which have different community values or hostile to individual autonomy.
- Our Constitution upholds the principle of social justice without compromising on individual liberties.
- Constitution upholds its commitment to group rights against the background of internal communal disputes.
- Secularism, according to our Constitution means freedom of religion of both individuals and communities and the state has the power to intervene in religiously sanctioned customs which deprive individuals of basic dignity and self respect.

4. On what basis Indian Constitution was criticised?

Ans. The Indian Constitution is subjected to many criticisms such as

- **Unwieldly** This criticism is based on the assumption that the entire Constitution of a country must be found in one compact document. But this is not true even of countries such as US which do have a compact Constitution.

- **Unrepresentative** Here, we must distinguish two components of representation, voice and opinion. People must be recognised in their own language or voice and not in the language of masters. From this dimension, the Indian Constitution is unrepresentative because members of the Constituent Assembly were chosen by a restricted franchise and not by universal suffrage.

  However, if we examine the other dimensions, we may not find it unrepresentative, as the debates in the Constituent Assembly are not only based on their individual concern but based on perceived interests and concerns of various social sections as well.
- **Entirely an Alien Document** The final criticism affirms that the Indian Constitution is entirely of an alien document borrowed from Western Constitutions and it is not in parity with the Indian people.

Picture Based Question

1. Observe the cartoon below and answer the questions that follow.

(i) What does the cartoon represents?
(a) Indian cricket league match
(b) Different groups and sections playing together
(c) Different groups fighting with each other
(d) Politicians of different political parties playing a cricket match

Ans. (b) Different groups and sections playing together

(ii) Who among the following represents democracy in the above picture?
(a) The person holding the bat
(b) The bowler in the field
(c) The umpire observing the match
(d) The fielders aiming to catch the ball

Ans. (c) The umpire observing the match

(iii) The umpire in the above picture signifies that......... .
(a) everyone has given due representation in the Constitution
(b) a law is equal for everyone
(c) the importance of preventing cheating in a society
(d) All sports in our country should be fair for everyone

Ans. (a) everyone has given due representation in the Constitution

(iv) The democracy in real sense means.
(a) Government by the consent of citizens
(b) Free exchange of ideas and rule of law
(c) Government for the people, by the people and of the people
(d) All of the above

Ans. (d) All of the above

SELF ASSESSMENT TEST

Objective Type Questions

1. Which word was inserted in the preamble by the 42nd amendment that envisages the goal of a 'welfare state'?
   (a) Fraternity (b) Democratic (c) Socialist (d) Sovereign
2. What is known as the soul of the Constitution?
   (a) Articles (b) Amendments (c) Rights (d) The Preamble

Very Short Answer Type Questions

3. What do you mean by philosophy of the Constitution?
4. What is the political philosophy underlying the Constitution?
5. What do you understand by social justice?
6. Give a definition of secular state.
7. What is Universal Adult Franchise?
8. Why is Indian Constitution considered unwieldy?

Short Answer Type Questions

9. Constitution is a means of democratic transformation. Explain.
10. Why there is a need to think back about the Constituent Assembly to interpret the Constitution?
11. How does the Indian Constitution protect the rights for diversity and the minority?
12. Secularism in India is different from that of the Western countries. Explain.
13. Discuss how the Indian Constitution reflected the efforts to combine Western and traditional Indian values during its drafting.
14. What do you mean by the spirit of consensus and accommodation adopted by the Constituent Assembly in framing the Constitution of India?

Long Answer Type Questions

15. Laws and moral values are connected. Elaborate.
16. The Constitution of India is not a perfect and flawless document. Justify the statement.

01 CHAPTER

Political theory examines the organisation of society, the need of government, the ideal form of governance and the relationship between law and freedom.

Political Theory: An Introduction

YOUR STUDY GOALS

1.1 Meaning of Politics
1.2 Key Concept in Political Theory
1.3 Applying Political Theory in Practice
1.4 Importance of Studying Political Theory

YOUR PRACTICE GOAL

- Objective Type Questions (28 Qs ; MCQs, A-R, Statements, Matching, Passage Based)
- Subjective Type Questions (10 VSAs, 6 SAs, 5 LAs 1 Picture Based)

Political theory systematically explores core values of political life such as **freedom**[1], **equality**[2] and **justice**[3]. It clarifies the existing definitions of these concepts by focusing on some major political thinkers of the past and present. It examines the presence of freedom and equality in everyday institutions like schools, public transport and government offices.

It studies whether existing definitions are adequate and how institutions and policy practices can be modified to make them more democratic. The objective of political theory is to train citizens to think rationally regarding political issues and to assess contemporary political events.

1.1 Meaning of Politics

- Politics is an important and integral component of any society. No society can exist without some kind of political organisation and collective decision-making.
- A number of social institutions such as family, tribes and economic institutions have emerged to help people fulfill their needs and aspirations.

1 **Freedom** It refers to an ability to act, speak or think without external restraints.
2 **Equality** It refers to the state of being equal, especially in terms of right, opportunities and treatment.
3 **Justice** It refers to fair and impartial application of the law ensuring that the right of individuals are protected and respected.

- Such institutions help in finding ways of living together acknowledging our obligations to each other.
- Among such institutions, the government plays an important part. Thus, the formation and functioning of government is an important focus of politics.

Influence of Politics in Daily Life

Politics is not only limited to the affairs of government. It also influences our daily lives in the following ways

- Government determines the economic, foreign and education policy of a state. These policies can help to improve the lives of people but an inefficient or corrupt government can endanger people's lives and security.
- If the government in power allows any conflict to become violent, it disrupts our lives. For example, If markets and shops are closed down, we cannot buy things that we may need urgently. Those who are sick can not reach the hospital. Even the school schedule gets affected, syllabus cannot be completed and a student may have to take extra coaching for the exams and pay tuition fees.
- If the government makes policies to increase literacy and employment, a student may get an opportunity to go to a good school and get a decent job.

Citizens' Engagement with Government

Citizens have a keen interest in what governments do because the actions of the government affect their lives deeply. Citizens express their interest in the following ways

- People form associations and organise campaigns to express their demands. They negotiate with others and try to shape the goals that governments follow.
- People protest and organise demonstrations to persuade the government to change the existing laws. This happens when people disagree with the policies of the government.
- People debate about the actions of their representatives and discuss matters related to corruption and reservation. They try to understand why some parties and leaders win elections.
  In this way people try to understand the logic behind the prevalent chaos and decline. Through this, people aspire to create a better world.

Origin of Politics

- Politics emerges from the reality that people have different views about what is fair and desirable for them and society.
- Politics involves multiple **negotiations**[4] that take place in a society. Collective decisions are made through these multiple negotiations. These negotiations take place at the following two levels

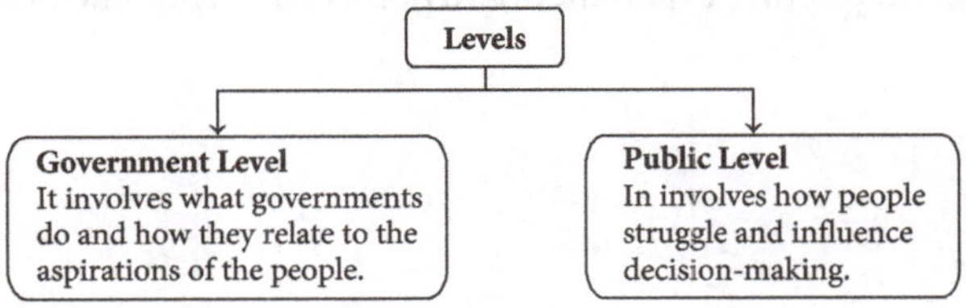

- Individuals engage in political activity when they
  - negotiate with each other.
  - participate in collective activities aimed at promoting social development.
  - work together to address and resolve common problems.

4 **Negotiation** It refers to discussion aimed at reaching an agreement.

Quick Test 1

1. Which core values poliatical theory explores?
2. Define the meaning of justice.
3. What are the two levels of negotiations in politics?

1.2 Key Concept in Political Theory

- Political theory deals with the ideas and principles that shape Constitutions, governments and social life in a systematic manner. These ideas include equality, freedom, justice, rights, dignity[5], etc.
- Constitutions are based on ideas and principles that have been debated since the times of **Kautilya** and **Aristotle.** These discussions continued with thinkers like **Jean Jacques Rousseau, Karl Marx, Mahatma Gandhi** and **Dr. B.R. Ambedkar.**
- The ideas of some thinkers are listed below
    - In the fifth century B.C., **Plato and Aristotle** discussed with their students whether monarchy[6] or democracy[7] was better.
    - In modern times, **Rousseau** first argued for freedom as a Fundamental Right of human kind.
    - **Karl Marx** argued that equality was as crucial as freedom.
    - **Mahatma Gandhi** discussed the meaning of genuine freedom or swaraj[8] in his book **Hind Swaraj.**
    - **Dr. Ambedkar** strongly argued that the Scheduled Castes must be considered a minority and must receive special protection.
- These above given ideas of thinkers are reflected in the Indian Constitution such as; The preamble of our Constitution guarantees freedom and equality, the chapter on the **Fundamental Rights** in our Constitution give equal rights to the people and abolished untouchability in any form, **Gandhian principles** based on welfare of weaker sections are reflected in Directive Principles[9].

Functions of Political Theory

- It clarifies the meaning of concepts such as freedom, equality, justice, democracy, secularism and so on. Different countries may try to protect such values by protecting them in their Constitutions. Examples of this are the American and Indian Constitutions.
- It examines the significance of principles such as rule of law[10], separation of powers[11], judicial review[12], etc. This is done by examining the arguments put forward by different thinkers in defence of these concepts.
- It also reflects upon current political experiences and points out trends and possibilities for the future.

5 **Dignity** It refers to the state or quality of being worthy of an honour or respect.
6 **Monarchy** It refers to a form of government in which a single person rules based on hereditary rights.
7 **Democracy** It is a system of government in which power is held by the people, either directly or through elected representatives.
8 **Swaraj** It refers to self-rule or independence.
9 **Directive Principles** It refers to guidelines in the Indian Constitution for the creation of social and economic policies aimed at achieving justice and equality.
10 **Rule of law** It refers to the idea that all members of society are equally subjected to laws and processes.
11 **Separation of powers** It refers to a governance model that divides the Government into organs where each organ has separate and independent powers.
12 **Judicial review** It refers to the power of a court to decide whether a law or decision by the government is Constitutional.

Challenges to Freedom and Equality

While India is free and independent, questions regarding freedom and equality have not stopped coming up. This is because of the following reasons

- Issues related to freedom, equality and democracy arise in various aspects of social life. Their implementation happens at different pace across different sectors.

  For example Although, equality exists in the political sphere in the form of equal rights to some extent but it may not always exist in the economic or social sphere.

- The Fundamental Rights guaranteed by our Constitution are re-interpreted by the respected courts in response to new circumstances.
- These rights have been amended and expanded over time through judicial interpretations and government policies which are designed to solve new problems and challenges faced by the society over time.

  For example The right to life was re-interpreted by the court and now this also includes the right to livelihood. Similarly, the right to information has been granted through a new law.

- With the new changes in our world, we discover new dimensions of freedom as well as new threats.

  For example Global communications technology making the networking easier and help the activists to network with each other across the world to protect the tribal culture.

  However, it also create threats for the people by allowing terrorists and criminals to form network easily. Thus, information which is shared online neeeds to be protected and this can be done only by government control.

  Although people recognise that some form of regulation is necessary to safeguard the security and privacy of the individual but **netizens**[13] (citizens of the internet) do not like government control in all sphere. As a result, questions are raised regarding the extent of freedom that should be given to people.

1.3 Applying Political Theory in Practice

Political theorists have provided diverse definitions of political ideas such as freedom and equality. We find multiple definitions of these ideas because of the human interaction with society. For example, the term equality focuses on our relationships with other human beings because they have many opinions regarding their needs, which should be understood and harmonised.

This can be understood through the following common experience of equality.

- **Equal Opportunity** People sometimes jump queues in public places like shops, doctor's clinics or government offices. When they get ahead, we feel cheated because we all want equal opportunity to access goods and services.
- **Special Counters for the Elderly and Disabled** Special provisions, such as separate counters for the elderly or disabled people are justified because they ensure equality for those who need extra support.
- **Poverty and Access to Basic Needs and Rights** Many poor people cannot afford basic services like healthcare because they have no money to pay for goods and services.
  - Many children are unable to attend school because they have to work to support their family.
  - Although the Indian Constitution guarantees the **Right to Primary Education** for all, but many of them cannot access this right.
  - Thus, the idea of equality is quite a complex subject. For example, if we are in a queue we want equal opportunity but if we suffer from some disability we want special provisions for us.
  - These above given common experiences of equality is not just about equal opportunity for all but also ensures fairness and give opportunities to the needy people.

---

13 **Netizens** It refers to people who actively participate in the online communities, forums, and social media platforms.

Role of Political Theorists

Political theorists may be academic or independent scholar. Their roles includes

- They clarify the meaning of political concepts for common people. This is done by looking at how these terms are understood and used in ordinary language.
- They also debate and examine the diverse meanings and opinions in a systematic manner.
- They examine complex questions, such as when equal opportunity is enough or when special treatment is necessary and how long such measures should last.

1.4 Importance of Studying Political Theory

It is important for students to study political theory for the following reasons

- Political theory is applicable to various professions, including politics, policy-making law and activism. Understanding these concepts can help students in their future careers.
- Students should have a foundational knowledge of political ideas to become a responsible voters. They will be able to make responsible decisions and express their interests.
- Political theory encourages students to analyse their own ideas and feelings about issues like discrimination and privilege. By looking at political things more carefully, students become moderate in their ideas and feelings.
- Political theory exposes students to think systematically on justice or equality. It helps students to improve their opinions and arguments. It enhances their ability to debate rationally and communicate effectively.

Quick Test 2

1. Write the name of the book in which Mahatma Gandhi discussed the meaning of genuine freedom.
2. What do you understand by the term rule of law?
3. Give one example of applying political theory in practice.

Mind Map

POLITICAL THEORY

1 Meaning of Politics

- It is an integral component of any society.
- Affects daily life including- Economic, education and foreign policies of a state.
- Explores core values of political life.
- Help in finding ways of living together and acknowledging our obligations.
- The formation and functioning of government is an important focus of politics.

Government Roles

- Formulates and implements policies.
- Manages collective decisions.

Influence of Politics in Daily Life

- An inefficient or corrupt government can endanger people's lives and security.
- Government in power allows any conflict to become violent.
- Government makes policies to increase literacy and employment.

2 Citizens Role in Politics

- Policies are influenced by citizens by activities like- Protest, campaign, and associations.
- Citizens analyse government actions and seek better solutions.

Citizens' Engagement with Government

- Associations and organise campaigns to express their demands.
- Protest and organise demonstrations to persuade the government to change the existing laws.
- Debate about the actions of their representatives and discuss matters related to corruption.

Origin of Politics

- The reality that people have different views about what is fair and desirable.
- Involves multiple negotiations that take place in a society.
- Collective decisions are made after multiple negotiations.
- Individuals engage in political activity when they negotiate with each other.
- Work together to address and resolve common problems.

3 Key Political Thinkers

- **Plato and Aristotle** Debated about monarchy and democracy.
- **Rousseau** Advocated freedom as a Fundamental Right.
- **Karl-Marx** Emphasised equality.
- **Mahatma Gandhi** Explored 'Swaraj'.
- **Dr. B.R. Ambedkar** Advocated rights for marginalised groups.

Key Functions of Political Theory

- Clarifies political concepts like Democracy, Secularism, Rule of Law.
- It reflects current political experience and modern trends.
- Suggests solutions for freedom and equality related challenges.

Challenges to Freedom and Equality

- Uneven applications of equality.
- Refined Fundamental Rights. (eg- Right to life).
- Balancing freedom and security in digital world.

4 Applying Political Theory in Practice

- Provided diverse definitions of political ideas such as freedom and equality.
- The human interaction with society.
- Equal opportunity to access goods and services.
- Special counters for the elderly and disabled. It ensure equality for those who need extra support.
- Poverty and Access to basic needs and rights.
- Right to primary education.

Role of Political Theorists

- They clarify the meaning of political concepts .
- They examine complex questions, about equality opportunity, and special treatment etc.

5 Importance of Studying Political Theory

- Applicable to various professions, including politics, policy-making law and activism.
- Able to make responsible decisions and express their interests.
- Encourages students to analyse their own ideas and feelings .
- By understanding political things carefully, students become moderate in their ideas and feelings.
- People start thinking systematically on justice or equality.
- Improve their opinions and arguments.
- Enhances their ability to debate rationally and communicate effectively.

Dr. B.R. Ambedkar

Aristotle, the Father of Political Science

NCERT Folder

Intext Questions

1. Write a short note on any of the political thinkers mentioned in the chapter. (Pg 5)

Ans. Jean Jacques Rousseau was a philosopher, writer and theorist, born in Switzerland. He was the first philosopher of modern times who argued for freedom. According to him, freedom is a Fundamental Right of humankind. He was a highly influential thinker who helped to shape the French revolution. He wrote **Social Contract,** in which he questioned the purpose of government and its responsibility for its citizens.

2. How does politics influence our daily life? Analyse a day's events in your life.

Or How does politics and government influence the daily lives of people?

Ans. Politics influences our daily lives in many ways. Let's analyse a typical day to see how this happens

(i) **Public Services** Services like electricity or water are often controlled by government policies. Decisions on supply, pricing and availability are shaped by political institutions.

(ii) **Education** In school, the curriculum and education system are influenced by the government's education policies.

(iii) **Transport** To travel anywhere, people use roads, buses or metro. These services are provided by the government. Fuel prices are all regulated by government policies. The traffic rules are enforced by law.

(iv) **Rights and Freedom** Throughout the day, people exercise freedoms granted by the Constitution-freedom to express opinions, assemble or engage in different activities. These are protected by political laws and systems.

(v) **Healthcare and Safety** If a person falls sick or faces an emergency, public health services and safety measures–like hospitals or police–are also controlled by the state.

Exercise

1. Which of the following statements are true/false about Political theory?

(i) It discusses ideas that form the basis of political institutions.

(ii) It explains the relationship between different religions.

(iii) It explains the meanings or concepts like equality and freedom.

(iv) It predicts the performance of political parties.

Ans. (i) True (ii) False (iii) True (iv) False

2. Politics is more than what politicians do. Do you agree with this statement? Give examples.

Ans. I agree with the statement. Politicians being a member of a party or a part of government are involved in politics. By giving following examples we can justify the statement that politics is more than what politicians do

- Politics is the practice and theory of influencing other people. Politics involves the making of a common decision for a group of people, i.e. a uniform decision applying in the same way to all members of the group.
- Politics is an art as well as a science of governance like governing of a political entity such as a nation or state and the administration.
- Politics involves actions of the government and its inter-relationship with aspirations of the people.
- Politics involves mass struggle and influence on decision-making. Generally, politics is understood as forming alliances, exercising power and protecting and advancing particular ideas or goals.

3. Vigilant citizens are a must for the successful working of a democracy. Comment.

Ans. Vigilant citizens are a must for the successful working of a democracy due to following reasons

- Vigilant citizens possess awakened reasoning and ability to reflect on the actions of their representatives.
- If vigilant citizens notice leaders defecting from parties, making false promises and false claims, manipulating specific group of the society, pursuing personal or group interest ruthlessly, they can organise associations, protests, etc.
- Organisation of demonstrations persuade the government to modify the existing outdated and false laws and to frame or pass new laws and regulations.
- They have the capability to check wrong policies and corruption persisting among government officials and leaders.

4. In what ways is the study of political theory useful for us? Identify four ways in which political theory can be useful to us.

Ans. The four ways in which study of political theory is useful for us are

(i) The knowledge gained by political theory helps in building good citizens.

(ii) Political theory provides good idea about government, administration and diplomacy.

(iii) Political theory provides information and idea about state and government.

(iv) It increases the political awareness of man, like, his freedom, rights and duties. It also reminds the government of its duty and responsibility towards the people.

5. Do you think that a good/convincing argument can compel others to listen to you?

Ans. Yes, I agree that a good/convincing argument can compel others to listen to one. Arguments prove the degree of reason of a proposition and the need to defend it. A good defence is a compelling factor in the audience listening to the speaker.

The knowledge of political theory enables an individual to think systematically on issues like justice, freedom, equality, fraternity, secularism, etc. Systematic thinking helps in polishing opinion of an individual. This helps the presentation of argument in an informed manner. A wise opinion is convincing and is for the sake of common interests. Therefore, it makes others listen to and agree with the individual who argues in a convincing manner.

6. Do you think studying political theory is like studying mathematics? Give reasons for your answer.

Ans. Every subject has its own language and terms. I think that studying political theory is not like studying mathematics due to following reasons

- Mathematics deals with precise concepts and patterns, while political theory studies human beings and their ideas in the context of power and decision-making.
- In mathematics, there are single definitions of terms while in political theory the definitions of terms vary according to the context. This is because the opinions of people changes unlike objects and carries different meanings of a single term in different contexts.
- The concepts that are dealt by mathematics are constant and derived through formulas, whereas the concepts of political theory are at variance and open to interpretation.

Exam Pattern Questions

Objective Type Questions

Multiple Choice Questions (MCQs)

1. The study that gives us information about the state and government is called ....

(a) Economic theory
(b) Political theory
(c) Social theory
(d) None of the above

2. The political theory explains the meaning of which of the following concept?

(a) Independence (b) Equality
(c) Democracy (d) All of these

3. Which of the following statements about political theory is incorrect?

(a) Politics is not confined to the affairs of government.
(b) Political theory systematically thinks about the values that inform political life-values such as freedom, equality and justice.
(c) Political theory clarifies the existing definitions of concepts by focusing on some major political thinkers of the past and present.
(d) None of the above

4. Which of the following is true to explain the importance of political theory? Diksha App

(a) Political theory exposes us to systematic thinking on justice and equality.
(b) Political theory is helpful to have a basic knowledge of political ideas and institutions.
(c) Study of political theory enhances political awareness.
(d) All of the above

5. 'Politics envelops us like the coils of a snake and there is no other way out but to wrestle with it'. Whose statement is this? Competency Based Que; Diksha App

(a) Mahatma Gandhi (b) M.N. Roy
(c) C. Rajagopalachari (d) Surendra Nath Tagore

6. Which of the following explains the importance of the political theory?
(a) Knowledge of person and state relations
(b) Knowledge of state and governance
(c) Knowledge of rights and duties
(d) All of the above

7. Which of the following are the subjects of studying political theory?
I. Knowing Principles and Ideas
II. Interpreting Principles and Ideas
III. Safeguarding Principles and Ideas
Select the correct answer using the codes given below.
(a) Only I (b) Only III
(c) Both II and III (d) I, II and III

8. The book "Hind Swaraj" was written by ....
(a) Dr. B.R. Ambedkar (b) Mahatma Gandhi
(c) Sardar Patel (d) Lala Lajpat Rai

9. Consider the following sentences regarding Dr. B.R. Ambedkar's views on Scheduled Castes (SCs). Competency Based Que
I. He argued that SCs must be considered as minority.
II. He argued for special protection to SCs.
III. He was against granting of reservations to SCs.
Which of the following statements is/are correct?
(a) Only I (b) Only II
(c) Both I and II (d) I, II and III

10. Arrange the following political thinkers in chronological order according to when they contributed their ideas.
I. Dr. B.R. Ambedkar II. Jean Jacques Rousseau
III. Kautilya IV. Plato
Codes
(a) IV, III, II, I (b) III, IV, II, I
(c) III, IV, I, II (d) IV, III, I, II

11. Consider the following statements related to the significance of political theory. Competency Based Que
I. The knowledge gained by political theory helps in building good citizens.
II. It establishes balance between state and individual.
Select the correct answer using the code given below.
(a) Only I (b) Only II
(c) Both I and II (d) None of these

12. Identify the incorrect pair related to the political values from the following options. Competency Based Que
(a) Democracy : A system of government where citizens exercise power directly or elect representatives.
(b) Justice : The principle of fairness and moral rightness in law.
(c) Secularism : The principle of separating religion from political and civic affairs.
(d) Censorship : The protection of citizens' rights to express their opinions freely.

13. Which of the following statements is correct? Diksha App
(a) Equality has one universally accepted definition.
(b) It is practically impossible to define equality.
(c) Equality is nothing but equal opportunities to all.
(d) There are many definitions for equality depending upon the context.

14. The .... has been interpreted by the Court to include the Right to Livelihood.
(a) Right to Religion
(b) Right to Life
(c) Right to Constitutional Remedies
(d) Cultural and Educational Rights

15. Who authored 'The Republic'?
(a) Plato (b) Aristotle
(c) Karl Marx (d) None of these

16. Special privileges to disabled and weaker sections is called. Diksha App
(a) Inequality
(b) Injustice
(c) Fairness and Social Justice
(d) Discrimination

17. Which of the following statements is correct regarding the relevance of studying political theory? Diksha App
(a) Political theory is relevant only for politicians.
(b) Political theory is not relevant for students.
(c) Political theory is relevant for people of all ages.
(d) None of the above

18. Match the following political values (List I) with their descriptions (List II).

List I	List II
A. Freedom	1. The state of being treated the same as others without discrimination.
B. Equality	2. The ability to act or think without hindrance or restraint.
C. Justice	3. The concept of fairness and the moral obligation to uphold individuals' rights.
D. Participation	4. The involvement of citizens in the decision-making processes of governance.

Codes

	A	B	C	D		A	B	C	D
(a)	2	1	3	4	(b)	3	4	1	2
(c)	1	2	4	3	(d)	4	3	2	1

19. Match the following thinkers (List I) with their associated ideas (List II).

List I	List II
A. Plato	1. Discussed genuine freedom (swaraj) in "Hind Swaraj".
B. Rousseau	2. Argued for freedom as a Fundamental Right of human kind.
C. Karl Marx	3. Emphasised the importance of equality alongside freedom.
D. Gandhi	4. Advocated for democracy over monarchy.

Codes

	A	B	C	D
(a)	2	1	3	4
(b)	3	4	1	2
(c)	1	2	3	4
(d)	4	2	3	1

20. There are two statements marked as Statement I and Statement II. Choose the correct alternative from the following options. **Competency Based Que**

Statement I Political theory only examines past political ideas and has no relevance to current political practices.

Statement II Political theory helps us understand and assess values such as freedom and equality in everyday life.

(a) Both Statement I and Statement II are true.
(b) Both Statement I and Statement II are false.
(c) Statement I is true, but Statement II is false.
(d) Statement I is false, but Statement II is true.

Assertion-Reason Questions

Directions (Q. Nos. 21-25) In the questions given below, there are two statements marked as Assertion (A) and Reason (R). Read the statements and choose the correct option.

Codes

(a) Both A and R are true and R is the correct explanation of A.
(b) Both A and R are true, but R is not the correct explanation of A.
(c) A is true, but R is false.
(d) A is false, but R is true.

21. Assertion (A) The unique ability of human beings to reason and communicate is fundamental to political theory.

Reason (R) This capacity allows individuals to express their thoughts, share ideas and engage in discussions about societal organisation and governance.

22. Assertion (A) Citizens actively engage with government actions.

Reason (R) This engagement includes forming associations, organising campaigns and debating policies to seek accountability and advocate for changes.

23. Assertion (A) Politics is very important for the progress and development of the society.

Reason (R) It is required to take fair decision and try to remove the injustices from the society.

24. Assertion (A) In modern times Rousseau first argued for freedom as a Fundamental Right of human kind.

Reason (R) Dr. B.R. Ambedkar discussed the meaning of genuine freedom or swaraj in his book "Hind Swaraj".

25. Assertion (A) Political theory tries to bring changes according to the circumstances.

Reason (R) Concepts like liberty and equality constantly developed as a result of political theory.

Passage Based Questions

26. Read the given passage and answer the following questions.

Political theory is concerned with understanding the values that guide society, such as freedom, equality and justice. It addresses fundamental questions like how society should be organised, why governments are necessary, and the best form of government. Political theory also explores whether the concepts of freedom and equality are present in our daily lives, like in schools, offices and government services. It asks whether the political institutions in place are truly democratic and how they can be improved. By studying political theory, we learn how to think critically about political events and participate in discussions about societal issues.

(i) Which of the following is a fundamental question that political theory addresses?

(a) How to set rules only ?
(b) How should society be organised and what form of government is best?
(c) What is the best way to understand freedom and equality only ?
(d) What is justice only?

(ii) What does political theory encourage us to do?

(a) Just follow orders
(b) Think critically about political events and discuss societal issues
(c) Avoid any form of discussion
(d) Focus only on personal interests

(iii) What does political theory examine about freedom and equality in the life of common people?

27. Read the given passage and answer the following questions.

Dr. Ambedkar vigorously argued that the Scheduled Castes must be considered a minority, and as such, must receive special protection. These ideas find their place in the Indian Constitution; our Preamble enshrines freedom and equality; the chapter on rights in the Indian Constitution abolishes untouchability in any form; Gandhian principles find a place in Directive Principles.

(i) Which principle advocated by Dr. Ambedkar for the scheduled castes is reflected in the Indian Constitution?
(a) Abolishment of untouchability
(b) Representation as a minority
(c) Right to freedom of speech
(d) Equal opportunity for education

(ii) What does the Preamble of the Indian Constitution emphasise according to the text?
(a) Abolishing untouchability
(b) Freedom and equality
(c) Special privileges for minorities
(d) Reservation of government jobs

(iii) Which chapter of the Indian Constitution specifically addresses the issue of untouchability?
(a) Fundamental Duties
(b) Preamble
(c) Directive Principles of State Policy
(d) Fundamental Rights

(iv) Which part of the Indian Constitution incorporates Gandhian principles?
(a) Fundamental Rights
(b) Preamble
(c) Directive Principles of the State Policy
(d) Fundamental Duties

28. Read the given passage and answer the following questions.

Although freedom is guaranteed in our Constitution, we encounter new interpretations all the time. The Fundamental Rights guaranteed by our Constitution are continually being reinterpreted in response to new circumstances. For instance, the right to life has been interpreted by the court to include the right to livelihood. The right to information has been granted through a new law. Societies frequently encounter new challenges which generate new interpretations. The Fundamental Rights guaranteed by our Constitution have been amended and expanded over time through judicial interpretations and government policies which are designed to address new problems.

(i) .... is the final interpreter of Indian Constitution.
(a) Supreme Court (b) High Court
(c) Parliament (d) President

(ii) .... is empowered to amend the Indian Constitution.
(a) Supreme Court (b) President
(c) State Government (d) Parliament

(iii) How have the Fundamental Rights in the Indian Constitution evolved over time?

Answers

1. (b) Political theory
2. (d) All of these
3. (d) None of the above
4. (d) All of the above
5. (a) Mahatma Gandhi
6. (d) All of the above
7. (d) I, II and III
8. (b) Mahatma Gandhi
9. (c) Both I and II
10. (b) III, IV, II, I
11. (c) Both I and II
12. (d) Censorship : The protection of citizens' right to express their opinions freely.
13. (d) There are many definitions for equality depending upon the context.
14. (b) Right to Life
15. (a) Plato
16. (c) Fairness and Social Justice
17. (c) Political theory is relevant for people of all ages.
18. (a) 2 1 3 4
19. (d) 4 2 3 1
20. (d) Statement I is false, but Statement II is true.
21. (a) Both A and R are true and R is the correct explanation of A.
22. (a) Both A and R are true and R is the correct explanation of A.
23. (a) Both A and R are true and R is the correct explanation of A.
24. (c) A is true, but R is false.
25. (a) Both A and R are true and R is the correct explanation of A.

26. (i) (b) How should society be organised and what form of government is best?

(ii) (b) Think critically about political events and discuss societal issues

(iii) Political theory examines whether the concepts of freedom and equality are present in the life of common people. For example, the actions of the government affect the life of people deeply, so they may take interest in what the government does. They form associations and organise campaigns to fulfill their demands and negotiate and try to shape the goals that the government pursues. They take part in collective activities which are designed to promote social development and help to resolve common problems.

27. (i) (b) Representation as a minority

(ii) (b) Freedom and equality

(iii) (d) Fundamental Rights

(iv) (c) Directive Principles of the State Policy

28. (i) (a) Supreme Court

(ii) (d) Parliament

(iii) The Fundamental Rights in the Indian Constitution have evolved through judicial interpretations and government policies. Courts have expanded these rights by including the right to livelihood under the right to life. The right to information was introduced to enhance transparency in governance.

Subjective Type Questions

Very Short Answer Type Questions

1. What is the main objective of political theory?

Ans. The main objective of political theory is to train citizens' to think rationally about political questions and assess the political events of our time.

It examines the values such as freedom, equality, justice and analyses the meaning and significance of these concepts in political life.

2. Why politics is significant for us?

Ans. Politics is significant for us due to the following reasons

- Politics binds diverse people together and it also gives opportunities to some specific social groups to express themselves.
- Politics is a process to establish equality and social harmony.

3. How government policies improve our lives?

Ans. Government policies improve our lives in the following ways

- By making policies for social security.
- By enacting laws for better education and maintenance of law and order.

4. If there is a corrupt government what could be possible consequences?

Ans. If there is a corrupt government, the possible consequences are as follows

- Law and order will be disrupted in the society.
- There will be fear of insecurity among people.

5. How do individuals engage in political activity ?

Ans. Individuals engage in political activity through the following

- By negotiating with one another.
- By participating in collective activities aimed at promoting social development.
- By working together to address and resolve common problems.

6. The government as a part of politics can affect on daily life of humans both in useful and a harmful way. How?

Competency Based Que

Ans. The government in a useful manner can frame foreign policy, education policy and economic policy to benefits the people.

The government in a harmful manner can lead to violent protest in response to various conflicts which may hamper the daily life of people.

7. What is the significance of studying political thinkers like Rousseau, Marx and Gandhi?

Ans. Studying political thinkers like Rousseau, Marx and Gandhi is significant because their ideas have greatly influenced political movements and policy decisions. Their theories on freedom, equality and justice have shaped political philosophies and the principles upheld by modern governments.

8. State the views of Dr. B.R. Ambedkar about Scheduled Castes.

Ans. The views of DR. B.R. Ambedkar about Scheduled Castes are as follows

- They must be considered as a minority.
- They must receive special protection under law.

9. What is the significance of equality in society?

Ans. Equality means treating all individuals fairly, without discrimination and ensuring equal opportunities for everyone. It is significant in society as it promotes justice, strengthens democracy and reduces socio-economic disparities, thus creates an inclusive and balanced community.

10. Why is political theory still relevant today?

Ans. Political theory remains relevant because issues concerning freedom, equality and democracy continue to arise in various areas of life. While some progress has been made, challenges and reinterpretations of Fundamental Rights still occur as societies evolve and new problems emerge.

Short Answer Type Questions

1. What do you mean by politics? How is politics significant for the society?

Or What is politics? Diksha App

Ans. Politics involves making common decisions for a group of people. It is considered that politics is a kind of public service.

It is important in resolving conflicts over distribution of resources and for development in society.

Significance of Politics

- Politics is important for the progress and development of the society.
- It is required to take fair decision and try to remove the injustices from the society.
- It involves the multiple negotiations that take place in society through which collective decisions are made.
- No society can exist without some form of political organisations and collective decision-making.

2. What does political theory deals with?

Or What is the scope of political theory? Diksha App

Ans. Political theory is closely related to the nature of state, the authority, the structure of the state and the interaction of the state with its environment.

- It critically evaluates values which influence political life like freedom, equality and justice.
- It explains the significance of principles such as rule of law, separation of powers, judicial review, etc.
- It examines the extent to which freedom should be granted to the citizens.
- It also examines whether existing institutions are adequate and how existing institutions can be made more democratic.

3. Discuss the role of political theory in understanding political systems and shaping political decisions.

Ans. Political theory plays a crucial role in understanding the structure and function of political systems by providing a framework for analysing the values, principles and ideas that guide political decision-making.

- It helps us to understand fundamental concepts such as freedom, equality, justice, democracy and the rule of law.
- By studying the works of political thinkers like Plato, Aristotle, Rousseau, Marx, Gandhi and other political theory, it allows us to examine different ideologies and political philosophies.
- Political theory also helps assess the functioning of political systems by questioning how institutions such as governmental and legal systems operate and whether they truly reflect the values they claim to uphold.

Thus, political theory encourages critical thinking, enabling citizens' to evaluate the policies and actions of political leaders, and to propose solutions for creating a more just and democratic society.

4. How can citizens express their interest in politics?

Ans. Citizens can express their interest in politics in the following ways

- People form associations and organise campaigns to express their demands. They negotiate with others and try to shape the goals that governments follow.
- People protest and organise demonstrations to persuade the government to change the existing laws. This happens when people disagree with the policies of the government.
- People debate about the actions of their representatives and discuss matters related to corruption and reservation. They try to understand why some parties and leaders win elections.

5. 'Equality must involve some kind of fairness'. Justify this statement. Competency Based Que

Ans. Equality must involve some kind of fairness, so that people are not unduly exploited and disadvantaged by economic factors.

In Indian society, there are many children who cannot go to school because they have to work to feed themselves. Most girl students in poor households are taken out of school to care for their younger siblings while parents go to work.

Hence, if there is no fairness in equality, there will be discrimination on the basis of gender, caste, religion, region, etc.

The fundamental principle of justice is that 'Equals should be treated equally and unequals unequally'. To achieve the objective of this principle, equality must be provided by giving fair opportunities.

6. "Meaning of freedom changes with context". Explain briefly. Competency Based Que

Ans. Meaning of freedom is changing with the changing context. This can be understand through the following.

Freedom means different things to many people. Some view freedom politically, as having the opportunity to vote for particular ideas, people or parties which best represent our views. Closely related to this is the notion of freedom of speech, where one has the liberty to voice their personal opinion or perspective.

While some understand freedom in a financial context, where people seek to free themselves from financial debt, outstanding credit and burden of loan. Thus, meaning of freedom changes with context and conditions of people.

Long Answer Type Questions

1. "Political theory plays a crucial role in society". Justify the statement. Competency Based Que

Ans. Political theory plays a crucial role in society. The statement can be justified through the following points

- It helps in understanding and analysing fundamental questions about governance, values and our relationships with one another.
- It explores concepts such as freedom, equality, justice and democracy. It offers clarity on their meanings and applications in both historical and contemporary contexts.
- It allows citizens to think critically and rationally about political issues. It enables them to engage responsibly in public life.
- It helps to understand and assess policies. It guides people to make informed decisions about societal problems and how they should be addressed.
- It helps people to engage with different perspectives on how society should function. This promotes informed participation in democracy. It also enhances the ability to advocate for justice, equality and fairness in everyday life.

2. How does political theory address the concepts of freedom and equality in modern societies?

Ans. Political theory addresses the concepts of freedom and equality in modern societies in the following ways

- It analyses their meanings and explores their practical implications in modern societies. For example, freedom is not limited to the absence of external restraints but also includes broader rights such as the right to life, livelihood and privacy.
- Courts and governments have continually re-interpreted and expanded the definition of freedom. This is in response to emerging challenges in society. Similarly, equality is also understood beyond equality of opportunity.
- Political theorists examine economic and social dimensions of inequality. They recognise that while political equality may exist, social and economic disparities still persist.
- Political theory argues for measures to achieve fairness. These measures include providing special provisions for disadvantaged groups or promoting equal opportunities for education and employment.
- Political theory highlights how freedom and equality are present in various institutions and everyday life. This encourages the development of policies that aim to create a more just and equitable society.

3. Why should students study political theory? Discuss its relevance. Diksha App

Ans. Students should study political theory because of the following reasons

- Political theory is applicable to various professions, including politics, policy-making, law and activism. Understanding these concepts can help students in their future careers.
- Students need a foundational knowledge of political ideas to be responsible voters. They will be able to make responsible decisions and express their interests.
- Political theory encourages students to analyse their own ideas and feelings about issues like discrimination and privilege. By looking at political things more carefully, students become moderate in their ideas and feelings.
- Political theory exposes students to systematic thinking. It helps students to improve their opinions and arguments. It enhances their ability to debate rationally and communicate effectively.

Thus, studying political theory is relevant for students as it provides a deeper understanding of key political concepts that shape society and governance. It provides them with critical thinking skills, enabling them to engage reasonably with issues of justice, freedom, equality and rights.

4. Discuss the ideas of significant historical thinkers which have guided political principles all around the world. **Competency Based Que**

Ans. The ideas of political thinkers which have guided political principles all around the world are given below

- In the fifth century B.C., Plato and Aristotle discussed the idea whether monarchy or democracy was better.
- In modern times, Rousseau first argued for freedom as a Fundamental Right of human kind.
- Karl Marx argued that equality was as crucial as freedom.
- Mahatma Gandhi discussed the meaning of genuine freedom or swaraj in his book "Hind Swaraj".
- Dr. Ambedkar strongly argued that the Scheduled Castes must be considered a minority and must receive special protection.

The ideas of these thinkers are also reflected in the Indian Constitution. The Preamble of the Indian Constitution enshrines freedom and equality. The chapter on rights in the Indian Constitution abolishes untouchability in any form. Gandhian principles are also reflected in Directive Principles.

5. What is the relevance of political theory in addressing modern issues such as global communication, privacy and the internet?

Ans. Political theory is highly relevant in addressing modern issues such as global communication, privacy and the internet, as it provides the philosophical and ethical frameworks needed to navigate the challenges posed by new technologies and the evolving global landscape.

Issue of Global Communication

- The rise of global communication technologies has led to greater interconnectedness, enabling activists, organisations and even governments to communicate and share information across borders.
- While this connectivity allows for the promotion of human rights, environmental protection and other causes, it also raises new challenges such as the spread of misinformation, cybercrime and the potential for state surveillance.
- Political theory helps to address these concerns by exploring the balance between freedom of expression and the need for regulation to protect individuals from harm, while also ensuring that governments do not overstep their authority in curbing free speech.

Issue of Privacy

- Privacy is another area where political theory is essential. With the increasing amount of personal data shared and stored online, issues surrounding data security and the right to privacy have become pressing concerns.
- Political theory explores the tension between the individual's right to privacy and the state's interest in protecting national security or preventing crime.
- It helps guide discussions on how much surveillance is acceptable, who has the right to access personal data, and what measures should be taken to protect individual privacy in the digital age.

Issue of Internet

- The internet has also raised questions about the regulation of online activities, such as whether governments or private corporations should control the flow of information.
- Political theory offers tools to critically assess these questions and evaluate how much freedom should be given to individuals for using of the internet and what kinds of ethical guidelines should be implemented.

Thus, information shared online needs to be protected and this can be done only through government control.

Picture Based Question

1. Study the cartoon given below and answer the question that follow.

(i) What is the central concern expressed through the image?

(a) The character's health
(b) The character's involvement in sports
(c) The character's political activities
(d) The character's financial situation

Ans. (c) The character's political activities

(ii) Based on the image, what might be the lady's main reason for advising the minister to retire from politics?

(a) Loss of public support
(b) Involvement in corrupt practices
(c) Desire to pursue another career
(d) Fear of political opposition

Ans. (b) Involvement in corrupt practices

(iii) In the context of the image, what political value might be considered at risk due to the politician's activities?

(a) Transparency and honesty
(b) Political equality
(c) National security
(d) Public health policy

Ans. (a) Transparency and honesty

(iv) The image suggests that the lady that believes politics can lead to which of the following problems?

(a) Encouraging unethical behaviour
(b) Promoting fair and free elections
(c) Improving education systems
(d) Strengthening international relations

Ans. (a) Encouraging unethical behaviour

SELF ASSESSMENT TEST

Multiple Choice Questions

1. Which of the following statements correctly defines politics?
   (a) Politics is just about what politicions do.
   (b) The purpose of politics is to advance self-interest.
   (c) Politics accomodates multiples needs and interests of various sections of the society.
   (d) Politics is a tool to establish dominance over weaker sections.
2. What are the two levels of negatiotion in politics?
   (a) The government level and the public level (b) The government level only
   (c) The public level only (d) None of these
3. In ancient Greece, who was described as the 'Wisest Man'?
   (a) Socrates (b) Plato (c) Aristotle (d) Cephalus

Very Short Answer Type Questions

4. Give two reasons as to why political theory is important.
5. Who firstly argued for freedom as a Fundamental Right of Human Being?
6. Why human beings are considered 'Unique'?
7. Write down the features of political theory?

Short Answer Type Questions

8. Why politics has become a negative word for some people?
9. Even though India has got independence, why do we need political theory?

Long Answer Type Questions

10. "Politics works as a pursuit of common good of people." Justify the statement.
11. Describe the contributions of any political thinkers in the study of political theory.
12. Politics affects daily life of human. Explain.

Competency Based Que

02
CHAPTER

Freedom is the desire of individuals to control their own lives and make their own decisions.

Freedom

▼ **YOUR STUDY GOALS**

2.1 Meaning of Freedom
2.2 The Sources of Constraints
2.3 Harm Principle
2.4 Negative and Positive Liberty

▼ **YOUR PRACTICE GOAL**

- Objective Type Questions (29 Qs ; MCQs, A-R, Statements, Matching, Picture Based)
- Subjective Questions (10 VSAs, 12 SAs, 5 LAs) 2 Picture Based

2.1 Meaning of Freedom

- Living in a society requires rules and regulations because people have different interests and goals, these rules limit individual freedom but also help in reducing insecurity and allow personal development.
- Political theory discusses how to distinguish between socially necessary constraints and other restrictions on freedom.
- **Freedom** is valuable as it allows individuals to make independent choices. It allows the use of rational thinking and judgement in decision-making.
- In simple terms, freedom means **absence of constraints**. However complete meaning of freedom has two aspects positive and negative.
  - **Positive Aspect** This means creating conditions that enable people to express themselves freely and develop their talents and potential.
  - **Negative Aspect** This means being free from outside control. It allows individuals to make their own choices and decisions.

The Ideal of Freedom

- The writings of **Nelson Mandela** and **Aung San Suu Kyi** emphasise the significance of the ideal of freedom.

- Freedom was crucial to India's national struggle and inspired movements in Asia and Africa against British, French and Portuguese colonialism[1].

Nelson Mandela

- Nelson Mandela in his autobiography, **Long Walk to Freedom**, describes his personal struggle against the apartheid[2] regime in South Africa.
- Mandela's struggle was against unjust constraints imposed under apartheid regime, which discriminated the citizens on the basis of race.
- Mandela aimed to free all the people of South Africa.
- Mandela spent twenty-seven years in jail to achieve freedom for his people.

The system of apartheid imposed many constraints on people. These were
- They were forced to move to separate town areas.
- They were denied freedom of movement across the country.
- They were not allowed to choose who they could marry.

Aung San Suu Kyi

- Aung San Suu Kyi was inspired by Mahatma Gandhi's ideas of non-violence.
- She saw her freedom as linked to the freedom of her people in Myanmar.
- She remained under house arrest[3] for many years to achieve this freedom.
- She wrote a book name, **Freedom from Fear.** In this book, she wrote that "For me real freedom is freedom from fear and unless you can live free from fear you cannot live a dignified human life".
- According to Aung San Sun Kyi living a **dignified human life,** requires us to be able to overcome such fear.

Swaraj

- Swaraj is concept similar to freedom. It combines two words—**Swa** (Self) and **Raj** (Rule), meaning both self-rule and rule over self.
- Swaraj was a key demand in India's freedom movement, which represented both political and Constitutional freedom.
- Mahatma Gandhi emphasised the idea of Swaraj as **'rule over the self,'** focusing on self-governance and self-discipline, as highlighted in his work **Hind Swaraj**.
- Swaraj signifies liberation from de-humanising institutions and emphasises self-respect, self-responsibility and self-realisation.
- Understanding the true-self and its connection to society is crucial in achieving Swaraj.

Quick Test 1

1 What is the positive aspect of freedom?

2 Which country practised apartheid system as a system of racial segregation?

3 "For me real freedom is freedom from fear and unless you can live free from fear you can not live a dignified human life". Who give this statement?

4 What is the meaning of 'Swaraj'.

1 **Colonialism** It is the practice of acquiring physical control over another country and taking ownership of its land.

2 **Apartheid** It refer to a system of institutionalised racial segregation and discrimination, where one group is treated unfairly and other has fewer rights than another.

3 **House Arrest** It is a legal condition in which a person is confined to their home as a form of punishment or restraint.

2.2 The Sources of Constraints

Individuals cannot avoid all constraints or restrictions while living in society. The sources of constraints on freedom are as follows

- **Domination and External Controls** Restrictions imposed by force, such as colonial rule of apartheid in South Africa.
- **Government Laws** Laws can restrict freedom, but democratic governments allow freedom to its citizens with some control to protect the freedom of all the citizens.
- **Social and Economic Inequality** Inequalities, like those in the caste system[4], also impose constraints on freedom.

Netaji Subhash Chandra Bose on Freedom

Netaji Subhash Chandra Bose believed that freedom should include

- Freedom for individuals and society
- Freedom for men and women
- Freedom from political bondage
- Freedom from religious intolerance and communalism
- Freedom of equal distribution of wealth
- Freedom for all classes
- Freedom from socio-economic inequalities

Bose's political views also included support for complete freedom for India, support for a **classless society** and support for state socialism.

The idea of Subhash Chandra Bose on freedom may appear **Utopian** (dream) but this idea alone can satisfy the hunger in the soul.

Need of Constraints

- We need some constraints to maintain the order in the society otherwise society would descend into chaos.
- They foster an environment where people can live together harmoniously while maintaining their individual beliefs. They encourage respect for differing views, opinions and beliefs.
- They help to manage differences in opinions and ambitions, thus reducing the likelihood of conflicts.
- They provide mechanisms for controlling violence and resolving disputes which are essential for peaceful co-existence. They provide protection against bullying or attempts to impose conformity.

2.3 Harm Principle

The **Harm Principle** was introduced by **John Stuart Mill** in his essay **On Liberty**. According to the principle, interference with liberty is justified only for self-protection and to prevent harm to others. The principle is explained as follows

- J.S. Mill divides the action into the the following categories

Self-Regarding Actions	Other-Regarding Actions
Actions that have consequences only for the individual actor and nobody else are called self-regarding actions.	Actions that have consequences for others are called Other-regarding actions.
The state (or any other external authority) can not interfere in such actions.	The State (or any other external authority) can interfere in such actions. It can constrain a person from behaving in a manner that harms another individual.
For Example, deciding to pursue a particular career based on personal interests and goals.	For Example, disposing waste in a way that harms the community's health and quality of life.

4 Caste System It is a hierarchical social structure traditionally found in India, where people are divided into different social groups (castes) based on their birth.

- If an action does not cause harm, it should not be restricted. However, in case of other-regarding actions restriction should depend on the level of harm caused. He recommends restriction on the basis of harm caused. This is explained as follows
  - **In case of minor harm** Mill has recommended only social dis-approval and not the force of law if minor harm is caused.
  - **In case of major harm** Mill has recommended constraining actions by the force of law. Still, very harsh constraints should not be imposed.
- Thus, freedom should only be constrained in special circumstances. Society must bear the inconvenience in the spirit of protecting freedom.

Restrictions to Freedom in Indian Constitution

- In the Constitutional discussions in India, the term **reasonable restrictions** is used for justifiable constraints on freedom.
- The conditions for a restriction is to be reasonable which are as follows
  - It must be fair and should be based on logic.
  - It should balanced and not to be too harsh.

Liberalism

- Liberalism, as a political ideology, is associated with tolerance. It defends the right of individuals to hold and express their opinions, even if others disagree.
- Modern liberalism prioritises the individual over entities like family, society or community. It values them only if they are important to the individual.
- Liberals prioritise individual liberty, advocating for personal choices (e.g., marriage decisions) over social or collective influences, such as family or community pressures.
- Historically, liberalism supported free markets and minimal state involvement. However, **modern liberalism** recognises the need for welfare measures and reducing social and economic inequalities.

2.4 Negative and Positive Liberty

In political theory there are two aspects of freedom, called negative and positive liberty. Difference between them is explained in the following table

Positive Liberty	Negative Liberty
It focuses on the individual's ability to self-govern and pursue personal development.	It focuses on the protection of an area where the individual is free from interference by external authorities.
It is based on the idea of the freedom to act, develop and improve oneself with enabling conditions.	It is based on the idea of the freedom from external interference or constraints.
It focuses on the conditions (education, material resources) needed for personal growth and development.	It focuses on the creation of a **minimum area of non-interference** where individuals are free to make their own choices.
Government should provide conditions like education, employment, to support individual development.	Government or external authority should be limited. It should not interfere with personal choices and actions.
Positive liberty is criticised because it can sometimes be misused by dictators. They may justify controlling actions by claiming it is to improve society.	Negative liberty is criticised for focusing only on the absence of interference. It neglects the necessary conditions for personal growth.
The goal is to create a society that supports individual capabilities and allows full self-expression.	The goal is to maximise the individual's area of personal freedom without compromising stability in society.

Freedom of Expression

- **Freedom of expression**[5] is one of the fundamental areas of non-interference. It should not be restricted without strong justification.
- J.S. Mill argued for protection of this freedom. **Voltaire** supported the right to express even with unpopular opinions.
- Over time many books, films, plays or articles have been banned after protests. Examples include bans on books like **The Satanic Verses** by Salman Rusdie and **Ramayana Retold** by Aubrey Menon, films like **The Last Temptation of Christ** and the play **Me Nathuram Boltey** were banned after protests.
- Banning is an easy solution in the short term as it satisfies immediate demands. However, it is harmful to the long-term future of freedom in society because once banning starts, it can become a habit.
- Partial ban like censorship is also crucial in a society. It ensures that inappropriate content is not accessible to certain audiences, such as children.

  In these cases, only specific portions of a film are restricted rather than the entire work being banned. This allows for a balanced approach, where content can still be shared but with necessary safeguards to prevent harm.

Freedom of thought and discussion

J.S. Mill defended the importance of **freedom of thought and discussion** in his book **On Liberty**. He gave the following reasons to support this idea

- Even false ideas contain some element of truth.
- Truth emerges from the clash of opposing views.
- Conflict of ideas ensures that truth remains dynamic and reliable.
- Suppressing ideas risks losing knowledge that may later prove valuable.

Role of Education

- Freedom includes the ability to make choices and with this comes the responsibility for the results of those actions.
- Education is essential to encourage the capacity to make informed choices and limit the interference of state and society.
- Most advocates of freedom and liberty argue that children must be placed in the care of parents. It is because their capacity for making rational decisions develops with time and education plays a key role in developing this ability.

Quick Test 2

1 Which system in India is an example of social inequality?
2 Who introduced Harm Principle?
3 Name the principle which justifies imposing constraints only to prevent harm to others.
4 Give the meaning of the term 'reasonable restrictions' used in the Indian Constitution.
5 What is a key requirement for individual development in positive liberty?

5 **Freedom of Expression** It is a right to express one's opinion without censorship, restraint or legal punishment.

Mind Map

FREEDOM

1 Meaning of Freedom

- Freedom means 'absence of constraints'.
- It allows individuals to make independent choices.

Aspects of Freedom

Positive Aspect
This means creating conditions for self-expression and personal growth.

Negative Aspect
There is absence of external control.

2 Ideal of Freedom

- **Nelson Mandela** Struggle against Apartheid.
- **Aung San Suu Kyi** Freedom from fear and Non-violence.
- **Mahatma- Gandhi** Self-rule or Swaraj.

3 Swaraj

- Swaraj is a concept similar to freedom.
- Key demand in India's freedom movement, representing both Political and Constitutional freedom.
- Mahatma Gandhi emphasised the idea of Swaraj as 'rule over self'.
- Emphasises self-respect, self-responsibility and self-realisation.
- Its connection to society is crucial in achieving Swaraj.

4 Sources of Constraints

- **Domination and External Control**
  For example Colonialism and Apartheid.
- **Government Laws**
  For example Balance between freedom and societal order.
- **Social Inequality**
  For example Caste system, economic disparity etc.

5 Need of Constraints

- To maintain the order in the society otherwise society would decline.
- Foster an environment for harmonious living of people.
- Encourage respect for differing views, opinions and beliefs.
- To prevent chaos and ensure societal order.
- To provide mechanisms for controlling violence and resolving disputes.
- To provide protection against bullying or attempts to impose conformity.

6 Harm Principle

- Introduced by J.S Mill.
- States that interference with liberty is justified only for self-protection.

Case of Harms

- **Minor Harms** Social dis-approval and not the force of law.
- **Major Harms** Constraining actions by the force of law.

Self-Regrading Actions
(No external interference).

Other-Regrading Actions
(Restrictions only when harm is caused).

7 Negative Vs. Positive Liberty

Negative Liberty

- Freedom from interference.
- Government or external authority should be limited.
- Negative liberty is criticised for focusing only on the absence of interference.

Positive Liberty

- Enables condition for personal development.
- Government should provide condition like education.
- Positive liberty is criticised because it can sometimes be misused by dictators.

8 Freedom of Expression

- Fundamental areas of non-interference.
- Voltaire supported the right to express even unpopular opinions.
- Over time many books, films, plays or articles have been banned after protests For example on books like 'The Satanic Verses' by Salman Rushdie.
- Banning is an easy solution in the short term.
- Partial ban like censorship is also crucial in a society.

9 Role of Education

- Empowers informed decision-making .
- Responsibility for the results of those actions.
- Encourage the capacity to make informed choices and limit the interference.
- Capacity for making rational decisions develops with time and education play an crucial role into it.

NCERT Folder

Intext Questions

1. Do only great men and women fight for great principles like freedom? What does this principle mean to you? (Pg 18)

Ans. It is not just great men and women who fight for big principles like freedom. Ordinary people also stand up for what is right and important. Everyone has the power to fight for freedom in their own way.

- Freedom means being able to live your life without being controlled unfairly by others.
- Freedom is a basic need for everyone and it is not just for a few people. This is important for all of us to protect our freedom. We don't need to be famous or powerful to fight for freedom. Even small actions, like speaking out against unfairness or helping other people, can make a big difference. Anyone can play a role in protecting freedom for themselves and others.

2. Do we have the freedom to destroy our environment? (Pg 27)

Ans. We do not have the freedom to destroy our environment because freedom comes with responsibility. While we are free to use the environment to meet our needs, we also must take care of it.

- Destroying the environment, such as polluting the air, cutting down trees or wasting water, not only affects us today but also affects our future generations.
- It also harms animals, plants and all living things that depend on nature to survive.
- Here in this context, true freedom means finding a balance between using the resources of earth and protecting them in a sustainable way.

Exercise

1. What is meant by freedom? Is there a relationship between freedom for the individual and freedom for the nation?

Ans. Freedom is a political term which allows an individual to make choices and to exercise independent judgement. Absolute freedom is not good for society. There should be reasonable constraints on freedom to maintain peace and harmony in society. There is a close relationship between the freedom for the individual and freedom for the nation, which are as follows

- In a free nation, every citizen is given freedom to develop his potentials with minimum social constraints.
- Freedom is crucial for overall development of a nation as well as of an individual. If a nation is free from any external influence, it can take better decisions for development of that nation and its citizens.
- A free nation gives opportunities to its citizens to enhance creativities and capabilities.

2. What is the difference between the negative and positive conception of liberty? **Diksha App**

Ans. For answer refer to text under the heading 'Negative and Positive Liberty' on page no. 235.

3. What is meant by social constraints? Are constraints of any kind necessary for enjoying freedom?

Ans. The domination and external controls on freedom of individual imposed by the society is known as social constraints. These controls may be imposed by the government through laws or Constitution which embody the power of the rulers over the people. Constraints of different kind exist and people are subject to them in different situations. Constraints on freedom can also result from social inequality of the kind implicit in the caste system. It can result from extreme economic inequality in a society.

Yes, the constraints are necessary for enjoying freedom because

- It is essential for the creation of a peaceful society.
- It develops respect for differences of views, opinions and beliefs.
- It is required to control violence and settle disputes.

4. What is the role of the state in upholding freedom of its citizens?

Ans. The role of the state in upholding freedom of its citizens is

- The state provides certain rights to its citizens.
- The state maintains reasonable restrictions on its citizens so that they cannot harm the rights of others.
- The state provides positive liberty to its citizens so that they can expand their ability and talent.
- The state puts reasonable restrictions on freedom of its citizens in order to maintain social stability.

5. What is meant by freedom of expression? What in your views would be a reasonable restriction on this freedom? Give examples.

Ans. Freedom of expression means the freedom to express one's views and ideas freely through speech, writing, books, plays, etc. It is considered to belong to the minimum area of 'non-interference'.

The examples of reasonable restriction on the freedom of expression are

- Censor boards restrict the freedom of speech by banning portion of the film to maintain peace and harmony in society. It also protects interests of various social groups.
- As per Indian Constitution, some of the Fundamental Rights are suspended during emergency by the President.

Exam Pattern Questions

Objective Type Questions

Multiple Choice Questions (MCQs)

1. What is apartheid?

(a) Gender discrimination (b) Facial discrimination
(c) Caste discrimination (d) Racial discrimination

2. What is the prerequisite for dignified human life as per Aug San Suu Kyi? Diksha App

(a) Freedom from fear (b) Freedom from inequality
(c) Freedom from poverty (d) Freedom from slavery

3. Which of the following are a source of constraints on individuals freedom? Diksha App

I. Constitution **II. Colonial laws**
III. Social inequality

Codes

(a) III only (b) I and II (c) I and III (d) I, II and III

4. In the context of Indian freedom struggle, 'Swaraj' refers to ....

(a) economic independence
(b) political and Constitutional freedom
(c) social equality
(d) military power

5. What is the key feature of a free society?

(a) Total absence of rules
(b) Enabling individuals to develop their potential with minimal constraints
(c) Imposing strict regulations to maintain order
(d) Elimination of all social conflicts

6. Freedom should be guaranteed with certain constraints because............ . Diksha App

(a) without constraints restrictions disagreements amongst people would lead to chaos
(b) it paves way for accomodation of differences and promotes co-existence
(c) acts as an mechanism to resolve differences amicably.
(d) All of the above

7. Liberalism as an idealogy can be best described as...... . Diksha App

(a) individualism (b) welfarism
(c) Both (a) and (b) (d) None of these

8. The concept of 'Harm principle' distinguishes between............ . Diksha App

(a) liberty and equality
(b) self regarding and other regarding actions
(c) equality and justice
(d) harming and non-harming actions

9. In the context of Indian Constitution, the term used for justifiable constraints is ....

(a) valid restrictions (b) justifiable restrictions
(c) true restrictions (d) reasonable restrictions

10. Which of the following statements is not correct with respect to positive freedom? Diksha App

(a) It is freedom in social context
(b) Freedom with reasonable restriction/constraints
(c) Non-interfering state
(d) None of the above

11. Negative freedom implies to .... Diksha App

(a) absence of external constraints
(b) expansion of oppournities to express one's self
(c) existence of minimum area of non-influence
(d) All of the above

12. It is concerned with examining the circumstances and essence of the individual-society relationship in order to improve the conditions. Competency Based Que

The above statement is related to

(a) Negative Liberty (b) Freedom
(c) Positive Liberty (d) Communitarian Liberty

13. What does the concept of 'freedom from' refer to in the negative liberty context?

(a) Freedom to choose any profession
(b) Freedom from interference in personal choices
(c) Freedom to express all opinions
(d) Freedom from societal expectations

14. In the context of freedom of expression consider the following statements. Competency Based Que

I. The freedom of expression is one of the topics that is regarded to fall under the maximum domain of 'non-interference'.

II. Freedom of expression is the freedom to communicate ideas without restraint, whether orally or in print or by any other means of communication.

Select the correct statements

(a) Only I (b) Only II
(c) Both I and II (d) None of these

15. Consider the following statements. **Competency Based Que**

I. No idea is completely false
II. Truth emerges by itself
III. Conflict of idea is valuable in all the times
IV. One cannot be sure that the ideas he considers true is actually true

Which of the following did John Stuart Mill consider as reason(s) for providing freedom of expression?

(a) I, II and IV
(b) I, III and IV
(c) I, II and III
(d) All of these

16. When should freedom be constrained according to Mill ?

(a) Whenever harm is caused
(b) In special circumstances when harm caused is serious
(c) Whenever it causes inconvenience
(d) When a majority disapproves

17. Two statements are given below

Statement I The apartheid regime discriminated between citizens based on their race.

Statement II Nelson Mandela's struggle was only focused on the rights of black people.

In the light of above statements choose the correct option

(a) Statement I and Statement II both are correct.
(b) Statement I and Statement II both are incorrect.
(c) Statement I is correct, but Statement II is incorrect.
(d) Statement I is incorrect, but Statement II is correct.

18. Match the following individuals with their views on freedom

List I	List II
A. John Stuart Mill	1. Advocated for Swaraj, emphasised self-rule and liberation from dehumanising institutions.
B. Voltaire	2. Believed in all-round freedom, including political, social and economic emancipation for all.
C. Mahatma Gandhi	3. Believed in individual liberty and the 'harm principle', which argues that freedom should only be restricted to prevent harm to others.
D. Netaji Subhash Chandra Bose	4. Advocated for freedom of speech and religious tolerance. He emphasised the importance of defending others' rights to express their views, even if we disagree.

Codes

	A	B	C	D
(a)	1	3	4	2
(b)	2	4	1	3
(c)	3	4	1	2
(d)	1	2	4	3

19. Find the incorrectly matched pair from the following

	List I		List II
(a)	Nelson Mandela	—	Long Walk to Freedom
(b)	Aung San Suu Kyi	—	Freedom From Fear
(c)	Salman Rushdi	—	Satanic Verses
(d)	Devdutta Pattnaik	—	Ramayana Re-told

20. Find the the correctly matched pair from the following

	List I (Statement)	List II (Given By)
(a)	'I disapprove of what you say but I will defend to death your right to say it'.	– Voltaire
(b)	Swaraj is my birth right and I shall have it.	– Mahatma Gandhi
(c)	It is Swaraj when we learn to rule ourselves.	– Bal Gangadhar Tilak
(d)	"For me real freedom is freedom from fear and unless you can live free from fear you cannot live a dignified human life".	– J.S. Mill

Assertion-Reason Questions

Directions (Q. Nos. 21-25) In the questions given below, there are two statements marked as Assertion (A) and Reason (R). Read the statements and choose the correct option.

Codes

(a) Both A and R are true and R is the correct explanation of A.
(b) Both A and R are true, but R is not the correct explanation of A.
(c) A is true, but R is false.
(d) A is false, but R is true.

21. **Assertion** (A)It is essential to determine which social constraints are justified in order to understand the concept of freedom.

Reason (R) Discussions on freedom should focus on the relationship between the individual and society, examining how certain societal features enable or restrict individual freedom.

22. **Assertion** (A) Mill distinguishes between 'self-regarding' actions, which only affect the individual and 'other-regarding' actions, which affect others, stating that the state should not interfere in self-regarding actions.

Reason (R) Mill believes that all actions, regardless of their impact on others, should be free from external authority.

23. **Assertion** (A) In India everyone has given some freedom rights under the Constitution but subjected to reasonable restriction.

Reason (R) Reasonable restriction is necessary in order to protect Security of the State, Friendly Relation with Foreign States, Public Order, etc.

24. **Assertion** (A) Freedom of speech is the most important civil liberty of people in a democratic polity.

Reason (R) State can regulate free speech in the interest of public order.

25. **Assertion** (A) Freedom of expression is the freedom to communicate ideas without restraint, whether orally or in print or by any other means of communication.

Reason (R) 'Negative liberty' allows an individual to develop his or her capability with reasonable constraints.

Passage Based Questions

26. Read the passage given below and answer the questions that follow

"If we are to bring about a revolution of ideas we have first to hold up before us an ideal which will galvanise our whole life. That ideal is freedom. But freedom is a word which has varied connotations and, even in our country, the conception of freedom has undergone a process of evolution. By freedom I mean all round freedom, i.e., freedom for the individual as well as for society, freedom for the rich as well as for the poor, freedom for men as well as for women, freedom for all individuals and for all classes. This freedom implies not only emancipation from political bondage but also equal distribution of wealth, abolition of caste barriers and social inequities and destruction of communalism and religious intolerance. This is an ideal which may appear Utopian to hard-headed men and women, but this ideal alone can appease the hunger in the soul".

(i) According to Bose , what is necessary to bring about a revolution of ideas?

(a) Political emancipation
(b) Economic reforms
(c) Holding up an ideal that galvanises our whole life.
(d) Abolition of social classes.

(ii) What does Subhash Chandra Bose mean by all round freedom?

(a) Freedom only for individuals.
(b) Freedom for both individuals and society.
(c) Freedom only for the rich.
(d) Freedom only for men.

(iii) How does Bose's concept of freedom address social inequalities?

27. Read the source given below and answer the questions that follow

"And liberalism is not the only modern ideology that supports tolerance. What is more distinctive about modern liberalism is its focus on the individual. For liberals entities like family, society, community have no value in themselves, but only if these are valued by individuals. They would say, for example, that the decision to marry someone should be taken by the individual rather than by the family, caste or the community. Liberals tend to give priority to individual liberty over values like equality. They also tend to be suspicious of political authority. Historically, liberalism favoured free market and minimal role to the state. However, present day liberalism acknowledges a role for welfare state and accepts the need for measures to reduce both social and economic inequalities".

(i) What is the primary focus of modern liberalism?

(a) Family (b) Community
(c) Individual (d) State

(ii) How do liberals view entities like family and community?

(a) As having inherent value
(b) As valuable only if individuals value them
(c) As more important than individuals
(d) As irrelevant to society

(iii) How has the liberal view on the role of the state evolved over time?

28. Read the passage given below and answer the questions that follow

"John Stuart Mill, a political thinker and an activist in the nineteenth century Britain, offered a passionate defence of freedom of expression, including freedom of thought and discussion. In his book 'On Liberty' he offered four reasons why there should be freedom of expression even for those who espouse ideas that appear 'false' or misleading today. First, no idea is completely false. What appears to us as false has an element of truth. If we ban 'false' ideas, we would lose that element of truth that they contain. This is related to the second point. Truth does not emerge by itself. It is only through a conflict of opposing views that truth emerges. Ideas that seem wrong today may have been very valuable in the emergence of what we consider right kind of ideas".

(i) What is the first reason Mill provides for the importance of freedom of expression?

(a) All ideas are completely false
(b) Every idea has an element of truth
(c) Only correct ideas should be expressed
(d) Truth is not valuable

(ii) **What danger does Mill highlight regarding the suppression of ideas considered false?**
(a) It leads to an increase in censorship
(b) It results in a lack of valuable knowledge
(c) It prevents society from evolving
(d) It encourages more false ideas

(iii) **According to Mill, how does truth emerge?**
(a) Through isolation of ideas
(b) By suppressing opposing views
(c) Through conflict of opposing views
(d) By accepting only popular ideas

(iv) **Why does Mill argue that exposing truth to opposing views is valuable?**
(a) To create confusion among people
(b) To ensure that the idea remains unchallenged
(c) To prevent ideas from becoming cliches
(d) To promote only accepted ideas

29. **Read the source given below and answer the questions that follow**

"A concept analogous to freedom in Indian political thought is 'Swaraj'. The term Swaraj incorporates within it two words — Swa (Self) and Raj (Rule). It can be understood to mean both the rule of the self and rule over-self. Swaraj, in the context of the freedom struggle in India, referred to freedom as a Constitutional and political demand and as a value at the social-collective level. That is why Swaraj was such an important rallying cry in the freedom movement. It is the understanding of Swaraj as Rule over the Self that was highlighted by Mahatma Gandhi in his work 'Hind Swaraj'.

(i) **What is the dual meaning of Swaraj as per the passage?**
(a) Rule by the self and rule over others
(b) Rule of the self and rule over self
(c) Self-governance and foreign rule
(d) Individual freedom and collective oppression

(ii) **How does the meaning of swaraj extend beyond political independe.**
(a) It also emphasises moral and social self-governance
(b) It focuses only on economic policies
(c) It is restricted to legal rights and law
(d) It solely advocates for military rule

(iii) **According to Mahatma Gandhi's interpretation in Hind Swaraj, what is the essence of Swaraj?**
(a) Achieving political independence
(b) Learning to rule ourselves
(c) Dominating other nations
(d) Rejecting all forms of governance

(iv) **How does the passage relate Swaraj to human development?**
(a) It focuses solely on economic growth
(b) It emphasises technological advancement
(c) It liberates individual and collective potentials guided by justice
(d) It promotes isolation from global influences

Answers

1. (d) Racial discrimination **2.** (a) Freedom from fear
3. (d) I, II and III
4. (b) political and Constitutional freedom
5. (b) Enabling individuals to develop their potential with minimal constraints
6. (d) All of the above **7.** (c) Both (a) and (b)
8. (b) self regarding and other regarding actions
9. (d) reasonable restrictions
10. (c) Non-interfering state
11. (d) All of the above **12.** (c) Positive Liberty
13. (b) Freedom from interference in personal choices
14. (c) Both I and II
15. (b) I, III and IV
16. (b) In special circumstances when harm caused is serious.
17. (c) Statement I is correct, but Statement II is incorrect.
18. (c) 3 4 1 2
19. (d) Devdutta Pattnaik-Ramayana Re-told
20. (a) Voltaire
21. (a) Both A and R are true, but R is not the correct explanation of A.
22. (c) A is true, but R is false.
23. (a) Both A and R are true and R is the correct explanation of A.
24. (b) Both A and R are true, but R is not the correct explanation of A.
25. (c) A is true, but R is false. 'Positive liberty' allows an individual to develop his or her capability with reasonable constraints.
26. (i) (c) Holding up an ideal that galvanises our whole life

(ii) (b) Freedom for both individuals and society

(iii) Bose's concept of freedom addresses social inequalities by advocating for equal distribution of wealth, abolition of caste barriers and elimination of communalism and religious intolerance. It aims to create a society with equal opportunities for all individuals and classes.

27. (i) (c) Individual

(ii) (b) As valuable only if individuals value them

(iii) Historically, liberalism favoured minimal state intervention and free markets. However, modern liberalism acknowledges the need for a welfare state and accepts measures to reduce social and economic inequalities. Thus, showing an evolution in its views on state involvement.

28. (i) (b) Every idea has an element of truth

(ii) (b) It results in a lack of valuable knowledge

(iii) (c) Through conflict of opposing views

(iv) (c) To prevent ideas from becoming cliches

29. (i) (b) Rule of the self and rule over self

(ii) (a) It also emphasises moral and social self-governance

(iii) (b) Learning to rule ourselves

(iv) (c) It liberates individual and collective potentials guided by justice

Subjective Questions

Very Short Answer Type Questions

1. What does Nelson Mandela's 'Long Walk to Freedom' represent in the context of the struggle against apartheid in South Africa?

Ans. Mandela's 'Long Walk to Freedom' represents the prolonged struggle against apartheid's unjust constraints and racial discrimination. It symbolises the sacrifices made to achieve freedom and equality for all South Africans, regardless of race. He spent twenty-seven years of his life in jail.

2. How does Aung San Suu Kyi define 'real freedom' and its connection to living a dignified human life?

Ans. Aung San Suu Kyi defines real freedom as 'freedom from fear'. She believes that overcoming fear of others' opinions, authority and community is essential to living a dignified human life and achieving true personal and collective freedom.

3. Explain in brief the meaning of freedom.

Ans. Freedom includes two dimensions: absence of external constraints allowing autonomous decision-making and the opportunity to express oneself and develop potential. It involves being free from constraints while having the ability to grow, create and realise one's capabilities fully.

4. State and define the two main dimensions of freedom.

Ans. Freedom has two main dimensions, which are

- **Negative Freedom** It refers to being free from external control, such as oppressive laws or social restrictions. For example, a person is free if they can make decisions without interference
- **Positive Freedom** It refers to having the conditions or opportunities to grow and achieve personal goals. For example, access to education allows individuals to realise their potential.

5. How does society decide which constraints are necessary?

Ans. Society uses laws and principles to identify necessary constraints that ensure safety, equality and order.

- Society imposes certain rules to protect people and maintain peace. For example, traffic rules are necessary to avoid accidents, even though they limit how people drive.
- Necessary constraints ensure that everyone's freedom is respected and no one's actions harm others.
- However, unjust constraints, like racial discrimination, should be removed as they violate the principles of equality and justice.

6. Give the meaning of the term 'reasonable restrictions' with example?

Ans. Reasonable restrictions are limits on freedom that are logical, proportional and necessary to protect others or society.

For example, banning loud music in public spaces at night is reasonable to ensure others' peace, but life imprisonment for playing music would be excessive. And the restrictions must strike a balance between protecting freedom and maintaining societal order.

7. Write two aspects of positive liberty.

Ans. Two aspects of positive liberty are as following

(i) Positive liberty is concerned with looking at the conditions and nature of the relationship between the individual and society.

(ii) The individual to develop his or her capability must get the benefit of enabling positive conditions in material, political and social domains.

8. Why were certain films, books and plays like, The Satanic verses and Me Nathuram Boltey, banned and what were the objections raised?

Ans. These works were banned due to protests from sections of society that felt they would harm the cultural or religious image of the community. For instance, The Satanic verses and The Last Temptation of Christ, were seen as offensive and were banned.

9. Why was Deepa Mehta's film about widows in Varanasi protested and what was the result of these protests?

Ans. Deepa Mehta's film about widows in Varanasi faced strong protests from some political groups who felt it would portray India negatively and cater to foreign audiences. Thus tarnishing the image of the ancient town. Due to these objections, the film was not allowed to be made in Varanasi and had to be filmed elsewhere instead.

10. Why does John Stuart Mill argue against banning the idea, even if they seem fable or harmful? Competency Based Que

Ans. John Stuart Mill provides four reasons against banning ideas

- **No idea is completely false** Even false ideas may contain elements of truth, which could be valuable.
- **Conflict of ideas reveals truth** Truth emerges through debates and opposing views.
- **Truth must be tested continuously** Even widely accepted truths may become common. Debating them ensures they remain relevant.
- **False ideas may become true later** History shows that suppressed ideas often turn out to be valuable over time.

Mill argues that banning ideas harms the development of knowledge and limits societal progress, making open discussion essential.

Short Answer Type Questions

1. What is the concept of 'Swaraj' in Indian political thought and why was it significant during the freedom struggle?

Ans. 'Swaraj' combines 'Swa' (self) and 'Raj' (rule).

- It signifies both self-rule and personal governance and emerged as a key demand for Constitutional freedom in India's struggle for independence.
- It emphasises individual self-respect and collective responsibility.
- Mahatma Gandhi highlighted this idea in 'Hind Swaraj', asserting that true freedom involves ruling oneself.
- Swaraj became a rallying demand and remains relevant today as it highlights the importance of justice and community in achieving liberation.

2. "Constraints are necessary in a society with differing opinions". Explain the statement. Competency Based Que

Ans. Constraints are essential in a diverse society to manage disagreements and prevent conflicts. They promote respect for differing views and create mechanisms to resolve disputes peacefully.

Legal and political restraints ensure that no group imposes its beliefs on others, allowing for open discussions. Without such constraints, there may be bullying or harassment, which will threaten individual freedoms.

Thus , these constraints support a society where everyone can express their opinions while maintaining harmony and protecting personal liberties.

3. Mention the sources of constraints on individual freedom, and tell how can they be addressed.

Ans. The sources of constraints on individual freedom are as followed

- **External Domination** Constraints are imposed by colonial rulers or oppressive governments through force or laws.
- **Government Constraints** Democratic governments allow citizens to retain some control over rulers, by protecting individual freedom.
- **Social and Economic Inequality** Constraints can arise from societal structures, like the caste system, that create unequal opportunities. Extreme disparities in wealth can limit access to resources and opportunities.

According to Subhash Chandra Bose these inequalities can be addressed by eliminating social and economic inequalities. This is essential for ensuring true freedom for all.

4. Define the positive dimension of freedom and state, why is it considered valuable in a free society?

Ans. The positive dimension of freedom refers to the ability of individuals, groups or nations to shape their own destinies and pursue their interests with minimal constraints.

A free society enables the full development of an individual's creativity, sensibilities and capabilities in areas like sports, science or art.

Freedom is valuable because it allows individuals to make choices, exercise judgement and reason, thus foster personal growth and self-expression.

5. "Democratic government is considered to be an important means of protecting the freedom of people". Justify this statement. **Competency Based Que**

Ans. Democratic government is considered to be an important means of protecting the freedom of people due to following reasons

- In democratic government, power and civic responsibility are exercised by all citizens, directly or through their freely elected representatives.
- Democratic government is a set of principles and practices that protect human freedom.
- Citizens in a democratic government have not only rights but they also have the responsibility to participate in the political system that in turn protects their rights and freedom.

6. Throw light on the views of Subhash Chandra Bose on freedom.

Ans. For Subhash Chandra Bose freedom means all round freedom i.e., freedom for the individual as well as for society; freedom for the rich as well as for the poor; freedom for men as well as for women; freedom for all individuals and for all classes.

For him, freedom implies not only liberation from political bondage but also equal distribution of wealth, abolition of caste barriers and social inequalities and destruction of communalism and religious intolerance.

7. What is the distinctive feature of modern liberalism and how has its stance on the role of the state evolved over time?

Ans. The distinctive feature of modern liberalism is its focus on the individual. Liberals believe that institutions like family, society and community only hold value if individuals choose to value them. They emphasise individual liberty over collective values like equality and are often cautious of political authority.

Historically, liberalism supported free markets and a minimal role for the state. However, contemporary liberalism has evolved to recognise the importance of a welfare state and the need for measures to address social and economic inequalities while still prioritising individual freedom.

8. Differentiate between Self-Regarding Actions and Other-Regarding Actions given by Mill. **Diksha App**

Ans.

Self-Regarding Actions	Other-Regarding Actions
Actions that have consequences only for the individual actor and nobody else are called self-regarding actions	Actions that have consequences for others are called other regarding actions.
The state (or any other external authority) can not interfere in such actions.	The state (or any other external authority) can interfere in such actions. It can constrain a person from behaving in a manner that harms another individual.
For Example, deciding to pursue a particular career based on personal interests and goals.	**For Example,** disposing waste in a way that harms the community's health and quality of life.

9. What do you mean by negative liberty?

Ans. Negative liberty is the absence of obstacles, barriers or constraints. Negative liberty explains the idea 'freedom from' which means freedom from state, family, community, authority, etc. An area where no authority can interfere is negative liberty.

In negative liberty, an individual can do whatever he/she wants to do. Political thinkers believe that state should not interfere in the choices of an individual, e.g. choices of dress, living, food, travelling, etc.

10. How is freedom defined in both negative and positive dimensions, and why is it considered valuable?

Ans. Freedom is defined as the absence of constraints, minimising social limitations on choices. However, it also has a positive dimension, where it empowers individuals and communities to shape their destinies and pursue their interests in areas like art, science and sports. A free society fosters creativity and personal growth. This dual understanding of freedom is valuable because it enables individuals to exercise their judgement, make informed choices and fully develop their potential in various fields.

11. **"Education plays a crucial role in the positive aspect of freedom". Justify the statement.** Competency Based Que

Ans. Education promotes individual freedom by enhancing the ability to make informed choices and promotes responsibility for one's actions. It plays a critical role in developing rational decision-making, especially in children, who need parental guidance as they grow.

By providing knowledge and skills, education empowers individuals to navigate societal influences and state interference, ultimately supporting personal and collective freedom.

12. **Do you think that freedom of expression is essential to protect the interests of every individual in society? Give examples to support your answer.** Competency Based Que

Ans. Freedom of expression is essential to protect the interests of every individual in society because it lays the foundation of a democratic society.

- Freedom of expression is a very significant freedom because it gives us opportunity to participate in democratic processes.
- Free, independent and diverse idea are essential for democracy. For example, ideas are expressed by films, books, movies, plays, paintings and social networking sites.
- Sometimes films, books, movies, paintings, etc are banned. Banning should be there, but it should not be politically motivated. There should be strong rationale behind it.
- Banning should not be regular, otherwise state gets into habit of banning every time.
- While enjoying this freedom, people should take care that there should not be hatred campaigns and hatred speeches against anyone.

Long Answer Type Questions

1. **Discuss the idea of freedom through the struggles of Nelson Mandela and Aung San Suu Kyi.**

Ans. Nelson Mandela and Aung San Suu Kyi are two prominent leaders who fought for freedom in their countries; South Africa and Myanmar, respectively. Their struggles highlight the importance of freedom and the sacrifices made to achieve it.

Struggle of Nelson Mandela

- Mandela fought against apartheid, a system of racial discrimination in South Africa. Black people were denied basic rights, such as freedom of movement and choice in marriage.
- Mandela believed that freedom was not just for Black people but for all citizens of South Africa.
- He spent twenty-seven years in prison, sacrificing his personal life and comforts for the freedom of his people.
- His struggle showed that freedom is worth fighting, even if it requires great personal sacrifices.

Struggle of Aung San Suu Kyi

- Aung San Suu Kyi fought for democracy and freedom in Myanmar, where military rulers restricted people's rights.
- She was Inspired by Gandhiji's principle of non-violence and spent many years under house arrest. She described freedom as 'freedom from fear,' emphasising that people must overcome fear to live a dignified life.
- Her struggle showed that freedom is not just about political rights but also about mental and emotional liberation.

Both leaders remind us that freedom is a powerful ideal that requires courage, perseverance and selflessness. Their sacrifices continue to inspire people across the world to fight against injustice and inequality.

2. **'A free society balances individual liberty with social constraints'. Explain the statement. What are the two main aspects of freedom?** Competency Based Que

Ans. Freedom has two main aspects: the absence of external constraints and the positive ability to develop one's potential.

- The absence of constraints means that individuals can make decisions and act autonomously without external coercion.
- However, freedom is also about providing conditions that allow people to express themselves, pursue their interests and fully develop their creativity and capabilities.
- A free society must strike a balance between allowing individual liberty and imposing necessary social constraints.
- While total freedom from constraints is impossible, it is essential to determine which constraints are justified and necessary for maintaining order and mutual respect.
- A free society minimises these constraints to allow individuals and groups to make their own destinies, while also ensures that such freedoms do not harm others.

This balance ensures that individuals can exercise their judgement, reason and choices while living harmoniously within a society.

3. Explain John Stuart Mill's harm principle and its application to the restriction of individual freedom. Diksha App

Ans. John Stuart Mill's harm principle suggests that the only justification for interfering with an individual's liberty is to prevent harm to others.

- Mill distinguishes between two types of actions 'self-regarding' and 'other-regarding'. Self-regarding actions affect only the individual and in such cases, neither the state nor external authorities have the right to interfere.
- An example of a self-regarding action is one's personal lifestyle choices, which do not impact others.
- In contrast, other-regarding actions affect others, and when these actions cause significant harm, state intervention may be justified.
- Mill emphasises that freedom is essential for human dignity, so any constraint must be limited to serious harm.
- For example, playing loud music may create inconvenience to neighbours, but it does not warrant legal punishment, only social disapproval is required.

However, actions that pose serious threats, such as hate speech, may require legal restrictions to protect others' freedoms. Mill warns that any imposed restrictions must not be so severe as to undermine the very essence of freedom.

4. Are constraints desirable on liberty? Give arguments to support your answer. Competency Based Que; Diksha App

Ans. Yes, constraints on liberty can be desirable, as no individual living in society can expect to enjoy total freedom without any restrictions.

- These constraints are necessary to maintain social order and balance the rights of individuals with the needs of the community.
- These are essential to determine which constraints are justified and beneficial and which should be removed.
- In a free society, not all social constraints are harmful; some are essential to protect the rights and freedoms of others. For example, laws that prevent violence or discrimination ensure that individuals do not harm one another. These necessary constraints enable society to function while safeguarding personal liberty.
- Moreover, freedom is not only about the absence of external controls but also about creating conditions that allow individuals to devlop their potential. Some social necessary constraints enable society to function while safeguarding personal liberty.

Some social constraints may be required to foster equality and justice, ensuring that everyone has the opportunity to fully realise their abilities and exercise their freedoms in a fair environment.

5. Why does John Stuart Mill advocate for freedom of expression, in his book of essays 'On Liberty' ?

Ans. John Stuart Mill strongly defends freedom of expression, arguing that even ideas that seem false or misleading should not be suppressed. He provides the following reasons for this

- No idea is entirely false; even incorrect ideas contain some element of truth. Banning these ideas would mean losing that truth.
- Mill believes that truth emerges only through the conflict of opposing views.
- Debating 'false' ideas helps strengthen our understanding of what is 'true'.
- The value of this conflict is ongoing. Without exposing ideas to opposing views, truths risk becoming stale cliches. Constant debate ensures that we remain critical and thoughtful about what we accept as true.
- Mill points-out that societies have often deemed ideas false, only to realise later that they were true. Suppressing all unacceptable ideas today could lead to the loss of valuable knowledge that may be proven beneficial in the future.

Therefore, freedom of expression is essential for intellectual and societal progress.

Picture Based Questions

1. Look at the picture given below and answer the questions that follow

(i) Who is the personality depicted in the image, and what is the title of his autobiography?

Ans. The personality is Nelson Mandela, a prominent anti-apartheid revolutionary. His autobiography is titled 'Long Walk to Freedom'.

(ii) What were some of the constraints faced by him and his people under the apartheid regime?

Ans. Under apartheid, Mandela and his people faced severe constraints, including forced relocation to townships, restricted movement and denial of personal choices like marriage. These discriminatory policies were rooted in racial segregation and systemic oppression.

(iii) What sacrifices did he make for the ideal of freedom? How did he view the struggle for freedom ?

Ans. Mandela sacrificed twenty-seven years of his life, often in solitary confinement, for the ideal of freedom. He gave up his youth, friendships and personal joys, enduring hardships to campaign for equality and justice for all South Africans.
Mandela viewed the struggle for freedom as essential for all South Africans, transcending racial boundaries. He believed it was vital not just for black or coloured individuals, but also for white citizens, aiming for collective liberation from oppression.

2. Look at the picture given below and answer the questions that follow

(i) Who is the personality depicted in the image?

(a) Malala Yousafzai
(b) Aung San Suu Kyi
(c) Nelson Mandela
(d) Wangari Maathai

Ans. (b) Aung San Suu Kyi

(ii) According to the personality given in the image what is required US to live a 'dignified human life'?

(a) Overcome from fear
(b) No need to overcome from fear
(c) Accept the authority of autocrats
(d) None of the above

Ans. (a) Overcome from fear

(iii) What does she consider as essential for living a dignified human life?

(a) Wealth and power
(b) Freedom from fear
(c) Popularity among peers
(d) Strong political alliances

Ans. (b) Freedom from fear

(iv) Who inspired thoughts of the personality given in the image on non-violence?

(a) The teachings of Nelson Mandela
(b) The principles of Mahatma Gandhi
(c) The philosophy of Martin Luther King Jr.
(d) The ideas of Nelson Rolihlahla Mandela

Ans. (b) The principles of Mahatma Gandhi

SELF ASSESSMENT TEST

Objective Type Questions

1. Freedom in its comprehensive sense implies............... . **Diksha App**
   (a) minimum external and social constraints
   (b) opportunities to develop one's pontential
   (c) state's intervention in individual's life
   (d) Both (a) and (b)
2. In the context of Indian Constitution, the term used for justifiable constraints is ....
   (a) valid restrictions
   (b) justifiable restrictions
   (c) true restrictions
   (d) reasonable restrictions
3. Who divided actions into 'other-regarding' & 'self-regarding'?
   (a) John Locke
   (b) Nelson Mandela
   (c) John Stuart Mill
   (d) Aubrey Menon
4. 'I disapprove of what you say, but I will defend to death your right to say it'. Who give this statement?
   (b) Mahatma Gandhi
   (b) J.S. Mill
   (c) Voltaire
   (d) Aung San Suu kyi

Very Short Answer Type Questions

5. Which country did Nelson Mandela belong to?
6. What do you mean by apartheid?
7. Which country did Aung San Suu Kyi belong to?

Short Answer Type Questions

8. Explain the importance of freedom in human prosperity?
9. Two kinds of actions are given by J.S. Mill. Does Mill call for law to interfere in all kinds of 'other regarding actions'?

Long Answer Type Questions

10. Explain the ideals of freedom according to Nelson Mandela and how they are relevent in today's globalising world?
11. Discuss the reasons given by J.S. Mill for protecting freedom of speech and expression?

03

CHAPTER

Equality as a political ideal states that all human beings are equal irrespective of their colour, gender, race or nationality. The notion of humanity is the basis of the notions of universal human rights or 'crimes against humanity'.

▼ YOUR STUDY GOALS

1.1 Introduction
1.2 Three Dimensions of Equality
1.3 Ways to Promote Equality

▼ YOUR PRACTICE GOAL

- Objective Type Questions (30 Qs ; MCQs, A-R, Statements, Matching, Passage Based)
- Subjective Questions (12 VSAs, 10 SAs, 3 LAs, 1 Picture Based)

Equality

1.1 Introduction

- Equality has inspired and guided human society for centuries as a powerful moral and political ideal.
- In modern period, equality was the rallying slogan against inequality. French revolutionaries used the slogan **'Liberty, Equality** and **Fraternity'** in the 18th century. People of Asia and Africa demanded equality during anti-colonial liberation struggles during the 20th century.
- Women and Dalits still demand equality. People want equality and it is an ideal. But it is a paradox or contradiction that we want equality but see inequality everywhere.

Meaning of Equality

- Equality does not mean treating people in an identical way, as people cannot be treated identically in all conditions. For the smooth functioning of society, sometimes people are treated differently, which is acceptable or necessary.
- For example, The Prime Minister of a country has some privileges that cannot be given to a common citizen. The fact that inequality is just or unjust should be considered.
- If people are treated differently on the basis of birth, caste, race, colour or gender, then it is unjust. If people are treated differently due to their talent, hard work, achievements, etc., then it is just.

Equality of Opportunities

As per the concept of equality, all human beings should get same rights and opportunities to develop their skills and talents. On the basis of equal opportunities, if a person becomes more or less successful, it is acceptable.

Natural and Social Inequalities

- Natural inequalities are those that emerge between people as a result of their different capabilities and talents. Natural inequalities are considered to be the result of the different characteristics and abilities with which people are born. Social inequalities are created by society.
- Social inequalities are those that emerge as a consequence of inequalities of opportunity or the exploitation of some groups in a society by others. The distinction between natural inequalities and social inequalities helps to distinguish between acceptable and unfair inequalities in society. However, it is not always clear or self-evident.
- For example, considering women as **'weaker sex'** due to natural differences between men and women, discrimination with **black people** in Africa on the basis of race was considered just by society. But it is an example of social inequality. Blacks and women were treated differently because they did not have power.
- With the development in medical science and technology, natural differences are now alterable or changeable. It will be unjust if people don't get help to overcome natural differences. For example, a blind person can get help from the computer.

Quick Test 1

1 What is the basis of the nation 'Universal human rights'?
2 Name the slogan used by French revolutionaries.
3 Name two groups which still demand equality.
4 What is the common belief of all religions about the creation of humans?

1.2 Three Dimensions of Equality

Based on different kinds of inequalities which exist in society, various thinker and ideologies have highlighted three main dimensions of equality as follows

Dimensions of Equality
- Political Equality
- Social Equality
- Economic Equality

Political equality

- In a democratic society, political equality includes granting equal citizenship to all the members of the state. **Equal citizenship** includes basic rights such as the right to vote, freedom of expression, movement and association and freedom of belief. These rights help citizens to develop themselves and participate in the affairs of the state.
- Rights enjoyed by people due to equal citizenship are legal rights guaranteed by the Constitution and laws. Despite legal rights, citizens can still face inequality due to differences in the resources and opportunities that are available to them in the social and economic spheres. So, people demand **'equality of opportunity'**.
- Political equality is not a guarantee of a just and **egalitarian**[1] society, but it is an important component of it.

1 **Egalitarian** It refers to a person or system that advocates for equality and equal opportunities among all individuals.

Social Equality

- Social equality refers to the equality of opportunity to all members of the society. Political equality is a way to ensure social equality. By political equality, it is ensured that all social groups get representation and have a voice in government.
- In India, lack of opportunities is not just due to lack of facilities but also due to some customs prevalent in different parts of the country or among different groups.
- For example, women face inequality due to social prohibitions.
- The state can play a role in ensuring social equality by making laws, but social groups and individuals can also play a role by raising awareness.

Economic Equality

- Economic inequality exists in a society due to significant differences in wealth, property or income between individuals or classes. It is measured
  - By measuring the relative difference between the richest and the poorest groups.
  - By estimating the number of people who live below the poverty line.
- Absolute equality of wealth or income has never been a reality. So modern democracies try to ensure equal opportunities for people.
- With equal opportunities, inequality can still exist, but, there is possibility that people improve their status due to available opportunities.
- Inequalities which remain untouched are dangerous for the society. They will divide the society between those classes and others who have remained poor over generations.

Feminism

- Feminism is a **political doctrine** of equal rights for women and men.
- Feminists are those who believe that inequalities in society are neither natural nor necessary and can be altered or changed.
- As per feminists, inequality between men and women is the result of patriarchy[2]. It is based on the assumption that men and women are naturally different so they should be treated unequally.
- Feminists differentiate between 'sex' and 'gender'. They show that inequality between men and women is social.
- As per division of work on the basis of patriarchy, women are responsible for **'private'** or **'domestic'** matters and men are responsible for **'public'** domain.
- Feminists say that women also work outside but still considered responsible for domestic work which creates 'double burden'.
- Feminists argue that difference between 'public' and 'private' and all forms of gender inequalities should be eliminated.

Liberals and Marixts on Economic Equality

- Marxism[3] and Liberalism[4] are two important political ideologies. **Marx**, a 19th century considered the private ownership of important economic resources like oil, land etc., and other forms of property as the root cause of inequality. Private ownership creates a class of wealthy people who have economic and political power.
- As per Marxists and socialists economic inequality supports other forms of inequality. Public control over essential resources and forms of property will create an egalitarian society.

2 Patriarchy It is a social system where men hold primary power in leadership, roles and decision making.
3 Marxism It is an ideology based on the ideas of Marx, which advocates for a classless and stateless society.
4 Liberalism It is a political ideology that gives importance to individual liberty and freedom.

- Liberals believe that principle of competition is the most efficient and fair way of distributing resources and rewards in society. State should ensure a minimum standard of living and equal opportunities for all. Liberals believe that political, economic and social inequalities are not linked with each other and can be tackled separately.

Socialism

- Socialism is a set of political ideas that emerged as a response to the inequalities present in, and reproduced by, the industrial capitalist economy.
- Just distribution of resources and minimisation of existing inequalities is the main concern of socialism.
- Advocates of socialism don't oppose market entirely but prefer some kind of government control over certain key areas such as education and health care.
- Socialist believe that only end of economic inequality will end all forms of inequality. Indian socialist thinker **Rammanohar Lohia** considered many inequalities which can be fought by **seven revolutions** or **Sapta Kranti**. These are
  - Revolution against inequality between men and women.
  - Revolution against inequality based on skin colour.
  - Revolution against caste-based inequality.
  - Revolution against colonial rule of some countries over others.
  - Revolution against economic inequality.
  - Revolution for civil liberties against unjust encroachments on private life and revolution for non-violence.
  - Revolution for renunciation of weapons in favour of satyagraha.

Quick Test 2

1. Name the three dimensions of equality.
2. What do you understand by the term egalitarian?
3. Name the two important political ideologies.
4. Who proposed the concept of Sapta Kranti?

1.3 Ways to Promote Equality

There are several ways suggested by liberals and socialists to achieve equality. However, liberals and socialists significantly differ with each other.

Establishing Formal Equality

- Formal equality is the first step in order to achieve equality. Inequalities all over the world have been protected by customs and legal systems, which resulted in discrimination.
- Laws, restrictions, customs, privileges, etc. should be ended to achieve equality.
- The Indian Constitution prohibits discrimination on the basis of religion, race, caste, sex or place of birth. It also abolished untouchability.
- Most modern Constitutions and democratic governments accept the principle of equality. They support the identical treatment of all citizens without any discrimination.

Equality through Differential Treatment

- Formal equality is necessary but not sufficient to achieve the goal of equality. Sometimes it becomes necessary to treat some groups differently due to their circumstances and give them special rights and privileges. So, they can develop themselves. For example, physically disabled people can demand special rooms in public spaces.

- Differences which hinder access to equal opportunities and how these differences can be overcome are being discussed in almost all societies today. Some countries use the policy of affirmative action, some have adopted the policy of reservations to promote equality of opportunity. For example, India adopted the policy of reservation[5].

Affirmative Action

- Affirmative action is based on the idea that to eliminate deeply rooted inequalities, some positive measures should be taken to minimise and eliminate entrenched forms of social inequalities. Most affirmative action policies are designed with the intention of correcting the cumulative effect[6] of past inequalities.

Forms of Affirmative Actions

- Affirmative action can be in many forms. For example, it can be in the form of scholarships to students from disadvantageous communities. In India, some groups have quotas or reserved seats in education and jobs. These groups faced the discrimination in the past and were denied equal opportunities.
- **Special Assistance** Special assistance in the form of affirmative action can be considered a temporary or time-bound measure. It is expected that disadvantaged groups will benefit from special assistance and develop themselves in order to compete with others in the future.
- **Critical View on Reservation** Critics point out that the policy of reservation is against equality. They argue that reservations do discriminate against other sections of society. They consider reservation as a form of reverse discrimination and support the identical treatment of all citizens.
- **Equal Rights of Individual and the Principle of Equality** It is necessary to make a difference between equal rights of individuals and the principle of equality. All individuals have the right to participate in competition, but competition should be fair. Fair competition will be ensured if disadvantaged groups get some special facilities.
- **Social and Econmic Inequalities** Most theorists recognise that lack of equal opportunities promotes social and economic inequalities. However, policies to ensure equal opportunities are a matter of debate. Some topics of debate are reservation for the deprived communities, definition of deprived, economic criteria to identify deprived, etc.
- **Differential Treatment** Differential or special treatment is a way to achieve equality, but it should have a proper justification and careful reflection. For example, women struggled for equal rights like the right to vote, the right to work, etc. After their entry into the workplace, they realised they needed some special rights to enjoy their rights.

  Differential treatment is essential to ensure equal right for certain groups of society. However, it should not create new structures of dominance and oppression. Neither it should become a way to reclaim special privileges and power in society by some dominant groups.

Quick Test 3

1. Mention three ways to promote equality.
2. What do you understand by the term cumulative effect?
3. Which treatment is essential to active equality?

5 **Reservation** It means policy of reserving seats in educational institutions and jobs for disadvantaged groups.
6 **Cumulative effect** It is a combined result of multiple events or actions happening over a period of time.

Mind Map

EQUALITY

1 Meaning of Equality

- Equality refers to the idea that all human being are equal regardless of colour, gender, race and Nationality.
- For example, The Prime Minister of a country has some privileges that cannot be given to a common citizen. The fact that inequality is just or unjust should be considered.

Equality of Opportunities

- All human beings should get same rights and opportunities to develop their skills and talents.
- A person becomes more or less successful, it is acceptable.

2 Three Dimensions of Equality

Political Equality

- Granting equal citizenship to all the citizens.
- Political equality is not a guarantee of a just and egalitarian society.

Social Equality

- Refers to the equality of opportunity to all members of the society.
- State can play a role in ensuring social equality by making Laws.
- Social groups and individuals can also play a role by raising awareness.

Economic Equality

- Measuring the relative difference between the richest and poorest groups.
- Estimating the Number of people who live below the poverty.

3 Liberals and Marxists on Economic Equality

- **Marxism** It emphasises public control over resources and supports egalitarian society.
- **Liberalism** It emphasises individual liberty, equality and the rule of law.

4 Ram Manohar Lohia's Sapta Kranti (Seven Revolution)

Addresses

- Gender inequality.
- Caste discrimination.
- Civil liberties.
- Renunciation of weapons.
- Racial inequality.
- Economic disparity.
- Violence.

5 Challenges to Equality

Natural Vs. Social Inequalities

- **Natural** - Result of the inborn characteristics and abilities of the people.
- **Social** - Result of the inequality of opportunity and exploitation.

6 Ways to Promote Equality

Establishing Formal Equality

- Prohibition of discrimination (e.g. untouchability abolished in India.)

Equality Through Differential Treatment

- Special rights for the disabled, women, minorities, etc.

Affirmative Actions

- It includes Quotas, reservations, scholarship to uplift disadvantaged group.

Forms of Affirmative Actions

- Special assistance.
- Critical view on reservation.
- Equal rights of individual and the principle of equality.
- Social and economic inequalities.
- Differential treatment.

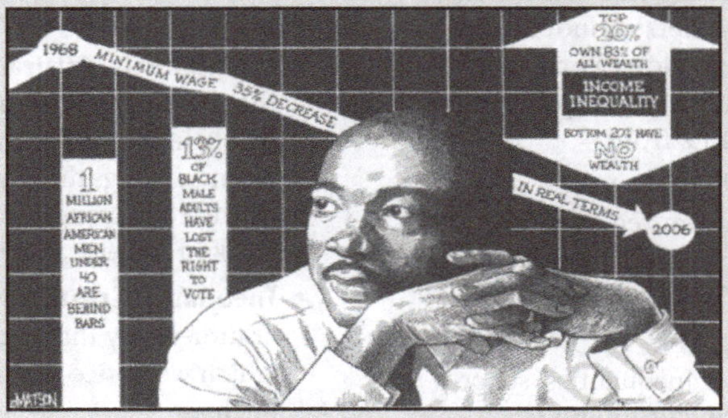

Martin Luther King Jr.

NCERT Folder

Intext Questions

1. Why we talk about global or national inequalities when all around us there are inequalities to which nobody seems to object? (Pg. 34)

Ans. We talk about global and national inequalities because they affect large groups of people and show how unfair systems are worldwide. However, it is also important to notice the inequalities around us, like differences in wealth, education or opportunities in our local communities.

These everyday inequalities often go un-noticed because they have existed for so long that people think they are normal. By addressing these local inequalities, we can take the first step toward creating a fairer society. If we ignore them, it becomes harder to fix larger inequalities on a national or global level.

2. Make a list of all the social and economic inequalities that you notice among the students of your own school? (Pg. 43)

Ans.
- **Economic Inequality** In my school economic inequality is reflected, when some students come from wealthy families and can afford expensive uniforms, books, gadgets and private tuition, while others struggle to buy basic school supplies.
- **Social Inequality** The following kinds of social inequalities are noticeable in my school.

(i) **Caste-based Discrimination** Where some students may face bias or exclusion because of their caste.

(ii) **Gender Inequality** Where girls may face restrictions from participating in certain activities or are not encouraged to pursue higher education. Students from rural areas often face challenges in adjusting to schools in urban areas due to language or cultural differences.

(iii) **Educational Opportunities** Some students attend extra coaching classes, while others cannot afford them, leading to unequal academic performance. Access to extracurricular activities, like sports or arts, may be limited for students from underprivileged backgrounds.

(iv) **Language Barriers** Students from regional or non-English-speaking backgrounds may face difficulties in understanding lessons and are often treated unfairly.

By identifying and addressing these inequalities, schools can work toward creating a more inclusive and fair environment for all students.

3. Make a list of all the facilities that students with various kinds of physical handicaps would need to learn as any other student. (Pg. 46)

Ans. Facilities needed by students with physical disabilities

(i) **Accessible Infrastructure**
- Ramps and elevators for easy movement.
- Wider doorways for wheelchair access.
- Accessible washrooms with proper support-bars.

(ii) **Assistive Devices**
- Hearing aids or audio systems for students with hearing impairments.
- Braille books and tactile learning materials for visually impaired students.

(iii) **Specialised Teaching Support**
- Teachers trained in sign language.
- Special educators for differently-abled students.

(iv) **Inclusive Classrooms**
- Comfortable seating arrangements.
- Peer support programs to encourage participation.

Facilities available in the school

In many Indian schools, facilities like ramps and basic accessible washrooms may be present, but assistive devices, special educators or advanced technologies like Braille or screen readers are often missing. Schools need to prioritise creating an inclusive environment to ensure that students with disabilities can learn equally.

Exercise

1. Some people argue that inequality is natural while others maintain that it is equality which is natural and the inequalities which we notice around us are created by society. Which view do you support? Give reasons. Diksha App

Ans. To support or discard these arguments we need to examine rationale behind it

- **Inequality is Natural** People with this argument say that inequality is natural because people are not equal by birth, they differ in traits, abilities and talents. Human beings differ in physical, mental and intellectual strength. There should be a division of work in society, as all people cannot do same work.
- **Inequality Created by Society** People with this argument say that equality is natural but inequalities which we notice around us are created by society. Such as

(i) Unequal distribution of wealth and resources.

(ii) Discrimination on the basis of gender, caste, region and religion, etc.

(iii) Unequal opportunity of employment.

I support neither of the arguments because both arguments are valid in different circumstances. Inequalities which are natural or socially created can be abrogated by giving special opportunities to needy people.

2. There is a view that absolute economic equality is neither possible nor desirable. It is argued that the most a society can do is to try and reduce the gaps between the richest and poorest members of society. Do you agree? **Diksha App**

Ans. Yes, I agree with the statement that absolute economic equality is neither possible nor desirable. Absolute economic equality has never been a reality. Poor people are not poor because they want to be. Not all wealthy people are wealthy due to their hard work. However, some became wealthy due to their hard work and talent. We should allow everyone to achieve wealth based on their individual talents. But society should help the poor and try to reduce the gaps between the richest and poorest members. Society should provide facilities and equal opportunities to the needy so they can develop themselves.

3. Match the following concepts with appropriate instances.

A.	Affirmative Action	1.	Every adult citizen has a Right to Vote.
B.	Equality of Opportunity	2.	Banks offer higher rate of interest to senior citizen.
C.	Equal Rights	3.	Every child should get free education.

Ans. (i) **Affirmative Action** Banks offer higher rate of interest to senior citizens.

Appropriate Instances After contributing for a long time in nation building process a person becomes senior citizen. It is generally considered that increasing age imposes several limitations on the elderly, biologically, socially and economically. To give them social security, banks offer higher rate of interest to senior citizen.

(ii) **Equality of Opportunity** Every child should get free education.

Appropriate Instances Due to socio-economic backwardness, a number of children do not get opportunity of education. Thus, it should be ensured that every child should get free education.

(iii) **Equal Rights** Every adult citizen has a Right to Vote.

Appropriate Instances Every citizen has right to enjoy political rights. Right to Vote is a good example of equal rights in our country.

4. A government report on farmers' problems says that small and marginal farmers cannot get good prices from the market. It recommends that the government should intervene to ensure a better price but only for small and marginal farmers. Is this recommendation consistent with the principle of equality? **Diksha App**

Ans. Yes, the government report regarding recommendation is consistent with the principle of equality because in this case, only small and marginal farmers are affected, as they do not have sufficient resources and knowledge about the prices of crops in the market.

5. Which of the following violate the principles of equality and why?

(i) Every child in class will read the text of the play by turn.

(ii) The Government of Canada encouraged white Europeans to migrate to Canada from the end of the Second World War till 1960.

(iii) There is a separate railway reservation counter for the senior citizens.

(iv) Access to some forest areas is reserved for certain tribal communities.

Ans. (i) Here, the principles of equality is not violated as every child is getting an opportunity to read text.

(ii) Yes, this is a violation of equality, as white Europeans were encouraged over coloured people on the basis of their colour differences.

(iii) No, there is no violation of equality, as they have special needs and requirements.

(iv) No, there is no violation of equality, as this is done to protect the livelihood, rights and culture of the tribal people.

6. Here are some arguments in favour of the Right to Vote for women. Which of these are consistent with the idea of equality? Give reasons. **Diksha App**

(i) Women are our mothers. We shall not disrespect our mothers by denying them the Right to Vote.

(ii) Decisions of the government affect women as well as men, therefore they also should have a say in choosing the rulers.

(iii) Not granting women the Right to Vote will cause dis-harmony in the family.

(iv) Women constitute half of humanity. You cannot subjugate them for long by denying them the Right to Vote.

Ans. (i) Right to vote is a political right and denying of such rights affect both men and women equally. Thus, this argument is consistent with the idea of equality.

(ii) Yes, this argument is consistent with the idea of equality as it is based on decision-making which affect both men and women.

(iii) No, this argument is not consistent with the idea of equality as giving right to vote has no connection with the family.

(iv) Yes, this argument is consistent with the idea of equality as it is based on rational thinking. The women constitute half population therefore, they must be given equal importance and opportunity to cast their vote.

Exam Pattern Questions

Objective Type Questions

Multiple Choice Questions (MCQs)

1. All faiths and religions proclaim all human beings to be the creation God. Which implication of equality is highlighted by this statement? Competency Based Que

(a) Economic implication of equality
(b) Political implication of equality
(c) Social implication of equality
(d) Moral implication of equality

2. The concept of ...., as a political ideal, implies that all human beings are of equal value, regardless of their colour, gender, ethnicity or nationality.

(a) liberty (b) freedom
(c) equality (d) justice

3. Revolutionaries of which country used the slogan 'Liberty, Equality and Fraternity' to revolt against landed feudal aristocracy and the monarchy. Diksha App

(a) France (b) England
(c) Germany (d) U.S.A.

4. The demand for equality was also raised during anti-colonial liberation struggles in Asia and Africa during the .... century.

(a) 20th (b) 19th
(c) 17th (d) 21st

5. Consider the following statements related to objective of the equality. Competency Based Que

I. All people are entitled to same rights and opportunities to develop their skills.

II. All people entitled to same rights and opportunities to pursue their goals and ambitions.

Which of the following statement is/are correct?

(a) Only I (b) Only II
(c) Both I and II (d) None of these

6. Which of the following inequalities cannot be altered?

(a) Social Inequalities (b) Natural Inequalities
(c) Political Inequalities (d) Inherent Inequalities

7. .... equality means that all people are equal before law.

(a) Political (b) Social (c) Civil (d) Positive

8. Political equality, also known as equality before the law, is a vital first step toward equality, but it is also complemented by ....

(a) social inequalities (b) equality of opportunity
(c) affirmative action (d) freedom of expression

9. It includes granting equal citizenship to all the members of the state. Competency Based Que

Which of the following equality the given statements is talking about?

(a) Political Equality (b) Social Equality
(c) Economic Equality (d) Both (a) and (c)

10. What kind of rights is 'Right to vote'?

(a) Constitutional Rights (b) Fundamental Rights
(c) Legal Rights (d) Both (a) and (c)

11. What do you mean by social equality?

(a) Freedom from fear of hunger.
(b) No discrimination should be made on the basis of caste, colour, race, creed, sex, religion, etc.
(c) All citizens are not equal before law.
(d) All citizens should have the means to meet their needs.

12. When there are no significant differences in wealth, income and property between individuals or classes, then it leads to ....

(a) political equality (b) economic equality
(c) social equality (d) All of these

13. Consider the following statements

I. A political doctrine which advocates unequal rights for women and men is called feminism.

II. According to Karl Marx inequality has come because of the private ownership and control of important economic resources like oil, land, forests and other forms of property. **Competency Based Que**

Select the correct statements?

(a) Only I (b) Only II
(c) Both I and II (d) None of these

14. Which of the following statements is incorrect? **Competency Based Que**

(a) Inequalities which are entrenched, that is, which remain relatively untouched over generations, are more dangerous for a society.
(b) Feminism is a political philosophy that advocates for equal rights of men and women.
(c) For liberals the principle of competition is the most just and efficient way of selecting candidates for jobs or admission to educational institutions.
(d) None of the above

15. .... argued that the root cause of inequality in society was private ownership of economic resources.

(a) Stephen Hawking (b) J.S. Mill
(c) Karl Marx (d) John Locke

16. Consider the following statements regarding socialism.

I. Socialism aims to minimise existing inequalities and distribute resources justly.

II. Rammanohar Lohia was an eminent socialist.

III. Lohia gave the concept of Sapta Kranti. **Competency Based Que**

Which of the following statement(s) is/are correct?

(a) Only I (b) I and II
(c) II and III (d) All of these

17. Select the wrong statement.

(a) Natural inequality and socially induced inequalities have been distinguished in political theory on occasion.
(b) Natural inequalities are considered to be the result of the different characteristics and abilities with which people are born.
(c) Social inequalities are those which are created by only an individual.
(d) In democratic societies, political equality would normally include granting equal citizenship to all the members of the state.

18. Which of the following grounds creates discrimination among the society?

I. Gender **II. Caste**
III. Region **IV. Religion**

Select the correct options?

(a) I, II and III (b) II, III and IV
(c) I, III and IV (d) All of these

19. Which of the following have been protected by customs and the legal system?

(a) Economic equality (b) Political equality
(c) Social equality (d) All of these

20. On which among the following grounds, does Indian Constitution prohibits discrimination?

(a) Religion (b) Caste
(c) Sex (d) All of these

21. Which of the following is a form of reverse discrimination?

(a) Reservation
(b) Racial prejudices
(c) Patriarchy
(d) Both (a) and (b)

22. Match List I correctly with List II

List I	List II
A. Liberalism	1. Equal rights for men and women
B. Marxism	2. Some kind of government regulation over certain key areas
C. Feminism	3. Principle of competition
D. Socialsim	4. Aboilation of private property

Choose the correct option.

	A	B	C	D
(a)	1	2	3	4
(b)	3	4	1	2
(c)	3	2	4	1
(d)	4	1	2	3

23. Consider the following statements.

Statement I Liberals are not completely against the market, but they want some government control over key resources.

Statement II Marx suggests seven revolutions to end inequalities in society.

In the light of above statements, choose the correct answer from the options given below

(a) Both Statement I and Statement II are true.
(b) Both Statement I and Statement II are false.
(c) Statement I is true, but Statement II is false.
(d) Statement I is false, but Statement II is true.

Assertion-Reason Questions

Directions (Q. Nos. 24-27) In the questions given below, there are two statements marked as Assertion (A) and Reason (R). Read the statements and choose the correct option.

Codes

(a) Both A and R are true and R is the correct explanation of A.
(b) Both A and R are true, but R is not the correct explanation of A.
(c) A is true, but R is false.
(d) A is false, but R is true.

24. **Assertion** (A) French revolutionaries used the slogan Liberty, Equality and Fraternity to protest against the democracy.

Reason (R) During anti-colonial independence movements in Asia and Africa in the 20th century, the demand for equality increased also.

25. **Assertion** (A) Natural inequalities are considered to be the result of the different characteristics and abilities with which people are born.

Reason (R) Social inequalities are created by society.

26. **Assertion (A)** The Constitutions of most of the democratic government around the world have incorporated provisions into constitution to prohibit discrimination.

Reason (R) There should not be discrimination on the ground of religion, race, caste to attain equality.

Competency Based Que

27. **Assertion (A)** In Indian Constitution, discrimination has been prohibited in Article 15.

Reason (R) 'Our Constitution also abolishes the practice of untouchability'.

Passage Based Questions

28. **Read the given passage and answer the following questions.**

Critics of positive discrimination, particularly policies of reservations, thus invoke the principle of equality to argue against such policies. They contend that any provision of reservations or quotas for the deprived in admissions for higher education or jobs is unfair as it arbitrarily denies other sections of society their right to equal treatment.

They maintain that reservations are a form of reverse discrimination and they continue with the practices that the principle of equality questions and rejects. Equality requires that all persons be treated alike and when we make distinctions between individuals on the basis of their caste or colour, we are likely to reinforce caste and racial prejudices.

For these theorists, the important thing is to do away with social distinctions that divide our society.

(i) .... is an act of giving advantage to those groups in society that are often treated unfairly because of their race, sex, caste, region or religion etc.

(a) Inequality (b) Social discrimination
(c) Biased sociality (d) None of these

(ii) What is equality?

(a) Equality means that all persons be treated alike.
(b) Equality requires distinctions between individuals on the basis of their caste or colour.
(c) Equality means dividing the society.
(d) All of the above

(iii) Why this passage suggests to do away with social distinction?

(a) Social distinction will reinforce caste and racial prejudice.
(b) Social distinctions will divide the society.
(c) Both (a) and (b)
(d) Neither (a) or (b)

(iv) Consider the following statements.

I. In the Indian Constitution there is no provision for reservation or quotas for deprived class in admission for higher education or jobs.

II. Equality requires that all person be treated alike.

Which of the statement given above is/are correct?

(a) Only I (b) Only II
(c) Both I and II (d) Neither I nor II

29. **Read the given passage and answer the following questions.**

The first step towards bringing about equality is, of course, ending the formal system of inequality and privileges. Social, economic and political inequalities all over the world have been protected by customs and legal systems that prohibited some sections of society from enjoying certain kinds of opportunities and rewards. Poor people were not granted the right to vote in a large number of countries. Women were not allowed to take up many professions and activities.

The caste system in India prevented people from the 'lower' castes from doing anything except manual labour. In many countries only people from some families could occupy high positions.

(i) The first step to bring equality should be to end the formal system of ....

(a) equality and discrimination
(b) social and economic
(c) inequality and privileges
(d) political and liberty

(ii) .... may take several forms, ranging from preferential spending on services for poorer groups, such as scholarships and hostels, to preferential treatment for admissions to educational institutions and employment opportunities.
(a) Freedom of expression
(b) Affirmative action
(c) Fundamental rights
(d) Directive principles of states policies

(iii) What steps can be taken for women to enable then to compete for jobs?

30. Read the given passage and answer the following questions.

Natural inequalities are considered to be the result of the different characteristics and abilities with which people are born. It is generally assumed that natural differences cannot be altered. Social inequalities on the other hand are those created by society. Certain societies may, for instance, value those who perform intellectual work over those who do manual work and reward them differently. They may treat differently people of different race, colour, gender or caste. Differences of this kind reflect the values of a society and some of these may certainly appear to us to be unjust.

(i) Which of the following equalities cannot be altered as per the general belief of people?
(a) Social inequalities (b) Economic inequalities
(c) Natural inequalities (d) Political inequalities

(ii) Which of these will get more respect in certain societies as per the given passage?
(a) Farmer (b) Labourer
(c) Engineer (d) Vegetable seller

(iii) What is the difference between natural inequalities and social inequalities on the basis of their origin?

Answers

1. (d) Moral implication of equality
2. (c) equality **3.** (a) France
4. (a) 20th **5.** (c) Both I and II
6. (b) Natural Inequalities
7. (a) Political
8. (b) equality of opportunity
9. (a) Political Equality
10. (d) Both (a) and (c)
11. (b) No discrimination should be made on the basis of caste, colour, race, creed, sex, religion, etc.
12. (b) economic equality
13. (b) Only II
14. (d) None of the above
15. (c) Karl Marx
16. (d) All of these
17. (c) Social inequalities are those which are created by only an individual.
18. (d) All of these
19. (d) All of these
20. (d) All of these
21. (a) Reservation
22. (b) 3 4 1 2
23. (b) Both statement I and Statement II are false.
24. (d) A is false, but R is true.
25. (b) Both A and R are true, but R is not the correct explanation of A.
26. (a) Both A and R are true and R is the correct explanation of A.
27. (b) Both A and R are true, but R is not the correct explanation of A.
28. (i) (d) Social discrimination
(ii) (a) Equality means that all persons be treated alike
(iii) (c) Both (a) and (b)
(iv) (b) Only II
29. (i) (c) inequality and privileges
(ii) (b) Affirmative action
(iii) To enable women to compete for jobs on an equal footing several steps can be taken which are as follows
(a) Equal pay for equal work.
(b) Provision of maternity leaves.
(c) Providing creches in the work place.
(d) Providing accus to medical facilities.
30. (i) (c) Natural inequalities
(ii) (c) Engineer.
(iii) Natural inequalities are considered to be the result of the different characteristics and abilities with which people are born, social inequalities on the other hand are those created by society.

Subjective Questions

Very Short Answer Type Questions

1. What is the concept of equality?

Ans. As per the concept of equality, all people are equal and should get the same rights and opportunities without facing any discrimination on the basis of gender, race, caste, religion, etc.

2. Why is equality important for us?

Ans. Equality is important for us because we can get equal treatment and cannot be discriminated on the basis of colour, race, gender, caste, religion and regions. This allows individual to cherish dignity and respect in society.

3. What do you mean by equality of opportunity?

Ans. The concept of equality of opportunity implies that every human being is entitled to the same rights and opportunities to develop their skills and talents and to pursue their goals and ambitions.

4. Define the term 'natural inequality'. How does it emerge?

Ans. Natural inequalities are those that emerge between people as a result of their different capabilities and talents. Natural equalities emerge as a result of the different characteristics and abilities with which people are born.

5. State the general assumption about natural inequality. Is that perception true according to you?

Ans. The general assumption about natural inequality is that it cannot be changed. According to me this assumption is wrong because natural inequalities can be changed with the help of medical science and technology.

6. How can men and women lead free and equal lives as per feminists?

Ans. Feminists believe that many of the inequalities we see in society between men and women are neither natural nor necessary and can be changed. So, both women and men can lead free and equal lives by changing these inequalities.

7. How can equality be established by following the formal system?

Ans. To establish equality by formal system, our political system needs to establish stringent laws and policies. For example, Indian Constitution abolished untouchability under Article 17.

8. Mention the importance of supplementing equality before law by equality of opportunity.

Ans. Equality before law should be supplemented by equality of opportunity. There will always be some groups who cannot enjoy their rights like others due to their substances. Only then, disadvantaged groups can compete with others.

9. Why do critics of positive discrimination consider it as a form of reverse discrimination?

Ans. Critics of positive discrimination consider it as a form of reverse discrimination because they believe that equality means treating all people alike. When distinction is made between individuals on the basis of caste or colour, caste and racial prejudices are reinforced.

10. Feminists are against the distinction between 'public' and 'private'. Justify. **Competency Based Que**

Ans. Feminists are against the distinction between 'public' and 'private' because they argue that women all over the world are employed in some form of work outside the home. They are active in the 'public' domain. But they are still, solely responsible for housework as well. This creates a 'double burden' on women.

11. What steps can be taken to promote equality?

Ans. Following steps can be taken to promote equality

(i) Equality through different treatment

(ii) By affirmative action

(iii) By giving equal opportunity

12. Ramesh and Reena are male and female employees who work for a company named ABC. Ramesh regularly works night shifts, whereas Reena occasionally works night shifts. If she works, she is provided convenience to reach the office. **Competency Based Que**

(i) Which equality is provided by company ABC to Reena?

(ii) Is discrimination with Ramesh justified?

Ans. (i) Reena is getting equality of opportunities by company ABC.

(ii) Discrimination with Ramesh is justified because he does not face the same challenges that Reena faces due to being a woman, like household work, safety concerns, etc.

Short Answer Type Questions

1. What are the the main features of equality?

Ans. Main features of equality are as follows

- Equality advocates an equitable and fair distribution of wealth and resources i.e. minimum possible gap between the rich and the poor.
- Equality implies the system of equal and adequate opportunities for all the people in society.
- Equality affirms the grant and guarantee of equal rights and freedoms to all the people.
- Equality does not stand for absolute equality. It accepts the presence of some natural inequalities.

2. "No society treats all its members in exactly the same way under all conditions". Explain this statement.

Competency Based Que

Ans. Equality is an ideal and practical, it is also challenging to apply it. It means no society can treat all its members in exactly the same way under all conditions. The smooth functioning of society requires division of work and functions where people often enjoy different status and rewards on account of it.

Many times these differences of treatment may appear acceptable or even necessary. For example, we usually do not feel that giving Prime Ministers or army generals, a special official rank and status against the concept of equality, until the privileges are not misused.

3. "Political equality or equality before the law is essential for us". Give your opinion on this statement.

Competency Based Que

Ans. Political equality or equality before the law is essential for us due to following reasons

(i) It grants equal citizenship to all members of the state.

(ii) It ensures conditions which allow the citizens to participate in the affairs of the state.

(iii) Political equality gives us certain rights such as Right to Vote, Right to Contest Elections, Right to Criticise the Government, etc.
These rights give opportunity to citizens to participate in the system of governance and decision-making.

4. What do you understand by 'Certain minimum conditions of life' in context of equality?

Ans. Equality means the state of being equal, specially in status, rights or opportunities. To achieve the objectives of equality certain minimum conditions are required to be provided to every member of the society.
Such minimum conditions refer to those conditions which are capable to live a dignified life.

These conditions are adequate health facility, the opportunity for good education, adequate nutrition and a minimum wage, etc.

5. "Patriarchy is based on the assumption that men and women are different by nature and this difference justifies their unequal positions in society". Comment on this statement based on your own experiences.

Competency Based Que

Ans. Patriarchy is the prime obstacle to women's advancement and development.

- Despite differences in levels of domination, the broad principles remain the same, i.e. men have the control.
- In the modern world where women go ahead by their merit, patriarchy creates these obstacles for women to go forward in society, because patriarchal institutions and social relations are responsible for the unequal positions of women in society.
- Patriarchy refers to the male domination both in public and in private sphere.
- In this way, feminists use the term 'patriarchy' to describe the power relationship between men and women as well as to find out the root cause of women's sub-ordination.

6. What are the seven kinds of inequalities identified by Rammanohar Lohia?

Ans. Eminent socialist thinker Rammanohar Lohia identified seven kinds of inequalities.

These are

(i) Inequality between men and women,
(ii) Inequality based on skin colour,
(iii) Caste-based inequality,
(iv) Colonial rule over some countries
(v) Economic inequality
(vi) Revolution for civil liberties against unjust encroachments on private life
(vii) Revolution for non-violence

These were the seven revolutions or **Sapta Kranti** which were the ideas of socialism for Lohia.

7. How does the Indian Constitution ensure social equality?

Ans. Since ancient times, the caste system in India prevented people from the 'lower' castes from doing anything except manual labour. These people faced social and economic inequalities. Some were treated as untouchables.

After independence, the Indian Constitution prohibited any discrimination on the basis of caste, gender, race or place of birth. It also abolished the practice of untouchability. Now, all citizens are equal and have equal rights as per the Indian Constitution.

8. Why do we need affirmative action?

Ans. We need affirmative action because our society has entrenched (rooted) inequality. Customs in our society since ages has deprived lower castes to minimum standard of living. Due to their continuous deprivation, they have been made more backward. In India, there has been inadequate facilities to provide good schooling and health services to all sections of the society.

Government has taken affirmative action and provided them reservations and other privileges, so that they get a level playing field in competition and live a dignified life with other people.

9. How can affirmative actions help in minimising social inequalities?

Ans. Indian society suffers from substantial inequalities in education, employment and income based on caste and ethnicity.

Affirmative actions help in minimising these sufferings or social inequalities in following ways

- It gives opportunities to socially and economically weaker sections of the society to enhance their talents and capabilities.
- It gives recognition to the needy people.
- It ensures minimum standard of living in society.
- It eliminates social prejudices from society.

10. What caution should be taken for differential treatment?

Ans. Differential treatment is given to people who are disadvantaged so they can develop themselves.

- However, we should take caution that differential treatment does not yield new structures of dominance and oppression or become a means for some dominant groups to reassert special privileges and power in society.
- Differential treatment is intended and justified only as a means to promote a just and egalitarian society.

Long Answer Type Questions

1. Explain the three dimensions of equality.

Ans. Based on different kinds of inequalities which exist in society, there are three dimensions of equality i.e. Political, Social and Economic.

(i) **Political Equality**

- It includes granting equal citizenship to all the members of the state. The rights which are considered necessary to enable citizen to develop themselves and participate in the affairs of state are right to vote, freedom of expressions, movement and association and freedom of belief.
- These rights are also considered as legal rights and Fundamental Right which are guaranteed by Constitution.

(ii) **Social Equality**

- Making equal laws is not sufficient, as we require equality in the access of resources.
- The pursuit of equality requires that people belonging to different groups and communities also have a fair and equal chance to compete for those goods and opportunities.
- So, there is a need for equal, social and economic conditions like adequate provision of health care, education, nutrition and minimum wages.

(iii) **Economic Equality**

- When there is no significant differences in wealth, income and property between individuals or classes, then it leads to economic equality.
- The relative disparity between the wealthiest and poorest classes is one way to quantify the degree of economic inequality in a society.
- Another method will be to measure the number of people living in poverty.
- If certain groups of citizens in a society have accumulated significant wealth and power that comes with it over centuries, the society will divided between those classes and those who have remained the poor.

2. What are the differences in the views of Karl Marx and liberals on equality?

Ans. Views of Karl Marx on Equality

- Karl Marx, a 19th century thinker says that inequality has arisen because of the ownership of important economic resources like oil, land, forests and other forms of property by rich class. By owning such great economic power, they have also got hold of political power.
- These rich classes make policies which are beneficial for rich class only and are dis-advantageous to poor class. So, only providing opportunities will not help the poor class.
- He believed that social, economic and political inequalities are interlinked to each other because rich people having control over wealth leads to control over political system and this also makes them powerful in society.

Views of Liberals on Equality

- Liberals believe that while state try to ensure a minimum standard of living and equal opportunities to all, this can not by itself bring equality and notice to society.

- They held that when people have attained minimum standard of living they should be allowed to compete between them and then everybody will get according to their hard work. As long as competition is there, inequalities will not be there in the system.
- They believe that political, social and economic inequalities are not linked. They want each sphere to be dealt individually to tackle its problems.
- For political inequality we need democracy, and for social and economic inequality, state can intervene to provide minimum standard of living.

3. Study the table and answer the following questions. The table given below shows the caste-community inequalities in higher education in India.

Competency Based Que

Caste/ Communities	Graduates per thousand persons
Schedule Caste (SC)	47
Muslim	61
Hindu-OBC	86
Scheduled Tribes (ST)	109
Christian	237
Sikh	250
Hindu-Upper Caste	253
Other Religions	315
All India Religions	155

Source: National Sample Survey Organisation, 55th round survey, 1999-2000

(i) What are the reasons for the data shown in the table?

(ii) What could be the reasons for the lowest number of graduates in SCs?

(iii) SCs, STs and OBCs have reservations in educational institutes and government jobs. What other steps can the government also take for their development? Suggest any two.

Ans. (i) The caste-community inequalities in higher education in India, as shown in the table, are the result of social and economic inequalities.

(ii) People of scheduled caste have faced discrimination for centuries. They don't face only economic inequality but social inequality also. In many parts of India, they still face discrimination. These could be the reasons for the lowest number of graduates in SCs.

(iii) The government can do the following things for the development of SCs, STs, and OBCs:
- Providing financial assistance : Government can provide financial assistance to SCs, STs and OBCs.
- Provide scholarship : Government can provide scholarships and free courses on skills development.

Picture Based Question

1. Study the cartoon given below and answer the Questions that follows.

(i) Which equality is being violated by the examiner in the picture?

(a) Equality of opportunities (b) Social equality
(c) Economic equality (d) Natural equality

Ans. (a) Equality of opportunities

(ii) What is not correct according to equality of opportunity?

(a) Access to education (b) Access to health
(c) Equality in ambition (d) Equality in safe housing

Ans. (c) Equality in ambition

(iii) What is the significance of equality?

(a) All humans deserve equal consideration.
(b) All citizen get equal treatment.
(c) No person will be discriminated on the basis of colour, caste gender and religion.
(d) All of the above

Ans. (d) All of the above

(iv) What can the examiner do to ensure fair selection?

(a) He can give the task of swimming to all animals.
(b) He can give the task of running to all animals.
(c) He can give different tasks to animals as per their natural abilities.
(d) He can choose the animal whom he considers best.

Ans. (c) He can give different tasks to animals as per their natural abilities.

SELF ASSESSMENT TEST

Objective Type Questions

1. Which of these were opposed by French revolutionaries?
   (a) Monarchy and feudal aristocracy
   (b) Democracy and monarchy
   (c) Justice and liberty
   (d) Feudal aristocracy and democracy
2. Who among the following was an eminent socialist?
   (a) Rammanohar Lohia
   (b) John Locke,
   (c) J.S. Mill
   (d) Adam Smith
3. .... refers to an ideology which values men more than women.
   (a) Socialism
   (b) Feminism
   (c) Patriarchy
   (d) Matriarchy

Very Short Answer Type Questions

4. Why is treating everyone equally in all conditions not equality?
5. What is political ideal of equality?
6. Why did black people face discrimination in Africa?
7. Mention some rights that a person will get as a result of political equality.
8. Define the term 'double burden' in the context of feminism.

Short Answer Type Questions

9. Political equality is not a guarantee of equality but still it is essential. Why?
10. Write about paradox of equality.
11. How will it be difficult to create an egalitarian society due to entrenched inequalities? Explain.
12. How can inequalities in society be removed as per Karl Marx? Discuss.
13. 'The commitment to the ideal of equality does not imply the elimination of all forms of differences'. Do you agree with this statement? Justify your answer. **Competency Based Que**

Long Answer Type Questions

14. Describe economic equality in detail.
15. Distinguish between political and social equality.
16. Mention some problems that women face due to customs. What role can states and social groups play to solve these problems?
17. Explain the doctrine of Sapta Kranti as given by Dr. Rammanohar Lohia.
18. 'Political liberty is meaningless without economic equality'. Elucidate. **Competency Based Que; Diksha App**

04
CHAPTER

Justice is the concept of ensuring the well-being of all people which involves giving each person what they deserve. The concept of justice is influenced by many fields and view points, including: ethics, morality, national thinking, law, equity and fairness.

Social Justice

▼ **YOUR STUDY GOALS**

▼ **YOUR PRACTICE GOAL**

- Objective Type Questions (27 Qs ; MCQs, A-R, Statements, Matching, Passage Based)
- Subjective Questions (10 VSAs, 7 SAs, 4 LAs 2 Picture Based)

4.1 Justice

- **Justice** has different interpretations by different cultures and traditions. In ancient Indian society, justice was associated with dharma. Maintaining **dharma** or a just social order was considered to be a primary duty of kings.
- Chinese philosopher **Confucius** argued that kings should maintain justice by punishing the wrongdoers or criminals and rewarding the virtuous or good.
- **Plato**, in his book **The Republic**, examined the concept of justice through a long dialogue between **Socrates** and his friends. Young people ask socrates why we should be just. They argue that why unjust people are more successful.
- **Socrates** explains that if everyone manipulated rules to fulfill their own interest then surely no one could benefit from injustice and no one would be secure. So, we should be just in our own long-term interest.
- He explains that justice does not only mean doing good to our friends and harm to our enemies or pursuing our own interests. Justice involves the well-being of all people.

- According to the German philosopher **Immanuel Kant**, human beings possess dignity. If all persons are granted dignity then they have the opportunity to develop their talents and pursue their chosen goals. Justice requires that we give due and equal consideration to all individuals.

4.2 Principles of Justice

The principle of justice is a set of concepts that address fairness, equality and equitable treatment. Here, we will discuss the three principles of justice i.e. Equal treatment for equals, Proportionate justice, Recognition of special needs.

Equal Treatment for Equals

- As per the principle of treating equals equally, all individuals share certain characteristics as human beings. So, they deserve equal rights and equal treatment.
- Most liberal democracies give many rights to citizens which include civil, political and social rights.

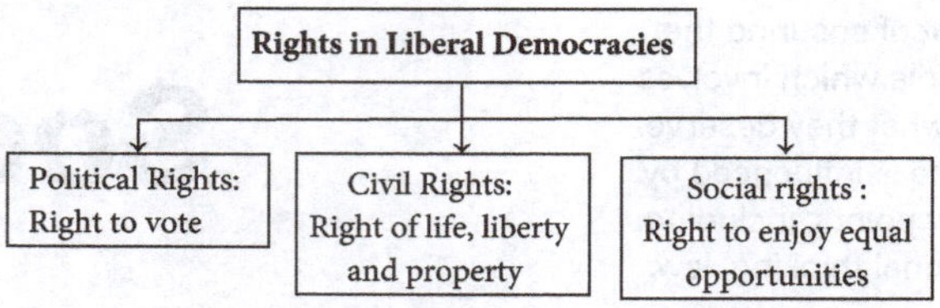

▲ *Rights in Liberal Democracies*

- Apart from equal rights, the principle of treating equals equally require that people should not face discrimination on the basis of class, caste, race or gender.
- They should be judged on the basis of their work and actions.
- **For example**, if a person receives one hundred rupees for some work and another receives only seventy five rupees for the same work because they belong to different caste, then it would be unjust.

Proportionate Justice

- The second principle of justice which states that people should be awarded on the basis of their skills, efforts and quality of their work is proportionate justice.
- Equal treatment is not the only principle of justice. There could be circumstances where treating everybody equally would be unjust.
- People should be awarded in proportion to the scale and quality of their effort.
- It would be fair and just to give the different rewards for different works.
- Workers should be paid differently based on the skills, effort and danger involved in their job.
- **For example,** a surgeon and a miner should be paid different salaries.

Recognition of Special Needs

- Recognition of special needs is the third principle of justice. Special needs of people should be recognised while distributing rewards and duties to promote social justice[1].
- Non-discrimination between people and rewarding them in proportion to their efforts are neither enough to ensure that people enjoy equality in other aspects of their lives in society nor that the society as a whole is just.

1 Social Justice It is the fair distribution of wealth and opportunities in a society.

- The principle of recognition of special needs does not oppose the principle of equal treatment. The principle of treating equals equally could imply that people who are not equal in certain important respects could be treated differently.
- **Physical disabilities** Age or lack of access to good education or healthcare, are some of the factors which are considered grounds for special treatment in many countries.
- An unequal society will be created if people who enjoy very different standards of living with people who have been deprived of even the basic minimum needs.
- **For example** In India, lack of access to facilities like health, education etc. is often found combined with caste discrimination. The Indian Constitution allowed for reservations of government jobs and quotas for admissions to educational institutions for people belonging to the Scheduled Castes and Scheduled Tribes.

Harmonising the Principles of Justice

- Governments might sometimes find it difficult to harmonise the three principles of justice which are: equal treatment for equals, proportionate justice and recognition of special needs.
- Pursuing equality of treatment by itself might sometimes work against giving due reward to merit. Emphasising rewarding merit as the main principle of justice might mean that marginalised sections would be at a disadvantage in many areas due to lack of basic facilities.
- Different groups in the country might favour different policies depending upon which principle of justice they emphasise. It is a function of governments to harmonise the different principles to promote a just society.

4.3 Just Distribution

- To achieve social justice in society, governments might have to do more than just ensure that laws and policies treat individuals in a fair manner. Social justice also concerns the just distribution of goods and services.
- If there are serious economic or social inequalities in a society, it might become necessary to try and re-distribute some of the important resources of the society to provide a level playing field for citizens.
- Social justice does not only require that people are treated equally in terms of the laws and policies of society but also that they enjoy some basic equality of life conditions and opportunities.
- The Indian Constitution abolished the practice of untouchability to promote social equality and ensure that people belonging to 'lower' castes have access to temples, jobs and basic necessities like water.
- Different State Governments have also taken some measures to re-distribute important resources like land in a more fair manner by instituting land reforms.
- Differences of opinion on matters such as whether and how to distribute resources and ensure equal access to education and jobs arouse fierce reactions in society and even sometimes provoke violence.

Quick Test 1

1. The king should uphold justice by punishing the wrongdoer and rewarding the good ones. Whose statement is this?
2. Who was the author of the book 'The Republic'?
3. What do human beings possess as per Immanual keant?
4. Name the three principles of justice.
5. Which principle of justice should a teacher use to reward marks to students in an examination?

4.4 John Rawls' Theory of Justice

- **John Rawls** presents the theory of justice with the help of a 'veil of ignorance'[2]. This theory is based on the 'veil of ignorance' expects people to just be to their usual rational selves.
- They are expected to think for themselves and choose what they regard to be in their interest.
- It will be evident that rational persons will try to ensure that the policies they frame benefit the society as a whole. Rawls argues that **rational thinking,** not morality, could lead us to be fair and judge impartially regarding how to distribute the benefits and burdens of a society.
- As in his example, people decide rules on the basis of reason that they could be in the best or worst situation. People act for their own self-interest, not on the basis of morality.

4.5 Pursuing Social Justice

- Justice does not mean absolute equality and uniformity in the way in which people live. A society will be unjust if poor people have no chance to improve their lives due to deep differences between rich and poor.
- A just society should provide people with the basic minimum conditions to enable them to live healthy and secure lives and develop their talents, as well as equal opportunities to pursue their chosen goals in society.
- There are disagreements about the best ways to help disadvantaged members of society.
- In India, different approaches are being supported by different political groups who debate the relative merits of different schemes for helping marginalised sections of the population.

> A just society is that society in which an ascending sense of reverence and descending sense of contempt is dissolved into the creation of a compassionate society. **–Dr. B.R. Ambedkar**

Free Markets Vs. State Intervention

- Supporters of the free market[3] suggest that, as far as possible, individuals should be free to own property and enter into contracts and agreements with others regarding prices, wages and profits.
- In a free market, people will compete with each other. Competent people would get a higher reward, whereas incompetent people would get a lesser reward.
- Many supporters of the free market accept that the intervention of state can ensure a basic minimum standard of living for all people so that they are able to compete on equal terms. The state can encourage and support private agencies to ensure basic facilities.
- In a free market, private agencies will provide only those services that are profitable for them to people who can bear the cost. There may be people who cannot afford these services due to the high cost. In such cases, state intervention is necessary.
- In a democractic society disagreements about issues of distribution and justice are inevitable and even healthy because they force us to examine different points of view and rationally defend our own views.

> Justice implies something which it is not only right to do and wrong not to do; but which some individual person can claim from us as his moral right. **–J. S. Mill**

Quick Test 2

1. What is 'veil of ignorance'?
2. According to Rawls' theory, which thinking could lead us towards fair judgement?
3. Mention two features of a just society.
4. Which problem does a poor person face in a free market?

---

2 **Veil of ignorance** It is a hypothetical state where people make decision without knowing their position in society.

3 **Free market** It is an economic system based on supply and demand with little or no government interference.

Mind Map

1 Justice

- Justice is the ethical idea that people are to be treated fairly and impartially.
- Maintain dharma or a social order was considered to be a primary duty of kings.
- Different State Government abolished the practice of untouchability to promote social equality.

2 Principles of Justice

Equal Treatment for Equals
- Equal rights for everyone and forbids discrimination.

Rights in Liberal Democracies
- **Political Rights** Right to vote.
- **Civil Rights** Right of life, liberty and property.
- **Social Rights** Right to enjoy equal opportunities.

Proportionate Justice
- People should be awarded on the basis of their skill's, efforts and quality of work.
- Equal treatment is not only the principle of justice.

Recognition of Special Needs
- It is the third principle of justice.
- Special duties of people should be taken care to promote social justice.
- Physical disabilities, requires special treatments.
- For example, In India, lack of access to facilities like health, education etc.

SOCIAL JUSTICE

3 Harmonising the Principles of Justice

- Harmonise the three principles of justice.
- Equal treatment for equal.
- Proportionate justice.
- Recognition of special needs.
- Emphasising rewarding merit as the main principle of justice.
- Different policies depending upon which principle of justice they emphasise.
- Governments to harmonise the different principles to promote a just society.

4 Just Distribution

- Justice also means fair distribution of goods and services.
- Different State Government abolished the practice of untouchability to promote social equality.
- Some measures like re-distribute important resources becomes necessary to provide equal developmental opportunities.
- Difference on manner of distribution of resources and equal access to education and jobs arouse fierce reactions in society.

5 John Rowl's Theory of Justice

- Presented Principles of Justice by the 'veil of ignorance'.
- This theory says that people should think for themselves and choose according to their interest.
- Rawls argues that rational thinking, is important then morality.
- For example, people decide rules on the basis of reason that they could be in the best or worst situation. People act for their own self-interest, not on the basis of morality.

6 Pursuing Social Justice

- Justice does not mean absolute quality and uniformity in the way in which people live.
- There are disagreement about the best ways to help disadvantages member of society.

Free Markets Vs. State Intervention
- **Free Market** Suggest individual should be free to own property.
- **State Intervention** Suggest the involvement of government in economic affairs.

A Just society is that society in which ascending sense of reverence and descending sense of contempt is dissolved into the creation of a compassionate society.

Dr. B.R. Ambedkar

Social Justice

NCERT Folder

1. What does it mean to give each person his/her due? How has the meaning of 'giving each his due' changed over time?

Ans. Giving each person his/her due means that providing justice by ensuring the well being of the people. This idea continues to be an important part of our understanding of justice.

- However, our understanding of what is due to a person has changed from time of Plato. Today, our understanding of what is just is closely linked to our understanding of what is due to each person as a human being.
- According to the German philosopher Immanuel Kant, if all persons are granted dignity then, what is due to each of them is the opportunity to develop their talents and pursue their chosen goals.

2. Briefly discuss the three principles of justice outlined in this chapter. Explain each with examples.

Ans. The three principle of justice are

(i) **Equal Treatment for Equals**

- This indicates the principle of treating people equally.
- All individuals share certain characteristics as human beings. Therefore, they deserve to be treated equally and equal rights should be provided.
- It includes civil rights like Right to life, liberty and property, political rights like Right to vote and social rights related to equal social opportunities.
- It also prohibits discrimination on the grounds of class, caste, gender and race. For example, two individuals from different backgrounds should be paid same reward for the same kind of job.

(ii) **Proportionate Justice**

- This principle indicates rewarding people in proportion to the scale and quality of their effort.
- It is just to reward different jobs differently on the basis of efforts, skills required and the danger involved.
- Proportionality provides balance to the principle of equal treatment. For example, the reward and compensation for a surgeon and an architect varies according to their skills which are required in their job.

(iii) **Recognition of Special needs**

- This principle is based on distributing rewards and duties on the basis of special needs of people.
- On the basis of factors such as age, physical disabilities and lack of access to good education or health care, special treatment is given in many countries.
- People with special needs or disabilities are treated unequal in some particular respect and therefore, are provided with some deserving and special help. A physically challenged person getting a reserved seat is an example of principle of recognition of special needs.

3. Does the principle of considering the special needs of people conflict with the principle of equal treatment for all?

Ans. The principle of considering the special needs of people does not raise a conflict with the principle of equal treatment for all because

- People with special needs are given special treatment to facilitate their participation in the running of the society.
- People with special needs also require special treatment for integration with society and for securing opportunities and basic needs that would be otherwise denied to them.
- The senior citizens, women and socially backward people are given special treatment due to their special needs.

4. How does Rawls use the idea of veil of ignorance to argue that fair and just distribution can be defended on rational grounds?

Ans. Rawls uses the ideal of a veil of ignorance to argue that fair and just distribution can be defended on rational grounds in following manners

- He says that if a person keeps himself/herself under the veil of ignorance then he/she would come up with the just distribution, fair laws and policies that would affect the whole society.
- A person under the veil of ignorance is unaware of his/her possible position and status in the society, therefore, he/she would rationally decide from the point of view of the worst-off.
- It will be clear to a person who can reason and think for himself, that those who are born privileged will enjoy certain special opportunities.
- It would make sense for each person, acting in his or her own interest, to try to think of rules of organisation that will ensure reasonable opportunites to the weaker sections.

- In this way, Rawls with his idea of 'veil of ignorance' is able to prove that fair and just distribution can be defended on rational grounds with the help of this idea.

5. What are generally considered to be the basic minimum requirements of people for living a healthy and productive life? What is the responsibility of governments in trying to ensure this minimum to all?

Ans. Housing, supply of clean water, basic amount of nourishment, education and minimum wage are the basic minimum requirements of people for living a healthy and productive life. Government is responsible for providing these services to all sections of the society irrespective of their class, caste, race and gender at a cost they can afford. Ways to ensure basic facilities are as follows

- Government should encourage private agencies to provide services such as health care, education etc and make policies that should try to empower people to buy those services.
- It might also be necessary for the government to give special help to the old and the sick who can not compete.
- It should make availability of good quality goods and services at a cost which people can afford.

6. Which of the following arguments could be used to justify state action to provide basic minimum conditions of life to all citizens?

(i) Providing free services to the poor and needy can be justified as an act of charity.

(ii) Providing all citizens with a basic minimum standard of living is one way of ensuring equality of opportunity.

(iii) Some people are naturally lazy and we should be kind to them.

(iv) Ensuring basic facilities and a minimum standard of living to all is a recognition of our shared humanity and a human right.

Ans. (i) No, this argument cannot be used to justify state action. All citizens have right to basic facilities to live a healthy and secure life. It is the responsibility of the government to provide basic facilities to the poor and needy. This is not an act of charity but its responsibility.

(ii) Yes, this argument can be used to justify state action. If people get a minimum standard of living, then people can live healthy and secure lives. Due to government policies, poor people also get access to facilities like health and education. Thus ensures equality in society.

(iii) No, this argument cannot be used to justify state action. Lazy people are not physically challenged and do not need special help like them. They can work. So, the state should not be kind to them.

(iv) Yes, this argument can be used to justify state action. All human beings are equal and should enjoy at least some basic rights and facilities to live a life with dignity as humans.

Exam Pattern Questions

Objective Type Questions

1. Citizen of a country gets proper justice in ....

(a) a non-democratic set up
(b) a democratic set up
(c) a dictatorship
(d) a monarchy

2. .... means fair treatment of people and the quality of being reasonable.

(a) Equality (b) Liberty
(c) Fraternity (d) Justice

3. Confucius was a philosopher who belonged to ....

(a) India (b) China
(c) Japan (d) South Korea

4. In which book Plato has given his idea of 'Justice'? **Diksha App**

(a) Das Kapital (b) Communist Manifesto
(c) The Republic (d) Mein Kampf

5. Which of the following statements is incorrect?

(a) Plato investigated why we should be concerned with justice.
(b) Socrates tells young people that if everyone is unfair, no one will profit from injustice.
(c) According to the German philosopher Immanuel Kant, human beings possess dignity.
(d) Justice requires that we should not give due and equal consideration to all individuals.

6. **Which German philosopher argued that human beings possess dignity?**
(a) Socrates (b) Plato
(c) Immanuel Kant (d) John Rawls

7. **Which one of the following is not the principle of justice?**
(a) Treating equals equally
(b) Treating unequal equally
(c) Recognition of special needs
(d) Proportionate justice

8. **People should be judged on the basis of their ....**
(a) group to which they belong
(b) work and actions
(c) region
(d) Both (a) and (c)

9. **Consider the following statements** Competency Based Que
I. Justice is based on the concept of fair treatment.
II. The principle of fair treatment must be matched with the principle of proportionality in order for society to be just.
Which of the following statement is/are correct?
(a) Only I (b) Only II
(c) Both I and II (d) None of these

10. **The principle of fair treatment must be matched with the .... in order for society to be just.**
(a) recognition of special needs
(b) justful distribution
(c) principle of proportionality
(d) free market intervention

11. **The Constitution has abolished the practice of untouchability to promote ....** Diksha App
(a) social equality (b) political equality
(c) economic equality (d) legal equality

12. **Which of the following resources has been mostly re-distributed by the government of different countries to ensure just distribution?** Diksha App
(a) Land (b) Crops
(c) Money (d) Property

13. **The term 'veil of ignorance' is attributed to ....**
Or **Who has given the concept of 'veil of ignorance'?** Diksha App
(a) Plato (b) Aristotle
(c) Socrates (d) John Rawls

14. **Under the veil of ignorance each person has to keep himself in a situation of complete ignorance about his possible ...., to establish just society?** Diksha App
(a) knowledge
(b) education
(c) wisdom
(d) position and status

15. **Which of the following agency of United Nation is responsible for giving the methods for calculating the basic needs of the people?** Diksha App
(a) World Health Organisation
(b) Security council
(c) Trusteeship council
(d) International Monetary Fund

16. **Identify the incorrect pair from the given options.** Competency Based Que
(a) John Rawls'- Veil of ignorance
(b) Confucius- Reward to virtuous
(c) Kant- Dignity
(d) Socrates- Punishment to wrongdoers

17. **Who has given the statement 'A just society is that society in which ascending sense of reverence and descending sense of contempt is dissolved into the Creations of the compassionate society'.** Diksha App
(a) Mahatma Gandhi (b) Bal Gangadhar Tilak
(c) Lala Lajpat Rai (d) Dr. B.R. Ambedkar

18. **Consider the following statements.** Competency Based Que
Statement I In 'veil of ignorance', people do not know about their position in future society.
Statement II In 'veil of ignorance' people take decision on the basis of morality.
In the light of above statements, choose the correct answer from the options given below
(a) Both Statement I and Statement II are true.
(b) Both Statement I and Statement II are false.
(c) Statement I is true, but Statement II is false.
(d) Statement I is false, but Statement II is true.

19. **Which of the following statements is correct?** Competency Based Que
I. In the free market, there will be competition.
II. Consumers have many choices in the free market.
III. Incompetent people can also survive in the free market.
IV. Everyone will get the same reward in the free market.
(a) I and II (b) III and IV
(b) I, II and IV (d) I and III

20. **Match the List I with List II.**

List I		List II	
A.	Equal treatment for equals	1.	Reservation in educational institutions for physically challenged students.
B.	Proportionate justice	2.	Regulation of fees in private hospitals.
C.	Recognition of special needs	3.	Rewarding of marks by teacher as per performance of student.
D.	State intervention to ensure social justice	4.	All adult citizens can vote.

Codes

	A	B	C	D		A	B	C	D
(a)	4	3	2	1	(b)	1	3	4	3
(c)	4	3	1	2	(d)	2	1	3	4

Assertion-Reason Questions

Directions (Q. No. 21-25) In the questions given below, there are two statements marked as Assertion (A) and Reason (R). Read the statements and choose the correct option.

Codes

(a) Both A and R are true and R is the correct explanation of A.
(b) Both A and R are true, but R is not the correct explanation of A.
(c) A is true, but R is false.
(d) A is false, but R is true.

21. Assertion (A) According to Chinese philosopher Confucius 'justice' does not only mean doing good to our friends and harm to our enemies or pursuing our own interests.

Reason (R) Justice was associated with dharma in ancient Indian culture and upholding dharma was considered a primary duty of kings.

22. Assertion (A) The Constitution allowed for reservations of government jobs and quotas for admissions to educational institutions for people belonging to the Scheduled Castes and Scheduled Tribes.

Reason (R) In our country, lack of access to good education or health care and other such facilities is often found combined with social discrimination on grounds of caste.

23. Assertion (A) The concept of legal justice is based on the belief that all human beings are equal and no discrimination should be made on any ground.

Reason (R) Political justice stands for a free and fair participation of people in the political sphere.

Competency Based Que

24. Assertion (A) In 'veil of ignorance' decisions taken by people about distribution of goods will be fair.

Reason (R) Humans are selfish and always prefer self-interest. **Competency Based Que**

25. Assertion (A) One of the duties of a democratic government is to meet the basic needs of its people.

Reason (R) According to Rawls 'a just society is that society in which ascending sense of respect and descending sense of disrespect is dissolved into the creation of a compassionate society'.

Passage Based Questions

26. Read the given passage and answer the following questions.

Differences of opinion on matters such whether, and how, to distribute resources and ensure equal access to education and jobs arouse fierce passions in society and even sometimes provoke violence. People believe the future of themselves and their families may be at stake. We have only to remind ourselves about the anger and even violence which has sometimes been roused by proposals to reserve seats in educational institutions or in government employment in our country. As students of political theory however we should be able to calmly examine the issues involved in terms of our understanding of the principles of justice.

(i) What is the ultimate result of differences of opinion on matters of distribution of resources?

(a) Fierce passion in society
(b) It can provoke violence
(c) Both (a) and (b)
(d) None of the above

(ii) What does the concept of a 'just distribution' involve?

(a) Ensuring fair laws but ignoring economic inequalities.
(b) Equal distribution of wealth among all citizens.
(c) Re-distribution of resources to provide a level playing field.
(d) Avoiding the re-distribution of resources to maintain social harmony.

(iii) When does re-distribution of resources become necessary?

27. Read the given passage and answer the following questions.

Wearing the imagined veil of ignorance is the first step in arriving at a system of fair laws and policies. It will be evident that rational persons will not only see things from the perspective of the worst-off, they will also try to ensure that the policies they frame benefit the society as a whole. Both things have to go hand-in-hand. Since no one knows what position, they will occupy in the future society, each will seek rules that protect them in case they happen to be born among the worst-off. But it would make sense if they also try to ensure that their chosen policy does not also make those who are better-off weaker because it is also possible that they could be born into a privileged position in the future society.

(i) .... means that resources and goods should be so distributive that everybody can enjoy minimum quality of life.

(a) Resource distribution (b) Distributive justice
(c) Political need theory (d) None of these

(ii) **What is the primary objective of the 'veil of ignorance'?**
(a) To eliminate personal biases when designing social rules.
(b) To promote wealth for the privileged class.
(c) To ensure that only the weak benefit from societal resources.
(d) To prioritise moral beliefs over rational thinking.

(iii) **Which of the following can help us regarding how to distribute the benefits and burdens of a society as per John Rawls?**
(a) Morality
(b) Sprituality
(c) Rationality
(d) Humility

(iv) **Consider the following statement**
I. Rational people will see things from perspective of the worst off.
II. Rational person try to ensure that the policies they frame benefits the society as a whole.
Which of the following is/are true? **Competency Based Que**
(a) Only I
(b) Only II
(c) Both I and II
(d) Neither I nor II

Answers

1. (b) a democratic set up
2. (d) Justice
3. (b) China
4. (c) The Republic
5. (d) Justice requires that we should not give due and equal consideration to all individuals.
6. (c) Immanuel Kant
7. (b) Treating unequal equally
8. (b) work and actions
9. (c) Both I and II
10. (c) principle of proportionality
11. (a) social equality
12. (a) Land
13. (d) John Rawls
14. (d) position and status
15. (a) World Health Organisation
16. (d) Socrates- Punishment to wrongdoers
17. (d) Dr. B.R. Ambedkar
18. (c) Statement I is true, but Statement II is false.
19. (a) I and II
20. (c) 4 3 1 2
21. (d) A is false, but R is true. According to Socrates 'Justice does not only mean doing good to our friends and harm to our enemies, or pursuing our own interests. Justice involves the well-being of all people'.
22. (a) Both A and R are true and R is the correct explanation of A. People face caste discrimination along with a lack of basic facilities. To ensure social justice, the Constitution allowed reservations of government jobs and quotas for people belonging to the Scheduled Castes and Scheduled Tribes. So, they can enjoy equal opportunities like others.
23. (d) A is false, but R is true. The concept of social justice is based on the belief that all human beings are equal and no discrimination should be made on the ground of race, religion, caste, gender and place of birth.
24. (a) Both A and R are true and R is the correct explanation of A.
25. (c) A is true, but R is false. According to Dr. B.R. Ambedkar, a just society is that society in which ascending sense of respect and descending sense of disrespect is dissolved into the creation of a compassionate society.
26. (i) (c) Both (a) and (b)
(ii) (c) Re-distribution of resources to provide a level playing field.
(iii) If there are serious economic or social inequalities in a society, it might become necessary to try and redistribute some of the important resources of the society to provide something like a level playing field for citizens.
27. (i) (b) Distributive justice
(ii) (a) To eliminate personal biases when designing social rules.
(iii) (c) Rationality
(iv) (c) Both I and II

Subjective Questions

Very Short Answer Type Questions

1. What do you mean by justice?

Ans. Justice is the proper administration of the law and the fair and equitable treatment of all individuals under the law.

2. How was the understanding of justice seen in ancient Indian society?

Ans. In ancient Indian society, justice was associated with dharma. Maintaining dharma or a just social order was considered to be a primary duty of kings.

3. Do the views of Confucius give a complete understanding of justice?

Ans. Confucius argued that kings should maintain justice by punishing wrongdoers and rewarding the virtuous. No, his views do not give a complete understanding of justice because justice is a broad concept. It is not just limited to reward and punishment.

4. What is the importance of dignity as per Immanuel Kant?

Or **How does German philosopher Immanuel Kant relates human dignity with the concept of justice?** Diksha App

Ans. Immanuel Kant has argued that human beings possesses dignity. If all persons are granted dignity, then they will have equal opportunity to develop their talents and pursue their chosen goals.

5. Give an overview of the principle of treating equals equally.

Ans. Principle of treating equals equally means that people should not be discriminated on grounds of class, caste, race and gender. They should be judged on the basis of their work and actions and not on the basis of the group to which they belong.

6. 'However, equal treatment is not the only principle of justice'. Comment. Competency Based Que

Ans. There could be circumstances where people need to be rewarded on the basis of their talent and hard work. There could also be people who need special help to compete with others. So, equal treatment with all people would be unfair.

7. What do you mean by basic needs of life? Name some basic needs of life.

Ans. Basic needs of life refer to those things that are needed to live a healthy and secure life. Some basic needs of life include housing, nourishment, clean drinking water, education and a minimum wage.

8. Give the meaning of an unjust society.

Ans. In an unjust society the differences between rich and poor are so great that they seem to be living in different worlds altogether. In such societies, the relatively deprived people have no chance at all to improve their condition despite their persistent hard work.

9. What do you mean by 'veil of ignorance'?

Ans. Rawl in his theory puts all individuals behind the 'veil of ignorance'. 'Veil of ignorance' means that individuals are put in a position where they do no know what is their status, wealth, class, ability, talent, etc.

10. Many private pharma companies have increased the price of life-saving drugs, citing production costs. Suggest any two things that the government can do in this case to ensure social justice. Competency Based Que

Ans. The government can do the following things

(i) The government can increase the production of government-owned pharma companies.

(ii) The government can provide many tax exemptions to private pharma companies.

Short Answer Type Questions

1. Why do young people Glaucon and Adeimantus in The Republic think that we should be unjust?

Ans. In 'The Republic', young people like Gaucon and Adeimantus ask Socrates why we should be just. They argue that there is no benefit in being just. People who are unjust live a better life than just people.

Unjust people who twist rules, avoid paying taxes, speak lies and deceitful are more successful than just people.

So, if we are unjust and avoid getting caught, then we can live a better life.

2. Explain the concept of protective discrimination.

Ans. Protective discrimination is the policy of granting special privileges to the downtrodden and the under-privileged sections of society, most commonly women and socially weaker classes.

- Some of citizens are depressed due to discriminatory social practices prevalent in the past and such a depression has hampered their right to basic dignified life.
- They are considered to be a case fit for being treated preferentially.
- For example, the Constitution allowed for reservations of government jobs and quotas for admissions to educational institutions for people belonging to the Scheduled Castes and Scheduled Tribes.

3. Akshat is a student of class XI. He usually notices questions that are for visually impaired students. Questions for visually impaired students are objective and descriptive in nature, whereas questions for normal students are map-based, where they need to locate places on the basis of given information. Akshat believes that questions for visually impaired students are easy and it is an injustice to normal students.

(i) Which principle of justice is used in providing different questions for visually impaired students?

(ii) Is the belief of Akshat regarding injustice to normal students correct? Discuss.

Competency Based Que

Ans. (i) The principle of recognition of special needs is used in providing different questions for visually impaired students.

(ii) No, the belief of Akshat is incorrect. Visually impaired students and normal students study the same syllabus. But, due to physical challenges, visually impaired students cannot answer map-based questions properly. So, it would be fair to design other questions for them as per their ability. Normal students have no such challenges and can answer map-based questions.

4. Which conditions in India have affected minimum condition of life needed by people?

Ans. Continuous increase in India's population and the growth of the population residing in slums and small towns, has resulted in over burdened infrastructure and a deterioration in public health.

- Inadequate civic amenities, lack of purchasing power and lack of knowledge and awareness among the poor have resulted in grave poverty.
- A few government policies have specifically targeted the poor, but they are neither sufficient nor effective.
- The deteriorating health status of people in many parts of country needs urgent attention because many of recent health problems have potential to take an epidemic form if neglected.
- A resurgence of malaria, dengue and tuberculosis indicates that much of the poor health emanates (arise) from a lack of basic amenities such as sanitation, clean water and housing.

5. Explain the meaning of 'Just distribution of resources'.

Ans. A society requires just distribution of goods and services for maintaining law and order. If there are deep inequalities in society, then it requires redistribution of goods and resources.

For example, when India was under British rule, then zamindars had acquired vast areas of land. But after independence, land reforms were introduced and land was redistributed among poor peasants.

Thus, just distribution means that resources and goods should be so distributed that everybody can enjoy minimum quality of life. If everybody does not have basic minimum resources, then it should be redistributed from rich classes to poor classes.

6. 'Social justice is lacking in society'. Justify this statement with your real life experiences.

Competency Based Que

Ans. Social justice is based on the value of fairness, equality, respect for diversity, access to social protection and the application of human rights in all spheres of life, including in the work place.

- In society, lack of social justice is noticeable in every spheres of life such as distribution of resources, disrespect towards weaker and tribal people and women.
- On one hand, some people enjoy too much power, while on the other hand rights of deprived people are suppressed.

7. 'Justice delayed is justice denied'. Justify the statement and give suggestions for fast redressal of justice.

Competency Based Que

Ans. 'Justice delayed is justice denied' is an old saying, which means that if timely justice is not provided to the sufferer, it loses its importance and violates human rights. The Indian Judicial System still lives in old age. It has been observed that a number of cases are pending in courts for a very long time.

Following are the suggestions for fast redressal of justice

- Number of judges should be increased.
- All existing vacancies of judges should be filled immediately.
- Artificial intelligence system should be introduced in court of law which would accelerate the process of administration of justice and also aid in giving flawless justice, thur reduces burden of judiciary.

Long Answer Type Questions

1. According to Socrates if everyone is unjust, everyone manipulates rules to suit their own interest, no one would be sure of benefiting from such injustice. Justify the above statement with the help of an example.

Competency Based Que; Diksha App

Ans. It is true that no one would be sure of benefiting from injustice. May be in the beginning some people might get benefits, but the end of doing injustice is always disastrous for all.

It is in our own interest first to obey the rules and to facilitate others in order to facilitate ourselves.

For example, if a person breaks the traffic rule and crosses the red signal, then it is possible that other people follow. They think that we can also reach early by breaking traffic rules. They might reach their destination early also. One by one, each person will break traffic rules. This action will cause the traffic jams and the road accident, which can result in the loss of lives. No one will benefit from unjust actions.

2. Explain the Rawls' theory of justice.

Ans. John Rawl was an important political thinker, who had given a theory of justice to achieve a just state. He puts all individuals behind the 'veil of ignorance'.

'Veil of ignorance' means that individuals are put in a position where they do not know their status, wealth, class, ability, talent etc. So these individuals will choose privileges which will affect them once they come out of 'veil of ignorance'.

Rawl believed that these individuals are rational and will choose privileges which will help them in developing their fuller personality. So, they will

- First, choose liberty, because if an individual has liberty then he/she will be able to achieve anything by his/her hard work.
- Secondly, they want equality of opportunity, which means that all individuals should get the equal opportunity.
- Thirdly, they will demand difference based principles. It means that if any individual, after 'veil of ignorance', comes out is disable or unfortunate, then society should help the least advantaged person.

This is Rawls' theory of justice where rationality rather than moral thinking can lead us to have a fair and just society.

3. How is the just distribution of goods and services is a guarantee of social justice in a society? **Diksha App**

Ans. To achieve social justice in society, governments might have to do more than just ensure that laws and policies treat individuals in a fair manner.

- Social justice also concerns the just distribution of goods and services, whether it is between nations or between different groups and individuals within a society.
- If there are serious economic or social inequalities in a society, it might become necessary to try and re-distribute some of the important resources of the society to provide something like a level playing field for citizens.
- Therefore, within a country social justice would require not only that people be treated equally in terms of the laws and policies of the society but also that they enjoy some basic equality of life conditions and opportunities.
- This is seen as necessary for each person to be able to pursue his/her objectives and express himself/herself.
- In our country for instance, the Constitution abolished the practice of untouchability to promote social equality and ensure that people belonging to 'lower' castes have access to temples, jobs and basic necessities like water.
- Different state governments have also taken some measures to re-distribute important resources like land in a more fair manner by instituting land reforms.

4. Discuss the importance of the role of state in the free market.

Ans. The state plays a very important role in the free market. The main work of the state is to ensure a basic minimum standard of living for all people so that they are able to compete on equal terms.

- Supporters of the free market state argue that to provide basic services, the state can allow markets in services like health and education.
- Private agencies should be encouraged to provide such services, while state policies should try to empower people to buy those services.
- It might also be necessary for the state to give special help to the old and the sick who cannot compete.
- But apart from this, the role of the state should only be to maintain a framework of laws and regulations to ensure that competition between individuals remains free of coercion and other obstacles.
- Private agencies mainly work for profit. They step into only those services where they can earn huge profit.
- Due to the high cost, many people cannot afford their services.
- For example, poor children cannot study in a private school due to high fees. In such cases, the state has to ensure that people get these basic services.
- The state can open government schools for poor children. It can set up government hospitals in rural areas.
- So, in the free market, the state acts as a regulator. It can also intervene to ensure basic facilities for people.

Picture Based Questions

1. Study the cartoon given below and answer the question that follow.

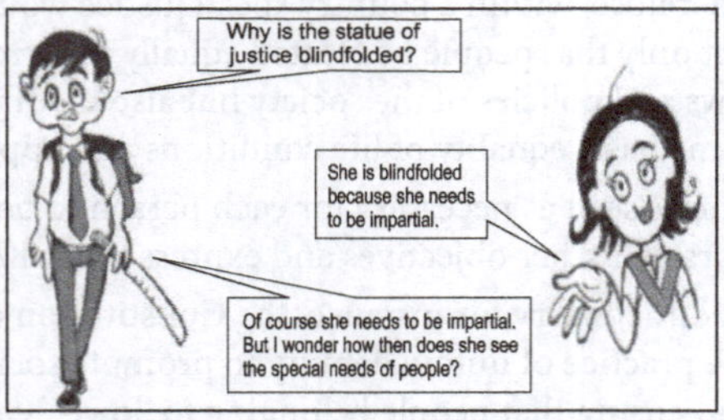

(i) Which of the following statement is incorrect in the context of principles of justice?
(a) People should not be discriminated against on grounds of class, race or gender.
(b) Justice is based on the concept of fair treatment.
(c) Physical disabilities, age or lack of good education are factors which are considered ground for special treatment.
(d) The state does not need to make harmony between three principles of justice and can follow any one of the three principles to ensure social justice.

Ans. (d) The state does not need to make harmony between three principles of justice and can follow any one of the three principles to ensure social justice.

(ii) The essential principles of modern judiciary is that........ .
(a) judges should be part of executive.
(b) judges should be under the control of the head of the state.
(c) there should be independence of judiciary.
(d) judges should be under the control of the electorate.

Ans. (c) there should be independence of judiciary.

(iii) What does the statue of justice blind folded symbolise?
(a) Impartial justice
(b) Determination of innocence or guilt made without bias
(c) Treating equally
(d) All of the above

Ans. (d) All of the above

(iv) Justice is essentially a ....
(a) legal concept
(b) moral concept
(c) social concept
(d) All of the above

Ans. (d) All of the above

2. Observe the cartoon given below and answer the questions that follow.

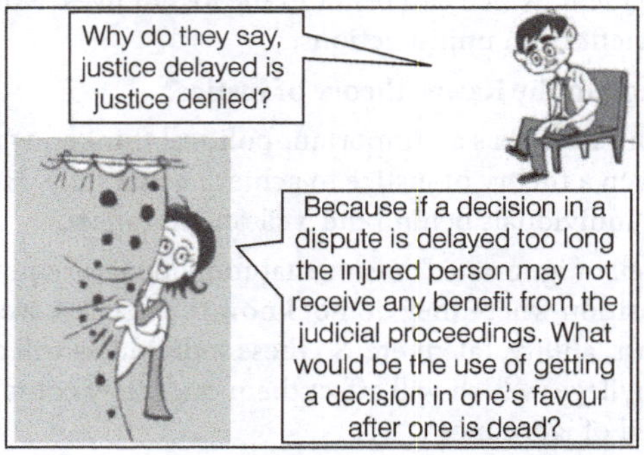

(i) What are the suggestion should be adopted so that justice should not delayed hence not denied?
(ii) What do you mean by a just society?
(iii) What is protective discrimination?

Ans. (i) The Indian Judicial System still lives in old age. It has been observed that a number of cases are pending in courts for a very long time.
Following are the suggestions for fast redressal of justice
- Number of judges should be increased.
- All existing vacancies should be filled immediately.

(ii) A just society is that society in which ascending sense of respect and descending sense of disrespect is dissolved into the creation of a compassionate society.

(iii) Protective discrimination is a policy of granting special privileges to the downtrodden and the underprivileged sections of society.

SELF ASSESSMENT TEST

Objective Type Questions

1. In ancient Indian society, justice was associated with ....
   (a) moksha (b) dharma
   (c) astha (d) None of these
2. In which of these cases should the state intervene to ensure social justice?
   (a) Golf clubs have increased their membership fees by 10%.
   (b) Industrial units are giving 25% reservation in jobs to local people.
   (c) Workers who do overtime get a higher salary.
   (d) A power company has increased the electricity charges by 20% in rural areas.
3. 'Justice implies something which it is not only right to do and wrong not to do; but which some individual person can claim from us as his moral right'. Which of these has said this statement?
   (a) Immanuel Kant (b) Dr. B.R. Ambedkar **Competency Based Que**
   (c) J.S. Mill (d) Socrates

Very Short Answer Type Questions

4. What was considered to be the primary duty of kings in ancient India?
5. Why does a teacher give grace marks to the weaker students in class?
6. Briefly explain the meaning of eqalitarian society?
7. Give two examples of treating equals equally.
8. Give two examples of proportionate justice.

Short Answer Type Questions

9. 'Justice involves the well-being of all people'. Elucidate. **Competency Based Que**
10. Explain the contribution of reservation in promoting social justice.
11. Analyse the essence of state intervention in market.
12. Is justice all about fairness? Explain your views with examples.
13. What do you mean by social justice? To what extent India has implemented it? Explain with examples.

Long Answer Type Questions

14. Do you think that state intervention is good option for newly independent countries? Examine and give reasons in support of your answer.
15. Explain the concept of proportionate justice. Justify it with the help of an example. **Diksha App**

05

CHAPTER

Rights are those guarantees which the state provide to every citizen in order to attain best self in society.

Rights

YOUR STUDY GOALS

YOUR PRACTICE GOAL

- Objective Type Questions (33 MCQs, A-R, Statements, Matching, Passage Based)
- Subjective Questions (12 VSAs, 10 SAs, 4 LAs)
  2 Picture Based Question

5.1 Meaning of Rights

- A right is essentially an entitlement or a justified claim that is recognised by society. Rights are primarily those claims that are considered necessary to live a life of respect and **dignity**[1]. For example, right to livelihood, freedom of expression, etc.
- Right are necessary for our well-being. They help individuals to develop their skills and talents.
- For example, right to education, helps to develop the capacity of an individual and enables us to make informed choices in life.
- Activities which are harmful for us or others cannot be claimed as rights. For example, smoking cannot be claimed as a right due to its bad effect on our lungs and others.

History of Rights

- In the 17th and 18th centuries, political theorists argued that rights are given by nature or God.
- Natural rights cannot be taken by anyone because human beings are born with them.
- Political theorists considered **three natural rights** as the basis of all rights, which are the right to life, **liberty**[2] and property.
- In recent years, the term human rights has been used more. The idea that rights are given by nature or god is unacceptable today.

---

1 **Dignity** It means the fact of being given honor and respect by people.

2 **Liberty** It refers to the state of being free from oppressive restrictions, constraints, or control, allowing individuals freedom to make choices.

- The basic assumption behind human rights is that human beings are entitled to certain rights because they are human beings. Every person is unique and equally valuable.
- The idea of human rights is supported by the **UN declaration of human rights**.
- The list of human rights has expanded due to new threats and challenges faced by society.

Kant on Human Dignity

- As per German philosopher **Immanuel Kant**, human beings possess dignity. They are valuable in themselves. Every person has dignity and should be treated with dignity because he is a human being. Kant's views represent the moral conception of rights.
- The moral conception of human rights is based on two arguments. First, we should treat people like the way , we want to be treated ourselves. Second, we should treat other persons not as a medium to fulfill our interests. We should respect people because they are humans.

5.2 Legal Rights and the State

- Many countries have enshrined a **bill of rights** in their Constitutions.
- Rights mentioned in the Constitution are those that are considered to be of basic importance. In some cases, they are supplemented by claims that gain importance due to the history and customs of a country.
- Some theorists define rights as claims that are recognised by the state.
- People make demands from the state by rights.
- Rights place a responsibility on the state to ensure that people enjoy their rights. For example, the right to education directs the state to ensure conditions where every citizen can get access to education irrespective of their economic condition.
- Rights also suggest what the state must **refrain**[3] from doing. For example, a person cannot be jailed as per the wish of the state without any offense.

Quick Test 1

1. What do we cannot claim as rights?
2. Mention the three natural rights considered by the political theorists.
3. State the basic assumption behind human rights.
4. Who supported the idea of human rights?
5. What is enshrined in the Constitution of many countries?

5.3 Kinds of Rights

Rights are those aspects of social life that are necessary for an individual to function successfully. There are three types of rights i.e. political rights, economic rights and cultural rights.

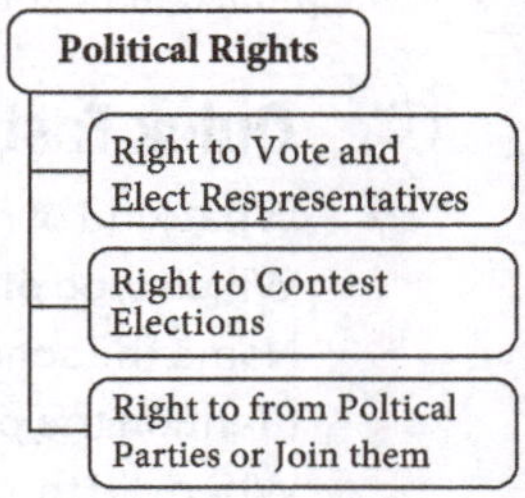

Political Rights

- Political rights give citizens the right to equality before law and the right to participate in political process.
- Political rights are supplemented by **civil liberties.**
- Collectively, civil and political rights form the basis of a democratic system of government.

3 **Refrain** It means to stop yourself from doing something.

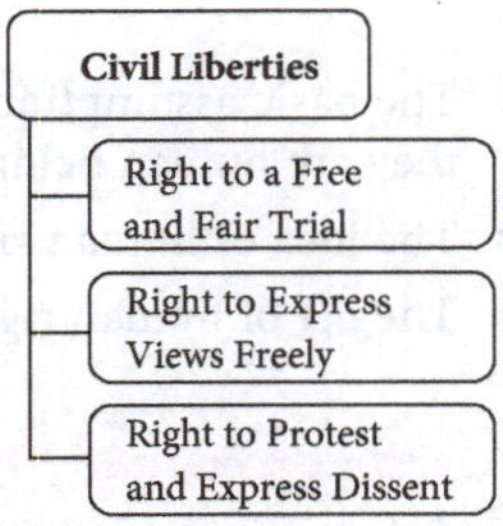

- Political rights make government accountable to the people by
  - giving greater importance to the concern of the individual over the rulers.
  - ensuring that all persons have an opportunity to influence the decisions of the government.

Economic Rights

- Political rights can be fully enjoyed by people only when their basic needs are met. Hence, democratic societies provide economic rights.
- In some countries, people with low incomes, receive housing and medical facilities; in others unemployed persons receive certain minimum wage to meet their basic needs.
- In India, the government has introduced a **Rural Employment Guarantee Scheme** to help the poor.

Cultural Rights

- In addition to political and economic rights, more and more democracies are recognising the **cultural claims** of their citizens.
- Rights like the right to have primary education in one's mother tongue and the right to establish institutions for teaching one's language and culture are recognised as being necessary for leading a good life.

5.4 Rights and Responsibilities

- Rights not only place **obligations**[4] on the state but also on people.
- Rights force us to think not just about our own personal needs and interests but to protect some things that are good for all. For example, protecting the environment will benefit all the people.
- Our rights are limited by the principle of equal and same rights for all. We cannot deprive a person of his rights and enjoy our rights.
- Rights of a person should be balanced when they come into conflict with rights of others. For example, a person cannot take pictures of others without their consent, affecting their privacy.
- Citizens must be careful about limitations that may be placed on their rights. Many times, the government imposes restrictions on civil liberties in the name of national security. People should be careful as governments can become **authoritarian**[5].

Universal Declaration of Human Rights

- The General Assembly of the United Nations adopted and proclaimed the Universal Declaration of Human Rights on **10th December, 1948**.
- The General Assembly urged all member nations to distribute and display the declaration and taught it in schools and other educational institutions in all countries.
- The General Assembly proclaimed the Universal Declaration of Human Rights as a **common standard** for all people and all nations. Every person and nation should keep the declaration in mind and promote the rights mentioned in the declaration.

Quick Test 2

1. What kind of rights are supplemented by civil liberties?
2. Which type of the rights form the basis of a democratic system of government collectively.
3. Name the scheme that has been introduced by the government to help the poor.
4. Mention the principle that limits our rights.
5. When did the United Nations adopt the Universal Declaration of Human Rights?

4 **Obligation** It refers the state of being forced to do something.
5 **Authoritarian** It is a system which enforces strict control, limits freedom, suppress dissent and prioritises power over democracy.

Mind Map

RIGHTS

1 Meaning of Rights

- A demand made by an individual, which is accepted by the society and recognised by the state.
- Right are necessary for our well-being. They help us to develop our skill and talents. For example, right to education.
- Activities which are harmful for us or other cannot be claimed as rights. For example, smoking.

2 Origin of Rights

In 17th - 18th Century

- Focus was on the Natural rights (Rights given by Nature/God) For example, Right to life, liberty and property.

In Modern Era

- Natural rights are slightly blurred now and human rights are given more importance.
- Human Rights were supported by the UN Declaration of human rights.
- Human Rights has expanded due to new threats and challenges faced by society.

3 Legal Rights and the State

- A bill of rights is enshrined in the Constitutions of many countries.
- Rights allows people to make demands from the state.
- Rights ensures the proper working of the state without violating individuals life and liberty.
- Rights as claims that are recognised by the state.
- Rights place a responsibility on state to ensure that people enjoy their rights.

4 Kinds of Rights

Political Rights

- Provides right to equality before law and right to participate in political processes.
- Political rights are supplemented by civil liberties.
- Rights make government accountable.

Economic Rights

- Rights that guarantee people of economic security.
- Democratic societies provides economic rights.
- The Government has introduced a rural employment guarantees scheme to help the poor.

Cultural Rights

- Rights that aim to assure the enjoyment of culture.
- Right to have primary education in one mother longue.
- Right to establish institutions for teaching one language and cultures.

5 Right and Responsibilty

- Rights not only place obligations on the state but also on people.
- One should respect rights of the other also.
- We must balance our rights when they came to conflicts.
- Citizens must be vigilant about limitation which are placed on their rights.

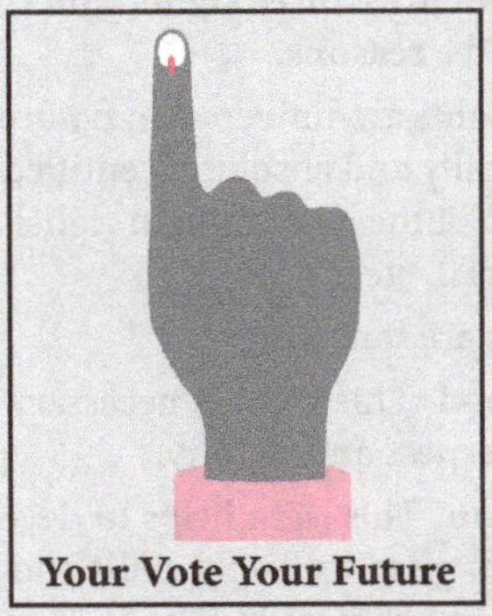

Voting Rights

Human Rights

NCERT Folder

Intext Questions

1. Go through recent newspapers and make a list of people's movements that have made proposals for new kinds of rights? (Pg 69)

Ans. In India, there have been several people's movements advocating for new kinds of rights, responding to the evolving needs of society. Some of these include

(i) **Environmental Rights** Movements such as the Chipko and Narmada Bachao Andolan have pushed for the right to a healthy environment, calling for sustainable development and the protection of natural resources.

(ii) **Women's Rights** Women's movements, particularly in the wake of issues like sexual harassment, have called for better legal protections, safety and equal opportunities. For example, the right to live free from violence has been championed by an organisations like the All India Democratic Women's Association (AIDWA)

(iii) **Digital Rights** With increasing internet access, there has been a call for digital rights, including privacy and freedom of expression online. Movements like the one for net neutrality have emerged to ensure that the internet remains open and accessible to all.

These movements reflect a broader shift toward recognising and safeguarding both individual and collective rights that respond to contemporary challenges.

2. Go through the newspapers of the last few days and identify cases of rights violations which have been discussed. What should the government and civil society do to prevent such violations? (Pg 73)

Ans. In recent months, there have been several significant cases of rights violations. One case is given below

In Manipur, ethnic violence between the Meitei and Kuki communities has led to the death of many people in 2023.

To prevent such violations both the government and civil society must take several measures

(i) **Government Accountability** The government should ensure that laws are used fairly. Proper investigations should be conducted into cases of violence and justice should be swiftly delivered.

(ii) **Civil Society Vigilance** Civil society organisations and media must continue to push for transparency, report on human rights abuses and raise awareness about these violations both domestically and internationally.

(iii) **Judicial Oversight** Courts must actively protect the rights of citizens by challenging unjust laws and ensuring that activists are not wrongfully imprisoned.

Both government actions and civil society advocacy are crucial in maintaining and protecting human rights in the country.

Exercise

1. What are rights and why are they important? What are the basis on which claims to rights can be made?

Ans. Rights are those claims which are necessary for leading a life of respect and dignity.

Rights are important due to following reasons

- Rights help individuals to develop their talents and skills.
- Rights give useful skills to individuals and enable us to make informed choices in life.
- Rights promote our creativity and originality.
- Rights are essential for survival of democracy.

The basis on which claims to rights can be made are

- They represent conditions that we collectively see as a source of self-respect and dignity.
- They are necessary for our well-being.
- They are necessary to earn livelihood.

2. On what grounds are some rights considered to be universal in nature? Identify three rights which you consider universal. Give reasons.

Ans. Some of the human rights are universal in nature. All human beings are equally and absolutely entitled to universal rights. Some of the basic human rights are right to life, right to a fair trial, etc.

Three universal rights are following

(i) **Right to Livelihood** This right is necessary for leading a life of respect and dignity.

(ii) **Right to Education** This right helps to develop our capacity to reason, gives us useful skills and enables us to make informed choices in life.

(iii) **Freedom of Expression** This right is important for the free expression of beliefs and opinions.

3. Discuss briefly some of the new rights claims which are being put forward in our country today, for example, the rights of tribal people to protect their habitat and way of life or the rights of children against bonded labour.

Ans. Some of the new rights claims are being put forward in our country today which are

- **The Rights of Tribal People** Tribal people are dependent on forest and land for their livelihood since ancient times. Tribal people do not want any interference in their habitat and way of life which is going on in the name of modernisaton. According to them, their demands are justified and essential for leading a secure and respectful life.
- **The Rights of Children Against Bonded Labour** Children are future of the country, they must be free from any kind of exploitation or bonded labour.
- **The Right to Education** Every child between the age of 6 to 14 years must have right to receive the basic education, as it helps in the development of their potential.

4. Differentiate between political, economic and cultural rights. Give examples of each kind of right.

Ans. Difference between the political, economic and cultural rights are given below

Political Rights Political rights treat all citizens equally. They give opportunity to every citizen to participate in political process. Political rights give opportunity to every citizens to participate in decision-making process of the government directly or indirectly. For example, political rights are right to vote and elect representatives, right to contest elections, the right to form political parties or join them.

Economic Rights Economic rights are those rights that ensure the entitlement of basic needs of food, shelter, etc. Economic rights help in fulfilling the political rights. For example, right to minimum wage is an economic right.

Cultural Rights Cultural rights are given to citizens to preserve their culture, its essence and its dignity. Political rights and economic rights help in ensuring cultural rights of citizens. For example, right to establish institutions to preserve one's language is a cultural right.

5. Rights place some limits on the authority of the state. Explain with examples.

Ans. Some limits that rights place on the authority of the state are

- They make the state responsible for its actions.
- They place an obligation upon the state to act in a certain way. The state is expected to make such policies which are capable to provide clean environment. They also place an obligation on the state to ensure that its polices should provide basic needs to all its individuals.
- They suggest that the state must refrain from doing certain things. The state cannot make such laws which violate the Fundamental Rights of the citizens and go against the Constitution.
- Freedom of expression is a basic right of individual, therefore, the state cannot stop anyone from expressing himself/herself.
- The state cannot arrest any individual unnecessarily as that would mean violating his/her right to liberty.

Exam Pattern Questions

Objective Type Questions

Multiple Choice Questions (MCQs)

1. Civil rights are provided to us by ....

(a) the people (b) the state
(c) nature (d) king

2. A .... is fundamentally an entitlement or a legitimate assertion.

(a) duties
(b) principles
(c) right
(d) None of the above

3. Which of the following rights are universal in nature?

(a) Right to livelihood (b) Freedom of expression
(c) Right to citizenship (d) Both (a) and (b)

4. A right such as the right to education, for example, aids in the development of our reasoning abilities, provides us with valuable skills and allows us to make educated decisions in life. In this context, education can be considered as the .... right.

(a) social (b) universal
(c) cultural (d) All of the above

5. Which of the following statements is/are correct?

(a) Rights are claims or entitlements necessary to lead a dignified life.
(b) Right to livelihood and freedom of expression are the only universal rights.
(c) Earlier, political thinkers argued that rights are given by the nature.
(d) Both (a) and (c)

6. .... provided the foundation for men's rights. This meant that our rights were not bestowed upon us by a monarch or a state, but rather that we were born with them.

(a) Universal Law
(b) Natural Law
(c) Fundamental Law
(d) Both (a) and (b)

7. What is the source of natural rights? Diksha App

(a) Nature (b) Constitution
(c) Parliament (d) King

8. Which of the following is/are consider as natural rights?

(a) Right to life (b) Right to liberty
(c) Right to property (d) All of these

9. Consider the following statements.

I. Natural rights are given to us by nature and they are inalienable.
II. Natural rights are derived from other basic rights.
III. Right to life, liberty and protest are the three natural rights. Competency Based Que

Codes

(a) Only I (b) I and II
(c) II and III (d) I, II and III

10. Given below are two statements. Competency Based Que

Statement I Natural rights are given by nature to us.
Statement II In the 21st century, the belief that nature is the source of all rights is unacceptable.

In the light of the above statements, choose the correct answer from the options given below.

(a) Both Statement I and Statement II are true.
(b) Both Statement I and Statement II are false.
(c) Statement I is true, but Statement II is false.
(d) Statement I is false, but Statement II is true.

11. What is the basis of Kant's conception of moral rights? Diksha App

(a) We should treat others as we would like to be treated ourselves and does not treat the other persons as means to our ends.
(b) We should treat others in a selfish manner.
(c) We should treat others in a like manner.
(d) We should treat others differently.

12. Consider the following statements related to moral conception of right. Competency Based Que

I. We should treat others as we would like to be treated ourselves.
II. We should not treat the other person as means to our ends.

Select the correct statements.

(a) Only I (b) Only II
(c) Both I and II (d) None of these

13. Which of the following is not an obligation upon each of us placed by rights? Diksha App

(a) Rights compel us to follow our duties as citizens.
(b) Rights require us to respect the rights of others.
(c) Rights are required to balance their rights with our duties.
(d) Rights require us to save the international community.

14. .... is one of our political rights.

(a) Right to get proper wages
(b) Right to vote
(c) Right to family life
(d) Right to freedom of press

15. Right to criticise the government is a/an ....

(a) civil right (b) political right
(c) economic right (d) natural right

16. Which of the following is not a natural right of a man?

(a) Right to life (b) Right to liberty
(c) Right to vote (d) Right to property

17. What is the coercive power behind legal rights? Diksha App

(a) Public opinion (b) Mortality
(c) Law (d) Nature

18. Which of the following is not a political right? Diksha App

(a) Right to contest election
(b) Right to cast vote
(c) Right to form political parties
(d) Right to free and join trail

19. Which of the following is/are our civil rights?

(a) Right to education (b) Right to personal liberty
(c) Right to life (d) All of these

20. Which type of security is given by the government to rural people by introducing a rural Employment Guarantee Scheme? Diksha App

(a) Social security (b) Legal security
(c) Economic security (d) Political security

21. Which of the following is not a part of economic rights?

(a) Right to equality (b) Right to property
(c) Right to work (d) Right to economic security

22. **The right to establish educational institutions for teaching one's language and culture is called as .... right.**

(a) cultural (b) social
(c) philosophical (d) economic

23. **The .... proclaims Universal Declaration of Human Rights as a common standard of achievement for all people and for all nations.**

(a) General Assembly (b) International Court of Justice
(c) UNESCO (d) WHO

24. **Identify and write the incorrect pair.** **Competency Based Que**

(a) Political right-Right to vote
(b) Natural right- Right to property
(c) Economic right- Right to minimum wage
(d) Cultural right- Right to education

25. **Match List-I with the List-II and choose the correct option.**

	List I		List II
A.	Natural right	1.	Sustainable development
B.	Civil liberty	2.	Primary education in mother tongue
C.	Human right	3.	Free trial
D.	Cultural right	4.	Property

Codes

	A	B	C	D		A	B	C	D
(a)	3	4	1	2	(b)	2	4	3	1
(c)	4	2	1	3	(d)	4	3	1	2

Assertion-Reason Questions

Directions (Q. Nos. 26-30) In the questions given below, there are two statements marked as Assertion (A) and Reason (R). Read the statements and choose the correct option.

Codes

(a) Both A and R are true and R is the correct explanation of A.
(b) Both A and R are true, but R is not the correct explanation of A.
(c) A is true, but R is false.
(d) A is false, but R is true.

26. **Assertion (A)** Fundamental Rights are important rights which is provided in the Constitution of India.
Reason (R) They provide the citizens of a country with human dignity and development of personality of every individual.

27. **Assertion (A)** The government imposed a heavy penalty on colleges charging fees more than the limit set by the government.
Reason (R) The right to education is a Fundamental Right. **Competency Based Que**

28. **Assertion (A)** The right of everyone to education has been recognised in the UDHR.
Reason (R) Education is the most powerful weapon you can use to change the world.

29. **Assertion (A)** Right to life, liberty, equal treatment and the right to political participation are our basic rights.
Reason (R) They serve as a reminder to the citizens that while enjoying their rights, they should also be conscious of duties.

30. **Assertion (A)** A right is essentially an entitlement or a justified claim.
Reason (R) The right to vote, right to form political parties and right to contest elections are the parts of economic rights.

Passage Based Questions

31. **Read the given passage and answer the following questions.**

Rights are essential for every person to live a fair and happy life. They protect our freedom and ensure equality in society. For example, the right to education helps us learn and grow, while the right to freedom of speech allows us to share our thoughts. Rights also come with responsibilities. We must respect others' rights and use our freedoms without harming anyone. Governments play an important role in protecting these rights and providing basic needs like health care and safety. By understanding and respecting rights, we can create a peaceful and just society where everyone can thrive.

(i) **What is the primary purpose of rights?**
(a) To limit freedom
(b) To protect freedom and ensure equality
(c) To create rules for society
(d) To give the government more power

(ii) **Which right helps people learn and grow?**
(a) Right to freedom of speech
(b) Right to education
(c) Right to vote
(d) Right to safety

(iii) **Why are rights important for individuals?**

32. Read the given passage and answer the following questions.

Most democracies today begin by drawing up a charter of political rights. Political rights give the citizens the right to equality before law and the right to participate in the political process. They include such rights as the right to vote and elect representatives, the right to contest elections, the right to form political parties or join them. Political rights are supplemented by civil liberties. The latter refers to the right to a free and fair trial, the right to express one's views freely, the right to protest and express dissent. Collectively, civil liberties and political rights form the basis of a democratic system of government. Political rights contribute to it by making the government accountable to the people, by giving greater importance to the concerns of the individual over that of the rulers and by ensuring that all persons have an opportunity to influence the decisions of the government.

(i) The rights of primary importance are called .... in India.

(a) Political rights
(b) Socio-economic rights
(c) Directive principles of State Policy
(d) Fundamental Rights

(ii) Political rights give the citizens the right to equality before ....

(a) President
(b) Prime minister
(c) law
(d) lower house of Parliament

(iii) How should a person not express his dissent against government policies in a democracy?

(a) By peaceful protests

Competency Based Que

(b) By raising slogans against the government in rallies
(c) By expressing his views on the internet
(d) By using violent methods to overthrow the government

(iv) What is the aim of the rights?

(a) Political rights give to the citizens the right to equality before law and the right to participate in the political process.
(b) Rights aim to protect the well-being of the individual.
(c) Political rights make the government accountable to the people
(d) None of the above

33. Read the given passage and answer the following questions.

Rights not only place obligations upon the state to act in a certain way for instance, to ensure sustainable development — but they also place obligations upon each of us. Firstly, they compel us to think not just of our own personal needs and interests but to defend some things as being good for all of us. Protecting the ozone layer, minimising air and water pollution, maintaining the green cover by planting new trees and preventing cutting down of forests, maintaining the ecological balance, are things that are essential for all of us. They represent the 'common-good' that we must act to protect for ourselves as well as for the future generations who are entitled to inherit a safe and clean world without which they cannot lead a reasonably good life.

(i) .... is a term which refers to those things which are shared and beneficial for all or most members of the community.

(a) Rights
(b) Common-good
(c) Liberty
(d) Sustainable development

(ii) The .... of our claims is so critical that some theorists describe rights as claims recognised by the state. The legal endorsement gives our rights a special status in society, but it is not the basis for claiming rights.

(a) fundamental and social recognition
(b) social and cultural recognition
(c) legal and Constitutional recognition
(d) None of the above

(iii) Why do rights come with responsibilities? Explain.

Answers

1. (b) the state
2. (c) right
3. (d) Both (a) and (b)
4. (b) universal
5. (d) Both (a) and (c)
6. (b) Natural Law
7. (a) Nature
8. (d) All of these
9. (a) Only I
10. (a) Both Statement I and Statement II are true.
11. (a) We should treat others as we would like to be treated ourselves and does not treat the other persons as means to our ends.
12. (c) Both I and II
13. (d) Rights require us to save the international community.
14. (b) Right to vote

15. (b) political right
16. (c) Right to vote
17. (c) Law
18. (d) Right to free and fair trail
19. (d) All of these
20. (c) Economic security
21. (a) Right to equality
22. (a) cultural
23. (a) General Assembly
24. (d) Cultural right- Right to education
25. (d) 4 3 1 2
26. (a) Both A and R are true and R is the correct explanation of A. The Fundamental Rights are the basic claims of the people for their well-being and all-round development. The Fundamental Rights are important because they provide the citizens of a country with human dignity and development of personality of every individual.
27. (a) Both A and R are true, and R is the correct explanation of A. The government has set a fee limit to ensure access to education for all people, but colleges charged more fees. The right to education is a Fundamental Right and colleges violated it by charging so they faced a penalty.
28. (a) Both A and R are true and R is the correct explanation of A. The right to education has been recognised in the UDHR because it is the most powerful weapon you can use to change the world.
29. (a) Both A and R are true and R is the correct explanation of A. Right to life, liberty, equal treatment and the right to political participation are our basic rights due to following reasons, they serve as a reminder to the citizens that while enjoying their rights, they should also be conscious of duties.
30. (c) A is true, but R is false. The right to vote, right to form political parties and right to contest elections are the parts of political rights.
31. (i) (b) To protect freedom and ensure equality
    (ii) (b) Right to education
    (iii) Rights are important because they protect our freedom, dignity and equality. They ensure that every person has the ability to live their life with respect and without fear of being treated unfairly. For example, the right to education helps individuals gain knowledge, while the right to freedom of speech allows people to express their opinions. Rights also make sure that governments take care of people's basic needs, such as health care and safety.
32. (i) (d) Fundamental Rights
    (ii) (c) law
    (iii) (d) By using violent methods to overthrow the government
    (iv) (b) Rights aim to protect the well-being of the individual.
33. (i) (b) Common-good
    (ii) (c) legal and Constitutional recognition
    (iii) Rights always come with responsibilities. We cannot enjoy rights in isolation. If people respect our rights, then we can enjoy our rights. Similarly, it is our responsibility to respect the rights of others. For example, if we want no interference in our lives, then it is our responsibility to not interfere in anyone's life.

Subjective Questions

Very Short Answer Type Questions

1. What is the meaning of claims?

Ans. Claims are those previliges for which we are entitled as citizens, as individuals and as human beings. Everything that we think necessary desirable are not claim, there are certain limitations on our claims.

2. Why 'Right to Education' should be recognised as a universal right?

Ans. The Right to Education should be recognised as a universal right, because it is necessary for our well-being and helps to develop our talents, skills and capacity to reason which enables us to make choices in life.

3. Why is the term 'human rights' being used more than the term 'natural rights' in recent years?

Ans. The term 'human rights' is being used more than the term 'natural rights' because a set of norms given by nature or God has been disapproved.

Rights are seen as guarantees that human beings themselves seek or arrive at in order to lead a good life.

4. What was Kant's view on human dignity?

Ans. Kant believes that each and every person has dignity and ought to be so treated by virtue of being a human being. A person may be uneducated, powerless or poor yet he deserves some dignity.

5. What is the significance of Right to Freedom of Religion?

Ans. Right to Freedom of Religion gives freedom to adopt any religion, to manage the religious affairs in one's own way to which their conscience allows. This right is significant for survival of a secular society and democracy.

6. Distinguish between Constitutional rights and natural rights.

Ans. Following are the differences between Constitutional rights and natural rights

Constitutional Rights	Natural Rights
Constitutional rights are coded in law.	Natural rights are considered universal and afforded to all people at birth by God or by nature.
Constitutional right is an agreement between the individual and the state that limits the individual's action, the state action or both usually for mutual benefit.	A natural right is a right that all creatures have or should have, merely by the fact of their existence.

7. Why is fulfillment of basic needs a right?

Ans. Fulfillment of basic needs is our legitimate claim. There are some basic needs like food, water, a house, education, health and livelihood without fulfilling these basic needs, we cannot live a life of respect and dignity.

8. Bhupesh is a factory worker. In his factory, machines are old and outdated, which need replacement and repair. Many accidents have happened, but the owner did not take any actions regarding machines.

(a) Which kind of right is violated by the owner?

(b) Justify your answer given in part (a).

Competency Based Que

Ans. (a) The owner is violating the right to life and right to safe working conditions.

(b) The right to safe working condition is fundamental aspect of the right to life. The factory owner's failure to replace and repair old and outdated machines, despite many accidents violates Bhupesh's right to a safe working environment.

9. How do rights differ from personal desires?

Ans. Rights are claims necessary for living a life of dignity and respect, while personal desires are things we want for our own comfort or enjoyment. For example, wanting to stay out late at night is a personal desire, but it is not a right. Rights are universally accepted and recognised by society, whereas personal desires are subjective and vary from person to person.

10. Why should rights be balanced when they conflict?

Ans. Rights need to be balanced to ensure fairness. For example, while a person has the right to freedom of expression, they cannot use it to harm others or violate their privacy. Balancing rights ensures that everyone enjoys equal rights without infringing on others' freedoms.

11. Should rights be absolute? Give your opinion.

Ans. Rights should not be absolute. Many times, it becomes necessary for the government to put restrictions on rights for the welfare of people.

For example, people have the right to information, but they cannot demand sensitive information about national security from the government.

12. Why is the freedom of speech and expression considered a universal right?

Ans. Speech makes humans different from animals. Through speech, a human being conveys his thoughts, sentiments and feelings to others.

Without the freedom of speech and expression, he cannot express his human nature freely. So, the freedom of speech and expression is considered a universal right.

Short Answer Type Questions

1. What are civil rights? Explain any two civil rights.

Diksha App

Ans. The rights which are essntial for the civilised existence are knows as civil rights. They are granted, protected and infurent by the state.

- **Right to life** It mean that the state must afford protection to the individual against all inimical forces.
- **Right to personal liberty** It mean that are individual must be given the freedom to enjoy his/her personal life. He/she must not be interfered with by the laws of the state till he remains within the boundary of the state law.

2. "Rights are necessary for leading a life of respect and dignity". Explain. **Competency Based Que**

Ans. Rights are necessary for leading a life of respect and dignity. It is so because, if we are deprived of some of our rights like right to livelihood, we will have to beg for buying basic necessities which will affect our dignity.

Rights are also necessary because they help individuals to develop their skills and talents.

For example, right to education helps us to develop our skills and gives us opportunity to progress in life.

3. Why is the right to livelihood more important than the political rights? Explain.

Ans. Right to livelihood includes basic needs such as food, shelter, clothing and health. Our rights of political participation can only be exercised meaningfully, if our basic needs are met.

A person living on the pavements and struggling to arrange one meal a day for his family, will not think about voting or contesting elections. For him, political rights by themselves will have little value.

Thus, right to livelihood is more important than political rights.

4. 'This conception of natural rights has been used widely to oppose the exercise of arbitrary power by states and governments and to safeguard individual freedom'. Explain the statement. **Competency Based Que**

Ans. In the seventeenth and 18th centuries, political theorists argued that rights are given to us by nature or God. The rights of men were derived from natural law. This meant that rights were not conferred by a ruler or a society; rather, we are born with them.

As such, these rights are inalienable and no one can take them away from us.

- They identified three natural rights of man: the right to life, liberty and property.
- All other rights were said to be derived from these basic rights. The idea that we are born with certain rights is a very powerful notion because it implies that no state or organisation should take away what has been given by the law of nature.

5. What is the basis and importance of human rights?

Ans. Human rights are those rights which all human beings are entitled by virtue of being human. It is based on the principle of respect for the individual. The following are some of the features human rights

- The fundamental assumption behind the concept of human rights is that every person is a moral and rational being who deserves to be treated with dignity.
- Human rights are both universal and fundamental; these are universal in the sense that they belong to all human beings irrespective of race, nationality, religion, gender, etc; these are also fundamental because once given, these cannot be taken back.
- They apply to everyone, regardless of where they come from, what they believe or how they live their lives.
- They can never be taken away, but they can be limited in some circumstances, like as when someone breaks the law or in the interests of national security. These ideals are legally defined and protected.

6. What are the two major arguments upon which Immanuel Kant's moral conceptions of rights rests?

Ans. According to Immanuel Kant, treating people with dignity is to treat them morally. This idea became the guiding principle for those struggling against social hierarchies and for human rights. He believe that every person has dignity and ought to be so treated by virtue of being a human being. His views represent the moral conception of rights based on two arguments

First, we must treat others as we would like to be treated ourselves.

Second, we should make sure that we don't treat the other person as a means to our ends. We should respect people not because they are useful to us, but because they are human beings.

7. What makes Fundamental Rights the most important and valued rights for the citizens?

Ans.
- The Fundamental Rights are the basic claims of the people for their well-being and all round development.
- The Fundamental Rights are important because they provide the citizens of a country with human dignity and development of personality of every individual.
- They guarantee civil liberties in order to sustain peace and harmony among the citizens of a nation.
- The Fundamental Rights are also defined as the basic human rights given to enjoy the freedom.

8. How does bonded labour of children deny their right to life?

Ans. Children are regarded as the future citizens of every nation. They must be freed from bonded labour. They are not born to serve others. In case of bonded labour, they are given minimum facilities to live and are involve in monotonous, streneous job. Bonded labour deny the right to life of children in the following way

- They are staying in an unhygienic environment with minimum opportunities to live a normal life. They cannot avail education.
- The Fundamental Rights, Right Against Exploitation demand their protection. Not only this Fundamental Right is denied but universal human right, right to life is also denied here.

Bonded labour of children is a curse to the society. It must be banned. All the children must have equal opportunities to be free and realise their full potential.

9. 'We must balance our rights when they come into conflict'. Explain. **Competency Based Que**

Ans. Right to freedom of expression allows an individual to express his ideas and beliefs freely. For example, right to express allows an individual to take pictures.

However, if an individual takes objectionable pictures of another person without his consent and shares it on different media, it would be a violation of another person's right to privacy.

Rights should be exercised in a way that they do not interfere with the rights of other. Therefore, we must balance our rights when they come into conflict.

10. 'National security is important, but it should not become a way to curb civil liberties'. Analyse.

Competency Based Que

Ans. Rights are not absolute and are subject to control and restrictions. Many times, the government puts restrictions on civil liberties in the name of national security. Such restrictions are justified for the general welfare of people and the country. But it should be examined whether the restrictions are really due to national security.

- Even people arrested in the name of national security should be allowed legal aid to present their case.
- We need to be extremely cautious about giving governments powers that could be used to curtail the civil liberties of individuals, for such powers can be misused. Governments can become authoritarian and undermine the very well-being of the members of the state.

Hence, even though rights can never be absolute, we need to be vigilant in protecting our rights and those of others, for they form the basis of a democratic society.

Long Answer Type Questions

1. What are the responsibilities that rights call for to action in a certain way?

Ans. The responsibilities that rights call for to action are as follows

- **Firstly,** Rights oblige or force us to think not only of self interest but also defending things as being good for all of us. Protecting ozone layer, minimising air and water pollution represents common good as they are essential for all of us.
- **Secondly,** Rights also require that an individual must respect the rights of others. In exercising individual's own right, he cannot deprive others of their rights. One's own rights are limited by the principle of equal and same rights for all.
- **Thirdly,** there is a need to maintain balance of rights, so that there are no conflicts. For example, an individual's right to freedom of expression must not violated other's sentiment.
- **Fourthly,** citizens must be careful about limitations which may be placed on their rights. Sometimes, the government imposes restriction on civil liberties of the citizens on the grounds of national security.

  On the other hand, we need to be cautious about giving powers to government, as it can misuse the power and may become authoritarian.

2. Discuss how the concept of rights has expanded to address modern challenges like environmental protection and social justice.

Ans. The concept of rights has evolved to include modern challenges as societies face new problems and develop a deeper understanding of dignity and equality. Initially, rights focused on basic freedoms like life, liberty and property. Over time, as issues like poverty, inequality and environmental degradation became significant thus the scope of rights expanded.

- **Environmental Protection** Growing concerns about pollution and climate change have led to demands for rights to clean air, water and sustainable development. These rights are essential for ensuring a healthy environment for future generations.
- **Social Justice** Rights have been reinterpreted to address discrimination based on gender, caste, race and religion.

  For example, women's rights and children's rights emphasise equality and protection from exploitation.
- **Economic Rights** The right to livelihood, housing and healthcare has gained prominence, recognising that economic security is necessary for a dignified life.

These expansions reflect society's commitment to ensuring that all individuals can live with dignity and that emerging challenges are addressed collectively. Rights are now seen as dynamic, adapting to the needs of the time while maintaining their core purpose of ensuring equality and respect for all.

3. 'Rights operate within a world of duties'. Explain.

Competency Based Que

Ans. Right and duties are closely related and cannot be separated from one another. If the state gives the right to life to a citizen, it also imposes an obligation on him to not expose his life to dangers, as well as to respect the life of others.

Rights can be enjoyed only in the world of duties. Rights are not the monopoly of a single individual. Everyone gets these equally.

This means that "Others also have the same rights which I have, and it is my duty to see that others also enjoy their rights".

It is our duty to respect the rights of others as well as the duty to use our rights in the interest of society. Since, state protects and enforces rights, it also becomes the duty of all citizens to be loyal to the state.

It is the duty of citizens to obey the laws of the state and to pay taxes honestly. Citizens should always be ready to defend the state. Thus, a citizen has both rights and duties. He enjoys rights and performs his duties.

4. Sudha is a 60 years old patient who has been in the hospital for the last two years. She is suffering from various diseases and feels immense pain. She filed a petition to the court to allow doctors to give her some medicine that would end her life. The court rejected the petition of Sudha.

(a) Why did the court reject the petition of Sudha? Is it justified?

(b) What can the court do for Sudha?

(c) If a person wants to harm himself, why should he not be allowed to harm himself? Is not it a violation of his rights? **Competency Based Que**

Ans. (a) Allowing to consume some medicine that would end her life will be a violation of her rights. The state, which also includes the court, has an obligation to protect the rights of citizens.

(b) The court can order the government to provide the best treatment to Sudha to cure her diseases. It can also order to provide a counselling session by a psychologist to Sudha to make her mentally strong.

(c) Every person has some basic rights, which include the right to life. A person cannot be allowed to harm himself or others. It is necessary to understand the reasons why he wants to harm himself. We should try to find out the reasons and try to help him. Right to life, like other rights, also needs some conditions like health, education, livelihood, etc. So, we should not only enjoy our rights but also help others to enjoy their rights.

Picture Based Questions

1. Study the picture given below and answer the question that follow.

(i) In the picture given below, the people are raising the demand for ....

(a) rights (b) duties (c) to get shelter (d) housing

Ans. (a) rights

(ii) Which of the following cannot be claimed as right? **Diksha App**

(a) Right to education
(b) Right to privacy
(c) Right to express yourself freely
(d) Right to take banned drugs

Ans. (d) Right to take banned drugs

(iii) Which of these is responsible for the enforcement of rights?

(a) State (b) Army
(c) Government officials (d) President

Ans. (a) State

(iv) Civil liberties and political rights form the basis of a......... .

(a) democratic goverment
(b) monarchical rule
(c) totalitarian government
(d) dictator rule

Ans. (a) democratic goverment

2. Study the cartoon given below carefully and answer the questions that follow.

(i) Which right is discussed in above picture?

(ii) What is the purpose of the right given in above picture?

(iii) What is the basis on which rights are claimed?

Ans. (i) Right to Information is discussed in the above picture.

(ii) The main purpose of the Right to Information Act is to empower citizens, promote openness and accountability in government operations, combat corruption and make our democracy truly function for them. A citizen can ask any questions from the government or seek any information.

(iii) The representation of conditions that individuals collectively regard as a source of self-respect and dignity are the basis on which claims to rights can be made. Every person's well-being necessitates it.

SELF ASSESSMENT TEST

Objective Type Questions

1. Which rights makes us aware about all other rights? **Diksha App**
   (a) Right to privacy (b) Right to life
   (c) Right to education (d) Right to contest election
2. What are rights? **Diksha App**
   (a) Justified claims and entitlements (b) Justified reviews
   (c) Justified manuals (d) Justified opinions
3. Two primary grounds on which rights are claimed are .... and ....
   (a) self respect and dignity (b) beliefs and thoughts
   (c) integrity and liberty (d) None of these

Very Short Answer Type Questions

4. Define the term rights.
5. How do political rights make government accountable to the people?
6. Why does the state cannot take away natural rights?
7. Why is right to property an important right? Explain briefly.

Short Answer Type Questions

8. Distinguish between right and claim and given examples.
9. Examine any two political rights of a citizen.
10. How are rights and duties inter related? Give two examples. **Diksha App**
11. How can we say that rights implies duties? Elaborate.

Long Type Questions

12. How can understanding and respecting rights contributing to a better society.
13. Analyse why are rights considered as the betterment of individuals?
14. What are human rights? Explain the different kinds of rights claimed by individuals. **Diksha App**

06

CHAPTER

Citizenship

Citizenship has been defined as full and equal membership in a political community. In the contemporary world, states provide a collective political identity to their members as well as certain rights.

YOUR STUDY GOALS

YOUR PRACTICE GOAL

- Objective Type Questions (32 Qs ; MCQs, A-R, Statements, Matching, Passage Based)
- Subjective Questions (10 VSAs, 6 SAs, 3 LAs, 2 Picture Based)

6.1 Citizenship and Rights

Rights enjoyed by citizens vary from state to state. Most democratic countries provide rights like

- Political rights such as the right to vote
- Civil rights such as freedom of speech or belief
- Socio-economic rights such as right to minimum wage, right to education, etc.
- The rights enjoyed by the citizens are the result of long struggle like the **French Revolution** in 1789. In Asian and African colonies, demand for equal citizenship became a part of independence struggle. Struggles to achieve equal membership and rights still continue in many parts of the world.
- Citizenship is about more than the state-citizen relationship. It is also about citizen-citizen relations and involves certain obligations of citizens to each other and to the society.

  Citizens are also considered to be the inheritors and trustees of the culture and natural resources of the country.

T.H. Marshall on Citizenship

- **T.H. Marshall** provides the formulation of relationship between equality, rights and citizenship in his book **Citizenship and Social Class.**

- He defines citizenship as "A status granted to those who are full members of society. All who possess the status are equal with respect to the rights and duties with which the status is endowed".
- The key concept in Marshall's idea of citizenship is equality. It implies two things
  - improvement in the quality of given rights and duties.
  - increase in the number of people who are granted these rights.
- **Marshall** sees citizenship as involving three kinds of rights: Civil, Political and Social.
- **Marshall** saw social class as a 'system of inequality'. Citizenship ensures equality by countering the divisive effects of class hierarchy.

6.2 Full and Equal Membership

- In India, one of the important rights that citizens have is **freedom of movement**. This right is of particular importance for workers who need to migrate in search of jobs. Many times resistance builds up among the local people against the jobs going to outsiders, sometimes at lower wages.
- Resistance against the outsiders can result in the form of organised violence against outsiders.
- There may be a difference between our response to poor migrants and skilled migrants. It raises the question of whether poor and unskilled workers should have the same right to live and work anywhere in the country as do skilled workers.
- Disputes may arise sometime in democratic societies. The Indian Constitution allows protest without harming the life or property of other people or the state.
- Citizens are free to try and influence public opinion and government policies by forming groups, holding demonstrations, using the media, appealing to political parties or by approaching the courts.
- In a democracy, all disputes should be settled through negotiation and discussion rather than power.

Martin Luther King

- The 1950s witnessed the emergence of **Civil Rights Movements** against inequalities that existed between black and white populations in the Southern states of the USA. Such inequalities were maintained by Segregation Laws[1].
- **Martin Luther King Jr.** was a black leader of the Civil Rights Movement against segregation laws. He gave many arguments against these laws
  - In terms of self-dignity and worth, all human beings are equal regardless of race or colour.
  - Segregation is like 'social leprosy or social stigma' on the body politic[2] because it inflicts deep psychological wounds on the people who suffer as a result of such laws.
  - Segregation laws create artificial boundaries between people and prevent them from co-operating with each other for overall benefit of the country.

  Martin Luther King gave a call for peaceful and non-violent resistance against the segregation laws.

Equal Rights

- As per citizenship, all citizens get equal rights. But in practice, reality is different. In every Indian city, there is a large population of slum-dwellers and squatters. They do useful work but may be blamed for exhausting resources of the city or for spreading crime or diseases. They live in slums with lack of basic facilities like water and sanitation.
- Awareness about the condition of urban poor is growing among governments, NGOs and other agencies and among the slum-dwellers themselves. In January 2004, a **national policy on urban street-vendors** was framed. Slum-dwellers are now aware and fighting for their rights. They have sometimes even approached the courts.

1 Segregation Law It is the law through which people were seperated and formed into different groups on the basis of race, religion and sex.

2 Body politic It means all the people of a nation, state or society considered collectively as an organised group of citizens.

Citizenship, Equality and Rights

- The Supreme Court gave an important decision regarding the rights of slum-dwellers in Bombay in response to a **Public Interest Litigation** filed by a social activist, olga tellis against Bombay Municipal Corporation in 1985.
- The Supreme Court gave the verdict that **Article 21** of the Constitution which guarantees the right to life also include right to livelihood.

- Another group which is becoming marginalised are tribal people and forest dwellers. They depend on forests and other natural resources for their basic needs. They face threat to their way of life and livelihood due to
  - search for land and resources to fulfil the needs of increasing population.
  - commercial interests like extraction of resources present in forests or coasts.
  - tourist industry.
- The government has a dual challenge which is protecting the rights of tribal people by without disturbing the development of the country. Ensuring equal rights and opportunities is not an easy task for the government. Different groups have different needs and problems which cannot be solved by uniform policies.

Quick Test 1

1 Name a civil right that is provided by most democratic countries.
2 How does Marshall see social class?
3 What is segregation law?
4 For which things are slum-dwellers blamed by people?

6.3 Citizen and Nation

The Concept of nation state[3] emerged in the modern period. French revolutionaries in 1789, asserted the sovereignty[4] of the nation state and democratic rights. Nation states claim that their boundaries define unique culture and shared history and not just territory.

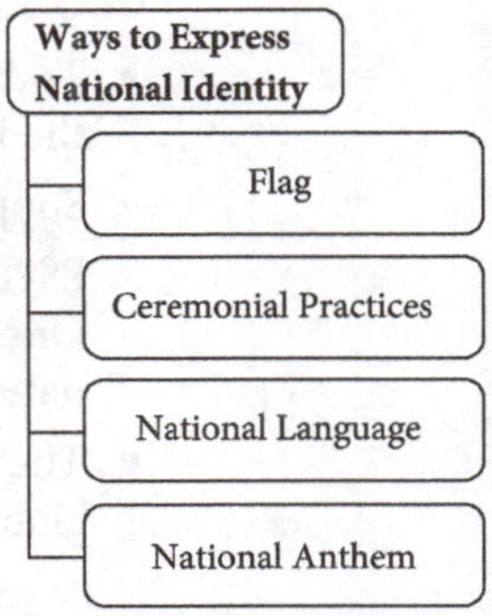

▲ *National Identity*

- Most modern states include diverse people, but the national identity of a democratic state provides a political identity to citizens, which can be shared by all citizens. Democratic states try to define their citizenship as inclusive as possible, but inclusivity can vary. France is a country that claims to be both **secular** and **Inclusive**, where citizens can assimilate publicly while retaining their beliefs in private. However, there are issues like use of religious symbols in public life.
- Naturalisation[5] is the criteria for granting citizenship to new applicants that vary from country to country. For Example, religion or ethnic origin is given priority while granting citizenship in countries like Israel or Germany.
- India defines itself as a secular, democratic, nation state. The Indian Constitution attempted to accommodate a very diverse society. It provided citizenship to all people without any discrimination. The provisions about citizenship in the Constitution can be found in **Part Two** and subsequent laws made by the Parliament. All citizens have equal rights along with protection for religious and linguistic minorities.

3 Nation state It is a group of people with the same culture, language, etc. who have formed an independent country.
4 Sovereignty It refers to the supreme authority and power of a state or nation to govern itself, make its own laws, and control its own affairs, free from external influence or interference.
5 Naturalisation It is the legal process by which a non-citizen becomes a citizen of a country they were not born in.

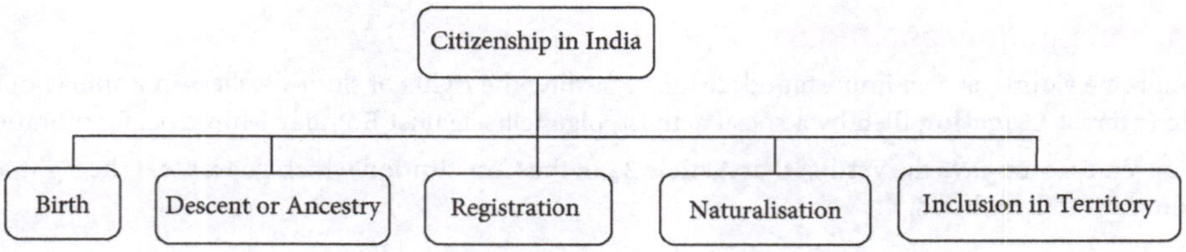

▲ *Criteria for Citizenship in India*

- However, despite inclusive provisions, there are some people who feel that they are being denied full rights of citizenship, like women, Dalits and people displaced by development projects who are struggling for equal rights.

Universal Citizenship

- Many states support the idea of universal and inclusive citizenship; however, each state fixes criteria for the grant of citizenship.
- Despite efforts to restrict migration, considerable migration of peoples still takes place due to wars, persecution, famine or other reasons.
- People unable to find refuge become stateless people or **refugees**[6]. They live in camps or as illegal migrants with a lack of rights and basic facilities.
- The U.N. has appointed a **high commissioner for refugees** to help people who suffer due to migration.
- Decisions about how many people can be absorbed as citizens pose a difficult humanitarian and political problem.
- Many countries have a policy of accepting people suffering due to persecution or war. However, countries may not want to accept an unmanageable number of people or expose the country to security risks.

Global Citizenship

- Today, people of different countries feel inter-connected due to new means of communication such as the internet, television and cell phones.
- Supporters of global citizenship argue that although a world community and global society do not exist, people already feel linked to each other across national boundaries.
- One of the attractions of global citizenship is that solutions to many problems that extend across national boundaries can be found due to combined efforts.
- The concept of global citizenship reminds us that national citizenship might need to be supplemented by global citizenship to work with people and governments across national boundaries.

Quick Test 2

1. What do nation states claim?
2. How does India define itself?
3. What has the U.N. appointed to help refugees?
4. Why are people interconnected in the present world?

6 **Refugee** It is a person who leaves his country due to war, persecution or natural disaster and seek safety in another country.

Mind Map

CITIZENSHIP

1 Meaning of Citizenship

- It means full and equal membership of a political community.
- Citizenship is about more than the state-citizen relationship.
- Citizens are also considered to be the inheritors and trustees of the culture and natural resources of the country.

Citizenship and Rights

- **Political Rights** Such as right to vote.
- **Civil Rights** Such as freedom of speech or belief.
- **Socio - economic Right** Such as right to minimum wage, right to education.

2 T.H. Marshall's View on Citizenship

- Key concept in Marshall's idea of citizenship is 'Equality'.
- Involved three kinds of rights- Civil, Political and Social.

3 Full and Equal Membership

- The important right that citizens have includes, freedom of Movement, right to life.
- Disputes may arise sometime in democratic societies.
- Citizens are free to try and influence public opinion and government policies.
- All disputes should be settled through negotiation and discussion rather than power.
- The Indian Constitution allows protest without harming the life or property of other people or the state.

4 Citizen and Nation

- Nationality of a citizen is identified by its flag, anthem, and language.
- India provides citizenship to all people without any discrimination.
- Naturalisation is the criteria for granting citizenship to new applicants vary from country to country.
- It provided citizenship to all people without any discrimination.
- The Constitution provisions can be found in part two.
- All citizens have equal rights along with protection for religious and linguistic minorities.
- Rights of citizenship, like women, Dalits and people displaced by developmental projects who are struggling for equal rights.

Universal Citizenship

- Citizenship provided to the citizens of a nation in all the country in which he is being present.
- Many people can be absorbed as citizens, it pose a difficult humanitarian and political problem like policy of accepting people suffering due to persecution or war.
- To accept an unmanageable number of people or expose the country to security risks.

Global Citizenship

- Citizenship provided to every citizen by any nation in which he is being present.
- Different countries feel inter-connected due to new means of communication.
- A world community and global society do not exist, people already feel linked to each other across national boundaries to support.
- Global citizenship reminds us that national citizenship might need to be supplemented by global citizenship to work.

Equality Rights

- All the citizens rich or poor should be guaranteed certain basic rights and a minimum standard of living.
- Awareness about the condition of urban poor is growing among governments.
- National policy on urban street-vendors was framed in 2004 .
- Tribal people and forest dwellers face threat to their way of life and livelihood due to.
  - Search for land and resources to fulfill growing population needs.
  - Commercial interests.
  - Tourist industry.

Citizenship is a status conferred upon an individual by virtue of his or her being full member of a community. In his study called Citizenship and Social Class (1950), one of the purposes of Marshall is to trace the historical evolution of the institution of citizenship in England since the latter part of the seventeenth century till the end of nineteenth century.

-T.H. Marshall

NCERT Folder

Intext Question

1. Write about the street vendors (Protection of Livelihood and Regulation of Street Vending) Act, 2014. (Pg. 89)

Ans. The Street Vendors (Protection of Livelihood and Regulation of Street Vending) Act, 2014 is a law in India aimed at protecting the rights of street vendors and regulating street vending in urban areas.

- **Protection of Livelihood** The Act recognises that street vending is an important source of livelihood for millions of people. It protects street vendors from harassment and eviction by local authorities, as long as they follow the rules set by the government.
- **Vending Zones** It provides for the creation of designated 'vending zones' where vendors can carry out their business without any issues.
- **Survey and Registration** Local governments are required to conduct a survey of street vendors in their areas and issue licenses to them. This helps in properly regulating the vendors and providing them with legal recognition.

Thus, the act is meant to ensure that street vendors have a legal right to earn and protect them from forced eviction.

Exercise

1. Citizenship as full and equal membership of a political community involves both rights and obligations. Which rights could citizens expect to enjoy in most democratic state today? What kind of obligation will they have to their state and fellow citizens?

Ans. The rights that citizens could expect to enjoy in most democratic state are Right to Equality, Right to Vote in political elections, Freedom of Expression, Right to have basic facilities, Right to Security and Equal Treatment by Laws.

There are legal and moral obligations on citizens to participate in and contribute to the shared life of the community as well as the state. Citizens are also expected to preserve the culture and natural resources of their country.

2. All citizens may be granted equal rights but all may not be able to equally exercise them. Explain.

Ans. All citizens may be granted equal rights but all may not be able to equally exercise them due to following reasons

- There are huge socio-economic inequalities which are obstacles in the way of equality of opportunity.
- There is a lack of awareness about accessibility to legal remedies.
- A large number of citizens are unaware of their rights.
- A lot of people are greedy and they make our administrative system a corrupt machinery. Thus, corruption prevents the delivery of services and that is how citizen's rights are hampered.

All the above factors have certain consequences which can be seen as following

- Right to Education is a Fundamental Right of every child but some children are not sent to school due to poverty and gender biasness and they are engaged in exploitative child labour.
- Domestic violence is a common social evil today. A number of women are unaware about the laws associated with it. Therefore, they are not able to seek legal remedies.
- Politicians or powerful administrative officers misuse their powers by which other people are deprived of their rights.

3. Write a short note on any two struggles for full enjoyment of citizen rights which have taken place in India in recent years. Which rights were beings claimed in each case?

Ans. The Indian Constitution attempts to guarantee equal membership to diverse groups such as Dalits, Scheduled Tribes and women, among others.

- Even those distant settlements in the Andaman and Nicobar Islands that had little touch with contemporary society have been covered.
- Various movements have taken place for the above-mentioned groups, namely women, SCs, STs and those displaced as a result of government development projects and 33 per cent seats have been reserved for all of them.
- The aspirations of marginalised people have been negotiated in a democratic society, for example, OBCs have 27 per cent reservation in all educational institutions.
- Women have also asked that 33 per cent of seats in State Legislatures and the Lok Sabha be reserved for them.

4. What are some of the problems faced by refugees? In what ways could the concept of global citizenship benefit them?

Ans. A refugee is an individual who is fleeing his country to escape persecution based on race, religion, nationality or membership of a certain group or political opinion.

Problems faced by refugees are as follows

- Refugees face the challenges of starvation, abduction (arrogation), violence and obtaining admission into a protected country.
- Refugees are forced to adopt the local customs and language of the sheltering country.
- Due to their history of persecution, many refugees are uncomfortable dealing with legal paperwork in a foreign country, especially if it is in a language that they cannot understand.
- Many refugees suffer from post-traumatic stress disorder after escaping from conditions of oppression and persecution.
- Adjusting to life in a different country is difficult for refugees and they face many unexpected hardships.
- There are often cultural and language barriers, as well as a feeling of alienation.

Global citizenship would be beneficial to refugees, as it will be easier to deal with problems that extend across national boundaries and require co-operation of other states. It would also help refugees and stateless people by providing them basic rights and solutions to their problems so that they can lead a moral dignified life.

5. Migration of people to different regions within the country is often resisted by the local inhabitants. What are some of the contributions that the migrants could make to the local economy?

Ans. Migrants contribute greatly towards the economy of the state where they work.

Following are the contributions that the migrants could make to the local economy.

- Migrants play a significant role to increase the workforce of local economy.
- Migrants contribute significantly to labour- market flexibility.
- Migrants contribute more in taxes and social services.
- Employment is the single biggest determinant of migrants net fiscal contribution.
- Migrants boosts the working-age population.
- Migrants also contribute to technological progress.

6. Democratic citizenship is a project rather than an accomplished fact even in countries like India which grant equal citizenship. Discuss some of the issues regarding citizenship being raised in India today.

Ans. In democratic countries, people are still far behind in enjoying the full rights associated with democratic citizenship.

- In the context of India, Equality of Rights is ensured for all citizens by the Constitution, but does not always translate on the ground.
- Socio-economic inequality is a major factor preventing the access of all citizens to basic rights.
- Citizens have the right to move and work freely anywhere within the territory.
- They have the right to enjoy basic facilities that are needed to survive and lead a healthy life but migrants are exempted from these rights as Indian citizens at some places.
- Many poor children are forcefully engaged in child labour. Though, these children have got certain Fundamental Rights in democratic India, but they are not able to enjoy it.
- The issues of dual citizenship for people who reside outside the country is also a matter of debate and shows the dynamic nature of the concept of citizenship.

Therefore, it can be said that democratic citizenship is a project that has still to meet its goal rather than having accomplished it.

Exam Pattern Questions

Objective Type Questions

Multiple Choice Questions (MCQs)

1. …………….. is the state of being a member of a particular community.

(a) Naturalisation (b) Citizenship
(c) Migration (d) Nationalisation

2. What is citizenship? Diksha App

(a) Half membership of a political community.
(b) Full and equal membership of a political community.
(c) Membership of a particular district.
(d) Membership of a regional organisation.

3. Citizenship is characterised as complete and fair participation in a ……. society.

(a) political (b) democratic
(c) economic (d) All of these

4. The precise nature of the rights granted to citizens may vary from state to state but in most democratic countries today they would include some ………….. like the right to vote.

(a) cultural rights (b) political rights
(c) social rights (d) economic rights

5. Which of the following is consider as a civil rights?

(a) Right to vote (b) Right to minimum wage
(c) Right to an education
(d) Freedom of expression or belief

6. Which of these statements is not correct?

(a) Many European countries experienced violent struggles by people against monarchies, some of them non-violent like the French Revolution in 1757.
(b) In South Africa, the black population had to undertake a long struggle against the ruling white minority for equal citizenship.
(c) Struggles to achieve full membership and equal rights continue even now in many parts of the world.
(d) In India, women and Dalit are still struggling to achieve full membership and rights.

7. What is not included in the concept of citizenship. Diksha App

(a) Relationship between states and their members.
(b) Relationship between citizen and the other fellow citizens.
(c) Obligations of citizens to each other and society.
(d) Duties of human beings towards animals.

8. What moral obligation is associated with citizenship?

(a) To compete for individual benefits.
(b) To participate in and contribute to the shared life of the community.
(c) To follow state-imposed restrictions without question.
(d) To avoid taking part in governance.

9. Citizens are also considered to be the inheritors and trustees of the culture and ………….. of the country.

(a) backbone (b) natural resources
(c) biological factors (d) None of these

10. Which of these countries witnessed the emergence of Civil Right Movement in 1950s?

(a) South Africa (b) United States of America
(c) India (d) Canada

11. Inequalities were maintained in Southern states of USA by a set of laws called ……. laws through which the black people were denied many civil and political rights.

(a) segregation (b) differentiation
(c) humanity (d) defective

12. Who fought against the segregation laws in the USA during the Civil Rights Movement? Diksha App

(a) Martin Luther (b) Martin Luther King
(c) Abraham Lincoln (d) Nelson Mandela

13. Consider the following statements.

Statement I Political parties do not take any interest in the resistance of local population against outsiders.

Statement II No region in India has experienced organised violence against 'outsiders'.

Competency Based Que

In the light of the above statements, choose the correct answer from the options given below

(a) Both Statement I and Statement II are true.
(b) Both Statement I and Statement II are false.
(c) Statement I is true, but Statement II is false.
(d) Statement I is false, but Statement II is true.

14. The right to protest is an aspect of the …………….. guaranteed to citizens in our Constitution, provided protest does not harm the life or property of other people or the state.

(a) freedom of religion (b) right to equality
(c) freedom of expression (d) freedom of conscience

15. **Consider the following statements.**

I. T.H. Marshall was an American sociologist.

II. He wrote a book called 'Citizenship and Social Class'.

III. According to Marshall, citizenship involves two kinds of rights: civil and political.

Which of the following statement(s) is/are correct?

Competency Based Que

(a) I and II (b) Only II
(c) Only I (d) I, II and III

16. **Who gave an important decision regarding the rights of slum-dwellers in Bombay?**

(a) Supreme Court
(b) High Court of Bombay
(c) State Legislature of Maharashtra
(d) Parliament

17. **Which of the following articles of the Indian Constitution guarantees the rights to life?**

(a) Article 20 (b) Article 21
(c) Article 22 (d) Article 23

18. **In which of these were the earliest assertions made regarding sovereignty of the nation state and democratic rights of citizens?**

(a) French Revolution
(b) American Revolution
(c) Indian Independence Movement
(d) None of the above

19. **What are the different ways to get the citizenship of India?**

(a) By birth (b) By naturalisation
(c) By registration (d) All of these

20. **Which of the following people are not facing the problem of statelessness in today's scenario?** **Diksha App**

(a) Illegal migrants
(b) Refugees
(c) People displaced by wars
(d) Students

21. **Which of the following organisations helped in strengthening global citizenship?** **Diksha App**

(a) United Nations
(b) National Banks
(c) Regional Organisations
(d) National Rescue Agencies

22. **Which of the following is a drawback of global citizenship?** **Diksha App**

(a) People feel close to each other across national boundaries.
(b) Global citizenship helps in spreading awareness about the prevention of diseases.
(c) It leads to international network links among the terrorists throughout the world today.
(d) It leads to the co-operation among the National Governments during pandemics.

23. **Identify and write the incorrect pair.** **Competency Based Que**

(a) France- Secular and inclusive
(b) U.S.A. - Country of refugees
(c) India- Secular and democratic
(d) South Africa- Discrimination with black population

24. **Match List-I with the List-II and choose the correct option.**

List I	List II
A. France	1. Civil Rights Movement in 1950s.
B. U.S.A.	2. Earliest assertions regarding the sovereignty of nation state.
C. India	3. Demand for citizenship by Turkish workers.
D. Germany	4. Provided asylum to Dalai Lama in 1959.

	A	B	C	D
(a)	4	2	1	3
(b)	2	1	4	3
(c)	3	1	4	2
(d)	1	3	2	4

25. **Arrange the following in chronological order**

I. President of Zimbabwe announced the plans to take ove 1500 farms.

II. Suprme Court gave decision regarding the rights of slum-dwellers in Bombay.

III. Martin Luther King witessed the emergence of civil rights movement.

IV. France struggled to assert independence and right.

Choose the correct option

(a) I, II, III, IV
(b) II, IV, I, III
(c) IV, III, II, I
(d) IV, III, I, II

Assertion-Reason Questions

Directions (Q. Nos. 26-30) In the questions given below, there are two statements marked as Assertion (A) and Reason (R). Read the statements and choose the correct option.

Codes

(a) Both A and R are true and R is the correct explanation of A.
(b) Both A and R are true, but R is not the correct explanation of A.
(c) A is true, but R is false.
(d) A is false, but R is true.

26. **Assertion (A)** Citizenship is characterised as complete and fair participation in a political society.

Reason (R) Citizens demand certain rights from their government, as well as assistance and security everywhere they go.

27. **Assertion (A)** Indian Constitution has included citizenship in Part-I.

Reason (R) The state provides rights to citizens so that they can enjoy a free and dignified life provisions regarding.

28. **Assertion (A)** The Constitution established a fundamentally democratic and inclusive concept of citizenship.

Reason (R) Citizenship in India can be obtained by birth, descent, registration, naturalisation or territorial inclusion.

29. **Assertion (A)** Illegal migrants are not granted any rights by any state and live in generally unstable circumstances.

Reason (R) Government has a limited resources and hence these days government are not looking out itself globally.

30. **Assertion (A)** Refugees should not be granted citizenship in any condition.

Reason (R) In a group of refugees, there could be some terrorists or spies of hostile countries. **Competency Based Que**

Passage Based Questions

31. Read the given passage and answer the following questions.

The 1950s witnessed the emergence of Civil Rights Movements against inequalities that existed between black and white populations in many of the Southern states of the USA. Such inequalities were maintained in these states by a set of laws called Segregation Laws through which the black people were denied many civil and political rights. These laws created separate areas for coloured and white people in various civic amenities like railways, buses, theatres, housing, hotels, restaurants, etc. Martin Luther King Jr. was a black leader of the movement against these laws. King gave many arguments against the prevailing laws of segregation. First, in terms of self-worth and dignity every human person in the world is equal regardless of one's race or colour.

(i) .... refers to discriminations which are present in society, these discriminations are based on race, religion, caste, gender etc.

(a) Civil liberties (b) Social leprosy
(c) Economic rights (d) All of these

(ii) What were the reasons of Civil Rights Movements of 1950 in USA?

(a) Existence of inequalities between Black and White which was maintained by segregation laws.
(b) Denial of civil and political rights to black people.
(c) Both (a) and (b)
(d) Neither (a) nor (b)

(iii) What were the arguments of Martin Luther King against segregation laws?

(a) Every human being is equal regardless of one's race or colour.
(b) Practice of segregation diminishes the quality of life.
(c) The segregation laws create artificial boundaries between people and prevent them from co-operating with each other for the overall benefit of the country.
(d) All of the above

(iv) Which of these was supported by Martin Luther King?

(a) Peaceful protests
(b) Physical violence
(c) Discrimination with white people after getting power
(d) Separate buses for black population

32. Read the given passage and answer the following questions.

Most modern states include people of different religions, languages and cultural traditions. But the national identity of a democratic state is supposed to provide citizens with a political identity that can be shared by all the members of the state. Democratic states usually try to define their identity so that it is as inclusive as possible — that is, which allows all citizens to identify themselves as part of the nation. But in practice, most countries tend to define their identity in a way which makes it easier for some citizens to identify with the state than others. It may also make it easier for the state to extend citizenship to some people and not others. This would be as true of the United States, which prides itself on being a country of immigrants, as any other country.

(i) Which of the following statements is correct about nation state?

(a) The concept of nation state evolved in the medieval period.
(b) Nation states claim that their boundaries define not just a territory but also a unique culture and shared history.
(c) One of the earliest assertions regarding the sovereignty of the nation state was made by the Russian revolutionaries in 1917.
(d) None of the above

(ii) Which of these is not used to express national identity?

(a) Flag (b) Films
(c) Ceremonial practices (d) Language

(iii) Why do controversies related to inclusivity arise in France?

Answers

1. (b) Citizenship
2. (b) Full and equal membership of a politcal community.
3. (a) political 4. (b) political rights
5. (d) freedom of expression or belief
6. (a) Many European countries experienced violent struggles by people against monarchies, some of them non-violent like the French Revolution in 1757.
7. (d) Duties of human beings towards animals.
8. (b) To participate in and contribute to the shared life of the community.
9. (b) natural resources
10. (b) United States of America
11. (a) segregation
12. (b) Martin Luther King
13. (b) Both Statement I and Statement II are false.
14. (c) freedom of expression
15. (b) Only II
16. (a) Supreme Court
17. (b) Article 21
18. (a) French Revolution
19. (d) All of these
20. (d) Students
21. (a) United Nations
22. (c) It leads to international network links among the terrorists throughout the world today.
23. (b) U.S.A. – Country of refugees
24. (b) 2 1 4 3
25. (c) IV, III, II, I
26. (b) Both A and R are true, but R is not the correct explanation of A.
    Both are not interrelated to each other. Citizenship is characterised as complete and fair participation in a political society because it allows an individual to enjoy all the basic rights guaranteed by the country.
27. (d) A is false, but R is true.
    Indian Constitution has included citizenship in Part-II.
28. (a) Both A and R are true and R is the correct explanation of A.
    A is about the principles of citizenship while R is about how to acquire a citizenship of India.
29. (a) Both A and R are true and R is the correct explanation of A.
    Illegal migrants are not granted any rights by any state and live in generally unstable circumstances because government has a limited resources and hence these days government are not looking out itself globally.
30. (d) A is false, but R is true.
    Not granting citizenship to any refugee who is suffering due to war, persecution or natural disaster will be against human values. Some refugees could be terrorist or spies which is a possibility. A more balanced approach is needed while granting citizenship.
31. (i) (b) Social leprosy
    (ii) (c) Both (a) and (b)
    (iii) (d) All of the above
    (iv) (a) Peaceful protests
32. (i) (b) Nation states claim that their boundaries define not just a territory but also a unique culture and shared history.
    (ii) (b) Films
    (iii) France claims to be a secular and inclusive country. Citizens are expected to assimilate into national identity, keeping their beliefs and practices private. Sometimes religious symbols and practices may enter in public lives which creates and roversies. For example, demand to wear turbon in school by a sikh student and demand by Muslim girls to wear the head scarf with their school uniforms.

Subjective Questions

Very Short Answer Type Questions

1. What is the importance of full membership of a state?

Ans. If a state does not give full membership to an individual, in that case he/she has to live as a refugee or stateless individual. That individual does not enjoy any rights granted by the state. Thus, full membership of a state is important.

2. Name some rights that are enjoyed by citizens in most democratic states.

Ans. Citizens in most democratic states enjoy some political rights like the right to vote and civil rights like the freedom of speech or belief and some socio-economic rights, which could include the right to a minimum wage, or the right to education.

3. Is citizenship a guarantee to enjoy equal rights? Express your opinion.

Ans. No, citizenship is not a guarantee to enjoy equal rights. Many sections of society, like poor people, slum-dwellers and tribals, do not enjoy equal rights due to a lack of basic facilities.

Citizenship gives a political identity and rights, but the benefits of full membership are subject to many things, like economic condition, equal opportunities, etc.

4. In Bangalore, contractors hired outsiders for construction work as they were ready to work at lower wages. Due to this, local workers lost their jobs. This gave rise to a conflict between local workers and outsiders, which became violent. How can this conflict be resolved by the government? Suggest any two ways. Competency Based Que

Ans. The government can resolve the conflict between local workers and outsider workers by

(i) The government can organise a meeting between local workers and outsiders to promote dialogue and co-operation.

(ii) The government fix the minimum wages that would be applicable for both local workers and outsider workers. If contractors pay less wages, then they should be jailed.

5. What benefits does a state provide to citizens?

Ans. A state provides a collective political identity to its members as well as certain rights. It is also expected from the state to provide help and protection wherever citizens travel outside the country.

6. According to T.H. Marshall, citizenship involves three kinds of rights- Civil, Political and Social. What are relation between these rights and citizenship? Competency Based Que

Ans.
- Civil rights protect the individual's life, liberty and property.
- Political rights enable the individual to participate in the process of governance.
- Social rights give the individual access to education and employment.

Together they make it possible for the citizen to lead a life of dignity. All these rights are fully enjoyed by citizens only. In this way, these rights are related with citizenship.

7. 'The conditions in slums are often shocking'. Analyse the statement. Competency Based Que

Ans. People in slums live in very difficult circumstances. Many people may have to live in a single room. People have to face lack of basic facilities like water and sanitation.

Life and property are insecure in a slum. Slum-dwellers can be removed from their place by the government anytime.

8. What do you mean by naturalised citizenship? Diksha App

Ans. Naturalised citizenship is a process of acquiring citizenship by foreigners. Naturalisation means that an individual who lives in a country for a certain minimum period and acquires the citizenship of that country.

9. 'Refugees live a miserable life'. Analyse the statement. Competency Based Que

Ans. Refugees migrate from their country due to war, natural disaster or persecution. If no state is willing to accept them, their lives become miserable. They may be forced to live in camps or as illegal migrants. Often they cannot legally work, educate their children or acquire property.

10. Do tribes enjoy the same equal rights as other citizens enjoy?

Ans. Tribal people do not enjoy equal rights. Their forests are being cut by rich people for their own commercial interests. They build hotels, playgrounds and their own beautiful localities and destroy the tribal people's area of living. They have been rendered homeless and been rooted out from their traditional place.

Short Answer Type Questions

1. What is the importance of citizenship in a person's life? Give your opinion. **Competency Based Que**

Ans. Citizenship is very important in the life of a person. Citizenship provides a political identity to a person. Then, a person can think of himself as Indian, German, Japanese, etc.

- States also provide certain rights to citizens. The state is also expected to help and protect the citizens wherever they travel outside the country.
- Rights vary from state to state. In most democratic states, citizens enjoy various political, social and economic rights.
- Without citizenship, the life of a person would be miserable. He/she will have no protection of state. He/she may have to live in refugee camps with a lack of basic facilities and no future.

2. How would you justify the statement that "Education plays a crucial role in making individuals into better citizens"? **Competency Based Que**

Ans. "Education plays a crucial role in making individuals into better citizens", this statement can be justified with following arguments

(i) Education enables an individual to possess three qualities viz intelligence, self control and conscience. With these qualities, an individual turns into a better citizen.

(ii) Education enables an individual to be careful about the rules of health and observe them accurately.

(iii) Education enables an individual to play his role in the society more successfully.

(iv) Education prepares an individual to fight for his rights and rights of others and take active part in all public activities.

3. What is the importance of equality and rights in Marshall's concept of citizenship?

Ans. The key concept in Marshall's idea of citizenship is that of 'equality'. This implies two things

- First, that the quality of the given rights and duties improves.
- Second, that the quantity of people upon whom they are bestowed grows.

Marshall sees citizenship as involving three kinds of rights: Civil, Political and Social.

- Civil rights protect the individual's life, liberty and property.
- Political rights enable the individual to participate in the process of governance.
- Social rights give the individual access to education and employment.

Together they make it possible for the citizen to lead a life of dignity.

4. Why ensuring equal rights and opportunities for all citizens is not an easy task for government? Explain.

Ans. Ensuring equal rights and opportunities for all citizens is not an easy task for the government. Different groups may have different needs and problems and the rights of one group may conflict with the rights of another. For example, every person has the right to a livelihood and freedom of movement in India.

Migrant workers move to different cities for jobs. Many times, they work at lower wages. Local workers may become jobless.

Here, the rights of migrant workers come into conflict with the rights of local workers. So, while framing policies, the needs and claims of people should be considered.

5. Raman is a Mauritian citizen who lives with his wife Shrishti in Port Louis, Mauritius. Ancestor of Raman and Shrishti came as workers in Mauritus in the 1800s. Later, they settled in the Mauritus permanently. Raman and Srishti want to take Indian citizenship. They are ineligible for citizenship by registration. How can they take Indian citizenship? Justify your answer. **Competency Based Que**

Ans. In India, citizenship can be acquired by birth, descent, registration, naturalisation and inclusion in territory. Raman and Srishti are ineligible for citizenship by registration and birth since they were not born in India and Mauritius is an independent country. They cannot claim citizenship by descent either, as they would need to prove ancestry of over 200 years, which is difficult.

Therefore, the best option for them to obtain Indian citizenship is through naturalisation, requiring them to live in India for a certain period before applying.

6. Why do we need global citizenship?

Ans. We need global citizenship due to the following reasons

- We are living in an interdependent world, so our problems are common.
- World is affected by global problems like war, migration, hunger, devastation and weapons and environmental problems.
- We need an inclusive idea of citizenship so that everybody is respected only because they are humans.
- Boundaries have been redefined by advancement in technology and communications.

Long Answer Type Questions

1. 'Each of the rights now enjoyed by citizens has been won after struggle'. Explain the statement. **Competency Based Que**

Ans. Earlier, people did not have equal rights. Today, rights enjoyed by us as citizens have been won after struggle.

- Some of the earliest struggles were fought by people to assert their independence and rights against powerful monarchies.
- Many European countries experienced such struggles, some of them violent, like the French Revolution in 1789.
- In the colonies of Asia and Africa, demands for equal citizenship formed part of their struggle for independence from colonial rulers.
- In South Africa, the black African population had to undertake a long struggle against the ruling white minority for equal citizenship. This continued until the early 1990s.

Struggles to achieve full membership and equal rights continue even now in many parts of the world. In India, women and dalits are fighting to get benefits of full membership.

2. **Discuss the ideas of Martin Luther King.**

Ans. Martin Luther King Jr. was a black leader of the movement against the segregation laws in U.S.A.. King gave many arguments against the prevailing laws of segregation.

(i) In terms of self-worth and dignity every human person in the world is equal regardless of one's race or colour.

(ii) King argued that segregation is like 'social leprosy' on the body politic because it inflicts deep psychological wounds on the people who suffer as a result of such laws.

King argued that the practice of segregation diminishes the quality of life for the white community also. He illustrates this point by following examples.

- The white community, instead of allowing the black people to enter some community parks as was directed by the court, decided to close them.
- Similarly, some baseball teams had to be disbanded, as the authorities did not want to accept black players.
- Thirdly, the segregation laws create artificial boundaries between people and prevent them from co-operating with each other for the overall benefit of the country.
- For these reasons, King argued that these laws should be abolished. He gave a call for peaceful and non-violent resistance against the segregation laws. He said in one of his speeches: "We must not allow our creative protest to degenerate into physical violence".

3. Do you agree that slum-dwellers are enjoying equal rights? Justify your answer. **Competency Based Que**

Ans. No, slum-dwellers are not enjoying equal rights like other citizens because of several reasons such as

- There is a large population of slum-dwellers and squatters in every city in India. They do necessary and useful work, often at low wages. They are seen as unwelcomed visitors by the rest of the town population. They may be blamed for straining the resources of the city or for spreading crime and disease.
- The conditions in slums are often shocking. Many people live in a single small room with a lack of basic facilities like sanitation, water, etc. Life and property are insecure in a slum. They are not considered owners of their property.
- Slum-dwellers provide a singular contribution to the city through their labour. They provide basic services by working as hawkers, petty traders, plumbers, domestic workers, etc.
- Street vendors are often exploited by police and town authorities. They have to pay a bribe for their livelihood.
- Besides economic rights, slum-dwellers are also not able to enjoy political rights like the right to vote. To be included in the list of voters, they need a permanent address, which they do not have.
- So, it is clear that slum-dwellers are not able to enjoy their rights. However, the situation is improving with the efforts of the government and slum-dwellers themselves.

Picture Based Questions

1. **Observe the cartoon given below and answer the question that follow.**

(i) What does the above cartoon depict?

(ii) Explain the meaning of equal membership of citizens.

(iii) From the above picture describe the impact on life of urban people if immigrant workers stop coming into cities.

Ans. (i) The above cartoon depicts a day in the life of Urban Indian middle class without immigrant workers.

(ii) Equal membership means that all citizens have got equal rights. Nobody is discriminated on the basis of caste, religion, region and gender etc.

(iii) Above picture illustrates that if immigrant workers stop coming to cities, then life of urban people would be influenced drastically.

There will be scarcity of workers for cleaning, shops, household works, etc. In that situation, basic services in the cities would be compromised. There will be imbalance of demand and supply of labour force.

2. Study the cartoon given below and the question that follow.

(i) The main theme of the cartoon could be

(a) An adventurous journey
(b) Struggle for civil rights
(c) Citizenship
(d) Insiders Vs. Outsiders

Ans. (d) Insiders Vs. Outsiders

(ii) The bus in the cartoon can be compared to a ....

(a) village
(b) city
(c) forest
(d) mill

Ans. (b) city

(iii) Which of these rights is of particular importance for workers?

(a) Right to vote (b) Right to property
(c) Freedom of movement (d) Cultural rights

Ans. (c) Freedom of movement

(iv) Which of these can be a way to resolve the conflict between the local population and outsiders in a democratic society?

(a) Restricting the entry of outsiders
(b) Dialogue and co-operation
(c) Arrest of outsiders
(d) By paying less wages to outsiders

Ans. (b) Dialogue and co-operation

SELF ASSESSMENT TEST

Objective Type Questions

1. Which kind of rights are not involved in T.H .Marshall's concept of citizenship? **Diksha App**
   (a) Civil rights (b) Political rights
   (c) International rights (d) Social rights
2. Which part of the Indian Constitution contains the provision of citizenship? **Diksha App**
   (a) Part 1 (b) Part 4
   (c) Part 2 (d) Part 3
3. Which of the following is not the means of acquiring citizenship in India? **Diksha App**
   (a) Birth (b) Naturalisation
   (c) By descent (d) Private job

Very Short Answer Type Questions

4. "He who has the power to take part in deliberative or judicial administration of any state is said by us to be a citizen of that state". Briefly explain. **Competency Based Que**
5. What do citizens expect from the state?
6. Write the importance of slum-dwellers in a city.
7. 'France, for instance, is a country which claims to be both secular and inclusive'. Analyse this statement. **Competency Based Que**

Short Answer Type Questions

8. How is the condition of urban poor improving? Explain.
9. Why are tribals not able to enjoy full benefits of membership? Explain.
10. Explain the provisions for citizenship given in the Indian Constitution.
11. How can you participate in nation building as a good citizen?

Long Answer Type Questions

12. Examine the claims made by nation states and their reality in practice.
13. What steps are taken by Indian Constitution makers and governments to accommodate a very diverse society? **Diksha App**
14. Do we need to try and evolve a more genuinely universal identity than national citizenship? Examine.

07

CHAPTER

Nationalism is a political ideology that emphasises the interest and culture of a particular nation or group of people and promotes the idea of national unity and independence.

Nationalism

▼ **YOUR STUDY GOALS**

▼ **YOUR PRACTICE GOAL**

- Objective Type Questions (36; MCQs, A-R, Statements, Matching, Passage Based)
- Subjective Questions (12 VSAs, 9 SAs, 4 LAs, 2 Picture Based)

7.1 Introducing Nationalism

Nationalism has emerged as one of the most strongest political beliefs which has shaped history during the last two centuries. It has passed through many phases.

- In the 19th century Europe, nationalism led to unification of a large number of small kingdoms into larger-nation states. The present day Germany and Italy were formed through such unification.
- A large number of new states were also formed in Latin America.
- Nationalism accompanied and contributed to the
  - Break up of large empires such as Austro-Hungarian and Russian empires in the early 20th century.
  - Break up of the British, French, Dutch and Portuguese empires in Asia and Africa.
- It inspired nationalist struggles in India and other colonies.

Challenges to the Nationalism

- Today, in many parts of the world, nationalist are struggling with separatist movement, who threaten to divide the existing states.
- Such separatist movements have developed among
  - Quebecois in Canada
  - the Basques in Northern Spain
  - the Kurds in Turkey and Iraq
  - the Tamils in Sri Lanka

- Arab nationalism today may hope to unite Arab countries in a pan-Arab union, but separatist movements like the Basques or Kurds struggle to divide existing states.

7.2 Nation and Nationalism

- Nationalism is a powerful force in the world. But it is difficult to arrive at an agreement regarding the definition of term like **nation or nationalism.**
- It is commonly believed that nations are constituted by a group who share certain features such as descent or language, or religion or ethnicity. But in fact there is no common set of characteristics which is present in all nations. Many nations do not have a common language, religion, race or descent.

Assumptions about Nation

- A nation is to a great extent an 'imagined' community, held together by the collective beliefs, aspirations and imaginations of its members.
- It is based on certain assumptions which people make about the collective whole with which they identify.

There are some assumptions about nations

Shared Beliefs

- A nation is constituted by a belief. People as a nation refer to the collective identity and vision for the future of a group which aspires to have an independent existence.
- A nation exists when its members believe that they belong together.

History

- People who see themselves as a nation represent a sense of continuing historical identity. They feel connected to the past while also looking toward the future.
- People express the continuing identity of the nation by using collective memories, legends, historical records. For example, India has had a long and continuing history as a civilisation and this civilisational continuity and unity is the basis of the Indian nation.

Territory

- Nations identify with a particular territory.
- A shared history and living together on a particular territory over a long period of time gives people a sense of collective identity. That territory has a special significance for them and they refer to it as their homeland.
- People refer to their homeland as motherland, fatherland or holy land. For example, Jewish people refer to Palestine as their 'promised land'.
- The aspiration for a homeland has been a major cause of conflict in the world because more than one set of people may claim to the same territory.

Shared Political Ideals

- Members of a nation share common vision for the state they want to build. They support a group of values like democracy, secularism[1] and liberalism[2].
- In a democracy, it is shared commitment to a set of political values and ideals that is the most desirable basis of a political community or a nation-state. Within it, members of political community are bound by a set of obligations.
- A nation is strengthened when people recognise and accept their obligations to their fellow members.

1 **Secularism** It is a philosophical movement that separates religion from civil affairs and the state.
2 **Liberalism** It is a political and philosophical ideology to establish individual freedom, consent and equality.

Common Political Identity

- Many people believed that a shared political vision about the state is not enough to bind individuals together as a nation. Instead shared **cultural identity** such as common language or common descent can bind individuals together as a nation in a better way.
- But it is difficult to bind the nation through religion or language. There are two reasons for this
  - All the religions in the world are internally diverse.
  - Most of the societies are culturally diverse.

So, because of both these reasons, it is desirable to imagine the nation in political terms rather than cultural terms.

Quick Test 1

1. Name any two countries facing separatist movement.
2. What is the concept of homeland?
3. When a nation is strengthened?

7.3 National Self-Determination

- Nations seek the right to govern themselves and determine their future development. This is called **self-determination**. For the claim of self-determination, a nation seeks recognition and acceptance by the international community of its status as a political entity or state.
- The notion of **one culture-one state** began to gain acceptance in 19th century Europe due to the frequent demands for the formation of states based on culture.
- The idea of one culture-one state was employed while reordering state boundaries after World War I. The Treaty of Versailles established a number of small, newly independent states.
- Re-organisation of state boundaries to satisfy the demands of one culture-one state, led to mass migration of population across state boundaries along with causing communal violence.
- Even newly-created states had more than one ethnic and cultural community, which left minorities disadvantaged.
- The right to national self-determination has also been asserted by national liberation movements in Asia and Africa when they were struggling against colonial domination. Most of these movements were inspired by the goal of bringing justice, rights and prosperity to the nation.
- Today every state faces the dilemma of how to deal with self-determination movements, raising questions about its legitimacy. The solution do this, does not lie in creating new states but in making existing states more democratic and equal.

Demand for National Self-Determination in Basque

- Demand for national self-determination has been raised in different parts of the world. Here we will study about the Basque region, where the demand for self-determination has been raised.
- Basque is a hilly region in Spain. This region is recognised by the Spanish Government as an 'autonomous'[3] region within the Spanish federation.
- But the leaders of Basque nationalist movement are not satisfied and they want a separate country.
- Basque nationalists say that their culture is very different from Spanish culture. They have their own language and also the hilly topography of this region makes it geographically distinct from the rest of the spain.
- The Spanish rulers tried to abolish their unique identity but the leaders of this movement raised their demand for a separate country.

3 Autonomous It refers to the state or condition of being self-governing, independent, and having the freedom to make decisions without external control or influence.

Nationalism and Pluralism

Nationalism and **Pluralism**[4] both are political ideologies. Nationalism emphasises loyalty for the nation and pluralism allows people to live together in a society while maintaining their own traditions.

- Many democratic nations today have introduced some measures for recognising and protecting the identity of the communities of cultural minorities, which are living in their territory.
- For example, the Indian Constitution has an elaborated set of provisions for the protection of the rights and identity of the religious, linguistics and the cultural minorities.
- In some countries, minorities also have the right to represent themselves as a group in legislative bodies and other institutions of the state.
- But despite recognition and protection, some groups may continue to demand separate statehood and this seems paradoxical (contradictory) in the present globalising world.
- It is impossible to grant statehood to every group, who sees themselves as a distinct cultural group.
- Therefore, the world we live in is one that is deeply conscious of the importance of giving recognition to identities.
- There are many struggles for the recognition of identities using the language of nationalism.
- Identity should not be allowed to create divisions.
- A person, as long as he can express his identities, has no need to make claims to the state for political recognition and concessions for any one identity.

Tagore's Critique of Nationalism

- Tagore asserted the independence of India from British rule.
- He made a distinction between opposing western imperialism and rejecting western civilisation. He supported that Indians should be proud of their culture, but they should not resist learning freely and profitably from abroad.
- He was very critical of narrow expressions of nationalism.
- Tagore feared that rejecting the west in favour of Indian tradition will limit Indians and could easily turn into hostility to other influences from abroad.

Quick Test 2

1. When did the notion of one culture-one state begin to gain acceptability in Europe?
2. Which region of Spain demanded for a separate country?
3. What do you understand by the term pluralism?
4. What was the fear of Tagore about nationalism?

4 **Pluralism** It is a political philosophy that allows people from different backgrounds, beliefs and life styles to co-exists in a society.

Mind Map

1 Introduction to Nationalism

- Nationalism means loyalty and devotion to a nation.
- **For example:** Patriotism, sacrifice for country.

Phases of Nationalism

- 19th Century unification of large number of small kingdoms.
- New nations were formed in Latin America.
- Nationalism resulted in breakup of Austro-Hungarian and Russian empire in 20th century.
- Nationalist struggle started in India and other countries.

2 Challenges to the Nationalism

- Struggles faced by separatist. (e.g. The Tamils in Sri-Lanka, the Kurds in Turkey and Iraq.
- Separatist movements like, Basques struggle to divide Arab nationalism.

3 Nation and Nationalism

- Nationalism is a powerful force in the world.
- Nations are constituted by a group who share certain features like descent or language.
- Many nations do not have a common language, religion, race or descent.

Assumption about Nation

- **Shared Belief** A nation is constituted by a belief identity.
- **Historical Identity** People who see themselves as a nation represent a sense of continuing historical identity.
- **Territory** Nations identify themselves with a particular territory and people refer it as homeland or mother land.
- **Shared Political Ideals** Members of a nation share common vision for the state they want to build.
- **Common Political Identity** Instead people shared cultural identity such as a common language or common decent can bind individuals together as a nation in a better way.

NATIONALISM

4 Nation Self-Determination

- A process where individual within a political community determine their own political institutions based on shared identities, common interests etc.
- The idea of one culture-one state was employed after World War I.
- The Treaty of Versailles established a number of small, and new independent states.
- The right to national self-determination has also been asserted by national liberation movements.
- Every state faces the dilemma of how to deal with self-determination movements.

5 Nationalism and Pluralism

- **Nationalism** Emphasises loyalty for the nation.
- **Pluralism** Allows people to line together in a society while maintaining their own traditions.

6 Tagore's Critique of Nationalism

- Tagore asserted the independence of India from British rule.
- He supported that Indians should be proud of their culture.
- He was very critical of narrow expressions of nationalism.
- Tagore feared that rejecting the west in favour of Indian tradition will limit Indians.

Rise of Nationalism in India

The Republic Day Parade in New Delhi is a prominent symbol of Nationalism

NCERT Folder

1. How is a nation different from other forms of collective belonging?

Ans. A nation is not any casual collection of people. It is different from other groups or communities found in human society and different from the family, which is based on face to face relationship with members having direct personal knowledge of the identity and character of others. It is also different from tribes, clans and other kinship groups in which ties of marriage or descent link them to each other.

As a member of a nation, we may never come face to face with most of our fellow nationals, nor need we share, ties of descent, language, religion or ethnicity with them.

Nation to a great extent is an 'imagined community' held together by the collective beliefs, aspirations and imaginations of its members. It is based on certain assumptions like shared beliefs, common history, common territory, shared political ideals and common political identity.

2. What do you understand by the right to national self-determination? How has this idea resulted in both formation of and challenges to nation-states?

Ans. National self-determination is when people as a whole try to gain, or keep the power to control their own affairs.

Self-determination means right to govern oneself. Nations always seek to govern themselves. It is worthy to mention that a nation get international acceptance and recognition. Because of it, nations lay claim to self government so that they may protect their culture and beliefs of their own people.

Aims of right to national self-determination are

- Bringing justice, liberty and equality.
- To protect the collective interest and culture of people.
- Prosperity to nation.
- Political recognition.
- Right to govern themselves.

Challenges of national self-determination are

- It is difficult to provide each cultural group as a separate statehood status.
- Such struggles for the demand of self-determination by different groups led to increased number of violence, mass-migration and riots.

Since, a cultural group gets right to govern themselves and establish their statehood, people from other cultural groups or minority groups start feeling marginalised and discriminated. This paradoxal situation leads to violence and backlash.

3. "We have seen that nationalism can unite people as well as divide them, liberate them as well generate bitterness and conflict". Illustrate your answer with examples.

Ans. The idea of nationalism can liberate people from the bond of various smaller groups to a wider and common group of nation where they share common interests and goals.

Nationalism is like a glue which unites people into a bond on the basis of same territory, shared beliefs, common history, shared political ideals, common political identity and aspirations.

The demand for a separate nation-state by the people of different lingual or cultural group can also be divided. Since, demands for separate nation-state by smaller groups often leads to conflict and it can generate bitterness and conflict.

4. Neither decent, nor language, nor religion or ethnicity can claim to be common factor in nationalisms all over the world. Comment.

Ans. A nation is a large group of collective people with shared culture, traditions, history usually language and ethnicity. But, this is the definition of nation in narrow terms. There is infact no common set of characteristics which present in all nations.

For example, in Canada, English speaking and French speaking people live together. India also shows lots of diversity based on language, culture, traditions and ethnicity.

A nation is more impersonal, abstract and openly political than an ethnic group. The term 'nation' emphasises the physical dimensions and boundaries of a geographical area and a self-governing legal and political entity. Therefore, neither decent, nor language, nor religion or ethnicity can claim to be common factor in nationalisms all over the world.

5. Illustrate with suitable example the factors that lead to the emergence of nationalist feelings.

Ans. The factors that lead to the emergence of nationalist feelings are given as follows

Shared (Common) Beliefs It is a common belief of people for their nation and give rise to extremely strong feeling of devotion. It is refer to collective identity and independent political existence. In a nation, people have common will to live together.

History People in a nation, share common historical identity by focusing on collective memories, legends, historical records. As in India, ancient civilisation and cultural heritage shows its grand history and give the feeling of oneness.

Territory People living in a particular region of the land for a long period share common history and culture. This habitated territory is termed as homeland for them.

Shared Political Ideals The real sense of oneness is felt by the people of a nation when they share collective aspiration to have an independent political existence. It is a commitment to a set of political values and principles such as democracy, secularism and liberalism.

Common Political Identity A common political identity is necessary for the real sense of collective identity.

6. How is a democracy more effective than authoritarian governments in dealing with conflicting nationalist aspirations?

Ans. A democratic government is more effective than an authoritarian government, as it respects the feeling and opinion of people and provides opportunity and right to every cultural group to their future development.

All cultural groups as well as those who are in minority have the opportunity to represent their people at the highest levels of decision making i.e. state legislature in a democratic system of government.

Thus, it provides a platform for all groups to express their aspirations. While, an authoritarian government will create an oppressive and authoritative society in which minority groups cannot survive. The dominance of the majority gives rise to nationalist aspirations among other groups in such situations.

Therefore, a democratic government can solve the conflicting nationalist aspirations by taking decisions through consensus that benefit all groups which are included in the democratic system, as it respects the rights and cultural identity of every group.

7. What do you think are the limitations of nationalism?

Ans. The limitations of nationalism can be pointed as follows

- Most nationalist ideals are representative of the goals of a single cultural group. Thus, they fail to incorporate the broader vision of inclusiveness.
- Since it is not possible for every cultural group to create its own nation-state, therefore every nation-state has more than one cultural group.
- The different cultural groups often get involved in conflicts due to their separate nationalist aspirations based upon a desire for homogenous identity.
- The role of nationalism in a globalised world is yet to be completely evaluated, as nationalist tendencies acquire a different meaning in an interconnected world.

Exam Pattern Questions

Objective Type Questions

Multiple Choice Questions (MCQs)

1. .... is defined as loyalty and devotion of the people to their nation.

(a) Nationalism (b) Secularism
(c) Citizenship (d) Development

2. The republic day in Delhi is a striking symbol of Indian ....

(a) secularism (b) pluralism
(c) liberalism (d) nationalism

3. Which of the following statements is correct about nationalism?

(a) Nationalism has always promoted war and destruction.
(b) Nationalism has been a factor in the break up of empires and states.
(c) Nationalism emerged in a single phase.
(d) Nationalism is about hating neighbouring countries.

4. Which of the following is an example of the unification process influenced by nationalism?

(a) Fomation of Canada (b) Partition of India
(c) Formation of Germany and Italy
(d) Creation of the United Nations

5. The present-day German and Italian states were formed through such a process of ....

(a) unification (b) consolidation
(c) Both (a) and (b) (d) disintegration

6. Which among the following empire ruled in Europe in the early 20th Century?

(a) Austro-Hungarian (b) British
(c) Dutch (d) Portuguese

7. Which of the following activities is not a true expression of nationalism? **Diksha App**

(a) Taking part in Republic Day parade
(b) Taking part with other fellow citizens in freedom struggle
(c) Taking part in separatist movements to develop new nation states
(d) Deny to do military service at the time of external attack

8. Identify the continents whose countries took part in National Liberation movements to assert their right to national self determination against colonial domination. **Competency Based Que; Diksha App**

(a) Africa and Asia
(b) Asia and Europe
(c) North America and South America
(d) Australia and New Zealand

9. Indian struggle for freedom to establish nation-states and independent foreign control was also the result of ....

(a) Irwin Pact (b) nationalism
(c) Shimla Conference (d) Cabinet Mission

10. Which of the following separatist movement has not taken place/ occurred in the country mentioned after it? Pick the odd one out. **Diksha App**

(a) Quebecois in Canada (b) Kurds in Iraq
(c) Kurds in Turkey (d) Tamils in India

11. What do you understand by the term nation?

(a) Sovereignty (b) Government
(c) Population (d) Imagined Community

12. A country is largely a.........., kept together by the members' shared values, hopes and imaginations.

(a) unimagined society (b) imagined society
(c) disguised society (d) sovereign society

13. What makes a citizen to be nationalist?

(a) To cast a vote and to pay taxes on time
(b) To respect the laws of the country
(c) To feel pride in belongingness with country
(d) All of the above

14. Select the wrong statement.

(a) Nationalism has emerged as one of the most convincing political creeds in the last two centuries, helping to form history.
(b) Nationalist struggles have contributed to the drawing and redrawing of the boundaries of states and empires.
(c) Today's Arab nationalism aspires to unite Arab countries in a pan-Arab union, but nationalist movements such as the Basques and Kurds fight to keep established states divided.
(d) A nation is only constituted by belief. Nations are not like mountains, rivers or buildings which we can see and feel.

15. What do nations use to create a sense of identity?

(a) Shared beliefs and aspirations
(b) Common physical traits
(c) Single dominant religion
(d) Exclusive economic interests

16. Who among the following has written the book 'The Discovery of India'?

(a) Dr. B.R. Ambedkar
(b) Jawaharlal Nehru
(c) S. Radhakrishnan
(d) V.P. Singh

17. .... play an important role in creating a sense of oneness, it is a shared vision of the future and the collective aspiration to have an independent political existence that distinguishes groups from nations.

(a) Political belief and ideals
(b) Fraternity and shared beliefs
(c) Territory and shared historical identity
(d) Integrity and dignity

18. Which of the following is not a true assumption made by people about the nation? **Diksha App**

(a) People having common shared beliefs
(b) People having common historical background
(c) People sharing common anti civilian intentions
(d) People sharing a particular territory

19. Which of the following promotes the feeling of nationalism?

(a) Common motherland and culture
(b) Common language
(c) Common religion
(d) All of the above

20. Which of the following treaty led to the formation of number of small states?

(a) Treaty of Versailles
(b) Treaty of Tordesillas
(c) The Peace of Westphalia
(d) The Treaty of Paris

21. Which of the following statement(s) is/are correct about the merits of self-determination?

(a) They can determine their own future developments.
(b) They get recognition as distinct political entity.
(c) They can protect their own cultural group.
(d) All of the above

22. Which of the following is not a difference between state and nation?

(a) Sovereignty is essential for a nation and not for a state.
(b) Idea of oneness is essential for the nation not for the state.
(c) State has four essential elements but nation has none.
(d) Sovereignty is essential for a state and not for a nation.

23. **Consider the following statement(s) is/are correct about the need to make nations more democratic and inclusive.** CBQ

(a) We love democracy.
(b) It will lead to financial inclusion.
(c) Democracy will give equal rights to all citizens whether majority or minority.
(d) It will lead to global citizenship.

24. **Which of the following statements is correct?**

I. The process of redrawing state boundaries ended in 1950s.
II. Today, in many parts of the world we witness nationalist struggles that threaten to divide existing states.
III. Some separatist groups in India use the language of nationalism. Competency Based Que

Choose the correct option.

(a) I and II (b) Only II
(c) II and III (d) I and III

25. **Which problem would arise if every distinct cultural group is given the grant of an independent state?** Diksha App

(a) Every group will become satisfied.
(b) Every group will get a distinct political identity.
(c) It would lead to a number of small economically and politically unstable states.
(d) Each group will become more tolerant.

26. **Match List I with List II and choose the correct option.**

List I	List II
A. India	1. French speaking population
B. Cananda	2. Spain
C. Palestine	3. Large number of languages
D. Basque	4. Homeland of Jews

Codes

	A	B	C	D		A	B	C	D
(a)	3	1	4	2	(b)	4	3	2	1
(c)	3	4	1	2	(d)	4	1	2	3

27. **Consider the following statements.** Competency Based Que

Statement I Nationalism is the spirit or aspirations of one's own country.

Statement II Nationalism unites as well as divides people.

In the light of above statements, choose the correct answer from the options given below.

(a) Both Statement I and Statement II are true.
(b) Both Statement I and Statement II are false.
(c) Statement I is true, but Statement II is false.
(d) Statement I is false, but Statement II is true.

Assertion-Reason Questions

Directions (Q. Nos. 28-32) In the questions given below, there are two statements marked as Assertion (A) and Reason (R).
Read the statements and choose the correct option.

Codes

(a) Both A and R are true and R is the correct explanation of A.
(b) Both A and R are true, but R is not the correct explanation of A.
(c) A is true, but R is false.
(d) A is false, but R is true.

28. **Assertion** (A) Nationalism is deeply associated with patriotism, national flags, sacrificing for the country.

Reason (R) The concept of nationalism emerged through the series of incidences took place in the world history.

29. **Assertion** (A) India does not share a common religion and linguistic identity.

Reason (R) India has diverse religions and, in these religions, also, there are different sects.

30. **Assertion** (A) In India, ancient civilisation and cultural heritage shows its grand history and give the feeling of oneness.

Reason (R) This idea of oneness reflects in the book 'The Discovery of India' which was written by Motilal Nehru.

31. **Assertion** (A) In the 19th century Europe, demand of one culture one state got acceptance and re-organisation of state boundaries took place after World War II.

Reason (R) A number of small states were formed by the Treaty of Versailles.

32. **Assertion** (A) Promoting pluralism is necessary in a country like India.

Reason (R) Nationalism can divide people and create so many problems.

Passage Based Questions

33. **Read the given passage and answer the following questions.**

Nations identify with a particular territory. Sharing a common past and living together on a particular territory over a long period of time gives people a sense of their collective identity. It helps them to imagine themselves as one people. It is therefore not surprising that people who see themselves as a nation speak of a homeland. The territory they occupied and the land on which they lived has a special significance for them, and they claim it as their own. Nations however characterise the homeland in different ways, for instance as motherland, fatherland or holy land. The Jewish people for instance, in spite of being dispersed and scattered in different parts of the world always claimed that their original homeland was in Palestine, the 'promised land'.

(i) What gives people a sense of collective identity as a nation?

(a) Following the same religion
(b) Sharing a common past and living together on a territory for a long time
(c) Speaking the same language
(d) Having the same political leader

(ii) What is the Jewish term for their original homeland?

(a) Holy land (b) Father land
(c) Promised land (d) Land of faith

(iii) Why is the homeland significant to a nation?

34. Read the given passage and answer the following questions.

Many people believe that a shared political vision about the state and society we wish to create is not enough to bind individuals together as a nation. They seek instead a shared cultural identity, such as a common language, or common descent. There is no doubt that speaking the same language makes it easier for us to communicate with each other and sharing the same religion gives us a set of common beliefs and social practices. Observing the same festivals, seeking the same holidays and holding the same symbols can bring people together, but it can also pose a threat to the values that we cherish in a democracy.

(i) Which of the following statements is correct?

(a) If the state declares an official religion, it will solve many problems.
(b) All religions are internally uniform.
(c) If one culture is promoted, people will feel more devotion towards the nation.
(d) All religions are internally diverse.

(ii) Which of these can bind individuals in a democratic nation?

(a) Religion (b) Festivals
(c) Values like liberty, equality, justice etc.
(d) Pride in the ancient history of the nation

(iii) Why does religion cannot bind individuals together as a nation? Explain.

35. Read the given passage and answer the following questions.

The world we live in is one that is deeply conscious of the importance of giving recognition to identities. Today we witness many struggles for the recognition of group identities, many of which employ the language of nationalism. While we need to acknowledge the claims of identity, we should be careful not to allow identity claims to lead to divisions and violence in the society. We need to remember that each person has many identities. For instance, a person may have identities based on gender, caste, religion, language or region and may be proud of all of them. So long as each person feels that he/she can freely express the different dimensions of his/her personality, they may not feel the need to make claims on the state for political recognition and concessions for any one identity.

(i) Which of the following is true regarding grant of an independent state to every district cultural group?

(a) Every state will become economically prosperous.
(b) It would make those states economically and politically unstable.
(c) Every such state will become more tolerant towards different cultures.
(d) It would lead to a feeling of fraternity among those states.

(ii) Which of the following is an example of pluralism?

(a) Separate colonies for minorities
(b) Imposition of one language for all
(c) Promoting regional languages and literature
(d) Declaration of state religion

(iii) The right to national .... was often understood to include the right to independent statehood for nationalities.

(a) nationalism (b) multi-culturalism
(c) self-determination (d) pluralism

(iv) Which of the following are the obstacles in the path of nationalism?

(a) Religious differences (b) Language differences
(c) regionalism and racism (d) All of these

36. Read the given passage and answer the following questions.

Once we abandon the idea of one-culture-one-state, it becomes necessary to consider ways by which different cultures and communities can survive and flourish within a country. It is in pursuit of this goal that many democratic societies today have introduced measures for recognising and protecting the identity of cultural minority communities living within their territory. The Indian Constitution has an elaborate set of provisions for the protection of religious, linguistic and cultural minorities.

(i) What becomes necessary once the idea of one-culture-one-state is abandoned?

(a) Enforcing uniform cultural practices
(b) Finding ways for different cultures to coexist and flourish
(c) Ignoring cultural differences
(d) Promoting one culture over others

(ii) What does the Indian Constitution do for religious, linguistic and cultural minorities?

(a) It ignores them
(b) It restricts their rights
(c) It provides provisions to protect them
(d) It enforces their assimilation into the majority culture.

(iii) What measures have been taken in many democratic societies to protect cultural minorities?

Answers

1. (a) Nationalism
2. (d) nationalism
3. (b) Nationalism has been a factor in the break up of empires and states.
4. (c) Formation of Germany and Italy.
5. (c) Both (a) and (b)
6. (a) Austro-Hungarian
7. (d) Deny to do military service at the time of external attack
8. (a) Africa and Asia
9. (b) nationalism
10. (d) Tamils in India
11. (d) Imagined Community
12. (b) imagined society
13. (d) All of the above
14. (d) A nation is only constituted by belief. Nations are not like mountains, rivers or buildings which we can see and feel.
15. (a) Shared beliefs and aspirations
16. (b) Jawaharlal Nehru
17. (c) Territory and shared historical identity
18. (c) People sharing common anti civilian intentions
19. (d) All of the above
20. (a) Treaty of Versailles
21. (d) All of the above
22. (a) Sovereignty is essential for a nation and not for a state.
23. (c) Democracy will give equal rights to all citizens whether majority or minority.
24. (c) II and III
25. (c) It would lead to a number of small economically and politically unstable states.
26. (a) 3 1 4 2
27. (a) Both Statement I and Statement II are true.
28. (b) Both A and R are true, but R is not the correct explanation of A. Assertion is about the definition of Nationalism whereas Reason is about its origin.
29. (a) Both A and R are true and R is the correct explanation of A. India does not share a common religion and linguistic identity. This is because India has diverse religions and, in these religions, also, there are different sects.
30. (c) A is true, but R is false. This idea of oneness is reflected in the book 'The Discovery of India' which was written by Jawaharlal Nehru.
31. (d) A is false, but R is true. In the 19th century in Europe, demand of one culture one state got acceptance and reorganisation of state boundaries took place after World War I.
32. (a) Both A and R are true and R is the correct explanation of A. Nationalism can unite as well as divide people. So, for a diverse country like India, pluralism can help in keeping its diversity.
33. (i) (b) Sharing a common past and living together on a territory for a long time
    (ii) (c) Promised land
    (iii) A homeland is significant because it represents the territory of a nation where a people has lived and built its history. It holds cultural, emotional and symbolic value for the people. People often refer to nations as their homeland, a motherland, fatherland or holy land, highlighting its importance as the foundation of their identity and heritage.
34. (i) (d) All religions are internally diverse.
    (ii) (c) Values like liberty, equality, justice, etc.
    (iii) All religions are internally diverse. They have survived and evolved through a dialogue within the community. As a result there exists a number of sects in each religion who differ significantly in their interpretation of the religious texts and norms. So, religion cannot bind individuals together as a nation.
35. (i) (b) It would make those states economically and politically unstable.
    (ii) (c) Promoting regional languages and literature.
    (iii) (c) self-determination
    (iv) (d) All of these
36. (i) (b) Finding ways for different cultures to coexist and flourish
    (ii) (c) It provides provisions to protect them
    (iii) Many democratic societies have introduced laws, policies and constitutional provisions to protect the identity of cultural minorities. These measures include granting rights to preserve their language, religion and cultural practices.

    For example, some countries provide recognition to their language, ensure representation in government and create spaces where minority communities can maintain their traditions.

Subjective Questions

Very Short Answer Type Questions

1. Write two merits of nationalism.

Ans. (i) Nationalism makes an individual feel that the nation is above all and raises the standard of living and unity among its citizens.

(ii) Nationalism creates a sense to make a country free from colonial rule and from those who rule over the nation from outside.

2. What are the two demerits of nationalism?

Ans. The two demerits of nationalism are as follows

(i) Nationalism based on one nation one state concept may lead to separatist struggles.

(ii) It creates a feeling of hatred for other nation which is injurious for world peace in this time of globalisation.

3. Name some groups which are involved in the separatist movements around the world.

Ans. Separatist movements have developed among the Quebecois in Canada, the Basques in Northern Spain, the Kurds in Turkey and Iraq, and the Tamils in Sri Lanka, etc.

4. How is a nation different from a family?

Ans. A family is based on face-to-face relationships, with each member having direct personal knowledge of the identity and character of others.

But a member of a nation may never come face-to-face with most fellow nationals. He does not have personal knowledge of the identity and character of others.

5. What constitutes a nation?

Ans. A nation constitutes of shared beliefs, common history, particular territory, shared political ideas and common political identity.

6. Briefly explain the meaning of the term 'imagined community' in the context of nationalism?

Ans. The term 'imagined community' refers to the idea that nations are not formed by direct personal relationships but by shared beliefs, aspirations and a sense of belonging. People feel connected as members of a nation even though they may never meet or know most of their fellow citizens.

7. How does the common history play a vital role in nation building?

Ans. People in a nation share common historical identity by focusing on collective memories, legends and historical records.

As in India, ancient civilisation and cultural heritage shows its grand history and give the feeling of oneness and thus, help in nation building.

8. What is the homeland or motherland for the people of a nation?

Ans. People who live together on a particular territory over a long period make sense of their collective identity. It has special significance to them, so, they claim it as their homeland or motherland.

9. How people were affected by the re-organisation of state boundaries based on 'one culture-one state'?

Ans. Re-organisation of state boundaries to satisfy the demands of 'one culture-one state', led to mass migration of population across state boundaries.

Millions of people as a consequence were displaced from their homes and expelled from the land which had been their home for generations. Many others became victims of communal violence.

10. Mention two differences between nationalism and pluralism.

Ans. Difference between nationalism and pluralism are as follows

Nationalism	Pluralism
Nationalism seeks to preserve the nation's culture and often involves a sense of pride in nation's achievements.	Pluralism is the recognition and affirmation of diversity to permit peaceful co-existence of different cultures/ethnicities within a land.
Nationalism accords a lot of importance to a homogenous setup where love for one's state should come before everything else.	Pluralists celebrate diversity and feel that the authority of state should be limited.

11. What was Rabindranath Tagore's critique of nationalism?

Ans. Rabindranath Tagore believed that patriotism should not overshadow humanity. Although he supported India's independence but he was very critical of narrow expressions of nationalism that excluded other cultures. He advocated learning from Western civilisation while preserving Indian traditions, emphasising the value of human relationships over rigid patriotism.

12. Due to heavy floods in Pakistan, thousands of people got displaced. The Indian government provided relief measures and monetary help. Some people opposed this move and protested against the government, accusing the government of compromising with nationalism. Is the Indian government's help to Pakistan against nationalism? Give your opinion. Competency Based Que

Ans. No, the Indian government's help to Pakistan is not against nationalism. As per humanity, every nation should help other nations during the time of crisis. Nationalism includes devotion towards one's own nation but not hatred against others.

Besides this, helping people of other nations increases the respect of one's own nation among people around the world.

Short Answer Type Questions

1. 'It has been a factor in the break up of empires and states'. Explain the statement. Competency Based Que

Ans. The given statement refers to nationalism. Nationalism has been a factor in the break up of empires and states.

It accompanied and contributed to the break up of large empires such as the Austro-Hungarian and Russian empires in the early 20th century in Europe as well as the break-up of the British, French, Dutch and Portuguese empires in Asia and Africa.

The struggle for freedom from colonial rule by India and other former colonies were nationalist struggles, inspired by the desire to establish nation-states which would be independent of foreign control.

2. Explain the concept of nationalism and its impact on history.

Ans. Nationalism is a political and social ideology where people feel a sense of unity and belonging to their nation. It is based on shared history, culture, language or aspirations. Nationalism has had both positive and negative impacts on history, which are given below

Positive Impacts

- Nationalism helped to unify small states into larger nations, such as Germany and Italy in the 19th century.
- It inspired freedom movements in colonies, like India's struggle for independence from British rule.
- It fostered a sense of identity and pride among citizens of a nation.

Negative Impacts

- Nationalism has also divided countries, leading to conflicts and wars. For example, it has contributed to the breakup of empires like the Austro-Hungarian empire.
- Separatist movements, such as those by the Basques in Spain or the Kurds in Turkey, show how nationalism can lead to divisions.

Thus, nationalism is a powerful force, which helps in shaping both unity and conflict around the world.

3. 'But there is in fact no common set of characteristics which is present in all nations'. Comment on this statement. Competency Based Que

Ans. It is commonly believed that nations are constituted by a group who share certain features such as descent, or language or religion or ethnicity. But, no common set of characteristics is present in all nations.

For example, many nations do not have a common language. Canada includes English speaking as well as French speaking peoples. India also has a large number of languages which are spoken in different regions and by different communities.

Similarly religion also cannot unite individuals because people of all religions live in many nations. People have different descent. So, nations do not have common set of characteristics.

4. Discuss the role of shared beliefs and history in building a nation.

Ans. Shared beliefs and history are essential for building a nation as they create a sense of unity and identity among its people.

Shared Beliefs Nations exist because people believe they are part of a collective group. These beliefs can include political ideals like democracy, secularism and freedom. For example, the Indian Constitution emphasises equality and liberty, which binds its citizens together.

Shared History Nations often draw upon historical events and collective memories to create a sense of identity. In India, nationalists referred to its ancient civilisation and cultural achievements to show its long history and unity.

5. What are the four differences between the state and a nation? Diksha App

Ans. A state has four essential elements: population, territory, government and sovereignty.

(i) A nation is an association organised through cultural and spiritual feelings, and it comes into existence with the consciousness of uniting the people into oneness either through common language or cultural conventions etc. But a state has a fixed territory where a nation is connected with the feelings of unity.

(ii) The idea of oneness or unity is essential for a nation only, but it is not essential for a state, which should be politically organised.

(iii) A state enjoys sovereignty as it is an essential element where a nation attempts at attaining freedom and gets sovereignty to become a state.

6. Provide the merits and demerits of national self-determination.

Ans. Merits of national self-determination are

- It maintains that political independence would provide dignity and recognition to the colonised people.
- It helps them to protect the collective interests of their people.
- Most national self-determination movements were inspired by the goal of bringing justice and rights and prosperity to the nation.

Demerits of national self-determination are

- It is difficult to provide each cultural group a separate statehood status.
- Such struggles for the demand of self-determination by different groups led to increasing amount of violence, mass-migration and riots.

Since, a cultural group gets right to govern themselves and establish their statehood, people from other cultural groups or minority groups start feeling marginalised and discriminated. This paradoxal situation leads to violence and backlash.

7. Why is pluralism relevant in dealing with conflicts in the present world? Express your opinion.

Competency Based Que

Ans. Pluralism is very relevant in dealing with conflicts in the present world. Pluralism refers to the idea that people live together as a nation despite their differences like race, religion, descent, ethnicity, etc.

At present, the world is witnessing separatist movements in many countries like Canada, Sri Lanka, etc. Creation of a new state for every group that feels itself different is impossible.

Pluralism can act as a path saver. Many democratic countries have introduced measures for cultural minority communities. Minority groups are getting rights and protection from the state.

In these ways, minorities will not feel alienated. This will resolve and avoid many conflicts.

8. How creation of new states on the basis of one culture-one state not helpful?

Ans. Re-organisation of state boundaries to satisfy the demands of one culture-one state, led to many problems such as

(i) The mass migration of population across state boundaries. Millions of people as a consequence were displaced from their homes and expelled from the land which had been their home for generations. Many others became victims of communal violence.

(ii) Besides this, it was not possible to ensure that newly created states contained only one ethnic community living within its boundaries.

Those communities, which were often small in number and constituted a minority within the state were often disadvantaged.

Hence, the problem of accommodating minorities as equal citizens remains unsolved.

9. Discuss the implications of the 'one culture-one state' principle. Why is it difficult to implement?

Ans. The 'one culture-one state' principle presumes that each cultural group should have its own independent state. While this idea aims to preserve and promote cultural identities, its implementation has proven to be highly problematic.

Most states are culturally diverse with multiple ethnic, linguistic and religious groups co-existing within their boundaries. Creating states based solely on cultural lines can lead to the displacement of minorities. For example, The Treaty of Versailles aimed to align state boundaries with cultural groups, resulting in mass-migrations and communal violence.

Complete cultural purity within state boundaries is impossible. Modern nation-states are inherently multicultural and attempts to enforce a singular cultural identity often lead to the marginalisation of minority communities. This can foster social inequalities.

Thus, the 'one culture-one state' principle aims to respect different cultures but its implementation can lead to significant social and political challenges.

Long Answer Type Questions

1. Examine the importance of territory as an assumption about nation.

Ans. Nations identify with a particular territory. It shares a common past and living together on a particular territory over a long period of time which gives people a sense of their collective identity.

- It helps them to imagine themselves as one people. It is therefore not surprising that people who see themselves as a nation speak of a homeland.
- The territory they occupied and the land on which they have lived has a special significance for them, and they claim it as their own.
- Nations however characterise the homeland in different ways, for instance as motherland, fatherland, holy land.

- The Jewish people for instance, in spite of being dispersed and scattered in different parts of the world always claimed that their original homeland was in Palestine, the 'promised land'.
- The Indian nation identifies with the rivers, mountains and regions of the Indian subcontinent.

However, since more than one set of people may lay claim to the same territory, the aspiration for a homeland has been a major cause of conflict in the world.

2. Why is it desirable to imagine the nation in political rather than cultural terms? Explain.

Ans. It is desirable to imagine a nation in political terms rather than cultural terms because

- It can ensure that all members of a nation are treated equally.
- A nation in political terms helps to protect democratic values by exphasising loyalty to act of values enshrined in the Constitution, rather than to a particular religion, race or language.

But imposing a single religious or linguistic identity as a condition for belonging to a particular state would necessarily exclude some groups. It might restrict the religious liberty of the excluded group or disadvantage those who do not speak the national language.

Either way, the ideal that we cherish most in democracy —namely, equal treatment and liberty for all—would be severely limited.

For both of these reasons, it is desirable to imagine the nation in political rather than cultural terms.

3. Discuss about national self-determination with examples.

Ans. National self-determination is when people as a whole try to gain, or keep the power to control their own affairs. Self-determination means right to govern oneself. Nations always seek to govern themselves.

It is worthy to mention that a nation get international acceptance and recognition. Because of it, nations lay claim to self government so that they may protect their culture and beliefs of their own people.

Demand for Self-Determination

- In the 19th century in Europe, demand of one culture one state got acceptance and reorganisation of state boundaries took place after World War I.
- A number of small states formed by the Treaty of Versailles. India also carried out long independence movement to claim right to self-determination.
- Such type of movements were also took place in other parts of Asia and Africa when they were struggling against colonial domination.
- Even today, there are groups who are fighting for separate statehood and self-determination. For example, Quebecois in Canada, Basque in Spain, Tamilians in Sri Lanka, etc.

4. Analyse the case of the Basque Nationalist Movement. What are their demands and how has the Spanish government responded?

Ans. The Basque Nationalist Movement in Spain is a significant example of a regional group seeking self-determination based on distinct cultural and historical identity.

- The Basque people, residing in a hilly and prosperous region in northern Spain, have long asserted their unique identity, which includes their own language, customs and historical governance systems.
- The Basque Nationalist Movement demands full independence from Spain, arguing that their distinct culture and language merit the formation of a separate state. They believe that despite the autonomy granted to the Basque region, it does not fully protect or promote their unique identity.
- Historically, the Spanish government's efforts to centralise control, particularly under the dictatorship of Francisco Franco, who banned the Basque language and suppressed their autonomy, have fueled these demands.
- In response, the Spanish government has recognised the Basque region as an autonomous community within Spain, granting it considerable self-governance. However, Basque nationalists argue that this autonomy is insufficient and they continue to demand for complete independence.

Thus, the Basque nationalist movement underscores the complexities of self-determination within a modern state. While autonomy has been granted, the demand for full independence highlights the ongoing tension between regional identities and national unity.

Picture Based Questions

1. Observe the picture given below and answer the following questions.

"Patriotism cannot be our final spiritual shelter; my refuge is humanity. I will not buy glass for the price of diamonds, and I will never allow patriotism to triumph over humanity as long as I live".

(i) What does Tagore's quote 'I will not buy glass for the price of diamonds' imply about his view of patriotism?

(a) Patriotism is more valuable than humanity
(b) Patriotism is a mere illusion compared to the deeper value of humanity
(c) Patriotism should be pursued above all else
(d) Patriotism is of equal value to humanity

Ans. (b) Patriotism is a mere illusion compared to the deeper value of humanity.

(ii) What aspect of British colonial administration did Tagore criticize?

(a) Lack of economic development
(b) The present of dignity in human relationships
(c) The absence of dignity in human relationships
(d) The promotion of western civilisation

Ans. (c) The absence of dignity in human relationships

(iii) What was the distinction Tagore made between opposing Western imperialism and rejecting Western civilisation?

(a) Western civilisation should be fully embraced
(b) Opposing imperialism doesn't mean rejecting all aspects of Western civilisation
(c) India should abandon both imperialism and Western civilisation
(d) Western civilisation must be entirely rejected

Ans. (b) Opposing imperialism doesn't mean rejecting all aspects of Western civilisation.

(iv) How did Tagore feel about Indians learning from abroad?

(a) Indians should reject all foreign influences.
(b) Indians should learn freely and profitably from abroad while remaining rooted in their culture.
(c) Indians should only focus on Indian traditions.
(d) Indians should adopt Western civilisation entirely.

Ans. (b) Indians should learn freely and profitably from abroad while remaining rooted in their culture.

2. Study the cartoon given below and answer the following question.

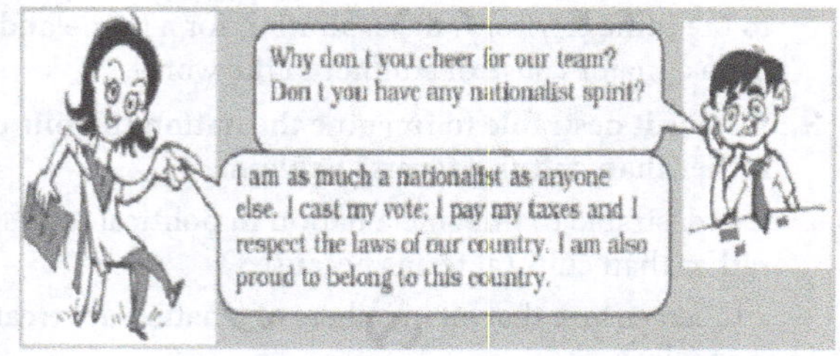

(i) What are the views of the boy in the cartoon show?

(ii) How can a person show nationalism in times of war?

(iii) Can we consider the girl in the cartoon nationalist? Justify your answer.

Ans. (i) The views of the boy in the cartoon show very narrow view of nationalism.

(ii) In times of natural disaster, a person can show nationalism by joining army. He can also help family members of soldiers and motivate them.

(iii) Yes, the girl in the cartoon can be considered nationalist. She is paying taxes and respecting the laws of the country. Tax money collected by the government is used for development works and running schemes for poor citizens. A nation needs law abiding citizens. She is also fulfilling her responsibilities by casting a vote.

SELF ASSESSMENT TEST

Multiple Choice Questions

1. Which of the following traits cannot be essentially called nationalism? **Diksha App**
   (a) Paying taxes in time
   (b) Casting your vote
   (c) Respecting the laws of the country
   (d) Love for money more than country
2. The .... is a feeling of sentiment for having an independent nation.
   (a) nationalism (b) self-determination
   (c) liberalism (d) nation
3. Which type of minorities are not protected by the provisions of Indian Constitution? **Diksha App**
   (a) Linguistic minorities (b) Educational minorities
   (c) Religious minorities (d) Cultural minorities

Very Short Answer Type Questions

4. How is a nation different from tribes, clans and other kinship groups?
5. What is Basque? **Diksha App**
6. Mention two differences between pluralism and nationalism.
7. Why did Rabindranath Tagore prefer humanity over patriotism? **Diksha App**

Short Answer Type Questions

8. Examine the importance of pluralism for India. **Competency Based Que**
9. Discuss the developments in Europe and Latin America due to nationalism.
10. 'A nation is constituted by belief'. Analyse this statement. **Competency Based Que**
11. How does history help in binding individuals together as a nation?

Long Answer Type Questions

12. "Nationalist struggles have contributed to the drawing and redrawing of the boundaries of states and empires". Explain the statement. **Competency Based Que**
13. 'It has united people as well as divided them, helped to liberate them from oppressive rule as well as been the cause of conflict and bitterness and wars'. Explain this statement with examples. **Competency Based Que**
14. Discuss and analyse the positive and negative aspects of the national self-determination.

08

CHAPTER

Secularism is the separation of religion from the state and the idea that the government should treat all the citizens equally, regardless of their religion.

Secularism

▼ **YOUR STUDY GOALS**

8.1 Introduction

8.2 Secular States

8.2 Criticism of Indian Secularism

▼ **YOUR PRACTICE GOAL**

- Objective Type Questions (41 Qs; MCQs, A-R, Statements, Matching, Passage Based)
- Subjective Questions (11 VSAs, 7 SAs, 3 LAs, 1 Picture Based)

8.1 Introduction

The Constitution declares that every Indian citizen has a **right to live with freedom and dignity** in any part of the country. Yet in reality many forms of discrimination can be seen, such as

Inter-religious Domination

It refers to targeting of members of one religion due to its religious identity. For example, incidents like sikhs massacre in Delhi in 1984 reflects inter religious domination.

Intra-religious Domination

It refers to discrimination within the community of the same religion. For example, Discrimination of some sections in Hindu religion such as

- Barring Dalits from entering Hindu temples.
- Hindu women cannot enter temples in some parts of the country.

Secularism is a doctrine that opposes all such forms of inter religious and intra religious dominations. It promotes freedom within religions and equality.

8.2 Secular States

- One way of preventing religious discrimination is to work together for **mutual understanding**. Education is one way of changing the mindset of people.
- Individual examples of sharing and mutual help can also contribute towards reducing suspicion between communities.

- State can prevent the domination by any religious group in following ways
  - State must not be **theocratic**[1]. Religious institutions and state institutions must be separated. However many states which are non-theocratic continue to have a close alliance with a particular religion.
  - State need to have **no formal and legal alliance** with any religion.
  - State must be committed to principles and goals such as peace, equality, religious freedom, freedom from religious oppression, discrimination and exclusion. There should be inter-religious and intra-religious equality.

  Thus, to promote secularism, state must be separated from organised religion and its institutions.

The Western Model of Secularism

- Western model of secularism is inspired by the **American model**. In this, there is separation of religion from the state.
- It means that the state will not interfere in the affairs of religion and in the same manner, religion will not interfere in the affairs of the state.
- No state policy can favour any particular religion and also no religious classification can be the basis of any public policy.
- Similarly, the state cannot aid any religious institution. It cannot give financial support to educational institutions run by religious communities. Nor can it obstruct the activities of religious communities, as long as they are working within the limits set by the law of the land.
- In this model, religion is a **private matter** and not a matter of state policy or law.
- It interprets **freedom and equality** in an individualistic manner. There is little scope for community based rights or **minorities**[2] rights.
- Finally, this form of secularism has no place for the idea of state supported religious reform.

Kemal Ataturk's Secularism

A very different type of secularism practiced in Turkey in the first half of the 20th century CE.

- Kemal Ataturk, the founder of modern Turkey, played a key role in establishing a secular state in Turkey.
- His secularism emphasised on Westernisation.
- Ataturk's secularism involved separating religion from all aspects of 'public life, including politics, education, society and jurisprudence'.
- Ataturk changed his own name from Mustafa Kemal Pasha to Kemal Ataturk.
- He banned the traditional cap **Fez** by the Hat law.
- Western clothing was encouraged for men and women.
- Also, the Western (Gregorian) calendar replaced the traditional turkish calender.

The Indian Model of Secularism

- Indian secularism is fundamentally different from Western secularism.
- In India, there is a deep religious diversity and a culture of **inter-religious tolerance** already exists prior to the coming of Western modern ideas.
- Indian secularism does not focus only on **religion-state separation** and the idea of **inter-religious equality** is also important in this model.

---

1 **Theocratic** It refers to a state directly run by the head of any particular religion.

2 **Minorities** A culturally, ethnically or racially distinct group that co-exists in society with other groups but it is sub-ordinate to more diminant group.

- Indian model of secularism equally focus on inter-religious and intra-religious dominations. It opposes the oppressions of minorities like Dalits and women within Hinduism.
- It protects from possible threats that a majority community might pose to the rights of the minority religious communities. This is its first important difference from mainstream Western secularism.
- Indian secularism provides individuals the **right to profess the religion** of their choice. It not only protects the religious freedom of individuals but also of minority communities. Thus, religious minorities also have a right to exist and to maintain their own **culture and educational institutions.**
- The Indian model of secularism provides for **state supported religious reforms.** For example, Indian Constitution bans untouchability[3] and **abolished child marriage.**
- The secular character of the Indian state is established by the fact that it is neither theocratic nor has it established any one or multiple religions.This allows it either to disengage with religion in American style or engage with it if required.
- Indian secularism allows for **principled state intervention** in all religions. It means that the state can interfere in the religious matters to carry out the reforms and to maintain peace and equality.

  The sailent features of Indian secularism are as follows
  - Equal respect and recognitions for all religions by the state.
  - No discrimination by the state on the basis of religion.
  - Non-interference in the functioning of any religion by the state.
  - No official religion in India. An individual has the right to practice propagate and profess any religion.

Nehru on Secularism

- Jawaharlal Nehru was in favour of 'Equal protection by the state in all religions'.
- He wanted a secular state to be one that protects all religions, but does not favour one at the expense of others and does not itself adopt any religion as the state religion.
- Nehru was not in favour of a **complete separation between religion and state**. According to him, a secular state can interfere in matters of religion to bring about social reform.
- Nehru himself played a key role in enacting laws abolishing caste discrimination, dowry and sati and extending legal rights and social freedom to Indian women.
- Secularism for him meant a complete opposition to communalism[4] of all kinds.
- For him secularism means only guarantee of **unity and integrity** of India.

Quick Test 1

1 Define secularism.
2 What is theocratic state?
3 Western model of secularism is inspired from which state?
4 In which state Kemal Ataturk's model of secularism was followed?
5 What led to the distinct form of secularism in India compared to the West?

---

3 **Untouchability** It is a social practice in which certain groups of people are considered impure or untouchable based upon race, caste etc.

4 **Communalism** It is a political ideology that prioritises the interests and identity of a particular religious or ethnic community over others ledding to conflict and division between different communities.

8.2 Criticism of Indian Secularism

Indian secularism has been criticised by following arguments

Anti Religious

- The first critism of Indian secularism is that it is anti-religious.
- It has been argued that secularism threatens religious identity. However as we studied earlier, secularism promotes religious freedom and equality. Thus, it protects **religious identity** rather than threatening it.

Western Import

- A second criticism is that secularism is a Western concept and therefore, may not fit well with Indian society.
- The mutual exclusion of religion and state, which is supposed to be the ideal for Western secular societies, but it is also not the defining feature of all secular states.
- A secular state may keep a principled distance from religion to promote peace between the communities and it may also intervene to protect the rights of specific communities.
- This is exactly happened in India. India evolved a distinctive form of secularism, which is not an import from the West.
- The fact is that, the secularism has both Western and non-Western origins.

  For example, in the West-the separation of religion (the church) from the state is central of Western secularism, but in India-the idea of peaceful co-existence of different religious communities is important.

Minoritism

- Third accusation against Indian secularism is the charge of advocating minority rights. According to the Indian Constitution, most fundamental interests of minorities must not be harmed and be protected by Constitutional law.
- Minority rights are justified as long as these rights protect their fundamental interests.

Interventionist

- Fourth criticism is that, Indian secularism interferes excessively with the religious freedom of communities. But it is a misconception about the Indian secularism.
- Although, Indian secularism rejects non-interference in religion, but it does not mean that it interferes excessively.
- Indian secularism follows the concept of **principled distance**, which allows the state to support necessary reforms in the religion.
- India support reform by encouraging liberal voices within religions, without being too harsh.

Vote Bank Politics

- The fifth criticism of Indian secularism is encouraging vote bank politics, where politicians seek votes from specific groups, often minorities, for short-term gains.
- This is not a major issue in a democratic nation as in a democracy the politicians are bound to seek votes. But, if a politician is promising to initiate a policy with the motivation to secure their vote, it is unfair.

- But if a secular politician, who sought the vote of minorities and managed to give them what they want, then this is a success of secularism, which aims to protect the interest of minorities.
- And also, politician should not neglect the interests of majority groups of the nation and maintain the balance and justice.

Impossible Project

- The last criticism says that Indian secularism can not work because it tries to do much, to find a solution to a contrary problem.
- A criticism of secularism claims it is unrealistic, as people with deep religious differences can't live together peacefully. However, Indian history disproves this and Indian secularism is seen as a model for the future.
- Thus, the Indian secularism mirrors the future of the world. With the intensification of **globalisation** the europeen countries, America and the beginning to resemble India in the diversity of cultures and religions.

Quick Test 2

1. Mention any two criticisms of the Indian model of secularism.
2. How Indian secularism differs from Western secularism.
3. What does Indian secularism allow regarding religious practices?
4. Name the term used for seeking vote from specific groups for short term gains by politicians.

Mind Map

SECULARISM

1 Meaning of Secularism

- Provides freedom to all people to follow propagate their religion without any discrimination.

Forms of Discrimination

Inter-Religious Domination
- Target members of one religion due to its religious identity.
  For example Incidents like Sikhs Massacre in Delhi in 1984.

Intra-Religious Domination
- Targets discrimination within the community of the same religion.
  For example Dalits in Hindu religion were banned from entering temples.

2 Secular State

- A state where no religion has been given official recognition by the government.
  Includes ways
- No formal and legal alliance.
- Commitment to principles and goals such as peace and equality.

Models of Secularism

Western-Model
- Inspired by American model.
- States do not interfere in religious affairs.
- Religion is a private matter.
- Interprets freedom and equality.

Indian-Model
- Deep religious diversity.
- Does not focus only on religion and state-separation.
- Right to profess the religion.
- Secularism provides for state supported religious reforms.

3 Criticism of Indian Secularism

Anti-religion
- According to the some opponents, Indian Secularism is anti-religious. It poses a threat to religious identity.

Western Import
- Secularism is a Western concept and may not fit well with Indian society.
- A secular state may keep a principled distance from religion to promote peace between the communities.

Minoritism
- Second accusation against Indian Secularism is the charge of advocating minority rights.
- Minority rights are justified as long as these rights protect their fundamental interests.

Interventionist
- Misconception that Indian Secularism interferes excessively with religious freedom.
- Although, Indian Secularism rejects non-interference in religion, but it does not mean that it interferes excessively.

Vote Bank Politics
- Secularism encourages Vote Bank Politics.
- Democratic nation is not a problem but if a politician is promising some people to initiate a policy to with secure their vote is unfair.

Impossible Project
- It tries to do too much, to find a solution to an intractable problem.
- The Indian Secularism mirrors the future of the world.

4 Nehru on Secularism

- He was in favour of 'Equal protection by the state to all religions'.
- He was not in favour of a complete separation between religion and state.
- Played a key role in enacting laws abolishing caste discrimination, dowry and sati and extending legal rights and social freedom to Indian women.
- A complete opposition to communalism of all kinds.
- For him secularism means only guarantee of unity and integrity of India.

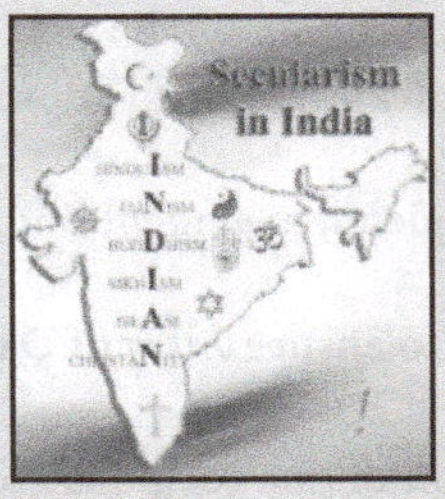

India is a secular country

All religions have a place in it.

NCERT Folder

Intext Question

1. List some of the ways in which you feel communal harmony could be promoted? (Pg. 114)

Ans. Communal harmony could be promoted by the following ways

Encourage Interfaith Dialogue Organise discussions and meetings where people from different religious backgrounds can share their beliefs and values. This helps in building mutual respect and understanding.

Celebrate Festivals Together People from different communities can celebrate each other's festivals. This fosters goodwill and strengthens social bonds, showing respect for each other's traditions.

Educate on Tolerance Schools and communities can teach the importance of respecting all religions and cultures. Education about diversity can promote peaceful co-existence.

Promote Equal Rights Ensuring that everyone, regardless of their religion, has equal access to resources, opportunities and justice is essential for maintaining harmony in society.

Government Intervention The government can create laws that protect the rights of all communities and take action against those who promote hatred or violence.

Thus, by implementing these above given steps, communities can work together to create a more peaceful and harmonious society.

Exercise

1. Which of the following do you feel are compatible with the idea of secularism? Give reasons

(i) Absence of domination of one religious group by another.

(ii) Recognition of a state religion.

(iii) Equal state support to all religions.

(iv) Mandatory prayers in schools.

(v) Allowing separate educational institutions for any minority community.

(vi) Appointment of temple management bodies by the government.

(vii) Intervention of state to ensure entry of Dalits in temples.

Ans. (i) Absence of domination of one religious group over another is compatible with the idea of secularism, as it allows freedom to all religious groups.

(ii) Recognition of a state religion is not compatible with the idea of secularism, because there will be clash between state religion and other religions.

(iii) Equal state support to all religions is compatible with the idea of secularism, as it provides a chance to every religion to preserve its traditions and flourish.

(iv) Mandatory prayers in schools is a feature of communal state. Thus, it is not compatible with the idea of secularism.

(v) Allowing separate educational institutions for any minority is compatible with the idea of secularism, as this will provide right to minority to maintain it's cultural identity and a chance to develop.

(vi) It is not compatible with the idea of secularism because it is concerned with only one religious group.

(vii) Intervention of state to ensure entry of Dalits in temples is compatible with the idea of secularism as it prevents discrimination and provides equal rights to every social group.

2. Some of the key characteristics of Western and Indian model of secularism have got mixed up. Separate them and make a new table.

Western Secularism	Indian Secularism
Strict non-interference of religion and state in each other's affairs.	State supported religious reforms allowed.
Equality between different religious groups is a key concern.	Equality between different sects of a religion is emphasised.
Attention to minority rights.	Less attention to community based rights.
Individual and his rights at the centre.	Rights of both individuals and religious community protected.

Ans.

Western Secularism	Indian Secularism
Strict non- interference of religion and state in each other's affairs.	State supported religious reforms allowed.
Less attention to community based rights.	Attention to minority rights.
Equality between different sects of a religion is emphasised.	Equality between different religious groups is a key concern.
Individual and his rights at the centre.	Rights of both individual and religious community protected.

3. What do you understand by secularism? Can it be equated with religious tolerance?

Ans. Secularism is a normative doctrine which seeks to realise a secular society. It opposes all forms of inter-religious domination. It gives opportunity to an individual to practice religion of his choice.

Secularism cannot be equated with religious tolerance, as tolerance may be compatible with religious domination by one group. However, religious tolerance is one of the components of secularism.

4. Do you agree with the following statements? Give reasons for supporting or opposing any of them.

(i) Secularism does not allow us to have a religious identity.

(ii) Secularism is against inequality within a religious group or between different religious groups.

(iii) Secularism has a Western-Christian origin. It is not suitable for India. **Competency Based Que**

Ans. (i) I do not agree with the statement because secularism allows us to have a religious identity. Indian Constitution allows its citizens to have a religious identity, so that the citizens can represent their religious institution whenever required in order to preserve and develop it.

(ii) Yes, I agree with the statement because secularism is against inequality both within a religious group and between different religious groups. The Indian Government tries to maintain equality within religious groups to prevent discrimination and eradicate practices that are derogatory to human dignity.

(iii) I do not agree with the statement because secularism may have a Western-Christian origin, but it is also have non-Western origin. This fits with the fact that India is a multi-cultural and religious society.

Thus, it is necessary to ensure equal treatment to all groups both within and between different religions to maintain harmony and integrate the country.

5. Indian secularism focuses on more than the religion-state separation. Explain. **Competency Based Que**

Ans. Indian secularism focuses on more than the religion-state separation in following ways

- All the religions are equally protected by the state.
- State shall not discriminate against any particular religion. It means that the state shall not prefer, favour or dis-favour any particular religion.
- Indian state has not any religion of its own.
- Indian secularism is not funded upon the principle of 'Separation of the state from religion'.

6. Explain the concept of principled distance. **Diksha App**

Ans. Principled distance is different from Western model of secularism which is the separation of government institutions and persons mandated to represent the state from religious institutions and religious dignitaries.

According to the concept of principled distance, a secular state may keep a principled distance from religion to promote peace between communities and it may also intervene to protect the rights of specific communities. The state gives equal preference to every religion and respects them all equally.

However, the state may interfere if religious groups try to exercise their power on the political and social life of the people. This balanced distance of state from religious groups is called principled distance.

Exam Pattern Questions

Objective Type Questions

Multiple Choice Questions (MCQs)

1. Secular state means ....

(a) the state has a religion
(b) the state is impartial in the matters of religion
(c) the state is against religion
(d) the state is irreligious

2. .... faced discrimination for centuries throughout Europe.

(a) Muslim (b) Christians
(c) Sikhs (d) Jews

3. In ...., the Arab minorities both Christians and Muslims are excluded from social, political and economic benefits?

(a) Israel (b) Pakistan
(c) Bangladesh (d) Sri Lanka

4. .... is a situation in which members of one religion are targeted and victimised because of their religious affiliation.
(a) Intra-religious domination
(b) Inter-religious domination
(c) Social inequalities
(d) Political inequalities

5. Which one of the following is an example of Inter-religious domination?
(a) Anti-Sikh Riots
(b) Godhra Riots
(c) Massacre of Kashmiri Pandits
(d) All of the above

6. If Muslims are killed by some other religious community in a nation. It is an example of......... .
Diksha App
(a) Inter-religious domination
(b) Intra-religious domination
(c) State-religious domination
(d) Inter-state religious domination

7. .... is an example of Intra-religious domination.
(a) Anti-Sikh Riots (b) Ill treatment of Dalits
(c) Godhra Riots (d) None of these

8. If untouchables are prevented from entering a temple. It is an example of
Diksha App
(a) Intra-religious domination
(b) Inter-religious domination
(c) Sectarian domination
(d) Majority domination

9. Who among the following were prevented from entering the temple?
I. Women **II. Dalit**
III. Adivasis
Select the correct answer using the codes given below.
(a) Only I
(b) I and II
(c) II and III
(d) I, II and III

10. Consider the following statement.
I. Indian secularism equally opposed the oppression of Dalits and women within Hinduism, the discrimination against women within Indian Islam or Christianity.
II. Indian secularism deals not only with religious freedom of individuals but also with religious freedom of minority communities.
Competency Based Que
Select the correct answer using the code given below.
(a) Only I (b) Only II
(c) Both I and II (d) None of these

11. A state governed directly by a priestly order is called .... state.
(a) nation (b) classic
(c) theocratic (d) political

12. Which of the following is not a way to stop religious discrimination?
Diksha App
(a) Promote fraternity
(b) Education
(c) Promoting religious harmony
(d) Hate speech against other religions

13. Which of the following is a theocratic state?
Diksha App
(a) Pakistan (b) India
(c) England (d) USA

14. India is a ....
(a) religion state (b) political state
(c) secular state (d) hindu state only

15. What is the Western model of secularism?
Diksha App
(a) State and religion will not interfere in each other's affair.
(b) State can aid any religious institution.
(c) All religions are considered as official religions.
(d) State can interfere in religious matters.

16. Statement I Western model of secularism was inspired mainly by the American model.
Competency Based Que
Statement II In this model separation of religion and state is understood as mutual exclusion.
In the light of above statements, choose the correct answer from the options given below
(a) Both Statement I and Statement II are true.
(b) Both Statement I and Statement II are false.
(c) Statement I is true, but Statement II is false.
(d) Statement I is false, but Statement II is true.

17. Which of the following statement(s) is/are correct about secularism propounded and practiced by Mustafa Kemal Ataturk?
(a) He set out in an aggressive manner to modernise and secularise Turkey.
(b) Western clothing was encouraged for men only.
(c) In 1938, the new Turkish alphabet was adopted.
(d) He did not put an end to the institution of Khalifa.

18. In western model of secularism the state cannot give any financial support to .... run by religious communities.
(a) educational institutions (b) minority institution
(c) political institution (d) All of these

19. Which of the following steps was not taken by Kemal Ataturk to modernise Turkey ?
Diksha App
(a) He banned the traditional cap worn by Muslim.
(b) He encouraged Western clothing for men and women.

(c) He adopted traditional Turkish calendar in in place of Western calendar.
(d) The new Turkish alphabet in a modified form was adopted by him.

20. Which of the following statements about Jawaharlal Nehru on secularism is incorrect?
(a) Nehru was the philosopher of Indian secularism.
(b) For Nehru secularism meant a complete opposition to communalism of all kinds.
(c) Nehru believed in Hindu religion and Hindu Gods.
(d) For Nehru secularism did not mean hostility to religion.

21. He was especially harsh in his criticism of the majority community's communalism, which he saw as a challenge to national unity for him, secularism was not only a matter of faith, but also the only way to ensure India's stability and dignity.

Who is referred as 'he' in the passage? **Competency Based Que**

(a) Nehru (b) Gandhi (c) Ambedkar (d) Patel

22. Which of the following is not the feature of secularism according to Jawaharlal Nehru? **Diksha App**
(a) Secularism didn't mean hostility to religion.
(b) Equal protection by state to all religions.
(c) State will not favour one religion at the expense of other.
(d) State will adopt one of the most popular religions.

23. Which of the following is Not the feature of Indian secularism? **Diksha App**
(a) It protects the rights of religious minorities.
(b) It gives special rights to religious majorities.
(c) In Indian secularism an individual has the freedom to profess the religion of his/her choice.
(d) There is room for state supported religious reforms.

24. Which of the following statements is correct about the Indian model of secularism?
(a) Indian secularism supports religious reforms.
(b) Equality between different sects of a religion is emphasised.
(c) State supported religious reforms are allowed.
(d) Less attention to community-based rights.

25. The Indian Constitution bans which of the following practices as part of its secular principles?
(a) Freedom to practice religion
(b) Untouchability
(c) Establishment of religious institution
(d) Use of religious symboles in public spaces

26. Which of the following level in India reflect the state's engagement in intra-religious reforms?
(a) Law banning child marriage
(b) Promotion of majority religious festivals
(c) Imposition of dress codes for religious communities
(d) Encouragement of religious conversions

27. Which of the following is/are threats to Indian secularism?
(a) Vote-bank politics (b) Anti-religious
(c) Social inequalities (d) All of the above

28. Which type of religious identities are undermined in Indian secularism? **Diksha App**
(a) Which promote equality
(b) Which promote religious freedom
(c) Dogmatic and violent religious identities
(d) Peaceful and co-operative

29. Statement I Indian secularism is an imitation of Western secularism.

Statement II Indian secularism deals not only with religious freedom of individuals but also with religious freedom of minority communities. **Competency Based Que**

In the light of above statements, choose the correct answer from the options given below
(a) Both Statement I and Statement II are true.
(b) Both Statement I and Statement II are false.
(c) Statement I is true, but Statement II is false.
(d) Statement I is false, but Statement II is true.

30. .... refers to privileges given to a specific community based on their religion, language, culture and ethnicity.
(a) Nationalism (b) Secularism
(c) Minoritism (d) Democracy

31. What is the major criticism of Indian secularism?
(a) It allows for the dominance of one religion.
(b) It promotes complete separation between religion and state.
(c) It permits state internention in religious matters.
(d) It eliminates all forms of religious practices.

32. The inclusion of secularism in the Indian Constitution was not aimed ....
(a) to offer religious freedom.
(b) to gaining minority votes.
(c) to unify a heterogeneous nation.
(d) to set the nation on the path to progress.

33. Match the following.

List I	List II
A. Western model of secularism	1. Targeting members of any religion
B. Intra-religious domination	2. American model
C. Inter-religious domination	3. Targeting of any community within the religion

Codes

	A	B	C		A	B	C
(a)	1	2	3	(b)	1	3	2
(c)	2	3	1	(c)	2	1	3

Assertion-Reason Questions

Directions (Q. Nos. 34-38) In the questions given below, there are two statements marked as Assertion (A) and Reason (R). Read the statements and choose the correct option.

Codes

(a) Both A and R are true and R is the correct explanation of A.
(b) Both A and R are true, but R is not the correct explanation of A.
(c) A is true, but R is false.
(d) A is false, but R is true.

34. **Assertion (A)** Secularism is invaluable in India.
Reason (R) India is a multi-religious and multi-cultural country.

35. **Assertion (A)** Secularism questions not only inter-religious but also intra-religious dominance.
Reason (R) Secularism opposes all forms of institutionalised religious supremacy.

36. **Assertion (A)** No person has a right to profess, practise and propagate the religion he or she believes in.
Reason (R) A secular state is one that does not establish any one religion as official religion.

37. **Assertion (A)** India is a secular state.
Reason (R) Secularism dictates that there is no official religion of the state.

38. **Assertion (A)** Western model of secularism is based on separation of religion and politics.
Reason (R) The state gives financial support to educational institutions run by religious communities.

Passage Based Questions

39. Read the given passage and answer the following questions.

Perhaps one way of preventing religious discrimination is to work together for mutual enlightenment. Education is one way of helping to change the mindset of people. Individual examples of sharing and mutual help can also contribute towards reducing prejudice and suspicion between communities.

It is always inspiring to read stories of Hindus saving Muslims or Muslims saving Hindus in the midst of a deadly communal riot. But it is unlikely that mere education or the goodness of some persons will eliminate religious discrimination. In modern societies, states have enormous public power.

(i) .... refers to ideological differences based on religious rigidity. It arises when a community feels that their sentiments are being hated by another community.

(a) Intra-community conflict
(b) Rational conflict
(c) Inter-community conflict
(d) None of the above

(ii) One way of preventing religious discrimination is to work together for............. .

(a) mutual exclusion (b) social exclusion
(c) mutual enlightenment (d) mutual inclusion

(iii) .... such as the Papal states of Europe in medieval times or in recent times the Taliban-controlled state, lacking separation between religious and political institutions, are known for their hierarchies and oppressions.

(a) Autocratic states (b) Theocratic states
(c) Both (a) and (b) (d) Neither (a) nor (b)

(iv) Consider the following statement.

I. Education is the only way of helping to change the mindset of people.
II. In modern societies, states have emormous public power.

Select the correct option using the code given below?

(a) Only I (b) Only II
(c) Both I and II (d) Neither I nor II

40. Read the given passage and answer the following questions.

Let us look at a very different kind of secularism practised in Turkey in the first half of the 20th century. This secularism was not about principled distance from organised religion, instead it involved, active intervention in and suppression of religion. This version of secularism was propounded and practised by Mustafa Kemal Ataturk. He came to power after the First World War. He was determined to put an end to the institution of Khalifa in the public life of Turkey. Ataturk was convinced that only a clear break with traditional thinking and expressions could elevate Turkey from the sorry state it was in. He set out in an aggressive manner to modernise and secularise Turkey.

(i) This secularism was not about principled distance from organised religion, instead it involved, active intervention in and suppression of religion. This version of secularism was propounded and practised by ....

(a) Jawaharlal Nehru (b) Mustafa Kemal Ataturk
(c) Dr. B.R. Ambedkar (d) None of the above

(ii) Ataturk was inspired by the ....

(a) middle East culture (b) traditional Turkish culture
(c) Western culture (d) None of the above

(iii) How did Ataturk try to promote secularism in Turkey?

41. Read the following passage and answer the following questions

'Equal protection by the state to all religions'. This is how Nehru responded when a student asked him to spell out what secularism meant in independent India. He wanted a secular state to be one that "Protects all religions, but does not favour one at the expense of others and does not itself adopt any religion as the state religion". Nehru was the philosopher of Indian secularism. Nehru did not practice any religion, nor did he believe in God. But for him secularism did not mean hostility to religion. In that sense Nehru was very different from Ataturk in Turkey. At the same time Nehru was not in favour of a complete separation between religion and state. A secular state can interfere in matters of religion to bring about social reform. Nehru himself played a key role in enacting laws abolishing caste discrimination, dowry, sati and extending legal rights and social freedom to Indian women. While Nehru was prepared to be flexible on many counts, there was one thing on which he was always firm and uncompromising. Secularism for him meant a complete opposition to communalism of all kinds. Nehru was particularly severe in his criticism of communalism of the majority community. Secularism for him was not only a matter of principles, it was also the only guarantee of the unity and integrity of India.

(i) According to Nehru, what was the key characteristic of a secular state?

(a) Complete separation of religion and state.
(b) Hostility towards religion.
(c) Protection of all religions without favoring any particular religion.
(d) Adoption of majority religion.

(ii) How did Nehru's approach to secularism differ from Ataturk's?

(a) Nehru promoted religious discrimination.
(b) Nehru was not hostile to religion despite being non-religious.
(c) Nehru supported state religion.
(d) Nehru opposed social reforms.

(iii) How did Nehru's vision of secularism balance religious freedom with social reform, and why did he consider it crucial for India's unity?

Answers

1. (b) the state is impartial in the matters of religion
2. (d) Jews
3. (a) Israel
4. (b) Inter-religious domination
5. (d) All of the above
6. (a) Inter-religious domination
7. (b) Ill treatment of Dalits
8. (a) Intra-religious domination
9. (b) I and II
10. (c) Both I and II
11. (c) theocratic
12. (d) Hate speech against other religions
13. (a) Pakistan
14. (c) secular state
15. (a) State and religion will not interfere in each other's affair.
16. (a) Both Statement I and Statement II are true.
17. (a) He set out in an aggressive manner to modernise and secularise Turkey.
18. (a) educational institutions
19. (c) He adopted traditional Turkish calendar in in place of Western calendar.
20. (c) Nehru believed in Hindu religion and Hindu Gods.
21. (a) Nehru
22. (d) State will adopt one of the most popular religions.
23. (b) It gives special rights to religious majorities.
24. (b) Equality between different sects of a religion is emphasised.
25. (b) Untouchability
26. (a) Law banning child marriage
27. (d) All of the above
28. (c) Dogmatic and violent religious identities
29. (d) Statement I is false, but Statement II is true.
30. (c) Minoritism
31. (c) It permits state interventions in religious matters.
32. (b) to gaining minority votes.
33. (c) 2 3 1
34. (a) Both A and R are true and R is the correct explanation of A. Secularism is invaluable in India because India is a land of diversity with multiple religions, cultures and geographical diversity. This diversity is a unique feature of Indian society.

35. (a) Both A and R are true and R is the correct explanation of A. Secularism questions not only inter-religious but also intra-religious dominance because it opposes all forms of institutionalised religious supremacy.

36. (d) A is false, but R is true. Secular states protect religious freedom, allowing individuals to profess, practice an propagate thier faith. They do not establish any official religion, ensuring neutrality and equality for all religions.

37. (a) Both A and R are true and R is the correct explanation of A. Secularism is an ideology that says religion should not be involved with the ordinary social and political activities of a country. It dictates that there is no official religion of the state. The Preamble to the Constitution asserts that India is a secular state.

38. (c) A is true, but R is false. The state cannot give any financial support to educational institutions run by religious communities.

39. (i) (c) Inter community conflict
(ii) (c) mutual enlightenment
(iii) (b) Theocratic states (iv) (b) Only II

40. (i) (b) Mustafa Kemal Ataturk
(ii) (c) Western culture
(iii) He declare Turkey a secular state and put an end to institution of Khalifa. He promoted secularism in the following ways

- The Fez, a traditional cap of Muslims was banned by Hat law.
- The Western (Gregorian) calender replaced the traditional Turkish calender.

41. (i) (c) Protection of all religions without favoring any particular religion.
(ii) (b) Nehru was not hostile to religion despite being non-religious.
(iii) Nehru's secularism balanced religious tolerance with progressive social reform. While protecting all religions equally, he supported state intervention to address religious social practices like caste discrimination and sati.

He viewed secularism as essential for India's unity, particularly oppossing majority communalism. This approach allowed for religious freedom while enabling necessary social changes through legislative action.

Subjective Questions

Very Short Answer Type Questions

1. What do you understand by the term 'Secularism'?

Ans. Secularism is the first and foremost doctrine that opposes all such forms of inter-religious domination. This is however only one crucial aspect of the concept of secularism.

An equally important dimension of secularism is its opposition to intra-religious domination.

2. What do you mean by inter-religious domination? Give example.

Ans. Inter-religious domination is a situation where one religion dominates and suppresses the other religion. For example, in 1984, there were anti-Sikh riots and in 2004, there were anti-Muslim riots in Godhra, Gujarat.

3. Brief intra-religious domination with the help an example.

Ans. Intra-religious domination is a situation where a community/religion dominates its own members. For example, Dalits are at lowest in social hierarchy. They were treated inhumanly and like slaves by upper castes in Hindu religion.

4. In which ways religious discrimination can be prevented?

Ans. Religious discrimination can be prevented in the following two ways
(i) By working together for mutual enlightenment.
(ii) By changing mind-set of people through education.

5. Why is the separation of religion and state important in a secular state?

Ans. Separating religion and state ensures that no religion receives special treatment or power. It prevents the state from favouring one religion over others and guarantees equal rights to all citizens, regardless of their beliefs. This helps to maintain peace and harmony in a diverse society.

6. What is the Western model of secularism?

Ans. Western model of secularism is based on separation of religion and politics. According to the Western model of secularism, state will not intervene in the affairs of religion and religion will not intervene in the affairs of the state. Each has separate sphere of its own. No public policy will be drafted on the basis of religion, and the state institution. The state cannot give any financial support to educational institutions run by religious communities.

7. Who was Kemal Ataturk? How did he try to promote secularism in Turkey? Diksha App

Ans. Ataturk came to power after the defeat of Turkey in the First World War and he was determined to put an end to the Institution of Khalifa in the public life of Turkey.

- He was involved in active intervention and suppression of Islamic religion.
- He set out in an aggressive manner to modernise and secularised Turkey.
- He declared Turkey a secular state putting an end to the institution of Khalifa. The Fez, a traditional cap of Muslim was banned by him. The Western calendar (Gregorian) replaced the traditional Turkish calendar.

8. Which type of secularism was propounded by Mustafa Kemal Ataturk.

Ans. According to Mustafa Kemal Ataturk, secularism was not about principled distance from organised religion. Instead, it involved active intervention in and suppression of religion.

9. What kind of secularism Pandit Jawaharlal Nehru wanted?

Ans. Nehru wanted a secular state to be one that protects all religions, but does not favour one at the expense of others and does not itself adopt any religion as a state religion.

10. Write two distinctive features of Indian secularism.

Ans. The two distinctive features of Indian secularism are following

(i) Indian secularism deals not only with religious freedom of individuals but also with religious freedom of minority communities.

(ii) Since a secular state must be connected equally with intra-religious domination, Indian secularism has made room for it and is compatible with the idea of state supported religious reform.

11. Do you agree that Indian secularism is an interventionist? Competency Based Que

Ans. Indian secularism is criticised by the critics arguing that Indian secularism is interventionist because it is coercive and it interferes excessively with the religious freedom of communities.

In fact, Indian secularism allows interference in religious affairs, particularly in the management of religious activities of the communities. But this interference is not negative, it is positive.

Indian secularism rejects non-interference in religion but it does not mean that it is excessively interventionist. Indian secularism follows the concept of principal distance.

Short Answer Type Questions

1. What are the characteristics of a secular state?

Ans. Following are the characteristics of a secular state

- A secular state is neutral towards all religions and doesn't favor and doesn't allow religion to interfere in politics.
- A secular state treats religion as only a personal matter.
- Secular state does not have any state religion, like India is a secular state and the people can follow any religion of their choice.
- In a secular state, the government is not concerned with the relation between citizens and god. It is concerned only with relation between citizens.

2. How does secularism in India address the issue of social inequality, particularly caste discrimination?

Ans. Secularism in India addresses social inequality, particularly caste discrimination by allowing the state to intervene in religious practices that perpetuate such inequalities. For centuries, the caste system in India was justified by religious doctrines, leading to the oppression of lower-caste communities, especially the Dalits. Indian secularism rejects caste-based discrimination, as it goes against the principles of equality and justice enshrined in the Indian Constitution.

The state's intervention in matters of religion, such as the abolition of untouchability through the Constitution is a key example of how secularism works to eliminate social inequality. Indian secularism does not simply tolerate religious practices; it actively works to ensure that religious doctrines or social customs do not reinforce harmful social hierarchies.

3. Being a secular state, several forms of exclusion and discrimination continue in India. Give examples of such exclusion and discrimination. Competency Based Que

Ans. India has been declared a secular state by the Constitution of India. Being a secular state, several forms of exclusion and discrimination continue in India. These are as follows

- Due to violence and terrorism in Kashmir valley, thousands of Hindu Kashmiri Pandits have been forced to leave their homes. They have not been able to return their homes for a long time. Still they are living in many parts of India and are victims of discrimination.
- In anti-Sikh riots of 1984, thousands of Sikhs were massacred in Delhi and other parts of the country.
- In 1992, Babari Masjid was demolished and there was widespread communal violence in many parts of the country.
- In 2002 in Godhara, Gujarat, many Muslims were killed in communal violence.

4. Discuss the relationship between secularism and religious freedom in India.

Ans. In India, secularism and religious freedom are closely related. Secularism ensures that the state does not favor any religion. It allows citizens to practice and follow their faith without fear of discrimination. Religious freedom is a Fundamental Right under the Indian Constitution, guaranteeing individuals the liberty to choose, change or propagate their religion.

However, secularism in India is not about complete separation of religion and state. The state can intervene in religious matters when required to protect the rights of individuals and promote equality. For example, India banned practices like untouchability and intervene in matters like child marriage, which harm individuals and society. Secularism in India aims to protect religious freedom while ensuring that harmful practices or discrimination under the guise of religion are eliminated. Thus, Indian secularism seeks to balance the freedom of religion with the principles of justice and equality.

5. Why is the protection of minority rights important in a secular state like India?

Ans. Protecting minority rights is crucial in a secular state like India because the country is home to a diverse range of religious, linguistic and cultural communities.

Secularism in India is not only about religious neutrality but it also involves ensuring that the rights of smaller or less powerful groups are safeguarded against discrimination by the majority. The Indian Constitution provides specific provisions for the protection of minority rights, ensuring that these groups can live freely, practice their religion and preserve their culture.

These protections help maintain social harmony by preventing the domination of one community over others. For example, the government can take affirmative action or legal protections to support minority groups, ensuring they are not excluded from economic, educational or political opportunities.

6. Indian secularism has been accused of being 'interventionist' and creating 'vote bank politics'. Explain and give your views. Competency Based Que

Ans. According to the Interventionist school of critics, Indian secularism is coercive and it interferes excessively with the religious freedom of communities.

This criticism misleads Indian secularism. It is true that by rejecting the idea of separation as mutual exclusion, Indian secularism rejects non-interference in religion.

Indian secularism also follows the concept of principled distance which allows for non-interference.

Indian secularism has also been accused of encouraging the politics of vote banks as an empirical (provisional) claim, that is not entirely false.

However, we need to put this issue in perspective. In a democracy, politicians are bound to seek votes. That is part of their job and that is what democratic politics is largely about. To blame a politician for pursing a group of people or promising to initiate a policy with the motivation to secure their votes is unfair. But if a secular politician who sought the vote of minorities and managed to give them what they want, then this is a success of secularism, which aims to protect the interest of minorities.

Thus, Indian secularism is based on freedom and equality.

7. What is the critique of 'AVote-bank politics' in relation to secularism?

Ans. The criticism of 'Vote-bank politics' in relation to secularism is that some politicians target specific religious or minority groups to get their votes, often by making promises to fulfill their demands. This can lead to the neglect of other communities and social issues.

Critics argue that such politics may exploit religious divisions for short-term political gain, rather than addressing the broader needs of society. This undermines the principles of equality and fairness that secularism seeks to uphold.

Long Answer Type Questions

1. Is secularism suitable for India? Explain.

Competency Based Que

Ans. Secularism is suitable for societies where religion continues to exercise a strong influence on people, for example, democratic society like India. A true secularism can play a great role in filling the religious and communal gap between the different communities.

Secularism is most suitable for India due to following reasons

- India is a multi- religious country. Every religion has its own culture and belief.
- Since ancient times diverse religious movements flourished in different parts of India, which promoted tolerance. So, the framers of the Constitution felt that secularism was the best option to continue the spirit.
- India is a democratic state. So it grants freedom of religion and equality of all religions to every individual.
- The partition of the country forced India to adopt secularism to maintain peace and prosperity.
- There is no official state-religion.
- Indian Constitution ensures the rights of minority community.
- Supreme Court in its judgment said secularism is the basic structure of the Indian Constitution, even Parliament cannot amend the basic structure of Indian Constitution.

Hence it is suitable in the context of India.

2. Secularism deals both with inter religious domination and intra religious domination. Elaborate.
Competency Based Que

Ans. Secularism is a doctrine that aims to establish a society without religious domination, whether between or within religions. It promotes equality and freedom within and between religions, and opposes any form of religious domination.

Here are some ways that secularism deals with inter-religious and intra-religious domination

- **Separation of religion and state** A secular state does not have a formal alliance with any religion and does not enforce any particular religion.
- **Freedom of religion** A secular state protects the religious freedom of individuals, and does not compel citizens to pay taxes for the promotion of any particular religion.
- **Equality of opportunity** A secular state ensures equal opportunities for followers of all religions and does not discriminate on the basis of religion.
- **Non-religious goals** A secular state has goals that are at least partly derived from non-religious sources, such as peace, religious freedom and freedom from discrimination.
- **Tolerance** Secularism includes religious tolerance, but it is not the same as religious tolerance, which can be compatible with religious domination.

In India, the Constitution mandates that the state to be secular, and prohibits the government for the promotion of any particular religion in government spaces.

3. Indian secularism is based on Western model of secularism. Critically analyse. **Competency Based Que**

Ans. Indian secularism diverges notably from the Western model. While Western secularism, particularly in countries like the United States and France, emphasises a strict separation between religion and state, Indian secularism seeks to maintain a 'principled distance' from all religions.

- The Indian model involves state intervention in religious affairs to ensure equality, which is less common in Western secularism.
- In practice, the Indian government intervenes in religious issues to promote social reform, as seen in laws addressing untouchability, Hindu personal law and other religious practices.
- The aim is not to privatise religion but to promote religious harmony and protect minority rights.
- For instance, the Indian state financially supports religious pilgrimages, including Haj subsidies and funding for temples, which contrasts with the hands-off approach in Western secularism.

However, critics argue that such interventions risk state favoritism and can sometimes lead to selective secularism, where majoritarian or politically convenient groups receive preferential treatment.

Thus, while inspired by the Western model, Indian secularism reflects a more nuanced approach, aiming to foster inclusivity in a diverse religious landscape.

Picture Based Question

1. Study the given cartoon and answer the questions that follow

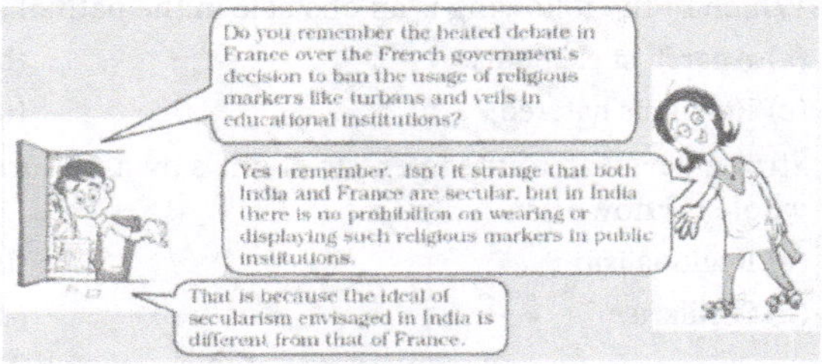

(i) What fundamental difference is highlighted between French and Indian secularism?

(a) France practices aggressive secularism with strict religious restrictions, while India follows accommodative secularism.
(b) India prohibits all religious symbols while France allows them.
(c) Both countries have identical secular policies.
(d) Neither country practices secularism.

Ans. (a) France practices aggressive secularism with strict religious restrictions, while India follows accommodative secularism.

(ii) The French government's ban on religious markers in educational institutions exemplifies

(a) positive secularism. (b) negative secularism.
(c) religious tolerance. (d) religious favoritism.

Ans. (b) negative secularism.

(iii) Indian secularism as depicted in the image can be best described as............ .

(a) state-sponsored religiosity.
(b) equal respect for all religions.
(c) anti-religious ideology.
(d) religious fundamentalism.

Ans. (b) equal respect for all religions.

(iv) The discussion in the image primarily addresses which aspect of secularism?

(a) Constitutional provisions regarding secularism
(b) Public expression of religious identity
(c) Role of religion in politics
(d) Religious discrimination

Ans. (b) Public expression of religious identity

SELF ASSESSMENT TEST

Objective Type Questions

1. On which of the following ground Indian secularism can be criticised?
   (a) Anti-religious (b) Western Import
   (c) Vote Bank Politics (d) All of these
2. Which of the following is an obstacle in the path of secularism.
   (a) Anarchist elements (b) Communalism
   (c) Religious hatered (d) All of these
3. Strong devotion to the interests of one's own minority or ethnic group rather than those of society as a whole is known as ....
   (a) Regionalism (b) Communalism
   (c) Secularism (d) Pluralism

Very Short Answer Type Questions

4. What is considered as 'Opium of the masses'?
5. Briefly explain the two ways to maintain secularism.
6. Write two features of a secular state.
7. What is the meaning of communalism? What are the ways to prevent this?
8. How did Turkey adopt secularism in the 20th Century?
9. Is secularism allowed for a minority community to make its own educational institution? Give reasons?

Short Answer Type Questions

10. Explain how did the concept of secularism emerge?
11. Mention any two weaknesses of secularism.
12. How does secularism guarantee freedom of religion? Is secularism based on morality?
13. Who laid foundations of a secular state in India? Why do we need a secular state?
14. What were Kemal Ataturk's views on secularism?
15. How can we promote communal harmony in India?

Long Short Answer Type Questions

16. Indian secularism focuses more on the religion-state separation. Explain. **Competency Based Que**
17. Explain the concept of principled distance in context of India. **Competency Based Que**
18. 'Secularism is against inequality within a religious group or between different religious groups'. Justify this statement. **Competency Based Que**

PROJECT WORK

Election and Representation

Declaration

I hereby declare that this document, titled "Elections in India," is an original work completed by me. The information presented has been gathered from various sources, including textbooks, online research, and official reports, to provide an insightful understanding of the election system in India.

I affirm that this work has not been copied from any existing material, and all sources of information have been duly acknowledged.

Signature: ________________

Name: ________________

Date: ________________

Acknowledgement

I would like to express my sincere gratitude to everyone who contributed to the completion of this project. First and foremost, I extend my thanks to my teachers and mentors for their valuable guidance and encouragement throughout this project. Their insights have helped me understand the importance of elections and democracy in India.

I would also like to acknowledge the efforts of the Election Commission of India and various scholars whose research and reports provided essential information for this study. Additionally, I am grateful to my family and friends for their continuous support and motivation.

Lastly, I appreciate the efforts of all those who work to ensure free and fair elections, as their dedication strengthens democracy in our country.

Date...........

....

Name of Student

Certificate

This is to Certify that the project work

.... is the

bonafide work of .... (Name of the

student) who carried out the work under my supervision

....

Name and Signature of
Teacher/Supervisor

Contents

Elections

Introduction

Elections are the foundation of democracy. They allow people to choose their representatives who will make decisions on their behalf. In a large country like India, it is not possible for every citizen to participate directly in decision-making. Instead, people elect leaders to represent them. This makes elections an essential part of the democratic system. However, not all elections are truly democratic, and different systems of elections impact representation in various ways.

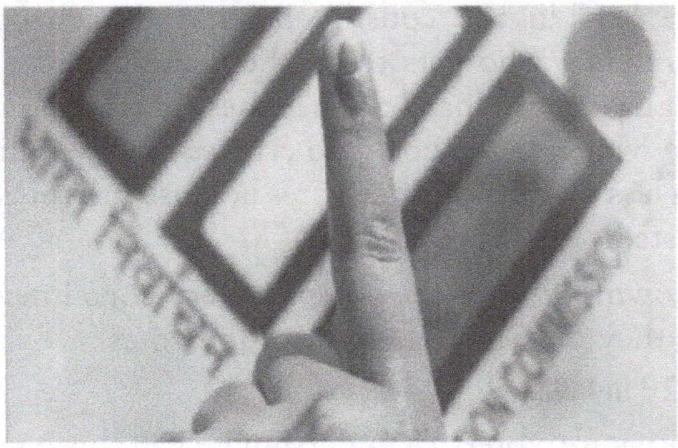

Direct and Indirect Democracy

There are two main types of democracy: direct and indirect. In direct democracy, citizens participate directly in decision-making. Ancient Greek city-states practiced direct democracy, where people voted on laws themselves. In modern times, local government bodies like gram sabhas in India come closest to direct democracy. However, for large populations, direct democracy is not practical. Instead, countries follow indirect democracy, where people elect representatives who make decisions for them. **This is the system India follows, where elections decide who will govern at different levels.**

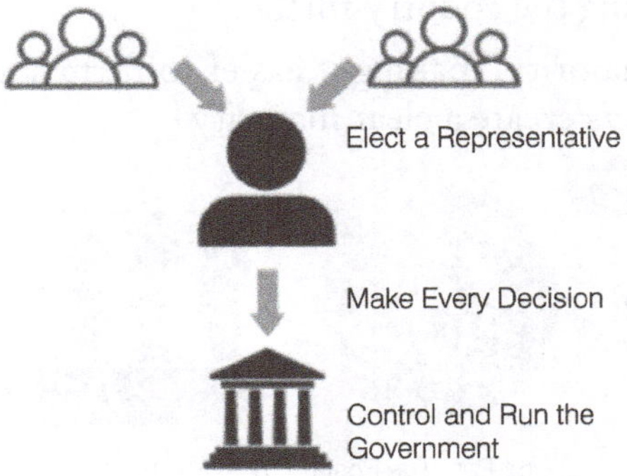

Election System in India

First Past The Post (FPTP) System

The 1984 Lok Sabha elections in India are a historic example of how the First Past The Post (FPTP) system works. In that election, the Congress Party won 415 out of 543 seats, over 80% of the total seats in Parliament. However, this result doesn't mean that 80% of Indian voters voted for the Congress Party. In fact, Congress received only 48% of the votes, but still won more than 80% of the seats. On the other hand, the BJP, with 7.4% of the votes, won less than 1% of the seats.

Working of the FPTP System

In India, elections are held in 543 constituencies, and each constituency elects one representative. The candidate who gets the highest number of votes in a constituency wins, even if they don't have more than half the votes. This is known as the First Past The Post system, where the winner is the one who crosses the "winning post" first. Often, a candidate can win with less than 50% of the votes because the votes of all other candidates who don't win are wasted.

For example, if a party wins 25% of the votes in every constituency, they could win all the seats, even though they only got a quarter of the votes.

Reasons for Choosing FPTP in India

- FPTP is simple and easy for voters to understand, even those with little knowledge of politics. Voters can clearly choose a candidate or a party.
- Each constituency elects one representative, making it easy for voters to know who they can hold accountable.
- The system helps form stable governments by giving the largest party or coalition more seats than their share of votes. This ensures that the executive (government) has the support of the majority in the legislature (Parliament).
- FPTP encourages different communities to work together to win elections. If India used Proportional Representation (PR), it could lead to the formation of separate parties for each community, dividing the country further.
- FPTP ensures a clear majority, making it easier to form stable governments, while PR systems might not always create a clear majority

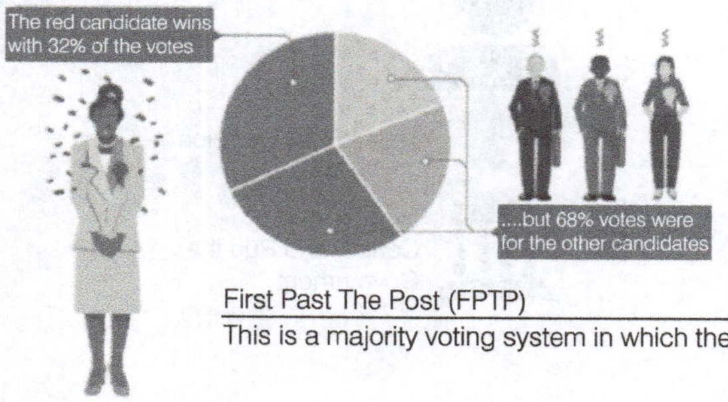

First Past The Post (FPTP)

This is a majority voting system in which the 'winner takes all'

Project Work

Results of the FPTP System

The FPTP system has proven effective in India. It has helped larger parties win clear majorities at the national and state levels. It also discourages parties that only represent one caste or community. While the FPTP system usually leads to a two-party system, India's experience has been different. After independence, the Congress Party dominated, but many smaller parties also emerged. Since 1989, coalition governments have become more common, with different parties joining together to form a government. Despite the FPTP system, smaller parties can still play an important role in elections, especially at the state level, where some two-party competition is beginning to develop.

Proportional Representation (PR)

In some countries like Israel, elections are conducted using a system called Proportional Representation (PR). This system is different from the First Past The Post (FPTP) system used in India.

How PR Works

- In PR, parties are allocated seats in the Parliament based on the percentage of votes they receive. For example, if a party gets 30% of the votes, it gets 30% of the seats.
- Voters in PR systems vote for a party, not individual candidates.
- The seats a party gets in the legislature directly match their share of votes.
- This system helps smaller parties get representation even if they don't have a large base of support.

Types of PR

- In some countries like Israel or the Netherlands, the whole country is treated as one large constituency, and the seats are given to parties based on the total votes they get.
- In other countries like Argentina and Portugal, the country is divided into multi-member constituencies. Each party provides a list of candidates, and seats are distributed based on the percentage of votes each party gets in each constituency.

Example from Israel

- Israel uses the PR system for its elections to the Knesset (Parliament).
- Voters vote for parties, not candidates, and the number of seats each party gets in the Knesset depends on how many votes they receive.
- Even smaller parties with a small support base can get representation in the legislature.
- This often results in coalition governments made up of multiple parties.

Proportional Representation in Rajya Sabha Elections

- In India, a special version of PR called the **Single Transferable Vote (STV)** system is used for electing members to the Rajya Sabha (Council of States).
- Members are elected by the members of the State Legislative Assemblies (MLAs).

- Voters rank candidates in order of preference. To win, a candidate must receive a certain number of votes, which is calculated based on a formula.
- If no candidate gets enough votes, the candidate with the least votes is eliminated, and their votes are transferred to the next preferred candidate. This continues until the required number of candidates are elected.

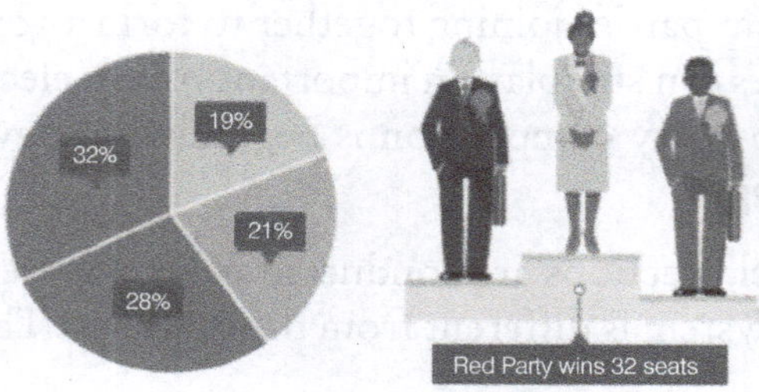

Comparision of FPTP and PR System of Election

FPTP	PR
The country is divided into small geographical units called constituencies or districts.	Large geographical areas are demarcated as constituencies. The entire country may be single constituency.
Every constituency elects one representative.	More than one one representative may be elected from one constituency.
Voter votes for a candidate.	Voter votes for the party.
A party many get more seats than votes in the legislatue.	Every party gets seats in the legislature in proportion to the percentage of votes that it gets.
Candidate who wins the election may not get majority (50%+1) votes.	Candidate who wins the election gets majority of votes.
For examples, U.K. India	For examples, Israel, Netherlands

Reservation of Constituencies

India has reserved seats for Scheduled Castes (SC) and Scheduled Tribes (ST) in the Lok Sabha and State Assemblies to ensure fair representation.

- These reserved constituencies are decided by the **Delimitation Commission.**
- SC and ST candidates can contest elections in these constituencies, but all voters can vote.

Project Work

- Currently, **84 seats** in Lok Sabha are reserved for SCs and **47 seats** for STs.
- Reservation has been extended until 2030 and can be renewed by Parliament.

There has also been a demand for **women's reservation** in Parliament, similar to the system in local governments, but this has not yet been passed as law.

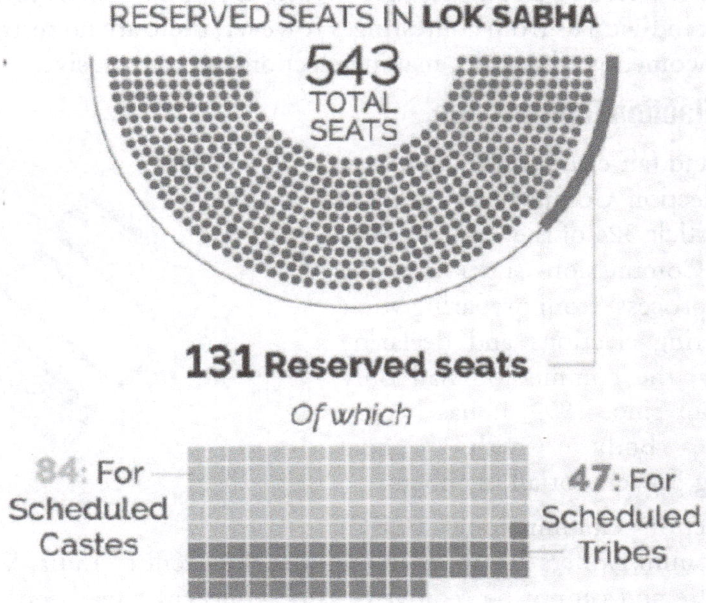

Free and Fair Elections

Elections are the backbone of any democracy. They ensure that citizens have the right to choose their representatives and hold them accountable. A truly democratic election system must be free, fair, impartial, and transparent so that the will of the people is reflected in governance. The Indian Constitution has established a robust electoral system that upholds these principles. Over the years, India has taken several measures to enhance the credibility of elections, but challenges remain.

> **Fact**
>
> The Universal Adult Franchise, the basis on which the first general elections were held, is considered as the biggest experiment in democracy anywhere in the world.

Universal Adult Franchise and Right to Contest

A fundamental feature of democracy is universal adult franchise, which means that all adult citizens have the right to vote. In India, this right was granted from the very beginning, unlike many other countries where people had to struggle for it. Initially, the voting age was 21, but in 1989, it was lowered to 18, allowing greater participation in the democratic process. This reflects the principle of equality and non-discrimination.

Similarly, the right to contest elections is open to all citizens. Any Indian citizen can contest elections if they meet the age criteria: 25 years for Lok Sabha and State Assembly elections. There are certain disqualifications, such as imprisonment for more than two years, which bar individuals from contesting. However, there are no restrictions based on gender, caste, income, or education, making elections more inclusive.

Independent Election Commission

To ensure free and fair elections, India has an Independent Election Commission (IEC) as mandated by Article 324 of the Constitution. The Election Commission supervises the entire electoral process, from preparing voter lists to conducting elections and declaring results. Initially, the commission had only one member, but since 1993, it has been a multi-member body with equal decision-making powers for all members.

The Chief Election Commissioner (CEC) and Election Commissioners are appointed by the President of India. While they enjoy security of tenure and cannot be removed easily, concerns have been raised about the appointment process, as the ruling government has significant influence. Many experts suggest that appointments should be made through a more transparent process involving the Leader of the Opposition and the Chief Justice of India.

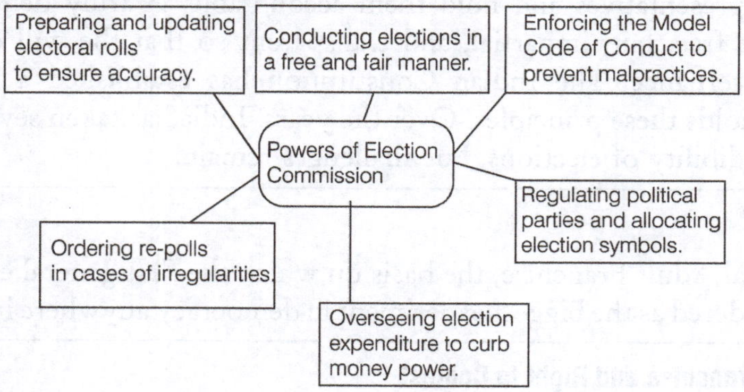

Electoral Reforms

The Election Commission, political parties, various independent groups, and many scholars have come up with proposals for electoral reform. Some of the proposed reforms are

- **Proportional Representation (PR) System** Some experts suggest replacing the First Past The Post (FPTP) system with a PR system, where seats are allocated based on the percentage of votes received. This would ensure fairer representation of smaller parties.
- **Reservation for Women** A proposal for one-third reservation for women in Parliament and Assemblies has been discussed for years. Increasing women's representation can make the political process more inclusive.
- **State Funding of Elections** To reduce the influence of money, some experts recommend that the government should fund elections. This could limit excessive spending and create a level playing field.
- **Stricter Laws on Criminal Candidates** Barring candidates with pending criminal cases from contesting elections can help reduce the criminalisation of politics.
- **Regulation of Political Parties** There should be laws ensuring that parties function democratically and maintain transparency in funding.
- **Stronger Action Against Electoral Malpractices** The Election Commission should have more powers to punish parties and candidates engaging in corrupt practices.

Conclusion

Free and fair elections are the foundation of democracy. India has made significant progress in ensuring transparent and impartial elections through universal suffrage, an independent Election Commission, and electoral reforms. However, challenges such as money and muscle power, criminalisation of politics, and misuse of media continue to threaten the integrity of the electoral process. Strengthening election laws, promoting political awareness, and encouraging active participation by civil society can help make Indian elections more democratic and inclusive. The responsibility lies not only with the Election Commission and political parties but also with voters, who must remain vigilant and choose their representatives wisely.

Bibliography

The following sources have been referred to in the preparation of this project on elections in India

1. NCERT Class 11 Political Science . Indian Constitution at Work
2. Election Commission of India (ECI) Official Website . https://www.eci.gov.in/
3. Britannica Electoral Systems & Democracy
4. The Constitution of India
5. Reports and Publications by the Association for Democratic Reforms (ADR) . https://adrindia.org
6. Books and Articles on Indian Democracy

Viva Voce Questions

1. ***What is the role of elections in a democracy?***

Ans. Elections allow people to choose their representatives who make decisions on their behalf.

2. ***What is the difference between direct and indirect democracy?***

Ans. In direct democracy, citizens make decisions directly, while in indirect democracy, they elect representatives to make decisions for them.

3. ***What system does India follow for elections?***

Ans. India follows the First Past The Post (FPTP) system for elections.

4. ***How does FPTP help in forming stable governments?***

Ans. FPTP helps form stable governments by giving the largest party or coalition more seats than their share of votes.

5. ***What is the main difference between FPTP and Proportional Representation (PR)?***

Ans. In PR, seats are allocated based on the percentage of votes each party receives, whereas in FPTP, the candidate with the most votes wins.

6. ***In which countries is Proportional Representation (PR) commonly used?***

Ans. Countries like Israel, the Netherlands, and Argentina use PR.

7. ***How are Rajya Sabha members elected in India?***

Ans. Rajya Sabha members are elected using the Single Transferable Vote (STV) system by the members of the State Legislative Assemblies (MLAs).

8. ***What is the purpose of reserving seats for SCs and STs in India?***

Ans. Reserved seats ensure fair representation for Scheduled Castes (SCs) and Scheduled Tribes (STs) in Parliament and State Assemblies.

9. ***How many seats in the Lok Sabha are reserved for SCs and STs?***

Ans. 84 seats in the Lok Sabha are reserved for Scheduled Castes (SCs) and 47 seats for Scheduled Tribes (STs).

10. ***What is universal adult franchise?***

Ans. Universal adult franchise means that all adult citizens have the right to vote, regardless of gender, caste, or other factors.

11. ***What is the minimum age to contest in Lok Sabha elections?***

Ans. The minimum age to contest in Lok Sabha elections is 25 years.

12. ***What does Article 324 of the Indian Constitution relate to?***

Ans. Article 324 empowers the Election Commission of India to supervise elections.

13. ***Who appoints the Chief Election Commissioner (CEC) in India?***

Ans. The President of India appoints the Chief Election Commissioner (CEC).

14. ***What is the role of the Election Commission of India (ECI)?***

Ans. The ECI supervises the entire electoral process, from preparing voter lists to conducting elections and declaring results.

SAMPLE QUESTION PAPER 1

A Highly Simulated Sample Question Paper for CBSE Class XI Examination

POLITICAL SCIENCE

General Instructions

Read the following instructions very carefully and follow them.

1. This question paper contains 30 questions. All question are compulsory.
2. Question paper is divided into Five Sections. Section A, B, C, D & E.
3. Section A : Question numbers 1 to 12 are Multiple Choice type questions. Each question carries 1 mark.
4. Section B : Question numbers 13 to 18 are Short Answer type-I questions. Each question carries 2 marks. Write answer to each question in 50 to 60 words.
5. Section C : Question numbers 19 to 23 are Long Answer type-I questions. Each question carries 4 marks. Write answer to each question in 100 to 120 words.
6. Section D : Question numbers 24 to 26 are Passage, Cartoon and Map-based questions. Answer each question accordingly.
7. Section E : Question numbers 27 to 30 are Long Answer type-II questions. Each question carries 6 marks. Write answer to each question in 170 to 180 words.
8. There is no overall choice in the question paper. However, an internal choice has been provided in few questions. Only one of the choice in such questions has to be attempted.

Section A

1. Which of the following elections in India is not conducted by the Election Commission of India? (1)

(a) Rajya Sabha elections
(b) Municipal elections
(c) State legislative assembly elections
(d) Lok Sabha elections

2. Which of the following is not an obligation upon each of us placed by rights? (1)

(a) Rights compel us to follow our duties as citizens.
(b) Rights require us to respect the rights of others.
(c) Rights are required to balance their rights with our duties.
(d) Rights require us to save the international community.

3. "It means that the court orders that the arrested person should be presented before it. It can also order to set free an arrested person if the manner or grounds of arrest are not lawful or satisfactory". Name the writ mentioned above. (1)

(a) Mandamus (b) Prohibition
(c) Habeas Corpus (d) Quo-Warranto

4. Democratic elections require that all adult citizens of the country must be eligible to vote in the elections. This is known as.................... (1)

(a) First Past The Post System
(b) Panchayati Raj System
(c) Universal Adult Franchise
(d) None of the above

5. **Assertion** (A) Secularism is invaluable in India.
Reason (R) India is a multi-religious and multi-cultural country. (1)

Codes

(a) Both A and R are true and R is the correct explanation of A.
(b) Both A and R are true, but R is not the correct explanation of A.
(c) A is true, but R is false.
(d) A is false, but R is true.

6. What among the following may be a consequence of a corrupt government? (1)

(a) Disruption of law and order
(b) Feeling of insecurity among people
(c) Transformation of republic into monarchy
(d) Both (a) and (b)

7. Which of the following describes the principles on which Constitution of India is based? **(1)**
(a) Cabinet Mission Plan (b) Wavell Plan
(c) August Offer (d) Objective Resolution

8. Which of the following statements is incorrect? **(1)**
(a) Inequalities which are entrenched, that is, which remain relatively untouched over generations, are more dangerous for a society.
(b) Feminism is a political philosophy that advocates for equal rights for men and women.
(c) For liberals the principle of competition is the most just and efficient way of selecting candidates for jobs or admission to educational institutions.
(d) None of the above

9. Match the following. **(1)**

A.	15th Amendment	1.	Minimum age of voting
B.	52nd Amendment	2.	Local government
C.	73rd Amendment	3.	Fundamental duties added in the Constitution
D.	61st Amendment	4.	Anti Defection
E.	42nd Amendment	5.	Increase age of retirement of High Court judges

Select the correct codes

	A	B	C	D	E		A	B	C	D	E
(a)	2	5	1	3	4	(b)	3	4	1	2	5
(c)	5	3	1	2	4	(d)	5	4	2	1	3

10. The term 'Veil of Ignorance' is attributed to .... **(1)**
(a) Socrates (b) Dr. B.R. Ambedkar
(c) John Rawls (d) Immanuel Kant

11. Arrange the following in chronological order. **(1)**
I. Adoption of the Constitution
II. The Constitution came into force
III. The Constituent Assembly held its first meeting

Codes
(a) I, II, III (b) II, I, III
(c) III, I, II (d) III, II, I

12. Give below are two statement.

Statement I Parliamentary system is based on the principles of collective leadership.

Statement II Presidential system is based on the system of individual leadership. **(1)**

Codes
(a) Both Statement I and Statement II are true.
(b) Both Statement I and Statement II are false.
(c) Statement I is true, but Statement II is false.
(d) Statement I is false, but Statement II is true.

Section B

13. Why do we need a Constitution? **(2)**

14. What is the role of the state in upholding freedom of its citizens? **(2)**

15. "John Rawls' theory of justice, is based on three principles that aim to create a just and fair society ". Explain these three principles. **(2)**

16. Explain any two writs issued by the Supreme Court of India. **(2)**

17. How is 'pocket-veto' availed by the President? **(2)**

18. Write any two prejudices which exist in Indian society. **(2)**

Section C

19. Why is local government important in a democracy? Explain with two suitable points. **(4)**

20. Mention the electoral reforms suggested by the various groups and organs of India. **(4)**

21. What are the functions of the legislature? **(4)**

Or 'The true test of any election system is its ability to ensure a free and fair electoral process'. Justify the statement by giving the importance for free and fair elections.

22. How can independence of judiciary be protected? **(4)**

Or "Rights place an obligation upon the state to act in certain kinds of waye". Do you agree with the statement?

23. What are the seven kinds of inequalities identified by Ram Manohar Lohia? **(4)**

Section D

24. Observe the cartoon given below and answer the questions that follow. **(1 + 1 + 1 + 1 = 4)**

(i) What aspect of Parliamentary democracy is being described in this cartoon?
   (a) Electoral process
   (b) Coalition politics
   (c) Political survival through confidence votes
   (d) Public voting system

(ii) The statement "My troubles are not over" despite winning the confidence vote suggests.
   (a) Temporary nature of political victories
   (b) Complete resolution of political crisis
   (c) Strengthening of government
   (d) Popular support for the leader

(iii) In the context of Parliamentary democracy, what does a confidence vote primarily determine?
   (a) Public opinion
   (b) Government's right to continue in office
   (c) Election results
   (d) Constitutional Amendments

(iv) The cartoon's underlying message about confidence votes suggests they are ....
   (a) effective tools for democratic governance.
   (b) procedural formalities that may not address core issues.
   (c) perfect indicators of government performance.
   (d) unnecessary Parliamentary procedures.

25. In the given map of India, four states have been marked as (A), (B), (C), (D). Identify these states and write their correct names in your book, along with the respective social number of the information used and concerned alphabet, as per the format given below. **(1 + 1 + 1 + 1 = 4)**

S.No. of the Information used	Alphabet concerned	Name of state
(i)		
(ii)		
(iii)		
(iv)		

(i) The state, where Pandit Jawaharlal Nehru born.
(ii) The state, related to Dr. Rajendra Prasad's birth.
(iii) The state related to Dr. B.R. Ambedkar's birth.
(iv) The state related to Mahatma Gandhi's birth.

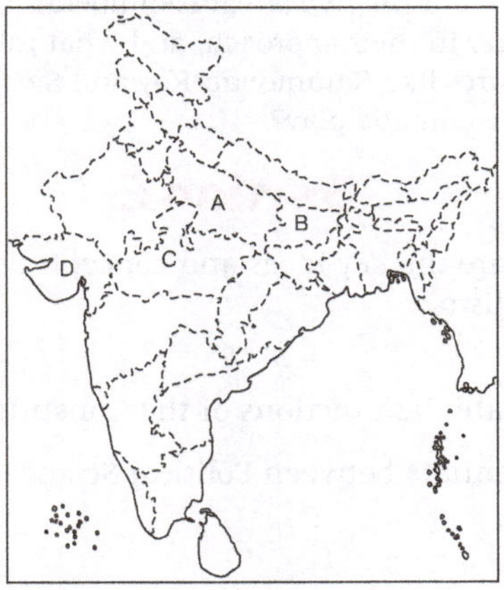

26. Read the following passage carefully and answer the question that follow. **(1 + 1 + 2 = 4)**

India liberalism has two streams. The first stream began with Rammohan Roy. He emphasised individual rights particularly the rights of women. The second stream included thinkers like K.C. Sen, Justice Ranade and Swami Vivekanada. They introduced the spirit of social justice within orthodox Hinduism. For Vivekanada, such a recording of Hindu society could not have been possible without liberal principles. K.M. Panikkar, In Defence of Liberalism, Bombay, Asia Publishing House, 1962.

(i) Which of the following best describes the primary focus of the first stream of liberalism in India led by Rammohan Roy?
   (a) Integrating Western education into traditional Hindu practices.
   (b) Emphasising individual rights, especially those of women.
   (c) Promoting Hindu orthodoxy and spiritual discipline.
   (d) Establishing democratic political institutions in India.

(ii) What was the primary contribution of thinkers like K.C. Sen, Justice Ranade and Swami Vivekananda in the second stream of Indian liberalism?
   (a) They introduced the spirit of social justice within Hindu orthodoxy.
   (b) They opposed any reform within Hindu society.
   (c) They advocated for the complete abandonment of traditional Hindu practices.
   (d) They focused exclusively on promoting Western values in India.

(iii) How did the two streams of liberalism in India differ in their approach, and what roles did key figures like Rammohan Roy and Swami Vivekananda play?

Section E

27. What are the key ideas and concepts associated with federalism? (6)

Or

Elucidate the functions of the Constitution.

28. Differentiate between Political Science and Politics. (6)

Or

'Gandhian principles of politics are relevant in Indian politics'. Justify this statement.

29. What are the salient features of the Western model of secularism? (6)

Or

Provide the arguments of Martin Luther King against the prevailing laws of segregation.

30. What are the differences in the views of Karl Marx and liberals on equality? (6)

Or

Explain the three dimensions of equality.

Answers

1. (b) Municipal elections

2. (d) Rights require us to save the international community.

3. (c) Habeas Corpus

4. (c) Universal Adult Franchise

5. (a) Both A and R are true and R is the correct explanation of A.

6. (d) Both (a) and (b)

7. (d) Objective Resolution

8. (d) None of the above

9. (d) 5 4 2 1 3

10. (c) John Rawls

11. (c) III, I, II

12. (a) Both Statement I and Statement II are true.

13. We need a Constitution because
- Constitution is a set of legal document according to which a nation is governed.
- Constitution guarantees Fundamental Rights to citizen against any subversion of power.

14. The role of the state in upholding freedom of its citizens is
- The state maintains reasonable restrictions on its citizens so that they cannot harm the rights of others.
- The state provides positive liberty to its citizens so that they can expand their ability and talent.

15. Following are the three principles in John Rawls' theory

(i) Liberty (ii) Equality of opportunity

(iii) Difference based principle

16. Two writs issued by the supreme court of India are

(i) **Habeas Corpus** It is an order of the court to present the arrested or detained person before the court to examine the cause and legality of arrest.

(ii) **Mandamus** This writ is issued by the court when it finds that a public office is unable or failed to perform his official duties.

17. The veto in which the President can keep the bill pending with him without any time limit and enjoys informal power to use this veto in effective manner is referred to as 'pocket-veto'.

18. Two prejudices which exist in Indian society

(i) Female should confine to household works.

(ii) Some castes are privileged in Indian society.

19. Local government is important in a democracy because of the following points

(i) **Representation and Participation** Local governments provide citizens a platform to participate in decision-making processes that affect their daily lives. This ensures that people's voices are heard, and their interests are represented.

(ii) **Effective Delivery of Services** Local governments are responsible for providing essential services such as water supply, sanitation, roads, and public health. They are better equipped to understand local needs and deliver services effectively.

20. The Election Commission, various independent groups, scholars and political parties have come up and suggested about changing the Constitutional provisions such as
- Our system of election should be changed from FPTP to some form of the PR system to ensure that parties get seats in proportion to the votes secured.
- One-third seats are to be reserved for women in Parliament and State Assemblies.
- Provisions to control the role of money in electoral politics and election expenses should be paid by the government out of special funds.
- Complete ban on the use of caste and religious appeals in the campaign. One candidate with any criminal background should be barred from contesting elections, even if the appeal is pending in court.

21. The main functions of the legislature are

(i) The legislature has the power to make laws for the country.

(ii) The legislature exercises control over the finances of the country by approving the budget, discussing financial policies, and exercising control over public expenditure.

(iii) The legislature checks the actions of the executive through various mechanisms, such as questions, debates, and committee inquiries.

Or In order to achieve democracy in a true sense, it is crucial that the election system is impartial and transparent. The true test of any election system is its ability to ensure free and fair electoral process. Free and fair elections are important because

(i) It allows the aspirations of the voters to find a legitimate expression through the electoral results.

(ii) Elections serves as a tool for the citizens to hold the government accountable.

(iii) It is a process through which a stable government is formed at the centre, state and local level.

(iv) Election provides the rights to caste vote and the right to contest elections to all the citizens of the country.

(v) Elections serves as the tool for the democratic setup of a country.

22. The independence of the judiciary can be protected in the following ways

(i) **Security of Tenure** Judges should have security of tenure to prevent them from being removed arbitrarily, which would help them to give judgments impartially.

(ii) **Separation of Judiciary from Executive** The judiciary should be separated from the executive to prevent executive interference in judicial decisions.

(iii) **Financial Independence** The judiciary should have financial independence to prevent any external influence on its decisions, and it should be allocated sufficient funds to function efficiently.

Or

Yes, I agree with the statement. Rights place an obligation upon the state to act in certain ways, ensuring that individuals' rights are protected and promoted. This means the state has a duty to

- Enact laws that uphold and safeguard rights
- Implement policies that promote and protect rights
- Ensure that its actions and decisions do not violate rights

In other words, the state has a responsibility to create an environment where individuals can exercise their rights freely and without fear of violation.

23. Eminent socialist thinker Ram Manohar Lohia identified seven kinds of inequalites. These are

(i) Inequality between men and women

(ii) Inequality based on skin colour

(iii) Caste-based inequality

(iv) Colonial rule over some countries

(v) Economic inequality

(vi) Revolution for civil liberties against unjust encroachments on private life

(vii) Revolution for non-violence

These were the seven revolutions or Sapta Kranti which was the ideas of socialism for Lohia.

24. (i) (c) Political survival through confidence votes.

(ii) (a) Temporary nature of political victories.

(iii) (b) Government's right to continue in office.

(iv) (b) Procedural formalities that may not address core issues.

25.

S.No. of the Information Used	Alphabet Concerned	Name of State
(i)	A	Uttar Pradesh
(ii)	B	Bihar
(iii)	C	Madhya Pradesh
(iv)	D	Gujarat

26. (i) (b) Emphasising individual rights, especially those of women.

(ii) (a) They introduced the spirit of social justice within Hindu orthodoxy.

(iii) The first stream of Indian liberalism, led by Rammohan Roy, focused on individual rights, notably advocating for women's rights and challenging oppressive traditions. The second stream, represented by thinkers like Keshab Chandra Sen, Justice Ranade, and Swami Vivekananda, worked to embed social justice within Hindu orthodoxy. Vivekananda, in particular, believed Hindu society's reform required liberal values, thereby linking tradition with progressive principles to inspire change from within. Both streams shared a vision of a more equitable and inclusive society.

27. Key ideas and concepts associated with federalism include

(i) **Division of Power** Federalism involves a division of power between the Central Government and constituent units, such as states or provinces.

(ii) **Dual Polity** Federalism has a dual polity, meaning there are two levels of government: national and regional.

(iii) **Written Constitution** Federalism is based on a written Constitution that outlines the powers and responsibilities of each level of government.

(iv) **Independent Judiciary** Federalism requires an independent judiciary to interpret the Constitution and resolve disputes between different levels of government.

Or

The functions of the Constitution are as follows

- A Constitution is to provide a set of basic rules that allows for minimal co-ordination amongst all members of a society.
- To provide assurance to the sections of the society against the violation of the basic rules and accommodate peacefully.
- A Constitution is to specify who has the power to make decisions in the society. It decides the formation of the government.
- A Constitution is to set some limits on the powers of the government against its citizens so that the government cannot trespass the Fundamental Rights of the people which is guaranteed by the Constitution.
- To enable the government to fulfil the aspirations and goals of the society in common, irrespective of caste, creed, colour, sex, religion, etc. and create conditions for a just society.

28. There are following differences between Political Science and Politics

- Politics means the issues, problems and political activities which are actually taking place in society. Against it, Political Science is a social science which studies the state and government.
- Politics is concerned with the day to day actual activities of the government. Political Science seeks to study the origin, nature and functions of the state, government and its all organs.
- Politics differs from state to state and within a state from time to time.
- The principles of Political Science are universal. Politics in India and Britain is different but the theory of Political Science is same in both the countries.
- Politics refers to the actual process of how humans interact in groups and Political Science is the scientific study of politics.

Or

Gandhian principles of politics are relevant in Indian politics due to following reasons

- Gandhi acknowledged traditional concepts and symbols. He introduced interpretations and ideas from foreign to Indian culture that shows the importance of Western humanism in his approach.
- He tried out different modes of political action and different types of political programme, which remained successful and are still motivating factors for politicians.
- Gandhi developed the political methods and campaigned the movements to capture the state's power through the prolonged Mass Movement.
- The theory of trusteeship is a major and new contribution of Gandhi in the arena of political philosophy.
- The main drive is on treating resources as a public trust with man being the trustee, so that the riches of nature and society are fairly used.
- Gandhi had proposed for Independent India, a policy that would be based on the belief of democratic self-government or self-rule.
- Democracy can function efficiently and according to the concept of Swaraj, only if it is decentralised. Due to relevancy of Gandhian principles of politics, the framers of Indian Constitution incorporated his political ideas in Directive Principles of State Policy and in some other parts of Indian Constitution.

29. The Western model of secularism has the following salient features

(i) **Mutual exclusion** The state and religion have separate spheres with independent jurisdiction.

(ii) **No State Intervention in Religion** The state will not intervene in the affairs of religion.

(iii) **No Religious Interference in State Affairs** Religion will not interfere in the affairs of the state.

(iv) **No Religious Rationale for State Policies** No policy of the state can have an exclusively religious rationale.

(v) **No State Aid to Religious Institutions** The state cannot aid any religious institution or provide financial support to educational institutions run by religious communities.

(vi) **Religion as a Private Matter** Religion is considered a private matter, not a matter of state policy or law.

Or

Martin Luther King Jr. presented several arguments against segregation laws

(i) **Equality and Human Dignity** Every human being has equal self-worth and dignity, regardless of race or color.

(ii) **Segregation as 'Social Leprosy'** Segregation inflicts deep psychological wounds on those who suffer under these laws.

(iii) **Diminished Quality of Life** Segregation diminishes the quality of life for both Black and white communities.

(iv) **Artificial Boundaries** Segregation creates artificial boundaries, preventing co-operation for the country's benefit.

(v) **Need for Non-Violent Resistance** King called for peaceful and non-violent resistance against segregation laws.

30. Views of Karl Marx on Equality Karl Marx, a 19th century thinker says that inequality has arisen because of the ownership of important economic resources like oil, land, forests and other forms of property by rich class. By owning such great economic power, they have also got hold of political power.

These rich classes make policies which are beneficial for rich class only and are disadvantageous to poor class. So, only providing opportunities will not help the poor class.

Karl Marx says that the need is to have state or public control over the resources and property of the society. He believes that social, economic and political inequalities are interlinked to each other because rich people having control over wealth leads to control over political system and this also makes them powerful in society.

Views of Liberals on Equality Liberals believe that while state try to ensure a minimum standard of living and equal opportunities to all, this can not by itself bring equality and notice to society. They held that when people have attained minimum standard of living they should be allowed to compete between them and then everybody will get according to their hard work. As long as competition is there, inequalities will not be there in the system.

They believe that political, social and economic inequalities are not linked. They want each sphere to be dealt individually to tackle its problems. For political inequality we need democracy, and for social and economic inequality, state can intervene to provide minimum standard of living. Liberals do not have problem, as such with inequality, but they want that inequality should not disturb us while achieving our capabilities.

Or

Based on different kinds of inequalities which exist in society, there are three dimensions of equality i.e. Political, Social and Economic.

Political Equality It includes granting equal citizenship to all the members of the state. The rights which are considered necessary to enable citizen to develop themselves and participate in the affairs of two state are right to vote freedom of expressions, movement and association and freedom of belief. These rights are also considered as legal rights, which are guaranteed by Constitution. Even in countries where all people have equal rights, significant inequalities will occur. Inequalities in the social and economic worlds are often the product of disparities in the wealth and opportunities available to people. As a result, demands for fair rights or a 'level playing field' are often made. However, we must note that, political and legal equality will not be sufficient and to create a just and equitable society, it is un-questionably a necessary component.

Social Equality Making equal laws are not sufficient, as we require equality in the access of resources (social goods), the pursuit of equality requires that people belonging to different groups and communities also have a fair and equal chance to complete for those goods and opportunities. So, there is a need for equal, social and economic conditions like adequate provision of health care, education, nutrition and minimum wages. Unequal opportunities do not arise only from lack of goods but also from customs. For example, women are not given equal rights in inheritance by some groups and also are denied the opportunity of higher education in India. Thus, we need to make policies to prevent discrimination and harassment of women in public places or employment. The state has a significant role in such matters.

Economic Equality When there is no significant differences in wealth, income and property between individuals or classes, then it leads to economic equality. The relative disparity between the wealthiest and poorest classes is one way to quantify the degree of economic inequality in a society. Another method will be to measure the number of people living in poverty. Entrenched inequalities or those that have remained largely unchanged over centuries, are more detrimental to a community. If certain groups of citizens in a society have accumulated significant wealth and the power that comes with it over centuries, the society will become divided between those wealthy class and those who have remained poor.

SAMPLE QUESTION PAPER 2

A Highly Simulated Sample Question Paper for CBSE Class XI Examination

POLITICAL SCIENCE

General Instructions

Same as Sample Question Paper 1

Section A

1. Which of the following is NOT a feature of rights? (1)

(a) Rights are necessary for leading a life of respect and dignity.

(b) Rights are justified claims.

(c) Smoking can be claimed as a right.

(d) Taking banned drugs cannot be claimed as a right.

2. In the question, a statement of Assertion (A) is followed by statement of Reason (R). Choose the appropriate answer from the options given below as the correct answer. (1)

Assertion (A) In Indian Constitution prohibition of discrimination has been mentioned in Article 15.

Reason (R) Our Constitution also abolishes the practice of untouchability.

Codes

(a) Both A and R are true and R is the correct explanation of A.

(b) Both A and R are true, but R is not the correct explanation of A.

(c) A is true, but R is false.

(d) A is false, but R is true.

3. Match the List I with the List II. (1)

	List I		List II
A.	Civil Rights	1.	Rights to reasonable conditions of work
B.	Economic Rights	2.	Rights to primary education in mother tongue
C.	Political Rights	3.	Rights to free and fair trial
D.	Cultural Right	4.	Right to context election

Codes

	A	B	C	D		A	B	C	D
(a)	3	1	4	2	(b)	2	1	3	4
(c)	2	1	3	4	(d)	4	2	3	4

4. Who among the following is not involved in policy making process in indirect or representative democracy? (1)

(a) Executive (b) Bureaucracy

(c) Citizens (d) None of these

5. **Statement I** One of the duties of a democratic government is to meet the basic needs of its people.

Statement II According to Rawls, a just society is that society in which ascending sense of respect and descending sense of disrespect is dissolved into the creation of a compassionate society. (1)

In the light of above statements, choose the correct answer from the options given below

(a) Both Statement I and Statement II are true.

(b) Both Statement I and Statement II are false.

(c) Statement I is true, but Statement II is false.

(d) Statement I is false, but Statement II is true.

6. Who said that if everyone were to be unjust then nobody would be secure, and it would harm all of them? (1)

(a) Confucius

(b) Plato

(c) Karl Marx

(d) Socrates

7. According to the Nehru report of 1928, what was the minimum age of the person who is entitled to vote. (1)

(a) 18 (b) 21 (c) 25 (d) 28

8. Arrange the following in chronological order. (1)

I. Congress dominance ended and era of coalition government started.

II. Left Front Government in West Bengal brought out a document demanding a restructuring of Centre-State relation.

III. There were agitations in some state against the imposition of the Hindi Language.

Codes

(a) I, III, II (b) III, II, I (c) I, II, III (d) III, I, II

9. Which type of executive system does India follow? (1)

(a) Semi-Presidential
(b) Parliamentary
(c) Presidential
(d) Semi-Parliamentary

10. What is the principle that needs to be balanced with equal treatment for justice in society ? (1)

(a) Equality
(b) Proportionality
(c) Fairness
(d) Rights

11. ………… equality means that all people are equal before law. (1)

(a) Political (b) Social (c) Civil (d) Positive

12. What do supporters of free markets believes ensures a just distribution of benefits and duties. (1)

(a) State
(b) Market
(c) Society
(d) Government

Section B

13. What is Preventive Detention? (2)

14. Why is the roles of Governors a source of controversy between the center and states? (2)

15. What does Immanuel Kant say about justice? (2)

16. In which ways citizenship can be acquired in India? (2)

17. Mention the two characteristics of class struggle? (1 + 1 = 2)

18. What do mean by the term 'federalism'? (2)

Section C

19. 'Justice delayed is justice denied'. Justify the statement and give suggestions for fast redressal of justice. (4)

Or Critically examine the features of the 73rd amendment of the Constitution.

20. In what way does secularism promote democracy? (4)

21. Discuss some of the conflicts in India's federal system. (4)

Or "Equality must involve some kind of fairness". Justify this statement.

22. What are the main characteristics of the method of amendment to the Constitution of India? (1 + 1 + 1 + 1 = 4)

23. What is the difference between 'self regarding actions' and 'other regarding actions'? (2 + 2 = 4)

Section D

24. Observe the cartoon given below and answer the questions that follow. (1 + 1 + 1 + 1 = 4)

(i) What aspect of Parliamentary democracy does this cartoon primarily satirise?
(a) Regular Parliamentary proceedings
(b) Suspension/expulsion of opposition members
(c) Voting procedures
(d) Legislative debates

(ii) The dialogue in the cartoon implies
(a) Voluntary exit by Parliamentarians
(b) Forced removal of members
(c) Routine Parliamentary break
(d) Protest by members

(iii) Which democratic concern is being highlighted through this cartoon?
(a) Strengthening of democratic processes
(b) Weakening of Parliamentary opposition
(c) Efficient Parliamentary functioning
(d) Successful legislative process

(iv) The cartoon's critique of Parliamentary proceedings suggests
(a) Healthy democratic debate
(b) Suppression of opposition voices
(c) Effective governance
(d) Parliamentary efficiency

25. In the given map of India, four states have been marked as (A), (B), (C), (D). Identify these cities and write their correct names in your book along with their respective serial number of the information used and the concerned alphabets as per format that follows. (1 + 1 + 1 + 1 = 4)

S.No. of the Information used	Alphabet concerned	Name of state
(i)		
(ii)		
(iii)		
(iv)		

(i) The state, having bicameral legislature.
(ii) The state, to which Bhimrao Ambedkar belonged, whom we call Father of Indian Constitution.
(iii) The state, also having bicameral legislature and also called economic capital of India.
(iv) The state, which was related to Subhash Chandra Bose's birth.

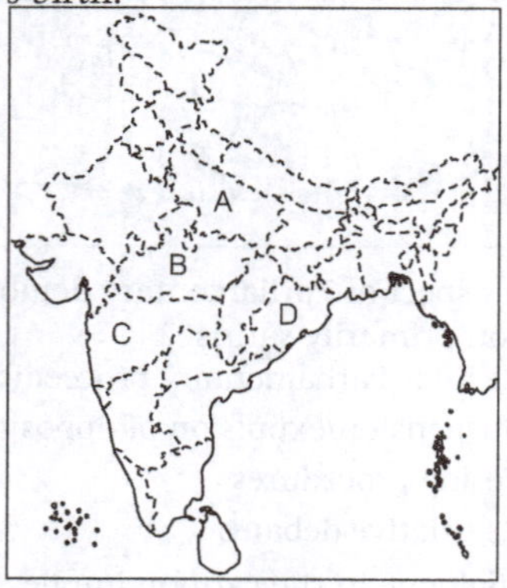

26. Read the following passage carefully and answer the question that follow. (1 + 1 + 2 = 4)

But I have come to say a few words on behalf of the Adibasis of India .... In the past thanks to the major political parties, thanks to the British Government and thanks to every enlightened Indian citizen we have been isolated and kept, as it were, in zoo .... .We are willing to mix with you, and it is for that reason, ... that we have insisted on a reservation of seats as far as the legislatures are concerned.We have not asked ...... (for) separate electorates .....Under the 1935 Act, throughout the legislatures in India, there were altogether only 24 Adibasi MLAs. Out of total of 1585, ... and not a single representative at the centre.

(i) Whose words are depicted in the passage?
(a) Jaipal Singh
(b) Mahatma Gandhi
(c) Dr. B.R. Ambedkar
(d) Jawaharlal Nehru

(ii) How have Adivasis been treated by the political parties, the British Government, and Indian citizens?
(a) They have been given adequate representation in the government.
(b) They have been empowered through separate electorates.
(c) They have been isolated and treated as though they are in a zoo.
(d) They have been integrated fully into mainstream society.

(iii) What concerns does the speaker express about the representation of Adivasis in the government, and how does he justify the demand for reserved seats?

Section E

27. What were the main provisions of the Cabinet Mission Plan? (6)

Or

Elucidate the functions of the Constitution.

28. Differentiate between Political Science and Politics. (6)

Or

'Gandhian principles of politics are relevant in Indian politics'. Justify this statement.

29. What are the criticism of Indian secularism? Explain. (6)

Or

What are the characteristics of a secular state?

30. Illustrate with suitable example the factors that lead to the emergence of nationalist feelings. (6)

Or

Why is it desirable to imagine the nation in political rather than cultural terms? Explain.

Answers

1. (c) Smoking can be claimed as a right.
2. (b) Both A and R are true, but R is not the correct explanation of A.
3. (a) 3 1 4 2
4. (c) Citizens
5. (c) Statement I is true, but Statement II is false.
6. (d) Socrates
7. (b) 21
8. (b) III, II and I
9. (b) Parliamentary
10. (b) Proportionality
11. (a) Political
12. (b) Market

SAMPLE QUESTION PAPER 3

A Highly Simulated Sample Question Paper for CBSE Class XI Examination

POLITICAL SCIENCE

General Instructions

Same as Sample Question Paper 1

Section A

1. The amendments which can be passed by simple majority are **(1)**

(a) Formation of new states
(b) Impeachment of President
(c) Removal of Speaker
(d) Removal of Vice-President

2. In the following question, a statement of Assertion (A) is followed by a statement of Reason (R). Choose the appropriate answer from the options given below.

Assertion (A) In India, people elect their own representations to govern the nation.

Reason (R) India is a democratic country. **(1)**

Codes

(a) Both A and R are true and R is the correct explanation of A.
(b) Both A and R are true, but R is not the correct explanation of A.
(c) A is true, but R is false.
(d)A is false, but R is true.

3. What is the primary basis for claiming human rights? **(1)**

(a) State laws and regulations
(b) Naturals laws or God
(c) Collective recognitions of dignity and well-being
(d) Individual desires and interest

4. What are the measures to protect liberty? **(1)**

(a) Provision of Fundamental Rights
(b) Independent judiciary
(c) Law or rule of law
(d) All of the above

5. According to Immanuel Kant , what is the moral conception of rights based on? **(1)**

(a) Treating others as means to our end
(b) Treating others with dignity and respects
(c) Pursuing individual self-interest
(d) Maintaining social hierarchies

6. Consider the following statements. **(1)**

I. A political doctrine which advocates unequal rights for women and men is called feminism.

II. According to Karl Marx inequality came because of the private ownership and control of important economic resources like oils, land, forest and other forms of property.

Select the correct statements?

(a) Only I (b) Only II
(c) Both I and II (d) None of these

7. Protecting the ozone layer and maintaining the ecology balance are essential for all of us. Which of the following is NOT TRUE regarding these actions? **(1)**

(a) They represent the 'common-good' that we must act to protect .
(b) They are necessary for the well-being of future generations.
(c) They can be achieved without individual effort.
(d) They are essential for leading a reasonably good life .

8. Identify and write the incorrect pair. **(1)**

(a) Political right-Right to vote
(b) Natural right- Right to property
(c) Economic right- Right to minimum wage
(d) Cultural right- Right to education

9. Which of the following body is responsible for drawing up the boundaries of the constituencies all over the country. (1)

(a) President
(b) Parliament
(c) Delimitation Commission
(d) Election Commission

10. **Statement I** The President also has a Veto-Power by which he can withhold or refuse to give assent to Bills passed by the Parliament.

Statement II If the Parliament passes the same Bill again after reconsideration and sends it back to the President, then the President is not bound to give assent to the Bill. (1)

In the light of above statements, choose the correct answer from the options given below.

(a) Both Statement I and Statement II are true.
(b) Both Statement I and Statement II are false.
(c) Statement I is true, but Statement II is false.
(d) Statement I is false, but Statement II is true.

11. Who among the following leaders do not represent the second stream of Indian liberalism? (1)

(a) K. C. Sen
(b) Rammohan Roy
(c) Justice Ranade
(d) Swami Vivekananda

12. Match the List I with the List II. (1)

	List I		List II
A.	Original Jurisdiction	1.	Supreme Court under Article 32.
B.	Appellate Jurisdiction	2.	Advises the President on matters of public importance
C.	Writ Jurisdiction	3.	Appeals from lower courts in civil criminal and Constitutional cases
D.	Advisory	4.	Settles disputes between Union states and other States

Codes

	A	B	C	D		A	B	C	D
(a)	4	3	1	2	(b)	2	1	3	4
(c)	2	1	3	4	(d)	4	2	3	1

Section B

13. Name the writs issued prescribly against the lower courts. (2)

14. Who enjoys the power to amend the Constitution and how? (2)

15. What steps can be taken to promote equality? (2)

16. State some of the conditions in India that have affected the minimum condition of life needed by the people. (2)

17. What constitutes a nation? (2)

18. How is the Governor of a state appointed? (2)

Section C

19. State the difference between Ordinary Bill and Money Bill. (2 + 2 = 4)

20. What is modern liberalism? (4)

Or "Freedom is valuable for human progress". Write your views on this statement.

21. Distinguish between Gram Panchayat and Gram Sabha. (4)

22. In what ways the study of political theory can impact the life of people? (4)

Or 'Social justice is lacking in society'. Justify this statement with your real life experiences.

23. Which conditions in India have affected minimum condition of life needed by people? (4)

Section D

24. Observe the cartoon given below and answer the questions that follow. (1 + 1 + 1 + 1 = 4)

(i) What does the instruction given by the examiner ("You must all climb that tree") primarily illustrate
(a) Fairness in assessment for all participants.
(b) Equality in testing without considering individual abilities.
(c) Encouragement for all animals to try new tasks.
(d) Emphasis on teamwork and collaboration.

(ii) Which of the following is the best interpretation of the message conveyed by the cartoon?
(a) All individuals should be given the same test to maintain fairness.
(b) Different beings require different methods of assessment based on their unique abilities.
(c) The strongest will always succeed, regardless of the task.
(d) Trees are a good measure of physical ability for all animals.

(iii) Why would the elephant likely find the test unfair compared to the monkey?
(a) The elephant is less interested in climbing trees.
(b) The monkey has a natural ability to climb trees, while the elephant does not.
(c) The elephant is afraid of heights.
(d) The elephant is unable to understand the instructions given.

(iv) What concept in education or assessment could this cartoon be used to criticise?
(a) Standardised testing without considering individual strengths and weaknesses.
(b) Practical skills testing in a controlled environment.
(c) Individual competition in group settings.
(d) Using animals as an example in educational settings.

25. In the given outline political map of India, four states have been marked as A, B, C, D. Identify these states and write their correct names in your answer-bool along with their respective serial number of the information used and the concerned alphabets as per the following format. **(1 + 1 + 1 + 1 = 4)**

S.No. of the Information used	Alphabet concerned	Name of state
(i)		
(ii)		
(iii)		
(iv)		

(i) A state which have bicameral legislature system.
(ii) A state in which Lala Lajpat Rai was born.
(iii) A state in which Dr. Rajendra Prasad was born.
(iv) A state in which Father of Nation, Mahatma Gandhi was born.

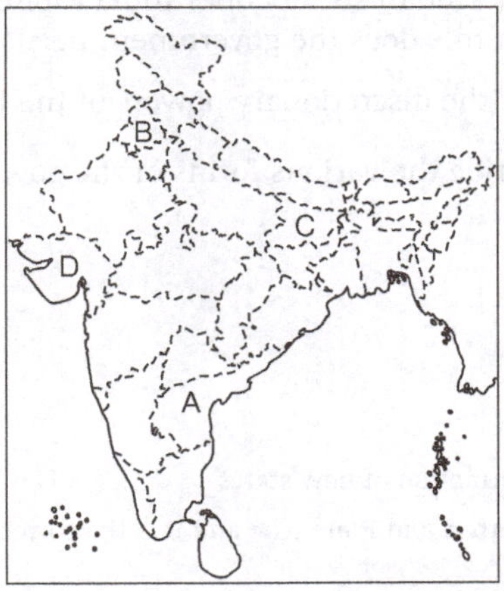

26. Read the following passage carefully and answer the questions that follow. **(1 + 1 + 2 = 4)**

"Separate electorates have been a curse to India, have done incalculable harm to this country.... Separate electorates have barred our progress.... We (Muslims) want to merge in the nation. ...for God's sake keep your hands off reservation for the Muslim community".

(i) According to the speaker, what impact have separate electorates had on India?
(a) They have improved social harmony and progress.
(b) They have caused great harm and hindered the country's progress.
(c) They have increased representation for all communities equally.
(d) They have helped Muslims gain more rights in India.

(ii) What does the speaker request regarding reservations for the Muslim community?
(a) To ensure reservations are provided to the Muslim community.
(b) To avoid giving any form of reservations or separate electorates to Muslims.
(c) To provide reservations only for Muslims in education.
(d) To reduce the existing reservations for Muslims.

(iii) Why does the speaker believe separate electorates are harmful, and what is their stance on reservations for Muslims?

Section E

27. Discuss the special features of the Indian Constitution considered as an important achievements. (6)

Or What kind of society does India aspires to be? What role does the government needs to play?

28. State the discretionary powers of the President. (6)

Or Describe the various forms of the government in details.

29. The problem of stateless people is an important one confronting the world today. Explain with example. (6)

Or International networks link terrorists today. Explain?

30. Distinguish between Western and Indian models of secularism. What are the criticism of the Indian model of secularism? (6)

Or Indian Constitution is federal in form but unitary in spirit. Comment.

Answers

1. (a) Formation of new states
2. (a) Both A and R are true and R is the correct explanation of A.
3. (c) Collective recognitions of dignity and well-being
4. (d) All of the above
5. (b) Treating other with dignity and respects
6. (b) Only II
7. (c) They can be achieved without individual effort.
8. (d) Cultural right- Right to education
9. (c) Delimitation Commission
10. (c) Statement I is true, but Statement II is false.
11. (b) Rammohan Roy
12. (a) 4 3 1 2